The Law Student's Dictionary

The Law Student's
Dictionary

J. E. Penner
Professor of Law, King's College London

This is the 13th edition of *Mozley and Whiteley's Law Dictionary* and continues its tradition of accuracy and reliability to provide an invaluable reference work for students of law

OXFORD
UNIVERSITY PRESS

OXFORD

UNIVERSITY PRESS

Great Clarendon Street, Oxford OX2 6DP

Oxford University Press is a department of the University of Oxford.
It furthers the University's objective of excellence in research, scholarship,
and education by publishing worldwide in

Oxford New York

Auckland Cape Town Dar es Salaam Hong Kong Karachi
Kuala Lumpur Madrid Melbourne Mexico City Nairobi
New Delhi Shanghai Taipei Toronto

With offices in

Argentina Austria Brazil Chile Czech Republic France Greece
Guatemala Hungary Italy Japan Poland Portugal Singapore
South Korea Switzerland Thailand Turkey Ukraine Vietnam

Oxford is a registered trade mark of Oxford University Press
in the UK and in certain other countries

Published in the United States
by Oxford University Press Inc., New York

© Oxford University Press 2008

British Library Cataloguing in Publication Data

Data available

Library of Congress Cataloging in Publication Data

Data available

Typeset by Newgen Imaging Systems (P) Ltd, Chennai, India
Printed in Great Britain
on acid-free paper by
Ashford Colour Press Ltd, Gosport, Hampshire

ISBN 978–0–19–921899–8

1 3 5 7 9 10 8 6 4 2

Preface

To learn any specialised body of knowledge is, in part, to learn its terms of art. The purpose of this dictionary is to provide an introduction to those terms in the law, bearing in mind what was said in the preface to the first edition:

> The primary object of this Work is to give an exposition of legal terms and phrases of past and present use. But, as the mere exposition of a word or phrase would often be barren and unsatisfactory, we have in many cases, especially when dealing with the legal terms of the present day, added an exposition of the law bearing upon the subject matter of this Entry.

In keeping with this object I have provided a number of longer entries in the form of brief essays on some of the major areas of law, particularly those whose doctrines exercise a substantial conceptual influence over the law generally: administrative law, constitutional law, commercial law, company law, contract law, criminal law and criminal procedure, equity, European Union law, intellectual property law, land law, property, public international law, remedies, torts, trusts, and unjust enrichment. In general, I have tried to emphasise the conceptual, rather than the more technical, aspects of the meanings of the terms, so as to give some idea of how these terms have been shaped by, and in turn shape, how lawyers think. There remains, as ever, the problem of deciding what to include and what to jettison in a new edition, and I have tried to strike the right balance between historical terms which demand attention even though they are no longer used to frame the current law, and terms which are in everyday lawyerly use. In particular I have tried to be sensitive in preserving entries for the terms of civil procedure overthrown by the Civil Procedure Rules 1998 while marking the terms that replace them. Practicality alone demands this. The word 'plaintiff', for example, will be a term of English law as long as we read cases.

I happily record my thanks to Simon Blackett for originally encouraging me to undertake this, and to all at OUP for their efficiency, understanding, and good humour.

J. E. Penner
November 2007

List of Abbreviations

Bl	Sir William Blackstone's Commentaries
Cowel	Cowel's Interpreter
Hals Laws	Halsbury's Laws of England
Hals Stats	Halsbury's Statutes of England
Hill and Redman	Hill & Redman's Law of Landlord and Tenant
May	May's Parliamentary Practice
RSC	Rules of the Supreme Court
Stone	Stone's Justices Manual
TL	Termes de la ley, or Terms of the Law

ACAS. The Advisory, Conciliation and Arbitration Service.
See ADVISORY, CONCILIATION AND ARBITRATION SERVICE.

ADR. *See* ALTERNATIVE DISPUTE RESOLUTION.

AGM. Annual general meeting.

ASBO. *See* ANTI-SOCIAL BEHAVIOUR ORDER.

A communi observantia non est recedendum. What is commonly observed, or common usage, should not be departed from. A maxim applying to the practice of the courts whose aim was to ensure uniformity in decision-making.
See PRECEDENTS.

A fortiori (from a stronger reason). All the more.

'A' list. A list of the present members of the company made out by the liquidator in the course of winding up who are primarily liable to contribute to the assets of the company.
See CONTRIBUTORY.

A mensa et thoro. From table and bed.
See JUDICIAL SEPARATION.

A 100. In shipping phraseology, denotes a first-class vessel.

A posteriori. An argument derived from considerations of an abstract character, or which have only a remote and possibly indirect (though none the less real) bearing on the point under discussion, is called an argument *a priori*; whereas an argument derived from actual observation or other direct consideration is called an argument *a posteriori*.

A R. *Anno regni*—in the year of the reign.

A, Table. *See* TABLE A.

A verbis legis non recedendum est (from the words of the law there should not be any departure). A rule to be applied in the interpretation of Acts of Parliament whereby the words of the statute rather than the intention of the Legislature are to be the primary guide for the Court.

A vinculo matrimonii. From the bond of matrimony.

Ab antiquo. From ancient time.

Ab initio (from the beginning), specially in relation to trespass. If a man abuses the authority given him by the law, he becomes, by the Common Law, a trespasser *ab initio* , so that the legality of his first proceedings is vitiated by his subsequent illegal acts.

Ab intestato (from an intestate). Succession *ab intestato* means the succession to the property of a person dying intestate, ie, without a will.

Abandonment. 1 Of RIGHT(s) or CLAIM(s). The giving up or WAIVER of a legal right or claim by failing to pursue it or prosecute it in a timely fashion, often inferred from the right- or claim-holders acting inconsistently with it, eg inferring a LESSOR'S abandonment of his right to evict a LESSEE following his giving a notice to his lessee to quit the leased property by thereafter accepting further rent under the LEASE.

2 In marine insurance, abandonment is the act of cession, by which, in case of the constructive total loss of a vessel or goods, the owners give to the insurers or underwriters what remains of the vessel or goods on condition of receiving the whole amount of insurance. Notice of such abandonment must be given to the underwriters within a reasonable time after the loss (see Marine Insurance Act 1906, s 62).
See TOTAL LOSS.

3 Service of a notice of DISCONTINUANCE OF ACTION OR CLAIM enables a party to abandon an action in the High Court.

4 Abandonment of a child or young person is an offence under the Children and Young Persons Act 1933, s 1. A local authority must provide accommodation for an abandoned child: Children Act 1989, s 20.

5 Of Property. Strictly speaking, property cannot be abandoned, in the sense that an owner may relinquish his or her title to land or goods by leaving occupation or discontinuing possession of property. His or her title remains until such time as another takes possession, and then gains a better title by the passage of time. At this point, the previous owner's title is extinguished. (*See* LIMITATION, STATUTES OF.) However, the belief that property which is appropriated has been abandoned is a good defence to a charge of theft.

Abatement. 1 *In commerce* it means a deduction made from payments due, and it is also used to denote the allowance sometimes made at the custom-house for damages received by goods in warehousing or during importation.

2 *Abatement amongst creditors* takes place where the assets of a debtor are not sufficient to pay his creditors in full, so that they are compelled to share the assets in proportion to their debts.

3 *Abatement amongst legatees* in like manner is enforced where there are not sufficient assets to pay the legacies in full. But pecuniary or general legacies abate proportionally before specific legacies and before demonstrative legacies until the fund out of which the latter are payable is exhausted; and 'in addition' a legacy may be expressly preferred to another of the same class.
See LEGACY.

4 *Abatement of an action or suit* takes place when, from some supervenient cause, one of the parties is no longer before the Court; so that, unless his place is supplied, there is no one to proceed in it. Where a party dies or becomes bankrupt, but the action survives, eg such as an action for DAMAGES for breach of CONTRACT, it does not abate by reason of the death or bankruptcy, and the action may be maintained by the party's PERSONAL REPRESENTATIVE or TRUSTEE in BANKRUPTCY.

5 *Abatement of nuisances,* ie, their removal. A SELF-HELP remedy allowed to one injured by a nuisance. The abatement must be done peaceably and without causing unnecessary damage.

Abdicate. To renounce or give up the throne or government. See eg, His Majesty's Declaration of Abdication Act 1936 which gave legal effect to the abdication of Edward VIII.

Abduction. The leading away of any person. More strictly, the taking away of a wife from her husband, a child from its parent, a ward from her guardian.

In some cases the act is criminal, and in others a civil action will lie against the abductor; and see Sexual Offences Act 1956, ss 19, 20 as to girls under the ages of 16 and 18 years respectively. A person connected with a child, eg a parent or guardian commits an offence if he takes or sends the child out of the United Kingdom without the appropriate consent: Child Abduction Act 1984, s 1.

Abet (Fr *Bouter*; Lat *Impellere, Excitare*). To encourage or set on. Thus, an abettor of a crime is one who, being present either actually or constructively, aids in the commission of the offence. A person who supplies the instrument for a crime or anything essential to its commission aids in the commission of it; if he does so knowingly and with intent to aid, he abets it as well and is guilty of aiding and abetting (see *National Coal Board v Gamble* [1959] 1 QB 11). Aiding and abetting almost inevitably involves a situation in which the secondary party and the main offender are together at some stage discussing the plans which they may be making in respect of the alleged offence, and are in contact so that each knows what is passing through the mind of the other (see *A-G's Reference (No 1 of 1975)* [1975] 2 All ER 684, CA).
See ACCESSORY.

Abeyance (probably from the Fr *Bayer*, to expect).

1 An ESTATE in land is said to be in *abeyance* when there is no person presently in existence (IN ESSE) who has a present right to possession of the land; though the law considers the estate as always potentially existing, and ready to vest whenever a proper owner appears. This estate has also been called *in nubibus* (in the clouds) and *in gremio legis* (in the bosom of the law). The law 'abhors' an abeyance of SEISIN (the rightful possession of land), for it defies the logic of property ownership by which the root of title is present possession of land, and transactions concerning land which did or might lead to an abeyance of seisin, where the ownership of land was in suspense for a time, were treated as void or invalid.

See LAND LAW.

2 The doctrine of abeyance of a peerage relates to the state of suspense into which a peerage falls when co-heirship occurs in the succession.

See PEERAGE.

Abode. A man's residence, where he lives with his family and sleeps at night. It may include a place where the person in question works and has his business.

Abolish. To annul, rescind, or repeal. Typically used to describe the statutory abolition of a long-standing doctrine of the common law.

Aboriginal title. A form of land title, distinct from an estate in fee simple, giving aboriginal peoples exclusive rights to occupy ancestral lands. Recognised to different extents in Australia, Canada, New Zealand, and the USA.

Abortion. A miscarriage, or the premature expulsion of the living foetus before the term of gestation is completed. To procure an abortion was an offence but it has now been legalised under certain circumstances by the Abortion Act 1967, Human Fertility and Embryology Act 1990.

See CHILD DESTRUCTION.

Abridgment. A short comprehensive treatise or digest of the law eg, the works of Fitzherbert, Brooke and Rolle Viner, Comyns and Bacon.

Abrogate. To annul or repeal.

Abscond. To go out of the jurisdiction of the courts, or to conceal oneself to avoid legal process.

Absence. 1 Non-appearance of a party to an action.

2 Unheard of for seven years, a presumption of death; absence of husband or wife for seven years is in certain circumstances a defence to an indictment for bigamy.

Absolute. Complete, unconditional. A rule or order absolute is one which is complete and can be put into force at once, in contradistinction to a rule or order *nisi*, which is made on the application of one party only (*ex parte*) to be made absolute unless the other party appears and shows cause why it should not be made absolute. Formerly

the dissolution of marriages was effected by decrees *nisi* followed by decrees absolute.

See DECREE ABSOLUTE; DIVORCE.

Absolute discharge. Where, in view of the circumstances, including the nature of the offence and the character of the defendant, the court may, instead of imposing the punishment to which the guilty defendant would otherwise be liable, discharge the defendant absolutely, or conditionally (a conditional discharge) upon the defendant's committing no other offence within a specified period (three years or less under the Powers of Criminal Courts (Sentencing) Act 2000, s 12).

Absolute privilege. A defence to an action for defamation. A statement otherwise actionable is privileged where it is made in:

(i) judicial proceedings by any Judge, advocate, juryman, party, or witness;

(ii) a fair, accurate and contemporaneous report in a newspaper of judicial proceedings (Law of Libel Amendment Act 1888, s 3);

(iii) Parliament by a member of either House;

(iv) reports and papers published by order of either House of Parliament (Parliamentary Papers Act 1840).

See DEFAMATION.

Absolute title. Under the Land Registration Act 2002, land may be registered with an absolute title. The first registration of any person as proprietor of freehold land with such a title vests in the person so registered an estate in fee simple in possession in the land, together with all rights, privileges, and appurtenances, belonging or appurtenant to it subject to the following rights and interests:

(i) To the incumbrances, and other entries, if any, appearing on the register; and

(ii) Unless the contrary is expressed on the register, to such overriding interests, if any, as affect the registered land; and

(iii) Where the first proprietor is not entitled for his own benefit to the registered land, as between himself and the persons entitled to minor interests, to any minor interests of such persons of which he has notice but free from all other estates and interests whatsoever, including estates and interests of the Crown (see Land Registration Act 1925, s 5).

For the effect of registration of leaseholds with an absolute title, see ibid, s 9.

See REGISTERED LAND.

A

Abstract of title, Abstract and epitome of title. Under the old system of deeds-based conveyancing, a summary or abridgment of the deeds constituting the title of an estate, furnished by a vendor or mortgagor to an intending purchaser or mortgagee, which operated to provide a narrative history of the sequence of ownership of the property. The 'abstract' provides the history of title, the 'epitome' a schedule of the various deeds and documents which gives proof of it. This is usually perused by the purchaser's or mortgagee's solicitor and verified by an examination of the original deeds. This is followed by requisitions on title.

See CONVEYANCING; REQUISITIONS OF TITLE; CURTAIN CLAUSES; TITLE.

Abundans cautela non nocet. Excess of caution does no harm.

Abuse of distress. The using of an animal or chattel distrained. This renders the distrainer liable as for a conversion.

See DISTRESS; CONVERSION.

Abuse of process. The malicious and improper use of some regular legal proceeding to obtain some advantage over an opponent.

Abuttals, or **Abbuttals** (Fr *Abutter*). The buttings or boundings of lands, showing to what other lands, highways, or places they belong, or are abutting.

Acceleration. The hastening of the vesting in possession of a REVERSION or REMAINDER by the determination of the prior particular ESTATE by SURRENDER, etc, before its natural termination.

Acceleration clause. A provision in a credit agreement, such as a mortgage, which specifies that upon an event occurring, the borrower must pay all or part of the outstanding loan sooner than specified in the schedule of repayment, eg at once. Typically the event specified will be the borrower's default in making timely repayments under the schedule.

Acceptance. 1 'A thing in good part, and as it were a kind of agreeing to some act done before, which might have been undone and avoided if such acceptance had not been.' *Cowel.* If, for instance, a LEASE for more than three years is made verbally it is normally invalid for not being in writing, but acceptance of rent from the LESSEE if he obtained possession will create a tenancy from year to year binding on the LESSOR;

and on the same principle, acceptance of rent may confirm a lease, which has been put an end to by notice, the acceptance here operating as a withdrawal, WAIVER or ABANDONMENT of the notice.

2 A buyer is deemed to have accepted goods when he intimates to the seller that he has accepted them, or when the goods have been delivered to him, and he does any act in relation to them which is inconsistent with the ownership of the seller, or when after the lapse of a reasonable time he retains the goods without intimating to the seller that he has rejected them (see Sale of Goods Act 1979, s 35).

3 In CONTRACT law, acceptance of an offer may be made by express words or may be inferred from conduct showing an unqualified intention to accept. A mere intention to accept not shown by words or conduct is insufficient.

Acceptance of a bill. *See* BILL OF EXCHANGE.

Accepting service is where the solicitor for a defendant on his behalf accepts service of a writ or other process of a Court, and undertakes to appear, so as to avoid the necessity of such writ or process being served on his client. *See* SERVICE, 3. This undertaking the Courts will enforce, if necessary, by attachment.

See ATTACHMENT.

Acceptor. A person who accepts a bill of exchange.

See BILL OF EXCHANGE.

Access. Approach, or the means of approaching. (i) The presumption of a child's legitimacy is rebutted if it is shown that the husband had not access to his wife within such a period of time before the birth as admits of his having been the father; (ii) the court may grant a 'contact order' enabling a child to visit or stay with the person named in it. *See* CONTACT ORDER.

Access land. Areas of land defined under s 1(1) of the Countryside and Rights of Way Act 2000 to which members of the public are entitled to have access for the purposes of open-air recreation.

Accession. 1 A mode of acquiring property by right of occupancy; whereby the original owner of anything which receives an accession by natural or artificial means, eg by the growth of vegetables, etc, the pregnancy of animals, etc, is entitled to it. But if the thing itself, by such operation, is changed into a different species, eg by making wine, oil, or bread, out of another's grapes, olives, or wheat, it belongs to the new operator, who is only to make a satisfaction to the former proprietor for the materials which he has so converted.

2 In international law, accession is occasionally used as a technical expression denoting the absolute or conditional acceptance, by one or several States, of a treaty already concluded between other sovereignties.

3 The word means also the coming of a King or Queen to the throne on the death of the prior occupant of it.

Accessory. A person who is not the chief actor in an offence, nor present at its performance, but is in some way concerned in it, either *before or after* the fact committed. An accessory *before* the fact is one who, being absent at the time of the crime committed, yet procures, counsels, or commands another to commit a crime.

The Criminal Law Act 1967, s 4 provides penalties for assisting any person who has committed an arrestable offence, with intent to impede his apprehension or prosecution. *See* ARRESTABLE OFFENCE.

Accident. As a ground for seeking the assistance of a court of EQUITY, eg, for relief against the consequences arising from the accidental loss or destruction of a deed, accident means not merely inevitable casualty, or the act of God, or *vis major* but also such unforeseen events, misfortunes, losses, acts, or omissions as are not the result of negligence or misconduct. (*See* VIS MAJOR.) (In the case of the loss of a negotiable instrument see Bills of Exchange 1882, ss 69, 70.)

In the Social Security Contributions and Benefits Act 1992 the word is used in the popular and ordinary sense and means a mishap or untoward event not expected or designed.

Accommodation bill. A bill of exchange to which a person has put his name, whether as DRAWER, ACCEPTOR, or INDORSER, without CONSIDERATION, for the purpose of accommodating some other party who desires to raise money on it. The accommodation party thus becoming liable on it, may, if compelled to pay, have his remedy over against the person accommodated.

See BILL OF EXCHANGE.

Accommodation land. Land bought by a builder or speculator who erects houses on it and then leases portions of it on an improved ground rent.

Accommodation works. Works such as gates, bridges, etc, which the railways are required to make and maintain for the accommodation of the owners and occupiers of land adjoining the railway.

Accomplice. A person associated with another in the commission of a criminal offence, whether as principal or accessory before the fact, or committing, procuring, or aiding and abetting (See *Davies v Director of Public Prosecutions* [1954] 1 All ER 507, HL). *See* ACCESSORY.

Accord and satisfaction. An agreement between the party injuring and the party injured, by reason of any trespass or breach of contract; which, when performed, is a bar to all actions on account of the injury, the party injured having thereby received satisfaction for, or redress of, the injury. *See* SATISFACTION.

Account. A statement of the transactions concerning a fund of property, especially the funds of a trust or a company, or of credits and liabilities between contracting parties. Regarding the latter, an open, or current, account is one of which the 'balance', ie the concluding statement of the account which expresses the current position of the account is not 'struck' ie not accepted by all interested parties. A stated account, or 'account stated', is no longer open or current, but closed by the statement, agreed to by both the parties, of a balance due to the one or other of them. A stated account is settled where balances due to one party or another are paid, closing the account.

Account, action of, claim for an. An action of account or claim for an account is an ACTION (CASE) in which the PLAINTIFF (CLAIMANT) demands an accounting by the defendant of his stewardship over a fund of property, most typically, a claim by the BENEFICIARY of a TRUST for an accounting by his TRUSTEE of the latter's transactions with the trust property. The trustee will be liable for any misdealings with the trust property that the account reveals, and so the action of account is typically brought as a means of remedying a breach of trust, and a trustee's general liability to beneficiaries can be called his 'liability to account.'

Accretion. Generally synonymous with accruer. But the word is specially used to denote an accession to an owner of land on the sea shore, or of fresh land recovered from the sea by alluvion or dereliction.

See ACCRUE; ALLUVION; DERELICTION.

Accrue. *Lit* to grow to, as interest accrues to principal. It also means to arise, eg when a cause of action is said not to have accrued to the plaintiff within six years. An accruing is referred to as an 'accruer'; the accruing of an action may be referred to as an 'accruer of action'.

Accumulation. When the income of a TRUST fund, eg bank account interest or dividends on shares, instead of being paid over to some person or persons as it arises, is invested so as to be reserved for the benefit of some person or persons in the future, the income is said to be accumulated. Restrictions are imposed on accumulation, partly by the rules against perpetuities, and partly by the Law of Property Act 1925, ss 164–166.

See PERPETUITY; TRUST.

Acknowledgment. 1 Of debt, if in writing signed by the debtor or his agent, will prevent the limitation period from running except as from the date of such acknowledgment. Similarly, as regards acknowledgment of title to land (see Limitation Act 1980, s 29).
2 Of signature to a will by testator. If the signature is not made in the presence of two witnesses, its subsequent acknowledgment in their presence will satisfy the Wills Act 1837.

Acquiescence. A version of consent, in particular to the violation of one's strict legal RIGHT(s), and a means by which a right may be lost: if a person acquiesces in another's violation of his or her rights over a period of time, he or she may lose that right though he or she might have asserted it successfully if he or she had pursued the right in a timely fashion.

See PROPRIETARY ESTOPPEL.

Acquis communantaire. The body of norms of the EU wider than the law as applied and interpreted by the European Court of Justice, in particular including the political norms expressed in opinions and actions of the EU institutions; under MAASTRICHT TREATY

Art 3, the EU must respect and build upon the *acquis communautaire*.

Acquisitive prescription. Prescription whereby a right is acquired. Sometimes called positive prescription.

See PRESCRIPTION.

Acquittal (Fr *Acquitter*; Lat *Acquietare*, to discharge, or keep in quiet). A deliverance, and setting free from the suspicion or guilt of an offence. Thus, a person who is discharged of a criminal offence by judgment, on its merits, is acquitted, and if subsequently charged with the same, or legally the same offence, may plead *autrefois acquit*.

See AUTREFOIS ACQUIT.

Act of God. An extraordinary occurrence or circumstance which could not have been foreseen and which could not have been guarded against; an accident due to natural causes, as eg a destructive storm, or a sudden and unforeseen death.

Cf VIS MAJOR.

Act of indemnity. *See* INDEMNITY ACT.

Act of Parliament. A statute; a law made by the Legislature, the Queen, Lords, and Commons in Parliament assembled.

Acts of Parliament are of three kinds:
(i)   Public.
(ii) Local or special.
(iii) Private or personal.

See STATUTE.

Act of Settlement 1700. An Act by which the Crown was settled (on the death of Queen Anne) upon Sophia, Electress of Hanover, and the heirs of her body being Protestants.

Act of State. An act committed by the sovereign power of a country which cannot be challenged in the Courts; the exercise of the Royal Prerogative.

See PREROGATIVE.

Act of Supremacy 1558. An Act by which the supremacy of the Crown in ecclesiastical matters was established.

Acta exteriora indicant interiora secreta. Acts indicate the intention.

Acte claire. A doctrine of EU law under which a court of a member state may decide a dispute on the basis of EU legislation without referring the matter to the European Court of Justice (ECJ), even though the provision in question has not been the subject of previous interpretation by the ECJ, where the provision is reasonably clear and free from doubt.

Actio personalis moritur cum persona.
A personal action dies with the person.

Action (Lat *Actio*). The lawful demand of one's right; thus an individual legal action is the prosecution or pursuit through the legal process of a legal claim founded upon one CAUSE OF ACTION, from the initiation of proceedings to the FINAL PROCESS.

A *civil* action is brought to enforce a civil right, eg if a person seeks to recover a sum of money lent, etc. *See* CASE.

A *penal* action aims at some penalty or punishment in the party sued, whether corporal or pecuniary; specially an action brought for the recovery of the penalties given by statute.

Criminal actions, ie prosecutions, are of a public nature, in the name of the Queen, against one or more persons accused of a crime.

Actionable *per se*. Words that are defamatory in themselves, such as those imputing criminality, promiscuity, or fraudulent activity. Claims for libel or slander based on such words do not require proof of damages.

Active trust. A trust requiring some active duties on the part of the trustee.
See BARE TRUST; TRUST.

Acts of sederunt. Ordinances for regulating judicial procedure in the Court of Session in Scotland.
See COURT OF SESSION.

Acts of Union. The incorporation of Wales into the realm was effected by two statutes of Henry VIII, 1535 and 1542. The Union with Scotland Act 1706 united England and Scotland in the reign of Queen Anne. The Union with Ireland Act, 1800 (George III) united Great Britain with Ireland from 1st January, 1801; but much of the Act was virtually repealed by legislation consequential on the establishment of the Irish Free State (Eire) in 1922.

Actual total loss. A term in marine insurance describing the situation 'where the subject-matter is destroyed or so damaged as to cease to be a thing of the kind insured, or where the assured is irretrievably deprived thereof' (see Marine Insurance Act 1906, s 57(1)). In the case of an actual total loss no notice of abandonment need be given (ibid, s 57(2)).

See ABANDONMENT.

Actuary (Lat *Actuarius*). A person who calculates the risks and premiums for fire, life, and other insurances.

Actus non facit reum nisi mens sit rea.
See ACTUS REUS.

Actus novus interveniens. A new act which intervenes to break the chain of causation.

Actus reus. A guilty act, ie an act which, if committed with the requisite malicious intent, counts as a criminal act, thus the particular act required for the commission of a crime, eg the actual appropriation of property necessary to commit a THEFT. Consider, however, the following: 'I desire to make an observation on the expression *actus reus* … Strictly speaking, though in almost universal use, it derives, I believe, from a mistranslation of the Latin aphorism: *Actus non facit reum nisi mens sit rea*. Properly translated, this means, "An act does not make *a man guilty* of a crime, unless his mind be also guilty". It is thus not the *actus* which is *reus*, but the man and his mind respectively. Before the understanding of the Latin tongue has wholly died out of these islands, it is as well to record this as it has frequently led to confusion' (see *Haughton v Smith* [1973] 3 All ER 1109, HL, per Lord Hailsham of St Marylebone, LC).

Ad hoc. For this; for this particular purpose. Thus, an action taken ad hoc is one taken to deal with a particular matter only, and one which does not reflect a consistent strategy or course of dealing.

Ad idem. Tallying in the essential point. There must be *consensus ad idem* for a valid CONTRACT.

Ad litem (for the suit). A guardian appointed by the court to defend a suit on behalf of a minor is called a LITIGATION FRIEND, formerly a guardian *ad litem*.
See CIVIL PROCEDURE; GUARDIAN; INFANT.

Ad medium filum acquae. To the centre line of the stream. *See* FILUM AQUAE MEDIUM.

Ad medium filum viae. To the centre of the road.

Ad valorem (according to the value). A duty, the amount of which depends on the value of the property taxed, is called an *ad valorem* duty.

Ad vitam aut culpam (for life or until misbehaviour).
See QUAMDIU BENE SE GESSERIT.

Adaption. In the case of a literary or dramatic work, this means (i) the conversion of a

non-dramatic into a dramatic work, or vice-versa; (ii) a translation of the work; (iii) the conversion of the work into picture form; or (iv) in relation to a musical work, an arrangement or transcription of the work: Copyright, Designs and Patents Act 1988, s 21 (3).
See LITERARY WORK; MUSICAL WORK.

Addition. A title given to a person besides his proper name and surname, ie of what estate, degree, or profession he is, and of what town, hamlet, or country.

Address for service. Address given by one party to an action or proceedings for service of notices, etc, by the other.

Ademption of a legacy. The implied revocation of a BEQUEST in a WILL by some subsequent act of the testator, eg when a specific CHATTEL is bequeathed, and the testator afterwards sells it, the gift is said to adeem, and can, of course, not take effect; ademption also occurs when a parent bequeaths a legacy to his child and afterwards makes a separate provision for the child in satisfaction of it.
See SATISFACTION.

Adherent. Being *adherent* to the Queen's enemies, eg by giving them aid, intelligence, or the like, constitutes high treason, by the Treason Act 1351.
See TREASON.

Adjectival or adjective law. As opposed to the 'substantive' law, the rules of practice and procedure in the courts.

Adjourn. To put off the hearing of a case to a future day or *sine die*. Usually in the discretion of the Court.
See SINE DIE.

Adjudication. 1 The giving of judgment; a sentence or decree; eg in the expression, it was adjudged for the plaintiff, etc.
2 An adjudication of bankruptcy.
See BANKRUPTCY.

Adjustment. In INSURANCE law, the settling of the amount of the loss, and of the INDEMNITY which the assured is entitled to receive, and, in the case of several UNDERWRITER(s), of the proportion which each underwriter is liable to pay in respect thereof.

Administration has several meanings. The Queen's ministers, or collectively the Government, are often called the *Administration*, as charged with the administration or management of public affairs. The administration of justice by judges, magistrates, etc.

The affairs of a bankrupt may be said to be *administered* by his trustee; and the affairs of an absent person, by his agent, factor, or attorney, etc. But the word is specially used in reference to the following case:

The administration of a deceased's estate; ie, getting in the debts due to the deceased, and paying his creditors to the extent of his assets, and otherwise distributing his estate to the persons who are by law entitled to it. The person charged with this duty is spoken of as 'executor' or 'administrator', according as he has been appointed by the deceased in his will, or by the Chancery Division. See also the Administration of Estates Act 1925, and the Supreme Court Act 1981. Also applied to the execution of a trust.
See ADMINISTRATION SUIT; ADMINISTRATOR; EXECUTION; EXECUTOR.

Administration order. An order directing that, during the period for which it is in force, the affairs, business, and property of a company are to be managed by an administrator appointed for the purpose by the Court (see Insolvency Act 1986, s 8(2)). The Court may make such an order if it is satisfied that a company is or is likely to become unable to pay its debts and considers that the making of an order would be likely to achieve eg the survival of the company as a going concern or a more advantageous realisation of its assets than would be effected on a winding up (see ibid, s 8(1), (3)).

Administration suit. A SUIT instituted for the ADMINISTRATION of a deceased's ESTATE. This suit may be instituted by an executor or administrator, or any person interested in the deceased's estate as CREDITOR, LEGATEE, NEXT OF KIN, etc.

Administrative law. A branch of PUBLIC LAW which deals with the rightful exercise of the powers of the various organs of the state or other public bodies, in particular the power of courts to control the action of these bodies by reviewing their actions or decisions by the process known as judicial review, ie the assessment by a judge or judges of a superior court of the legality or correctness of an inferior tribunal or administrative agency's actions. It is closely related to CONSTITUTIONAL LAW, for the powers of action allocated to different organs and branches of the state is determined ultimately by the extant political settlement embodied in the constitution. Roughly, then, while constitutional law concerns the ultimate rules which reflect the current political settlement, administrative law concerns the rules and procedures by which the courts give effect to that settlement in a detailed way as a matter of day-to-day oversight to ensure that particular organs of the state do not act in excess of their powers, or fail to act to carry out their duties. In particular, administrative law concerns the power of the courts to control the conduct of various local authorities, commissions, tribunals, agencies, and other bodies given powers to act under statutes, ie by Act of Parliament, to ensure that they act in accordance with the powers granted them, and so many cases in administrative law concern claims by affected individuals that a public body has acted *ultra vires*, ie in excess of the powers granted it by Parliament. With respect to administrative agencies or tribunals which are not courts of justice but which act in a *quasi*-judicial capacity, ie render decisions which have an adjudicative nature, the courts have sometimes required such bodies to observe the rules of 'natural justice', chiefly to act fairly in good faith, and in particular so as to ensure that adjudicators are not biased in favour of one side or the other and that each party has an opportunity to adequately state his case (the principle of *audi alteram partem*, hear the other side). There is no general rule of natural justice that an administrative decision-making body must give reasons for the actual decisions it renders. Traditionally, the three most important administrative law actions were actions for the prerogative orders of *certiorari*, *mandamus*, and prohibition (called prerogative because they originated in the residual jurisdiction of the royal courts to do the King's justice in extraordinary circumstances, in particular to ensure that the King's own officials were exercising properly the authority over his subjects granted to them by him). An order of *certiorari* (to be more fully informed of) commanded proceedings to be removed from an administrative or inferior tribunal to a superior court for a review of the action taken by it. The court might review such an action on all of its merits, and either declare it valid, or invalid as having been taken *ultra*

vires, or quash the decision as somehow bad though taken *intra vires*. In the last case, the court might substitute its own decision, or command the inferior by an order of *mandamus* to itself undertake the decision-making process again in accordance with criteria which the superior court declared to properly reflect the scope and nature of its authority. Generally, the court will not undertake to review (or substitute its own judgment for) a decision on the facts by an administrative tribunal or body if the decision is within the proper scope of the latter's discretion, unless the body unreasonably refused to take into account facts material to making its decision, or the decision on the facts was so unreasonable that nobody acting reasonably could have come to that decision. An order of prohibition commands a body or tribunal to refrain from acting illegally, in particular to refrain from acting in particular circumstances for to do so would be *ultra vires*.

Administrator. A person to whom the administration of the estate of a deceased is committed by letters of administration from the Chancery Division in cases where the deceased left no will, or when the executor acting under a will is out of the realm, where the validity of the will itself is questioned, or *cum testamento annexo*, where the testator has left a will and has not appointed an executor, or where the testator has appointed an executor who is either unable or unwilling to act.

If a stranger, ie a person who is neither administrator nor executor, takes the goods of the deceased, and administers of his own wrong, he may be charged and sued not as an administrator but as an executor *de son tort*.
See EXECUTOR DE SON TORT.
See ADMINISTRATION.

Administratrix. A woman to whom administration is granted.
See ADMINISTRATION; ADMINISTRATOR.

Admiralty. The Probate, Divorce and Admiralty Division of the High Court of Justice, created by the Judicature Act 1873, so far as regards admiralty, succeeded to the *civil* jurisdiction of the High Court of Admiralty. It had jurisdiction over claims for salvage, damage arising by collision or otherwise on the high seas and other maritime causes. There were two divisions of the jurisdiction of the Admiralty Division of the High Court, the Prize Court and the Instance Court. The admiralty jurisdiction of the High Court was later set out in the Administration of Justice Act 1956, s 1 and included jurisdiction to hear claims to the possession and ownership of ships or stores therein, claims for damage done or received by a ship, claims for death or injury arising from any defect, etc, in a ship, claims for loss of or damage to cargo or goods, etc.

Part I of the Administration of Justice Act 1956 was amended by the Administration of Justice Act 1970, which established a new Admiralty Court as part of the Queen's Bench Division of the High Court.

Admissions, in *evidence*, are the testimony which the party admitting bears to the truth of a fact against himself. In practice, these are usually made in writing by the solicitors in an action, in order to save the expense of formal proof.

Admonition. A judicial reprimand to an accused person on being discharged from further prosecution.

Admortisation. *See* AMORTISATION.

Adoption. An act by which the rights and duties of the natural parents of a child are extinguished, and equivalent rights and duties (eg, as to custody, maintenance, education, etc) become vested in the adopter or adopters, to whom the child then stands in all respects as if born to them in lawful wedlock. The rules governing, and effect of, adoption have been extensively altered over the 20th century; see Adoption Acts 1926 to 1976, Children Act 1989, Adoption and Children Act 2002. Under INTERNATIONAL LAW, the incorporation, eg by customary usage, of norms of international law into municipal law.

Adoptive Acts. Acts of Parliament which come into operation in particular districts on being adopted, in the manner prescribed in them, by the local authorities or inhabitants of that district.

ADR Convention. The European Agreement Concerning the International Carriage of Dangerous Goods by Road (Geneva, 30th September 1957).

Adult. A person who has attained full age, now 18. *See* FULL AGE; INFANT.

Adulteration. The mixing with an article intended for food or medicinal use of any other substance, whether noxious or harmless, or the abstraction of any constituent part whereby the quality,

substance or nature of the article is injuriously affected and the purchaser is prejudiced. The law relating to the 'adulteration' of food was consolidated by the Food Act 1984. The term 'adulteration' is now obsolete, having been replaced by 'rendering food injurious to health' under the Food Safety Act 1990, s 7.

Adultery. Voluntary sexual intercourse during the subsistence of the marriage between one spouse and a person of the opposite sex not the other spouse. It is one of various facts which may be put before a divorce court in proof that a marriage has irretrievably broken down (see Matrimonial Causes Act 1973, s 1). *See* DIVORCE.

Advance freight. Freight payable to a shipowner on the signing of bills of lading or on shipment instead of on the delivery of the goods. Such freight is usually not returnable even in the event of the ship or the goods being lost before she starts on her voyage. *See* FREIGHT.

Advancement. 1 That which is given to a child by a father, or other person standing *in loco parentis*, in anticipation of what the child might inherit. The term advancement derives from two senses: the payment 'advances' the child's receipt of an expected interest, in that he or she receives it earlier than he or she would in the normal course of events, and secondly, the payment is taken to 'advance' the child in life, by making provision for obtaining a suitable role or occupation; thus advancements were typically made to purchase a son's commission in the army or a clerical living, or to a daughter upon her marriage. Payments of capital from a trust fund to a beneficiary before their interest in the capital VESTS are also called advancements, and a TRUSTEE's power to make advancements of this kind are implied in the Trustee Act 1925, s 32.

2 A trustee may have a power of advancement, which allows the expenditure of trust capital for the benefit of a beneficiary with a capital interest.

3 A presumption of advancement, ie a presumption that a gift was intended, arises when a man transfers property to, or purchases property in the name of, his wife or child or someone to whom he stands *in loco parentis*.
See PORTION; SATISFACTION.

Adverse possession. Where one person is in possession of property under any title, and another person claims to be the rightful owner of the property under a different title, the possession of the former is said to be an 'adverse possession' with reference to the latter. A rightful owner neglecting to assert his claim within a given period (defined, according to the circumstances of the case, by the Limitation Act 1980) is henceforth barred of his right to it. The acquisition of title to REGISTERED LAND by adverse possession has been made more difficult under Part 9 of the Land Registration Act 2002. *See* LIMITATION, STATUTES OF; OCCUPANCY. This is to be distinguished from prescription. *See* PRESCRIPTION.

Adverse witness. A witness hostile to the party calling him, who may, with the leave of the Court, cross-examine him.

Advice, letter of. A notification by one person to another in respect of a business transaction in which they are mutually engaged, eg, by consignor to consignee, of goods having been forwarded to him; or by one merchant to another of the drawing of bills of exchange on him.

Advice on evidence. Advice given by counsel, after the close of pleadings, on the evidence which it will be necessary to call to support his client's case.

Advisory Committee on Legal Education and Conduct. A committee appointed by the Lord Chancellor having the general duty of assisting in the maintenance and development of standards in the education, training and conduct of those offering legal services: Courts and Legal Services Act 1990, ss 19, 20.

Advisory, Conciliation and Arbitration Service. A body set up under the Employment Protection Act 1975, Part I, to promote the improvement of industrial relations. As well as arbitrating in trade disputes and giving free advice, it may issue codes of practice.

Advocate. A person privileged to plead for another in court. Formerly, in England, confined to those who practised in the Ecclesiastical and Admiralty Courts, but now that these courts have been thrown open to all barristers-at-law, the title has lost its distinctive meaning. In Scotland, barristers practising before the Supreme Court are called advocates. *See* ADVOCATES, FACULTY OF.

Advocate General (of the European Court of Justice). A lawyer, whose role is to assist the judges, privileged to advise the EUROPEAN COURT OF JUSTICE in the form of learned opinions on the law of the case before it. His submissions are given after those of the parties.

Advocate, Lord. *See* LORD ADVOCATE.

Advocates, Faculty of. In Scotland the barristers practising before the Supreme Court are called *advocates*. The Faculty of Advocates is a corporate body, consisting of the members of the bar in Edinburgh, founded in 1532, the members of which are entitled to plead in every court in Scotland, and in the House of Lords.

Advowson (Lat *Advocatio*). The right to present to a benefice (Stat West 2, 1285), the *jus patronatus* of the Canon Law. Advowsons are either *appendant* or *in gross*, or partly the one and partly the other. An advowson is *appendant* when it is annexed to the possession of a manor and passes with it; *in gross*, belonging to the person of its owner. Or if a partial right of presentation is granted to a stranger, the advowson may be *appendant* for the term of the lord, and *in gross* for the term of the stranger. Advowsons are also said to be *presentative* or *collative*. An advowson *is presentative* when the patron has the right to present his clerk to the bishop, and to demand his institution if he is so qualified; *collative* when the bishop and patron are one and the same person so that the bishop performs by one act (*collation*), the separate acts of presentation and institution. There was formerly a third species, viz, *donative*, when the patron by a *donation* could place the clerk into possession without presentation, institution, or induction; but all *donative* benefices were converted into *presentative* by the Benefices Act 1898. As to restrictions on the sale of advowsons, see the Benefices Act 1898 (Amendment) Measure 1923.

Affiant. The technically correct term for one who makes and swears an affidavit, who is more often nowadays termed a 'deponent' (one who makes a deposition).

Affidavit (Lat *Affido*). A statement in writing and on oath, sworn before a person who has authority to administer it.

Affinity. The relationship resulting from marriage, between the husband and the blood relations of the wife; and also between

A

the wife and the blood relations of the husband. By the Marriage Act 1949, s 1 marriages between certain degrees of kindred and affinity are prohibited. The prohibited degrees of relationship are set out in Sch 1 to that Act.

See CONSANGUINITY.

Affirm. To ratify or confirm a former law or judgment. Hence a Court of Appeal is said to *affirm* the judgment of the court below. To *affirm* also means to make a solemn declaration, equivalent to a statement upon oath.

See AFFIRMATION.

Affirmanti non neganti incumbit probatio. The burden of proof is on the person who alleges, and not on the person who denies.

Affirmation. The testimony given either in open court, or in writing, of those who are permitted to give their evidence without having an oath administered to them, as all persons objecting to take an oath are now enabled by law to do (see the Oaths Act 1988).

Affirmative, the (as opposed to the negative). Some positive fact or circumstance which is alleged to be or to have been, and which is generally therefore to be proved, according to the rule of law 'that the affirmative of the issue must be proved'.

See RIGHT TO BEGIN.

Affray. A person is guilty of affray if he uses or threatens unlawful violence towards another and his conduct is such as would cause a person of reasonable firmness present at the scene to fear for his personal safety (see Public Order Act 1986, s 3(1)).

Affreightment (Lat *Affretamentum*). The freight of a ship. The contract of affreightment is either by charter-party or bill of lading.

See BILL OF LADING; CHARTER-PARTY; FREIGHT.

Aforethought. A word used to define the premeditation which generally distinguishes murder from manslaughter. It is irrelevant for how short a time this premeditation may have been conceived in the mind.

Age. The periods of life when men and women are enabled by law to do that which before, for want of age and consequently of judgment, they could not legally do.

See FULL AGE; INFANT.

Agent. A person authorised, expressedly or impliedly, to act for another (called the principal) and who is, in consequence of, and to the extent of, the authority delegated by him, bound by the acts of his agent. This term includes most kinds of agents, eg factors and brokers, and the stewards of landowners. It is also usually applied to designate the London solicitor acting on the instructions of the solicitor in the country. Agents may be either *general*, who can bind their principals in all matters of a class, or *special*, in a particular transaction only. The agent is not usually personally liable.

See DEL CREDERE COMMISSION.

Agent of necessity. A person who pledges the credit of another when urgent reasons make it necessary to do so, eg, the master of a ship purchasing goods necessary for the continuance of the voyage. Such acts are binding on the principal.

Aggravated assaults. Distinguished from common assaults, eg, offences against boys under 14, or women (see the Offences against the Person Act 1861, s 43).

Aggravated burglary. *See* BURGLARY.

Aggravation, or *matter of aggravation*, is that which is introduced into a pleading for the purpose of increasing the amount of damages, but which does not affect the right of action itself.

Agist (Fr *Giste*, a bed or resting place; Lat *Stabulari*). Agistment now generally means the taking in by any one of other men's cattle to graze in his ground at a certain rate per week, or the payment made for so doing. See the Agricultural Holdings Act 1986, s 18, as to privilege of agisted cattle from distraint. There is also an *agistment* of seabanks, viz, where lands are charged to keep up the sea-banks, and are hence termed *terrae agistatae*.

Agreement (said to be from the Latin *Aggregatio mentium*). The consent or joining together of two minds in respect of anything done or to be done; also the written evidence of such consent. An agreement, or *contract*, exists either where a promise is made on one side, and assented to on the other; or where two or more persons enter into an engagement with each other, by a promise on either side.

See CONTRACT.

Agreement to sell. A contract of sale whereby the transfer of the property in the goods is to take place at a future time or subject to some condition later to be fulfilled: Sale of Goods Act 1979, s 2(5). The agreement becomes a sale when the time elapses or the conditions are fulfilled subject to which the property in the goods is to be transferred: ibid, s 2(6).

Agricultural holding. A tenancy of land used for the purpose of agriculture under which the tenant receives various protections under the Agricultural Holdings Act 1986.
See SECURITY OF TENURE.

Aid and abet. *See* ABET.

Aid and comfort. The giving of aid and comfort to the Queen's enemies in her realm, or elsewhere, is treason under the Treason Act 1351.
See TREASON.

Air. The enjoyment of air free and unpolluted is a natural right, and interference with such right is actionable unless such interference is by virtue of an easement.
See EASEMENT.

Alderman (Sax *Ealdorman,* elder man). A local official who formerly presided with the bishop in the Saxon council of *schyregemote,* taking cognizance of civil questions while the latter attended to spiritual ones. There were anciently alderman of the county, of the hundred, etc. By the Local Government Act 1888 the title was revived for some members of county councils. The title is now obsolete, except that by the Local Government Act 1972, s 249 the title of honorary alderman may be conferred on any person who has, in the opinion of a county or district council, rendered eminent services to that council as a past member. No alderman may now serve *as such* on any council.

Aleatory contract. A contract whose effect depends on an uncertain event, eg. an indemnity insurance contract for loss caused by fire or theft.

Alias. *Alias dictus,* 'otherwise called'. An assumed name, or other name by which one is called.

Alibi (elsewhere). When an accused person, in order to show that he could not have committed the offence with which he is charged, sets up as his defence that he was *elsewhere* at the time when the crime is alleged to have taken place, this defence is called an *alibi.*

Alien (Lat *Alienus*). Generally a person born outside the dominions of the Crown of England, ie out of the allegiance of the Queen. But to this rule there are some exceptions. Thus, the children of the Sovereign, and the heirs of the Crown, wherever born, have always been held natural-born subjects; and the same rule applies to the children of our ambassadors born abroad. And by various statutes the restrictions of the Common Law have been gradually relaxed, so that many, who would formerly have come under the definition of an alien, may now be regarded as natural-born subjects to all intents and purposes (see the British Nationality Act 1981).

Alien enemy. An alien born in, or the subject of, a hostile State.

Alienation. A transferring of property, or the voluntary resignation of an estate by one person, and its acceptance by another.

Alieni juris (of another's right). An expression applicable to those who are in the keeping or subject to the authority of another, and have not full control of their person and property. In English law there are generally reckoned two classes of such persons; infants (ie, minors) and persons suffering from mental disorder.
See SUI JURIS.

Alimentary trust. *See* PROTECTIVE TRUST.

Aliter (otherwise). A phrase used for the sake of brevity in pointing out a distinction.

Aliud est celare—aliud tacere. Silence is not equivalent to concealment.

Aliunde (from another source, from another place, in another way). Thus if, when a case is not made out in the method anticipated, it may be proved *aliunde,* ie by other and different evidence.

All fours. A phrase, often used to signify that a case or a decision agrees in all its circumstances with some other case or decision.

'All risks' insurance. A type of insurance designed to protect the insured against loss or damage however caused. Policies of this type are used in marine insurance, jewellery insurance, contractors' insurance, and cash or goods in transit insurance policies.
See MARINE INSURANCE.

Allegation. The assertion or statement of a party to a suit or other proceeding (civil or criminal) which he undertakes to prove.

Allegiance. 'The tie which binds the subject to the Sovereign, in return for that protection

A

which the Sovereign affords the subject.' *Bl.* Allegiance is either *natural* and perpetual, or *local* and temporary; the former being such as is due from all men born within the Sovereign's dominions immediately on their birth; the latter, such as is due from an alien during the time that he continues within the Queen's dominion and protection and, in certain circumstances, even after he leaves it. For form of oath of allegiance, see the Promissory Oaths Act 1868, s 2.

See ALIEN; OATH OF ALLEGIANCE.

Allodial land. Land held otherwise than by feudal tenure, ie under a tenure ultimately 'of the King'. Such land was held absolutely, or outright, no allegiance to a superior being a requirement of continuing possession. Following the Norman Conquest all land in England was incorporated under the system of feudal tenures; thus allodial land ceased to exist in England thereafter.

See LAND LAW.

Allonge. A slip of paper applied to a bill of exchange, on which indorsements are written where there is no room for them on the bill itself (see Bills of Exchange Act 1882, s 32(1)).

Allotment. Share of land assigned on partition or under an enclosure award. As to provision of allotment gardens, etc, for labourers and others, see the Allotments Acts 1908 to 1950.

Allotment letter. Of shares in a company concluding the contract to take shares.

Alluvion. Land which is gained from the sea by the washing up of sand and earth, so as in time to make *terra firma*.

See DERELICTION.

Almshouse. A house provided for the reception or relief of poor persons. To make a place an almshouse it is not necessary that the inmates should be entirely destitute, or that it should supply all their wants (see *Mary Clark Home Trustees v Anderson* [1904] 2 KB 645).

Alteration in deeds or other documents generally vitiates the instrument if made in a material part after execution. In deeds an alteration is presumed to have been made before or at the time of execution; in wills, after execution; and see Wills Act 1837, s 21. As to bills of exchange, see the Bills of Exchange Act 1882.

Alternative Dispute Resolution. Procedures for settling disputes outside, or alongside, litigation in courts, favoured in certain sorts of cases, such as commercial, labour, and family disputes, for their lower costs and expedition. *See* ARBITRATION.

Alumnus. A foster child. A person educated at a school or college is called an *alumnus* of it.

Amalgamation. The combination of two or more companies or their businesses into one company or into the control of one company. See Companies Act 1985, ss 425–427.

Ambassador. A representative sent by one sovereign power to another, with authority conferred on him by letters of credence to treat on affairs of state; the highest rank among diplomatic officials. His person is protected from civil arrest, and his goods from seizure under distress or execution, by the Diplomatic Privileges Act 1964.

Ambiguity. Uncertainty of meaning in the words of a written instrument. Where the doubt arises on the face of the instrument itself, eg a blank is left for a name, the ambiguity is said to be *patent*, as distinguished from a *latent* ambiguity, where the doubt is introduced by collateral circumstances or extrinsic matter, the meaning of the words alone being *prima facie* sufficiently clear and intelligible.

Ambulatoria est voluntas defuncti usque ad vitae supremum exitum. The will of a person who dies is revocable up to the last moment of life.

Ambulatory. Able to walk. Existing as a legal act, but not taking effect until some future event, eg death. Revocable until it takes effect. Used to describe the nature of a person's last will.

Amendment. A correction of any errors in writ or pleadings in actions or prosecutions. Large powers of amendment have been given by modern statutes.

Amenity. *See* LOSS OF AMENITY.

Amicus curiae (a friend of the court). A bystander, usually a barrister, who informs a Judge in court on a point of law or fact on which the Judge is doubtful or mistaken.

Amnesty. An act of pardon by which crimes against the Government up to a certain date are condoned so that a person can never be charged with committing them. It originates with the Crown, and may be general, to all concerned, or particular.

Amortisation. The redemption of stock by a sinking fund.

Ancient lights. Windows through which the access and use of light have been actually enjoyed without interruption for twenty years, unless enjoyed by express consent or agreement in writing: Prescription Act 1832.

Ancient monument. Any structure, work, site, garden, or area which in the opinion of the Historic Buildings and Monuments Commission is of historic, architectural, traditional, artistic, or archaeological interest (see National Heritage Act 1983, s 33(8)). See also Ancient Monuments and Archaeological Areas Act 1979.
See HISTORIC BUILDINGS AND MONUMENTS COMMISSION.

Ancient writings. Deeds and other documents which are more than thirty years' old. These when adduced in evidence 'prove themselves', ie they do not ordinarily require proof of their execution when coming from the proper custody.

Ancillary (Lat *Ancilla*, a slave). Auxiliary, or subordinate.

Ancillary relief. Phrase used in divorce proceedings to refer to orders for financial support, the division of property, and so on, ie relief ancillary to the main relief sought, the decree of divorce.

Angling. Fishing. Angling in the daytime (that is, in the period beginning one hour before sunrise and ending one hour after sunset) is not *per se* an offence under the Theft Act 1968. But angling in the daytime in water which is private property or in which there is any private right of fishery is an offence for which the angler is liable to a fine.

Animals. Either (i) *domitae naturae*, of a tame nature, which are the subject of absolute ownership, are considered personal property and may be the subject of theft; or (ii) *ferae naturae*, of a wild nature, which are to be regarded as property, but they cannot be stolen unless they have been reduced into possession by or on behalf of another person (see Theft Act 1968, s 4(4)). Qualified ownership may be acquired in them either *per industriam*, by taming or keeping them under control, *proper impotentiam*, by their being too weak to get away, or *propter privilegium*, by franchise from the Crown, eg, in warren.

For the rules imposing strict liability in tort for damage done by an animal on the ground that the animal is regarded as *ferae naturae*, or that its vicious or mischievous propensities

are known or presumed to be known, see Animals Act 1971, ss 2–5. Those sections cover, respectively: liability for damage done by dangerous animals; liability done by dogs to livestock; liability for damage and expenses due to trespassing livestock; and exceptions from liability.

Animus. Intention, in particular, the intention with which an act is done.

Animus cancellandi. Animus revocandi. The intention of cancelling. The intention of revoking, specially in relation to a will.

Animus furandi. The intention of stealing—at Common Law it must be present at the time of taking.

Animus manendi. The intention of remaining, which is material for the purpose of ascertaining a person's *domicile*.
See DOMICILE.

Animus possidendi. The intention of possessing as a full owner. Necessary for an occupant of land to establish a title by ADVERSE POSSESSION.

Animus revertendi. The intention of returning.

Animus revocandi. *See* ANIMUS CANCELLANDI.

Animus testandi. The intention of making a will.

Annual general meeting. *See* MEETING.

Annual return. A return to be made by a company every year giving various details relating to eg its registered office, registers of members and debenture holders, shares, director, and secretary (see Companies Act 1985, ss 363 and 364).

Annual value. A value placed upon hereditaments for the purpose of assessing liability to income tax or rates.

Annuity. A yearly sum payable. A life annuity is an annual payment, eg under the terms of a will, during the continuance of any life or lives.

Ante-date. To date a document before the day of its signature or execution. As to BILLS OF EXCHANGE, see the Bills of Exchange Act 1882, s 13(2).

Ante litem motam. Before a suit is put in motion.

Ante-nuptial. Before marriage.

Ante-nuptial agreement. An agreement made before marriage as to the division of assets, etc, should the parties divorce. Not generally regarded by the Court as binding in English law.

A

Anti-social behaviour order. Order made by a magistrate under the Crime and Disorder Act 1988 against a person of at least 10 years of age who has behaved in ways causing or likely to cause harassment, alarm, or distress, specifying behaviour from which he or she must in future desis.

Antique (or **Vetera**) **statuta** (ancient statutes). The Acts of Parliament from Richard I to Edward III.

Anton Piller order. An order permitting an individual to search and take possession of the property of another in order to further justice in a civil action (which takes its name from *Anton Piller KG v Manufacturing Processes Ltd* [1976] 1 All ER 779, CA). Following the CIVIL PROCEDURE RULES 1998, such an order is to be known as a 'search order'.

Apology in actions for libel may operate as a defence, or in mitigation of damages (see Libel Act 1843, ss 1, 2; Defamation Act 1996 s 2).

Appeal. A complaint to a superior court of an injustice done by an inferior one. The party complaining is styled the appellant, the other party the respondent.

In *civil* cases, appeals from the Chancery, Queen's Bench, and Family Divisions of the High Court lie to the Court of Appeal (civil division); from the Court of Appeal, to the House of Lords. The Judicial Committee of the Privy Council is also the ultimate court of appeal in ecclesiastical matters, and from certain Commonwealth courts. Leave in many cases necessary for appeal. As to appeals in *criminal* cases, these are to the Court of Appeal (criminal division), and thence to the House of Lords.

Appellant. *See* APPEAL.

Appellate Committee of the House of Lords. *See* HOUSE OF LORDS.

Appellate jurisdiction. The jurisdiction exercised by a court of appeal.

Appendant. Annexed to, or belonging to, some principal right or CORPOREAL HEREDITAMENT. Eg, a COMMON of fishing may be *appendant* to a freehold, which is to say that the right to fish in some body of water is linked to or 'runs with' ownership of the freehold; appendant rights, or *appendants* are naturally and originally joined to the principal right, as distinguished from *appurtenances,* which may be created at any time, and either by express GRANT or PRESCRIPTION.

Appointed day. The day appointed for bringing into force an Act of Parliament or part of it.

Appointee. A person to whom or in whose favour 'a power of appointment' is exercised. *See* APPOINTMENT; POWER.

Appointment. Besides its ordinary meaning, to appoint is to cause to be transferred property, under a *power of appointment.* Eg, under a TRUST, an individual given a power of appointment (called the 'donee' of the power of appointment) is entitled to have the TRUSTEE transfer (some amount of the) property held on trust to persons who are referred to as the OBJECTS of the power. *See* POWER.

Apportionment. The dividing of a legal right into its proportionate parts, according to the interests of the parties concerned. The word is generally used with reference to the adjustment of rights between two persons having SUCCESSIVE INTERESTS in the same property, eg a TENANT FOR LIFE and the REMAINDERMAN. By the Apportionment Act 1870 it is provided that all rents, annuities, dividends, and other periodical payments in the nature of income, are to be considered as accruing from day to day, and are apportionable in respect of time accordingly.

Appraisement. Valuation.

Apprentice (Fr *Apprendre*, to learn). One who is bound by deed indented, or indentures, to serve his master and be maintained and instructed by him.

Approbate and reprobate. To take advantage of the beneficial parts of a deed, and reject the rest. This the law does not generally permit. *See* ELECTION.

Appropriation. 1 The perpetual annexation of an ecclesiastical benefice to the use of some spiritual corporation, sole or aggregate, being the patron of the living. The patrons retained the tithes and glebe in their own hands, without presenting any clerk, they themselves undertaking to provide for the service of the church. When the monasteries and religious houses were dissolved, the appropriations belonging to them became vested in the Crown, and many of these were afterwards granted out to subjects, and came into the hands of lay persons, called by way of distinction *lay impropriators.* *See* VICAR.

2 The application of a particular payment for the purpose of paying a particular debt. The debtor at the time of paying has the right of appropriation, but, as a general rule, the creditor may apply the payment if the debtor does not; if neither does so, the law usually appropriates earliest payment to earliest debt (*Clayton's case*).

3 Any part of the real or personal estate of a deceased person may be appropriated in its actual conditions in or towards satisfaction of a legacy or share of residue. See Administration of Estates Act 1925, s 41.

4 The Theft Act 1968, s 1 provides that a person is guilty of theft if he dishonestly 'appropriates' property belonging to another with the intention of permanently depriving the other of it. In this connection 'appropriation' is defined (by s 3) as any assumption by a person of the rights of an owner. This includes any later assumption of such rights after having come into the possession of the property lawfully or without actually having stolen it, as eg wrongful appropriation by a bailee. *See* THEFT.

Appropriator. A spiritual corporation entitled to the profits of a benefice.
See APPROPRIATION, 1.

Approve (Lat *Approbare*). To improve; especially of land.

Approvement. 1 The improvement or partial inclosure of a common. Consent of the Secretary of State for the Environment is now necessary (see Law of Commons Amendment Act 1893). For further restrictions on approvements, see Law of Property Act 1925, s 194.
See COMMON, RIGHTS OF.

2 The profits arising from the improvement of land approved.

Appurtenances, or **Things appurtenant** (Lat *Pertinentia*). Things both corporeal and incorporeal belonging to another thing as the principal, but which have not been naturally or originally so annexed, but have become so by grant or prescription, e g hamlets to a manor, common of pastures, turbary, piscary, and the like.
See APPENDANT.

Common appurtenant may arise not only from long usage but from grant. It may extend to beasts not generally commonable,

thus differing in some degree from *common appendant*.

Arbitration is where two or more parties submit all matters in dispute to the judgment of *arbitrators*, who are to decide the controversy; and if they do not agree, it is usual to add, that another person be called in as *umpire*, to whose sole judgment it is then referred. Frequently there is only one arbitrator originally appointed. The decision, in any of these cases, is called an *award*. But sometimes, when the umpire gives the decision, it is termed *umpirage*. The Arbitration Act 1950 consolidated the earlier law with respect to arbitration. Amendments to it were made by the Arbitration Act 1979, concerning the judicial review of arbitration awards and the abolition of the procedure of stating a case for the decision of the High Court.

An international Convention on the settlement of investment disputes between States and nationals of other States was implemented by the Arbitration (International Investments Disputes) Act 1966.

Arbitration agreements with an international element may be recognised and enforced in the United Kingdom (see Arbitration Act 1975). Where a 'consumer' enters into an arbitration agreement, the Consumer Arbitrations Agreement Act 1988 applies.
See ADVISORY, CONCILIATION AND ARBITRATION SERVICE; CONSUMER ARBITRATION AGREEMENT.

Arbitration clause. Contractual provision requiring the parties to seek arbitration to resolve certain or all disputes concerning the contract before resorting to litigation.

Archbishop. The chief of all the clergy in his province. He has the inspection of the bishops of that province, as well as of the inferior clergy; or, as the law expresses it, the power to *visit* them. There are two archbishops for England: Canterbury, styled Primate of all England; and York, Primate of England.
See VISITOR, 1.

Archdeacon. An ecclesiastical officer subordinate to the bishop throughout the whole of a diocese or in some particular part of it. He is usually appointed by the bishop, and has a kind of episcopal authority. He *visits* the clergy, and has his separate court for punishment of offenders by spiritual

A

censures, and for hearing all other causes of ecclesiastical cognisance. As a general rule, the jurisdictions of the archdeacon and the bishop are concurrent, but with appeal from former to latter. He also examines for ordination, induction, etc.

See INDUCTION; ORDINATION.

Arches, Court of. A court of appeal belonging to the Archbishop of Canterbury, of which the judge, who sits as deputy to the archbishop, is called the *Dean of the Arches*, because he anciently held his court in the Church of St Mary-le-Bow (*Sancta Maria de arcubus*). This court was afterwards held in the hall at Doctor's Commons, and subsequently at Westminster. Its proper jurisdiction is only over the thirteen peculiar parishes belonging to the archbishop in London. But the office of Dean of the Arches having been for a long time united with that of the archbishop's principal official, he now, in right of the last-mentioned office (as does also the official principal of the Archbishop of York, who since the Public Worship Regulation Act 1874 is the same judge as for Canterbury), receives and determines appeals from the sentences of all inferior ecclesiastical courts within the province. Many original suits are also brought before him, in respect of which the inferior judge has waived his jurisdiction.

From the Court of Arches and from the parellel court of appeal in the province of York, an appeal lies to the Judicial Committee of the Privy Council.

See JUDICIAL COMMITTEE OF THE PRIVY COUNCIL.

Arm's length, at. A transaction at arm's length is a transaction between unrelated parties, each acting out of their own self-interest. The terms of such a transaction are generally presumed to reflect the fair market value of the goods or services concerned. When a person is not, or having been, ceases to be, under the influence or control of another, he is said to be 'at arm's length' from him, eg, a CESTUI QUE TRUST and TRUSTEE.

Arraign, arraignment (Lat *Ad rationem ponere*, to call to account). To arraign is to call a prisoner to the bar of the court to answer the matter charged in the indictment. The prisoner is to be called to the bar by his name. The indictment is to be read to him, after which it is to be demanded of him whether he is guilty of the crime of which he stands indicted, or not guilty. He may

then either confess, plead not guilty, or stand mute.

See MUTE.

Arrangements between debtors and creditors are agreements under which the debtor's affairs are to be conducted so as to provide for the payment of debts owing to creditors, so as to maximise the payment of those debts, but by which the agreeing creditors will not proceed at law to have the debtor declared bankrupt. Arrangements must be in accordance with the Deeds of Arrangement Act 1914, Insolvency Act 1986.

As to arrangements within the bankruptcy law, see Insolvency Act 1986, Part VIII.

Arrears. Debts outstanding after the date when they should have been discharged, ie money still owing after the date on which it should have been paid.

Arrest. A restraint of a man's person, obliging him to be obedient to the law. An arrest is the beginning of imprisonment, whereby a man is first taken, and restrained of his liberty, by a lawful warrant; also it signifies the decree of a court, by which a person is arrested. An arrest consists of the actual seizure or touching of the person's body with a view to his detention. The mere pronouncing of words of arrest is insufficient unless the person sought to be arrested submits to the process.

Any person may, without warrant, arrest anyone whom he, with reasonable cause, suspects to be committing an arrestable offence. See, generally, as to arrest without warrant the Criminal Law Act 1967, s 2. As to the use of force in making an arrest, see ibid, s 3.

Arrest without warrant is also allowed in certain other criminal cases. When a person is arrested without warrant, he must be informed of the reason.

A warrant of arrest may also be obtained in Admiralty proceedings to detain the ship or other *res*, the subject of the action.

Arrest of judgment. A staying or withholding of judgment, although there has been a verdict in the case, on the ground that there is some error on the face of the record, from which it appears that the plaintiff has at law no right to recover in the action, or that the prisoner should not be sentenced.

Arrest of ship. A judicial process by which claims against a ship owner are commenced by bringing a claim *in rem* (a claim against the thing itself) for the ship, by which the

Admiralty Marshal takes custody of the ship until the determination of the proceedings.

Arrestable offence. An offence for which the sentence is fixed by law or for which a person (not previously convicted) may be sentenced to imprisonment for five years, or the attempt to commit any such offence. A person committing or suspected to be committing an arrestable offence may be arrested without warrant (see Police and Criminal Evidence Act 1984, s 2).

See SERIOUS ARRESTABLE OFFENCE.

'Arrived' ship. A ship which has reached the port (*E L Oldendorff & Co GmbH v Tradax Export SA: The 'Johanna Oldendorff'* [1973] Lloyd's Rep 285 at 291, HL (per Lord Reid)) or berth (*Stag Line Ltd v Board of Trade* [1950] 1 All ER 1105, CA), as the case may be, specified in a charter-party.

Arson. The malicious and wilful burning of a house or other building. Formerly a Common Law offence only, it was made a statutory offence, with liability to imprisonment for life, by the Criminal Damage Act 1971.

Articled clerk. Formerly, a person bound by articles to serve with a practising solicitor, previously to being admitted himself or herself as a solicitor. Now 'trainee' solicitors enter contracts of traineeship with solicitors in the way of acquiring practical experience as a requirement for being admitted as a solicitor.

Articles. A word used in various senses.

1 Agreements between different persons expressed in writing, SEALED or unsealed, are often spoken of as 'articles'. A contract made in contemplation of marriage is, in general, spoken of as 'marriage articles', if it contemplates a further instrument, ie, settlement, to carry out the intention of the parties. So also 'articles of partnership', 'articles of association', etc.
See ARTICLED CLERK.

2 Rules are sometimes spoken of as 'articles'; as, for instance, 'articles of war', 'articles of the navy', 'articles of a constitution', 'articles of religion'. The Thirty-nine Articles drawn up by the Convention in 1562, which must be subscribed to on taking holy orders.

3 The complaint of the promoter in an ecclesiastical cause is called 'articles'. So, an impeachment by the House of Commons is expressed in what are called 'articles of impeachment'.

4 The paragraphs of an order or instrument made under statutory powers.

Articles of association. Regulations governing the mode of conducting the business of an incorporated company and its internal organisation. These must usually accompany the Memorandum of Association, which sets out the objects and capital, etc, of the company. In the case of a company limited by shares, Table A of the Companies Act 2006 may be taken as the articles of the company. *See* TABLE A.

Articles of religion. *See* ARTICLES, 2.

Artificial person. *See* PERSON.

Artistic work means (i) a graphic work, photograph, sculpture, or collage, irrespective of artistic quality; (ii) a work of architecture being a building; (iii) a work of artistic craftsmanship: Copyright, Designs and Patents Act 1988, s 4(1).

As against. An expression indicating a partial effect or influence. Thus, an action may be dismissed as against certain parties to it, who have been wrongfully made parties, while maintained against others.

Ascendant. *See* DESCENT.

As of. A judgment *as of* Trinity Sittings is a judgment not delivered in Trinity Sittings, but having the same legal effect.
See SITTINGS.

Assault (Fr *Assailler*). Defined by Blackstone 'to be an attempt or offer to beat another, without touching him': and though no actual suffering is proved, yet the party injured may have redress by action for damages as a compensation for the injury, or nominally by criminal prosecution. A *battery* is the unlawful beating of another, and includes the least touching of another's person wilfully or in anger. Practically, however, the word assault is used to include the battery.
See BATTERY.

Assay (Fr *Essayer*). A proof, a trial. Thus, the *assay* of weights and measures is the examination of them by officials.

The *assay* of metals is the testing of the fineness of the precious metals and their alloys. The principal assay offices are: (i) the Wardens and Commonalty of the Mystery of Goldsmiths of the City of London; (ii) the Incorporation of Goldsmiths of the City of

Edinburgh; (iii) the Guardians of the Standard of Wrought Plate in Birmingham; and (iv) the Guardians of the Standard of Wrought Plate within the town of Sheffield.

See CARAT; HALLMARK.

Assent. Consent. The executor's assent to a bequest is essential to perfect a legatee's title. Provisions as to assents are contained in the Administration of Estates Act 1925, s 36. To pass the legal estate it must be in writing, signed by the personal representative, and must name the person in whose favour it is given. The statutory covenant against incumbrances may be implied if the assent is expressed to be given 'as personal representative' (see s 36(3)).

Assessment of costs. The settlement by a costs judge or costs officer of the amount payable by a party in respect the of costs of a case, action, or suit. Prior to the Civil Procedure Rules 1998, this was called the 'taxation of costs' and was carried out by a 'taxing master'.

See COSTS.

Assessors. Persons who assess the public rates or taxes, also persons who assist a judge with their special knowledge of the subject which he has to decide: eg, 'legal assessors', 'nautical assessors', 'mercantile assessors'.

See NAUTICAL ASSESSORS.

By the Supreme Court Act 1981, s 70 the High Court or Court of Appeal may call in the aid of one or more assessors specially qualified, and may try and hear the matter in question with their assistance. Largely employed in the Admiralty Court and the Judicial Committee of the Privy Council in ecclesiastical matters (Appellate Jurisdiction Act 1876, s 14). See now the Civil Procedure Rules 1998, 35.15.

Assets (Fr *Assez*, enough). By *assets* is meant such property as is available for the payment of the debts of an individual or company, or of a person deceased.

Formerly, it was important that the assets of a deceased person were divided into *real estate*, and *personal assets*, consisting of what is called *personal estate*, which were administered according to different rules.

Under the Administration of Estates Act 1925, s 32, the real and personal estate, whether legal or equitable, of a deceased person, are made assets for the payment of his debts, whether by specialty or simple contract. This section virtually abolishes any

distinction between legal and equitable assets. Realty and personalty are alike equally liable for the payment of debts, and vest in the personal representatives, who have a power of sale. See generally Administration of Estates Act 1925, as amended by Administration of Estates Act 1971.

See MARSHALLING OF ASSETS.

Assign (Lat *Assignare*) means: (i) to make over a right or interest to another; (ii) to point out, or set forth.

Assignee, or **Assign.** A person who is appointed by another to do any act in his own right, or who takes the rights or title of another by assignment, as distinguished from a *deputy* who acts in the right of another. Such an assignee may be either *by deed*, ie, by act of party, eg when a lessee assigns his lease to another, or *in law*, the person whom the law so makes, without any appointment of the person, as an administrator who is the assignee in law to the intestate.

Assignor. One who transfers or assigns property to another.

See ASSIGNEE.

Assisted person. *See* LEGALLY ASSISTED PERSON.

Assize Courts, or **Assizes.** 1 Ancient form of court composed of a body of men sitting together (*assideo*) to try a dispute.

2 Prior to the establishment of Crown Courts, the Assizes were the circuit courts which tried indictable offences throughout England and Wales. Abolished by the Courts Act 1971.

3 A synonym for 'Act' or 'statute', as in the Assize of Clarendon 1166.

Association, Articles of. *See* ARTICLES OF ASSOCIATION.

Association, Memorandum of.

See MEMORANDUM OF ASSOCIATION.

Assurance. 1 The legal evidences of the transfer of property are called the *common assurances* of the kingdom. They are also called *conveyances*, and are, in general, effected by an instrument called a *deed*.

2 Insurance.

See INSURANCE.

Assured shorthold tenancy. A statutory form of residential tenancy providing for six months SECURITY OF TENURE: Housing Acts 1988, 1996.

Assured tenancy. A statutory form of residential tenancy heavily protected by statute as regards SECURITY OF TENURE. Now incapable of being created, those that remain will eventually end: Housing Acts 1988, 1996.

Asylum. A place in which offenders could find refuge. To seek *political asylum* means to ask admission to another country in order to obtain refuge from political persecution or harassment.

Attachment. The taking into the custody of the law the person or property of one already before the Court, or of one whom it is sought to bring before it. This was done by means of a writ, called a *writ of attachment*. An attachment differs from an *arrest* or *capias*, as it may extend to a man's goods as well as to his person; and from a *distress*, as it may extend to his person as well as his goods. The process of attachment is the method which was used by the superior courts for the punishment of all cases of CONTEMPT OF COURT.

Attachment of debts. *See* GARNISHEE.

Attachment of earnings. A court may make an attachment of earnings order to secure payment of an order of the court, such as a JUDGMENT DEBT. The debtor must give particulars of his earnings and anticipated earnings, and attend the court hearing at which the deduction rate from earnings will be decided. The debtor's employer must then, under the court order, deduct the specified amounts from the debtor's wages or salary, and pay them to the collecting officer of the court (see Attachment of Earnings Act 1971).

Attempt to commit a crime. One of the series of acts necessary to the commission of the crime, and directly approximating to it. Not punishable more heavily than if the attempted crime had been completed (see Powers of Criminal Courts Act 1973, ss 18(2), 30(2) and Criminal Attempts Act 1981).

Attendance centre. A place at which offenders under 21 may be required to attend and be given supervision, appropriate occupation or instruction in pursuance of a court order: Powers of Criminal Courts (Sentencing) Act 2000, s 60.

Attestation. The subscription by a person of his name to a deed, will, or other document executed by another, for the purpose of testifying to its genuineness.

1 Deed of document *inter vivos*. A deed ought to be duly attested, ie show that it was executed by the party in the presence of a witness or witnesses. In most cases this is rather for preserving the evidence, than for constituting the essence, of the deed, but attestation is essential for the validity of bills of sale (Bills of Sale Act 1878, and Bills of Sale Act (1878) Amendment Act 1882), and for deeds executing powers of appointment (Law of Property Act 1925, s 159), and in a few other cases.
See BILL OF SALE.

2 Will. Every will except a military will must, by the Wills Act 1837, be made in the presence of two or more witnesses present at the same time, such witnesses *attesting* and subscribing the will in the presence of the testator, though not necessarily in the presence of each other.
See MILITARY WILL.

Attestation clause. The clause in which a witness to a deed, will, or other document certifies to its genuineness. It is not legally essential, even for a will (Wills Act 1837, s 8), but it is the simplest evidence of due execution and is universally included.
See ATTESTATION.

Attested copy. A copy of a document verified as correct.

Attorn. To *turn over* or entrust business to another. Hence the word *attorney* is used to signify a person entrusted with the transaction of another's business.
See POWER OF ATTORNEY.

Attorney. One appointed by another man to do something in his stead.
See ATTORN; POWER OF ATTORNEY.

Attorney-General. The principal law officer of the Crown, and the head of the Bar of England. It is his duty, among other things, to prosecute on behalf of the Crown, and to file, *ex officio*, information in the name of the Crown.
See INFORMATION.

Auctioneer. A licensed agent to sell property and conduct sales or auctions. He is deemed the agent of both parties. *See* AGENT.

Audi alteram partem (hear the other side). Both sides should be heard before a decision is given.
See ADMINISTRATIVE LAW.

Audience, right of. The right to appear as an advocate before the court.

Auditor. A person appointed to check the accounts of local authorities, companies, partnerships, trusts, etc.

Auditor General. *See* COMPTROLLER AND AUDITOR GENERAL.

Auditors' report. A report prepared by the auditors relating to the financial state of a company.

It must state whether the annual accounts have been properly prepared in accordance with the Companies Act 1985, s 235(1). It must be signed by them: ibid, s 236. In preparing the report the auditors must carry out such investigations as will enable them to form an opinion as to whether proper accounting records have been kept by the company: ibid, s 237(1).

Authentication. A certificate of an act being in due form of law, given by proper authority.

Authorised capital. The total amount of capital which a COMPANY is authorised by its memorandum of association to offer to subscribers, as distinguished from its *issued* capital, or capital actually taken up by such subscribers.

Authorised share capital. *See* NOMINAL SHARE CAPITAL.

Authority. **1** Power given by one person to another enabling the latter to do some act. *See* AGENT.

2 a governing body, eg, county council or local authority;

3 grounds for some legal proposition, eg, judicial decisions, or opinions of authors. *See* LOCAL AUTHORITY.

Autre droit, in. In right of another. A person may hold property in his own right or in right of another, eg, trustee in right of *cestui que trust*, or an executor or administrator in right of the deceased and his legatees, devisees, or the persons entitled on his intestacy.

Autre vie. The life of another, eg an estate *pur autre vie* is an estate for the life of another.

Autrefois acquit (beforetime acquitted). By this plea a prisoner charged with an offence pleads that he has been tried before and acquitted of the same offence. The plea, however, is only good in reference to a verdict of *acquittal* by a *jury* or on a final determination by a court of summary jurisdiction. Therefore, if a man is committed for trial and the jury having him in charge is discharged by the Judge before verdict, he is still liable to be indicted for the same crime. The first indictment must have been such that he could have been lawfully convicted

on it. The true test whether such a plea is a sufficient bar in any particular case is, whether the evidence necessary to support the second indictment would have been sufficient to procure a legal conviction on the first (see Criminal Procedure Act 1851, s 28, and Evidence Act 1851, s 13).

Where an accused pleads *autrefois acquit*, it is for the Judge, without the presence of a jury, to decide the issue: Criminal Justice Act 1988, s 122.

Autrefois convict. A plea by an accused person that he has been previously convicted of the same crime of which he is accused. This plea is a good plea in bar to an indictment. It depends on the same principle, and is governed by the same rules as *autrefois acquit*. As to the form of the plea, see Criminal Procedure Act 1851, s 28.

Where an accused pleads *autrefois convict*, it is for the Judge, without the presence of a jury, to decide the issue: Criminal Justice Act 1988, s 122.

See AUTREFOIS ACQUIT.

Average. **1** *General average* is the contribution which the owners, in general, of a ship, cargo, and freight, make towards the loss sustained by any individual of their number, whose property has been sacrificed for the common safety. The proportion which the value of the property so sacrificed bears to the entire value of the whole ship, cargo, and freight, including what has been sacrificed, is first ascertained. Then the property of each owner contributes in the proportion so found. Under the usual marine insurance policies the underwriters are liable for these payments made by the assured (see Marine Insurance Act 1906, s 66).

2 *Particular average*, as distinguished from general average, is a loss of the ship, cargo, or freight, severally, to be borne by the owner of the particular property on which it happens. In cases where the loss is not total, it is called *average* or *partial* loss. In every case of partial loss the underwriter is liable to pay such proportion of the sum he has subscribed as the damage sustained by the subject of insurance bears to the whole value at the time of insurance (see Marine Insurance Act 1906, ss 69–71).

Average clause. A clause in an insurance policy stating that if at the time of the loss the sum insured is less than the value of the subject-matter of insurance, the assured is to be regarded as his own insurer for the difference and is to bear a rateable proportion of the loss accordingly.

Averment (Lat *Verificatio*) has various meanings:

1 A positive statement of facts as opposed to an argumentative or inferential one.

2 The technical name (in pleading) for allegations, such as occur in declarations on contracts, of the due performance of all the conditions precedent, which the form and effect of each contract show to be necessary.

Avoidance. 1 A vacancy; especially of the vacancy of a living by the death of the incumbent.

2 Destroying the effect of a written instrument, or of any disposition in it.

3 Avoidance of tax, which is permissible if done legally: as opposed to *evasion* of tax.

Avulsion. The sudden removal of soil from the land of one person, and its deposit on the land of another, by the action of water. The soil in such a case belongs to the owner from whose land it is removed.

Award. The decision of an arbitrator. *See* ARBITRATION.

Away-going crop. A crop sown during the last year of tenancy, but not ripe till after its expiration. The out-going tenant is generally entitled to compensation either by the express terms of his contract or by the custom of the country or in accordance with the Agricultural Holdings Act 1986, s 65, Sch 8. *See* EMBLEMENTS.

B

B. A baron, ie a Judge of the Court of
Exchequer.
See BARON, 2.

BBC. The BRITISH BROADCASTING CORPORATION.

Back freight. Freight consisting of expenses
claimed by the shipowner from the cargo
owner where the master is unable to deliver
the goods to the consignee because, eg, the
consignee refuses to take delivery, and the
master deals with the goods as he thinks fit for
the benefit of the shipowner and may even take
them back to the port of loading (see *Cargo ex
Argos, Gaudet v Brown* (1873) LR 5 PC 134).

Backing a warrant. The indorsement by
a justice of the peace, in one county or
jurisdiction of a warrant issued in another.
Now unnecessary. A warrant 'backed for bail'
entitled the police, having arrested the person
accused, to release him on bail.

Bad (in substance). The technical word for an
unsound plea.

Bail (Fr *Bailler*, to deliver). The freeing or setting
at liberty one arrested or imprisoned, on
others becoming sureties by recognisance for
his appearance at a day and place certainly
assigned, he also entering into his own
recognisance. The party is delivered (or
bailed) into the hands of the sureties, and is
accounted by law to be in their custody.

They may, if they like, surrender him to
the Court before the date assigned and free
themselves from further responsibility. Under
the Magistrates' Courts Act 1980, justices
are empowered to grant bail with or without
sureties (see Bail Act 1976).

Bailable offence. An offence for which justices
may or are bound to take bail. *Stone.*

Bailee. A person to whom goods are entrusted
by way of bailment.
See BAILMENT.

Bailiff (Lat *Baillivus*). **1** An officer, appointed
to execute writs and processes of the court,
and to do other ministerial acts.

2 In Guernsey, a judge of the Royal Court is
styled 'Bailiff'.

Bailiff-errant. A bailiff's deputy.

Bailment. A delivery of goods by one person,
called the *bailor*, to another person, called
the *bailee*, for some purpose, under an
agreement, express or implied, either for
CONSIDERATION or GRATUITOUSLY that, after
the purpose has been fulfilled, they shall be
redelivered to the bailor, or otherwise dealt
with according to his directions, or kept until
he reclaims them.

Bailments are of six kinds:
 (i) the bare deposit of goods with another,
for the exclusive use of the bailor.
 (ii) the lending of goods for the use or
convenience of the bailee.
 (iii) the placing of goods with the bailee on
hire.
 (iv) the pawning or pledging of goods.
 (v) the delivery of goods to a carrier to a
person who is to carry out some services
in respect of them for payment.
 (vi) similar to the last, but where the carriage
or services are to be gratuitous.

Bailor. A person who entrusts goods to another
by way of bailment.
See BAILMENT.

Ballot, vote by. A method of secret voting, so
called from the fact that originally voting for
or against was made by placing a white or
black 'ball' in a box. This method of voting is
regulated by the Representation of the People
Acts.

Bank credit. Accommodation allowed to a
person on security given to a bank to draw on
the bank up to a certain amount agreed on.

Bank-note. A promissory note issued by a bank, undertaking to pay to the bearer on demand the amount of the note.
See MONEY; LEGAL TENDER.

Bankruptcy. A debtor, who by reason of some act or circumstance indicating a failure to meet his liabilities may be adjudged a 'bankrupt' by the High Court or by a County Court exercising bankruptcy jurisdiction. Proceedings are commenced by the presentation of a bankruptcy petition by a creditor or by the debtor himself. The Court may then make a bankruptcy order. The bankruptcy order continues until the bankrupt is discharged. On the making of the order the bankrupt's estate vests in his trustee in bankruptcy or, in the case of the Official Receiver, on his becoming trustee. There are restrictions on a bankrupt disposing of his property. The duties of the trustee in bankruptcy are to acquire, control, realise, and distribute the bankrupt's estate among his creditors. Bankruptcy is regulated by the Insolvency Act 1986 as amended.

Banneret, or **Knight banneret** (Lat *Miles vexillarius*). A knight made in the field, with the ceremony of cutting off the point of his standard, and making it, as it were, a banner; and accounted so honourable that if created in the King's presence, he ranked next to a baron and before a baronet.
See BARON; BARONET.

Banns. The publishing of matrimonial contracts in church before marriage. They must be published on three Sundays before the solemnisation of the wedding, in the parish (or each of the parishes) where the parties to be married reside. They must be published in an audible manner and in accordance with the form prescribed in the rubric prefixed to the office of matrimony in the Book of Common Prayer. Banns may also be published by the chaplain or captain or commanding officer of one of Her Majesty's ships at sea (see Marriage Act 1949, ss 6–14).

Bar. A term used in several senses:
1 Of the place where prisoners stand to be tried; hence the expression 'prisoner at the bar'.
2 Of the place where barristers stand in court to speak for their clients; hence, the term *barristers*.
3 Of the profession of a barrister, and the person who practises it.

4 A legal impediment, eg a near blood relationshop is a bar to marriage; the expiration of a limitation period bars a claim or action.

Bar Council (The General Council of the Bar). A committee of barristers established in 1894. The members are partly elected and partly co-opted. The duty of the Council is to protect the interests and etiquette of the Bar.

Bar of the House. The place at which witnesses before either House of Parliament are examined, and to which persons guilty of a breach of privilege are brought to receive judgment.

Bare (or mere) licencee. One whose presence on land is merely tolerated or permitted by the owner; an invitee. Such a person must quit the land as soon as practicably possible upon the owner withdrawing permission.

Bare trust. A trust under which the TRUSTEE, called a bare trustee, has no duty to perform other than, on request, to transfer the legal trust property to the BENEFICIARY or deal with it according to the latter's direction.
See TRUST.

Bargain and sale. Traditional form of transfer of land for valuable consideration, in which the contract (the bargain) is first agreed, and then on some later date the transfer of title to the buyer and the purchase price to the seller (the sale) takes place, hence 'bargain and sale'. Also called 'contract and conveyance'.

Barnard's Inn. *See* INNS OF CHANCERY.

Baron has the following meanings:
1 A degree of nobility next to a viscount. Barons hold (i) by prescription, (ii) by patent. Includes a life peer under the Life Peerages Act 1958.
2 A judge of the Court of Exchequer. These judges were superseded by justices of the Queen's Bench Division, under the Judicature Acts.

Baronet (Lat *Baronettus*). A dignity or degree of honour created by letters patent and descendible to issue male, with precedency before bannerets, knights of the bath, and knights bachelors, excepting only such bannerets as are made *sub vexillis regis in aperto bello, et ipso rege personaliter praesente*.
See BANNERET.
This order was created by James I in 1611.

Barony. The honour and territory which give title to a baron.

Barrator, or Barretor. 1 A deceiver, a vile knave or unthrift.

2 A person guilty of barratry.

See BARRATRY.

Barratry. 1 Barratry, or common barratry, was the common law offence of habitually or frequently inciting or stirring up suits and quarrels, in particular so as to lead to the initiation or continuation of legal proceedings. Abolished by the Criminal Law Act 1967.

2 Any wilfully wrongful or fraudulent act committed by the master of a ship or the crew, causing damage to the ship or cargo, to which the owner is not a consenting party.

3 It is also applied to the simony of clergymen going abroad to purchase benefices from the see of Rome.

See SIMONY.

Barring of/the entail. *See* ENTAIL.

Barrister. A person called to the bar by the benchers of the Inns of Court. Formerly, barristers had exclusive right of audience in the Supreme Court except in bankruptcy; now solicitors may also acquire such right of audience.

See SOLICITOR.

Base fee. *See* FINE, 3.

Basilica. A body of law framed in AD 880 by the Emperor Basilius.

Bastard, in English law, is one who is born of parents not legally married.

Bath, knight of the. *See* KNIGHT, 3.

Battery. A violent striking or beating of any person. In law this includes any touching or laying hold of another, however slight.

See ASSAULT.

Bawdy house. *See* BROTHEL.

Bearer. Money payable under a cheque or security may be expressed to be payable to a certain person or bearer, in which case anyone who presents the cheque or security may claim payment, and, in case of transfer, endorsement will not be necessary.

Begin, right to. *See* RIGHT TO BEGIN.

Bench. A word often used with reference to judges and magistrates; thus, 'judges on the bench', 'the judicial bench', 'a bench of magistrates'. Also the bishops of the Episcopal bench.

Bench warrant. A warrant issued by the presiding judicial officer of a court for the apprehension of an offender; so called in opposition to a justice's warrant, issued by a justice of the peace or stipendiary magistrate.

Benchers. Principal officers of each Inn of Court, in whom the government of the Inn is vested.

See INNS OF COURT.

Benefice. An ecclesiastical living of a parish (see Benefices Act 1898).

Beneficial interest. A right of substantial enjoyment or interest, as opposed to merely nominal ownership or interest. Thus if A holds lands in trust for B, A holds the legal title, and B, who is called the BENEFICIARY or CESTUI QUE TRUST, holds the equitable title or equitable interest. Because, under the rules of trust law, the trustee must hold his legal title to secure the benefits of the property to the beneficiary (or beneficiaries) under the terms of the trust, the beneficiary is said to have the beneficial interest or beneficial title in the property. Where, however, A holds the legal title to property for his own benefit, ie not as a trustee for anyone else, A is said to have a beneficial legal interest or title in the property.

See EQUITY.

Beneficial occupation. Occupation of land which is to the benefit of the occupier. The word 'beneficial' does not connote pecuniary profit, but means 'to the advantage of'.

Beneficiary. 1 Generally, one who benefits from a circumstance or legal arrangement. Thus a third-party beneficiary of a contract is one who, though not a party to a contract, benefits from the performance of it.

2 The modern term used in place of CESTUI QUE TRUST, ie a person for whom trust property is held, having rights against the TRUSTEE to enforce the trust, ie ensure that the trustee carries out the trust according to its terms.

See BENEFICIAL INTEREST; TRUST.

3 The person in possession of a benefice.

See BENEFICE.

Benelux. *See* EUROPEAN COMMUNITY.

Benevolent society. *See* FRIENDLY SOCIETY.

Bequeath. To dispose of personal property by will. In reference to real property the word 'devise' is generally used.

See DEVISE.

Bequest. A disposition by will of personal property; a legacy.

Berne Convention for the Protection of Literary and Artistic Work. An international convention giving copyright protection in all countries which are signatories to it. Ratified by the United Kingdom and given effect to by the Copyright, Designs and Patents Act 1988. *See* COPYRIGHT.

Berth note. A form of contract used by shipbrokers by which the broker notifies the shipowner that his ship has been engaged to carry a specified cargo.

Bestiality. The crime of having carnal intercourse with beasts.

Bet. A wager, under which money or money's worth is made payable on the result of some future uncertain event. A betting contract, though not illegal, is void at law, binding in honour only. Money paid in satisfaction of a betting contract is, however, irrecoverable at law: see Gaming Act 1845, s 18 (see Betting, Gaming and Lotteries Acts 1963 to 1971). Bets or wagers are to be distinguished from (i) contracts of insurance, in which an assured, though he will be paid upon the occurrence of some uncertain future event, such as the burning down of his house, is regarded as being indemnified for a loss—in view of the possibility of that loss he is regarded as having an INSURABLE INTEREST; and (ii) investments, although the value of and profits accruing from particular investments may vary.

Better equity. Where A has, in the contemplation of a court of equity, a superior claim to land or other property than B has, he is said to have a *better equity*. Thus, a second mortgagee, advancing his money without knowledge of a prior mortgage, has a better equity than the first mortgagee who has not secured for himself the possession of the title deeds, or has parted with them, so as to enable the mortgagor to secure the second advance as upon an unencumbered estate. After 1925 the priority of all mortgages depends on registration except where the mortgage is protected by a deposit of title deeds, in which case the mortgage has the priority given by the old law (see Law of Property Act 1925, s 97). *See* MORTGAGE.

Bid. To offer a price for a thing which is being sold. May be withdrawn before acceptance except where under SEAL.

Bigamy (Lat *Bigamia*). The offence of marrying a second time, by one who has a former husband or wife still living and not divorced (see Offences Against the Person Act 1861, s 57).

Bilateral contract. One in which the parties are under an obligation reciprocally towards each other, eg sale, where one party becomes bound to deliver the thing sold and the other to pay the price. *See* UNILATERAL CONTRACT.

Bill. This word has several meanings:
1 An account delivered by a creditor to his debtor in respect of goods supplied or work done. Thus, a *bill of costs* is a bill furnished by a solicitor to his client, as to which see the Solicitors Act 1974.
2 Bill in Parliament. A measure submitted to either House of Parliament for the purpose of being passed into law. When a measure has been actually passed into law, it is called an 'Act'.

Bills are divided into public and private bills. It may be laid down generally (though not without exception) that bills for the particular interest or benefit of any person or persons, of a company or corporation, a parish, a city, a county, or other locality, are treated as *private bills,* to be distinguished from measures in which the whole community is interested, which are called *public bills.*

Bill of costs. *See* BILL, 1.

Bill of entry. An account of the goods entered at the custom house both inwards and outwards. It must state the name of the merchant, the quantity and kind of the goods, etc.

Bill of exchange. Bills of exchange are written documents which facilitate dealing with credit, the payment of debts, etc. A bill of exchange is defined by the Bills of Exchange Act 1882, s 1 as an unconditional order in writing, addressed by one person (the drawer) to another (the drawee, and afterwards acceptor), signed by the person giving it, requiring the person to whom it is addressed to pay on demand, or at a fixed or determinable future time, a sum certain in money to, or to the order of, a payee, who is either a specified person, or the bearer of (anyone who possesses) the bill. For example, a cheque is an unconditional order by a person (the drawer) to a banker (the drawee) to pay money; the bank

'accepts' the cheque when it honours the order and makes payment, to the payee, generally a third party. The bank will accept the order embodied in the cheque in view of its pre-existing contractual relationship with the drawer, usually the contractual relationship whereby the drawer maintains a current account with the bank providing the drawer with a cheque-writing facility. Bills of exchange are typically negotiable instruments, though by various forms of writing and marking (ie by 'crossing' cheques) their negotiability can be curtailed.
See CHEQUE; NEGOTIABLE INSTRUMENT.

Bill of health. A certificate, signed by a consul and given to the ship's master on leaving a port, showing the sanitary condition of the port at the time the ship sailed. It may be clean, suspected (or touched), or foul.

Bill of lading. A mode of authenticating the transfer of property in goods sent by ship. It is, in form, a receipt from the captain given to the shipper or consignor, undertaking to deliver the goods, on payment of the freight, to some person whose name is expressed in it, or INDORSED on it by the consignor. The delivery of this instrument will transfer to the party so named (usually called the consignee), or to any other person whose name is indorsed thereon, the property in the goods. It is thus used both as a contract for carriage and as a document of title (see Carriage of Goods by Sea Act 1971 and Carriage of Goods by Sea Act 1992). Although a document of title that can be transferred by endorsement and delivery, so that a holder to whom it has been indorsed (a 'transferee') can demand the goods on payment of freight, and can sue upon it where this demand is not met, it is not a NEGOTIABLE INSTRUMENT, so a transferee can have no better title to the goods than had the transferor who indorsed it.

Bill of Rights. A declaration delivered by the Lords and Commons to the Prince and Princess of Orange, 13th February, 1688, and afterwards enacted by Parliament, when they became King and Queen. It declared illegal certain acts of the late King James II, and insisted on the rights and liberties asserted in it as being the 'true, ancient, and indubitable rights of the people of this kindgom'.

Bill of sale. An assignment under seal of chattels personal, ie a DEED by which title to chattels is transferred without a transfer of possession. The Bills of Sale Act 1878 applies now only to absolute bills of sale, eg, a transfer where the donor remains in possession, but the retention of possession is not to secure the payment of a debt, in which case the bill of sale is one 'by way of mortgage'. The Bills of Sale (1878) Amendment Act 1882 applies to every bill of sale by way of mortgage. Both classes must be registered within seven days and re-registered every five years, and those under the Act of 1882 must set out the consideration for which it was made, and must not be for less than £30 or they will be void. The Act of 1882 also makes void every bill of sale unless it is made in a form scheduled to the Act. See also Bills of Sale Acts 1890, 1891; also Law of Property Act 1925, s 189(1), which provides that a power of distress given by way of indemnity against a rent payable in respect of any land, or against the breach of any covenant or condition in relation to land, is not a bill of sale within the meaning of the above Acts.

Bill of sight. A document furnished to the customs officer by an importer of goods, who, being ignorant of their precise quality and quantity, describes them to the best of his knowledge and information (see Customs and Excise Management Act 1979, s 38).

Bill of sufferance. A licence granted at the custom-house to a merchant, to allow him to trade from one English port to another without paying customs duty.

Billeting. The quartering of members of Her Majesty's forces in inns, hotels, and other dwellings. Statutory provision for billeting in times of emergency is made in Part IV of the Army Act 1955, the relevant sections dealing, among other matters, with the provision of billets, payment for accommodation, appeals against billeting, etc.

Bind over. To order a person to enter into a recognisance, binding himself under a penalty to do some particular act, eg, on being granted bail, to appear and stand his trial at a later date; or to abstain from committing some offence, eg causing a breach of the peace (see Magistrates' Courts Act 1980, s 7).
See RECOGNISANCE.

Bi-partite. Of two parts.

Bishop. The principal officer of the Church in each diocese. All Church of England bishops are to be chosen by a Crown Appointments Commission, which makes nominations for presentation to the Prime Minister and appointment by the Queen. A *suffragan* bishop is a deputy or assistant bishop in spiritual matters, a *coadjutor* in temporal matters.

Bishop's court. The consistory court in each diocese, held under the authority of the bishop, by his chancellor.

Bissextile, commonly called Leap-year, every fourth year. It is called bissextile because formerly, in each such year, the *sixth* day before the calends of March was *twice* reckoned, viz, on the 24th and 25th February. By a statute of Henry III these days were, in each leap-year, to be counted one day, and the extra day in leap-year is now added to the end of February and called the 29th.

Blackacre. A fictitious piece of land, used as an example in much legal discourse.

Blackmail. The attempt to extract money by threatening letters or threats to accuse of crime. It is defined by the Theft Act 1968, s 21(1) as follows: 'A person is guilty of blackmail if, with a view to gain for himself or another or with intent to cause loss to another, he makes any unwarranted demand with menaces; and for this purpose a demand with menaces is unwarranted unless the person making it does so in the belief (i) that he has reasonable grounds for making the demand; and (ii) that the use of the menaces is a proper means of reinforcing the demand.'

Black Rod. The usher belonging to the most noble order of the Garter; so called because of the black rod he carries in his hand. He is also usher of the House of Lords. He is also called the *gentleman usher*, as opposed to his deputy, who is called the *yeoman usher*. He is appointed by letters patent from the Crown. He executes the orders of the House, for the commitment of parties guilty of breaches of privilege and of contempt, and assists at the introduction of peers, and other ceremonies.

Blackstone, Sir William (1723–1780). English jurist and judge, first Vinerian professor of law at Oxford, and author of the famous *Commentaries on the Laws of England.*

Blank acceptance. An acceptance written on blank stamped paper, and acting as a *prima facie* authority by the acceptor to complete a bill of exchange for any amount the stamp will cover (see Bills of Exchange Act 1882, s 20).
See ACCEPTANCE OF A BILL.

Blank indorsement. *See* INDORSEMENT.

Blank transfer. A transfer form relating to shares without the name of the transferee being inserted.

Blasphemy. Denying in some scandalous way the being or providence of the Almighty, or contumelious reproaches of our Saviour Jesus Christ; also all profane scoffing at the Holy Scripture, or exposing it to contempt and ridicule.

Blight notice. A notice served by a person requiring the appropriate public authority to purchase blighted land: Town and Country Planning Act 1990, s 149(5).
See BLIGHTED LAND.

Blighted land. Land disadvantageously affected by planning proposals of public authorities: Town and Country Planning Act 1990, s 149(1).

Blockade. An operation of war by which one of the belligerents is able so to apply his force to one of the enemy's ports or coastlines as to render it dangerous to attempt to enter or leave. A blockade to be binding must be effective. A party violating it must be proved to have been aware of its existence. Any attempt on the part of a neutral ship to enter or leave a blockaded place with goods or forbidden information is deemed a breach of blockade, and exposes her to seizure and confiscation.

Blue chips. Shares in well established and regarded public companies.

Board. A body of persons having delegated to them certain powers of central government, or set up for the purposes of local government, or elected as directors by the shareholders in a company.

Board of Trade. A committee of the Privy Council, charged with the consideration of matters relating to trade and industry which were not dealt with by other departments and other matters of a miscellaneous character. In practice, the Board never meets and is an administrative Government department presided over by a President.

The functions of the Board of Trade are now exercised by the Secretary of State for Trade and Industry.

Body of an instrument. The main and operative part, as opposed to the recitals, etc, in a deed, to the title and jurat in an affidavit.

See RECITAL; JURAT.

Bona fides. Good faith, without fraud or deceit. Eg a *bona fide* holder of a bill of exchange or other security is one without knowledge of any defect in title (see the Bills of Exchange Act 1882, s 29).

See NEGOTIABLE INSTRUMENT; BILL OF EXCHANGE.

Bona fide purchaser. Common abbreviation of '*bona fide* purchaser for value of a legal interest without notice, actual, imputed, or constructive, of an equitable interest'. Also known as 'equity's darling'. In general, a person who gives valuable CONSIDERATION for a legal title, or a legal interest in property, such as a legal mortgage over land, will take that title or interest free of any pre-existing equitable interests in the property, so long as he was, at the time of the sale, actually unaware of such interests, and had no constructive notice of them, ie knowledge of them he would have acquired through diligent investigation of his seller's title prior to sale, and no imputed notice of them, ie the actual or constructive notice of them of any agent acting for him in the transaction (eg a solicitor). Thus the owner of this unnoticed equitable interest will not be able to enforce his prior rights in the property against this purchaser. By contrast, a purchaser will be bound to give effect to any pre-existing legal interests in the property. This regime of notice, by which interests in property are protected or may be lost in the course of transactions with the property, is now largely obsolete with respect to transactions with land, having been replaced by a system under which interests and titles to land are protected by registration in public registers. However, with respect to personal property held on trust this rule of bona fide purchase, sometimes called the 'doctrine of notice', continues to operate.

See EQUITY LAND LAW, REGISTRATION OF TITLE, LAND CHARGES.

Bona vacantia. 1 Goods found without any apparent owner. They belong to the first occupant or finder, unless they are royal fish, shipwrecks, treasure trove, waifs and estrays, which belong to the Crown.

See FISH ROYAL; TREASURE TROVE; ESTRAYS.

2 Under the rules for the division of real and personal estate on intestacy which are contained in the Administration of Estates Act 1925, the residuary estate belongs (in default of certain relatives specified in the Act) as *bona vacantia* to the Crown or to the Duchy of Lancaster or the Duke of Cornwall (as the case may be).

3 Under the Companies Act 1985, s 654(1), certain property of dissolved companies.

Bond. An instrument under SEAL, whereby a person binds himself to do or not to do certain things; this is a *single* bond. The person so binding himself is called the *obligor*. The person to whom he is bound, who is entitled to enforce the bond, is called the *obligee*. In some cases the obligor binds himself to pay a certain sum, called a *penal sum* or *penalty*, to which a condition is added, that, if he does or does not do a particular act (ie, if he complies with the conditions which the bond is intended to secure), the bond shall be void, otherwise it is to be of full force and effect. This is a *double* bond. The obligee, however, cannot recover the whole penalty, but only the actual loss proved to have been suffered.

Bonds are frequently issued by governments and companies as security for money borrowed by them.

See SEAL; DEED.

Bond creditor. A creditor whose debt is secured by a bond.

See BOND.

Bonded goods. Imported goods deposited in a government warehouse until the duty on them is paid.

Bonus. A sum added to that insured under a policy accruing after the policy has been in force for a specified period (see *Prudential Insurance Co Ltd v IRC* [1904] 2 KB 658 (per Channell, J)).

Bonus share. A share given by the company free to a shareholder, usually in proportion to his present shareholding, eg one bonus share for every share at present held by him.

Book of Common Prayer. The book prescribed by the Act of Uniformity 1662, constituting the standard of faith, worship, and discipline in the Church of England (see Church of England (Worship and Doctrine) Measure 1974, s 1(1)).

Bookmaker. Any person who, whether on his own account or as servant or agent to any other person, carries on, whether occasionally or regularly, the business of receiving or negotiating bets or conducting pool betting operations. See Finance Act 2004, s 15.

Booty of war. Prize of war on land, as opposed to prize at sea. It belongs by right to the Crown, but was at one time usually given to the captors.

Borough. As used in the Reform Act 1832 the term 'borough' meant a town entitled to send a member to Parliament, or 'parliamentary borough', and in the Municipal Corporations Act 1882 a town incorporated for the purposes of internal government, or 'municipal borough'. A town or city which was granted a charter of incorporation became known as a borough, the corporation consisting of a mayor, aldermen, and councillors. Under the reorganisation of local government areas, boroughs existing before 1st April 1974 ceased to exist (though the London boroughs were maintained) (see Local Government Act 1972, s 20(6)). Their rights and privileges were preserved, however, by Part XII of the Act of 1972, under which the status of borough may also be conferred on certain districts.

Borstal, Borstal institution. Formerly, name given to a place in which offenders not less than 16 but under 21 years of age were detained and given training and instruction conducive to their reformation and the prevention of crime (see Prison Act 1952, s 43).

Bote, Bot. Ancient law relating primarily to rights necessary for husbandry on land, eg house-bote, a sufficient allowance of wood from the estate to maintain a house in repair; fire-bote, a sufficient allowance of wood for fuel; hedge-bote, wood to repair hedges, etc.

Bottomry, Bottomry bond. A maritime bond in the nature of a mortgage of a ship, when the owner borrows money to enable him to carry on his voyage, and pledges the keel or bottom of the ship as a security for the repayment. If the ship is lost, the lender loses the whole of his money; but, if she returns safely, then he receives back his principal, and also the premium or interest agreed on.
See RESPONDENTIA.

Bought and sold notes. Copies of entries and memoranda made by brokers of their transactions in buying and selling stock, or shares, and delivered to the sellers and purchasers for whom they act. The copy of any such entry, delivered to the purchaser, is called the *bought* note; the copy delivered to the seller is called the *sold* note.

Boundary Commission. A Commission whose purpose is to keep the distribution of seats at Parliamentary elections under continuous review (see Parliamentary Constituencies Act 1986, s 2(1)). There are separate Commissions for England, Scotland, Wales, and Northern Ireland (see ibid, s 2(1)). For their constitution, see ibid, Sch 1. See further, Boundary Commissions Act 1992, which makes additional provision for the members of the Commission and the time limits for the submission of their reports.

Bracton. A famous lawyer in the reign of Henry III, renowned for his knowledge both of the Common and Civil Law. He wrote a celebrated book, *De Legibus et Consuietudinibus Angliae* (Concerning the Laws and Customs of England).

Breach. An invasion of a right or violation of a duty. The word is specially used in the following expressions:
1 *Breach of covenant or contract.* A non-fulfilment of a covenant or contract.
2 *Breach of the peace.* A disturbance of the public peace.
3 *Breach of pound.* Taking by force, out of a pound, things lawfully impounded.
4 *Breach of prison.* The escape from arrest of a person lawfully arrested for a crime.
5 *Breach of privilege.* An act or default in violation of the privilege of either House of Parliament, eg by false swearing before a committee of the House, or by resisting its officers in the execution of their duty.
6 *Breach of promise (of marriage).* Failure to fulfil a promise to marry. Formerly gave rise to an action for breach of promise (abolished Law Reform (Miscellaneous Provisions) Act 1970, s 1.
7 *Breach of trust.* A violation by a trustee of the duty imposed on him by the instrument creating the trust.

Break clause. A provision in a fixed-term lease giving the option of terminating the lease prior to the end of the full term.

Breakdown of marriage. The sole ground for a petition for divorce is no longer that of a specific matrimonial offence, as eg adultery, but is that of the irretrievable breakdown of the marriage. Breakdown may be *proved* by

evidence of adultery, desertion, unreasonable behaviour, or the fact that the parties have lived apart for a number of years (see Matrimonial Causes Act 1973, s 1).
See DIVORCE.

Bribery. The taking or giving of money for the performance or non-performance of a public duty.

By the Representation of the People Act 1983, s 113 a person is guilty of bribery if he gives money or procures any office in order to induce a voter to vote or refrain from voting, etc. Bribery is a corrupt practice under the Act.

See also Prevention of Corruption Acts 1889 to 1916; Honours (Prevention of Abuses) Act 1925, under which any person who attempts to obtain a grant of honours by the provision of gifts or money is guilty of an offence.

Brief. A statement of a client's case written out by the solicitor for the instruction of counsel in a civil or criminal proceeding.

Britannia. A description of silver of a standard of fineness of 958.4 parts per 1000 (see Hallmarking Act 1973, Sch 2).

British Broadcasting Corporation. A corporation incorporated by Royal Charter in 1926, and operating under a licence from the Secretary of State.

British citizenship. A person born in the United Kingdom is a British citizen if at the time of the birth his father or mother is (i) a British citizen; or (ii) settled in the United Kingdom (see British Nationality Act 1981, s 1(1)).

British citizenship may also be acquired by adoption, descent, registration, and naturalisation (see ibid, ss 1–6). British citizenship may be renounced (see ibid, s 12). It may also be resumed (see ibid, s 13).

British Dependent Territories citizenship. A person born in a dependent territory is a British Dependent Territories citizen if at the time of the birth his father or mother is (i) a British Dependent Territories citizen; or (ii) settled in a dependent territory (see British Nationality Act 1981, s 15(1)).

Such citizenship may also be acquired by adoption, descent, registration, and naturalisation (see ibid, ss 15–18). It may be renounced or resumed (see ibid, s 24).

British Islands unless the contrary intention appears, means the United Kingdom, the Channel Islands, and the Isle of Man (see Interpretation Act 1978, s 5, Sch 1).
See UNITED KINGDOM.

British Library. A national library formed by bringing together four libraries: (i) the British Museum Library (including the National Reference Library for Science and Invention); (ii) the National Central Library; (iii) the National Lending Library for Science and Technology; and (iv) the British National Bibliography. It is under the control and management of 'The British Library Board' (see British Library Act 1972, s 1(2)) and consists of a comprehensive collection of books, manuscripts, periodicals, films, and other recorded matter whether printed or otherwise.

British Overseas citizenship. Any person who was a citizen of the United Kingdom and Colonies at the commencement of the British Nationality Act 1981 and who does not become either a British citizen or a British Dependent Territories citizen becomes a British Overseas citizen (see British Nationality Act 1981, s 26). Such citizenship may be renounced (see ibid, s 29).
See BRITISH CITIZENSHIP; BRITISH DEPENDENT TERRITORIES CITIZENSHIP.

British subject. A person who has the status of a Commonwealth citizen under the British Nationality Act 1981 (see British Nationality Act 1981, s 51(1)(b)).

Britton. A famous treatise of the reign of Edward I, at whose command it was apparently written; founded on Bracton and Fleta.
See BRACTON; FLETA.

Brocage, or **Brokerage.** The wages or hire of a *broker*. Brokerage for procuring a marriage is contrary to public policy, and not recoverable.

Broker (from the French word *Broieur*). A grinder or breaker into small pieces; because he that is of that trade draws the bargain into particulars. Now usually an agent between the contracting parties in business transactions, paid by a commission, or brokerage.
See FACTOR; STOCKBROKER.

Broker's cover note. A note issued by a broker pending the preparation of the policy certifying that the insurance has been effected and setting out its terms. By issuing the cover note the broker does not incur liability on the insurance since he does not purport to be an insurer. If there is no insurance, in fact, he will be liable to the proposer for breach of duty.

Brothel. A place resorted to by persons of both sexes for prostitution, not a house occupied by one woman where she receives a number of men. By the Sexual Offences Act 1956, s 33 it is an offence for a person to keep or to manage or to assist in managing a brothel. Sections 34, 35 of the Act also make it an offence for a landlord to let premises for use as a brothel, or for a tenant to permit such use.

Budget. The financial statement of the national revenue and expenditure for each year, submitted to Parliament by the Chancellor of the Exchequer.

Building lease. A LEASE of land for a long term, usually ninety-nine years, at a rent called a ground rent, the lessee covenanting to build on it.

By the Law of Property Act 1925, s 99 either a mortgagor or mortgagee in possession can (in case of mortgage made after 1925) make a valid building lease for 999 years. Under the Settled Land Act 1925, s 41 a tenant for life may make a building lease for 999 years (see also ss 44 and 46 of that Act).

Building society. A society whose purpose or principal purpose is that of raising, primarily by the subscriptions of the members, a stock or fund for making to them advances secured on land for their residential use (see Building Societies Act 1986, s 5).

Bullion. The ore or metal of which gold is made. It signifies gold or silver in mass or billet.

Burden of proof (or *onus probandi*). The duty of proving one's case. It is a rule of evidence that the point in issue is to be proved by the party who asserts the affirmative, according to the maxim, *ei incumbit probatio qui dicit, non qui negat.*

Thus, in general, the burden of proof lies on the PLAINTIFF (CLAIMANT) or prosecutor. But he or she may adduce evidence sufficient to establish a *prima facie* case, and the burden of proof is then said to be *shifted* on to the other side, although this is not actually correct. By adducing sufficient evidence to establish a *prima facie* case, the trier of fact, either the judge or a jury, may properly decide in favour of the plaintiff unless evidence rebutting the plaintiff's evidence is presented by the defendant. Thus, while the burden

rests with the plaintiff, the presentation of a *prima facie* case makes imperative the presentation of evidence by the defendant, and in this sense only, he bears a (practical) burden of proof.

See RES IPSA LOQUITUR.

In criminal cases it is exceptional for the burden to rest on the defence. Even when it does, the burden is lighter than that which rests on the prosecution.

The burden of proof is to be distinguished from the *standard of proof*, ie the certainty with which the trier of fact concludes that the plaintiff's or prosecutor's evidence establishes the facts necessary for liability. In civil cases, the usual standard of proof is that the evidence must show that, *on the balance of probabilities*, the defendant is liable. The criminal standard is higher, ie the evidence must be more convincing: the evidence must show, *beyond any reasonable doubt*, that the defendant (or 'the accused') is guilty as charged.

Burglary. Section 9 of the Theft Act 1968 provides that a person is guilty of *burglary* if he enters any building or part of a building as a trespasser with intent to commit certain offences (eg stealing, inflicting grievous bodily harm, etc); or having so entered, commits or attempts to commit such offences. Penalty: imprisonment for up to fourteen years.

Furthermore, by s 10, a person is guilty of *aggravated burglary* if he commits any burglary and at the time has any firearm or imitation firearm, any weapon of offence, or any explosive. Penalty: liability to imprisonment for life.

Burial in some part of the parish churchyard is a Common Law right of all parishioners (and a moral right of strangers, *Kempe v Wickes* (1809) 3 Phil 265, 274).

Burial authorities are the councils of districts, London boroughs, parishes, the Common Council of the City of London, and the parish meetings of parishes having no parish council (see Local Government Act 1972, s 214).

Business name. A name used by a person in the course of his business.

Certain business names are prohibited eg if they are likely to give the impression that the business is connected with the Government or a local authority: Business Names Act 1985, s 2. Some words or expressions for use as part of a business name require the Secretary of State's approval: ibid, s 3.

Where a business name is used, the actual name of the person, company or partnership using it must be stated on all business letters and on invoices and receipts issued in the course of the business: ibid, s 4(1). A notice to the same effect must be displayed in a prominent position in any premises where the business is carried on: ibid, s 4(1).

Business tenancy. A tenancy of land used for the carrying-on of a trade, profession, or employment under which the tenant receives various protections under the Landlord and Tenant Act 1954 Part II.

See SECURITY OF TENURE.

By-laws, or **Byelaws.** Laws made by councils, boards, corporations, and companies, under powers conferred by Acts of Parliament, for the government of their members and the management of their business. And, independently of statutory powers, byelaws made by a corporation aggregate are binding on its members unless contrary to the law of the land, or contrary to and inconsistent with their charter, or manifestly unreasonable.

See CORPORATION.

The council of a district or of a London borough may make byelaws for the good rule and government of the whole or any part of the district or borough, and for the prevention and suppression of nuisances (see Local Government Act 1972, ss 235–238).

C

CA. COURT OF APPEAL.

CAA. CIVIL AVIATION AUTHORITY.

CAP. COMMON AGRICULTURAL POLICY.

CAV. CUR ADV VULT.

CB. CHIEF BARON.

CGT. CAPITAL GAINS TAX.

CIF. Cost, insurance, freight. A term describing a typical basis upon which the price in a shipping contract is determined. A price quoted 'cif' at a certain place usually includes everything up to delivery at the port or place of destination.
Cf FOB.

Cabinet. Those Privy Councillors who, under the name of cabinet ministers or cabinet council, actually transact the immediate business of the Government, and assemble for that purpose from time to time as the public exigencies require. The cabinet is a body first established by Charles I.

Cab-rank rule. The principle of impartiality which requires a practising barrister to accept any brief to appear in his professed area of expertise, as provided for in the *Code of Conduct for the Bar.*

Cadit quaestio. There is an end to the argument.

Calendar. *See* MONTH.

Call. 1 Instalments whereby the capital in companies is gradually paid up by the shareholders (see Companies Act 1985, s 8(1)).
2 The conferring on students of the degree of barrister.
3 The right to demand the allotment or transfer of shares at or before a given date at a given place.
See OPTION, 2.

Call of the House. The calling over the names of members in either House of Parliament, pursuant to a resolution of the House ordering the attendance of the members of it. The order may be enforced by fine and imprisonment.

Calling the jury. This consists in successively drawing out of a box, into which they have been previously put, the names of the jurors on the panels annexed to the record, and calling them over in the order in which they are so drawn. The twelve persons whose names are first called, and who appear, are sworn as the jury unless some just cause of challenge or excuse, with respect to any of them, is brought forward.
See CHALLENGE.

Calling upon a prisoner. When a prisoner has been found guilty on an indictment, the clerk of the Court calls on him to say why judgment should not be passed on him.
See INDICTMENT.

Calls on contributories. Demands made by a company, or its official liquidator, on persons liable to contribute to its assets.
See CONTRIBUTORY.

Camera. The judge's private room behind the Court.
See SITTINGS IN CAMERA.

Campbell's Acts. *See* LORD CAMPBELL'S ACTS.

Cancellation. The striking out or revocation of the contents of an instrument by drawing lines (*cancelli*) across it. Mere cancellation does not revoke a will.

Cancelling clause. A clause entitling a charterer to cancel the charter-party if the vessel is not ready to load at the port of loading by the date stated in a voyage charter-party (*see* CHARTER-PARTY), or is not delivered to the charterer at the date stated in a time charter-party.

Cancelling date. *See* CANCELLING CLAUSE.

Candlemas Day. The feast of the Purification of the Blessed Virgin Mary (2nd February), so called from the custom of blessing and distributing candles, of eleventh-century origin. A quarter day in Scotland.

Canon. 1 A cathedral dignitary, appointed sometimes by the Crown and sometimes by the bishop. The benefice attached to it is called a *canonry.*
See CHAPTER.
2 A law or ordinance of the Church.
3 In Civil Law a rule, eg, the canons of inheritance.

Canon Law. A body of Roman ecclesiastical law, compiled in the twelfth, thirteenth and fourteenth centuries, from the opinions of the ancient Latin fathers, the decrees of General Councils, and the decretal epistles and bulls of the Holy See, and first codified by Gratianus in 1139.

In 1603 certain canons were enacted by the clergy under James I. But, as they were never confirmed in Parliament, it has been held that, where they are not merely declaratory of the ancient canon law, but are introductory of new regulations, they do not bind the laity, whatever regard the clergy may think proper to pay them. They were revised again in 1865.

Cap of maintenance. One of the regalia or ornaments of State belonging to the Sovereign.

Capax doli. *See* DOLI CAPAX.

Capita, distribution per. A distribution of an intestate's estate, in which each claimant has a share in his own right as in equal degree of kindred to the deceased, and not as representing another person, ie, distribution *per stirpes.*
See STIRPES, DISTRIBUTION PER.

Capital. The net amount of property belonging to a merchant, after deducting the debts he owes. This term, however, is more strictly applied, either to the sum of money which he has invested in his business at first, or to the available sum he may afterwards have at his command for carrying it on.

Capital allowance. An allowance which may be made for the purpose of income tax and corporation tax in respect of capital expenditure in case of eg machinery and plant, ships, agricultural buildings. See Capital Allowances Act 1990.
See CORPORATION TAX; INCOME TAX.

Capital clause. A clause in a company's memorandum of association stating the amount of share capital with which the company proposes to be registered and the division of it into shares of a fixed amount.

Capital gains tax. Tax charged in respect of capital gains, that is, chargeable gains accruing to a person on the disposal of assets. Certain kinds of property are exempt. See Taxation of Chargeable Gains Tax Act 1992.

Capital messuage. *See* MANSION OR MANSION-HOUSE.

Capital punishment. Death by hanging. Abolished as a punishment for murder by the Murder (Abolition of Death Penalty) Act 1965. It remained a punishment for treason, piracy with violence, or setting fire to HM ships until abolished by the Crime and Disorder Act 1998, s 36.
See MURDER; PIRACY.

Capital transfer tax. Tax charged upon the transfer of assets, either by way of gift *inter vivos* or under a will. Roughly, a gift tax, chargeable to the donor. See, eg, Capital Transfer Tax Act 1984 (now abolished).

Capitation tax, fee, grant, etc, is one raised or paid on each individual or according to the *heads,* eg, for each child in a school.

Capitulary. A code of laws.

Caption. That part of a legal instrument, eg, of an indictment, which shows where, when, and by what authority it is taken, found, or executed.

Capture. A seizure; a word especially used with respect to the seizure of a ship or cargo, etc, at sea by a belligerent in time of war.

Carat. A description indicating that an article, or the metal in an article, is of so many carats, is to be presumed to be an indication that the article or metal is of gold, and that its fineness is that specified in the following table for that number of carats (not applicable if, as in a case where the article is a precious stone, the word 'carat' is used as a measure of weight for precious stones, and not as a measure of fineness).

Table 1	
Number of carats	Indicates gold of a standard of fineness of
9	375 parts per thousand
12	500 parts per thousand
14	585 parts per thousand
15	625 parts per thousand
18	750 parts per thousand
22	916.6 parts per thousand

and so in proportion for any other number of carats (see Hallmarking Act 1973, Sch 1, Part III, para 2).

See ASSAY; HALLMARK.

Care and supervision order. An order placing a child in the care of a designated local authority: Children Act 1989, s 31(1)(a).

Cargo. Goods and merchandise shipped for carriage by water.

Carrier. A person who carries goods for another for hire.

A *common carrier* is one who undertakes to carry goods for all persons indiscriminately. The law casts on the common carrier a duty (i) to carry for everyone who offers to pay his charges; (ii) to answer for everything carried as an insurer; this liability, however, is restricted by the Carriers Acts 1830 and 1865.

Carrier's lien. Common law right of a carrier to retain possession of goods carried until paid.

See LIEN.

Carry over. A term used on the Stock Exchange signifying the postponement of the completion of a contract to buy or sell shares.

See CONTANGO.

Carte blanche. A white sheet of paper; a phrase used especially to mean a paper given by one person to another with nothing on it except the signature of the former, so that the latter may fill it up at his discretion. Hence, the figurative expression, 'to give any one *carte blanche*', ie unlimited authority.

Cartel, or **Chartel. 1** An instrument executed between two belligerent powers for settling the exchange of prisoners of war and other like matters. Also a challenge to a duel to decide a legal controversy.

2 A combination of companies or businesses with the object of eliminating competition and so maintaining high prices for goods.

Legislation against cartel agreements, overriding the laws of Member States, is a feature of the European Economic Community legislation (see Competition Act 1980)

See EUROPEAN COMMUNITY.

Cartel ship. A ship employed in effecting the exchange of prisoners of war.

Case. A whole or entire proceeding at law from the initiation of proceedings to FINAL PROCESS concerning one substantial CAUSE OF ACTION giving rise to a claim for a REMEDY by a PLAINTIFF (or CLAIMANT) (or several acting together) against one or more DEFENDANTs. The term to be preferred in lawyerly use over 'action' following the CIVIL PROCEDURE ACT 1997 and CIVIL PROCEDURE RULES.

Case, action on the, or **trespass on the.**

See TRESPASS ON THE CASE; NEGLIGENCE.

Case Management Conference. A proceeding at an early stage of litigation under the CIVIL PROCEDURE RULES in which the court issues directions to the parties so as to efficiently manage the case, giving directions eg re production of witness statements, disclosure of documents, settling of issues. Replaces the proceeding under the old rules known as a summons for directions.

See DIRECTIONS, SUMMONS FOR.

Castigatory. *See* SCOLD.

Casting vote. The vote given by the chairman of a deliberative assembly, where the votes are equally divided.

Casus belli. An occurrence giving rise to or justifying or giving a pretext for war.

Casus omissus. A case inadvertently left unprovided for by a statute.

Catching bargain. A bargain which unfairly traps, or catches, another. By the Law of Property Act 1925, s 174, no acquisition made in good faith, without fraud or unfair dealing, of any reversionary interest in real or personal property, for money or money's worth, is liable to be opened or set aside merely on the ground of undervalue. Equity, however, retains its right to relieve an heir or reversioner from a 'catching bargain' in cases where the transaction is unconscionable.

Cathedral. The principal church of a diocese.

See DIOCESE.

Cattlegate. Common for one beast.

Cattle-grid. A device designed to prevent the passage of animals but to allow the passage of all or some other traffic: Highways Act 1980, s 82(6).

Causa causans. The immediate cause, the *causa proxima*, the last link in the chain of causation.

Causa mortis. *See* DONATIO MORTIS CAUSA.

Causa proxima et non remota spectatur. The immediate and not the remote cause is to be looked at.

Causation. One thing's causing another. The law's understanding of causation provides a basis for its determining that, eg, the defendant's act caused the plaintiff's injury. In particular, since different factors can work together to cause something, for a defendant's act or omission to act where he ought to have acted to have caused a plaintiff's injury his act or ommission must be a, or the, 'proximate', ie more or less direct, cause of the injury.

Cause. 1 A general term covering a SUIT or ACTION or CASE at law. *See* CASE; SUIT. (*Cf* CAUSE OF ACTION.)

2 That which produces or effects a result. *See* CAUSATION.

Cause book. The book or other record kept in the Central Office, Chancery Chambers, the Principal Registry of the Family Division, the Admiralty and Commercial Registry, and every district registry in which the letter and number of, and other details relating to, a cause or matter are entered.

Cause of action. The factual circumstances giving rise to a legal claim, ie a claim that can be pursued by an ACTION or SUIT. So, for example, one's being carelessly injured by another is the cause of action giving rise to a legal action for DAMAGES or NEGLIGENCE.

Cause-list. The printed list of causes made out for each day during the sittings of the courts; the causes being tried in the order of their entry.

Caution. 1 In ecclesiastical, admiralty, and Scots law, signifies *surety* or *security*. It is also called *cautionary*.

2 Under the Land Registration Acts 1925 to 1966 a person interested could place on the register a caution preventing the proprietor from dealing with the land without notice to the cautioner. Abolished by the Land Registration Act 2002 and replaced by 'unilateral notices'.
See LAND REGISTRATION; LAND LAW.

3 A warning to an accused person that any statement made by him may be used in evidence.

Caveat (let him beware). An intimation made to the proper officer of a court of justice to prevent the taking of any step without intimation to the party interested (caveator) to appear. See Supreme Court Act 1981, s 108 as to caveats against grants of probate or administration.

Caveat emptor (let the buyer beware). A maxim implying that the buyer must be cautious, as the risk is his and not that of the seller. If a person sells goods as his own, and the price is paid, and the *title* proves deficient, the seller may be compelled to refund the money. But for the *soundness* of the goods, the seller is not usually bound to answer; but there are several exceptions embodied in the Sale of Goods Act 1979, ss 13–15.
See SALE OF GOODS, CONTRACT FOR.

Censure. A condemnatory judgment, or, more especially, a reprimand from a superior.

Census. A numbering of the people, first taken in 1801 in England, and now taken every ten years. For particulars required to be given, see the Census Act 1920. It is an offence to disclose, without lawful authority, any census information which relates to an identifiable person or household: Census (Confidentiality) Act 1991, s 1.

Central Criminal Court. The court originally established by the Central Criminal Court Act 1834 (repealed) for the trial of offences committed in London, Middlesex, and certain parts of Essex, Kent, and Surrey.

The Courts Act 1971 provides that when the Crown Court sits in the City of London, it is to continue to be known as the Central Criminal Court. The former courthouse and accommodation also continue to be known by that name, or, colloquially, as the 'Old Bailey'.

Central Office of the Supreme Court consists of the following departments: (i) the Masters' Secretary's and Queen's Remembrancer's Department; (ii) the Action Department; (iii) the Filing and Record Department; (iv) the Crown Office and Associates' Department; and (v) the Supreme Court Taxing Office (see RSC 1965, Ord 63).

Certificate. A writing made in any court, to give notice to another court of anything done in it. *Cowel.*

Certificate, land. A certificate drawn up by the Land Registry and containing particulars of registered land, and delivered to the registered proprietor or deposited in the Registry as the proprietor may prefer. *See* LAND REGISTRATION.

Certificate, share. *See* SHARE CERTIFICATE.

Certificate of incorporation. A document signed by the Registrar of Companies showing that the company to which it relates has been formed.

On the registration of a company's memorandum, the Registrar must give a certificate that the company is incorporated and, in the case of a limited company, that it is limited (see Companies Act 1985, s 13(1), (2)). Where he registers a company's memorandum which states that the company is to be a public company, the certificate of incorporation must contain a statement that the company is a public company (see ibid, s 13(6)). *See* LIMITED COMPANY; PUBLIC COMPANY.

Certificate of insurance. A certificate stating that in accordance with an authorisation granted to the person signing the certificate the insurers are liable to the insured, subject to the terms and conditions stated in it.

Certification of transfer. A certification indorsed on a transfer form showing that a share certificate has been lodged with a company representing more shares than the transferor wants to transfer.

Certified cheque. *See* CHEQUE.

Certified copy. One signed and certified as true by the official in whose custody the original is.

Certiorari (to be more fully informed of). An order commanding proceedings to be removed from an inferior court into a superior court for review. *See* ADMINISTRATIVE LAW.

Certum est quod certum reddi potest (Id certum est quod potest reddi certum) (that is certain which can be easily rendered certain). The law imposes requirements of certainty upon the terms of various transactions in order for those transactions to be valid, eg terms of contracts, of trusts, of leases, and so on. However this does not entail that all aspects of a transaction must be known in their particulars from the outset; it is sufficient that all necessary particulars will be certain when it is essential that they are known. For example, an *income* BENEFICIARY under a TRUST is entitled to be paid income on the trust property; nevertheless that the amount of income on property is not known in advance before it arises (eg the exact value of dividends on shares before they are declared, etc) does not make the trust void for uncertainty of subject matter (uncertainty about the property which is the subject of the trust), because the income will be known exactly when it arises and must be paid to the beneficiary.

Cessante ratione legis, cessat ipse lex. Where the reasoning behind a law ceases to exist, the law itself ceases to exist.

Cesser. The ceasing or termination, in particular of a legal right, obligation, or property interest upon the happening of some event or the end of some stipulated period of time.

Cestui que trust. The person for whose benefit property is held on trust; the person entitled to the equitable, as opposed to the legal, estate. Thus, if land is granted to A in trust for B, B is the *cestui que trust* and A is the trustee. *See* TRUST; BENEFICIARY; EQUITY.

Cestui que use. The person for whose benefit property was held 'on use', the use being the forerunner of the trust. *See* USE; TRUST; BENEFICIARY; EQUITY.

Cestui que vie. The person for whose life any land is granted. Thus, if A is the tenant of lands for the life of B, B is called the *cestui que vie.*

Chairman. The person elected by the directors of a company to be chairman of their meetings, including a person who, though not so elected, holds any office carrying similar functions. Generally, any person elected to take charge of and control meetings, as, eg, of a local council. He may have a casting vote. *See* CASTING VOTE.

Challenge. An objection taken against jurors.

In proceedings for the trial of any person for an offence on indictment:
- (i) that person may challenge all or any of the jurors for cause, and
- (ii) any challenge for cause must be tried by the Judge before whom that jury is to be tried: Juries Act 1974, s 12(1).

Formerly, a person was entitled to a peremptory challenge of jurors, needing to show no cause why they should be excluded from the jury, but the right of peremptory challenge was abolished by s 118 of the Criminal Justice Act 1988.

A challenge for cause must be made after the juror's name has been drawn by ballot and before he is sworn.

An accused person may also make a challenge to the 'array', ie by objecting to the whole panel of jurors on the ground of the partiality of the Lord Chancellor or his officer who arrayed it.

Chamberlain. The word is variously used in our chronicles, laws, and statutes, as:
1 The Lord Great Chamberlain of England, to whose office belongs the government of the palace at Westminster and of the House of Lords during session.
2 The Lord Chamberlain of the Queen's House, the Queen's Chamberlain, to whose office it especially appertains to look to the Queen's furniture, pictures and plate, and to govern the employees belonging to the Queen's House.

Chambers. The offices of a judge in which a large part of the business of the Superior Courts is transacted by a judge or a master. Applications by way of summons, and inquiries incidental to a suit, are made in chambers.
See JUDGE; MASTERS OF THE SUPREME COURT.

Champerty. Formerly a criminal offence and a tort, wherein a stranger maintains (assists in or pays the legal expenses of) the legal action of another for a share of any resulting judgment proceeds. CONDITIONAL FEE ARRANGEMENTS are not champertous.
See MAINTENANCE.

Chancel. That part of a church where the communion table stands. The rector or impropriator is bound to repair it.
See APPROPRIATION.

Chancellor. A word used in several senses:
1 The Lord High Chancellor, who is the highest judicial functionary in the kingdom, and prolocutor or Speaker of the House of Lords by prescription. He is a Privy Councillor and Cabinet minister by virtue of his office, and usually (though not necessarily) a peer of the realm. He goes out of office with the Government.
See PRIVY COUNCIL.

2 The Chancellor of the Duchy of Lancaster, an official of the Crown as owner of the Duchy of Lancaster. The duties are now little more than nominal.
3 The Chancellor of the Exchequer is the minister who has control over the national revenue and expenditure.
4 The Chancellor of a University, who is the principal officer of the University. His office is for the most part honorary. The Chancellor's Court of Oxford has a jurisdiction over the members of the University, and the judge of the court is the vice-chancellor or his deputy. A similar privilege formerly enjoyed by the University of Cambridge has been abolished.
5 The Chancellor of a Diocese is the officer appointed to assist a bishop in matters of law, and to hold his consistory courts for him.
See CONSISTORY COURTS.
6 The Chancellor of the Order of the Garter and other military orders is an officer who seals the commissions and keeps a register of proceedings, etc.

Chancery Chambers. The offices of the Chancery Division.

Chancery Court of York. The court of the Archbishop of York, for ecclesiastical matters in the province. From it, faculty appeals lie to the Judicial Committee of the Privy Council.
See JUDICIAL COMMITTEE OF THE PRIVY COUNCIL.

Chancery district registries. The district registries of Birmingham, Bristol, Cardiff, Leeds, Liverpool, Manchester, Newcastle upon Tyne, and Preston.

Chancery Division. One of the three Divisions of the High Court of Justice, superseding the former High Court of Chancery. The causes and matters assigned to the Division include the administration of estates, partnership actions, actions relating to mortgages, portions and charges on land, trusts, etc, and bankruptcy business. The companies court and the patents court are also situated in this Division.

The Division consists of the Lord Chancellor, who is president, and not less than five puisne Judges, one of whom may be nominated as Vice-Chancellor.

Chapel is of two sorts: (i) adjoining to a church as a parcel of the same (as in the case of a lady chapel), or (ii) separate from the mother church, where the parish is wide, and commonly called a chapel of ease, because it is built for the ease of one or more parishioners who dwell too far from the church. *Cowel.*

Chapter (*Capitulum*). A body of dignitaries called canons, appointed sometimes by the Crown, sometimes by the bishop and sometimes by each other, attached to a cathedral church and presided over by a dean. This body constitutes the council of the bishop in both the spiritual and temporal affairs of the see.

Charge. A word used in various senses:
1 The address delivered by the presiding judicial officer to the jury instructing them in their duties.
2 The bishop's address to his clergy at a visitation.
   See VISITATION.
3 A criminal accusation against anyone.
4 A charge on land is a SECURITY INTEREST in land. Charges on land are typically called INCUMBRANCES, for they 'incumber' the title to land. Charges on land are mortgages, either legal or equitable (*See* LAND LAW), or charging orders, made by a court to secure the payment of a JUDGMENT DEBT. As to the only charges on land which are capable of subsisting at law, see Law of Property Act 1925, s 1(2), and as to mortgages, see the Law of Property Act 1925, Part III, and Sch 1, Parts VII and VIII.
5 A commission.
6 Expenses or costs.

Charge by way of legal mortgage. A mortgage created by charge. One of the only two ways in which a legal mortgage can be created. The mortgagee, under such a charge, does not get any legal term. But the effect of such a charge is to give him the same protection, powers and remedies as if a mortgage term by demise or sub-demise were vested in him (see Law of Property Act 1925, s 87, and Form No 1 in Sch V to the Act).
See MORTGAGE; LAND LAW; SECURITY.

Chargé d'affaires. A resident minister of a lower grade accredited by the Government of one State to the Minister of Foreign Affairs of another. He may be either originally sent and accredited by his government, or merely temporarily substituted in the place of the minister of his nation during his absence.

Charge sheet. The paper on which are entered the charges intended to be brought before a magistrate.

Charging order. An order imposing on any such property of a judgment debtor a charge for securing the payment of any money due or to become due under the judgment: Charging Orders Act 1979, s 1(1).

Charitable appeal. An appeal to members of the public to give money or other property which is made in association with a representation that the whole or any part of the proceeds is to be applied for charitable, benevolent or philanthropic purposes: Charities Act 2006, s 45(2)(b).

Charitable, benevolent, or philanthropic institution. A charity or an institution which is established for charitable, benevolent, or philanthropic purposes: Charities Act 2006, s 47(1).

Charitable purposes. Purposes recognised in law as being of a charitable nature. CHARITIES may only direct their funds to such purposes. Charitable purposes are of a varied nature, and until the Charities Act 2006 derived from a list of such purposes found in the Preamble to the Charitable Uses Act 1601, sometimes known as the Statute of Elizabeth. The scope of charitable purposes grew by analogy from the list in the Preamble, any purpose mentioned in the Preamble being charitable, the courts having expanded the list to include those purposes analogous to those found there. Charitable purposes were characterised as falling under four heads: (i) the relief of poverty; (ii) the advancement of education; (iii) the advancement of religion; and (iv) other purposes beneficial to the community not falling under the above heads: *Income Tax Special Purposes Commissions v Pemsel* [1891–4] All ER 28 at 55 (per Lord Macnaghten). Under the Charities Act 2006, s 2, charitable purposes are the prevention or relief of poverty, the advancement of education, the advancement of religion, the advancement of health or the saving of lives, the advancement of citizenship or community development, the advancement of the arts, culture, heritage, or science, the advancement of amateur sport, the advancement of human rights, conflict resolution or reconciliation or promotion of religious or racial harmony or equality and diversity, the advancement of environmental protection or improvement, the relief of those in need by reason of youth, age, ill-health, disability, financial hardship or other disadvantage, the advancement of animal welfare, the promotion of the efficiency of the armed forces of the Crown, or of the efficiency of the police, fire, and rescue services or ambulance services, and purposes analogous thereto.

Charitable trust. A trust for charitable purposes. Unlike trusts for persons, charitable trusts may be perpetual. Charitable trusts are also relieved of many tax liabilities to which trusts for persons are subject.

Charity. Any institution, corporate or not, which is established for charitable purposes and is subject ultimately to the control of the High Court in the exercise of the Court's jurisdiction with respect to charities.

Charities are governed by rules developed in the court of EQUITY and by the Charities Act 2006, which governs the registration of charities, the institution of the Charity Commissioners and their powers to register, supervise, obtain information about, and administer charities.

Charity Commissioners. A body of commissioners for England and Wales, originally established by the Charitable Trusts Acts 1853–1860. The Commissioners have the general function of promoting the effective use of charitable resources by encouraging the development of better methods of administration, by giving information and advice, and by investigating and checking abuses, and determining which institutions are charities and maintaining a register of charities.

Charity Tribunal. Established by the Charities Act 2006, a tribunal which hears appeals from the decisions of the Charity Commissioners.

Charta. A charter, for the holding of an estate; also a statute.

Charta, Magna. *See* MAGNA CARTA.

Charter. Taken in law for written evidence of things done between man and man.

1 Royal charters either to persons, eg, letters patent for title, or to corporations, eg, to a company, giving sovereign rights, as to the former British North Borneo Company, British South Africa Company.

2 Charters of private persons are deeds and instruments under SEAL for the conveyance of lands, etc.

Charterer. 1 One who 'charters' or hires a ship under a charter-party; also called 'freighter'. *See* CHARTER-PARTY.

2 An owner of freehold land in Cheshire.

Charter-party (Lat *Charta partita*, a writing divided). A commercial instrument, by which a person who wishes to export goods from this country or to import them from abroad, engages for hire an *entire* vessel for the purpose, for an agreed sum.

See BILL OF LADING.

Chase. 1 The driving of cattle to or from any place. Also droveway.

2 A place for receiving deer, etc. It was commonly less than a forest, and larger and better supplied with keepers and game than a park. Also a chase differs from a park in not being enclosed.

3 A right of keeping and hunting beasts of chase, or royal game, either in one's own ground, or in that of another.

Chastisement. The Common Law right of a parent, teacher, or other person having the lawful control or charge of a child or young person to administer punishment. A parent has the defence of 'reasonable chastisement' against the charge of assaulting a child.

Chattels (Lat *Catalla*). The name given to things which in law are deemed personal property. Chattels are divided into *chattels real* and *chattels personal*; chattels real being interests less than a freehold in land which devolved (after the manner of personal estate) as leaseholds. As opposed to freeholds, they are regarded as personal property. But as being interests in real estate, they are called *chattels real* to distinguish them from movables, which are called *chattels personal*.

Formerly, the distinction between real and personal property was important for the devolution of estates on intestacy (*see* SUCCESSION), but now the rules as to devolution apply equally to real and personal property.

In normal legal parlance, chattels do not comprise the entire spectrum of personal property, but only CHOSES in possession, ie tangible objects. Thus intangible personal property, CHOSES in action of various kinds, intellectual property, and so forth, are not chattels.

The Administration of Estates Act 1925, s 55(1)(x) defines 'personal chattels' as meaning carriages, horses, stable furniture and effects (not used for business purposes), motor cars and accessories (not used for business purposes), garden effects, domestic animals, plate, plated articles, linen, china, glass, books, pictures, prints, furniture, jewellery, articles of household or personal use or ornament, musical and scientific instruments and apparatus, wines, liquors, and consumable stores.

See REAL AND PERSONAL PROPERTY.

Cheat. To defraud another of his rights or property by means of some deceitful practice, eg by using false weights and measures, or by dishonestly obtaining by deception property belonging to another (see Theft Act 1968, ss 15, 25(5)).

Cheating at play is punishable in like manner as obtaining money by false pretences (see Gaming Act 1845, s 17).

Cheque. A written order addressed by a person (the drawer) to a banker (the drawee) to pay money, generally to some third party (the payee). It is defined by the Bills of Exchange Act 1882, s 73 as a bill of exchange drawn on a banker payable on demand.

See BILL OF EXCHANGE.

A cheque may be drawn in favour of a specified person, or payable to his order, in which case it may be transferred to another party by endorsement and delivery, or payable to bearer (ie to any one currently holding it), in which case it is transferable by mere delivery. If properly transferred to him or her, the transferee acquires the same right as had the original payee or bearer to demand payment from the drawee.

The law of cheques is codified in the above-mentioned Act, and in the Cheques Acts 1957 and 1992, all of which are to be construed as one.

A *certified* cheque is a cheque which the bank on which it is drawn has certified that it will accept and pay on presentation.

Uncrossed cheques are transferable, and count as NEGOTIABLE INSTRUMENTS. The transferee may demand payment from the drawee (the bank upon which a cheque is drawn) upon presentation of the cheque. However, by various means the transferability of cheques may be restricted. A *crossed* cheque is a cheque crossed with two lines, between which may be inserted *either* the name of a bank *or* the words 'and company' in full or abbreviated. In the former case the banker on whom it is drawn must not pay the money

for the cheque to any person other than the banker named; in the latter case he must not pay it to any person other than a banker. A *non-transferable* cheque is a crossed cheque bearing the words 'account payee' or 'a/c payee' either with or without the word 'only', and operates similarly to the latter-mentioned crossed cheque. In all of these cases an individual may only receive payment under the cheque via a banker, who will present the cheque to the drawee bank.

Chicago Convention. An international Convention signed on 7 December, 1944. Its object is to lay down principles and make arrangements in order that international civil aviation may be developed in a safe and orderly manner and that international transport services may be established on the basis of equal opportunity and may be operated soundly and economically. The Civil Aviation Act 1982 gives effect to it.

Chief, examination in. The examination of a witness by the party who calls him.

Chief Baron. The title given to the Judge who presided in the Court of Exchequer (*see* COURT OF EXCHEQUER). Now superseded by Lord Chief Justice of England.

Chief Child Support Commissioner. A Commissioner appointed by the Secretary of State: Child Support Act 1991, s 22(1). He is assisted by Child Support Commissioners: ibid s 21(1).

Chief Child Support Officer. An officer appointed by the Secretary of State. His duty is to (i) advise child support officers on the discharge of their functions in relation to maintenance assessments; (ii) keep under review the operation of the provision made by the Child Support Act 1991 with respect to such assessments; and (iii) report to the Secretary of State annually on the matters with which he himself is concerned: Child Support Act 1991, s 13(1),(4).

See MAINTENANCE.

Chief Clerk. *See* MASTERS IN CHANCERY.

Chief Constable. 1 Used by Sir Edward Coke as synonymous with *high constable*.
2 Now a person at the head of a constabulary force.

See CONSTABLE.

Child. The meaning varies, eg in the Children and Young Persons Act 1933, the word means a person under the age of 14 years (s 107(1)).

But in the Children Act 1989 it means a person under the age of 18 years (s 105(1)).

Child, age of criminal responsibility of. It is conclusively presumed that no child under the age of 10 years can be guilty of any offence: Children and Young Persons Act 1933, s 50.

Child, legitimacy of. *See* LEGITIMACY OF CHILD.

Child, legitimation of. *See* LEGITIMATION OF PERSON.

Child assessment order. An order requiring an assessment of a child's health and development or of the way in which he has been treated, to determine whether or not the child is suffering, or is likely to suffer, significant harm: Children Act 1989, s 43(1).

Child benefit. A benefit payable to a person who is responsible for one or more children: Social Security Contributions and Benefits Act 1992, s 141. For 'child', see ibid, s 142.

Child destruction. Wilfully causing the death of a child capable of being born alive before it has an existence independent of its mother (see Infant Life (Preservation) Act 1929, s 1). See also Abortion Act 1967, which legalises abortion in certain circumstances.

Child in need. A child
(i) who is unlikely to achieve or maintain a reasonable standard of health or development without the provision for him of services by a local authority;
(ii) whose health or development is likely to be significantly impaired without the provision for him of such services; or
(iii) who is disabled: Children Act 1989, s 17(10).
As to 'disabled', see ibid, s 17(11).

Child minder. A person who looks after one or more children under the age of 8 for reward for a period exceeding 2 hours in any day: Children Act 1989, s 71(2).
Child minders must be registered: ibid, s 71(1).

Child of the family, in relation to the parties to a marriage, means:
(i) the child of both of those parties;
(ii) any other child, not being a child who is placed with those parties as foster parents by a local authority or voluntary organisation, who has been treated by both of those parties as a child of their family: Children Act 1989, s 105(1).

Child Support Appeal Tribunal. A tribunal whose function is to hear appeals from the decision of a child support officer: Child Support Act 1991, s 21.
See CHILD SUPPORT OFFICER.

Child Support Commissioner. A Commissioner whose function is to hear appeals on a question of law from a Child Support Appeal Tribunal: Child Support Act 1991, s 24. An appeal on a question of law lies to the Court of Appeal from a decision of a Child Support Commissioner: ibid, s 25.

Child support maintenance. Periodical payments which are required to be paid in accordance with a maintenance assessment: Child Support Act 1991, s 3(6).
See MAINTENANCE.

Child Support Officer. An officer appointed by the Secretary of State to carry out functions conferred by the Child Support Act 1991, s 13(1). These functions include maintenance assessments (ibid, ss 11, 12), periodical reviews (ibid, s 16) and reviews on changes of circumstances (ibid, s 17).

Children's home. A home which provides care and accommodation for more than three children at any one time: Children Act 1989, s 63(2). Such a home must be registered: ibid s 63(1).

Chiltern Hundreds. Her Majesty's hundreds of Stoke, Desborough, and Burnham. The office of steward or bailiff of these hundreds, a sinecure office with only nominal duties and remuneration, is ordinarily given by the Treasury to any member of the House of Commons who wishes to retire from the House. It is a settled principle of Parliamentary law that a member, after he is duly elected, cannot relinquish his seat. In order to evade this restriction, a member, who wishes to retire, accepts an office under the Crown which legally vacates his seat, and obliges the House to order a new writ (see House of Commons Disqualification Act 1975, s 4).

Chinese walls. Invisible divisions between different functions of financial conglomerates. They are designed to prevent CONFLICTS OF INTEREST.

Chivalry (*Servitium militare*), from French chevalier; in Common Law a tenure of land by knight-service. *Cowel*; 2 Bl.
See TENURE; LAND LAW.

Choice of law clause. A clause in a contract, trust, or other instrument which indicates which jurisdiction's law will govern the contract, trust, etc.
See CONFLICT OF LAWS; PROPER LAW.

Choice of law principles. The principles by which is determined which country's law applies to settle a dispute. For example, disputes over the ownership of land are determined by the *lex situs*, the law of the jurisdiction in which the land is found.
See CONFLICT OF LAWS; PROPER LAW.

Chose. A thing, specifically, any asset other than land. *Choses* are of two kinds— *choses in possession* and *choses in action*. A *chose in possession* is an item of property which can be possessed, and therefore all objects, clothes, furniture, food, animals, books, and so on are *choses in possession*. A *chose in action* is a thing of which a person has not any means of possessing, but merely a right to claim it (if withheld) by action, ie by process of law. Thus, the right to be paid the balance of one's account at a bank, or the right to be paid money owed one by a debtor, is a *chose in action*. *Choses in possession* are transferred by delivery with the intention that the receiver shall henceforward be the owner, or by DEED of gift. *Choses in action* are transferred by assignment in writing, signed by the assignor, absolute in terms, and to be effective notice must be given in writing to the debtor (see Law of Property Act 1925, s 136(1)).

Church. Apart from its architectural meaning (*a building for* religious worship) the expression 'church' has two distinct meanings: (i) the aggregate of the individual members of a church; or (ii) the quasi-corporate institution which carries on the religious work of the denomination whose name it bears, eg the Church of England, the Catholic Church, etc (*Hals Laws*).
See GUILD CHURCH.

Church Commissioners were set up by the Church Commissioners Measure 1947 for the purpose of uniting Queen Anne's Bounty with the Ecclesiastical Commissioners, both of which bodies were dissolved and their functions, etc, transferred to the new Commissioners.

Churchwardens. The guardians or keepers of the church, and representatives of the body of the parish. In general, the parson chooses one, and the parishioners another. They are chosen yearly in or about Easter week. They have the care and management of the goods belonging to the church, eg the organ, the Bible, and parish books.

Cinque Ports. The five ports of Hastings, Romney, Hythe, Dover, and Sandwich; to which Winchelsea and Rye were later added. They have a governor or keeper, called the Lord Warden of the Cinque Ports, and various privileges granted to them. The jurisdiction of the Lord Warden in civil suits was taken away in 1855, but he still possesses a maritime jurisdiction.

Circuit. The Supreme Court and the County Courts are administered by the Lord Chancellor, through a unified court service, which is organised on a circuit basis. England and Wales are divided into six circuits: (i) the Midland and Oxford Circuit; (ii) the North Eastern Circuit; (iii) the Northern Circuit; (iv) the South Eastern Circuit; (v) the Wales and Chester Circuit; and (vi) the Western Circuit. A circuit administrator is responsible to the Lord Chancellor for the administration of the courts in each circuit.

The Lord Chief Justice appoints, for each circuit, two judges of the High Court to be presiding judges. They have overall responsibility for the conduct of judicial business and matters generally affecting the judiciary.

The Crown appoints additional circuit judges to serve in the Crown Court and County Courts. Deputy circuit judges may also be appointed (*Hals Laws*).
See CROWN COURT; JUDGE.

Circuity of action is a longer course of proceeding than is necessary to effect any result.

Circumstantial evidence. Proof of circumstances from which, according to the ordinary course of human affairs, the existence of some fact may reasonably be presumed. It is thus opposed to direct evidence of the fact itself.
See DIRECT EVIDENCE.

Citation. A summons to a party to appear; applied particularly to process in the Scots courts, and in the ecclesiastical courts; also to the commencement of probate proceedings.

The word is also applied to the quoting of legal cases and authorities in the Courts.

City is defined by Cowel as being such a town-corporate as has a bishop and a cathedral church; by Blackstone, as a town incorporated, which is or has been the see of a bishop.

City Code on Take-overs and Mergers. A code operated by the Stock Exchange relating to the take-overs and mergers of listed companies. It is not a code of law but of business practice. A Panel on Take-overs and Mergers is responsible for its operation.

City of London Court. A court in the City of London, formerly called the Sheriff's Court, later amalgamated with the Mayor's Court. *See* MAYOR'S AND CITY OF LONDON COURT.

City of London police. *See* CONSTABLE, 3.

Civil. A term variously opposed to criminal, ecclesiastical, military, or common law. The civil law and procedure and civil actions, etc as opposed to the criminal law and procedure and actions, etc, concerns non-penal actions under which individuals seek redress for wrongs, eg damages for breach of contract. The civil law as opposed to the ecclesiastical law is the law generated by the law courts and Parliament, rather than the law generated by the Church. As opposed to military law, the civil law is the law applying to civilians, ie those not serving in the army, navy, or airforce. As opposed to the laws of England, the members of the Commonwealth, and the United States, whose legal systems are based on the COMMON LAW, civil refers to those systems of law, such as the French or German, whose law derives from Roman CIVIL LAW and is generally embodied in 'civil codes'.

Civil Aviation Authority. A body corporate whose functions include the licensing of air transport, the licensing of the provision of accommodation in aircraft, the provision of air navigation services, the operation of aerodromes, the provision of assistance and information, the registration of aircraft, the safety of air navigation and aircraft (including airworthiness), the control of air traffic, the certification of operators of aircraft, and the licensing of air crews and aerodromes (see Civil Aviation Act 1982, s 3).

Civil commotion. An insurrection of the people for general purposes, though not amounting to rebellion. The elements of turbulence or tumult are essential. A stage intermediate between a riot and civil war.

Civil Law. 1 is defined in Justinian's Institutes as 'that law which every people has established for itself'; in other words, the law of any given State. But this law is now distinguished by the term *municipal law*, the term *civil law* being applied to the Roman civil law, or systems of law deriving therefrom.

2 The non-criminal law. *See* CORPUS JURIS CIVILIS.

Civil List. An annual sum granted by Parliament to the King or Queen and certain members of the Royal Family Crown at the commencement of each reign in lieu of hereditary revenues, for the expenses of the royal household and establishment. The Civil List Act 1972 fixed the sum at £980,000, which has been supplemented from time to time under the Civil List Act 1975.

Civil remedy. A remedy available to a person by action, as opposed to a criminal prosecution. *See* PROSECUTION.

Civil procedure. The procedures by which litigants initiate and maintain proceedings in a civil action or case, and the specific means of governing of this process by judges and other officials of the court. The day to day processes of litigation, from the filing of claims, the setting down of hearing dates, the specifying of particular forms for different documents, time periods for the giving of notices, and so on, are generally set down in the 'rules of court' for particular courts which are amended from time to time, and usually published anew annually.

Civil Procedure Act 1997. An Act embodying reforms in the law of civil procedure proposed by a Committee headed by Lord Woolf (generally known as the 'Woolf Reforms'), which are intended to promote the early settlement of claims and to expedite the legal process in advance of trial and make it less expensive, in particular through the greater oversight of judges.

Civil Procedure Rules. The new form of the rules of court, made under the Civil Procedure Act 1997, which apply both to county courts and to the High Court generally.

Civil responsibility. To be *civilly* responsible for any act or omission means to be liable in an action or other proceeding at the suit of a person or corporation, or (in certain cases) at the suit of the Crown suing as for a private wrong. This is opposed to criminal responsibility, which means liability to answer in a criminal court. The action, etc, is styled a civil remedy, in opposition to a prosecution, which is brought by the Crown.

Civil Service. This term includes all servants of the Crown, other than holders of political or judicial offices, who are employed in a civil capacity and whose remuneration is paid wholly and directly out of monies voted by Parliament.

Civil side. The side of a court devoted to civil cases.

Claim (Lat *Clamare*). **1** A challenge of interest in anything that is in the possession of another person, or at least out of the possession of the claimant. *Cowel.*
2 Under the CIVIL PROCEDURE RULES 'claim' is the new term for 'action'.
See STATEMENT OF CLAIM; ACTION.

Claim form. Under the CIVIL PROCEDURE RULES, the filing of a claim form becomes the sole means of initiating a CASE in the High Court and county courts, replacing the writ, originating summons, and all other originating processes.

Claimant. One who makes a legal claim. In accordance with the CIVIL PROCEDURE RULES, claimant is to be the preferred term in lawyerly use for the party previously called the PLAINTIFF.

Clarendon, Constitutions of. Enacted 1164. Confirmed 1176. Their object was to limit the pretensions of the clergy within the realm.

Claves insulae. The House of Keys of the Isle of Man.
See KEYS.

Clayton's case. *See* APPROPRIATION, 2.

Clean hands are required from a plaintiff in Equity, ie he must be free from reproach, or taint of fraud, etc, in his conduct *in respect of the subject matter of his claim.*
See EQUITY.

Clear days. A phrase used to indicate the calculations of days from one day to another excluding both the first and last day.

Clearance. A certificate given by the collector of a port, that a ship has paid dues and been cleared at the customs house and may sail. Clearance has, therefore, been defined as *a permission to sail.*

Clearing house. The place where the operation termed 'clearing' is carried on; 'clearing' being a method adopted by London banks for exchanging the drafts of each other's businesses and settling the difference.

Clement's Inn. *See* INNS OF CHANCERY.

Clergy refers to clerks in Holy Orders of the Church of England.

Clerk of the Crown in Chancery. An officer whose duty is (i) to issue writs for elections on receiving the Lord Chancellor's warrant; (ii) to deliver to the Clerk of the House of Commons the list of Members returned to serve in Parliament; (iii) to certify the election of representative peers for Scotland and Ireland, etc. (*see* HOUSE OF LORDS). Provision was made by the Lord Chancellor's Pension Act 1832 for the abolition of this office when it should become vacant. The office has, however, been continued, and the duties and salary of the Clerk are now regulated by the Great Seal (Offices) Act 1874, s 8.

Clerk of the House of Commons. One of the officers of the House of Commons, appointed by the Crown for life, by letters patent, in which he is styled 'Under Clerk of the Parliaments, to attend upon the Commons'. *May.*

Clerk of the Parliaments. The chief officer of the House of Lords, appointed by the Crown, by letters patent. *May.*

Client. A person who consults a solicitor. A solicitor, also, in reference to the counsel he instructs is spoken of as a client. The word is also used in reference to other professions.

Clifford's Inn. *See* INNS OF CHANCERY.

Clogging equity of redemption. In a mortgage, no clog or fetter may be imposed on the equity of redemption, ie the equitable right to regain the mortgaged land unencumbered following the payment of the mortgage loan. The maxim is 'Once a mortgage, always a mortgage' and any stipulation contained in a mortgage transaction, the object of which is either to deprive the mortgagor of his right to redeem, or to prevent him from getting his property back in substantially the same state as at the beginning of the transaction, is void as being repugnant to the nature of a mere security.
See EQUITY OF REDEMPTION; MORTGAGE; SECURITY INTEREST.

Close company. With some exceptions, a company that is under the control of five or fewer participators, or of participators who are directors (see Income and Corporation Taxes Act 1988, s 414).

Close season. A season in which hunting or fishing is prohibited. See, eg, Salmon and

Freshwater Act 1975, Sch 1, for close seasons for salmon and trout. The close seasons for various types of game are laid down in the Game Act 1831, s 3: eg partridges, from 1st February to 1st September in any year; pheasants, 1st February to 1st October; grouse, 10th December to 12th August, etc. Hares and leverets are preserved during March to July by the Hares Preservation Act 1892.

Closure. The procedure whereby a debate is brought to a close. In Parliamentary debates, if the notion 'that the question be now put' is voted on and carried (provided that not less than one hundred members vote in favour), the debate must cease.

Club. A voluntary association, for social and other purposes, of a number of persons who pay a certain sum either to a common fund for the benefit of the members or to a particular individual. In the former case it is a 'members' club and in the latter a 'proprietary' club. In a proprietary club the expenses and risk are borne by a contractor who takes all profits. A members' club is usually managed by a steward under the superintendence of a committee, and the members, merely as such, are not liable for debts incurred by the committee or for goods supplied to the club. A club as a body has no position recognised in law. It is not a partnership, nor a company, nor a society subject to statutory rules, except under the Licensing Acts. As to the sale of intoxicating liquor in clubs, see Licensing Act 1964, ss 39 et seq.

Coadjutor bishop. A bishop appointed in aid of a bishop incapacitated by permanent mental infirmity from the due performance of his episcopal duties.
See SUFFRAGAN.

Coast. The land which bounds the sea; the limit of land jurisdiction. The limit varies according to the state of the tide. When the tide is in, and covers the land, it is sea; when the tide is out, it is land as far as low-water mark (*R v Forty Nine Casks of Brandy* (1836) 3 Hag Adm 257).

Coastal waters. Waters within the distance of three nautical miles from any point on the coast measured from low-water mark of ordinary spring tides: Public Health Act 1936, s 343(1); Water Resources Act 1991, s 104.

Coastguard. A body of officers and men formerly raised and equipped by the Commissioners of the Admiralty, for the defence of the coasts of the realm and for the more ready manning of the navy in case of war or sudden emergency, as well as for the protection of the Revenue against smugglers.

By the Coastguard Act 1925 the coastguard was transferred from the Admiralty to the Board of Trade, to be employed as a coast-watching force. Provision was made for the transfer of land held by the Admiralty in connection with the coastguard service to the Ministry of Works.

Code. A system or collection of laws.

Code Napoléon, otherwise called the *Code Civil*, is a code composed of thirty-six laws, the first of which was passed in 1803 and the last in 1804, which were united in one body under the name of *Code Civil des Français*.

Sometimes, however, the name is extended to the whole of Napoleon's legislation.

Codicil. A schedule or supplement to a will, when the testator desires to add, explain, alter, or retract anything. It must be executed with the same formalities as a will under the Wills Act 1837.
See WILL.

Codifying statute. A statute whose purpose is to put in statutory form all the existing rules of statute and common law governing an area, eg Sale of Goods Act 1979, replaced by Sale of Goods Act 1983.
See CONSOLIDATION ACT.

Coercion. The threat of taking away from another person something which he possesses, or of preventing him from obtaining an advantage which he would otherwise have obtained, by influence or duress (see *Ellis v Barker* (1871) 40 L J Ch 603). '"Coercion" involves something in the nature of negation of choice' (see *Hodges v Webb* [1920] 2 Ch 70).

Cognisance, judicial. Knowledge on which a Judge is bound to act without having it proved in evidence; eg the public Acts of Parliament, the several seals of the Sovereign, etc. A Judge is not bound to take cognisance of current events, however notorious, nor of the law of other countries.
See JUDICIAL NOTICE.

Cohabitation. Living together as husband and wife, whether or not legally married.

Coinage standards. Standards of the weight of each coin for the time being authorised by the enactments relating to coinage: Weights and Measures Act 1985, s 3(4).

Coke, Sir Edward. Lord Chief Justice of the King's Bench in the reign of James I. He compiled reports, and was the author of four volumes of 'Institutes' on the Common Law, and of an edition of *Littleton's Treatise on Tenures*.
See LITTLETON.

Collateral. That which hangs by the side. An assurance collateral to a deed is one which is made over and besides the deed itself. Thus, if a person covenants with another, and enters into a bond for the performance of his covenant, the bond is called a collateral assurance. *Cowel.*

Collateral descendant. *See* DIRECT DESCENDANT; DESCENT.

Collateral security. An additional security, eg for the better safety of a mortgagee.
See MORTGAGE.

Collation. The comparison of a copy with the original document, in order to ascertain its correctness.

Collation to a benefice. When the Ordinary is also the patron, and *confers* the living, the presentation and institution are one and the same act, and are called a collation to a benefice.
See ORDINARY.

Collative advowson. *See* ADVOWSON; COLLATION TO A BENEFICE.

Collective agreement. An agreement or arrangement made by or on behalf of one or more trade unions and one or more employers or employers' associations in relation to terms and conditions of employment, matters of discipline, membership or non-membership of trade unions, etc (see Trade Union and Labour Relations (Consolidation) Act 1992, s 178).

Collective investment scheme. Any arrangements with respect to property of any description, including money, the purpose or effect of which is to enable persons taking part in the arrangements to participate in or receive profit arising from the acquisition, holding, management, or disposal of the property or sums paid out of such profits or income (see Financial Services Act 1986, s 75(1)).

College of Arms. *See* HERALDS' COLLEGE.

Collegiate church. A church consisting of a body corporate of dean and canons, eg Westminster, Windsor, etc, independently of any cathedral.

Collusion. An agreement between two or more persons, to defraud another person or other persons of their right, or to frustrate a rule of public policy. The word is generally, though not necessarily, used with reference to collusive legal proceedings. Collusion in a petition for divorce was a bar to a degree, but this bar was removed (along with others) by the Divorce Reform Act 1969.

Some collusive legal proceedings, or 'collusive actions', achieved a legal result which could not be obtained by the parties otherwise, and which in time were no longer regarded as being against public policy, and so ripened into 'fictitious' legal actions positively facilitated by developments in court procedure. The most famous of these are the fine and the recovery, both methods of barring an entailed estate. These fictitious actions were abolished by the Fines and Recoveries Act 1833.
See ENTAIL.

Colonies. Possessions or dependencies of the British Crown in certain parts of the world. Colonies are not part of the mother country, but distinct, though dependent territories. In general, they were either acquired from other States by conquest or treaty, or else were acquired by right of occupancy only.

Most of the former British colonies have now been given their independence.

Colourable. Not real, the reverse of bona fide, eg, an alteration made only for the purpose of evading the law of copyright.

Combination, unlawful. An assembly of workmen or others met to perpetrate unlawful acts (see Conspiracy and Protection of Property Act 1875).

Combination order. Now known under the Powers of Criminal Courts (Sentencing) Act 2000 as a 'community punishment and rehabilitation order'. An order requiring a person of or over the age of 16, who is convicted of an offence punishable with imprisonment, (i) to be under the supervision of a probation officer for a specified period; and (ii) to perform unpaid work, 'community service' for a specified number of hours.

Comity of nations. An expression generally used to indicate the practice adopted by the

C

courts in one country of giving effect (within certain limits) to the laws of another country, and the judgments given by its courts.

Commercial Court. A court constituted as part of the Queen's Bench Division, to take causes and matters entered in the Commercial List (Civil Procedure Rules, Part 58).

The Judges of the Court are such of the puisne Judges of the High Court as the Lord Chancellor may from time to time nominate to be Commercial Judges.

Commercial law. Also known as mercantile law, a branch of the laws of CONTRACT and PROPERTY dealing with business transactions. The main subject areas are the SALE OF GOODS, the law of BILLS OF EXCHANGE, NEGOTIABLE INSTRUMENTS, and documents of title, and the law of credit transactions, in particular secured credit transactions. Sales of goods are the most common commercial contractual transaction, by which a money payment (or the promise to make one) is exchanged for a CHATTEL or chattels. They are thus contracts for the exchange of property, and so involve the law of both. The law of sale of goods is particularly concerned with the express or implied terms of the contract concerning the seller's good title to the goods or authority to sell them and the quality of the goods and their fitness for the buyer's purposes, in particular where sold (wholly or in part) on the basis of a description or sample; the property or title aspects of a contract for sale, in particular the time when and circumstances in which the buyer obtains title to the goods (eg at the time the contract is made and before actual delivery of the goods, or upon delivery, or sometime following delivery (eg when the purchase price is paid for goods transferred on credit), etc, and the rights of THIRD PARTY purchasers of the goods in these circumstances; and the seller's and buyer's remedy for breach of contract. Bills of exchange, negotiable instruments, and documents of title all concern the '*reification*' (the turning of an abstract thing into something tangible) *of rights* to be paid certain sums of money or to be delivered property, *into* documentary form. An example of the former is a PROMISSORY NOTE, which embodies the right to be paid a certain sum of money, and of the latter, a BILL OF LADING, which embodies the right to the cargo on board a ship. These documents are typically transferable so as to confer upon the

transferee the right they embody, and much of the law in this area concerns the rights of transferees to enforce such rights in different circumstances, eg where the transferee in good faith takes from a transferor who obtained the document fraudulently, or where the transaction or relationship between the original parties to the creation of the document is such as to affect the force of the right the document purportedly embodies. Notice again the connection between the law of contract and the law of property. Voluntarily-created contractual obligations, by being embodied in a document that may be transferred in theory to any one, become of a species of property right, and so the rights of THIRD PARTY transferees become an issue. The law of credit transactions concerns the rules governing the relationship of creditor and debtor, and in particular, the law of secured debt transactions, ie transactions by which the creditor takes a SECURITY INTEREST in the property of the debtor. This law is often much involved in the law of the sale of goods, for many sales of goods are also secured credit transactions. For example, a seller may deliver and pass title to goods to a buyer on credit, but take a security interest in the goods so delivered; if the buyer does not pay the price under the contract, ie his debt to the seller, in the specified time, the seller will be able to exercise a right to re-possess the goods, and sell them on to a THIRD PARTY to make up the deficiency in the price paid. (*Cf* RETENTION OF TITLE).

Following the creation of legislation to protect consumers in commercial dealings, commercial law can also encompass CONSUMER LAW.

Commission, assent to Bills by. Under the Royal Assent by Commission Act 1541, the Sovereign usually signified the royal assent by a commission of peers appointed by letters patent under the Great Seal. The Act of 1541 was repealed by the Royal Assent Act 1967, under which an additional method of signifying the royal assent was introduced. This is by pronouncing, in both Houses of Parliament, the fact of the Queen's assent by letters patent under the Great Seal. The necessity for the Commons to come to the Upper House to hear royal assents has been abolished.

Commission areas are areas for which there is a commission of the peace, ie the appointment

of persons to sit as magistrates (justices of the peace), and are (i) every county; (ii) every London commission area; and (iii) the City of London: Justices of the Peace Act 1997, s 1.
See LONDON COMMISSION AREA.

Commission del credere. *See* DEL CREDERE COMMISSION.

Commission of the peace. A Commission under the Great Seal addressed generally, and not by name, to all such persons as may from time to time hold office as justices of the peace for the commission area: Justices of the Peace Act 1997, s 3.
See COMMISSION AREAS; JUSTICE OF THE PEACE.

Commission to examine witnesses.
A commission issued to a foreign country or other place out of the jurisdiction of a court in which a suit is instituted, for the purpose of obtaining such evidence of witnesses residing in such foreign country or other place, as may be material to the question before the court.

Modern procedure is now generally regulated either by Conventions entered into between certain countries, to provide for the taking of evidence; or by the presentation of Letters of Request, through diplomatic channels, asking the government concerned that the required evidence be taken.

Commissioners for Local Administration. Commissioners appointed for the purpose of the investigation of administrative action taken by or on behalf of local authorities (see Local Government Act 1974, s 23). For provisions as to complaints about administrative action, see ibid, s 27.

Such a commissioner is often known as 'The Local Government Ombudsman'.

Commissioners for Oaths. Solicitors appointed by the Lord Chancellor to administer oaths to persons making affidavits to be used in law suits, etc.

Commitment. The sending of a person to prison. The word is also used of the document or warrant by which a commitment is directed.

Committal for trial. The sending for trial before a jury of a person charged before the examining justices with an indictable offence.

Committee, Judicial. *See* JUDICIAL COMMITTEE OF THE PRIVY COUNCIL.

Committee of Supply. A committee into which the House of Commons resolves itself for considering the amount of supply to be granted to Her Majesty. *May.*

Committee of the Whole House.
A Parliamentary committee composed of every member of the House. To form it in the Commons, the Speaker quits the chair, another member being appointed chairman. In the Lords, the chair is taken by the chairman of committees. In these committees, a Bill is debated clause by clause, amendments made, blanks filled up, and sometimes the Bill is entirely remodelled. *May.*

Committee of Ways and Means. A committee into which the House of Commons resolves itself, for the purpose of considering the ways and means of raising a supply. *May.*

Common, rights of includes cattlegates or beastgates (by whatever name known) and rights of sole or several vesture or herbage or of sole or several pasture, but do not include rights held for a term of years or from year to year: Commons Registration Act 1965, s 22(1). It is a PROFIT À PRENDRE which a person has in the land of another, eg to pasture beasts there, to catch fish, to dig turf, to cut wood, or the like. It is chiefly of five kinds: common of *pasture*, of *piscary*, of *turbary*, of *estovers*, and *in the soil*.

1 Common of *pasture* is the right of feeding one's beasts on another's land. This kind of common is either appendant, appurtenant, because of vicinage, or in gross.

  (i) *Common appendant* is a right belonging to the owners or occupiers of arable land, under the lord of a manor, to put commonable beasts on the lord's waste, and on the lands of other persons within the same manor. Commonable beasts are either beasts of the plough, or such as manure the ground.
     See WASTE, 2.

  (ii) *Common appurtenant* arises from no connection of tenure, but may be annexed to lands in other lordships; or may extend to such beasts as hogs, goats, or the like, which neither plough nor manure the ground. This kind of common can be claimed only by special grant or prescription.

     It should be noted with regard to common appendant and appurtenant that the enfranchisement effected by the Law of Property Act 1922, s 128 does not affect rights of common enjoyed by the owners of the tenements (see Sch XII (4) to the Act), and these continue to attach to their enfranchised tenements.

(iii) *Common because of vicinage* is where the inhabitants to two townships, which lie contiguous to each other, have usually intercommoned with one another; the beasts of the one straying mutually into the other's fields, without any molestation from either. This is only a permissive right; and therefore either township may inclose and bar out the other, though they have intercommoned time out of mind.

(iv) *Common in gross*, or at large, is such as is neither appendant nor appurtenant to the land, but is annexed to a man's person, being granted to him and his heirs by deed, or claimed by prescriptive right.

2 Common of *piscary* is a liberty of fishing in another man's water.

3 Common of *turbary* is a liberty of digging turf on another's ground.

4 Common of *estovers* or *estouviers*—ie necessaries; from *estoffer*, to furnish—is a liberty of taking necessary wood, for the use of furniture of a house or farm, from another's estate.

5 Common *in the soil* consists of the right of digging for coal, minerals, stones, and the like.

The inclosure of commons is regulated now by the Inclosure Acts and by the various Commons Acts from 1285 to 1908 (see also Commons Registration Act 1965).

See CATTLEGATE; HERBAGE; PASTURE; ACCESS LAND.

Common, tenancy in. One of the two basic forms of co-ownership, the other being joint tenancy. A tenancy in common is sometimes referred to as ownership of 'undivided shares', as its basic rationale is that though each co-owner is each an owner of the whole of the property, each holds his or her own interest in the property separately. Thus, upon death, a tenant in common's right to the property can be passed under his or her will, and if not given by will, devolves under the rules of intestate SUCCESSION.

As regards land, this tenancy is possible only in EQUITY, (see ss 34–39 and Sch 1,

Part IV to the Law of Property Act 1925 (as amended by the Law of Property (Amendment) Act 1926)), however, co-owners may hold movable property as tenants in common.

See JOINT TENANCY.

Common Agricultural Policy. A policy of the EU (i) to increase productivity by promoting technical progress; (ii) to ensure a fair standard of living for the agricultural community; (iii) to stabilise markets; (iv) to ensure the availability of supplies; and (v) to ensure that supplies reach consumers at reasonable prices: Treaty of Rome, Art 39(1).

Common assault. An assault unaccompanied by circumstances of aggravation.

See ASSAULT.

Common assurances. *See* ASSURANCE, 1.

Common Bench. A name sometimes given to the former Court of Common Pleas.

See COURT OF COMMON PLEAS.

Common carrier. *See* CARRIER.

Common employment, rule of. The common law rule by which a master was not liable to a servant suffering injury by the negligence of another of his servants, except where the master was careless in the selection of his servants or carelessly failed to take precautions for their safety. The rule was abolished by the Law Reform (Personal Injuries) Act 1948.

Commonhold. Established by the Commonhold and Leasehold Reform Act 2002, a species of title under which each owner of a unit of a larger development (eg a flat in a block of flats) holds a fee simple estate in his own unit, while the fee simple of the common parts of development (corridors, lifts, etc) are held in fee simple by a management or 'commonhold' association.

Common informer. An informer, ie one who provided an information to initiate a criminal proceeding, who sued on a penal statute which entitled any person to sue to recover the penalty imposed upon the accused, if convicted. The common informer procedure was abolished by the Common Informers Act 1951.

Common land means
(i) land subject to rights of common whether those rights are exercisable at all times or only during limited periods;

(ii) waste land of a manor not subject to rights of common;
but does not include a town or village green or any land which forms part of a highway: Commons Registration Act 1965, s 22(1). *See* TOWN OR VILLAGE GREEN; WASTE, 2.

Common Law. The ancient unwritten law of this kingdom. 1 *Bl.*
The term 'Common Law' is used in various senses:
1 Of the ancient law above mentioned embodied in judicial decisions as opposed to statute law, ie the law enacted by Parliament.
2 Of the original and proper law of England, formerly administered in the Common Law Courts, ie the superior court of Westminster, and the Nisi Prius Courts, as opposed to the system called Equity, which was administered in the Court of Chancery. Since the Judicature Act 1873 all courts administer law and equity concurrently (see now Supreme Court Act 1981, s 49).
3 Of the municipal law of England as opposed to the Roman Civil Law, or other foreign law.

Common Market. *See* EUROPEAN UNION.

Common of shack. *See* SHACK.

Common Pleas. *See* COURT OF COMMON PLEAS.

Common Prayer. *See* BOOK OF COMMON PRAYER.

Common prostitute. *See* PROSTITUTION.

Common recovery. *See* RECOVERY.

Common scold (Lat *Communis rixatrix*). *See* SCOLD.

Common seal. An expression used to denote the seal of a corporation or of a company.

Common Serjeant of London. A judicial officer of the City of London, next to the recorder. Any person appointed to be Common Serjeant is, by virtue of that appointment, a circuit judge (see Courts Act 1971).

Commonwealth. A word which signifies the common weal or public policy; sometimes it is used to designate a republican form of government: and especially the period of English history from the execution of Charles I in 1649 to the restoration of the monarchy under Charles II in 1660. Now used to describe the United Kingdom and the self-governing countries.

Commorientes. Persons dying of the same accident or on the same occasion. Under the provisions of the Law of Property Act 1925, s 184 the younger is deemed to have survived the elder.

Communis error facit jus. Common error sometimes makes right, ie will be reflected in law.

Community home. A home for the care and accommodation of children looked after by a local authority: Children Act 1989, s 53(1).

Community land. Land acquired for development by local or new town authorities under the provisions of the Community Land Act 1975.

Community service order. Where a person of or over sixteen years of age is convicted of an offence punishable with imprisonment, the Court by which he is convicted, may, instead make a community service order, requiring him to perform unpaid work for a specified number of hours (see Powers of Criminal Courts Act 1973, s 14(1)).

Company. A body of persons associated together for the purposes of trade or business. Companies are formed (i) by charter, (ii) by special Act of Parliament, (iii) by registration at Companies House.
Companies are regulated chiefly by the Companies Act 2006.
For the different types of companies, see the entries below.

Company, holding. *See* HOLDING COMPANY.

Company, private. *See* PRIVATE COMPANY.

Company, public. *See* PUBLIC COMPANY.

Company, subsidiary. *See* SUBSIDIARY COMPANY.

Company, unlimited. *See* UNLIMITED COMPANY.

Company law. The law governing companies, one of the two most prevalent forms of business organisation, the other being PARTNERSHIPS. Companies may be public, limited either by shares or by guarantee, or private, which may be limited by shares or unlimited.
See PUBLIC COMPANY; PRIVATE COMPANY; COMPANY LIMITED BY GUARANTEE; COMPANY LIMITED BY SHARES; UNLIMITED COMPANY.
There are two related, central principles which underlie the general shape of company law. The first is the principle of corporate personality. Companies are corporations, which means that the company has a distinct personality in law from those of its members (*cf* PARTNERSHIPS, LIMITED LIABILITY PARTNERSHIPS). Thus a company can sue or

be sued in its own name, and holds its own property. The members are not entitled to treat the company's property as property co-owned by them all. Their interest in the company is limited by the rights they have under the company's charter or rules of association: typically, the holder of ordinary shares in a company limited by shares has the right to be paid dividends as and when declared by the company's board of directors (ie governing officers) and the right to participate in the governance of the company at general meetings of the shareholders and in the election of the board of directors. So, for example, if a company brings an action against someone for breach of contract, any damages it receives become the property of the company—they are not distributed to the members as if they were joint plaintiffs (claimants) in the legal action. Similarly, if the company is itself liable to an outside party, only the assets of the company itself (including any rights it holds to make monetary demands, or *calls*, on others, eg its members) are available to meet that liability. The members are not themselves personally liable to the company's creditors. The second principle is limited liability. Although unlimited companies exist, the vast majority of trading companies exploit the facility of limited liability. This liability refers to the liability of members of the company to meet its liabilities after the company's own assets are used up. If one holds fully paid up shares in a company, one has no further liability to the company, and thus no liability indirectly to its creditors.

Besides dealing with the effects of limited liability and corporate personality in a company's dealing with outside parties, company law concerns the incorporation (or birth) of companies and their winding-up (termination), the law governing the issuance of shares, and the rights provided by different shares to shareholders and the relations between different classes of shareholders, the rights of shareholders vis-à-vis the company itself and against the directors, the election of directors and the taking over of control of a company, and the duties of directors.

The Companies Act 2006 consolidates and amends the previous statutory and common law relating to companies.

Company limited by guarantee. A company having the liability of its members limited by the memorandum of association to such amount as the members may respectively thereby undertake to contribute to the assets of the company in the event of its being wound up.

Company limited by shares. A company having the liability of its members limited by the memorandum of association to the amount, if any, unpaid on the shares respectively held by them.

Company secretary. An officer of a company dealing with the running of it from day to day and its general administration.

Compassing. Contriving or imagining.

Compensation. 1 An allowance for the apprehension of criminals.
2 The money paid by an authority taking land under an Act of Parliament, for the purchase of the interest in the land of the parties entitled to it.
See COMPULSORY PURCHASE ORDER.
3 Money paid for damage caused by any wrong or breach of contract, or to persons defrauded or injured by any criminal offence.

Compensation order. A court by or before which a person is convicted of an offence may, in addition to dealing with him in any other way, make an order requiring him to pay compensation for any personal injury, loss, or damage resulting from that offence (see Powers of Criminal Courts (Sentencing) Act 2000, s 130).

Complainant. One who commences a prosecution against another.

Complaint. The act by which civil proceedings are set in motion in the magistrates' courts, as distinguished from an information in respect of a criminal offence (see Magistrates' Courts Act 1980, ss 50, 51).
See CRIMINAL PROCEDURE.

Completion. The finalisation of a contract, especially one for the sale of land. The vendor delivers up the land contracted to be sold with a good title. The purchaser pays the price and takes possession. Completion normally takes place at the office of the vendor's solicitor at an agreed period after the exchange of contracts.

Compos mentis. Of sound mind.

Composition. A sum of money agreed to be accepted by the creditors of a debtor in satisfaction of the debts due to them from the debtor. A composition may be a private one effected by deed and registered under the Deeds of Arrangement Act 1914, when only creditors assenting to it will be bound; or a composition in bankruptcy proceedings under the Insolvency Act 1986, when, if passed by the creditors and approved by the Court, it will bind all creditors entitled to prove, and of course no registration under the Deeds of Arrangement Act 1914 is necessary.

Deeds of arrangement affecting land may be registered under s 7 of the Land Charges Act 1972, in the name of the debtor.
See ARRANGEMENTS.

Compound. To arrange, come to terms, especially in the settlement of a debt.

Compound settlement. Where land is settled by a series of separate deeds, the deeds together form one settlement which is called a 'compound settlement'. The commonest example of this occurs in the case of a resettlement, which requires several deeds. The fee simple is first settled on the father for life with remainder to his eldest son in tail; the entailed interest is barred by the son with the consent of his father as protector; and, finally, the land is resettled, generally, on the father for life, then on the son for life, with remainder to the son's eldest son in tail. In this case the three deeds may be read as one, being together called a 'compound settlement'. The Settled Land Act 1925, s 1(1), proviso, provides that the word 'settlement' is to be construed as referring to such a compound settlement where it exists.
See SETTLEMENT.

Compromise. An adjustment of claims in dispute by concession, either without resort to legal proceedings, or on the condition of abandoning them if already commenced.

Comptroller. One who observes and examines the accounts of collectors of public money.

Comptroller and Auditor General. An official appointed under the National Audit Act 1983 whose function is to carry out examinations into the economy, efficiency and effectiveness with which Government departments and bodies supported by public funds have used their resources in discharging their functions (see ss 6 and 7 of the Act).

He has a right of access to all such documents as he may reasonably require for carrying out an examination: National Audit Act 1983, s 8. He must report to the House of Commons the results of any examination: ibid, s 9.

Compulsory purchase order. An order, usually made by a local authority and confirmed by a Minister, for the compulsory acquisition of land. Provisions as to compensation for compulsory purchase of land, or for injurious affection where part of a person's land is taken for the purpose of works, are now largely combined in the Land Compensation Act 1973.

Computer misuse. Knowingly causing a computer to perform any function with intent to secure unauthorised access to any program or data held in it: Computer Misuse Act 1990, s 1.

Concealment. (i) *Suppressio veri* to the injury or prejudice of another; if fraudulent, it is ground for rescinding a contract; (ii) of birth is an offence (see the Offences against the Person Act 1861, s 60); (iii) of documents, with a view to gain for himself or another or with intent to cause loss to another (see Theft Act 1968, s 20; see also Law of Property Act 1925, s 183).

Conciliation. A settling of disputes without litigation.
See ADVISORY, CONCILIATION AND ARBITRATION SERVICE.

Concluded is often used in the same sense as estopped.
See ESTOPPEL.

Concurrent interests. The interests of co-owners, ie the interests of more than one person who hold identical kinds of interest in the very same right, eg tenants in common, joint tenants.
See SUCCESSIVE INTERESTS.

Concurrent jurisdictions. The jurisdiction of several different tribunals authorised to deal with the same subject-matter at the choice of the plaintiff.

Concurrent liability. Liability under two heads of law for the same act, eg liability in both contract and tort for an act causing an injury which amounted both to a breach of contract and negligence.

Concurrent/consecutive sentences. A judge may order that two or more terms of imprisonment are to be served concurrently (ie simultaneously) or consecutively.

Condemnation. The adjudging of a captured vessel to be lawful prize.
See PRIZE OF WAR.

Condition. The term condition has several meanings:

1 In contract law, a condition is a term of a contract. If a condition of a contract is not met, then the innocent party may treat the contract as at an end, refuse further performance of his obligations under it, and bring an action against the other party for DAMAGES for breach.

See CONTRACT LAW; WARRANTY.

2 In property law, a condition is a term of a GRANT, which either sets a requirement for the grant taking effect, a condition precedent, or provides for the termination of the estate granted upon the happening of an event, a condition subsequent.

See CONDITIONS PRECEDENT AND SUBSEQUENT.

Conditional Discharge. *See* ABSOLUTE DISCHARGE.

Conditional fee, otherwise called a fee simple conditional, properly comprises every estate in fee simple granted on condition. But the term is usually understood to refer to that particular species called a 'conditional fee' at Common Law, which is an estate restrained in its form of donation to some particular heirs (exclusive of others): eg, to the heirs of a man's body, or to the heirs male of his body. The judges of earlier days construed it, not as an estate descendible to some particular heirs, but as an estate on condition that the land was to revert to the donor, if the donee had no heirs of his body. Once, therefore, an heir was born to the donee, the court would hold that the condition was met, and on the principle that once a condition was met it was utterly gone, the donee would then be regarded as having a fee simple absolute. This construction of gifts of lands was put a stop to by the Statute of Westminster the Second (1285), commonly called the statute *De Donis Conditionalibus*, which provided that henceforth the will of the donor should be observed *secundum formam in carta doni expressam* (according to the form expressed in the charter of gift), under which entailed estates or fees tail could thenceforward be granted. Under the Law of Property Act 1925 legal estates tail are converted into equitable estates tail, and such last-mentioned estates may be created in any property, real or personal (see ss 1(1) and (3), 130, and Sch 1, Part i).

See ESTATE.

Conditional fee agreement. An agreement in writing between a person providing advocacy or litigation services and his client which provides for his fees and expenses to be payable only in specified circumstances: Courts and Legal Services Act 1990, s 58(1).

Conditional interest. An interest in property subject to a condition.

See CONDITIONS PRECEDENT AND SUBSEQUENT.

Conditional legacy. A bequest whose operation depends on the happening or not happening of some uncertain event, on which it is either to take effect or to be defeated.

See LEGACY.

Conditional limitation. A phrase used specially in the two following senses:

1 Of an estate or interest in land so expressly defined and limited by the words of its creation that it cannot endure for any longer time than until a particular contingency happens, ie a *present* interest, to be divested on a *future* contingency.

2 Of a future use or interest limited to take effect on a given contingency, in derogation of a preceding estate or interest. This is also called a *shifting* or *secondary* use, and also an *executory interest*. It is a future estate to come into possession on a given contingency.

See ESTATE; EXECUTORY INTEREST.

Thus, if land is granted to the use of A and his heir until B returns from Rome, and then to the use of B and his heirs, A's estate is a conditional limitation of the first sort, and B's estate is a conditional limitation of the second sort above mentioned. Under the provisions of the Law of Property Act 1925 any such limitations can only take effect as equitable interests (see s 1 and Sch 1, Part 1 of the Act). A limitation which would (before 1926) have taken effect as a shifting or springing use will take effect now as a shifting or springing trust (see s 4(1) of the Act).

Conditional sale agreement. An agreement for the sale of goods under which the purchase price or part of it is payable by instalments, and the property in the goods is to remain in the seller (notwithstanding that the buyer is to be in possession of the goods) until such conditions as to the payment of instalments or otherwise as may be specified in the agreement are fulfilled (see Consumer Credit Act 1974, s 189(1)).

See HIRE-PURCHASE AGREEMENT.

Conditions of sale. The terms stated in writing, on which an estate or interest is to be sold by public auction. The Law of Property Act 1925, s 45, applies certain conditions of sale to all contracts, unless otherwise expressly stated. In the exercise of his powers under s 46 of the Act, the Lord Chancellor has prescribed a Statutory Form of Conditions of Sale which also apply to contracts by correspondence, unless excluded or modified.

Conditions precedent and subsequent. A condition *precedent*, in a conveyance or disposition of an estate, is a condition which must happen or be performed before the estate or interest can vest. A condition *subsequent* is a condition on the failure or non-performance of which an estate already vested may be defeated.

Condonation. A pardoning, or remission, especially of a conjugal nature. The immediate effect of *condonation* was to bar the party condoning of his or her remedy for the offence in question. Condonation is no longer a statutory bar to divorce.

Coney. A rabbit.
See GAME.

Conference. 1 In Parliamentary practice, a mode of communicating important matters by one House of Parliament to the other by means of deputations of their own members. *May.*
2 A meeting between the counsel and solicitor to advise on the client's case.
See CONSULTATION.

Confession by a criminal may be in open court when called on to plead to the indictment or elsewhere.
See VOLUNTARY CONFESSION.

Confidential communications. *See* PRIVILEGED COMMUNICATION.

Confirmatio Chartarum (confirmation of the charters). A statute enacted in the reign of Edward 1 (1297), confirming and making some additions to Magna Carta.
See MAGNA CARTA.

Confirmation. 1 A conveyance of an estate or right, whereby a voidable estate is made sure and unavoidable or a particular estate is increased.
2 The ratification by the archbishop of the election of a bishop by the dean and chapter.
See CHAPTER.

Confiscate. To appropriate to the revenue of the Crown.

Conflict of interest, Conflict of interest and duty. In equity, the situation where a fiduciary's own interests conflict with his duty to act in the best interests of his principal. The 'no conflict rule' forbids a fiduciary from placing himself in a position where his own interest and his duty to his principal conflict in this way.

Conflict of laws. The discordance between the laws of one country and another, as applied to the same subject-matter; eg in the case of a contract made in one country and intended to be executed in another. Rules of law have been developed to deal with conflicts of laws, in particular rules for determining which country's courts are the appropriate forum for the dispute, and which country's law is the appropriate law for the resolution of the dispute. Because the law governing these disputes was developed largely in respect of PRIVATE LAW claims regarding contracts, torts, property, and the validity of marriages, the law of conflicts is also called 'private international law', to distinguish it from the law of nations, or 'public' international law.
See INTERNATIONAL LAW.

Confusion of goods. Where the goods of two persons are so intermixed that the several portions can be no longer distinguished; eg if the money, corn or hay of one person is intermixed with that of another. If the intermixture is by consent, it is supposed the owners have an interest in common in proportion to their shares, but if one person wilfully intermixes his property with another's without his consent, the law gives the entire property to him whose right is invaded and endeavoured to be rendered without his consent. 2 *Bl.*

Congé d'élire. The Queen's permission to a dean and chapter to choose a bishop. The dean and chapter are bound to elect such person as the Crown recommends, whose name is given in the letter missive which accompanies *the congé d'élire*.
See CHAPTER.

Consanguinity. Relationship by blood, as opposed to *affinity*, which is relationship by marriage.
See AFFINITY.

Consent presupposes a physical power, a mental power and a free and serious use of them. If consent is obtained by fraud or undue influence, it is not binding.

See UNDUE INFLUENCE.

A girl or boy under the age of 16 cannot in law give any consent which would prevent an act from being an indecent assault under the Sexual Offences Act 1956, ss 14, 15; otherwise consent, validly given, would be a good defence (see also *R v Woolaston* (1872) 26 LT 403).

Consequential damage or injury is damage or injury arising by *consequence* to one person, from the culpable act or omission of another.

Conservation area. An area of special architectural or historic interest, the character or appearance of which it is desirable to preserve or enhance (see Environmental Protection Act 1990).

See HISTORIC BUILDINGS AND MONUMENTS COMMISSION.

Consideration. A compensation, matter of inducement, or *quid pro quo*, for something promised or done. Valuable consideration is necessary to make an agreement binding in law, (though obligations may be made binding by expressing them in writing SEAL, ie in a DEED). It need not be adequate, but must be of some value in the eye of the law and cannot be illegal. It must also be present or future, but it must not be past, ie a value given before the agreement was made.

There is also a consideration called the consideration of 'blood', ie natural love and affection for a near relation. This is, for some purposes, deemed a *good* consideration, but it is not *valuable* consideration, so as to support an action on a simple contract. It is sometimes called *meritorious* consideration.

See CONTRACT LAW.

Consignment. The act of sending goods; also the goods themselves so sent. The person who consigns the goods is called the consignor, and the person to whom they are sent is called the consignee.

Consistory Courts. Courts held by diocesan bishops within their several cathedrals, for the trial of ecclesiastical causes arising within their respective dioceses. The bishop's chancellor, or his commissary, is the judge. From his sentence an appeal lies to the archbishop.

Consolato del Mare. An ancient collection of customs of the sea, including those relating to sea warfare. It was probably compiled in

the latter part of the fourteenth century, and seems to have been first published at Barcelona.

Consolidated Fund. A fund formed by the union, in 1787, of three public funds, then known as the *Aggregate* Fund, the *General* Fund, and the *South Sea* Fund. This Consolidated Fund of Great Britain was combined with that of Ireland by the Consolidated Fund Act 1816, s 1, as the *Consolidated Fund of the United Kingdom*. The United Kingdom now means Great Britain and Northern Ireland only.

The Consolidated Fund constitutes almost the whole of the ordinary public income of the United Kingdom, is pledged for the payment of the whole of the interest on the National Debt, and is also liable to several specific charges imposed upon it from time to time by Act of Parliament.

See NATIONAL DEBT.

Consolidation Act. An Act of Parliament which repeals and re-enacts with amendments, if and where necessary, a number of previous enactments. Statutory provision is made for making corrections and minor improvements in consolidation by the Consolidation of Enactments (Procedure) Act 1949.

See CODIFYING STATUTE.

Consolidation of actions. Two or more actions pending in the same Division between the same parties for the same cause of action may be consolidated, or put together for hearing as one action, by order of the Court or a judge (see RSC 1965, Ord, 4 r 10).

See CONSOLIDATION ORDER.

Consolidation of mortgages. A mortgagee, whether original or by assignment, who held more than one mortgage by the same mortgagor, had a right in equity to compel the mortgagor to redeem all the mortgages if he sought to redeem one of them, See as to consolidation of mortgages, Law of Property Act 1925, s 93.

Consolidation of shares. A conversion of a number of shares of a certain nominal value into a smaller number of shares of a larger nominal value, eg the conversion of twenty 5 pence shares into one £1 share.

Consolidation order. An order for consolidating the actions, invented by Lord Mansfield, the effect of which is to bind the plaintiff or defendants in several actions by the verdict in one, where the questions in dispute, and the evidence to be adduced, are the same in all. The application for such an order is most frequently made in actions against underwriters on policies of insurance.

See CONSOLIDATION OF ACTIONS.

Consols. Funds formed by the consolidation of Government annuities.

See CONSOLIDATED FUND.

Conspiracy. A combination or agreement between two or more persons to carry into effect a purpose harmful to some individual, or to particular classes of the community, or to the public at large (see, eg, Conspiracy and Protection of Property Act 1875).

Constable. An inferior officer to whom the service of maintaining the peace, and bringing to justice those by whom it is infringed, is more immediately committed.

1 *High and Petty Constables. High constables* were appointed at the courts leet of the franchise or hundred over which they presided, or, in default of that, by the justices at their special sessions. The proper duty of the high constable seems to have been to keep the peace within the *hundred*, as the petty constable did within the *parish* or *township*.

   Petty constables were inferior officers in every town and parish, subordinate to the high constable. Their principal duty was the preservation of the peace, though they also had other particular duties assigned to them by Act of Parliament, particularly the service of the summons and the execution of the warrants of the justices of the peace, relative to the apprehension and the commitment of offenders. The various regional police forces have now superseded them, and they have not been appointed since 24th March 1873.

2 *Metropolitan Police.* The Metropolitan Police Force is a body of men originally established by the Metropolitan Police Act 1829, and is under the immediate orders of the Commissioner of Police of the Metropolis, and two Assistant Commissioners.

   The Metropolitan Police District does not include the City of London, but otherwise it extends to a radius of about fifteen miles from Charing Cross.

   The Metropolitan Police Force is under the general control of the Home Secretary (see now Police Act 1964).

3 *The City of London Police.* The City of London Police Force was established by the City of London Police Act 1839. The management of the City Police is also in the hands of a Commissioner, appointed by the Lord Mayor, Aldermen, and Commons of the City, with the approval of the Queen. The police authority is the Common Council of the City of London.

4 *Police Areas.* Outside London, the police force is divided into police areas, under Chief Constables.

   Various local forces have been amalgamated into larger divisions, eg Thames Valley Division.

5 *The River Tyne.* This has its own police force under the authority of the Tyne Improvement Commissioners.

6 *Special Constables.* These are appointed by the magistrates to execute warrants on particular occasions, or to act in aid of the preservation of the peace on special emergencies. This office, in the absence of sufficient volunteers, is compulsory.

Constat. A certificate of what appears (*constat*) on the record touching the matter in question. An exemplification of the enrolment of letters patent under the Great Seal is called a constat.

See LETTERS PATENT; GREAT SEAL.

Constituency. An area having separate representation in the House of Commons (see Parliamentary Constituencies Act 1986, s 1(2)).

Constituent. 1 One who appoints an agent.

2 One who by his vote constitutes or elects a Member of Parliament.

Constitution is a word generally used to indicate the extant political settlement of a sovereign territory of state, ie the crystallised form in which political power is distributed and exercised. It thus determines the form of the government in a State. Where continuing allegiance is shown towards a constitution as set out in a written instrument, as in the United States, the written instrument is itself generally called the constitution.

   In countries having a written constitution, eg Switzerland and the United States, the word 'constitutional' usually means in conformity with the written constitutional instrument, and the word 'unconstitutional' means in violation of the written constitution; however ongoing political practice, in particular the practice of the courts in interpreting and modifying the principles embodied in the written constitution, generates a body of constitutional law and political practice which itself must ultimately be regarded as part of the constitution law of the State. When 'constitutional' or 'unconstitutional' are applied in the United Kindom, eg to the legislation of Parliament or to the conduct of a minister of the Crown, the words in question are words of a more vague and indefinite import. They are often used as signifying merely approval or disapproval from the perspective of one assessing how well the act in question reflects the supposed values or principles or logic underlying the extant political settlement. Sometimes they are used with greater precision, to mean 'legal' or 'illegal' in so far as the act in question indicates conformity with, or variation from, the accepted legal boundaries of political practice.

See CONSTITUTIONAL LAW.

Constitutional law. The law of the constitution, that is those understandings, rules, and principles of the extant political settlement which the law, ie lawyers and judges, regard as grounds for decision in the courts. In general, these are laws provided by various constitutionally significant statutes, ie Acts of Parliament, and rules of the common law.

There is no single written constitutional instrument of the United Kingdom outlining the rules and principles of political governance, and so no primary statement of constitutional law from which other rules and principles of constitutional law derive, or with which they must be compatible. Rather, there are a large number of statutes and cases. There are also a large number of unwritten rules and understandings, or 'conventions'. While together the rules found in statutes and the common law and the conventions together comprise the constitution of the United Kingdom, in general, a distinction is made between legal constitutional rules, ie constitutional *laws*, and non-legal conventions, though the boundary is not precise. Clear statutory rules and rules of the common law which govern political practice are considered constitutional laws, whereas conventions may not be enforced by the courts. Though the observance of a convention will not be enforced by the

courts, nor will the courts provide a remedy for its breach, the courts have often taken the opportunity to declare whether a particular principle or rule counts as a convention of the constitution. The breach of a convention will have one of three political effects (effects which may be enhanced by the court's exercising its declaratory function): (i) no political effect, in which case the convention will likely cease to have the status of a constitutional convention, unless general adherence to it is restored, the breach being regarded as exceptional; (ii) a political sanction, eg a government of the day might suffer politically for a breach of a convention, losing its support in the Commons or at a general election, or by having to resile from the breach at these prospects; (iii) where the breach is regarded as so serious that it amounts to a coup d'état, ie the illegitimate usurpation of political power, civil unrest, civil chaos, or civil war, until either the old political settlement or constitution is restored, or a new one established. Examples of conventions are the convention that the reigning King or Queen will not refuse assent to a bill passed by both the Lords and Commons, that he or she will ask the leader of the political party commanding a majority of the House of Commons to form a government, and that the judicial business of the House of Lords (ie acting as the highest court of appeal) will be assigned to its Appellate Committee made up of the Law Lords; however see Constitutional Reform Act 2005, below). It may be presumed that the failure to adhere to any of these conventions would result in a severe political sanction, in the first two cases, possibly the abolition of the monarchy, in the latter, by Parliament removing the appellate jurisdiction of the Lords by statute.

While the political settlement has altered in extreme ways over the centuries, the process has been more one of continual reform than revolution, and so the legal rules of the constitution have accumulated over a long period. The most important earlier statutes are those that settled important matters of principle between the Crown, Parliament, and the courts. Besides Magna Carta, whose constitutional significance today is slight, the Bill of Rights Act 1689 settled Parliament's authority, and in particular the House of Commons within it. The Act of Settlement continued this process, also establishing the Church of England by law and furthering the independence of the judiciary. More recently, the House of Lords Act 1999 altered the composition of the House of Lords by providing for the exclusion of most hereditary peers. Also of great importance are the Acts of Union with Wales, Scotland, and Ireland. The Reform Acts of the 19th century reformed elections to Parliament and extended the franchise, ie the right to elect members of the House of Commons, and this process continues in the several Representation of the People Acts, most recently in the Representation of the People Act 2000 which concerns the system for the registration of electors and provides for the trial of new voting methods. By the Constitutional Reform Act 2005, a new Supreme Court will assume the jurisdictions of the APPELLATE COMMITTEE OF THE HOUSE OF LORDS and the JUDICIAL COMMITTEE OF THE PRIVY COUNCIL. For an example of a particular case, the *Case of Proclamations* (1611) 12 Co Rep 74 established that the Crown was unable to exercise its PREROGATIVE power to alter the general law. However by far the greatest common law contribution to the law of the constitution concerns the development of ADMINISTRATIVE LAW, by which the courts assess the legality of the actions of public actors other than Parliament, in particular reviewing the decisions of administrative agencies and officials, inferior tribunals, and the exercise by ministers of their ministerial discretion. In so doing the courts have developed the doctrines of NATURAL JUSTICE. From this wealth of material, and in particular the analysis of it by the great constitution scholar AV Dicey in *The Law of the Constitution* (first published 1885), has emerged the most central principle of constitutional law, that of *Parliamentary sovereignty*, ie that in the constitutional order Parliament is supreme, and can, by statute, make or unmake any law, including laws concerning the constitution. The courts have consistently adhered stringently to this principle, although following the Human Rights Act 1998 the courts may declare that any legislation is incompatible with those protocols of the European Convention on Human Rights to which the United Kingdom is a signatory. Normally, international obligations of the United Kingdom undertaken by treaty become binding only upon incorporation in ordinary statutes of Parliament, but the United Kingdom's membership of the EUROPEAN UNION (the United Kingdom's membership was incorporated in law by the European Communities Act 1972), though likewise an incorporation of treaty obligations by statute, is arguably a more far-reaching, *constitutional* change in the legal order, such that at some stage, simple withdrawal from the European Union by statute would not be regarded as legally within the competence of Parliament acting alone, the constitution of the United Kingdom having since become inextricably intertwined with the European polity. It may already be a near-constitutional convention that any major change in the UK's status or membership within the European Union by Parliament be preceded by a general referendum.

See ADMINISTRATIVE LAW; EUROPEAN UNION LAW.

Construction. Interpretation as, for example, the construction of statutes or the construction of the terms of a contract reduced to writing.

Constructive. An adjective nearly synonymous with 'implied'; meaning that the act or thing to which it refers does not exist, though it is convenient, for certain legal purposes, to assume that it does. See the following entries.

Constructive desertion. In divorce proceedings, the doctrine of constructive desertion places the act of desertion on one spouse although it is the other spouse who has left the matrimonial home, eg where the conduct of a husband or wife has forced the other to leave. *See* DIVORCE.

Constructive dismissal. Where an employer unilaterally so alters the terms or conditions of employment, that the employee has no real choice but to resign, the employee is said to be constructively dismissed.

Constructive notice. Notice imputed by construction of law. Whatever is sufficient to put a person of ordinary prudence on inquiry is constructive notice of everything to which that inquiry might have led. See Law of Property Act 1925, s 199, which provides that a purchaser is not to be prejudicially affected by an instrument, matter, fact, or thing unless it is within his own knowledge, or would have come to his knowledge if such inquiries and inspections had been made as ought to reasonably have been made by him. *See* BONA FIDE PURCHASER.

Constructive treason. An act raised by forced and arbitrary construction to the crime of treason; eg the accroaching or attempting to exercise royal power was, in 1347, held to be treason in a knight of Hertfordshire, who forcibly assaulted and detained one of the King's subjects until he paid him £90. *See* TREASON.

Constructive trust. A trust arising by operation of law. It differs from an implied trust, which arises from the implied or presumed intention of a party. (*See,* eg RESULTING TRUST). A constructive trust may arise without reference to the presumed intention of any party. Thus, eg, a constructive trust may arise where a person, who is only joint owner, permanently benefits an estate by repairs or improvements. A trust may arise in his favour in respect of the sum he has expended in such repairs or improvements. Or a constructive trust may arise *in reference* to the intentions of parties, but without giving effect to their exact intentions. Thus a constructive trust may arise where A, the legal owner of an estate in land, is married to B, and A and B have some common intention to share the land, and in virtue of B's reliance on that intention, B acts to her detriment: A will be regarded as holding the legal estate on trust for himself and B in appropriate shares. Occasionally, in order to avoid a fraud, the courts will give effect to an intended trust which fails for want of compliance with a statute imposing formalities on the creation of a trust, for example a requirement that the declaration of trust be evidenced in writing under s 53(1)(b) of the Law of Property Act 1925; but this is better regarded as an express trust enforced by Equity despite the statute on the principle that Equity will not allow a statute intended to prevent frauds from being used as an instrument of fraud, rather than as a constructive trust. The most prevalent example of the constructive trust is the *contractual* constructive trust. Where A and B enter into a contract for the sale of land, or for a unique chattel, as soon as the contract is made, but before transfer of title to the property, equity will regard the seller as holding the property on trust for the buyer. The trust evaporates when the legal title to the property is transferred under the contract of sale, and B becomes the legal owner of it.

Consul. An agent appointed by a State to reside in a town belonging to another State, for the purpose of watching over the commercial interests of the subjects of the State from which he has received his commission. He is not clothed with diplomatic character. His appointment is communicated to the government of the State in which he is appointed to reside, and its permission is required to enable him to enter on his functions. This permission is given by an instrument called an *exequatur*. *See* EXEQUATUR.

Consultation. A meeting of one or more counsel and the solicitor instructing them for deliberating or advising. *See* CONFERENCE.

Consumer, dealing as. A party to a contract 'deals as consumer' in relation to another party if:
   (i) he neither makes the contract in the course of a business nor holds himself out as doing so; and
   (ii) the other party does make the contract in the course of a business; and
   (iii) in the case of a contract governed by the law of sale of goods or hire-purchase the goods passing under or in pursuance of the contract are of a type ordinarily supplied for private use or consumption (see Unfair Contract Terms Act 1977, s 12(1)).

But on a sale by auction or competitive tender the buyer is not in any circumstances to be regarded as dealing as a consumer (ibid, s 12(2)).

Consumer arbitration agreement. An agreement entered into by a consumer that future differences between the parties to a contract are to be referred to arbitration: Consumer Arbitration Agreements Act 1988, s 1. A person is a 'consumer' if (i) he neither makes the contract in the course of a business nor holds himself out as doing so; and (ii) the other party makes the contract in the course of a business; and (iii) in the case of a contract governed by the law of sale of goods or hire purchase or by the Unfair Contract Terms Act 1977, s 7, the goods are of a type originally supplied for private use or consumption: ibid, s 3(1). But on a sale by auction or by competitive tender the buyer is not to be regarded as a 'consumer': ibid, s 3(1). Such an agreement cannot be enforced against a consumer except (i) with his written consent signified after the differences in question have arisen; or (ii) where he has submitted to arbitration in pursuance of the agreement; or (iii) where the court makes an order disapplying s 1 of the Act where there is no detriment to the consumer: ibid, s 1.

Consumer Credit Act 1974 introduced a system for the protection of consumers, administered by the Director General of Fair Trading, of licensing and other controls of traders concerned with the provision of credit, or the supply of goods on hire or hire-purchase and their transactions.

Consumer credit agreement. A personal credit agreement by which the creditor provides the debtor with credit not exceeding £15,000: Consumer Credit Act 1974, s 8(2).

See PERSONAL CREDIT AGREEMENT; CREDIT.

Consumer hire agreement. An agreement made by a person with an individual ('the hirer') for the bailment of goods to the hirer which (i) is not a hire-purchase agreement; (ii) is capable of subsisting for more than three months; and (iii) does not require the hirer to make payments exceeding £15,000: Consumer Credit Act 1974, s 15.

See HIRE-PURCHASE AGREEMENT.

Consumer law. The law dealing with the rights of consumers, in particular their rights regarding commercial dealings with suppliers of goods and services, the obtaining of credit, and the liability of manufacturers and suppliers in respect of defective products.

See COMMERCIAL LAW.

Consumer Protection Act 1987 concerns (i) the liability for damage caused by defective products; (ii) consumer safety; and (iii) misleading price indications.

See PRODUCT LIABILITY.

Consumer Protection Advisory Committee. A committee established for the purpose of performing the functions assigned to it by Part II of the Fair Trading Act 1973, s 3(1). The Secretary of State or any other Minister or the Director General of Fair Trading may refer to it the question of whether a consumer trade practice specified in the reference adversely affects the economic interests of consumers in the United Kingdom: ibid, s 14.

See CONSUMER TRADE PRACTICE.

Consumer trade practice. Any practice carried on in connection with the supply of goods or services to consumers relating to (i) the terms on which goods or services are supplied; (ii) the manner in which those terms are communicated to consumers; (iii) the promotion of the supply of the goods or services; (iv) the methods of salesmanship employed; (v) the way in which goods are packed; and (vi) the methods of demanding or securing payment for goods or services: Fair Trading Act 1973, s 13.

See CONSUMER PROTECTION ADVISORY COMMITTEE.

Consummation. The completion of a thing, especially of a marriage by complete sexual intercourse.

Contact order. An order requiring the person with whom a child lives, or is to live, to allow the child to visit or stay with the person named in the order, or for that person and the child otherwise to have contact with each other: Children Act 1989, s 8(1).

Container includes any form of packaging of goods for sale as a single item, whether by way of wholly or partly enclosing the goods or by way of attaching them to, or winding them round, some other article, and in particular includes a wrapper or confining band: Weights and Measures Act 1985, s 94(1).

Contango. The sum paid per share or per cent on a settlement day of the Stock Exchange, for continuing a 'Bull' account to the next settlement day.

Contempt of court. Anything which plainly tends to create a disregard of the authority of courts of justice; eg the open insult or resistance to the Judges who preside there, or disobedience to their orders. Contempt of court is punishable by imprisonment of the offender or a fine (see Contempt of Court Act 1981).

Contempt of Parliament. Anything which is a breach of the privileges of either House of Parliament, according to the law and usage of Parliament, is a contempt of the High Court of Parliament, and punishable by the House by committal.

Contentious business. Legal business where there is a contest, as opposed to non-contentious business where there is no such contest. The term is most frequently used in connection with obtaining probate or administration.

Contingent legacy. One bequeathed on a contingency; eg, if the legatee shall attain the age of 21 years.

Contingent remainder. An estate in remainder on a prior estate, *limited* (ie marked out in a deed or other written instrument) to take effect, either to a dubious and uncertain person, or on a dubious and uncertain event.

Thus, if land is given to A, a bachelor, for life, and after his death to his eldest son, the remainder to the eldest son of A is contingent, as it is not certain whether A will have any son. So, if land is given to A for life, and after his death to B, in case C shall then have returned from Rome; B's interest during A's life, until C shall have returned from Rome, is a contingent remainder.

A contingent remainder was defined by Fearne, in a work first published in 1772, as a remainder limited to depend on an event or condition, which might never happen or be performed, or which might not happen or be performed until after the determination of the preceding estate.

A contingent remainder (i) cannot take effect until the 'prior particular estates' (ie, the interests for life, or otherwise, appointed to take effect before it) have come to an end; (ii) cannot take effect unless the requisite contingency has happened. In the former respect it resembles a *vested remainder*, and differs from an *executory interest*. In the latter, it differs from a *vested remainder*, and resembles an *executory interest*. It has the weakness of both these estates, and the strength of neither. Under the Law of Property Act 1925, remainders (whether vested or contingent) can only subsist as equitable interests (see ss 1, 4, and also Sch 1, Part 1).

See EXECUTORY INTEREST; REMAINDER.

Continuance, Notice of. Where a plaintiff could not be ready for trial on a day for which notice had been given, he might give notice of continuance, and continue his notice to any future sitting. It is now obsolete; notice of trial not being given now for any particular sittings.

Continuation clause. A clause used in marine insurance to extend the duration of a time policy beyond the date of its normal expiry until the vessel reaches her destination.

Continuing partners. Partners remaining and carrying on a partnership after the retirement of one or more of their fellow partners.

Contra bonos mores. Against good morals.

Contra pacem. 'Against the peace of our lord the King, his crown and dignity'; a form formerly necessary in indictments for offences against the Common Law. Obsolete.

See now, as to the form of indictment, Indictment Rules 1971, SI 1971 No 1253.

Contra proferentum. Against the person who proffers or puts forward a thing. A rule of construction of written documents by which an ambiguous provision is construed against the party responsible for its incorporation in those terms.

Contraband, in its primary sense denotes something prohibited by ban or edict, and indicates a prohibited trade.

But the most usual application of the term is to such goods as are contraband of war, ie munitions and such other goods carried in a neutral vessel in time of war as may be made directly available for hostile purposes by one belligerent against the other.

The latter belligerent is entitled to seize such goods *in transitu*, and in certain cases even to confiscate the ship in which they are carried. All belligerents have the right of visitation and search to prevent the conveyance of contraband goods to an enemy.

The definition of contraband goods has varied at different times, and on several occasions has been settled by treaties between States.

Contract. A contract has been variously defined. Thus, it is said to be 'an agreement between competent persons, upon a legal consideration, to do or abstain from doing some act'; or more shortly as 'an agreement enforceable at law'. The agreement may be by *parol*, ie by word of mouth, or writing not under seal, or it may be by specialty (ie, by writing under seal) (although see CONTRACT LAW for the fundamental distinction between contracts and obligations under seal); in which case it is more properly termed a *covenant*. Where a contract is not a specialty, it is called a *parol* or *simple contract*, to distinguish it from a contract by specialty. A simple contract may be either *written* or *verbal*. A simple contract must be made on a *consideration*, in order that an action may be founded on it.

See CONSIDERATION; DEED; SEAL.

An action of contract, or *ex contractu*, is an action in which the wrong complained of is a *breach of contract*, and is opposed to an action of *tort*, which is brought for a wrong *independent of contract*.

See TORT; CONTRACT LAW.

Contract law. The law governing agreements. A contract is an agreement that the law will enforce, and so by making a contract the parties undertake obligations to each other and confer rights upon each other that these obligations will be fulfilled, and upon failure to do so, to enforce these obligations at law. Contracts comprise one of the two branches of common law which enforce voluntarily-undertaken obligations, the other being the law of covenants, a covenant being a promise embodied in a document called a DEED; deeds were formerly required to be SEALed, hence the expression promise or obligation 'under seal'. The law of covenants arose earlier than the modern law of contract. Under the law of covenants, any promise formally expressed in a written deed is enforceable at law. The embodiment of the promise in a formally perfect deed was all important; if the seal fell off the deed, the promise was not enforceable; if the deed embodied a promise to pay a certain amount of money, and upon payment the one who made the promise by deed, the promisor or covenantor, failed to retrieve the deed or deface it, the promisee or covenantee could sue upon the deed again and receive payment a second time (though relief against this result was available in a court of EQUITY). In virtue of the law of covenants, many medieval commercial transactions one would nowadays regard as contractual were made legally enforceable by the use of a particular kind of deed called a penal bond (see BOND), which would embody a covenant that a party would pay a certain sum of money as a penalty if he failed to carry out his obligations to the covenantee. The modern law of contract arose entirely separately, by the evolution of an action in TORT, ie an action for damages for the commission of a civil wrong. The action was known as *assumpsit*, and framed the circumstances of the plaintiff's injury: the plaintiff claimed that the defendant, having *assumed* a task, or undertaken to carry out some task for the plaintiff, had done it so badly that the plaintiff suffered loss. This action in tort, then, would recognise an agreement to the extent of providing an award of damages to a party to an agreement to the extent that the other party committed *mis*feasance, ie performed badly so as to cause loss. The action evolved, however, to cover cases of pure *non*feasance, ie cases where a party failed altogether to fulfil his or her voluntarily-undertaken obligations, and by this process, the law came to enforce *informal* agreements, ie agreements not embodied in any particular form such as a written deed. Oral agreements are perfectly enforceable at common law, though by statute some contracts have been made invalid or unenforceable unless in writing (eg, contracts for the sale of land (see Statute of Frauds 1677, Law of Property (Miscellaneous Provisions) Act 1989)). The essence of a contract, then, lies in the actual agreement of the parties, not in any form such as a document, and so to speak of a 'written contract' is actually a misnomer. A contract may be 'reduced' to writing, ie expressed in writing, but the writing is still evidence of the agreement, not the agreement itself. However, contracts reduced to writing characteristically include a term specifying that the parties agree that the writing comprehensively expresses their agreement, in which case the writing is generally conclusive as to the terms of the contract.

Contracts are formed by the agreement of the parties, often expressed as a *consensus ad idem*, agreement in all essential matters. The standard analysis of the formation of contracts is in terms of offer and acceptance: a contract is formed when an offer by one party is accepted by another. An 'acceptance' in which a party accepts certain aspects of the offer but proposes changes to others is a counter-offer, not a true acceptance. Offers must be distinguished from 'invitations to treat', ie invitations to make an offer or negotiate. Generally, advertisements expressing the willingness to sell goods at specified prices, or the display of goods at specified prices, are at law invitations to treat only, not offers, thus the advertiser or displayer is not bound by contract to a person attending to buy the goods on the terms of the advertisement or display. In general, the law will not allow a party to be excused from contractual obligations because they were mistaken about, eg the quality of the goods offered for sale; the general rule is *caveat emptor*, buyer beware, and parties are responsible for negotiating the terms of their obligations and rights under contracts, though relief will be provided in cases where a party enters a contract on the basis of a material misrepresentation made by the other party.

While, as we have seen above, that there are generally no formality requirements in contract, the law will only enforce bargain agreements, ie agreements where each side provides value to the other, and in this context value is called CONSIDERATION. Generally, however, the law will not inquire into the 'adequacy' of consideration, so that one may undertake legally binding but essentially GRATUITOUS obligations by taking as consideration something of nominal value, eg £1 or a peppercorn. Agreeing to do something requested by the other party is, of course, valuable consideration, and is the basis of contracts of service and employment.

The particular provisions of an agreement are called its terms, and the law divides terms into two basic kinds, conditions and warranties. Conditions are terms which are essential to the functioning of the agreement, for example the implicit or express term that a seller of goods owns them or has authority to sell them. If a condition of a contract is breached, the innocent party is entitled to treat the contract as at an end, to refuse to further fulfil his or her side of the agreement, and claim for any damages arising on the breach. A warranty is a term the breach of which does not entitle the innocent party to treat the contract as at an end. For example, minor deficiencies in goods do not allow a buyer to refuse to accept them, but rather only to claim damages for their deficiency. More recently a third category of 'innominate' terms has been recognised; the consequences of the breach of such terms depends upon the seriousness in the particular circumstances. Terms of exclusion or exception clauses, aka exemption clauses, are terms by which a party is made not liable in a way he or she otherwise would be under the law of contract or other branch of law, eg a term of an agreement of sale whereby a manufacturer is made not liable for any injury caused by his negligent manufacturer of the goods sold. In general, one of the chief functions of the law of contract is to allow parties to alter the legal relationships they might otherwise have under the general law, though by principles of public policy and statute restrictions are placed on this; for example, the Unfair Contract Terms Act 1977, s 2 makes void any contractual term purporting to limit or exclude a person's liability for personal injury or death resulting from his or her negligence.

The contractual *doctrine of privity* flows from the nature of contracts as agreements; only those 'privy' to an agreement, ie the agreeing parties, have rights and obligations under it. Because of the inconvenience this rule causes in particular circumstances—if A buys a holiday for his whole family, and the holiday provider breaches the contract by failing to provide the holiday contracted for, it was not clear whether and how damages were to be determined for the losses suffered by the non-contracting members of A's family, and to whom such damages, if available, were to be paid—Parliament by the Contracts (Rights of Third Parties) Act 1999 has made the enforcement by third parties possible in certain circumstances.

Contracts end upon the completion of performance by both sides, by agreement of the parties, by frustration (by unexpected events making the contract impossible to perform), or by a serious breach by one party.

The standard remedy for breach of contract is DAMAGES, ie a money award which puts the innocent party, so far as money can do so, in the position he or she would have been in had the contract been performed. This is sometimes called the 'expectation' measure of damages, by which the innocent party is able to claim the profit he or she would have received had the contract been performed. In exceptional circumstances, a plaintiff may be awarded an order of specific performance, an injunction by the court to the defaulting party to perform his or her contractual obligations. This is only standardly given where the plaintiff contracted to buy land or a unique chattel, ie the seller defendant will be ordered to transfer the property, as money damages are considered an inadequate remedy.

Contract note. The note sent by a broker or agent to his principal advising him of the sale or purchase of any stock or marketable security.
See BOUGHT AND SOLD NOTES.

Contracted-out prison. A prison for the confinement of remand prisoners which is run by a person with whom the Secretary of State has entered into a contract for him to do so: Criminal Justice Act 1991, s 84(1),(2).
See REMAND.

Contracting out. Persons for whose benefit a statute has been passed may usually contract with others in such a manner as to deprive themselves of the benefit of the statute. In the case of certain statutes such 'contracting out' is forbidden, eg the Agricultural Holdings Act 1986, s 2.

Contractual voyage. The voyage from the port of loading to the port of discharge as declared in the charter-party or in the bill of lading.

Contribution, suit for. A TORTFEASOR may bring a claim for 'contribution' against any other tortfeasors who committed the tort with him or her and who would be jointly liable with him or her to an award of DAMAGES, in circumstances where that tortfeasor has alone discharged their joint liability by compensating the tort victim. The other tortfeasors will be liable to the first to pay a contribution representing their proportionate liability.

Contributory. Every person liable to contribute to the assets of a company in the event of its being wound up (see Insolvency Act 1986, s 79). In the case of a company limited by shares no contribution can be required from any member exceeding the amount unpaid on his shares (see ibid, s 74(2)). A past member is not liable to contribute if he has ceased to be a member for one year before the commencement of winding up (see ibid, s 74(2)).

Present members who are liable to contribute are placed on the 'A' list and are primarily liable. Past members who are liable to contribute are placed on the 'B' list and are secondarily liable.

Contributory negligence. Negligence, by which a person contributes to the happening of an accident to himself, for which others are partially, or even mainly responsible. It was formerly a complete defence to an action for damages to prove that the plaintiff's own negligence was the cause of the accident. Now, the injured person will not be entitled to recover full damages for the injury if it can be shown that, except for his negligence, the accident would not have happened. Damages are apportioned in accordance with the Law Reform (Contributory Negligence) Act 1945.

Controller. *See* COMPTROLLER.

Convention. 1 A name given to such meetings of the Houses of Lords and Commons as take place by their own authority, without being summoned by the Sovereign. This can only take place during great national crises. Thus, in 1660, the Convention Parliament met, which restored King Charles the Second; and in 1688, the Lords and Commons met to dispose of the Crown and kingdom in favour of the Prince of Orange.

2 A treaty with a foreign power.

3 A term applied to constitutional rules which are observed although they have not the force of law.

See CONSTITUTIONAL LAW.

Conversion. 1 The tort committed by a person by 'converting' to his own use the goods of another. This will be a ground for an action by the latter (formerly known as an action for *trover* and *conversion*). In criminal law the modern term is 'appropriation' (see Theft Act 1968, s 3(1)).

See APPROPRIATION; INTERFERENCE WITH GOODS.

2 The change in the nature of property by which, for certain purposes, real estate is considered as personal, and personal estate as real, and transmissible and descendible as such. Thus, money directed to be employed in the purchase of land, and land directed to be sold and turned into money, are to be considered as that species of property into which they are directed to be converted.

See REAL AND PERSONAL PROPERTY.

Conveyance. 1 Under the old system of deed-based transfer of title to land operating prior to the advent of land registration, the transfer of the ownership of property, especially land, from one person to another, by written instrument, typically a deed; or the written instrument whereby such transfer is effected.

2 As used in the Law of Property Act 1925, 'conveyance' includes a mortgage, charge, lease, assent, vesting declaration, vesting instrument, disclaimer, release, and every other assurance of property or of an interest therein by any instrument, except a will. 'Convey' has a similar meaning (see s 205(1)(ii)).

See ABSTRACT OF TITLE; ROOT OF TITLE; LAND REGISTRATION.

Conveyancer. One who draws conveyances; formerly, especially a barrister who confined himself to drawing conveyances, and other chamber practice.

Conveyancer, Licenced. One licenced to provide conveyancing services under the Administration of Justice Act 1985 and the Courts and Legal Services Act 1990. It is important to note that in this context 'conveyancing' includes the transfer of land under the system of registered titles to land, not just conveyancing under the old deed-based system.

See LAND REGISTRATION.

Conveyancing. The practice of drawing conveyances.

See CONVEYANCE.

Conveyancing Counsel are counsel appointed for the purpose of assisting the Court in the investigation of the title to any estate, and on whose opinion the Court or any Judge may act. By the Supreme Court Act 1981, s 131 conveyancing counsel of the Court are to be not more than six nor less than three in number, and are appointed by the Lord Chancellor. They must be conveyancing counsel in actual practice who have practised as such for not less than ten years.

Conviction is where a person, being indicted for a crime, admits it, or, having pleaded not guilty, is found guilty by the verdict of a jury. A summary conviction is where a person is found guilty of an offence on summary proceedings before a stipendiary magistrate or bench of justices.

Coparcenary, estate of. Former estate of land arising when an estate in fee simple descended to the female heirs of the deceased in the absence of living sons, the female heirs, or 'coparcenors', or 'parcenors' being treated as a single heir.

Copyhold. Former estate of land which historically originated from unfree (or villein) tenancies of land, the methods of establishing title to and conveyancing of which were entirely separate from those of freehold estates.

See LAND LAW.

Copyright. A property right subsisting in (i) original literary, dramatic, musical or artistic works; (ii) sound recordings, films, broadcasts; and (iii) the typographical arrangement of published editions: Copyright, Designs and Patents Act 1988, s 1.

See LITERARY WORK; MUSICAL WORK; ARTISTIC WORK; SOUND RECORDING; PUBLISHED EDITION.

Copyright in literary, dramatic, musical or artistic works expires 70 years from the end of the year in which the author dies: Copyright, Designs and Patents Act 1988, s 12, as extended by the European Union Duration of Copyright and Rights in Performance Regulations 1995.

The copyright owner has the exclusive right to (i) copy the work; (ii) issue copies of it to the public; (iii) perform, show or play the work in public; (iv) broadcast it; and (v) make an adaptation of it: ibid, ss 16–21.

In an action for infringement of copyright, all such relief by way of damages, injunctions or otherwise is available to him as is available in respect of the infringement of any other property right: ibid, ss 96–100.

It is an offence to make or deal with infringing articles: ibid, ss 107–110.

Certain acts are permitted in relation to copyright works, eg

(i) when the work is being used for research and private study (ibid, s 29), criticism, reviewing and news reporting (ibid, s 30);

(ii) things done for the purpose of education (ibid, ss 32–36);

(iii) copies made for libraries and archives (ss 37–44);

(iv) anything done for the purposes of parliamentary or judicial proceedings (ibid, s 45) or Royal Commissions (ibid, s 46); and

(v) the supply of copies of material which is comprised in public records (ibid, s 49).

Copyright is transmissible by assignment, by testamentary disposition or by operation of law as personal or movable property: ibid, s 90(1). An assignment of copyright is not effective unless it is in writing signed by or on behalf of the assignor: ibid, s 90(3).

The copyright owner may grant a licence to another person to do any acts restricted by copyright.

A licensing body (ie one whose main object is the negotiation or granting of a licence) may act as an agent for the copyright owner, and may draw up a 'licensing scheme' with regard, eg, to the copying of the work or performing it in public or broadcasting it.

The terms of a licensing scheme and applications with respect to entitlement to a licence may be referred to the Copyright Tribunal: Copyright, Designs and Patents Act 1988, ss 118–122.

See COPYRIGHT TRIBUNAL.

Copyright protection is afforded to performers and to persons having recording right (Copyright, Designs and Patents Act 1988, ss 180–212).

See PERFORMER'S RIGHTS; RECORDING RIGHTS.

Authors and film directors have certain 'moral rights' (Copyright, Designs and Patents Act 1988, ss 77–89).

See MORAL RIGHTS.

Crown and Parliamentary copyright is protected by ss 164, 165.
See CROWN COPYRIGHT; PARLIAMENTARY COPYRIGHT.

Copyright extends to protection in those countries which are parties to the Berne Convention.
See BERNE CONVENTION.

Copyright in respect of *Peter Pan* by JM Barrie is given to the trustees of the Hospital for Sick Children, Great Ormond Street, London for an indefinite period although the copyright in the play expired in 1987: Copyright, Designs and Patents Act 1988, s 301 and Sch 6.
See INTELLECTUAL PROPERTY LAW.

Copyright Tribunal. A tribunal with jurisdiction to determine proceedings concerning, eg, copyright licensing schemes, entitlement to licences, and royalty payments: Copyright, Designs and Patents Act 1988, ss 145–152. An appeal lies on a point of law arising from a decision of the Tribunal to the High Court, ibid, s 152.

Co-respondent. Any person made respondent to, or called on to answer, a petition, or other proceeding, jointly with another. The word was used of a person charged by a husband, petitioning for divorce, with adultery with the wife, and made jointly with her as a respondent to the suit.

Coronation oath. The oath administered to every King or Queen who succeeds to the imperial crown of this country at his or her coronation, whereby he or she swears to govern the kingdom of England and its dominions, according to the statutes of Parliament agreed on, and the laws and customs of the same, and to maintain the Protestant reformed religion established by law. The form of the oath is prescribed by the Coronation Oath Act 1688.

Coroner. The principal duty of a coroner is to inquire concerning the manner of the death of any person who is killed, or dies a violent or unnatural death or a sudden death, the cause of which is unknown, or has died in prison (see Coroners Act 1988, s 8). A coroner is empowered to hold an inquest without a jury, in certain cases; and is given certain other important powers. Concerning treasure trove, he has to inquire who were the finders, and where it is (see Coroners Act 1988, s 30)). He has power to order the exhumation of bodies (see Coroners Act 1988, s 23).

See TREASURE TROVE.

Coroner's verdict, coroner's jury's verdict. The coroner's or the coroner's jury's conclusion as to the manner of death of a person is called a 'verdict'. Although a coroner is not required to state his verdict in any form, verdicts of the following forms are suggested both by tradition and in legislation (see SI 1984/552 Coroner's Rules, Form 22): death by or as a result of: natural causes, industrial diseases, dependence on drugs, non-dependent abuse of drugs, want of attention at birth, lack of care, neglect, and/or self-neglect, suicide (which must be based upon a finding of intention, the standard of proof being that of the criminal law, beyond a reasonable doubt), as a result of an attempted or self-induced abortion, accident or misadventure (the latter taken by some to indicate the fatal consequence of the deceased's embarking on risky or hazardous behaviour), disaster, execution of a sentence of death (which would now only be given following the inquest which would be held in respect of a person lawfully executed abroad and whose body was returned to England and Wales, *see* CAPITAL PUNISHMENT), lawful killing (eg by someone acting in self-defence), unlawful killing (eg by murder, manslaughter, perhaps by the act of a dangerous driver), still-birth (although this verdict is anomalous, for if a child is 'born dead', it was never alive at law, and so it cannot have died); finally, there is the 'open' verdict, given in cases where the evidence does not support a conclusion as to the cause or circumstances of death. The categories of verdict are not exclusive. For example, a death might be caused both by industrial disease and neglect, or by abuse of drugs and misadventure, eg where a person accidentally overdoses on a recreational drug.

Corporate personality, principle of. A principle that a company is in law a different person from its members, eg (i) a member of a 'one-man' company can lend money to it on the security of its assets and gain priority over the unsecured creditors, for he and the company are separate persons (see *Salomon v Salomon & Co Ltd* [1897] AC 22, HL); (ii) a member has no insurable interest in the property of the company (see *Macaura v Northern Assurance Co* [1925] AC 619, HL); (iii) the nationality of a company does not depend on that of its members (see *Janson v Driefontein Consolidated Mines Ltd* [1902] AC 484, HL).

But in certain cases the Court will 'lift the veil' of corporate personality and look at the reality of the situation.

See COMPANY LAW; LIFTING THE VEIL.

Corporation. A number of persons united and consolidated together so as to be considered as one person in law, possessing the character of perpetuity, its existence being constantly maintained by the succession of new individuals in the place of those who die, or are removed. Corporations are either *aggregate* or *sole*. Corporations aggregate consist of many persons, several of whom are contemporaneously members of it, eg the mayor and commonalty of a city, or the dean and chapter of a cathedral. Corporations sole are such as consist, at any given time, of one person only, eg the Queen, a bishop, a vicar, etc. A corporation must sue, or be sued, in its corporate name.

See CHAPTER; COMPANY LAW.

Corporation tax. A tax payable in respect of the income of a company.

Corporeal hereditaments. Things having a real physical existence, eg, land and houses, which are subject to the rules governing property in land, as opposed to INCORPOREAL HEREDITAMENTS.

See LAND LAW.

Corpus. The capital of a fund, such as a TRUST fund as opposed to the income; the various properties making up a fund from time to time.

Corpus juris civilis. The body of Roman Civil Law, published in the time of Justinian, containing: (i) The Institutes or Elements of Roman Law, in five books; (ii) The Digest or Pandects, in fifty books, containing the opinions and writings of eminent lawyers; (iii) A new Code, or collection of Imperial Constitutions, in twelve books; (iv) The Novels, or New Constitutions, later in time than the other books, and amounting to a supplement to the Code.

Corroboration. Evidence in support of principal evidence. Required as to the evidence of an accomplice, in bastardy proceedings and some other cases.

See ACCOMPLICE; BASTARD.

Corrupt practices. Treating, undue influence, bribery, and personation are corrupt practices at elections (see Representation of the People Act 1983, ss 60, 113–115); and as to the appointment of Commissioners to

inquire into the existence of corrupt and illegal practices at elections, see the Election Commissioners Act 1949.

Corruption. The corrupt acceptance of bribes. The bribery of agents and other similar offences are punishable under the Prevention of Corruption Acts 1889 to 1916.

Costs. The expenses incident to a suit or action, paid, in general, by the losing party.

Costs in the case/costs in the cause. A judicial statement, expressing the decision that the costs of an INTERIM/INTERLOCUTORY proceeding will be included in the award of costs to the winning party upon FINAL JUDGMENT.

Couchant. Lying down.

See LEVANT AND COUCHANT.

Council tax. A tax introduced by the Local Government Finance Act 1992. A local authority must levy and collect it: Local Government Finance Act 1992, s 1(1). It is payable in respect of dwellings situated in its area (ibid, s 1(1)). There are different amounts for dwellings in different valuation bands (ibid, s 5). The persons liable to pay tax are set out in ibid, ss 6–9. The amount of tax payable is calculated in accordance with ibid, ss 10–13.

The local authority must compile a valuation list showing which of the valuation bands is applicable to the dwelling (ibid, ss 22, 23). It must set the amounts of tax for different categories of dwellings (ibid, s 30).

The Secretary of State has power to limit the amount of tax payable (ibid, s 53).

Counsel. A barrister.

See BARRISTER; QUEEN'S COUNSEL.

Counterclaim. A defendant in an action may set off or set up by way of counterclaim any right or claim whether such set-off or counterclaim sounds in damages or not. Such set-off or counterclaim has the same effect as a statement of claim in a cross action so as to enable the Court to pronounce a final judgment in the same action both on the original and on the cross claim. But if in the opinion of the Court such set-off or counterclaim cannot be conveniently disposed of in the same action or ought not to be allowed, the Court may refuse permission to the defendant to avail himself of it.

See SET-OFF.

Counterfeit. A thing is a counterfeit of a currency note (*see* CURRENCY NOTE), or of a protected coin (*see* PROTECTED COIN):
(i) if it is not a currency note or a protected coin but resembles a currency note or a protected coin (whether on one side only or on both) to such an extent that it is reasonably capable of passing for a currency note or protected coin of that description; or
(ii) if it is a currency note or protected coin which has been so altered that it is reasonably capable of passing for a currency note or protected coin of some other description (see Forgery and Counterfeiting Act 1981, s 28(1)).

Counterfeiting. The OFFENCE of making or causing to be made a COUNTERFEIT with the intention of passing off the counterfeit for the true item with an intention to defraud.
See FRAUD.

Counterpart. When the several parts of an indenture are interchangeably executed by the parties to it, that part of copy which is executed by the grantor is called original, and the rest are counterparts.
See INDENTURE.

Countersign. The signature of a secretary or other person to vouch for the authenticity of a document signed by a superior.

County. A division of the kingdom, originally made up of an indefinite number of hundreds. The word is derived from *Comes, the Count* of the Franks; ie the earl or *ealdorman* (as the Saxons called him) of a shire, to whom the government of it was entrusted.
Under the reorganisation of local government by the Local Government Act 1972, counties in England are classed as either metropolitan counties or non-metropolitan counties. The metropolitan counties are Greater Manchester, Merseyside, South Yorkshire, West Yorkshire, Tyne and Wear, and West Midlands. There are 39 non-metropolitan counties, which include most of the former well-known counties such as Kent, Surrey, etc, though generally with some boundary changes. A few new counties came into being (eg Avon, comprising Bath, Bristol, and parts of Gloucestershire and Somerset), whilst Rutland was swallowed up in Leicestershire.
Wales is divided into eight counties.

Each county is divided into districts, and each county and each district has its own council.
Greater London and the Isles of Scilly are excluded from the above provisions.

County Councils. The elective bodies established by the Local Government Act 1972, ss 2, 21. For every county (which may be metropolitan or non-metropolitan (*see* COUNTY)) there is a council consisting of a chairman and councillors. Elections are held every four years. Their functions, which include education, housing, town planning, etc, are listed in Part IX of the Act of 1972.

County Court. The modern County Courts were first established by the County Courts Act 1846. This Act and various amending Acts have been consolidated from time to time, the latest consolidation being that effected by the County Courts Act 1984.
There are at present about 300 County Courts, all co-ordinated in a system covering the whole of England and Wales, though each is a distinct, self-contained and autonomous tribunal. The courts, which are local courts of record of civil jurisdiction, are normally presided over by circuit judges. They are among the most important of the inferior courts.
Jurisdiction is either *general*, ie, given by the Act of 1984, which is wholly concurrent with that of the High Court in Common Law, equity, admiralty, and probate but subject to specified limitations as to consent, class or amount; or *special*, ie, conferred by various statutes dealing with particular branches of law. This special jurisdiction may be exclusive to the County Courts or may be exercised concurrently with the High Court or with the Magistrates' Courts or both.

County Rate. One levied on the occupiers of lands in a county for various local purposes. The present method of levying is for the county council to precept on the district councils who collect the rates from the occupiers.
See RATE; PRECEPT.

Coupons. Dividend and interest certificates. Generally attached to bonds or other certificates of loan. When the interest is payable, they are cut off and presented for payment.

Court (Lat *Curia*) has various meanings:
1 The house where the Queen remains with her retinue.

2 The place where justice is judicially administered.

3 The judges who sit to administer justice; and, in jury trials, the judge or presiding magistrate, as opposed to the jury.

4 A meeting of a corporation, or the principal members of it; eg the Court of Aldermen, Court of Directors, etc.

Court, County. *See* COUNTY COURT.

Court for Consideration of Crown Cases Reserved. A Court established in 1848 for the purpose of deciding any question of law reserved for its consideration by any Judge or presiding magistrate in any court of oyer and terminer, gaol delivery, or Quarter Sessions, before which a prisoner had been found guilty by verdict. Superseded by the Court of Criminal Appeal, which in turn has been superseded by the Criminal Division of the Court of Appeal under the Criminal Appeal Acts 1966 and 1968.

Court-martial. A court with jurisdiction to try and punish military offences.

By the Army Act 1955, s 84 courts-martial may be either general courts-martial, district courts-martial, or field general courts-martial. The powers of these different types of courts-martial are defined in s 85 of the Act.

Similar provisions are made in the Air Force Act 1955, ss 84, 85; and in the Naval Discipline Act 1957, ss 38, 53–66.

The Courts-Martial (Appeals) Act 1968 provides for the hearing of appeals against convictions by naval, army and air force courts-martial by the Courts-Martial Appeal Court, with a further appeal, on the certificate of the Attorney-General that a point of law of exceptional public importance is involved, to the House of Lords.

Court of Appeal. A court of appellate jurisdiction originally established under the Supreme Court of Judicature (Consolidation) Act 1925, s 1, but which was reconstituted under the Criminal Appeal Act 1966. The Court of Appeal is now a superior court of record consisting of two Divisions, the Civil Division and the Criminal Division. The Civil Division exercises the jurisdiction exercisable by the court prior to the Act of 1966; the Criminal Division exercises appellate jurisdiction under the Criminal Appeal Act 1968, the former Court of Criminal Appeal having been abolished.

The Court of Appeal consists of the Lord Chancellor (president of the Court); ex-Lord Chancellors; any Lord of Appeal in Ordinary who, at the date of his appointment, would have been qualified to be appointed to an ordinary judge of the Court of Appeal or who, at that date, was a judge of that court; the Lord Chief Justice; the Master of the Rolls; the President of the Family Division; and not more than 18 ordinary members of that court, called Lords Justices of Appeal (see Supreme Court Act 1981, s 2(2)). But this number may be increased by Order in Council (see ibid, s 2(3)).

Generally speaking, appeals lie to the Court of Appeal from all orders and judgments of the High Court; although in certain circumstances an appeal may lie directly to the House of Lords from proceedings in the High Court under the Administration of Justice Act 1969.

As to appeals from the County Court, see the County Courts Act 1984, s 77.

Court of Archdeacon. The most inferior ecclesiastical court, held before a judge appointed by the archdeacon himself, and called his *official*. Its jurisdiction comprises ecclesiastical causes in general arising within the archdeaconry. From the Archdeacon's Court an appeal generally lies to that of the bishop. Now virtually obsolete.
See ARCHDEACON.

Court of Arches. *See* ARCHES, COURT OF.

Court of Chancery. *See* CHANCERY DIVISION.

Court of Chivalry. A court held before the Earl Marshal of England, acting through his Surrogate, with jurisdiction relating to encroachments in the matter of coats of arms, etc. The court probably dates from the time of the Conquest.

After a lapse of 200 years, during which the court had not sat, a citation was issued under the seal of the Earl Marshal (the Duke of Norfolk) on 20th October 1954, citing the defendants (a theatre company) to enter an appearance in the High Court of Chivalry to answer the complaint of the plaintiff corporation. In this way proceedings were commenced in *Manchester Corpn v Manchester Palace of Varieties, Ltd* [1955] 1 All ER 387. At the hearing, before the Earl Marshal and the Lord Chief Justice (Surrogate), it was held that the Court (despite Blackstone having regarded it as obsolete) still had jurisdiction to deal with complaints relating to the usurpation of armorial bearings.

Court of Common Pleas, or, as it was sometimes called, the Court of Common Bench, was one of the superior courts of Common Law. It had cognisance of all actions between subject and subject, without exception. It formerly had an exclusive jurisdiction over real actions, which excelled all others in importance. It was also entrusted with exclusive jurisdiction in appeals from the decisions of revising barristers, and in some other matters.

By the Supreme Court of Judicature Act 1873, s 16, the business of the Court of Common Pleas was transferred to the Common Pleas Division of the High Court of Justice established under that Act. But by Order in Council of 16th December 1880, under s 32 of the Act, that Division was merged in the Queen's Bench Division.

Court of Criminal Appeal. A court formerly constituted under the Criminal Appeal Act 1907, s 1. Judges of the court were the Lord Chief Justice and all judges of the Queen's Bench Division.

Any person convicted on indictment had a right of appeal to the Court (i) against his conviction on any ground of appeal which involved a question of law alone; (ii) with the leave of the Court itself, or on the certificate of the Judge who tried him, that it was a fit case for appeal on a question of fact, or of mixed law and fact, or other sufficient ground; or (iii) with the leave of the Court itself against his sentence.

The Court of Criminal Appeal was abolished by the Criminal Appeal Act 1966, s 1, its jurisdiction being transferred to the Criminal Division of the Court of Appeal. *See* COURT OF APPEAL.

Court of Exchequer. One of the superior courts of Westminster, a very ancient court of record, intended principally to order the revenues of the Crown, and to recover the King's debts and duties. It was called the Exchequer, *scaccarium*, from the chequered cloth, resembling a chessboard, which covered the table there, and on which, when certain of the King's accounts were made up, the sums were marked and scored with counters.

The Exchequer consisted of two divisions, the *receipt* of the Exchequer, which managed the royal revenue, and the *court*, or judicial part of it. This court was originally subdivided into a court of equity and a court of Common Law. But by an Act of 1841, all the equity jurisdiction of the Court of Exchequer was transferred to the Court of Chancery.

The Court of Exchequer consisted, moreover, of a *revenue* side and of a Common Law or *plea* side. On the *revenue* side it ascertained and enforced the proprietary rights of the Crown against the subjects of the realm. On the *plea* side it administered redress between subject and subject in all actions personal.

By the Supreme Court of Judicature Act 1873 the business of the Court of Exchequer was transferred to the Exchequer Division of the High Court of Justice, and by Order in Council under s 32 of that Act the Exchequer Division was in turn merged in the Queen's Bench Division.

Court of Exchequer Chamber. An intermediate court of appeal between the superior courts of Common Law and the House of Lords. When sitting as a court of appeal from any one of the three superior courts of Common Law, it was composed of judges of the other two courts. The powers of this court were, by the Judicature Act 1873, s 18(4) transferred to the Court of Appeal established by that Act.

Court of Faculties. *See* FACULTY.

Court of King's (or Queen's) Bench. One of the superior courts of Common Law. It was so called because the Sovereign used to sit there in person. The Court might follow the Sovereign's person wherever he went; and, after Edward I had conquered Scotland it actually sat at Roxburgh. The Court kept all inferior jurisdiction within the bounds of their authority, and might either remove their proceedings to be determined before itself, or prohibit their progress below. It superintended all civil corporations in the kingdom. It commanded magistrates and others to do what their duty required, in every case where there was no other specific remedy. It protected the remedy of the subject by speedy and summary interposition. It had cognisance both of criminal and civil causes; the former in what was called the *Crown side* or *Crown office*; the latter in the *plea side* of the Court.

By the Judicature Act 1873, s 34 the jurisdiction of the Court was assigned to the Queen's Bench Division of the High Court of Justice, and by Order in Council under s 32 the Common Pleas and Exchequer Divisions were merged in the Queen's Bench Division in February 1881.

Court of Lord High Steward of the Queen's Household. A court created by the Offences within the Court Act 1541, with jurisdiction to inquire of, hear, and determine all treasons, misprisions of treason, murders, and bloodshed committed within any of the Queen's houses or palaces. The Act was repealed so far as relating to certain offences by the Statute Law Revision Act 1948. But generally it remains in force and the jurisdiction of the Court could still be invoked.

Court of Protection. The department of the High Court which dealt with the estates of persons incapable, by reason of mental disorder, of managing and administering their property and affairs.

Originally known as the Office of the Master in Lunacy, then as the Management and Administration Department, it is continued under its modern title by the Mental Health Act 1983, s 93.

Court of record. A court whose acts and judicial proceedings are enrolled for a perpetual memorial and testimony; whose rolls are the *records* of the courts. All courts of record are the Queen's courts, and no other court has authority to fine and imprison. The very establishment of a new jurisdiction with the power of fine or imprisonment makes it instantly a court of record. Such Common Law courts as are *not* courts of record are of inferior dignity, and in a less proper sense the Queen's courts. In these, the proceedings not being enrolled or recorded, as well their existence, as the truth of the matters contained in them, must, if disputed, be tried and determined by a jury. A court not of record, says Blackstone, is the court of a private man, whom the law will not entrust with any discretionary power over the fortune or liberty of his fellow-subjects.

Court of Session. The superior court, in Scotland, of law and equity, divorce and admiralty, having a general civil jurisdiction.

Court of Stannaries of Cornwall and Devon, established for the administration of justice among the tinners, was a court of record with a special jurisdiction, held before a judge called the vice-warden, with an appeal to the lord warden. All tinners and labourers in and about the stannaries (ie, the mines and works in Devon and Cornwall where tin was dug and purified) might sue and be sued in the court in all matters arising within the stannaries, except pleas of land, life, and member. By the Stannaries Court (Abolition) Act 1896 their jurisdiction was transferred to County Courts.
See COUNTY COURT.

Covenant. A clause of an agreement contained in a deed whereby a party stipulates for the truth of certain facts, or binds himself to give something to another, or to do or not to do any act.
See DEED; RECITAL.

Cover note. A note signed on behalf of the insurers by the agent through whom a proposal for insurance is submitted, and issued by him to the proposer giving interim cover while the proposal is being considered by the insurers.

Coverture. Prior to the reforms of the 19th century Married Woman's Property Acts, the condition or state of being a married woman under which a woman could not own property free from her husband's control.

Credit includes a cash loan and any other form of financial accommodation: Consumer Credit Act 1974, s 9(1).

Credit broker. A person acting in the course of a business of credit-brokerage carried on by him: Supply of Goods and Services Act 1982, s 18(1).
See CREDIT-BROKERAGE.

Credit-brokerage. The effecting of introductions of individuals to obtain
  (i) credit to persons carrying on any business so far as it relates to the provision of credit; or
 (ii) goods on hire to persons carrying on a business which comprises or relates to the bailment of goods under a contract for the hire of goods; or
(iii) credit, or to obtain goods on hire, to other credit-brokers: Supply of Goods and Services Act 1982, s 18(2).

Credit business, ancillary. Any business comprising (i) credit-brokerage (*see* CREDIT-BROKERAGE); (ii) debt-adjusting (*see* DEBT-ADJUSTING); (iii) debt-counselling (*see* DEBT-COUNSELLING); (iv) debt-collecting (*see* DEBT-COLLECTING); or (v) the operation of a credit reference agency (*see* CREDIT REFERENCE AGENCY): Consumer Credit Act 1974, s 145(1).

Credit insurance. Insurance against risks of loss arising from the insolvency of debtors or their failure to pay their debts when due: Insurance Companies Act 1982, Sch 2, Part I.

Credit reference agency. A person carrying on a business comprising the furnishing of persons with information relevant to the financial standing of individuals, being information collected by the agency for that purpose: Consumer Credit Act 1974, s 145(8).

Credit-token. A card, check, voucher, coupon, stamp, form, booklet or other document or thing given to an individual by a person carrying on a consumer credit business, who undertakes:
   (i) that on the production of it, he will supply cash, goods and services on credit, or
   (ii) that, where on the production of it to a third party, the third party supplies cash, goods and services, he will pay the third party for them, in return for payment to him by the individual: Consumer Credit Act 1974, s 149(1).

Credit union. A society whose objects are:
   (i) the promotion of thrift among its members by the accumulation of their savings;
   (ii) the creation of sources of credit for the members' benefit at a fair and reasonable rate of interest;
   (iii) the use of the members' savings for their mutual benefit; and
   (iv) the training and education of the members in the wise use of money: Credit Unions Act 1979, s 1(3).
   Credit unions can be registered under the Industrial and Provident Societies Act 1965, s 1(1).

Creditor. One to whom another person owes money.

Creditors' voluntary winding up. A winding up in the case of which a declaration of solvency has not been made in accordance with the Insolvency Act 1986.
See DECLARATION OF SOLVENCY.

Cremation. The disposal of a dead body by burning instead of burial. This is not illegal unless it is done so as to cause a nuisance, or with the intention of preventing a coroner's inquest (see Cremation Acts 1902 and 1952, and Local Government Act 1972, s 214).

Crime. A crime, as opposed to a civil wrong (*see* TORT), is an act which is forbidden, or the omission to perform an act which is commanded by the Common Law, by statute or by regulations made by a subordinate authority; the remedy for which is the punishment of the offender at the instance of the State.

Criminal bankruptcy order. An order made against a person convicted by the Crown Court where as a result of the offence loss or damage of over £15,000 has been suffered by identifiable persons. A criminal bankruptcy petition may then be presented to the High Court and a trustee of the criminal bankrupt's property may be appointed (see Powers of Criminal Courts Act 1973, ss 39–41, Sch 2).

Criminal damage. An offence committed by one who wilfully or recklessly damages, or threatens to damage another's property without lawful excuse. Criminal Damage Act 1971, which replaced the Malicious Damage Act 1961, the name under which the offence was formerly known.

Criminal Injuries Compensation Board.
   See CRIMINAL INJURIES COMPENSATION SCHEME.

Criminal Injuries Compensation Scheme. A non-statutory compensation scheme under which a person who has sustained personal injury directly attributable to:
   (i) a crime of violence (including arson and poisoning); or
   (ii) an arrest or attempted arrest of an offender; or
   (iii) the prevention or attempted prevention of an offence; or
   (iv) giving help to a constable attempting to arrest an offender.
may apply for an ex gratia payment.
   Application must be made to the Criminal Injuries Compensation Board.

Criminal law. The criminal law, as distinct from the entire law governing crime which would include the law of criminal procedure (*see* CRIMINAL PROCEDURE), is the substantive law which defines the various crimes or offences, the particular factual incidents of the offences which must be proven at trial for a verdict of guilty, and the sentences which may be passed following conviction. The criminal law is primarily the product of the common law (*see* COMMON LAW), not statute, and though over the centuries much legislation has been passed by Parliament to better define, modify, add or abolish particular offences and the sentences pertaining to them, much of the criminal law is still governed by rules and principles developed at common law. There is, therefore, no systematised 'criminal code'. Although nowhere defined by statute or by common law, for analytic purposes the criminal law may be conceptually divided into a 'general part' and a 'special part', the boundaries of which are vague. The general part of the criminal law comprises those rules and principles which apply more or less generally to all offences, eg the requirement of *mens rea*, ie a guilty mind, that is, that all criminal liability depends in some way upon the offender's having a malicious intention or knowledge that he or she was doing wrong, or, eg, the principles governing liability for *attempts* to commit crimes. The special part concerns the particular features of the various offences, for example the requirements for liability for arson, theft, murder, and so on. The various offences can be roughly grouped into five categories, though certain offences may fit more or less well into more than one category: offences against the Crown or the State (*see*, eg, TREASON, PIRACY, COUNTERFEITING); offences against the person (*see*, eg, MURDER, ASSAULT and BATTERY, RAPE); offences against property (*see*, eg, THEFT, CRIMINAL DAMAGE, ARSON); 'public order' offences (*see*, eg, AFFRAY, RIOT) including 'consensual' acts offending against the 'moral order' (*see*, eg, ABORTION, PROSTITUTION, drug possession, DRUG TRAFFICKING); and regulatory offences (*see*, eg, HIGHWAY CODE). Since the latter 19th century, judges have been given a broad discretion in determining punishments, usually limited only by a maximum sentence specified by the common law or statute. Sentencing is now governed by a statutory framework under the Criminal Justice Act 1991 and, in a controversial departure from recent tradition, the Crime (Sentences) Act 1997 sets certain minimum and mandatory sentences for repeat offenders and conviction for certain offences. The main sentences for adults convicted of an offence are IMPRISONMENT (sentences of which may be suspended), FINES, COMMUNITY SERVICE ORDERS, PROBATION, COMBINATION ORDERS, binding-over orders (see BIND OVER), CURFEW ORDERS, COMPENSATION ORDERS, and ABSOLUTE and CONDITIONAL DISCHARGES.

Criminal procedure. The law of criminal procedure establishes and governs the legal process by which those accused of offences, ie crimes, are brought before the court, tried,

and sentenced, and the subsequent recourse of the accused (also called the criminal defendant) and the prosecutor to an appeal either to the finding of guilt or the sentence. The origin of a specifically *criminal* legal procedure, as opposed to legal procedure generally, arises with the conceptual distinction of certain wrongs as involving a 'public' aspect, in addition to simply being wrongs generally, remedies which might be sought by the victim from the law. In other words, criminal procedure arose as a procedure distinct from civil procedure (*see* CIVIL PROCEDURE) as the notion of crime or offence became distinguished from that of tort (*see* TORT), wrongs merely giving the victim rights in law against the tortfeasor, or wrongdoer; as *offences*, the Crown or some other public authority took an interest, in particular, by levying punishments upon those convicted of offences. The English law of criminal procedure has historically been heavily influenced by divisions in the law between more and less serious offences and the punishments to which those convicted of them were liable, in particular the distinction between felonies and misdemeanours. Felonies were offences so serious that the Crown took an interest in the punishment of the offender, called a *felon*, and the measure of this seriousness by which these offences were regarded is manifest in the fact that all felonies were punished in the same way, by death and the forfeiture to the Crown of all the felon's real property (*see* ESCHEAT) and personal goods. The inflexibility of this application of one punishment to all felonies had a profoundly detrimental effect upon the substantive criminal law; lawyers and judges contrived to narrowly define felonies, and to introduce technicalities allowing an accused to avoid conviction and thus the punishment. The theoretical treatment of felons undoubtedly only persisted because of various practical means by which its severity could be mitigated; in particular 'the benefit of clergy', or 'claiming clergy', by which an individual claimed to be a member of the clergy and thus liable to the ecclesiastical jurisdiction, not the common law jurisdiction, became a fictionalised device by which an accused could escape liability at the court's discretion. Some offences were not 'clergiable', and much in the way of statutory penal reform up to the 19th century concerned the modifications of the list of offences which were and were not clergiable. Secondly, a system of pardons evolved whereby the judges would, typically at the end of a termly circuit, present recommendations for pardon to the Secretary of State; the most prevalent form of commutation of sentence was transportation. Finally, the unofficial practice of juries finding 'perverse' verdicts of not guilty is acknowledged to have had a significant effect.

Less serious offences, termed *misdemeanours*, were tried by local courts and local judicial officials, from whose jurisdiction derives that of the present day magistrates' courts in which justices of the peace preside. Punishment for misdemeanours was a matter for the discretion of the justices, though such punishments were to be proportionate to the gravity of the offence, and they could not inflict punishments that touched life or limb, fines and whipping being typical. In felony cases, prosecutions could be initiated in two ways: (i) by an *appeal*, either by the victim or by an *approver*, a felon who 'appealed' his accomplice(s) in a crime; an approver thus providing *King's (or Queen's) evidence* in this way would escape punishment should his accomplice(s) be convicted, but would suffer the punishment of a felon in the normal way if they were not. (The appeal was abolished in 1819); (ii) by way of a bill of indictment; formerly such bills were written accusations presented to a *grand jury* who would either commit the accused to trial by *approving* the bill (finding it to be a *true* bill), or dismissing it. Prosecution of misdemeanours was initiated by the presentation of an *information*, either by the victim, by an informer (*see* COMMON INFORMER) or, ex officio, by an officer of the law.

Forfeiture for felony was abolished by the Forfeiture Act 1870, and the distinction between felonies and misdemeanours was abolished by the Criminal Law Act 1967. Now offences are distinguished into three categories: summary offences triable by magistrates whose prosecution is initiated by an information; indictable offences whose prosecution is initiated by indictment and must be tried by jury in a Crown Court; and offences which may be initiated either by information or indictment, and tried either summarily or in a Crown Court. Presently, either the magistrates' court or the accused may insist upon an 'either way' offence being

tried in a Crown Court. Where the police decide to charge a person with an offence, the case is prepared and conducted by the Crown Prosecution Service, who may decide not to proceed, eg for want of sufficient evidence.

Early on, those accused of felony were generally tried by battle or by ordeal, but when these forms of trial were abolished or became unworkable English judges began the long evolution of the process of trial by jury. Originally juries were panels of locals who, like present day witnesses, could speak on the issue of the accused's guilt, but became over time members of the public sworn to render a verdict of guilty or not guilty on the basis of evidence given by witnesses in court. Historically, the verdict of a jury need be unanimous, but by the Juries Act 1974 juries may render a MAJORITY VERDICT. The rules of trial procedure, of evidence and the right to call a witness and the right to counsel were largely developed from the 18th century onward. Defendants in criminal trials were accorded the right to give evidence under oath by the Criminal Evidence Act 1898.

An accused who following a plea of not guilty to a charge is found guilty, or an accused who pleads guilty to a charge, is *convicted* of the offence. There is now a variety of sentences that may follow conviction (*see* CRIMINAL LAW). The practice of *plea-bargaining* is one whereby an accused will plead guilty to an offence, or to a lesser offence, rather than not guilty which would entail the expense and uncertainty of a trial, for the recommendation to the court by the lawyer appearing for the prosecution of a particular sentence.

See CRIMINAL LAW.

There was no specific appellate jurisdiction in criminal matters before the creation of the COURT FOR CONSIDERATION OF CROWN CASES RESERVED, which was superseded by Court of Criminal Appeal in 1907. Now appeals from trial decisions of the magistrates' courts are heard by judges of the Crown Courts, and appeals from decisions at trial in the Crown Courts in the Court of Appeal, Criminal Division.

Cross-appeal. If both parties to a judgment are dissatisfied by it, and each accordingly appeals, the appeal of each is called a cross appeal in relation to that of the other; it not being open to a respondent to an appeal, as such, to contend that the decision in the court below was not sufficiently favourable to him. But by RSC 1965, Ord 59, rr 6,7, a respondent will be allowed so to contend, if he has within due time given notice of his intention so to do to any parties who may be affected by such a contention.

Cross-examination. The examination of a witness by the opposing counsel. Leading questions are allowed, which is not the case in examination-in-chief.

Also, an examination of a hostile witness on behalf of the party producing him is sometimes called cross-examination.
See EXAMINATION, 1; LEADING QUESTIONS; HOSTILE WITNESS.

Crossed cheque. *See* CHEQUE.

Crown. A word often used for the King and Queen as being the Sovereign of the realm, ie in the public capacity of representative of the State as a constitutional monarchy. So understood, the Crown is distinguishable from the individual King or Queen, and in this respect, the 'Crown never dies'.

Crown Cases Reserved. *See* COURT FOR CONSIDERATION OF CROWN CASES RESERVED.

Crown copyright. Copyright existing where the Crown is the first owner of any copyright in a work: Copyright, Designs and Patents Act 1988, s 163. The Crown is entitled to copyright in every Act of Parliament or Measures of the General Synod of the Church of England: ibid, s 164.
See COPYRIGHT; SYNOD.

Crown Court. The Crown Court was established by the Courts Act 1971. It is part of the Supreme Court, with jurisdiction throughout England and Wales, and is a superior court of record.
See COURT OF RECORD.

Any High Court judge, circuit judge or recorder, sitting alone or with justices of the peace, may exercise its jurisdiction and powers. The Crown appoints circuit judges to serve in the Crown Court and County Courts.

Crown lands (Lat *Terrae dominicales regis*, the demesne lands of the Crown) include the share reserved to the Crown at the original distribution of landed property, and such as came to it afterwards by forfeitures or other means. In modern times the superintendence of the royal demesnes has been vested in the Commissioners of Woods, Forests, and Land Revenues, and it is now usual for the Sovereign to surrender these lands at the commencement of his reign for its whole duration in consideration of the Civil List settled upon him. And see Crown Lands Act 1927 (incorporating the Commissioners of Crown Lands) and Crown Estate Act 1961.
See CIVIL LIST.

Crown Office means the Crown Office and Associates' Department of the Central Office of the Supreme Court.
See CENTRAL OFFICE OF THE SUPREME COURT.

Crown privilege. *See* PUBLIC INTEREST IMMUNITY.

Crown proceedings. Any proceedings in contract or in tort which are brought by or against Crown. An action may now be brought as of right. See the Crown Proceedings Act 1947.

Crown Prosecution Service. A Service established under the Prosecution of Offences Act 1985 consisting of:
(i)   the Director of Public Prosecutions;
(ii) the Chief Crown Prosecutor; and
(iii) other staff appointed by the Director (see Prosecution of Offences Act 1985, s 1).

The Director is appointed by the Attorney-General and is subject to his supervision (see ibid, ss 2(1), 3(1)). It is his duty (i) to take over the conduct of all criminal proceedings instituted on behalf of a police force; and (ii) to institute and have the conduct of criminal proceedings in any case where it appears to him that (a) the importance or difficulty of the case makes it appropriate that proceedings should be instituted by him; or (b) it is otherwise appropriate for proceedings to be instituted by him (see ibid, s 3(2)).

Crown Prosecutor. A person, who is a barrister or solicitor, designated by the Director of Public Prosecutions as a member of the Crown Prosecution Service (see Prosecution of Offences Act 1985, s 1(3)).
See CROWN PROSECUTION SERVICE.

Cruelty. Conduct on the part of husband or wife which entitled the other party to judicial separation or divorce.

The sole ground for divorce is now the irretrievable breakdown of a marriage. One of the grounds is that the respondent has behaved in such a way that the petitioner cannot reasonably be expected to live with the respondent. Instances of cruelty may therefore be brought in evidence. Generally, as to divorce, see Matrimonial Causes Act 1973.

Legal cruelty has been defined (*Russell v Russell* [1897] AC 525) as conduct of such a character as to have caused danger to life, limb, or health (bodily or mental), or as to give rise to a reasonable apprehension of danger. No hard and fast rules can, however, be laid down. In determining what constitutes cruelty, regard must be had to the circumstances of each particular case, keeping always in view the physical and mental condition of the parties, and their character and social status.

For summary proceedings for persistent cruelty see Matrimonial Proceedings (Magistrates' Courts) Act 1960.

See DIVORCE.

Cruelty to animals. The making of painful experiments on animals, and the practice of vivisection, are restricted by various statutes (see principally Cruelty to Animals Act 1876, and Protection of Animals Acts 1911 to 1964, and Wild Animals (Protection Act) 1996, s 1).

Cruelty to children. For provisions for the prevention of cruelty to children see Children and Young Persons Act 1933, s 1.

Cujus est solum ejus est usque coelum et ad inferos. To whom belongs the soil, his it is, even to heaven, and to the middle of the earth. But by the Civil Aviation Act 1982, s 776(1) no action lies in respect of trespass or nuisance by reason only of the flight of an aircraft over property at a reasonable height.

Cum dividend. With the dividend. A term used in connection with the purchase of shares resulting in the buyer having a right to the dividend in respect of them.

See DIVIDEND; SHARE.

Cum rights. With the rights. A term used to denote the fact that a buyer of shares is entitled to subscribe for further shares in proportion to the number bought.

See RIGHTS ISSUE; SHARE.

Cum testamento annexo. With the will annexed.

See ADMINISTRATOR.

Cumulative legacy. A legacy which is to take effect in addition to another disposition whether by the same or another instrument, in favour of the same party, as opposed to a substitutional legacy, which is to take effect as a substitute for some other disposition.

See LEGACY.

Cumulative preference shares. Where preference shares are cumulative, then if the profits of the company in any year are insufficient to pay the fixed dividend on them, the deficiency must be made up out of the profits of subsequent years.

See PREFERENCE SHARES.

Preference shares are presumed to be cumulative and ambiguous language in the articles will not be enough to make them non-cumulative (see *Foster v Coles and MB Foster & Sons Ltd* (1906) 22 TLR 555).

See NON-CUMULATIVE PREFERENCE SHARES.

Cumulative sentence. A sentence passed on a person already under sentence for a crime; the second sentence to commence after the expiration of the first and not to run concurrently.

Cur adv vult. *See* CURIA ADVISARI VULT.

Curate. A person who has the cure of souls. The term is applied to one holding the lowest degree in the Church.

Curator. A person entrusted with the charge of an estate, or with the conduct of a minor who is past the age of pupillarity, or with the management of a lawsuit. Also used of the keeper of a museum.

Curfew order. An order requiring a person of or over the age of 16 who is convicted of an offence to remain for a period at a place specified in it: Criminal Justice Act 1991, s 12(1).

Curia advisari vult. An expression used in law reports to indicate that the Court wished to deliberate before pronouncing judgment.

Currency note means
1 any note which
   (i) has been lawfully issued in England and Wales, Scotland, Northern Ireland, any of the Channel Islands, the Isle of Man or the Republic of Ireland; and
   (ii) is or has been customarily used in the country where it was issued; and
   (iii) is payable on demand; or
2 any note which
   (i) has been lawfully issued in some country other than those mentioned above; and
   (ii) is customarily used as money in that country (see Forgery and Counterfeiting Act 1981, s 27(1)).

Curtain clauses. Those provisions of the Law of Property Act 1925 which relate to the modification of the equitable doctrine of notice. (Not to be confused with the 'curtain principle': see LAND REGISTRATION). Their general principle is that the legal estate in land should be vested in some person or persons authorised to sell, exchange, partition or lease it, and in certain cases to mortgage it so as to override all equities other than certain excepted ones. The overridden equities are transferred from the land itself to the purchase money, if sold, or to the land taken in exchange on a partition, or to rents and profits of the land leased.

See BONA FIDE PURCHASER; NOTICE; LAND LAW.

Curtesy. A species of life estate, now abolished, to which a widower was entitled in the lands of his wife upon her death.

See DOWER.

Curtilage. A garden, yard or field, or other piece of ground lying near or belonging to a house or messuage.

See MESSUAGE.

Custodian trustee. A trustee appointed to have the custody as distinguished from the management of the trust property.

Custom. Unwritten law established by long use. Custom is of two kinds:

1 General custom, ie the Common Law properly so called.

See COMMON LAW.

2 Particular custom, ie, the customs which affect only the inhabitants of particular districts. These it is usual to designate by the word customs, to distinguish them from the Common Law.

The requisites to make a particular custom good are: it must have been (i) used so long that the memory of man runs not to the contrary (*see* TIME IMMEMORIAL), (ii) continuous, (iii) peaceable, (iv) reasonable, (v) certain, (vi) compulsory, and (vii) consistent with other customs.

Custom house. A house in several cities and seaports, where the Queen's customs are received, and all business relating to them transacted.

See CUSTOMS ON GOODS.

Custom of merchants (*Lex Mercatoria*). The branch of law which comprises the rules relating to bills of exchange, partnership and other mercantile matters. In mercantile custom, universality is of far greater importance than immemorial antiquity.

See LAW MERCHANT.

Custom of the country means, in agriculture, the usage which, unless expressly excluded, formerly governed the relations of agricultural landlords and tenants. Now becoming obsolete (see Agricultural Holdings Act 1986, Agricultural Tenancies Act 1995).

Customs on goods. The duties, toll, or tariff payable on goods exported and imported. The law relating to customs and excise is now principally embodied in the Customs and Excise Management Act 1979.

Cy-près. When the intention of a donor or testator is incapable of being literally acted on, or where its literal performance would be unreasonable, or in excess of what the law allows, the Courts often allow the intention to be carried into effect *cy-près*, ie, *as nearly as may be* practicable, or reasonable, or consistent with law; (i) when a testator attempts to settle his property on future generations beyond the limits allowed by law; or (ii) where a gift for a charitable purpose is for some reason impossible to carry out. The *cy-près* doctrine, under wills, appears to be abolished. In the case of charities, the court will apply the charitable gift to a charitable purpose of the same kind as that intended by the donor. (See Charities Act 2006, ss 15–18).

D

DCL. Doctor of Civil Law.

DPP. *See* DIRECTOR OF PUBLIC PROSECUTIONS.

DTI. *See* DEPARTMENT OF TRADE AND INDUSTRY.

Damages. The pecuniary, ie monetary, satisfaction awarded by a Judge or jury in a civil action for the wrong suffered by the plaintiff.
See EXEMPLARY DAMAGES; LIQUIDATED DAMAGES; GENERAL DAMAGES; SPECIAL DAMAGES; NOMINAL DAMAGES.

Dame. The title of the wife of a knight or baronet. The equivalent of a knighthood for a woman.

Damnify. To injure, to damage, to cause loss to any person.

Damnosa hereditas. A burdensome inheritance; ie, an inheritance of which the liabilities exceed the assets.

Damnum absque injuria. A damage without injury, ie, effected without legal wrong. In such a case, no action is maintainable. Thus, if one has a mill, and one's neighbour builds another mill on his own ground, whereby the profit of one's mill is diminished, no action lies against him, for everyone may lawfully erect a mill on his own ground.

Data. Information recorded in a form in which it can be processed by equipment operating automatically in response to instructions given for that purpose (see Data Protection Act 1984, s 1(2)).

Data Protection Registrar. A registrar appointed under the Data Protection Act 1984 whose duty is to promote the observance of the data protection principles by data users (see Data Protection Act 1984, s 36(1)).

Day, weather permitting working. *See* WEATHER PERMITTING WORKING DAY.

Day, weather working. *See* WEATHER WORKING DAY.

Days. A term used in a charter-party to denote consecutive days including Sundays and holidays: *Nielsen & Co v Wait, James & Co* (1885) 16 QBD 67, CA. The word 'day' usually means a calendar day commencing at midnight, and not a period of 24 hours calculated from the moment of the vessel's arrival: *The Katy* [1895] P 56, CA.

Days, running. *See* RUNNING DAYS.

Days of grace. 1 Three days allowed for the payment of a bill of exchange or a promissory note after it has nominally become due. No such days of grace are allowed in the case of bills of exchange and promissory notes purporting to be payable on sight or on demand (see Bills of Exchange Act 1882, s 14).
2 A period after the expiry date of an insurance policy allowing the insured to renew it. In the absence of a stipulation he is not entitled to days of grace.

De bene esse. May perhaps be translated 'for what it is worth'. To take or do a thing *de bene esse* is to allow or accept for the present, provisionally, until it comes to be more fully examined, and then to stand or fall according to the merit of the thing in its own nature, so that *valeat quantum valere potest* (let it have its weight, in so far as it can be assessed). Thus, the taking of evidence in a Chancery action *de bene esse* is taking evidence out of the regular course, and is looked upon as a temporary and conditional examination, to be used only in case the witness cannot be afterwards examined in the action in the regular way.

De bonis non. *See* ADMINISTRATOR.

De die in diem. From day to day; thus, a sitting *de die in diem* is a sitting until a case is concluded.

De facto. In fact, in reality. An expression indicating the actual state of circumstances, independently of any question of right or title; thus, a King *de facto* is a person acknowledged and acting as King, independently of the question whether some one else has a better title to the Crown.

By the Treason Act 1495 subjects obeying a King *de facto* are excused from any penalties of treason to a King *de jure*.
See DE JURE.

De jure. As of right, legitimate. Sometimes used of a supposed right as opposed to actual fact; thus, a government *de jure* is a so-called government which is not a government, but which, according to the speaker or writer, ought to be a government.
See DE FACTO.

De minimis non curat lex. The law takes no account of very trifling matters.

De novo. Anew. Thus, to begin *de novo* is to begin again from the beginning.

De son tort. *See* EXECUTOR DE SON TORT; TRUSTEE DE SON TORT.

Deacon. The lowest degree of holy orders in the Church of England.

Dead freight. Damages claimable by a shipowner where a charterer has failed to provide a full cargo (see *Angfartygs AB Halfdan v Price and Pierce Ltd* [1939] 1 All ER 322).

Dead rent. A rent payable on a mining lease in addition to a royalty, so called because it is payable although the mine may not be worked.

Dealing as a consumer. *See* CONSUMER, DEALING AS.

Dean. The chief of the clergy appointed for the celebration of divine service in the bishop's cathedral.

Dean of the Arches. The Judge of the Arches Court, so called because he anciently held his court in the Church of St Mary-le-Bow (*Sancta Maria de arcubus*).
See ARCHES, COURT OF.

Death Duty. Duty paid from the assets of a deceased person's estate by the PERSONAL REPRESENTATIVE of the deceased, usually calculated as a percentage value of the estate.

Conceptually distinct from an INHERITANCE TAX.

Death-bed or **dying declarations.** As an exception to the general rule against hearsay evidence (see HEARSAY EVIDENCE), the statements of persons *in extremis* are admissible in evidence after their death as to the cause of it eg statements made by a person fatally wounded as to the identity of his assailant.

Debenture. 1 A custom-house certificate to the effect that an importer of goods is entitled to 'drawback'.
See DRAWBACK.

2 A form of loan secured by an interest in property (*see* SECURITY INTEREST), most typically entered into by companies to secure funds for their business operations. It is a charge in writing (usually under seal) of certain property with the repayment at a time fixed of the money lent at a given rate of interest. Being for a fixed sum and time it was found to be inconvenient to lenders, and has been superseded in some cases by *debenture stock,* whereby the creditors or debenture holders receive rights of periodic payment and rights to enforce the security where timely payment is not made. Debenture stock is frequently irredeemable and usually transferable in any amount. The issue of debenture stock in the case of companies incorporated by Act of Parliament is regulated either by their special Acts or by the Companies Clauses Act 1863. As to registration, see Companies Act 1985, ss 190, 191.

Debenture-holders' action. An action brought by a debenture-holder on behalf of himself and all other debenture-holders of the same class to enforce their rights under the debentures.

Debenture trust deed. A deed charging specific property of a company by a legal mortgage or legal charge in favour of trustees for the debenture-holders and charging the rest of the assets of the company by a floating charge.
See DEBENTURE; FLOATING CHARGE.

Debit card. A card the use of which by its holder to make a payment results in a current account of his at a bank, or at any other institution providing banking services, being debited with the payment.

Debt. A certain sum due from one person to another either (i) by *record*, eg, judgment, (ii) under *specialty*, or deed, or (iii) under *simple* contract by writing or oral. With the exception of certain preferred debts, all debts are payable *pari passu* in bankruptcy (see Insolvency Act 1986, s 328). In the administration of the estate of a deceased person the order is (i) Crown debts, (ii) rates, taxes, etc, (iii) judgments, (iv) recognisances and statutes, (v) specialty and simple debts, (vi) voluntary debts, but when the estate is insolvent the order follows that of bankruptcy (see Administration of Estates Act 1925, s 34(1), and Sch I, Part I).

Debt-adjusting, in relation to debts due under consumer credit agreements or consumer hire agreements, means:
  (i) negotiating with the creditor or owner terms for the discharge of a debt; or
  (ii) taking over the debtor's obligations to discharge a debt; or
  (iii) any similar activity concerned with the liquidation of a debt: Consumer Credit Act 1974, s 145(5).
  See CONSUMER CREDIT AGREEMENT; CONSUMER HIRE AGREEMENT.

Debt-collecting. The taking of steps to procure payment of debts due under consumer credit agreements or consumer hire agreements: Consumer Credit Act 1974, s 145(7).
See CONSUMER CREDIT AGREEMENT; CONSUMER HIRE AGREEMENT.

Debt-counselling. Giving advice to debtors or hirers about the liquidation of debts due under consumer credit agreements or consumer hire agreements: Consumer Credit Act 1974, s 145(6).
See CONSUMER CREDIT AGREEMENT; CONSUMER HIRE AGREEMENT.

Deceit. Fraud, craft, or collusion, employed for the purpose of gaining an advantage over another. A false statement of fact made by a person knowingly or recklessly with intent that it shall be acted on by another who does so act on it and thereby suffers damage. A tortious act, a plaintiff may bring an action for damages for deceit.
See FRAUD.

Deception. By the Theft Act 1968, s 15(4) 'deception' means any deception (whether deliberate or reckless) by words or conduct as to fact or as to law, including a deception as to the present intentions of the person

using the deception or any other person. It is an offence under the act to obtain goods or services by deception.
See CHEAT.

Declarant. A person who makes a declaration.

Declaration, statutory. *See* STATUTORY DECLARATION.

Declaration in lieu of oath. Prior to 1835 a large number of oaths had to be taken in the course of business affairs, with the result that the taking of an oath came to be regarded as a pure formality. To check the abuse of the oath the Statutory Declarations Act 1835 was passed, providing for the substitution of a statutory declaration, in a form set out in a Schedule to the Act, except (i) in the case of an oath of allegiance (*see* OATH OF ALLEGIANCE), and (ii) in the case of an oath, affirmation or affidavit in a court of justice.
See STATUTORY DECLARATION.

Declaration of solvency. A statutory declaration by the directors, where it is proposed to wind up a company voluntarily, to the effect that they have made a full inquiry into the affairs of the company, and that, having done so, they have formed the opinion that the company will be able to pay its debts in full within such period not exceeding twelve months from the commencement of the winding up as may be specified in the declaration (see the Insolvency Act 1986, s 89(1)).
  A declaration of solvency has no effect unless:
  (i) it is made within the five weeks immediately preceding the date of the passing of the resolution for winding up or on that date but before the passing of that resolution; and
  (ii) it embodies a statement of the company's assets and liabilities as at the latest practicable date before the making of the declaration: (ibid, s 89(2)).

Declaration of trust. The essential operative act by which a trust is created. A declaration of trust whereby a person admits that he holds property on trust for another is called a *self-declaration of trust*. Typically, however, a person who creates a trust will transfer property *on trust* to someone who will hold the legal title to the property as trustee, and before or at the time of transfer will declare the trust, either orally or in writing.

A trust is only *constituted*, made actual, when the trustee acquires the legal title to the trust property. A declaration of trust of land, whether freehold or leasehold, must, by the Law of Property Act 1925, s 53, be evidenced in writing, and signed by the party declaring the trust. But declarations of trust of money, or personal chattels, need not be so evidenced. For the form of trust instrument on settlement of land, see Settled Land Act 1925, Sch I, Form No 3.

Declaratory Act. An Act of Parliament which professes to *declare* existing law, and not to enact new law. Legislative declaration, however, like judicial, is sometimes deceptive, and enacts new law under the guise of expounding the old.

Declaratory Judgment. A judgment which states the court's opinion on the law or declares the rights of the parties, but makes no other order. A party seeking such a declaration by the court is said to seek declaratory relief.

Declaratory Relief. *See* DECLARATORY JUDGMENT.

Decree. A law. An order of the Court; the order of a Court of Chancery disposing of a suit was traditionally known as a 'decree in equity'.

Decree absolute. Final decree in suits for dissolution or nullity of marriage.
See DECREE NISI.

Decree in equity. *See* DECREE.

Decree nisi. The Matrimonial Causes Act 1973, s 1(5) provides that every decree of divorce shall, in the first instance, be a *decree nisi*, not to be made absolute until after the expiration of a fixed time.

After the pronouncement of the *decree nisi*, and before it is made absolute, any person may show cause why the decree should not be made absolute. Failing any such intervention, the party who has obtained the decree normally applies for, and is granted a *decree absolute*, upon which the parties are finally divorced.
See DIVORCE.

Dedication of way. The giving up of a private road to the use of the public.

Where a way over any land has been actually enjoyed by the public as of right and without interruption for a full period of 20 years, the way is deemed to have been dedicated as a highway unless there is evidence that there was no intention to dedicate it. See more fully Highways Act 1980, s 31. See also s 3 (dedication of highway by agreement with parish council) and s 7(3) (dedication of land for the widening of highways) of the same Act.

Deed. An ancient creature of the common law, the deed is a formal written instrument which *acted* at law to alter the rights and duties of the parties to it, hence the term *deed*. Deeds could, for example, bind someone at law to carry out a promise expressed in it, or transfer title to property. At common law a deed, to be effective, needed to be SEALed and delivered, hence the use of the phrase a document, promise, etc 'under seal'. The seal was all important—if the seal fell off, the deed was ineffective. As long as the parties to the deed were clear, and the party bound under the deed affixed his seal, there was no need for a signature, and rare was the person who could make one given the general inability to write. The requirement of signature came later, so that a deed to be effective needed to be signed, sealed and delivered. Delivery is also essential. The mere writing, signing, and sealing of a deed did not make it effective; a person obtaining an advantage under a deed needed to attain possession of it by delivery, ie the creator needed to transfer possession of the deed to that person with the intention of making it legally binding.
See DELIVERY OF A DEED.

Deeds no longer require a seal, so that strictly speaking it is now incorrect to refer to promises, etc. 'under seal'; by the Law of Property (Miscellaneous Provisions) Act 1989, deeds must be signed by the party or parties bound by them, and *attested* by two witnesses. The requirement of delivery remains. By properly signing, sealing, and delivering a deed, or now by signing, having attested, and delivering a deed, a person is said to *execute* a deed. Execution in the case of a corporation requires the affixing of the seal of the corporation.

Deeds are of two general forms, either a *deed poll* or a *deed indented*. If a deed is made by more parties than one, there ought to be as many copies of it as there are parties; multiple copies of the deed were thus made by copying, or engrossing, the words of the deed as many times as necessary on one parchment, and the copies then separated by cutting in irregular acute angles on the top or side, ie along *indented* lines, and such deeds are called indentures. Because the different copies of the deed could be shown to tally or correspond with one another by placing them side by side, this method of making deeds served as a device to prevent fraud. By the Law of Property Act 1925, s 56(2), a deed between parties, to effect its objects, has the effect of an indenture though not indented or expressed to be an indenture. A deed made by one party only is not indented, but *polled* or shaved quite even, and is therefore called a *deed poll*, or a single deed.

Deeds may be described as deeds, or as conveyances, trust instruments, settlements, mortgages, etc, according to their nature (see Law of Property Act 1925, s 57).

Deed of arrangement. *See* ARRANGEMENTS.

Deed of composition. *See* COMPOSITION.

Deed of covenant. Covenants are often entered into by separate deed, eg, a deed of covenant for production of deeds (now generally replaced by an acknowledgement).

Deed of separation. *See* SEPARATION.

Deed-poll. *See* DEED.

Deem. To consider something to be. See *R v Norfolk County Council* (1891) 60 L J QB 379, in which Cave J, said: 'Generally speaking, when you talk of a thing being deemed to be something, you do not mean to say that it is that which it is deemed to be. It is rather an admission that it is not what it is deemed to be, and that, notwithstanding it is not that particular thing, nevertheless…it is to be deemed to be that thing'. See also *St Aubyn v A-G (No 2)* [1951] 2 All ER 473 at 498, per Lord Radcliffe.

Defalcation. The act of an embezzler or misappropriator of funds in his care, such as a trustee who fraudulently appropriates trust funds.
See EMBEZZLEMENT.

Defamation. The general term for words which tend to injure a person's reputation by degrading him in the opinion of his neighbours or to make him ridiculous. Defamation is divided into (i) libel; and (ii) slander.

Libel consists of matter published in a permanent form, eg a newspaper, a film, a letter, a photograph.

Slander consists of matter published in an oral form. But the broadcasting of words by means of wireless telegraphy (ie by radio or television) is treated as publication in a permanent form.

To found an action for defamation, the offending matter must be published to a third party.

In the case of libel, no damage to the plaintiff has to be proved. In slander, special damage, ie actual loss consequent on the diminution of one's reputation, must be proved except where the statement is an imputation:

(i) of a criminal offence;
(ii) of a contagious or infectious disease;
(iii) of unchastity of a woman (Slander of Women Act 1891);
(iv) in respect of a person's profession or business.

Defences to an action for defamation are:
(i) absolute privilege (*see* ABSOLUTE PRIVILEGE);
(ii) justification (ie truth);
(iii) qualified privilege (*see* QUALIFIED PRIVILEGE);
(iv) fair comment (*see* FAIR COMMENT).

The defendant may offer an apology in mitigation of damages: Libel Act 1843, s 1. By the Defamation Act 1996, a defendant may make an *offer of amends*, to publish an appropriate correction to the defamatory statement and pay an amount to the plaintiff in compensation.

A person who maliciously publishes a libel, knowing it to be false, commits an offence: ibid, s 4.

Default. An offence in omitting that which one ought to do as in the expression 'wilful neglect or default'. It is often taken for non-appearance in court at a day assigned; and judgment given against a party by reason of such non-appearance, or other neglect to take any of the steps required of him within due time, is called *judgment by default*.

Default action. A procedure in the County Courts for the summary recovery of a debt or liquidated demand.

Default fine. A daily fine imposed where a person is convicted after continued contravention.

Default judgment. A resolution of a dispute by the court's decision in favour of the plaintiff or claimant where the defendant has failed to defend the action or case.

Defeasance. Defeat, ie termination or extinction, generally of a pre-existing legal right or interest upon the occurrence of an event specified when the right or interest was granted or created. Thus a *defeasible* interest in land is an interest granted or created on a condition of defeasance, eg a life estate to A so long as A does not leave the country.

Defeasance, deed of. A collateral deed, made at the same time with a conveyance, containing certain conditions, on the performance of which the estate then created may be defeated or totally undone. So, a defeasance on a bond or recognisance, or judgment recovered, is a condition which, when performed, defeats or undoes it. It is inserted in a separate deed in the same manner as the defeasance of an estate mentioned above.

Defect in a product occurs where the safety of the product is not such as persons generally are entitled to expect in relation to the risks of death, personal injury or damage to property: Consumer Protection Act 1987, s 3(1).

Defence. *See* STATEMENT OF DEFENCE.

Defendant. A person sued in a civil action or charged with a criminal offence. In the case of a criminal offence, he is also called the *prisoner* or the *accused*.

Defender of the Faith. The title 'Defender of the Faith' (*fidei defensor*) was first given by Pope Leo X to Henry VIII in 1521, Henry having written against Martin Luther on behalf of the Catholic church. Despite the subsequent events of the Reformation the title has continued to be used by the Kings and Queens of England to the present day. The title (expressed FD or Fid Def) is still stamped on coins of the realm.

Deferment of sentence. The Crown Court or a magistrates' court may defer passing sentence on an offender to enable the court to have regard to his future conduct or to any change in his circumstances. The offender must consent and deferment must be for not more than six months (see Powers of Criminal Courts Act 1973, s 1).

Deferred debt. A debt (eg one in respect of which a rate of interest varying with the profits of a business is payable) which has to be paid after the preferred debts and the ordinary debts have been paid in full.

Deferred shares or stock. Stock or shares in a company, the holders of which have a right to participate in the net earnings of the company, but the right is *deferred* until the prior claims of preferred and ordinary stock or shareholders have been met.

Definitive sentence. The final judgment of an ecclesiastical court, as distinguished from an interlocutory or provisional judgment. *See* ECCLESIASTICAL COURTS.

Degradation. 1 Of peers. Where a person who has been in the rank of peer has ceased to be such, eg when a peeress, who is such only by a former marriage, subsequently marries a commoner, or where a peer is deprived of his nobility by Act of Parliament.

2 Of ecclesiastics. As thus applied, the word signifies an ecclesiastical censure, whereby a clergyman is deprived of his holy orders. *See* HOLY ORDERS.

Degree. A step; in particular, the increments of distance between kindred for the purpose of applying the rules of devolution of property on the death of one intestate, ie with no valid will (*see* SUCCESSION). Those who are equally close or distance to the deceased, eg all of the deceased's children, are said to be kin or kindred of 'equal degree'.

Del credere commission. A commission for the sale of goods by an agent, who, for a higher reward than is usually given, becomes responsible to his principal for the solvency of the purchaser, ie the agent (who is then called a *del credere* agent) guarantees the due payment of the price of the goods sold.

Delegation. The assignment of a duty or power of action to another person.

Delegatus non potest delegare. An agent cannot delegate his authority.

Delicto, action ex. A phrase occasionally used to designate an action of *tort*; ie an action for a wrong which is such independently of contract, eg for libel, assault, etc. Delict as used in CIVIL LAW systems roughly corresponds to tort. *See* TORT.

Delicto, in pari. *See* IN PARI DELICTO.

Delivery. The transferring of possession from one person to another. It may be *actual*, as when, in fact, goods change hands, or *constructive*, eg where a buyer is already in possession of goods before sale, and afterwards pays for them.

Delivery clause. A clause in a time charter-party stating the port and the time at which the vessel is to be delivered to the charterer.

Delivery of a deed. This is held to be performed by the person who executes the

deed placing his finger on the seal, and saying 'I deliver this as my act and deed'. A deed takes effect only from delivery. A delivery may be either absolute, to the other party or grantee himself; or to a third person, to hold until some condition is performed by the grantee; in which latter case it is called an *escrow*.
See DEED.

Delivery order. An order addressed by the owner of goods to a bailee requiring him to deliver the goods to a named person. Included in the term 'document of title' as defined by the Factors Act 1889, s 1.

Delivery up of goods, order for. A remedy provided for by the Torts (Interference with Goods) Act 1977 by which a claimant may recover goods unlawfully in the possession of the defendant.
See CONVERSION.

Demise (Lat *Demittere*). To lease. The word implies an absolute covenant on the part of the lessor for quiet enjoyment. This implied covenant may be, and usually is, qualified by an express covenant more limited in extent.
See LEASE.

Demise charter-party. A charter-party under which the charterer puts his own stores, fuel oil, etc, on board and hires the crew. It is sometimes known as a 'bare-boat' charter-party. In such a charter-party the master and crew are the charterer's servants, and the possession and control of the vessel rest in him.

Demise of the Crown. A phrase used to denote the death or abdication of the King or Queen, because the kingdom is thereby transferred or *demised* to his successor.

Demolition order. Under the provisions of the Housing Act 1985 local authorities are empowered to make demolition or closing orders in respect of premises which they consider unfit for human habitation. The content of such a demolition order is specified in s 267; it must require vacation within a period to be specified (not less than 28 days), and that thereafter the premises shall be demolished within six weeks. As to what matters are to be taken into account in determining the question of fitness for human habitation, see ibid, s 604.

Demonstrative legacy. A gift by will of a certain sum to be paid out of a specific fund.
See LEGACY.

Demurrage. The daily sum payable by a charterer, who, having chartered a ship for a voyage, detains it for a longer time than he is entitled to do by the charter-party.

Demurrer. Formerly, a pleading by a defendant in a civil action that the facts stated by the plaintiff, even if assumed to be true, did not show a good CAUSE OF ACTION or, in other words, that the plaintiff was making a claim unknown to the law. The plea of demurrer was superceded by the application to 'strike out' the plaintiff's statement of claim (now, the claimant's 'statement of case') as disclosing no cause of action.

Department of Trade and Industry. A government department responsible for general overseas policy, commercial relations, exports, tariffs, companies, and insurance legislation.

Departure. In pleading, departure is the shifting of his ground by a party, or a variation from the title or defence which he has once insisted on.

Dependant. A person who to some extent depends on others for the provision of the ordinary necessities of life; a person to some extent maintained by another (*Re Ball, Hand v Ball* [1947] 1 Ch 228).

Deponent. A person who gives evidence, whether orally or by affidavit.
See AFFIANT; DEPOSITION.

Deportation. Transportation, banishment.

Depose. To make a deposition or statement on oath.
See DEPOSITION.

Deposit. 1 The act of entrusting money to a bank is called a *deposit* in a bank; and the amount of the money deposited is also called the *deposit*.
2 A type of bailment by which a person entrusts another with a chattel to keep it safely without reward.
See BAILMENT.
3 Money paid as earnest or security for the performance of a contract, eg, the money paid by the purchaser on signature of a contract for sale.
4 Of litter. An offence under the Environmental Protection Act 1990.

Deposit of title deeds. This is when the title deeds of an estate are deposited (generally with a bank) as a security for the repayment of money advanced. This operates as an equitable mortgage. The right to create equitable charges by deposit of deeds is preserved by the Law of Property Act 1925, ss 2(3) and 13.

See EQUITABLE MORTGAGE; MORTGAGE.

Deposit Protection Fund. A fund administered by the Deposit Protection Board under the Banking Act 1987. Its function is to pay compensation to depositors in the event of a bank becoming insolvent (see Banking Act 1987, s 58). All banks are liable to contribute to the Fund (ibid, s 52).

Deposition. A word to indicate written evidence or oral evidence taken down in writing, given by a 'deponent'. The general principle is that a witness statement may not be read at the trial as evidence except where the witness himself cannot be produced, for that denies the defendant the opportunity to cross-examine the witness on his evidence. In general, see Civil Procedure Rules 1998 for the circumstances in which depositions are ordered and may be used at trial.

Deprave. To pervert or morally corrupt.

See OBSCENITY.

Deprivation. A depriving or taking away: eg a bishop, parson, vicar, etc, is deposed from his preferment.

Deputy. One who acts for another in some office. Judges of the Supreme Court cannot act by deputy, but deputy circuit judges may be appointed under the Courts Act 1971, s 24(2). By the Sheriffs Act 1887 every sheriff must appoint a deputy having an office within a mile of the Inner Temple Hall for the receipt of writs, etc.

Derelict. Vessel or cargo which is abandoned to sea by those in charge of it without hope on their part of recovering it or without any intention of returning to it (*The Aquila* (1798) 1 Ch Rob 37 at 40). A vessel which is left only temporarily by her master and crew with the intention of returning to her is not a 'derelict' even though her management may have passed into the hands of salvors (*Cossman v West; Cossman v British America Assurance Co* (1887) 13 App Cas 160).

Dereliction. Where the sea shrinks back below low water-mark, so that land is gained from the sea. If this gain is gradual, it goes to the owner of the land adjoining; but if it is sudden, the land gained belongs to the Crown.

See ACCRETION.

Derivative action or **claim.** An action or claim brought by the shareholders of a company, on behalf of the company itself, who would normally be the proper plaintiff. It is an exception to the rule that only the company itself should have standing to bring claims on its own behalf. It is the essence of such a claim that the directors or officers have failed in their duty of directing the company by not themselves launching the action or claim in the company's name.

Derivative conveyance. A conveyance which presupposes some other conveyance precedent, and serves to enlarge, confirm, alter, restrain, restore, or transfer the interest granted by such original conveyance.

See PRIMARY CONVEYANCES.

Derivative settlement. *See* SETTLEMENT.

Derogate. To take away from or to evade. The maxim that 'No man can derogate from his own grant' means that a man, having contracted eg to sell land, cannot afterwards prejudice the purchaser by obstructing the easements, etc, implied in the grant.

See EASEMENT.

Descendant. A relation in a succeeding generation. A direct or lineal descendent is a child, a child of that child (ie grandchild) and so on. A collateral descendent is one whose relationship is traced through a common ancestor, ie one's nephew is one's relation as being a child of one's brother or sister, who shares one's parents.

Descent. One of the two main ways by which property in land was acquired before the Administration of Estates Act 1925, specifically, the way land was acquired upon intestacy, ie upon the death of an owner of the land where the land was not disposed of by will. Thus, acquisition of land by descent was opposed to acquisition of land at the direction of the owner, either by a grant *inter vivos*, or by will. Only the acquisition of land by descent is properly called 'inheritance', for the rules of descent reflected the system by which succeeding generations had claims *as heirs* upon the land of their ancestors. The rules of descent embodied the principles of primogeniture, by which male heirs were preferred to female heirs, and only the eldest son inherited if there were several. This system applied only to estates in land, the devolution of personal property upon intestacy operating by different rules. The devolution of all manner of property in an intestate's estate became subject to common rules by the Administration of Estates Act 1925.

Desertion. 1 The criminal offence of abandoning the naval, military or air force service without permission.

By the Naval Discipline Act 1957, s 15 a person is guilty of desertion if he leaves or fails to attend at his ship or place of duty with the intention of remaining permanently absent from duty without proper authority or if, having left or failed to attend at his ship or place of duty in any circumstances, he does any act with the like intention. Desertion is also dealt with under the Army Act 1955, s 37 and the Air Force Act 1955, s 37.

2 An abandonment of a wife or husband. Evidence of desertion may be given on a petition for divorce on the ground of irretrievable breakdown of marriage (see Matrimonial Causes Act 1973, s 1).

See DIVORCE.

Design. Features of shape, configuration, pattern, or ornament, applied to an article by an industrial process, being features which in the finished article appeal to and are judged by the eye, but does not include:

(i) a method of construction, or

(ii) features of shape or configuration of an article which

   (a) are dictated solely by the function which it has to perform; or

   (b) which are dependent on the appearance of another article of which the article is intended by the author of the design to form an integral part: Registered Designs Act 1949, s 1(1).

See DESIGN RIGHT.

Design, registered. *See* DESIGN RIGHT.

Design right. A property right which subsists in an original design: Copyright, Designs and Patents Act 1988, s 213(1). 'Design' means the design of any aspect of the shape or configuration of an article: ibid, s 213(2). A design is not 'original' if it is commonplace in the design field in question at the time of its creation: ibid, s 213(4). A design right does not subsist until the design has been recorded in a design document or an article has been made to the design: ibid, s 213(6).

The 'designer' is the person who creates it: Copyright, Designs and Patents Act 1988, s 214(1). In the case of a computer-generated design, the designer is the person by whom the arrangements necessary for the creation of the design are undertaken: ibid, s 214(2).

The designer is the first owner of any design right which is not created in pursuance of a commission (ie one for money or money's worth) or in the course of employment: Copyright, Designs and Patents Act 1988, s 215(1). Where a design is created in pursuance of a commission, the person commissioning it is the first owner: ibid, s 215(2). Where it is created by an employee in the course of his employment, his employer is the first owner: ibid, s 215(3).

Design right expires 15 years from the end of the calendar year in which the design was first recorded in a design document: ibid, s 216(1).

The owner of design right has the exclusive right to reproduce it for commercial purposes:

(i) by making the articles to that design; or

(ii) by making a design document recording the design for the purpose of enabling such articles to be made: ibid, s 226(1).

There is a primary infringement of a design right where a person without the licence of the owner of the design right does anything which is the owner's exclusive right: ibid, s 226(3).

Secondary infringement occurs where a person, without the licence of the owner of the design right:

(i) imports into the United Kingdom for commercial purposes; or

(ii) has in his possession for commercial purposes; or

(iii) sells, lets for hire, or offers or exposes for sale or hire, in the course of a business, an article which is, or which he knows or has reason to believe is, an infringing article: ibid, s 227(1).

The owner of a design right, in an action for infringement of design right, is entitled to all such relief by way of damages, injunctions, accounts or otherwise as is available in respect of the infringement of any other property right: ibid, s 229(1). He may apply for an order for the delivery up of an infringing article (ibid, s 230) or an order for the disposal of an infringing article (ibid, s 231).

D

Desuetude. A rule or practice that is no longer followed is said to fall into 'desuetude', or disuse. While desuetude is fatal to the existence of a custom, and perhaps to rules of the common law, desuetude does not per se affect the validity of statutory law.

Detainer. The forcible detention of a person's person or property.
See FORCIBLE DETAINER.

Detention of vessel clause. A clause in a time charter-party making the charterer liable for the detention of a vessel and expenses incurred thereby, eg in the event of the vessel being driven into port through stress of weather or suffering an accident to her cargo.

Determinable freeholds. Freehold estates, eg fees simple or life estates, which are limited by the possibility of termination on a given contingency, specified in the deed creating them. There is an extremely fine distinction between estates defeasible upon condition subsequent, and determinable estates. An estate defeasible upon condition subsequent is regarded as the gift of the whole freehold estate which may be extinguished upon the occurrence of an event, for example a life estate framed 'to A for life but if she marries, then to B for life'; a determinable life estate is one regarded as being limited to a lesser period than a life estate from the outset, eg 'to A during her widowhood' which may, should the determining event not occur, ripen into a full life estate. After 1925 they subsist only as equitable interests in land (see Law of Property Act 1925, s 1, and Sch I, Pt I).
See CONDITIONS PRECEDENT AND SUBSEQUENT; CONDITIONAL LIMITATION; ESTATES; LAND LAW.

Determinable interest. An interest in property which may come to an end on the happening of an event.

Determine. To come to an end, cease to exist; bring to an end or extinguish.

Detinue. A common law form of action for the recovery of goods from a defendant who rightfully acquired possession of them but wrongfully detained them, ie failed to return them to the true owner. Abolished by the Torts (Interference with Goods) Act 1977.
See INTERFERENCE WITH GOODS.

Devastavit. The waste or misapplication of the assets of a deceased person committed by an executor or administrator which makes him personally liable to those who have claims on the deceased's assets, eg creditors, legatees, etc.

Development. For the purposes of the Town and Country Planning Acts, development means, with certain exceptions, the carrying out of building, engineering, mining or other operations in, on, over or under land, or the making of any material change in the use of any buildings or other land. The latter includes the conversion of a single dwelling into two or more dwellings; the display of advertisements on buildings not normally so used, etc. Planning permission must be sought from the local planning authority before developments are carried out.

Local planning authorities themselves are required to carry out periodic surveys of their areas and to prepare 'structure plans', outlining their policies and general proposals for development, for the approval of the Minister of Housing and Local Government (see Town and Country Planning Act 1971, s 7(3)).

Deviation. A departure from a plan conceived and agreed on.

1 *Marine insurance.* Where a ship without lawful excuse deviates from the voyage contemplated by the policy, the insurer is discharged from liability as from the time of deviation (see Marine Insurance Act 1906, s 46(1)). It is immaterial that the ship may have regained her route before any loss occurs (ibid, s 46(1)). The intention to deviate is immaterial; there must be a deviation in fact to discharge the insurer from his liability under the contract (ibid, s 46(3)). Various excuses for deviation, eg where it is (i) reasonably necessary for the safety of the ship or subject-matter insured, or (ii) for the purpose of saving human life, are set out in s 49.

2 *Carriage by sea.* In voyage charter-parties (*see* CHARTER-PARTY) and bills of lading (*see* BILL OF LADING) to which the Hague–Visby Rules (*see* HAGUE–VISBY RULES) do not apply, deviation is allowed only (i) for the safety of the adventure; (ii) to save human life; or (iii) under an express clause in the contract.

Where the Hague–Visby Rules apply, the deviation is also excused in saving or attempting to save property at sea or where the deviation is reasonable (Art IV, r 4).

3 *Railway.* In the case of a railway under construction, deviation is allowed only

within certain limits (see Railways Clauses Consolidation Act 1845, ss 11 *et seq*).

Devise (Lat *Divisa*). A gift by a man of his lands and goods by his last will and testament in writing. The term 'devise' is principally used with reference to landed property, and 'bequeath' and 'bequest' with reference to personalty. The giver is called the *devisor* and the recipient the *devisee*.

Devolution. The transmission of title to property by operation of law, as opposed to by the act of the owner, to a PURCHASER; so, for example, property devolves when it becomes vested in the personal representative of the deceased upon death, or in the trustee in bankruptcy where an individual is bankrupt.

Devolve. *See* DEVOLUTION.

Dictum. 1 Arbitrament.
  2 A saying or opinion of a judge, during the hearing of a case.
  See OBITER DICTUM.

Die without issue. *See* DYING WITHOUT ISSUE.

Dies juridicus. An ordinary day in court, as opposed to Sundays and other holidays, on which the courts do not sit.

Dies non (*scil Juridicus*). A day on which legal proceedings cannot be carried on, eg Sundays, etc.
  See DIES JURIDICUS.

Dieu et mon droit ('God and my right'). The motto of the royal arms, introduced by Richard I, indicating that the Queen holds her dominions of no one except God.

Digest. 1 The Digest of the Emperor Justinian (otherwise called the Pandects) was a collection of extracts from the most eminent Roman jurists. In AD 530 Justinian authorised Tribonian, with the aid of sixteen commissioners, to prepare such a collection, and allowed ten years for the work. It was, however, completed in three years, and published under the name of the Digest or Pandects, on 16th December 533, and declared to have the force of law from the 30th of that month.
  See CORPUS JURIS CIVILIS.
  2 A digest of cases is a compilation of the head-notes or main points of decided cases, arranged in alphabetical order, according to the branches or subjects of law which they respectively illustrate. See, eg, *The English and Empire Digest*.

Dignitary. A dean or provost of a cathedral church; an archdeacon, canon, prebendary, etc (see Church Dignitaries (Retirement) Measure 1949, s 12 and Ecclesiastical Offices (Age Limit) Measure 1975).

Dignities. A species of incorporeal hereditament in which a person may have a property or estate. They were originally annexed to the possession of certain estates in land, and are still classed under the head of real property.
  See INCORPOREAL HEREDITAMENT.

Dilapidation. 1 The name for ecclesiastical waste committed by the incumbent of a living; which is either voluntary, by pulling down; or permissive, by allowing the chancel, parsonage-house, and other buildings belonging to them, to decay.
  See WASTE.
  2 Also used to signify a lack of repair for which a tenant who has agreed to give up the premises in good repair is liable.

Dimissory letters. Letters sent by one bishop to another, requesting him to ordain a candidate for holy orders, who has a title in the diocese of the former bishop, but is anxious to be ordained by the latter.
  See TITLE, 2.

Diocese. The circuit of a bishop's jurisdiction.

Diploma. 1 A royal charter or letters patent.
  2 A certificate less in status than a degree.

Diplomacy. The conduct of negotiations between nations, by means of correspondence or by ambassadors or the like.
  See AMBASSADOR.

Diplomatic privilege. The privilege of immunity from process, etc, accorded to ambassadors and representatives of foreign powers and the Commonwealth, and to their servants (see Diplomatic Privileges Act 1964).
  See COMMONWEALTH.

Direct descendant. A direct, or lineal, descendant is one who inherits property in a right line from generation to generation, ie a child from his parent, grandparent, great-grandparent, and so on. Opposed to a collateral descendent, who inherits by virtue of sharing a common ancestor, thus a brother might inherit from his childless brother, by tracing from the latter upwards to their shared parent, and then downwards to the former.

D

Direct effect, doctrine of. Doctrine of EU Law by which Community law creates rights and duties for EU citizens which are directly effective and enforceable in the courts of member states without those member states first having to pass implementing legislation.

Direct evidence. Evidence directly bearing on the point at issue, and which, if believed, is conclusive in favour of the party adducing it. It is opposed to *circumstantial* evidence, from which the truth as to the point at issue can be only inferentially deduced.

See CIRCUMSTANTIAL EVIDENCE.

Direction to a jury. Where a Judge instructs a jury on any point of law, in order that they may apply it to the facts in evidence before them. Misdirection may be a ground for a new trial if, in the opinion of the Court of Appeal, some substantial wrong or miscarriage has been thereby occasioned.

Directions, summons for. Formerly, a summons which is issued in most actions at an early stage of the proceedings for directions as to discovery and inspection of documents, mode and place of trial, and the like. (See RSC 1965, Ord 25). Under the new Civil Procedure Rules, this function is performed by CASE MANAGEMENT CONFERENCES.

Director. A person who *conducts* the affairs of a company.

A private company must have at least one director: Companies Act 1985, s 282(3). A public company must have at least two directors: ibid, s 282(1). The company must keep a register of directors: ibid, s 288. A director must hold a qualification share if the articles of association so require: ibid, s 291. Generally, a person cannot be appointed a director of a public company if he is aged 70 at the time of his appointment: ibid, s 293(2). A director can be removed: ibid, s 303.

Fair dealings by directors can be enforced, eg there are restrictions on a director taking financial advantage (ibid, ss 311–322A); certain share dealings by a director or his family are prohibited (ss 323–329); and there are restrictions on a company's powers to make loans to a director (ibid, ss 330–334).

Directors are not entitled to any remuneration apart from express agreement. But the articles of association usually provide that their remuneration shall be determined by an ordinary resolution of the company.

A director becomes disqualified if he does anything which by the articles of association amounts to a disqualification, eg if he becomes bankrupt or is suffering from mental disorder.

A court may make a disqualification order under the Company Directors Disqualification Act 1986.

See DIRECTOR, DISQUALIFICATION ORDER AGAINST.

A director is under a duty in the performance of his functions to have regard to the interests of the company's employees in general as well of those of its members: Companies Act 1985, s 309(1).

A director is under a duty of care towards the company, the standard of which is that of an ordinary person in the conduct of his own affairs.

Director, disqualification order against. An order by the court under the Company Directors Disqualification Act 1986. Such an order can be made if, eg

(i) he is convicted of an indictable offence (s 2);

(ii) he is guilty of persistent breaches of companies legislation (s 3);

(iii) he is guilty of fraudulent trading (s 4);

(iv) he has been a director of an insolvent company (s 6).

If a person acts in contravention of a disqualification order, he is guilty of an offence (s 13), and he is personally liable for the company's debts (s 14).

A register of disqualification orders is kept (s 18).

Director, managing. *See* MANAGING DIRECTOR.

Director, shadow. *See* SHADOW DIRECTOR.

Director General of Fair Trading. An officer appointed by the Secretary of State for the purpose of performing the functions stated in the Fair Trading Act 1973. These duties are (i) to keep under review the carrying on of commercial activities in the United Kingdom which relate to goods supplied to consumers or which relate to services supplied to them, and to collect information with respect to such activities, and the circumstances relating to practices which may adversely affect the interests of consumers; and (ii) to receive and collate evidence becoming available to him with respect to such activities: ibid, s 2(1).

Director of Public Prosecutions. An official whose duties include the instituting, undertaking, or carrying on of criminal proceedings under the directions of the Attorney-General (see now Prosecution of Offences Act 1985, ss 2, 3). He must be a barrister or solicitor of not less than ten years' standing (see Prosecution of Offences Act 1985, s 2).

Director's qualification share.
See QUALIFICATION SHARE.

Directory statute. A statute which directs anything to be done or omitted, without invalidating acts or omissions in contravention of it.

Disability. An incapacity for the full enjoyment of ordinary legal rights; eg, persons under age and mentally disordered persons are under disability. It may be either *absolute* or *partial*.

Sometimes the term is used in a more limited sense, eg when it signifies an impediment to marriage; or the restraints placed on clergymen by reason of their spiritual avocations.

Disabling statute. A statute which disables or restrains any person or persons from doing that which formerly was lawful or permissible.

Disbar. To deprive a barrister of his privileges and status as such.
See BARRISTER.

Disbench. To deprive a bencher of his privileges.
See BENCHERS.

Discharge. A word used in various senses:

1 Of the discharge of a bankrupt under the Insolvency Act 1986, s 280, by which he is freed of all debts and liabilities provable under the bankruptcy, with certain specified exceptions.

2 Of the discharge of a surety, whereby he is released from his liability as surety.
See SURETY.

3 Of the release of a prisoner from prison.

4 Of the payment of a debt whereby the debtor is freed from further liability.

5 Of the release of lands, or money in the funds, from an incumbrance, by payment of the amount to the incumbrancer, or otherwise by consent of the incumbrancer. As to discharge of mortgage by means of indorsed receipt, see Law of Property Act 1925, s 115, and Form No 2 set out in Sch III to that Act.
See INCUMBRANCE.

6 Of the reversal of an order of a court; thus, it is said that an order was 'discharged on appeal', etc.

7 A rule *nisi* is discharged where the court decides that it is not to be made absolute.

8 Of a jury, on the giving of a verdict, or on failure to agree to a verdict.

9 Of a person who is found guilty of an offence and, without further punishment, is discharged absolutely or conditionally (see Powers of Criminal Courts Act 1973, s 7).

Disclaimer. A renunciation, denial, or refusal. It is used:

1 Of any act whereby a person refuses to accept an interest in property, eg of estate which is attempted to be conveyed to him, as where land is conveyed to an intended trustee without his consent, and he refuses to accept it. This is called the disclaimer of an estate. Powers of disclaimer are given by the Administration of Estates Act 1925, s 23 to the personal representative of a tenant for life of the trust estate.

2 Of the refusal by the trustee in a bankruptcy to accept a burdensome lease or other onerous property of the bankrupt (see the Insolvency Act 1986, s 315).

3 Of disclaimer of a trade mark under the Trade Marks Act 1938, s 14.

4 Of disclaimer of powers. Under the Law of Property Act 1925, s 156 a person to whom any power, whether coupled with an interest or not, is given may by deed disclaim the power.

5 Of the refusal by a liquidator of a company to accept a burdensome lease or other onerous property (see the Insolvency Act 1986, s 178).

Disclosure. The revealing of information. More specifically, the disclosure of documents which may serve as evidence in a trial, by one side to the other in advance of trial. Disclosure of documents was formerly termed 'discovery of documents'. For the rules concerning disclosure the Civil Procedure Rules 1998, Part 31.
See DISCOVERY.

Discontinuance of action or claim. The breaking off of an action or claim, eg on withdrawal by consent. See generally the Rules of Civil Procedure 1998, Part 38.

D

Discount. 1 An allowance made to bankers or others for advancing money on bills of exchange before they become due.
See BILL OF EXCHANGE.

2 An allowance frequently made at the settlement of accounts, by way of deduction from the amount payable.

Discovery. The term describing the processes by which one party to an action discovered or acquired information from the other side about the evidence upon which that other would rely at trial. Discovery was:

1 Of *facts*, obtainable by either party to an action, in the form of answers on oath to questions known as interrogatories administered by the other party after approval of the court, and on payment of deposit as security for the costs. The answers, or any of them, might be put in as evidence at the trial, and are obtained with the object of getting admissions or discovery of such material facts as relate to the case of the party interrogating.
See INTERROGATORIES.

2 Of *documents*, obtained as above. The party against whom an order for discovery of documents was made was required to file an affidavit setting out all the documents relating to the action which are or have been in his possession or power.

Under the Civil Procedure Rules 1998, documentary discovery is called the disclosure and inspection of documents, found in Part 31, and rules concerning witness statements and depositions are found in Parts 32 and 34.

Discovery is also used in reference to the disclosure by a bankrupt of his property for the benefit of his creditors.

Discredit. To show to be unworthy of credit, or credibility. The term is employed chiefly in regard to witnesses in a court. As a general rule, a party is not entitled to discredit his own witness.

Discretionary trust. A trust under which the trustees have a discretion to apply the income and/or the capital of the trust as they wish.
See TRUST.

Discrimination. 1 Unlawful on grounds of colour, race, nationality or ethnic or national origins by the Race Relations Act 1976.

2 Sex discrimination is made unlawful (subject to certain exceptions) by the Sex Discrimination Act 1975. Sections 1, 2, 3, and 4 of that Act relate respectively to sex discrimination against women; sex discrimination against men; discrimination against married persons in the employment field; and discrimination by way of victimisation.
See EQUAL OPPORTUNITIES COMMISSION.

3 By the Human Rights Act 1998, courts of the UK will have the power to declare laws incompatible with the European Convention on Human Rights.

Disfranchise. To take away from a person his privilege or franchise or a constituency of its right of returning a member of Parliament. *May.*

Dishonest. It is enacted by the Theft Act 1968, s 1 that a person is guilty of theft if he 'dishonestly' appropriates property belonging to another with the intention of permanently depriving the other of it.
See THEFT.

Section 2 of the Act elaborates on the question of what is, and what is not, dishonesty. For example, a person's appropriation of property belonging to another is not to be regarded as dishonest if he appropriates the property in the belief that he has a legal right to deprive the other of it; nor if he believes that the other would have given his consent if he had known of the appropriation and the circumstances of it. On the other hand, a person's appropriation of property may be dishonest notwithstanding that he is willing to pay for it.

Dishonour. Where the drawee of a bill of exchange refuses to accept it, or, having accepted it, fails to pay it according to the tenor of his acceptance (see Bills of Exchange Act 1882, s 47).
See BILL OF EXCHANGE.

Dismissal of action or claim. This action by the court terminates legal proceedings, and may take place on defaults of various kinds by a claimant in pursuing his claim, eg non-appearance at trial, etc (see Rules of Civil Procedure 1998).

Disorderly house. A bawdy house or brothel. Provisions for the suppression of brothels are contained in the Sexual Offences Act 1956 ss 33–36.
See BROTHEL.

Disparagement. *Inequality* or unsuitability in marriage.

Dispatch money. Money payable by the shipowner to the charterer for any time saved in loading or discharging. The amount of dispatch money payable is often fixed at one-half of the demurrage rate.
See DEMURRAGE.

Dispensation. 1 An exemption from law.
2 An ecclesiastical licence.

Disposition (of property). An act by which an owner rids himself of his title to property, eg by transfer, or surrender.

Disseisin. To disseise is to dispossess a rightful occupier of land, by attacking and turning him out; the act is one of 'disseisin'.

Dissenters. Persons who do not conform to the Established Church. The word is usually confined to Protestant seceders from the Established Church, and their descendants.

Dissolution. The act of breaking up.
1 Of *Parliament* is where a final period is put to the existence of a Parliament by the Sovereign's will, expressed either in person or by representation, or by lapse of time.
2 Of a *partnership*, by proper notice, by effluxion of time as agreed in the articles of partnership, by order of a court, by death, insolvency, etc, of a partner.
3 Of a *marriage*, by a decree of divorce.
See DIVORCE.
4 Of *companies,* by winding up, etc (see Insolvency Act 1986, ss 201, 205).

Distrain. To execute a distress.
See DISTRESS.

Distraint. A distress.
See DISTRESS.

Distress. The taking of a personal chattel out of the possession of a wrong-doer into the custody of the party injured, to procure satisfaction for the wrong committed. The word is most frequently (though not at all exclusively) used with reference to the taking by a landlord of goods for the non-payment of rent.

Distribution. A word used specially for the division of the personal estate of an intestate among the parties entitled to it as next of kin.
The Administration of Estates Act 1925 contains a code of succession on intestacy, applying, in the case of deaths occuring after 1925, alike to real and personal estate.
See REAL AND PERSONAL PROPERTY.

District council. Under the Local Government Act 1972. Under that Act England and Wales are divided into local government areas known as counties (*see* COUNTY) and those counties are sub-divided into local government areas known as districts, each with its district council consisting of a chairman and councillors.

Disturbance. A form of real injury done to an incorporeal hereditament (*see* INCORPOREAL HEREDITAMENT), by hindering or disquieting the owners in their regular and lawful enjoyment of it. Blackstone enumerates five sorts of this injury: (i) Disturbance of *franchises*; (ii) Disturbance of *common*; (iii) Disturbance of *ways*; (iv) Disturbance of *tenure*; (v) Disturbance of *patronage*. It is also used in connection with a tenant who quits an agricultural holding.

Divest. Dispossess.

Dividend. 1 The periodic income arising from stocks, shares, etc.
2 The proportion of a creditor's debt payable to him on the division of a bankrupt's or insolvent's estate.

Divine right or **Divine right of Kings.** The patriarchal theory of government, according to which the Monarch and his legitimate heirs, being by *divine right* entitled to the sovereignty, cannot forfeit that right by any misconduct, however gross, or any period of dispossession, however long. It was by this right that the English Sovereigns in the seventeenth century claimed to reign.

Divisional Courts. Courts originally established in 1873, and continued under the provisions of the Supreme Court Act 1981, s 66. Such courts are normally constituted of two or three judges and proceedings before them are regulated by RSC 1965, Ord 52.
The principal jurisdiction of the Divisional Courts of the Queen's Bench Division consists of appeals by case stated from magistrates' courts and the Crown Court, appeals from inferior courts in respect of orders or decisions relating to contempt of court, election petitions and certain statutory appeals from inferior tribunals. To Divisional Courts of the Chancery Division come appeals from county courts in bankruptcy and land registration matters. Divisional Courts of the Family Division deal with appeals by case stated from the Crown Court or a magistrates' court relating to maintenance agreements, appeal from matrimonial orders made by magistrates' courts, etc.

Divisions of the High Court. The High Court is made up of three Divisions:

   (i) The Chancery Division, consisting of the Lord Chancellor (president) and a number of puisne judges, one of whom may be nominated as Vice-Chancellor;

  (ii) The Queen's Bench Division, consisting of the Lord Chief Justice (president) and a number of puisne judges;

 (iii) The Family Division, consisting of a president and a number of puisne judges (see Supreme Court Act 1981, s 5).

Causes and matters are distributed among the several Divisions as directed by rules of court; nevertheless, all jurisdiction vested in the High Court belongs to all Divisions alike (see Supreme Court Act 1981, s 5(5)). Within the particular divisions specific courts may be constituted to handle particular business, eg the Commercial Court and the Admiralty Court in the Queen's Bench Division, and the Companies Court and the Patents Court within the Chancery Division.

Power is given to alter the number of Divisions by Order in Council (ibid, s 7).

Divorce. The termination of a marriage otherwise than by death or annulment.
See NULLITY OF MARRIAGE.

The only ground on which a petition for divorce may be presented by either party to a marriage is that the marriage has broken down irretrievably (see Matrimonial Causes Act 1973, s 1).

Breakdown of the marriage is (by s 1(2) of the Act of 1973) proved by showing that: (i) the respondent has committed adultery and the petitioner finds it intolerable to live with him/her; (ii) the respondent has behaved in such a way that the petitioner cannot reasonably be expected to live with him/her; (iii) the respondent has deserted the petitioner for a continuous period of at least two years before the presentation of the petition; (iv) the parties to the marriage have lived apart for a continuous period of at least two years before the presentation of the petition and the respondent consents to a decree being granted; or (v) the parties to the marriage have lived apart for a continuous period of at least five years immediately preceding the presentation of the petition.

Under the Family Law Act 1996, an order of divorce was to be granted upon the irretrievable breakdown of a marriage, but prior to an order of divorce the Act encouraged parties to take 'all practical steps' to save the marriage. The Act was trialled from 1997 to 2000, but was not regarded as being on the whole successful. The Act will not now be implemented.

Dock. The place in court where a prisoner is placed while on trial. He may, from the dock, instruct counsel without the intervention of a solicitor.

Dock warrant. A document given to the owner of goods imported and warehoused in the docks, as a recognition of his title to the goods, on the bills of lading and other proofs of ownership being produced. Like a bill of lading, it passes by indorsement and delivery, and transfers the absolute right to the goods described in it.
See BILL OF LADING.

Doctrine of notice. *See* BONA FIDE PURCHASER.

Document. A written paper or something similar which may be put forward as evidence.

'Document' includes in addition to a document in writing:

   (i) any map, plan, graph or drawing;

  (ii) any photograph;

 (iii) any disc, tape, sound track or other device in which sounds or other data (not being visual images) are embodied so as to be capable (with or without the aid of some other equipment) of being reproduced from it; and

 (iv) any film, negative, tape or other device in which one or more visual images are embodied so as to be capable (as aforesaid) of being reproduced from it (see Civil Evidence Act 1968, s 10(1)).

Document of title. A document enabling the possessor to deal with the property described in it as if he were the owner, as eg, a bill of lading (*see* BILL OF LADING).

Doli capax (capable of crime). An expression used to indicate that a child between the ages of ten and fourteen has sufficient understanding to discern between good and evil, so as to be criminally responsible for his actions. This is otherwise expressed by the maxim, *Malitia supplet aetatem* (malice supplies the want of age).

Doli incapax. Incapable of crime. There is a conclusive presumption that children under ten years of age are *doli incapax*. Nothing, therefore, that they do can make them liable to be punished by a criminal court.

Domesday Book (Lat *Liber judiciarius*). An ancient record made in the reign of William the Conqueror, containing a survey of the lands in England. It was begun by five justices assigned for that purpose in each county in 1081, and was finished in 1086.

Domestic animal. Any horse, ass, mule, bull, sheep, pig, goat, dog, cat, or fowl, or any other animal of whatsoever kind or species, and whether a quadruped or not which is tame or which has been or is being sufficiently tamed to serve some purpose for the use of man: Protection of Animals Act 1911, s 15.

Domestic servants. Servants whose main or general purpose is to be about their employers' persons or establishments, residential or quasi-residential, for the purpose of ministering to the employers' needs or wants, or to the needs or wants of those who are members of such establishments, including guests (*Re Junior Carlton Club* [1922] 1 KB 166, per Roche, J).

Domicile. The place in which a person has his fixed and permanent home, and to which, whenever he is absent, he has the intention of returning. It is of three sorts: (i) by birth; (ii) by choice; (iii) by operation of law. On domicile depend questions of personal status and the devolution of movable property.

Dominant tenement. A tenement in favour of which a service or 'servitude' is constituted. Thus, an estate, the owner of which has, by virtue of his ownership, a right of way over another man's land is called the *dominant tenement* in respect of it. The land over which the right of way exists is called the *servient tenement*.
See EASEMENT; LAND LAW.

Dominion. Those former dependencies of the United Kingdom which had obtained complete self-government. First defined in the Statute of Westminster 1931 to include Canada, Australia, New Zealand, South Africa, Eire, and Newfoundland. Of these Eire and South Africa left the Commonwealth and Newfoundland became a province of Canada.

The term 'dominion', having come to be thought of as conveying a misleading impression of the constitutional and international status of the countries concerned, has now ceased to be used for official purposes.

Dominus litis. The controller of a suit or litigation.

Domitae naturae (of a tame dispostion). An expression applied to animals of a nature tame and domestic, eg, horses, cattle, sheep, poultry, and the like. In these a man may have as absolute a property as in any inanimate thing.
See ANIMALS.

Donatio mortis causa (a gift by reason of death). A gift of personal property made by a person who apprehends that he is in peril of death, and evidenced by a manual delivery by him, or by another person in his presence and by his direction, to the donee or to some one else for the donee, of the means of obtaining possession of the property, or of the writings whereby the ownership of it was created, and conditioned to take effect absolutely in the event of his not recovering from his existing disorder, and not revoking the gift before his death.

A *donatio mortis causa* differs from a legacy mainly in its being wholly independent of the donor's last will and testament. It therefore requires no assent on the part of his executor or administrator to give full effect to it. It is liable to the donor's debts in case of insufficiency of assets, and is subject to inheritance tax.
See DONOR.

Donee. *See* DONOR.

Donor. A person who makes a gift to another; and the person to whom the gift is made is called the *donee*.

Dormant partner. A person who takes no active part in the partnership affairs, and is not known to the world as a partner, but who receives the profits of the partnership.
See PARTNERSHIP.

Double complaint. *See* DUPLEX QUERELA.

Double entry. A system of bookkeeping in which the entries are made so as to show the debit and credit of every transaction.

Double insurance. Where a person, being fully insured by one policy, effects another with another insurer or insurers, the risk and interest being the same in both. He may recover the amount of his actual loss from either insurer, but not both, as the contract is one of indemnity only. The insurer who pays is entitled to contribution from the other. As to double insurance in marine insurance, see Marine Insurance Act 1906, s 32.

Double jeopardy, rule against. A person may not be tried twice for the same offence.

Double rent. Rent payable by a tenant who continues in possession after the time for which he has given notice to quit, until the time of his quitting possession (see Distress for Rent Act 1737, s 18).

Double value. Double the yearly value of lands payable by a tenant who wilfully 'holds over' (ie, continues in possession) after the expiration of his term, and after notice by the landlord requiring him to leave (see Landlord and Tenant Act 1730, s 1).

Double waste. When a tenant bound to repair allows a house to be wasted, and then unlawfully fells timber to repair it, he is said to commit double waste.
See WASTE.

Dowager. A queen dowager is the widow of the King. So, a duchess dowager, countess dowager, etc, is the widow of a duke, earl, etc.

Dower. A species of life estate which, formerly, a widow was able to claim in the lands of her husband upon his death.
See CURTESY.

Draft. A cheque or bill of exchange, or other negotiable instrument; also the rough copy of a legal document before it has been engrossed.

Drawback. The repayment of duties or taxes previously charged on commodities, from which they are relieved on export.

Drawee. A person on whom a bill of exchange is *drawn*, as one who may be expected to 'accept' it.
See BILL OF EXCHANGE.

Drawer. A person who draws a bill of exchange.
See BILL OF EXCHANGE.

Droit. A French word, corresponding to the Latin *jus*, and signifying either (i) a right; or (ii) law, as used in such phrases as 'the law of nations', etc.

Droits of admiralty. A word applied to ships and property of the enemy taken by a subject in time of war without commission frosm the Crown (*see* PRIZE OF WAR). Any such prize would, by the effect of the prerogative (*see* PREROGATIVE), become an admiralty *droit*,

or a right of the admiralty. The rights of the admiralty were relinquished in favour of the captors.
See PRIZE OF WAR.

Drug trafficking. Doing or being concerned in producing or supplying a controlled drug, transporting or storing a controlled drug, importing or exporting a controlled drug, contrary to the Misuse of Drugs Act 1971 (see Drug Trafficking Offences Act 1986, s 38(1)). The proceeds of drug trafficking are liable to confiscation (ibid, s 1).

Drunkenness. Intoxication with alcoholic liquor.

Dubitante (doubting). A word used in law reports to signify that a Judge cannot make up his mind as to the decision which he should give.

Duces tecum (bring with thee). A subpoena commanding a person to appear at a certain day in Court, and to *bring with him* some writings, evidences, or other things.
See SUBPOENA.

Duchy Court of Lancaster. A special jurisdiction held before the Chancellor of the Duchy or his deputy concerning equitable interests in lands held of the Crown in right of the Duchy of Lancaster. Although it has not been abolished, the Court last sat in 1835.
See CHANCELLOR, 2.

Duel. Where two persons engage in a fight with intent to wound or kill the other. If either of them is killed, the other and the seconds are guilty of murder. It is an offence to challenge another to fight or to provoke another to send a challenge.

Duke. The first title of nobility next to the royal family. No subject was honoured with this title until the time of Edward III, who, in 1337, created his son, Edward the Black Prince, Duke of Cornwall.

Dum bene se gesserit (so long as he shall behave himself well). Words used to signify that the tenure of an office is to be held during good behaviour, and not at the pleasure of the Crown or the appointer.

Dum casta vixerit (so long as she shall live chaste). Deeds of separation between husband and wife often provided that the allowance to the wife is to be paid only so long as she lives a chaste life. The clause to this effect is called the '*dum casta* clause'.

Dum sola (while single). An expression used to indicate the period of a woman being unmarried or a widow.

Dumping. To dump means to unload, to tip out rubbish. The word is used legally in two respects: (i) permanently depositing substances and articles in the sea from a vehicle, ship, aircraft, etc; (ii) exporting goods at a price lower than the comparable prevailing price in the country of origin.

Dunnage. Pieces of wood placed against the sides and bottom of the hold of a vessel to preserve the cargo from the effects of leakage. Other articles may be used, eg mats (*Hogarth v Walker* [1900] 2 QB 283, CA).

Duplex querela (double complaint or quarrel). A complaint in the nature of an appeal from the ordinary to his next immediate superior, eg, from a bishop to an archbishop. This complaint is available to a clergyman who, having been presented to a living, is refused institution by the ordinary.
See ORDINARY.

Duplicate. 1 Second letters patent granted by the Lord Chancellor in a case in which he had formerly done the same, when the first were void.
2 A copy or transcript of a deed or writing.
3 The ticket given by a pawnbroker to the pawnor.

Duplicate will. A will executed in duplicate, the intention usually being that the testator is to keep one copy himself, and that the other is to be deposited with someone else. On probate both copies must be deposited at the Probate Registry.

Durante bene placito. During the pleasure of the grantor.
See QUAMDIU BENE SE GESSERIT.

Durante lite, or **Pendente lite.** During the continuance of a suit.

Durante minore aetate. During minority.

Durante viduitate (during widowhood). Words used with reference to an estate granted to a widow until she marries again.

Duress (Lat *Durities*). A constraint. Of this there are two kinds.
1 Actual imprisonment, where a man actually loses his liberty.
2 Duress *per minas* (by threats), where the hardship is only threatened and impending.

A contract made under duress is voidable at the option of the person on whom it is exercised, but the person who has employed the force cannot avail of it as a defence if the contract is sought to be enforced by the other party.

During Her Majesty's pleasure. Phrase indicating the indefinite period during which a person found not guilty by reason of insanity may be detained at a specified hospital for the mentally ill.

Dutch auction. A so-called 'auction' in which the property is set up for sale at a price beyond its value, and the price is gradually lowered until a person takes it.

Dwelling. A building or part of a building occupied or intended to be occupied as a separate dwelling, together with any yard, garden, outhouses, and appurtenances belonging to or usually enjoyed with that building or part of it. It implies a building used or capable of being used as a residence by one or more families and provided with all necessary parts and appliances, eg floors, staircases, windows, etc.

'Dying without issue'. Dying without children. These words are held, under the Wills Act 1837, s 29, to refer only to the case of a person dying and leaving no issue behind him *at the date of his death*.

D

E

E converso. Conversely, contrariwise.

EC. EUROPEAN COMMUNITY.

ECJ. EUROPEAN COURT OF JUSTICE.

ECU. EUROPEAN CURRENCY UNIT.

EEC. European Economic Community.

EGM. Extraordinary general meeting.
See MEETING.

E&OE. Errors and omissions excepted. A phrase extended to an account stated, to excuse slight mistakes or oversights.

ER. An abbreviation for Elizabeth Regina.

EU. EUROPEAN UNION; *See* EUROPEAN UNION, LAW OF.

Earl. Title of nobility ranking between a marquess and a viscount.

Earl Marshal. The officer who (formerly jointly with the Lord High Constable) presides over the Court of Chivalry. Under him is the Heralds' College of Arms. The office is of great antiquity and has been for several centuries in the family of the Howards.
See COURT OF CHIVALRY; HERALDS' COLLEGE.

Earldom. The status of an earl.

Earmark. A mark for the purpose of identifying anything which is a subject of property.

Earnest. The evidence of a contract of sale; money paid as part of a larger sum, or goods delivered as part of a larger quantity; or anything given as security to bind a bargain.

Easement. A particular kind of INCORPOREAL HEREDITAMENT, ie an intangible right in land. An easement is a right enjoyed by a person over his neighbour's property, eg a right of way, or a right of passage for water, which is a privilege without a *profit*; that is, the easement owner enjoys some right over the land of another but which does not allow him to take anything away such as soil or timber.
See PROFIT À PRENDRE.

Generally an easement belongs to a person as being the owner of a specific house or land, which is then called the *dominant tenement*, the land in which the easement owner has a right being called the *servient tenement*.
See DOMINANT TENEMENT.

An easement may be positive or negative; a positive easement is a right to do some thing on the servient tenement, such as pass over it (a right of way) or park a car there, to run telephone lines over it, etc. A negative easement does not allow the easement owner to act in any way, but prevents the owner of the servient tenement from acting in a certain way, eg an easement of light prohibits the servient owner from building in a such a way as to prevent light reaching the dominant owner's windows.

Under the Law of Property Act 1925 an easement at law must be for an interest equivalent to an estate in fee simple absolute in possession or a term of years absolute. After 1925, all other easements are equitable only (see Law of Property Act 1925, s 1).
See LAND LAW; REGISTERED LAND.

Easement of necessity. Where a grantor of land grants part of the land so as to cut off the land he retains from any passage to a highway, there will be implied in his favour an easement of way across the land granted.

Eat inde sine die. A form of words indicating that a defendant may be dismissed from an action, and 'go without day', that is, without any future day appointed for his reappearance.

Ecclesia. A church or place set apart for the service of God. Sometimes it means a parsonage.
See PARSONAGE.

Ecclesiastical corporation. A corporation of which the members are entirely spiritual persons, eg bishops, parsons, deans and

chapters, archdeacons, etc. The visitor of an ecclesiastical corporation is the ordinary.
See ORDINARY.

Ecclesiastical Courts. The Archdeacon's Court (now practically obsolete) the Consistory Courts, the Provincial Courts (ie the Court of Arches of Canterbury and the Chancery Court of York), and the Court of Faculties. These are the ecclesiastical courts proper; but there is also the Court of Final Appeal, which used to be the Court of Delegates, but is now the Judicial Committee of the Privy Council.
See JUDICIAL COMMITTEE OF THE PRIVY COUNCIL; SUPREME COURT.

Edict. A proclamation, prohibition or command. A law promulgated.

Eggshell skull principle. A tortfeasor must take his victim as he finds him. It is no answer to a claim for damages for personal injury that the victim would not have suffered injury, or as great an injury, but for his unusual frailty, eg a weak heart.

Ei qui affirmat, non ei qui negat, incumbit probatio. The burden of proof lies upon the person who affirms and not on the person who denies.

Ejusdem generis (of the same kind or nature). Where in a statute, etc, particular classes are specified by name, followed by general words, the meaning of the general words is generally cut down by reference to the particular words, and the general words are taken to apply to those things not specifically mentioned in the statute, etc, that are *ejusdem generis* with the particular classes.

Election. When a person is left to his own free will to take or do one thing or another, as he pleases. But it is more frequently applied to the choosing between two rights by a person who derives one of them under an instrument in which an intention appears (or is implied by a court of law or equity) that he should not enjoy both, eg, where A gives B property but by the same instrument gives to C property which really belongs to B, B would have to elect between retaining his own property and to that extent abandoning what A gave him, or taking what A gave him and allowing his (B's) property to go to C.
See REMEDY.

The word is also applied to the choosing of officers or representatives; specially the choosing, by a constituency, of some person or persons to represent it in Parliament.

Election agent. The representative of a candidate at a Parliamentary or local government election under the Representation of the People Act 1983, s 67. As to his duties with regard to election expenses, etc, see ibid, ss 72 *et seq.*

Election Judges. Judges of the High Court selected in pursuance of Part III of the Representation of the People Act 1983 and the Supreme Court Act 1981, s 142 for the trial of election petitions. Such Judges are selected each year from the puisne Judges of the Queen's Bench Division, to be placed on a rota for the trial of petitions for the ensuing year.
See ELECTION PETITION.

Election petition. A petition complaining of an undue return of a member to serve in Parliament. Such a petition, in a prescribed form, must be presented in the Queen's Bench Division to be tried by two Judges on the rota (see Representation of the People Act 1983, s 123(1)). Local elections may similarly be questioned under ibid, ss 127 *et seq.*
See ELECTION JUDGES.

Eleemosynary. Charitable, in particular relieving poverty.
See CHARITY.

Embargo on ships. A prohibition issued by the Crown on ships, forbidding them to go out of any port.

The term 'embargo' is borrowed from Spanish law procedure and means *arrest* or *sequestration*. It is applied to the seizure or detention of persons or property which happens to be within the territory of the nation at the time of seizure. The seizure of ships and cargoes under the authority of municipal law is spoken of as a *civil* embargo. An *international* embargo, on the other hand, is an act not of civil procedure, but of hostile detention. It may be made for the same object as reprisals are made on the high seas, for the satisfaction of a debt or the redress of an injury; and it may also be made by way of prelude to war.
See REPRISAL.

Embezzlement. An act by which a clerk or servant or anyone employed in that capacity fraudulently intercepts money or goods before they come into his master's legal possession, and converts them to his own use.

Such an act is now 'theft' under the Theft Act 1968.

See FRAUDULENT CONVERSION; LARCENY; THEFT.

Emblements. The profits of a crop which has been sown, ie any products created by annual industry, eg corn as opposed to grass, *fructus industriales* not *fructus naturales*. The general rule as to emblements sown by an out-going tenant, whose estate ended before the harvest time, was, that the out-going tenant or his representatives should have the crop if the termination of the estate arose from the act of God or the will of the landlord, but not if the termination of the estate was due to effluxion of time, or any act of forfeiture committed by the tenant. See Agricultural Holdings Act 1986, s 21, which provides for an extension of tenancy in lieu of claims to emblements.

Emergency protection order. An order that a child is to be removed to accommodation provided by the applicant for the order or that he is not to remain in the place in which he is at present being accommodated: Children Act 1989, s 44(1).

Eminent domain (Lat *Dominium eminens*). The right which every State or Sovereign power has to the use of property of its citizens for the common welfare.

See EXPROPRIATION.

Empanel. *See* IMPANELLING A JURY.

Emphyteusis. A perpetual lease.

Employers' liability insurance. A type of insurance protecting the insured against his liability to pay damages for injuries sustained by persons in his employment.

Employment and indemnity clause. A clause in a time charter-party concerning the employment of a vessel and the circumstances in which the charterer is under a duty to indemnify the shipowner for loss or damage resulting from the master of the vessel complying with the charterer's orders.

Employment Appeal Tribunal. A tribunal which hears appeals from industrial tribunals on various matters relating to employment: Employment Protection (Consolidation) Act 1978, s 136.

Emptor. A buyer.

See CAVEAT EMPTOR.

En auter droit, or **En autre droit** (in another person's right); eg, an executor holds property and brings actions in right of those entitled to the testator's estate.

See EXECUTOR.

En banc. The full bench. A court sits '*en banc*' when all the members of a court sit as distinct from a single judge or smaller panel of judges. A form of a re-hearing on appeal in the Court of Queen's (King's) Bench prior to the creation of the Court of Appeal.

En ventre sa mere. In his mother's womb. An unborn child.

Enabling statute. A statute enabling persons or corporations to do that which, before it was passed, they could not do, as opposed to a prohibiting statute, under which acts are forbidden.

Encroachment. An unlawful gaining on the possession of another.

Encumbrance. *See* INCUMBRANCE.

Endorsement. *See* INDORSEMENT.

Endowment means:

1 The setting or severing of a sufficient portion for a vicar towards his perpetual maintenance.
  See PORTION.

2 Any permanent provision for the maintenance of schools or universities.

3 A permanent provision for any institution or person.

Endowment insurance. A type of insurance whereby a specified sum becomes payable not on the death of the insured but on the arrival of a specified date, the insured being still alive.

Endowment policy. *See* ENDOWMENT INSURANCE.

Enduring power of attorney. A power of attorney which is not revoked by any subsequent mental incapacity of the donor. Now called a 'lasting power of attorney' (see Capacity Act 2005, s 9).

See POWER OF ATTORNEY.

Enemy. Persons engaged in armed operations against any of Her Majesty's forces, including armed mutineers, armed rebels, armed rioters, and pirates (see the Army Act 1955, s 225).

Enfeoff. To invest a person with title to land by livery of seisin.

See FEOFFMENT; LIVERY OF SEISIN.

Enfeoffment. *See* ENFEOFF; FEOFFMENT.

Enfranchise. To make free, to incorporate a person into a society or body politic.

The word is now used principally in two different senses:

1 Of conferring a right to vote at a Parliamentary election.
   See FRANCHISE.
2 Of the conversion of leasehold into freehold.

See ENLARGE; LEASEHOLD ENFRANCHISEMENT.

Engagement. A betrothal, a mutual promise of marriage. Engagements to marry are not enforceable at law (see Law Reform (Miscellaneous Provisions) Act 1970, s 1).

Enlarge. To *enlarge* frequently means to put off or extend the time for doing anything. Thus, enlarging a rule signifies extending the time for doing that which by a rule of court is required to be done.

To *enlarge an estate* is to increase a person's interest in land, eg where there is an estate in A for life, with remainder to B and his heirs, and B releases his estate to A, A's estate is said to be *enlarged* into a fee simple.

Enquest. An inquisition by jurors.
   See INQUEST.

Entail. An estate in land, viz a fee tail, aka an estate tail, especially used with reference to the restraint which such an estate imposed upon its owner, ie the points in which such an estate differed from an estate in fee simple; the principal feature of the fee tail distinguishing it from the fee tail was that the estate would only endure so long as the original grantee's line of direct descendants continued. This made the estate subject to uncertain and sudden termination, which made it largely unsellable, though means at law, principally the fine and the recovery, were devised to 'bar' the entail and essentially convert the estate into one in fee simple (*see* ESTATE; FINE; RECOVERY). And this correct use of 'entail' was often its popular sense; but sometimes it was, in popular language, used differently, so as to mean a succession of life estates, eg it was said that 'an entail ends with A B', meaning that A B was the first person who was entitled to the estate as a tenant in tail, and therefore able to bar or cut off the entail. No legal estate tail can exist or be created after 1925. An equitable estate tail might be created after 1925 in real or personal property (see Law of Property Act 1925, s 130).
   See ESTATE; LAND LAW; STRICT SETTLEMENT.

Entering bills short. When a bank, having received a bill of exchange which has not yet matured for payment from a customer, does not carry the amount to his credit but notes down the receipt of the bill in the customer's account, with the amount and the time when due. Whether, however, any given bill is to be regarded as 'short bill' (that is, not to be treated as cash) must depend not so much on whether it has been 'entered short' as on the surrounding circumstances, and the general mode of dealing between the parties.
   See BILL OF EXCHANGE; MATURITY.

Enterpleader. *See* INTERPLEADER.

Entire contract. A contract in which everything to be done on one side is the consideration for everything to be done on the other. This is opposed to a severable or apportionable contract.
   See CONSIDERATION.

Entirety. The whole, as distinguished from a moiety, etc.
   See MOIETY.

Entirety, tenancy by the. A form of common law tenancy under which, formerly, a husband and wife were regarded as together the single owner, the control of the title being in the husband.
   See COVERTURE; COMMON, TENANCY IN; JOINT TENANCY.

Entrapment. The enticing or luring of a person into the commission of a crime in order to prosecute him. Showing entrapment does not provide a defence in English criminal law.

Entry signifies:

1 Putting down a business transaction in a book of account.
2 The taking possession of lands or tenements. See the following entries.

Entry, forcible. *See* FORCIBLE ENTRY.

Entry, right of. A right to enter and take possession of lands or tenements without bringing an action to recover them; a remedy allowed in various cases by common or statute law, or the deed by which an estate (ie, a person's interest in land) is marked out and limited.

Entry of judgment. The setting down of judgment by a registrar of the Chancery Division, or in the Action Department (Queen's Bench Division), in a book kept for the purposes.

Enumerators. Persons appointed to take the census.

See CENSUS.

Enure. To take effect, operate, result or be available. When it is said that a transaction enures to the benefit of A B, it means that A B gets the benefit of it.

Environment consists of the air, water and land; and air includes air within buildings and the air within other natural or man-made structures above or below ground: Environmental Protection Act 1990, s 1(2).

Environment, pollution of means pollution due to the release from any process of any substances which are capable of causing harm to man or any other living organisms supported by the environment: Environmental Protection Act 1990, s 1(3).

See ENVIRONMENT.

Environmental law. The body of law, mostly enacted by statute and recently often the result of law-making by institutions of the European Union, concerning the protection of the environment and provision, eg of clean water and clean air. See, eg, the Environmental Protection Act 1990, Water Resources Act 1991, Clean Air Act 1993, Environment Act 1995, Pollution Prevention and Control Act 1999.

Envoy. A diplomatic agent despatched by one State to another.

Eo nomine. In that name; on that account.

Epitome of title. *See* ABSTRACT OF TITLE.

Equal Opportunities Commission. A body set up under the Sex Discrimination Act 1975. Its duties are to work towards the elimination of discrimination and to promote equality of opportunity between men and women generally.

Equitable estate. Any estate, interest or charge in or over land which is not a legal estate takes effect as an equitable interest (see Law of Property Act 1925, s 1(3)).

See ESTATE; EQUITY; LAND LAW.

Equitable lien. *See* LIEN; EQUITY.

Equitable mortgage. A mortgage recognised in equity but not at law.

See MORTGAGE; EQUITY; LAND LAW.

Equitable mortgages may be effected either by a written instrument or by a deposit of title deeds with or without writing. The right to effect such an equitable mortgage is preserved by the Law of Property Act 1925, (see ss 2(3), 13).

See TITLE DEEDS.

Equitable waste. An unconscientious or unreasonable use of settled property, eg by a tenant for life, pulling down a mansion-house, or felling timber standing for ornament, or doing any other permanent injury to the inheritance. This kind of waste is forbidden, even to a tenant for life who holds *without impeachment of waste*.

The Law of Property Act 1925, s 135 provides that an equitable interest for life without impeachment of waste does not confer on the tenant for life any right to commit equitable waste, unless an intention to confer such a right appears in the instrument creating the equitable interest.

See WASTE; SETTLEMENT.

Equity. In its most general sense, equity is a term applied in most European legal orders for the inherent residual jurisdiction of the courts to depart from the rules of law in extraordinary cases where the strict application of the law would work injustice. Although this general equitable jurisdiction was never strictly speaking absent in the courts of common law, the courts of common law traditionally hesitate to depart from the settled rules in particular cases for fear of creating exceptions that would unsettle the law, making it less uncertain. For example, one principal of the common law courts was that the 'law would not bend to protect fools', even if the result of a party's foolishness at law was arguably harsh and unfair. A singular feature of the development of English law is that this general equitable jurisdiction came to form the basis of a body of law separate from the rules of common law, administered by a separate court, called the Court of Equity. In this sense, in which it is distinguished from the Common Law, Equity consisted originally in a body of rules and procedure which grew up separately from the Common Law and which was administered in different Courts. Where the Common Law courts might provide no remedy for a plaintiff in a just cause, or might otherwise provide a harsh result, it became customary for suitors to apply to the medieval Chancellor, who as 'keeper of the King's conscience' would give equitable relief. From the time of Edward II, or earlier, the Chancellor and his officials, later the

Court of Chancery, issued writs and exercised jurisdiction which, in theory at least, did not override the Common Law, but which was intended to remedy its imperfections in particular cases, and so, in theory at least, relief from a Court of Equity was regarded as discretionary. Over time the principles of equitable intervention crystallised into a second body of law, know as Equity; the principles of this body of law have often been framed in terms of a series of equitable maxims (see below); and it is important to realise that equity has always been a 'gloss' on the law, a departure from the common law in certain circumstances to better provide justice, but not a comprehensive body of law in its own right. Nevertheless, the Court of Chancery created one entire substantive branch of law, the law of trusts, as well the law of fiduciary obligations, and much of the current law governing property in land. The orders of the Court of Chancery also gave rise to legal remedies unavailable at common law, in particular the injunction.

See TRUST; REMEDY.

The power of Chancellors to depart from the rules of the common law was a source of continual friction during the medieval period, but by the end of the 17th century it became settled that the decrees of Chancery would prevail. By the Judicature Acts of 1873–75 the Court of Chancery and the Courts of Common Law were fused, so that the rules of both the Common Law and Equity were thenceforward applied in one court. The Court of Chancery became the Chancery Division of the High Court, and for convenience certain matters of equitable jurisdiction are still assigned to it; but by the Supreme Court Act 1981, s 49 both law and equity are to be administered in all Divisions of the High Court and in the Court of Appeal. But where there is any conflict between the rules of Common Law and the rules of equity, the latter are to prevail.

A few of the 'maxims' of equity may be briefly stated, as follows:

(i) 'Equity acts *in personam*', ie against a specific person rather than against property, and so compels performance of contracts, trusts, etc.

(ii) 'Equity follows the law', ie does not depart unnecessarily from Common Law principles.

(iii) 'Equity delights in equality', ie attempts to adjudicate fairly or equally between the parties.

(iv) 'He who seeks equity must do equity', or a plaintiff must himself be prepared to see justice done.

(v) 'He who comes into equity must come with clean hands', ie must not have been guilty of improper conduct in regard to the subject matter of litigation.

The most significant continuing effect of Equity is the law of trusts, a legal device essentially unknown outside the UK (save for Scotland, which derives its law from Roman Civil Law) and those countries like the United States, Canada, Australia, etc which received the common law and equity. Under a trust, there is a division in the title to property. The legal title to the property is held by a trustee, who holds it for the benefit of the beneficiary. Thus the trustee has all the legal powers to deal with the property as full owner, but must exercise those powers for the benefit of the beneficiary, whose equitable right that the trustee do this was enforced by Chancery who in the eyes of Equity was the true owner. As a result, in particular in the law of property, equity recognised a kind of indirect right in property, via the holding of another, the trustee. In consequence, equitable versions of the many different legal interests one might have in land could be created, interests which would be recognised not at law but in Equity. Thus one might have equitable rights as a co-owner, have an equitable mortgage in the land, or have an equitable easement, eg an equitable right of way, all of which will be enforced by equity against the legal owner of the land. The most important distinction between a legal interest in land and an equitable interest of the same kind was the relative frailty of equitable interests. If the legal owner of the land sold it, any subsequent purchaser would be bound by any legal interests in the land, whether he or she knew about them or not. Thus a buyer of a piece of land in which another had an easement of right of way would be bound to let the easement owner pass over his land. If the easement was equitable however, a buyer of the land who was unaware of the easement and who could not discover its existence by diligently inspecting the title deed and the land, would take free of it, and the equitable easement owner's right would be extinguished. *See* BONA FIDE PURCHASER.

Equity of a statute. The sound interpretation of a statute, the words of which may be too general, too special or otherwise inaccurate and defective.

Equity of redemption. The right which a mortgagor has, on payment of the mortgage debt, with interest and costs, to *redeem* the mortgaged estate, even after the right of redemption has gone at law.
See MORTGAGE.

Equity's darling. *See* BONA FIDE PURCHASER.

Equity share capital. Means a company's issued share capital excluding any part of it which, neither as respects dividends nor as respects capital, carries any right to participate beyond a specified amount in a distribution (see Companies Act 1985, s 744).

Errors excepted. A phrase appended to an account stated, to excuse slight mistakes or oversights. Sometimes 'Errors and omissions excepted'—E&OE.
See ACCOUNT.

Escape. At Common Law every person is guilty of an escape who (i) being a prisoner, without force, escapes from custody or prison; (ii) being a prison officer, intentionally or negligently allows a prisoner to escape from his custody; or (iii) being a private person, and having a person in his lawful custody, permits him to escape. A prisoner escaping by *force* is guilty of breach of prison.

By the Prison Act 1952, s 39 it is an offence to aid any prisoner in escaping or attempting to escape from a prison.

Escheat. Escheat was an incident of all freehold estates by which, upon the occurrence of certain events, the estate in the land would be extinguished, and the ownership of the land would revert to the original grantor of the estate (or to his SUCCESSORS IN TITLE) or to the Crown by whom all land was ultimately held.
See TENURE; ESTATE; LAND LAW.

The most important occasions for escheat were escheat *propter delictum tenentis*, escheat upon a tenant's commission of a felony, and escheat *propter defectum sanguinis*, escheat upon a tenant's dying without heirs. The various bases upon which escheat might occur have been abolished; land owned by an intestate which cannot be transmitted by the rules of intestate succession because of the absence of any near enough relation now

passes to the Crown as *bona vacantia*, goods without an owner.

Escrow (Lat *Scriptum*). A scroll or writing sealed and delivered to a person not a party to it, to be held by him until some condition or conditions were performed by the party intended to be benefited by it; and, on the fulfilment of those conditions, to be delivered to such party, and to take effect as a deed to all intents and purposes.
See DEED.

Essence of a contract. In contracts certain stipulations, eg as to time, are sometimes stated to be *of the essence of the contract*. This means that such stipulations must in all circumstances be strictly complied with.

Estate. 1 The largest kind of INTEREST in land, ie an ownership interest. An estate is 'time in the land', ie a period of rightful ownership. Before the reorganisation of LAND LAW by the PROPERTY ACTS 1925, three basic estates were recognised at law: the fee simple, the fee tail, and the life estate. The length of time in the land of each was determined by the terms under which the land could be inherited, and an estate the length of which was determined by inheritance was called a fee. A fee simple was the largest estate, and was created by a GRANT 'to A and his heirs.' Thus the estate lasted so long as any person could inherit from the current estate owner. (Originally, there was some question as to whether the estate depended on there being persons alive who might have inherited from A, the original grantee. Thus, if A sold the land to B, and during B's ownership A's genealogical line died out so A had no GENERAL DESCENDANTS or 'heirs', it might have been argued that the estate came to an end, as the original time in the land was determined by the continuing existence of A's line. However it was settled early on that 'and his heirs' would apply to any fee simple owner for the time being; thus the estate would only terminate if the present owner died without heirs, ie general descendants.) A fee tail was an estate created by a grant to 'A and the heirs of his body' (sometimes limited to male or female heirs only). This estate could only be inherited by direct, or lineal, descendants, and unlike the fee simple, by the statute *De Donis Conditionalibus* (see ENTAIL; CONDITIONAL FEE), when the lineal descendants of the original grantee failed, the estate terminated. A life estate was one granted to a person for his or her life only. Only fees and life estates were properly considered estates, and acquired the name of freeholds. Time in the land determined by a fixed period, ie a TERM OF YEARS, also called a LEASE, was distinguished as a leasehold interest, but came to be regarded as an estate of ownership in its own right.

By the Law of Property Act 1925, s 1, the only estates in land which are capable of subsisting or of being conveyed or created at law are:

(i) An estate in fee simple absolute in possession (ie a fee simple which is subject to no CONDITIONS, ie 'absolute', and one 'in possession', ie not a future interest);

(ii) A term of years absolute.
See LAND LAW.

2 The sum total of one's property available for distribution, either one's estate in bankruptcy which is available for distribution to one's creditors, or one's estate on death, distributable under one's WILL or, where there is no will, or the will is insufficient to dispose of all of one's estate, under the rules of intestate SUCCESSION.

Estate contract. A contract by an estate owner to convey or create a legal estate, eg contract for sale of a legal estate; because the vendor of such a contract is subject to an order of SPECIFIC PERFORMANCE, and because 'Equity looks upon that as done which ought to be done' (an Equitable maxim—*see* EQUITY) the beneficiary of an estate contract will be regarded as being the owner of the land in equity as soon as the contract is made under a contractual CONSTRUCTIVE TRUST. Thus the buyer of the land will have equitable ownership of the land from the time the contract is made. (See Land Charges Act 1972).

Estate owner. The owner of a legal estate as defined by ss 1(4) and 205(1)(v) of the Law of Property Act 1925. An infant cannot be an estate owner.
See ESTATE; INFANT.

Estates of the realm. According to *Blackstone and Hallam*, they are:
1 The Lords Spiritual (*see* LORDS SPIRITUAL);
2 The Lords Temporal—who sit together with the Lords Spiritual in one House of Parliament (*see* LORDS TEMPORAL);
3 The Commons—who sit by themselves in the other House.

Estop, to. *See* ESTOPPEL.

Estoppel. The law in some cases estops or prevents a person from alleging certain facts, which then cannot be proved by him. 'An estoppel' says Blackstone, 'happens where a man hath done some act or executed some deed which estops or precludes him from averring anything to the contrary.'
Estoppels may be divided into four kinds:
1 Estoppel by record. The rule that a person may not deny the fact of a judgment of a court which has previously been decided against him, appears to be based on two maxims—*Interest reipublicae ut sit finis litium* and *Nemo debet bis vexari pro eadem causa.* It applies generally to all civil and criminal courts.
See INTEREST REIPUBLICAE UT SIT FINIS LITIUM; NEMO DEBET BIS VEXARI PRO EADEM CAUSA.

2 Estoppel by DEED. The rule that a party to a deed is not permitted to deny facts stated in it affords an illustration of the importance of a seal in English law. There is no such estoppel in the case of ordinary signed documents, unless it comes within the definition of estoppel by conduct.

3 Estoppel by conduct. A person who, by his words or conduct, wilfully causes another person to believe in the existence of a certain state of things, and induces him to act in that belief, so as to alter his position for the worse, is estopped from setting up against the other person a different state of things as existing at the time in question.
See PROPRIETARY ESTOPPEL.

4 Estoppel *in pais*. A tenant of land is estopped from disputing the title of the landlord by whom he was let into possession of whom he has acknowledged by the payment of rent.

Estovers. A liberty of taking necessary wood for the use or furniture of a house or farm, from another's estate. This right is generally appurtenant to a house, though, of course, it may be attached to land for the purpose of repairing fences. Tenants for life and tenants for years are entitled to take estovers from the land. The right is limited by immediate necessity. A tenant cannot cut or store wood with a view to future requirements.
See BOTE.

Estrays. Such valuable animals as are found wandering in any manor or lordship, and no person knows the owner of them, in which case the law gives them to the King as the general owner and lord paramount of the soil.

Estreat (Lat *Extractum*). **1** A true copy, or duplicate, of an original writing.

2 The estreat of a recognisance means the extracting, or taking out from among the other records, of a recognisance or obligation which has become forfeited, and sending it to be enforced; or, in some cases, directing it to be levied by the sheriff and returned to the Lords of the Treasury. No recognisance removed into the Queen's Bench Division may be estreated without the order of a Judge. If it appears to the Judge that default has been made in performing the conditions of the recognisance, he may order it to be estreated.

See RECOGNISANCE.

Estuary. The tidal part of a river.

Et seq; Et sequentes. 'and that which follows.'

Euratom. *See* EUROPEAN ATOMIC ENERGY COMMUNITY.

Eurocontrol. The European Organisation for the Safety of Air Navigation established by the International Convention relating to co-operation for the safety of air navigation concluded at Brussels on 13th December 1960 (see Civil Aviation Act 1982, s 24).

European Atomic Energy Community.
An association of European States for the pooling of atomic knowledge and resources, established on 25th March 1957, and of which the United Kingdom became a member on 1st January 1973. Referred to as 'Euratom' (see European Communities Act 1972, Sch 1).

European Coal and Steel Community.
An association of European States for pooling resources of iron, coal and steel. It was established by the Treaty of Paris on 18th April 1951, and the United Kingdom became a member on 1st January 1973. Its principal functions are to supervise the formation of prices, to control investment, and to eliminate intra-zone tariffs. The Treaty provides for free and equal access of all users to the sources of production; anti-trust legislation and control of monopolies; and the financing of technical research.

European Commission. The term generally used now to describe the EUROPEAN COMMUNITY COMMISSION, following the Maastricht Treaty of 1992, 'The Treaty on European Union'. *See* EUROPEAN UNION; EUROPEAN UNION, LAW OF.

European Community. This association of European States, formerly known as the European Economic Community, and often referred to as 'the Common Market', was established by the Treaty of Rome on 25th March 1957. Following the successful customs union of the Benelux countries (Belgium, Holland, and Luxembourg) immediately following the war, the Treaty of Rome admitted France, Germany, Italy, the United Kingdom, Denmark, Greece, the Irish Republic, Spain, Portugal, Austria, Finland, and Sweden to membership.

The purpose was economic, with the aim of creating one big market area. The prime means of achieving this were the abolition of customs barriers and quantitative restrictions, the freedom of citizens of the community to work and establish businesses throughout the Community. There is a common agricultural policy, cartels and monopolies are controlled, and there is co-ordination of policies in the spheres of commerce and finance. With the creation of the monetary union with the euro as currency, the aim to establish a common currency is on its way to being met, though some member states, including the UK at present, are not currently participating.

Following the Maastricht Treaty of 1992, 'The Treaty on European Union' (see European Communities (Amendment) Act 1993), the term European Community has been more or less replaced by the term European Union, although the European Community, as well as the European Coal and Steel Community and the European Atomic Energy Community, have not been abolished or superseded as specific entities. *See* EUROPEAN UNION; EUROPEAN UNION, LAW OF.

European Community Commission.
The Commission must formulate recommendations or deliver opinions on matters dealt with in the Treaty of Rome: Art 155. It must exercise the powers conferred on it by the Council for the implementation of the rules laid down by the Council: ibid, Art 155. Following the Maastrict Treaty of 1992,

'The Treaty on European Union', generally called the European Commission.
See EUROPEAN COMMUNITY COUNCIL.

European Community Council (of Ministers). A council made up ministerial representatives of the various member states, the appropriate minister of the government from each state for the subject under discussion, eg the Council is composed of finance ministers when taxation policy is under discussion. The Council's duty is to ensure co-ordination of the general economic policies of the Member States: Treaty of Rome, Art 145. It can confer on the Commission powers for the implementation of the rules which it lays down: ibid, Art 145. Now called the Council of the European Union following the Maastrict Treaty of 1992, 'The Treaty on European Union', or commonly, just the Council.
See EUROPEAN COMMUNITY COMMISSION; EUROPEAN UNION; EUROPEAN UNION, LAW OF.

European Community directive. A directive issued by the Council or the Commission binding, as to the result to be achieved, on each Member State to which it is addressed, but leaving to the national authorities the choice of form and methods: Treaty of Rome, Art 189.
See EUROPEAN COMMUNITY COMMISSION; EUROPEAN COMMUNITY COUNCIL.

European Community margin of solvency. The margin of solvency of an insurance company computed by reference to the assets and liabilities of the business carried on by it in Member States (taken together): Insurance Companies Act 1982, s 32(5)(b).

European Community patent. A patent granted under the European Community Patent Convention: Patents Act 1977, s 130(1).

European Community Patent Convention. A convention signed at Luxembourg on 15th December 1973, giving protection of a patent in all Member States of the EC: Patents Act 1977, s 130(1).

European Community regulation. A regulation issued by the Council or the Commission having general application. It is binding in its entirety and directly applicable in all Member States: Treaty of Rome, Art 189.
See EUROPEAN COMMUNITY COUNCIL; EUROPEAN COMMUNITY COMMISSION.

European Court of Justice. A court whose duty is to ensure that in the interpretation and application of the Treaty of Rome the law is observed: Treaty of Rome, Art 164. It consists of 13 Judges: ibid, Art 165. It is assisted by 6 Advocates-General: ibid Art 166.

European Currency Unit. The unit of account defined in Council Regulation (EEC) No 3180/78 as amended: Insurance Companies Act 1982, s 96B(4).

European Investment Bank. A bank whose task is to contribute, by having recourse to the capital market and utilising its own resources, to the balances and steady development of the common market in the interests of the EC: Treaty of Rome, Art 130.

European Parliament consists of representatives of the peoples of the EC Member States and exercises the advisory and supervisory powers conferred upon it by the Treaty of Rome: Treaty of Rome, Art 107. It is, for the most part, a consultative body, which renders advice to the Council and Commission on proposed legislation, though via a new 'Co-decision Procedure' introduced in the Maastrict Treaty of 1992, the Parliament and the Council may, in effect, legislate together.

European patent. A patent granted under the Convention on the Grant of European Patents (which was signed at Munich on 5th October 1973): Patents Act 1977, s 130(1).
See PATENT.

European Patent Office. An office established under the Convention on the Grant of European Patents: Patents Act 1977, s 130(1).
See EUROPEAN PATENT.

European patent (UK). A patent designating the United Kingdom: Patents Act 1977, s 130(1). A 'designated' country is one in which protection is sought for the invention which is the subject of the application or patent: ibid, s 130(1).
See PATENT.

European Social Fund. A fund established by the EC to improve employment opportunities for workers and to contribute thereby to the raising of the standard of living: Treaty of Rome, Art 123.

European Union. The European Union came into being 1st November, 1993, superseding the association of European states known as the European Community, following the Maastrict Treaty of 1992, 'The Treaty on European Union'. However, the term is

E

broader than European Community, intended to form an umbrella term for it and the European Coal and Steel Community and the European Atomic Energy Community, and the European Union is said to be founded upon the other three communities, although it appears that initiatives which create new law, develop the institutions of the European Community, or create new bodies which further the political, economic, and monetary union of the member states, although the results of the acts of the European Community institutions may be regarded as initiatives of the European Union operating through the institutions of one of the communities. In this way, the European Community might eventually be regarded as having been superseded by the European Union.

See EUROPEAN UNION, LAW OF.

European Union, Law of. The Law of the European Union (or EU) is generally divided into two parts, the law of EU institutions, and substantive law of the EU. The former is the law governing the constitution, powers, and inter-relationships of EU bodies such as the European Commission, the Council, the European Parliament, and the European Court of Justice, and the general framework of the European polity as originally laid out in the Treaty of Rome and since modified by subsequent treaties, in particular the Maastrict Treaty of 1992. One can regard this as the *constitutional* law of the EU. Recent developments have concerned the rights of nationals of one Member State to vote in the national elections of another, so as to begin to create right for individuals as citizens not only of their member state but as citizens of the EU. The projected expansions of the EU will also involve changes in this part of EU law. The substantive law of the EU consists of those laws issuing from the institutions which govern the behaviour of the subjects of the European Union, either by EUROPEAN COMMUNITY REGULATION or by EUROPEAN COMMUNITY DIRECTIVE, eg environmental law, competition law, and so on, although this law is enforced by the regulatory agencies, courts, etc of the several Member States. Ultimately, questions concerning the meaning of EU laws and their interactions with the municipal laws of the Member States may be resolved by the European Court of Justice. The European Court of Justice has developed

and reinforced many times the doctrine of 'primacy', the doctrine that EU laws are superior to the municipal laws of the Member States, and so in any clash between them the law of the EU will prevail. The bulk of the substantive law of the European Union predominantly flows from the Union's origins in the European Economic Community, and is therefore concerned to ensure the operation of a single market for all member states, and other economic matters. In consequence, there has been much law generated on the free movement of persons, both to work as employees and to establish business throughout the Union, on the free movement of goods, freedom from restrictions on the provisions of services, competition, and the harmonisation of taxation. However, there is also EU law concerning the environment, social policy, and police cooperation.

Eviction. Dispossession; also a recovery of land by process of law.

Evidence. That which, in a court of justice, makes clear, or ascertains the truth of, the very fact or point in issue, either on the one side or on the other.

Any matter, lawfully deposed to on oath or affirmation, which contributes (however slightly) to the elucidation of any question at issue in a court of justice, is said to be *evidence*.

Evidence is either *written* or *parol*; written evidence consists of records, deeds, affidavits, or other writings: *parol* or *oral evidence* consists of witnesses personally appearing in Court, and in general swearing to the truth of what they depose. Evidence may also be primary, ie, best evidence, or secondary; direct, circumstantial, or hearsay; real or intrinsic.

See CIRCUMSTANTIAL EVIDENCE; DIRECT EVIDENCE; HEARSAY EVIDENCE.

Ex abundanti cautela. From excessive caution.

Ex aequo et bono. Deriving from the civil law, meaning in justice and fairness, and referring to the general 'equitable' jurisdiction of a court to apply, interpret, or occasionally depart from, the rules of law so as to achieve a just result in the particular case.

See EQUITY.

Ex cathedra. With the weight of one in authority; originally applied to the decisions of the Popes from their cathedra or chair.

Ex contractu. Actions *ex contractu* are actions arising out of breaches of contract, express or implied.

Ex debito justitiae. As a matter of right; as opposed to a matter for the favour or discretion of the Court. Thus, the improper rejection of evidence in an action is a ground for a new trial as a matter of right, or *ex debito justitiae*.

Ex delicto, or **Ex maleficio.** Actions *ex delicto*, or *ex maleficio*, are actions founded on some wrong other than a breach of contract, express or implied.

Ex dividend. Without the dividend. A term used in connection with the purchase of shares resulting in the buyer not having a right to the dividend in respect of them.
See CUM DIVIDEND; SHARE.

Ex dolo malo non oritur actio. No right of action arises out of a fraud.

Ex facto jus oritur. The law arises out of the fact.

Ex gratia. As a matter of favour.

Ex nudo pacto non oritur actio. No action arises from a bare pact, ie one made without consideration. This applies to simple contracts, not to specialty contracts, which are made by deed.
See CONSIDERATION; DEED.

Ex officio. By virtue of an office. Any prerogative or jurisdiction which a person in office has, by virtue of that office, he is said to exercise *ex officio*.

Ex officio information. 1 A criminal information filed by the Attorney-General *ex officio* on behalf of the Crown in the Queen's Bench Division.
2 The expression is also applied, though not very frequently, to information filed by the Attorney-General in the Chancery Division to have a charity properly established.
See INFORMATION; CHARITY.

Ex pacto illicito non oritur actio. No action arises on an illegal agreement.

Ex parte. 1 Of the one part, one-sided. Thus, an *ex parte* statement is a statement of one side only. So, an injunction granted *ex parte* is an injunction granted after hearing one side only.
See INJUNCTION.

2 The phrase '*ex parte*' preceding a name in the heading of a reported case indicates that the party whose name follows is the party on whose application the case is heard.

Ex parte application. An application to the court by one party without having informed the other side. Under the CIVIL PROCEDURE RULES such an application is now called a 'without notice' application.

Ex post facto. Something done so as to affect another thing that was committed before. An *ex post facto* law is one having a retrospective application.

Ex proprio motu. Of his own mere motion, spontaneously, eg when a Judge, without application from any party, orders a witness to be prosecuted for perjury, or commits him for trial.

Ex rights. Without the rights. A term used to denote the fact that a buyer of shares is not entitled to subscribe for further shares in proportion to the number bought.
See CUM RIGHTS; SHARE.

Ex turpi causa non oritur actio (no right of action arises from a base cause), eg on a contract founded on an immoral consideration.

Examination. 1 The interrogation of witnesses. The *examination-in-chief* of a witness is the interrogation of a witness, in the first instance, by the counsel of the party calling him. His examination by the opposing counsel is known as his *cross-examination*; and his further examination by his own side, on points arising out of the cross-examination, is his *re-examination*.
2 The examination of a bankrupt is the interrogation of a bankrupt, by a court having jurisdiction in bankruptcy, as to the state of his property.
3 The examination of a prisoner is the inquiry into the charge made against him by a stipendiary magistrate or justice of the peace, preparatory to his being committed for trial, in case there should appear to be a *prima facie* case against him.

Examiners of the court. Barristers of not less than three years' standing appointed by the Lord Chancellor to examine witnesses out of court.

Excerpta or Excerpts. Extracts.

Excess clause. A clause in an insurance policy specifying that the insured must bear liability up to a specified sum if a loss occurs, eg the first £200. Only after this limit has been reached are the insurers liable and then only for the sum by which the limit is exceeded.

Excess policy. A policy in respect of a subject matter which is also insured under another policy, stating that the insurer is under no liability until the insured has been paid in full under that other policy.

Exchange, bill of. *See* BILL OF EXCHANGE.

Exchequer. The Department of State having the management of the royal revenue. It consisted formerly of two divisions, the first being the office of the receipt of the Exchequer, for the collection of the royal revenue; the second being a court for the administration of justice.
See CHANCELLOR; COURT OF EXCHEQUER.

Exchequer Chamber. *See* COURT OF EXCHEQUER CHAMBER.

Excise. A name formerly confined to the imposition on beer, ale, cider, and other commodities manufactured within the realm, being charged sometimes on the consumption of the commodity, but more frequently on the retail side of it.

Under recent Acts of Parliament, however, many other imposts have been classed under excise. Such is the case with regard to the licence which must be taken out by every one who uses a gun, or deals in game. See particularly Customs and Excise Management Act 1979.

Exclusion clause. A term of a contract by which a party excludes a legal liability he would otherwise have, for example liability for negligently caused injury in the course of providing a service contracted for.
See CONTRACT.

Excommunication, or **Excommengement.** A spiritual censure for offences falling under the ecclesiastical cognisance. It is described in the books as twofold: (i) the lesser excommunication which is an ecclesiastical censure, excluding the party from the sacraments; (ii) the greater, which excluded him from the company of all Christians, and rendered him incapable of any legal act.

Exeat. Leave to depart.
See NE EXEAT REGNO.

Execute. *See* EXECUTION.

Executed and **Executory.** These words are used in a sense very nearly equivalent to past (or *present*) and *future* respectively. Thus,

1 A contract may be either *executed*, eg if A and B agree to exchange horses, and they do it immediately; here the possession and the right are transferred together; or *executory*, eg if they agree to exchange next week; here the *right* only vests, and their reciprocal *property* in each other's horse is not in *possession* but in *action*; for a contract executed, which differs nothing from a grant, conveys a *chose in possession*; a contract executory conveys only a *chose in action*.
See CHOSE.

2 So, a *consideration* for a promise may be *executed* or *executory*, according as the consideration precedes the promise or not; and its character in this respect is determined by the relation which it bears in point of time to the promise, as being prior or subsequent.
See CONSIDERATION.

3 So, a *devise* (ie a disposition of land by will), by which a future estate is allowed to be limited contrary to the rules of the old Common Law, is called an *executory devise*.
See EXECUTORY INTEREST.

4 Also, an estate in possession, whereby a present interest passes to the tenant, is sometimes called an *executed* estate, as opposed to the *executory* class of estates depending on some *subsequent* circumstances or contingency.

5 A trust may also be *executed* or *executory*. An *executed* trust is one where the trust estate is completely defined in the first instance, no future instrument of conveyance being contemplated. An *executory* trust is a trust where the party whose benefit is designed is to take through the medium of a future instrument of conveyance to be executed for the purpose. The importance of the distinction lies in this, that an *executed* trust is construed strictly according to the technical meaning of the terms used; an *executory* trust is construed according to the apparent meaning of the author of the trust, as gathered from the instrument by which it is created.

This is one of the most technical and difficult distinctions in English law. It might at first be supposed that an executed trust was a trust fully administered by the final distribution, on the part of the trustee, of the trust property among the parties entitled to it; and that an executory trust was a trust not yet fully administered. As Lord St Leonards said in the case of the *Earl of Egerton v Brownlow* (4HCL 210): 'All trusts are in a sense executory, because a trust cannot be executed except by conveyance, and therefore there is always something to be done. *But that is not the sense which a court of equity puts upon the term executory trust.*' And his Lordship went on to distinguish the two in this way: an *executory* trust is where the author of the trust has left it to the court to make out from *general expressions* what his intention is. An executed trust is where 'you have nothing to do but to take the limitations he has given you, and convert them into legal estates'. Or, perhaps, it may be expressed in this way: An *executory* trust is one of which the author indicates, either by the vagueness and generality of the words he has used, or by his intention expressed in the instrument creating the trust, that some further conveyance should be executed for expressing the trust in proper legal form. Whereas, an *executed* trust is a trust itself expressed in proper legal form. An executory trust thus bears to an executed trust the same relation which the heads of a settlement bear to the settlement itself. This use of the term 'executed' may, perhaps, be illustrated by such expressions as 'the execution of a will', 'execution of a deed'. *See* TRUST.

Execution. 1 The putting in force the sentence of the law in a judicial proceeding. It is styled *final process*.

2 The signing of a deed or will, or other written instrument, in such manner as to make it (so far as regards form) legally valid (see, eg Law of Property (Miscellaneous Provisions) Act 1989, s 1).

3 The carrying out of a trust.

4 The carrying out of the sentence of death.

Executive. The branch of government which is entrusted with carrying the laws into effect. The supreme executive power is vested in the King or Queen for the time being who by convention acts on ministerial advice. *See* CONSTITUTIONAL LAW.

Executor. One to whom another, by his last will and testament, commits the execution of his directions and dispositions of it. His duties are:

  (i) to bury the deceased in a manner suitable to the estate which he leaves behind him;

 (ii) to prove the will of the deceased;

(iii) to make an inventory of the goods and chattels of the deceased, and to collect the goods so listed; and for this purpose, if necessary, to take proceedings against debtors to his testator's estate;

(iv) to pay, *first*, the debts of his testator and *then* the legacies bequeathed by his will; and to distribute the residue, in default of any residuary disposition, among the persons entitled to it on an intestacy.

An executor is the legal personal representative of his testator, and the testator's rights and liabilities devolve (see DEVOLUTION) for the most part upon him. A person appointed executor is not on that account bound to accept the office. See, generally, Administration of Estates Act 1925 and Supreme Court Act 1981, Part V.

Executor de son tort. An executor by his own wrong. One who, without any just authority, intermeddles with the goods of a deceased person, as if he has been duly appointed executor. An *executor de son tort* is liable to the burden of an executorship without its advantages. He cannot bring an action himself in right of the deceased, but actions may be brought against him (see Administration of Estates Act 1925, ss 28, 29).

Executory interest. In one sense any future estate in land is an executory estate or interest (*see* EXECUTED AND EXECUTORY). But the term 'executory interest' is especially applied to such an interest in real estate as is 'limited' to commence at a future time, on some contingency not depending on the determination of a prior estate. Eg, if land be limited by deed to A and his heirs in trust for B and his heirs until C shall return from Rome, and then in trust for D and his heirs, D's interest is called an *executory interest*. After 1925 such an interest will only subsist as an equitable interest (see Law of Property Act 1925, Part 1). *See* ESTATE; LAND LAW.

Executrix. Feminine of executor.

E

Exemplary damages. Damages on a high scale, given mainly in respect of tortious acts, committed through malice or other circumstances of aggravation, which exceed the amount required merely to compensate the plaintiff for the loss or injury suffered by him or her.

Exempli gratia (abbrv ex gr or eg). For the sake of example.

Exemplification. 1 A copy.
2 A certified transcript under the seal of a court.

Exemption clause. *See* EXCLUSION CLAUSE.

Exequatur. A rescript or order given by the foreign department of a State to which a consul is accredited, authorising the functionaries of the home department to recognise the official character of the consul (*see* CONSUL). It may be revoked at any time at the discretion of the government of the country in which he is established.

Exhibit. A document or other thing shown to a witness while giving evidence and sworn by him.

Usually applied to a document referred to in an affidavit and shown to the deponent when being sworn. The exhibit is marked by the commissioner or other person before whom it is sworn.

Exoneration. Relieving part of the estate of a deceased person, charged with a debt, by the payment of the debt out of another part of it. This may be by law, or by the special direction of the deceased in his will.

Expatriation. Forsaking one's own country and renouncing allegiance, with the intention of becoming a permanent resident and citizen in another country. See British Nationality Act 1981, s 12, under which on registration of renunciation of citizenship, a person ceases to be a British citizen.

Expectancy, Estates in. Interests in land which are limited or appointed to take effect in possession at some future time.
See ESTATE.

Expectant heir. One who has a prospect of coming into property on the death of another person.
See DESCENT.

Such persons have always been under the protection of courts of equity, who have relieved them from unconscionable bargains.
See CATCHING BARGAIN.

Expectation of life. In matters of life insurance, and the granting of annuities, this expression means the length of time that any specified person may expect, according to the table of averages, to live.

Expert witness. A skilled witness called to give evidence in the subject with which he is specially conversant. As to the rules of court relating to, and the admissibility of, expert opinion, see Civil Procedure Rules 1998, Part 35.
See SKILLED WITNESS.

Expiring Laws Continuance Act. An Act passed for the purpose of continuing—usually for one full year more—temporary Acts which would otherwise expire.

Export Guarantees. Guarantees given by the Secretary of State for Trade and Industry to persons carrying on business in the United Kingdom in connection with the export, manufacture, etc of goods. There is an Export Guarantees Advisory Council (see Export Guarantees Act 1975).

Exposing. A term used for various purposes:
1 Exposing food for sale: an offence under the Food Act 1984, s 1, if it contains substances injurious to health or is unfit for human consumption.
2 Exposing a child: an offence under the Offences Against the Person Act 1861, s 27, and under the Children and Young Persons Act 1933, s 1.
3 Exposing the person.
See INDECENT EXPOSURE.

Express. That which is not left to implication, eg an express promise or covenant.

Express contract or convention. A contract or agreement expressed in words, or by signs which custom or usage has made equivalent to words.

Express malice. *See* MURDER.

Express trust. A trust which is clearly expressed by its author or may fairly be collected from a written document.
See TRUST.

Express warranty. In marine insurance, an 'express warranty' 'may be in any form of words from which the intention to warrant is to be inferred' (see Marine Insurance Act 1906, s 35(1)). 'An express warranty must be included in, or written upon the policy, or must be contained in some document incorporated by reference into the policy' (ibid, s 35(2)).

'An express warranty does not exclude an implied warranty, unless it be inconsistent therewith' (ibid, s 35(3)).

Expressio unius est exclusio alterius. The mention of one is the exclusion of another. A principle of CONSTRUCTION.

Expressum facit cessare tacitum (what is expressed makes what is implied to cease). A principle of CONSTRUCTION. Eg, an express covenant in a lease destroys that which would otherwise be implied by the use of the word 'demise'.
See DEMISE.

Expropriation. The compulsory taking of land by a public authority, with compensation to be fixed by a board or court.

Extension clauses. Clauses in motor insurance policies which: (i) afford cover to any person driving the insured's vehicle with his consent; and/or (ii) protect the insured whilst he is driving any other vehicle which does not belong to him.

Exterritoriality. A term used in international law to denote the condition of persons who are considered to be outside the territory of the State in which they reside and so are not amenable to its laws, eg an ambassador and the persons belonging to his suite, whose residence is exterritorial and protected by diplomatic privilege.
See DIPLOMATIC PRIVILEGE.

Extinguishment. An effect of consolidation. Thus, if a person purchases land out of which he has a rent, then the property and the rent are consolidated, and the rent is said to be *extinguished*. So, if a lessee or tenant for life purchases the reversion, his estate for years of life may be extinguished, being merged in the reversion unless there is a contrary intention (see Law of Property Act 1925, s 185).
See MERGER.

Also a parol contract is said to be *extinguished* by a contract *under seal* between the same parties to the same effect.

Extortion. An unlawful or violent extraction of money or money's worth from a person. The word is used especially as follows:
1 In reference to demanding money or other property by threats, and menaces of various kinds.
See BLACKMAIL.
2 In reference to the unlawful taking by an officer, under colour of his office, of money, not due to him, or more than

was due. This offence was abolished by the Theft Act 1968, s 32.

Extortionate credit bargain. A bargain which (i) requires the debtor to make payments that are grossly exorbitant; or (ii) otherwise grossly contravenes ordinary principles of fair dealing: Consumer Credit Act 1974, s 138(1). Such a bargain may be reopened by the court if it thinks just: ibid s 139.

Extra vires. *See* ULTRA VIRES.

Extradition. The surrender of a person by one State to another.
The Extradition Act 1989 sets out (i) the persons liable to extradition (s 1) (*see* EXTRADITION, LIABILITY TO); (ii) the meaning of 'extradition crime' (s 2) (*see* EXTRADITION CRIME); (iii) arrangements for the return of a person to a foreign State or a Commonwealth country or a colony (ss 3–5) (*see* EXTRADITION ARRANGEMENTS); (iv) restrictions on return (s 6); (v) procedure (ss 7–14) (*see* EXTRADITION PROCEDURE); (vi) treatment of persons returned by foreign States (ss 18–10); and (vii) special cases (ss 21–25).

Extradition, liability to. Where extradition procedures are available between the United Kingdom and a foreign State, a person in the United Kingdom who:
(i) is accused in that State of an extradition crime; or
(ii) is alleged to be unlawfully at large after conviction of an extradition crime by a court in that State,
may be arrested and returned to that State in accordance with those procedures: Extradition Act 1989, s 1(1).
A person in the United Kingdom who is accused of an extradition crime:
(i) in a Commonwealth country designated under s 5; or
(ii) in a colony
or who is alleged to be unlawfully at large after conviction of such an offence in any such country, or in a colony, may be arrested and returned to that country in accordance with extradition procedures: ibid, s 1(1).
See EXTRADITION CRIME.

Extradition, restrictions on return. A person must not be returned, or committed or kept in custody for the purposes of return if:
(i)   the offence of which the person is accused or was convicted is one of a political character;

(ii) it is an offence under military law which is not also an offence under the general criminal law;

(iii) the request for his return is in fact made for the purpose of prosecuting or punishing him on account of his race, religion, nationality or political opinions, or;

(iv) he might, if returned, be prejudiced at his trial or punished, detained or restricted in his personal liberty by reason of his race, religion, nationality or political opinions: Extradition Act 1989, s 6(1).

In relation to Commonwealth countries and colonies, 'race' includes tribe: ibid, s 6(10).

Extradition arrangements. Arrangements made with a foreign State under which extradition procedures under Part III of the Extradition Act 1989 will be available as between the United Kingdom and that State: Extradition Act 1989, s 3(1).

See GENERAL EXTRADITION ARRANGEMENTS.

Extradition crime means:

(i) conduct in the territory of a foreign State, a designated Commonwealth country or a colony, which if it occurred in the United Kingdom would constitute an offence punishable with imprisonment for a term of 12 months, or any greater punishment, and which is punishable under the law of the foreign State, Commonwealth country or colony;

(ii) an extra-territorial offence against the law of a foreign State, designated Commonwealth country or colony which is punishable with imprisonment for a term of 12 months, or any greater punishment, and which satisfies the conditions specified in the Extradition Act 1989, s 2(2), and all the conditions specified in s 2(3): Extradition Act 1989, s 2(1).

Extradition procedure consists of (i) an extradition request by the foreign State, Commonwealth country or colony (Extradition Act 1989, s 7(1)); (ii) an authority to proceed issued by the Secretary of State (ibid, s 7(4)); (iii) arrest for the purposes of committal (ibid, s 8); (iv) proceedings for committal (ibid, s 9); (v) statement of case by the court of committal for the opinion of the High Court (ibid, s 10); (vi) application for habeas corpus (ibid, s 11); (vii) order for return (ibid, ss 12, 13); and (viii) simplified procedure (ibid, s 14).

See EXTRADITION.

Extra-judicial. Any act done or word spoken by a Judge, outside the authority and jurisdiction which for the time being he is exercising, is called *extra-judicial*.

See OBITER DICTUM.

Extraordinary resolution. A resolution passed by a majority of not less than three-quarters of such members as (being entitled to do so) vote in person, or where proxies are allowed, by proxy, at a general meeting of a company, of which notice specifying the intention to propose the resolution as an extraordinary resolution has been given (see Companies Act 1985, s 378(1)).

Extra-territoriality. *See* EXTERRITORIALITY.

F

FCS. Free of capture and seizure. A term, exempting marine underwriters from liability for the acts of the Queen's enemies, pirates, etc.
See UNDERWRITER; ENEMY; PIRACY.

FOB (free on board). A term inserted in contracts for the sale of goods to be shipped. It signifies that the cost of shipping, ie, putting on board at a port or place of shipment, is to be paid by the seller.

Fac simile probate. This is where the probate copy of a will is a *fac simile* of the original will. It is allowed in cases where the construction of the will may be affected by the appearance of the original paper.

Facio ut des. I do that you may give; eg when I agree to perform anything for a price.

Facio ut facias. I do that you may do; eg when I agree with a man to do his work for him, if he will do mine for me.

Factor. An agent remunerated by a commission, who is entrusted with the possession of goods to sell in his own name as apparent owner. The Factors Acts were amended and consolidated by the Factors Act 1889.

Factorage. Also called 'commission'. An allowance given to factors by a merchant.
See FACTOR.

Factory. Any premises in which persons are employed in manual labour in any process for or incidental to (i) the making of any article or of part of any article, or (ii) the altering, repairing, ornamenting, finishing, cleaning or washing or breaking up or demolition of any article, or (iii) the adapting for sale of any article, or (iv) the slaughtering of cattle, etc, or (v) the confinement of such animals in certain premises whilst awaiting slaughter, being premises in which the work is carried on by way of trade or for purposes of gain,

and over which the employer has the right of access or control. See Factories Act 1961, s 175, which also specifies a number of classes of premises, eg, shipyards, dry docks, laundries, etc, which are to be included in the expression 'factory'.

Factum. An act or deed.

Facultative reinsurance. *See* REINSURANCE.

Faculty. **1** A privilege of special dispensation, granted to a person by favour and indulgence to do that which by the Common Law he could not do, to marry without banns, or erect a monument in a church, etc. For the granting of these there is a special court of the Archbishop of Canterbury called the Court of the Faculties with a chief officer called the Master of the Faculties (Lat *Magister ad Facultates*), whose power was given by the Ecclesiastical Licences Act 1533. Faculties are also granted by the ordinary Consistory Courts.
2 A department of a university.
3 In Scots Law, 'faculty' means a power which any person is at liberty to exercise.

Faculty of Advocates. The college of advocates in Scotland, ie the barristers entitled to practise in the Court of Session.
See COURT OF SESSION.

Fair. A sort of market granted to any town by privilege, for the more speedy and commodious provision of such things as the subject needs. *Cowel.* Fairs are controlled by various statutes, one of the earliest being the Statute of Northampton (1328) which required that fairs should be held according to charter and for the time limited by it. Old fairs are held annually as, eg, at Oxford, Banbury, Warwick, etc, under charters granted several centuries ago.

A 'pleasure fair' used for providing certain entertainments, including circuses, the exhibition of human beings or performing animals, merry-go-rounds, coconut shies, hoop-las, and so forth (see Public Health Act 1961, s 75) and Betting, Gaming and Lotteries Act 1963, s 75).

Fair comment. A defence to an action for defamation. The defendant must show that (i) the statement he has made was one of comment and not one of fact; (ii) the comment was fair; and (iii) the comment was on a matter of public interest.

The defence of fair comment can be defeated by proof of *malice* on the defendant's part, ie that the comment was made through an improper motive.

See DEFAMATION.

Fair Trading, Director General of.
See MONOPOLY.

Fair wear and tear. The deterioration to property caused by reasonable use. Tenants are typically required to return the property to the landlord in the condition in which it was first let, allowing for the deterioration resulting from fair wear and tear.

Fallow land. Land ploughed but not sown, and after summer's crops left uncultivated for a time.

Falsa demonstratio non nocet. A false demonstration does not injure.
See FALSE DEMONSTRATION.

Falsa grammatica non vitiat chartam. Bad grammar does not nullify a deed.

False demonstration. An erroneous description of a person or thing in a written instrument. The meaning of the maxim that 'a false demonstration does not injure', is that where there is an adequate naming or definition, with a convenient certainty, of any person or thing in a written instrument, a subsequent erroneous addition will not vitiate it.

False imprisonment. A trespass committed against a person by imprisoning him without lawful cause. Every confinement of a person is an imprisonment, whether it is in a prison, or in the stocks, or even by forcibly detaining him in the street. False imprisonment is usually made the subject of a civil action, but is also indictable at the suit of the Crown.

False personation. The offence of personating another for the purpose of fraud.

Personation of a voter is an offence under the Representation of the People Act 1983, s 60; personation of a master for the purpose of giving a false character to a servant is a misdemeanour by the Servants' Characters Act 1792, s 1; and impersonation of a husband in order to commit rape is an offence under the Sexual Offences Act 1956, s 1.

False pretence. Any false statement of fact whereby a person, knowing it to be false, obtained from another, for himself or for his own benefit, any chattel, money, or valuable security, with intent to cheat or defraud any person. The equivalent offence under the Theft Act 1968, s 15 is that of 'obtaining property by deception'.

False return of a writ. The return of a writ falsely indorsed to the effect that its directions have been complied with or are impossible of performance. False return by a sheriff, etc, to a writ, renders him liable to an action for damages.

False trade description. A trade description which is false to a material degree, or which is misleading (see Trade Descriptions Act 1968, s 3).

Falsify signifies, **1** To prove a thing to be false. **2** To tamper with any document, whether of record or not, by interlineation, obliteration, or otherwise. It is an offence to copy a false instrument (see Forgery and Counterfeiting Act 1981, s 2); to use a false instrument (see ibid, s 3); to use a copy of a false instrument (see ibid, s 4); and to have in one's custody a false money order, share certificate, passport etc (ibid, s 5). For the meaning of 'instrument', see ibid, s 8, and 'false', see ibid, s 9.

Fam D. Family Division. *See* FAMILY DIVISION.

Family. A word with various meanings, according to the context in which it is found. Thus, in one sense it may mean a whole household, including servants and perhaps lodgers. In another it means all persons descended from a common stock, ie all blood relations. In a third, the word includes children only; thus, when a man speaks of his wife and family, he means his wife and children (see *Re Makein* [1955] 1 All ER 57).

Family assistance order. An order requiring
 (i) a probation officer to be made available; or
 (ii) a local authority to make an officer of the local authority available, to advise, assist and (where appropriate) befriend any person named in the order: Children Act 1989, s 16(1).

Family Division. One of the three Divisions of the High Court. So named on the reorganisation of the courts in 1971 (see Administration of Justice Act 1970 and the Courts Act 1971). To it was assigned the High Court's matrimonial and domestic business (previously dealt with by the Probate, Divorce and Admiralty Division), as well as non-contentious or common form probate business. The Division consists of a President and not fewer than three puisne judges (Act of 1970, s 1).

Family law. The law concerning marriage, divorce, and the rights of spouses vis-à-vis each other, and children vis-à-vis their parents. In recent years, the rights of couples not married but cohabiting, including single-sex cohabitees, the law governing domestic violence, the economic support of former spouses and their children, the protection of children inadequately cared for, and the adoption of children have received increased attention.

Family provision. Provision for dependants which the Courts are empowered to make out of the estate of a deceased person under the Inheritance (Provision for Family and Dependants) Act 1975. Applicants for each provision include a surviving spouse, a former spouse who has not remarried, any child of the deceased, any person who, though not a child of the deceased, had been treated as a child of the family, and any person (even if not related) who was being wholly or partly maintained by the deceased at the time of his death.

Fare. Money paid for a passage by land or water.

Under railway bye-laws travelling without pre-payment, and with intent to defraud, is punishable.

Farriery. Any work in connection with the preparation or treatment of a horse's foot for shoeing: the fitting of a shoe to a horse's foot, and incidental work. See Farriers (Registration) Act 1975, which created a Farriers Registration Council, and was passed to prevent unnecessary suffering to horses through shoeing by untrained persons.

Faryndon Inn. The old name for Serjeants' Inn.
See INNS OF CHANCERY.

Fast day. A day of abstinence appointed by the Church.

Days of general fast may also be appointed by royal proclamation. Although such

appointment is very rare, such a day would be a day on which no legal business would be transacted (RSC 1965, Ord 64, r 7).

A fast day appointed by royal proclamation would similarly be a 'non-business day' for the purposes of computing time under the Bills of Exchange Act 1882.

Federal Government. A government formed by the aggregation of several States, previously independent, in such manner that the sovereignty over each of the States resides thenceforth in the aggregate of the whole, while each of the States, though losing its individual sovereignty, retains nevertheless important political powers within its own territory, and shares the sovereignty of the entire Federation with the other States, and (in general) with a new legislative or executive body having a limited jurisdiction over the entire area of the Federation, and called 'the general government'. If the individual States retain severally their sovereign character, the Federation is called a *permanent confederacy of supreme governments*.

Fee farm rent is where an estate in fee is granted subject to a rent in fee of at least one-fourth of the value of the land at the time of its reservation. It can be distrained for (see Law of Property Act 1925, ss 121, 205(1)(xxiii)).
See DISTRESS.

Fee simple. An estate limited to a man and his heirs; the most absolute interest which a subject can possess in land, ie equivalent to full ownership. A 'fee simple absolute in possession' is one of the two legal estates in land which are now capable of subsisting under the Law of Property Act 1925, s 1(1); and by s 60 of that Act, a conveyance of freehold land without words of limitation passes the fee simple, unless a contrary intention appears.
See ESTATE; LAND LAW.

Fee tail. An estate limited to a man and the heirs of his body, also called an *estate tail*.
See ESTATE; LAND LAW.

Felo de se. Self-murder, or suicide.
See SUICIDE.

Felony. At common law, criminal offences were either felonies, the more serious, or misdemeanours, the less serious. Originally all felonies were punishable by death and confiscation (escheat for felony) of property. Misdemeanours attracted less severe

F

punishments. The distinction was abolished in England under the Criminal Law Act 1967. *See* CRIMINAL PROCEDURE.

Feme (Fr *Femme*). A woman.

Feme covert (Lat *Femina viro co-operta*). A married woman; as opposed to *feme sole*, which means a single woman. *See* FEME SOLE.

Feme sole. A single woman, including those who have been married, but whose marriage has been dissolved by death or divorce, and (for most purposes) those women who are judicially separated from their husbands.

Feoffment, feoffor, feoffee. Ancient common law mode of transferring title to land. The feoffor, the grantor or transferor, performed the ceremony of livery of seisin, delivering possession of the land to the feoffee, the recipient or grantee. Now obsolete, replaced by transferring land by conveyance/ registration. *See* LIVERY OF SEISIN; CONVEYANCE; LAND REGISTRATION.

Feoffor to uses, feoffee to uses. *See* USE.

Ferae naturae. Of a wild disposition. An expression applied to animals which are generally found at liberty, although it may happen that they are sometimes tamed and confined by the art and industry of man. Regarded as property but not capable of being stolen unless first reduced into possession (see Theft Act 1968, s 4(4)).

Ferry. A liberty or franchise by prescription, or by the Queen's grant or Act of Parliament, to have a boat for passage on a great stream for the carriage of persons, etc, for a reasonable toll. This right, where it exists, involves a right of action on the part of the owner of the ferry against those who set up a new one so near as to diminish his custom. On the other hand, the existence of the right implies also a duty, on the part of the grantee, to keep up a boat over the stream, if not otherwise fordable, for the convenience of the public; and neglect of the duty will render him liable to criminal prosecution.

Feud. Implacable hatred, not to be satisfied except by the death of the enemy; and especially a combination of the family of a murdered man to avenge his death on the murderer and all his family.

Fi fa. *See* FIERI FACIAS.

Fiat. A short order or warrant of a Judge for making out and allowing certain processes; or an indorsement by the Lord Chancellor or Attorney-General, on behalf of the Crown, on a petition for any purpose for which the consent of the Crown is necessary.

Fiat justitia ruat coelum. Let justice be done though the heavens should fall.

Fidei defensor. *See* DEFENDER OF THE FAITH.

Fidelity insurance. A type of insurance giving cover against loss by an employer caused by the dishonesty of an employee.

Fiduciary. A person with a legal power to alter the legal position of another, generally called the fiduciary's *principal* and one who must use his or her discretion in exercising that power so as to serve the principal's best interests and, in particular, so as never to serve his own interests to the detriment of his principal. Examples are agents, who are fiduciaries to their principals, and trustees, who are fiduciaries to the beneficiaries of the trust, and company directors to their companies. The law of fiduciaries is the product of EQUITY, and one of its chief concerns is to prevent and deal with situations where the fiduciary's own interests conflict with his duty to serve the best interests of his principal. *See* AGENT; TRUSTEE; CONFLICT OF INTEREST; EQUITY.

Fiduciary estate. The estate or interest of a trustee in lands or money, as opposed to the beneficial interest or enjoyment thereof.

Fieri facias, or fi fa. A writ of execution available to a person who has recovered judgment in an action of debt or damages, addressed to the sheriff to command him to levy the debt or damages from the goods of the party against whom judgment is recovered.

Fieri facias de bonis ecclesiasticis. A writ of execution issued when a judgment debtor is a clerk in holy orders, and the sheriff returns (ie endorses on the writ) that the debtor has no lay fee within his country.

Fieri feci. A return to the writ of *fieri facias*, denoting that the sheriff or other officer to whom it is directed has levied the sum named in the writ, either wholly or as to that part to which the return is applicable. *See* FIERI FACIAS; RETURN.

Filius nullius. Filius populi. (Son of no man. Son of the people). Expressions used of a bastard. *See* BASTARD.

Film, in relation to copyright, means a recording on any medium from which a moving image may by any means be produced: Copyright, Designs and Patents Act 1988, s 5(1). Copyright does not subsist in a film which is a copy taken from a previous film: ibid, s 5(2).
See COPYRIGHT.

Filum aquae medium. The thread or middle part of a stream which divides the jurisdictions or properties. Riparian owners possess the bed of a river *usque ad medium filum.*
See RIPARIAN PROPRIETORS.

Final dividend. A dividend recommended by the directors of a company and approved at the annual general meeting. It may be paid in addition to one or more interim dividends.
See INTERIM DIVIDEND.

Final judgment. A judgment awarded at the *end* of an action, as opposed to an *interlocutory judgment.*
See INTERIM/INTERLOCUTORY JUDGMENT.

Final process. Execution on final judgment.
See FINAL JUDGMENT; PROCESS.

Finder of goods has a special property in them, good against everyone except the true owner.
See TREASURE TROVE.

Finding of a jury. The verdict of a jury.

Fine. 1 Any pecuniary penalty or pecuniary forfeiture or pecuniary compensation payable under a conviction (see the Magistrates' Courts Act 1980, s 150(1)).

2 A lump sum payment given in consideration for the grant of a lease, usually a long lease, and separate from periodic rent; also called a premium.
See LEASE.

3 A legal procedure, originally a Collusive action, which became a fictitious one facilitated by court practice, by which an entailed estate, or fee tail, could be 'barred', that is the rights of succeeding descendants in the original grantee's direct line (the 'issue in tail') line could be extinguished, turning the estate into a 'base fee', a fee simple determinable upon the extinction of the original grantee's direct line. Barring the entail by fine could be effected not only by the tenant in tail in possession, but one with only a future interest in tail.
See ENTAIL; RECOVERY; ESTATE; LAND LAW.

Firebote, otherwise called housebote. A sufficient allowance of wood to burn in a house.

See HOUSEBOTE.

Firm. Persons who have entered into partnership with one another (see Partnership Act 1890, s 4(1)).

Firm name. The name under which their business is carried on by persons who have entered into partnership with one another (see Partnership Act 1890, s 4(1)).

First impression. A case of *first impression* (Lat *primae impressionis*) is a case for which there is no precedent applicable in all respects.
See PRECEDENTS.

First instance, Court of. That before which an action is first tried. Thus distinguished from a court of appeal.

Fiscal. Belonging to the exchequer or revenue.

Fish royal. Whale and sturgeon which, when thrown ashore, or caught near the coast, are the property of the Sovereign.

Fishery. A right of fishing. The right is of three kinds: (i) A free fishery; (ii) A several fishery; (iii) A common piscary. A *free fishery* is an exclusive right of fishing in a public river. A *free fishery* differs from a *several* fishery, because a person who has a *several* fishery must be the owner of the soil, which in a free fishery is not requisite. It differs also from a *common of piscary* in that a *free fishery* is an exclusive right, and a *common of piscary* (the right of fishing in another person's waters) is not so.

Fishgarth. *See* GARTH.

Fixed penalty notice. A notice offering the opportunity of the discharge of any liability to conviction of the offence to which it relates by payment of a fixed penalty in accordance with Part III of the Road Traffic Offenders Act 1988, s 52(1).
For fixed penalties, see ss 51 to 90 of the Act.

Fixtures. Things of an accessory character, annexed to houses or lands; including not only such things as grates in a house, or steam engines in a colliery, but also windows and palings. To be a fixture, a thing must not constitute part of the principal subject, eg in the case of the walls or floors of a house; but on the other hand, it must be in actual union or connection with it, and not merely brought into contact with it, eg in the case of a picture suspended on hooks against a wall. As a general rule, the property, by being annexed to the land, immediately belongs to the freeholder, but there are three exceptions to the rule: (i) in favour of trade fixtures;

(ii) for agricultural purposes (see Agricultural Holdings Act 1986, s 13); (iii) for ornament and convenience.

See TRADE FIXTURES.

Flag of convenience. A flag of a country other than his own to which a shipowner transfers the registration of his ship for tax reasons or in order to avoid the safety provisions required of ships sailing under the flag of his own country.

Flagrante delicto. The apprehension of a man red-handed in the act of committing a crime.

Flat. A separate and self-contained set of premises, whether or not on the same floor, constructed for use for the purposes of a dwelling and forming part of a building from some other part of which it is divided horizontally.

Fleet. A place where the tide flows—a creek, hence Northfleet, etc.

Fleta. A nom de plume of a lawyer, who lived in the time of Edward I. He wrote a book of the Common Law of England, as it existed in his time. The work is entitled 'Fleta, seu Commentarius Juris Anglicani'. He is supposed to have been confined in the Fleet Prison, hence the name.

Floating capital. Capital retained for the purpose of meeting current expenditure.

Floating charge. A charge created by a company by a debenture on its assets for the time being. It gives the debenture-holders no immediate right *in rem* over the assets that it affects; but leaves the company a free power of disposition over the whole of its property.

See CHARGE; DEBENTURE; IN REM; SECURITY INTEREST.

'A floating charge is ambulatory and hovers over the property, until some event occurs which causes it to settle and crystallise into a specific charge' (see *Barker v Eynon* [1974] 1 All ER 900).

Floating policy. A type of marine insurance policy which describes the insurance in general terms, and leaves the name of the ship or ships and other particulars to be defined by subsequent declaration (see Marine Insurance Act 1906, s 29(1)).

Floor of the court. That part between the Judge and the first row of counsel. Parties who appear in person stand there.

Flotation. An issue on the Stock Exchange of shares in a new public company.

Flotsam, or **floatsam.** Any goods which are lost by shipwreck, and lie *floating* or swimming on the top of the water. The expression is included in the definition of 'wreck' in the Merchant Shipping Act 1894, s 510. Flotsam, with other wreck, belongs to the Crown if no owner appears to claim it within a year.

See WRECK.

Foenus nauticum. The extraordinary rate of interest, proportionate to the risk, demanded by a person lending money on a ship, or on *bottomry*. The agreement for such a rate of interest is also called *foenus nauticum*.

See BOTTOMRY.

Folio. Generally 72 words of a legal document. But for some purposes 90 words are reckoned to the folio.

Force generally means unlawful violence.

Force majeure. Irresistible compulsion or coercion.

Forcible detainer. A forcible holding possession of any lands or tenements, whereby the lawful entry of justices, or others having a right to enter, is barred or hindered.

Forcible entry. The violent entering and taking possession of lands or tenements with menaces, force, and arms, which is both a civil and a criminal injury.

Foreclosure. The forfeiture by a mortgagor of his equity of redemption, by reason of his default in payment of the principal or interest of the mortgage debt within a reasonable time. For a mortgagee to initiate proceedings for foreclosure is the most extreme remedy available to him or her for the mortgagor's default, for not only is the mortgagor's right to redeem the mortgaged land extinguished, the mortgagor remains liable to repay the whole of the outstanding mortgage debt. For this reason, mortgagees are typically limited to the remedy of an order for the possession of the property so as to exercise a power of sale, the proceeds of sale going to reduce the outstanding mortgage loan (after deduction of the costs of sale, etc) and so reducing the mortgagor's liability under the mortgage loan to the extent of the value of the land.

See EQUITY OF REDEMPTION; MORTGAGE.

Foreign. Any country which has a separate jurisdiction and law of its own.

Foreign attachment. A process by which a debt due to a judgment debtor from a person not a party to the action or suit is made available for satisfying the claim of the judgment creditor. Such a process has been immemorially used in London, Bristol and other cities.

See GARNISHEE.

Foreign Enlistment Acts. Statutes for preventing British subjects serving foreign States in war. The Foreign Enlistment Act 1870 provides that if any British subject, without the licence of Her Majesty, accepts any commission in the military or naval service of any foreign State at war with any friendly State (ie a State at peace with Her Majesty), he is punishable by fine or two years' imprisonment, or both. Any person who, without licence from the Crown, builds or equips any ship for the service of a foreign State at war with a friendly State, is punishable in like manner.

Foreign law. The law of a foreign state. In cases where the court determines that the law properly to be applied to the case is foreign law, eg where a contract is in dispute and the contract specifies that the contract will be governed by the law of a named foreign state, the court will hear from those with expertise of the foreign law and its application to the case; it is thus a question of fact which must be proved by the evidence of expert witnesses (see Foreign Law Ascertainment Act 1861). See also Civil Evidence Act 1972, s 4, Civil Procedure Rules 1998, 33.7.

See CONFLICT OF LAWS.

Foreman. The presiding member of a jury.

See JURY.

Forensic medicine. The science of medical jurisprudence, comprising those matters which may be considered as common ground to both medical and legal practitioners; eg inquiries relating to suspected murder or doubtful sanity.

Foreshore. That part of the shore which is covered by an ordinary tide. It *prima facie* belongs to the Crown.

Forest. A legal right. It was defined as the right of keeping, for the purpose of hunting, the wild beasts and fowls of forest, chase, park, and warren, in the safe protection of the King, in a territory or precinct of woody ground or pasture set apart for the purpose (see *Manwood's Forest Laws*, 1598).

Most of the ancient forest laws, the earliest still on the statute book being a charter of 1297, were repealed by the Wild Creatures and Forest Laws Act 1971. The statute abolished any franchises of forest, free chase, park or free warren, and abrogated the forest law except in so far as it relates to the appointment and functions of verderers.

Forfeiture is defined by Blackstone as a punishment annexed by law to some illegal act or negligence, in the owner of lands, tenements, or hereditaments, whereby he loses all his interest in them, and they go to the party injured, as a recompense for the wrong which either he alone, or the public together with himself, has sustained. Most commonly, today, forfeiture occurs when a lease is terminated for reason of the lessor's breach of covenant. Relief against forfeiture is provided for by the Law of Property Act 1925, s 146, and by the Landlord and Tenant Act 1927, s 18(2).

Forfeiture of share. An expropriation by a company of a member's share. Shares can only be forfeited for non-payment of calls (*see* CALL) or for similar reasons. An attempt to forfeit shares for other reasons is illegal (see *Hopkinson v Mortimer, Harley & Co Ltd* [1917] 1 Ch 646).

Forged transfer. A transfer, which is not a genuine one, made with a view of inducing the company to register shares standing in the name of the supposed transferor into that of the transferee.

If a transfer is forged and the company registers the transfer and gives a share certificate to the transferee, the true owner remains entitled to be put back on the register.

The company does not incur any liability in damages by putting the transferee's name in the register, but if it issues a certificate and any person acts on the faith of it and suffers damage, the company will be liable (see *Bloomenthal v Ford* [1897] AC 156, HL).

See also Forged Transfer Acts 1891 and 1892 which protect buyers of shares from losses by forged transfers.

Forgery. The making of a false document in order that it may be used as genuine, or the counterfeiting of a currency note or protected coin. See Forgery and Counterfeiting Act 1981, under which the law relating to forgery, counterfeiting and kindred offences was consolidated.

See CURRENCY NOTE; PROTECTED COIN; COUNTERFEIT.

Forma pauperis (the character of a pauper). Formerly, any person might be admitted to take or defend or be a part of any legal proceedings in the High Court as a poor person on proof of that fact. This procedure which has now been superseded by legal aid under the Legal Aid and Advice Acts 1974, 1988.

See LEGAL AID.

Fortune-teller. A person pretending or professing to tell fortunes, or using any subtle craft, means, or device, by palmistry or otherwise, to deceive and impose on any of Her Majesty's subjects. Such a person may be punishable as a rogue and vagabond under the Vagrancy Act 1824, s 4. Note however that persons who, with intent to deceive or by using any fraudulent device, purport to act as spiritualistic mediums or to exercise powers of clairvoyance, etc, are punishable under the Fraudulent Mediums Act 1951, s 1.

Forum. A word frequently used to signify the place where jurisdiction is exercised in a given case, eg if a person is sued in England, on a contract made in France, England in the given case is the *forum*, and the law of England is, accordingly, the *lex fori*.

Forum non conveniens. An inappropriate *forum*. A doctrine in the law of conflicts which entitles a court to refuse jurisdiction over a matter if accepting jurisdiction would lead to substantial inconvenience or injustice to one or more of the parties.

Forum originis. The court of the country of a man's domicile by birth.

See DOMICILE.

Forwarding agent. One who carries on the business of arranging for the carriage of goods for other people. He is entitled to be indemnified against all expenses incurred on behalf of his principal and to be paid his charges for his services. His duty is to exercise reasonable care.

Foul berth. A berth where sufficient space is not left for a vessel to swing at anchor without coming into contact with another vessel anchored nearby (see *The Northampton* (1853) 1 Ecc & Ad 152 at 160).

Founder's share. A share allotted to a person who first founded the company. The issue of such shares is now rare. The holder of such a share is usually entitled to a proportion of the profits if the dividend on the ordinary shares has been paid up to a specified amount.

Four corners of an instrument, ie that which is contained on the face of a deed (without any

aid from the knowledge of the circumstances in which it was made) is said to be within its four corners, because every deed is supposed to be written on one entire skin.

Four seas. The seas surrounding England; divided into the western, including the Scottish and Irish; the northern; the eastern or North Sea; and the English Channel.

Fraction of a day. The law does not recognise such a fraction, except in cases of necessity and for the purposes of justice. When, therefore, a thing is to be done on a certain day, the whole of that day is allowed for doing it.

Franchise. A royal privilege, or branch of the Queen's PREROGATIVE, vested in the hands of a subject. It arises either from royal grant or from PRESCRIPTION which presupposes a grant. It is an incorporeal hereditament and is synonymous with liberty. There are many kinds, eg bodies corporate, the right to hold fairs, markets, ferries, fisheries. At the present day, the word is most frequently used to denote the right of voting for a member to serve in Parliament, which is called the Parliamentary franchise; or the right of voting for a county or district councillor, which is called the local government franchise.

The term is also frequently used with reference to a contract whereby a businessman is permitted to use a well-known business name, and receives advice and assistance, in return for money and/or purchasing stock-in-trade from, or at the direction of, the other party to the contract.

See PREROGATIVE.

Frank. To *frank* a letter means to send it post-free, so that the person who receives it shall have nothing to pay. This is now done in the ordinary way by prepaying the postage.

Frater consanguineus. A brother by the father's side, as opposed to *frater uterinus*, a brother by the mother's.

Frater uterinus. A brother by the mother's side.

Fraud. The modes of fraud are infinite, and it has been said that the courts have never laid down what constitutes fraud, or any general rule, beyond which they will not go in giving equitable relief on the ground of fraud. Fraud is, however, usually divided into two large classes: (i) actual fraud; and (ii) constructive fraud.

An actual fraud may be defined as something said, done or omitted by a person with the design of perpetrating what he must have known to be a positive fraud.

Constructive frauds are acts, statements or omissions which operate as virtual frauds on individuals or which, if generally permitted, would be prejudicial to the public welfare, and yet may have been unconnected with any selfish or evil designs; eg bonds and agreements entered into as a reward for using influence over another, to induce him to make a will for the benefit of the obligor. For such contracts encourage a spirit of artifice and scheming and tend to deceive and injure others.

'To amount to fraud, conduct must be deliberately dishonest' (see *R v Sinclair* [1968] 3 All ER 241).

Fraud on a power. The use of a power of appointment in such a way as to benefit a person not within the class of proper appointees, so as to defeat the intention of the person granting the power. So, for example, if a power-holder appoints property to X, to whom the property may properly be appointed, but on condition that X transfer half of the property to Y, to whom property is not to be appointed, this exercise is a fraud on the power. As to the protection afforded to purchasers in good faith, see Law of Property Act 1925, s 157.

Fraudulent conversion. Where a person dishonestly appropriates or converts to his or her own use property which has been entrusted to him or her, that person commits a fraudulent conversion. Such an act is now 'theft' under the Theft Act 1968.
See EMBEZZLEMENT; LARCENY; THEFT.

Fraudulent conveyance. A conveyance of property made with intent to defraud creditors. Such a conveyance is voidable under the Law of Property Act 1925, s 172 unless it has been made for valuable consideration (or upon good consideration) and in good faith to a person without notice of the intent to defraud.

Fraudulent medium. *See* MEDIUM.

Fraudulent preference. *See* PREFERENCE, FRAUDULENT.

Fraudulent trading. Trading by a company in defraud of creditors or for a fraudulent purpose (see Insolvency Act 1986, s 213).

Free chapel. Places of worship of royal foundation exempted from the jurisdiction of the ordinary, or founded by private persons to whom the Crown has thought fit to grant the same privilege.
See ORDINARY.

Free fishery. *See* FISHERY.

Free warren. A franchise or royalty derived from the Crown, empowering the grantees to take and kill beasts and fowls of warren; also for the preservation and custody of them.

Freehold, or **frank tenement** (Lat *Liberum tenementum*). Freehold estates were those titles to the ownership of land worthy of acceptance by a free man during the medieval period when the basic structure of English land law was developed, being the fee simple, the fee tail, or the life estate.

The term freehold is used at present in opposition to leasehold.

A leasehold interest, being an estate for a term of years, is only a chattel interest, and in law is less than estate of freehold, however long the term may be.
See ESTATE; LAND LAW.

Freeman. An allodial proprietor, one born or made free to enjoy certain municipal immunities and privileges.

By former local government legislation, persons of distinction, or who had rendered eminent services, might be admitted to be honorary freemen of a borough. Under the Local Government Act 1972, s 20(6) the former boroughs (except for the London boroughs) ceased to exist. Section 248 of the Act, however, provides for the retention of the status and rights of the freemen of the former boroughs, and also for the admission, in the future, of persons to the freedom of cities and towns. The roll of freemen of any such city or town is to be kept by an officer of the relevant district council.

Freemen of London. The freedom of the City of London can be obtained in three different ways: (i) by *patrimony*, ie as the son of a freeman born after the father has acquired his freedom; (ii) *servitude*, ie by serving an apprenticeship to a freeman; and (iii) *redemption*, ie by purchase.

As to the second method, apprenticeship is to a member of one of the City livery companies, eg The Merchant Taylors' Company. On completion of his apprenticeship the former pupil is entitled not only to membership of the Company, but also to the freedom of the City.

The last method includes the case where the freedom of the City is obtained by

F

honorary gift, as a mark of distinction for public services.

Freezing order. *See* MAREVA INJUNCTION.

Freight. The sum payable for the carriage of goods in a vessel. It may also, in a policy of marine insurance, include the benefit which a shipowner expects to derive from carrying his goods in his own vessel. As to the shipowner's lien for freight, see Merchant Shipping Act 1894, ss 494, 495.

Freighter. The hirer of a vessel.

Friars. The name of an order of religious persons, of which there are four principal branches: (i) Minors, Grey Friars, or Franciscans; (ii) Augustines; (iii) Dominicans, or Black Friars; (iv) White Friars, or Carmelites.

Friendly Society. An association for the purpose of affording relief to the members in sickness, and assistance to their widows and children on their deaths (see Friendly Societies Act 1992).

Friendly suit. A suit brought not in a hostile manner, the object being to settle some point of law, or do some act which cannot safely be done except with the sanction of a court of justice.

From. Generally excludes the day from which the time is to be reckoned.

Frontager. One who owns property which fronts or abuts on a street, etc.

Fructus industriales. *See* EMBLEMENTS.

Frustration. The prevention of the carrying out of a contract, eg by reason of the destruction of the subject matter.

'The premature determination of an agreement between parties, lawfully entered into and in course of operation at the time of its premature determination, owing to the occurrence of an intervening event or change of circumstances so fundamental as to be regarded by the law both as striking at the root of the agreement, and as entirely beyond what was contemplated by the parties when they entered into the agreement' (see *Cricklewood Property v Leighton's Trust* [1945] AC 221 at 228, HL, per Lord Simon, LC).

See generally Law Reform (Frustrated Contracts) Act 1943.

Frustration clause. A clause used in marine insurance exempting the insurers from liability in the event of the frustration of the adventure.

Full age. The age of majority was formerly twenty-one, but is now eighteen: Family Law Reform Act 1969, s 1.

Functus officio. A person who has discharged his duty, or whose office or authority has come to an end, is said to be *functus officio*.

Fund, Consolidated. *See* CONSOLIDATED FUND.

Funeral expenses. It is the first duty of an executor or administrator to bury the testator in a manner suitable to the estate which he has left, and the expenses will form a first charge on the estate; if, however, he is extravagant, he commits a *devastavit*, for which he is answerable to the creditors or legatees.
See DEVASTAVIT.

Fungibles. Movable goods which may be estimated by weight, number or measure, eg grain or coin. They are opposed to jewels, paintings, etc.

Furandi animus. The intention of stealing; ie the intention, in one who takes goods, of unlawfully depriving the rightful owner of his property in them.
See THEFT.

Furnival's Inn. *See* INNS OF CHANCERY.

Further advance or **charge.** A second or subsequent loan of money to a mortgagor by a mortgagee, either on the same or on an additional security.
See MORTGAGE.

Further assurance. Covenant for further assurance, in a deed of conveyance, means a covenant to make to the purchaser any additional 'assurance' which may be necessary to complete his title. It is *implied* on the use of the appropriate words, eg 'as beneficial owner', in conveyances made on and after 1st January 1882, by virtue of the Conveyancing Act 1881 (see now, as to implied covenants for title, s 76 of, and Sch II to, the Law of Property Act 1925).
See ASSURANCE.

Future estate, future interest. An estate in land or interest in property to take effect in possession at a future time. The expression is most frequently applied to contingent remainders and executory interests; but it would seem to be also applicable to vested remainders and reversions.
See CONTINGENT REMAINDER; ESTATE; EXECUTORY INTEREST; LAND LAW.

Future goods. Goods to be manufactured or acquired by the seller after the making of the contract of sale: Sale of Goods Act 1979, s 61(1). Where by a contract of sale the seller purports to effect a present sale of future goods, the contract operates as an agreement to sell the goods: ibid, s 5(3).

See AGREEMENT TO SELL.

Game. A word used to denote animals and birds which are objects of the chase, *ferae naturae.*

See FERAE NATURAE.

The word is defined under the Game Acts as including hares, pheasants, partridges, grouse, heath or moor game, black game, and bustards; though some of the provisions of these Acts are directed to deer, woodcock, snipe, quail, landrails, and rabbits.

At Common Law game belongs to a tenant and not to a landlord, but the right to game is frequently reserved to the landlord in the lease.

A game licence must be taken out by anyone killing or taking game. As to the right of an occupier to kill hares and rabbits, see Ground Game Act 1880 and Ground Game (Amendment) Act 1906. See also Agricultural Holdings Act, 1986, s 20 for the compensation for damage by game.

Gaming, or **Gambling.** The playing of a game of chance for winnings in money or money's worth, whether any person playing the game is at risk of losing any money or money's worth or not; a 'game of chance' includes a game of chance and skill combined, but not any athletic game or sport (see Gaming Act 1968, s 52).

A gaming machine is a machine constructed or adapted for playing a game of chance by means of the machine, and which has a slot or other aperture for the insertion of money or money's worth in the form of cash or tokens (see ibid, s 26).

Gaming licence duty is payable under Part II of the Betting and Gaming Duties Act 1972, in respect of the following games: baccarat, punto banco, big six, blackjack, boule, chemin-de-fer, chuck-a-luck, craps, crown and anchor, faro, faro bank, hazard, poker dice, pontoon, French roulette, American roulette, trente-et-quarante, vingt-et-un, and wheel of fortune. A special duty is imposed on the game of bingo but gaming carried on both in a private dwelling and on a domestic occasion does not require a licence. Dominoes and cribbage may be played in public houses.

Garnishee. A person who is *garnished* or warned. The word is especially applied in law to a debtor who is *warned* by the order of a court to pay his debt, not to his immediate creditor, but to a person who has obtained a final judgment against such creditor. The order is called a *garnishee order.*

Garnishment. A term now generally used in connection with the attachment of debts in the hands of a third party.

See GARNISHEE.

Garter. The honourable ensign of a great and noble society of knights, called Knights of the Order of St George, or of the Garter. The Order was first instituted by Edward III, for good success in a skirmish, in which the King's garter, it is said, was used as a token. The Order of the Garter is the first dignity after the nobility.

Garth. A close in the north of England; and enclosure about a house or church; also a dam or weir in a river, for the catching of fish, often called a fishgarth.

Gazette. The official publication of the Government, also called the *London Gazette.* It is evidence of Acts of State, and of everything done by the Queen in her political capacity. Orders of adjudication in bankruptcy are required to be published in it; and the production of a copy of the *Gazette*, containing a copy of the order of adjudication, is conclusive evidence of the fact, and of the date of it.

See ACT OF STATE.

Gazump. To raise a price previously agreed on with a prospective purchaser of property.

General agent. An agent empowered to act *generally* in the affairs of the principal, or at least to act for him *generally* in some particular capacity; as opposed to one authorised to act for him in a particular manner.
See SPECIAL AGENT.

General average. *See* AVERAGE, 1.

General average act. In marine insurance, where any extraordinary sacrifice or extraordinary expenditure is voluntarily and reasonably made in time of peril for the purpose of preserving the property imperilled in the common adventure (see Marine Insurance Act 1906, s 66(4)).
See GENERAL AVERAGE CONTRIBUTION.

General average contribution. A term used in marine insurance to denote a rateable contribution from the other parties interested in the adventure to which a person on whom a general average loss falls is entitled, subject to the conditions imposed by maritime law (see Marine Insurance Act 1906, s 66(3).
See GENERAL AVERAGE ACT.

General average expenditure. Expenditure incurred by a shipowner for the common safety of the adventure, eg (i) expense of discharging the cargo; (ii) a payment made to salvors employed by him; and (iii) expenses in a port of refuge.

General average loss. In marine insurance, a loss caused by or directly consequential on a general average act. It includes a general average expenditure as well as a general average sacrifice (see Marine Insurance Act 1906, s 66(1)).
See GENERAL AVERAGE ACT.

General average sacrifice. A sacrifice of the cargo, ship or freight for the common safety for the purpose of preserving from peril the property involved in a common maritime adventure.

General damages. Damages that will be presumed to have arisen from the defendant's unlawful act, such as for pain, inconvenience, etc, and need not be specifically proved.
See SPECIAL DAMAGES.

General descendants. Both one's direct, or 'lineal', and one's collateral descendants, ie anyone who might inherit property from one on one's death.
See DESCENT.

General equitable charge. Any charge in the nature of a mortgage which is not secured by a deposit of documents relating to the legal estate affected, and does not arise, or effect an interest arising, under a trust for sale or a settlement (see Land Charges Act 1972, s 2(4), Class C (iii)).

General extradition arrangements. Arrangements of a general nature made with one or more States and relating to the operation of extradition procedures under Part III of the Extradition Act 1989: Extradition Act 1989, s 3(3).

General lien. The right of certain agents, eg solicitors, insurance brokers, to detain an article from its owner until payment is made, not only in respect of that particular article, but of any balance that may be due on a general account between the parties.
See BAILMENT.

General lighthouse authority. This expression means Trinity House (see Merchant Shipping Act 1894, s 634(1)). Subject to any powers or rights enjoyed by local lighthouse authorities, a general lighthouse authority is responsible for the superintendence and management of all lighthouses, buoys and beacons in England and Wales and the adjacent seas and islands (see Merchant Shipping Act 1894, s 634(1)).
See TRINITY HOUSE.

General Medical Council. A body established by the Medical Act 1983, s 1(1). As to its constitution, see ibid, Sch I. It is responsible for the medical education and registration of medical practitioners (see ibid, Parts II, III and IV). It has power to advise on conduct or ethics (see ibid, s 35). It may direct that a medical practitioner's name should be removed from the register on the ground of professional misconduct (see ibid, s 36).

General partner. A member of a limited partnership who is liable for all debts and obligations of the firm: Limited Partnerships Act 1907, s 4(2).
See LIMITED PARTNERSHIP.

General ship. A ship which is used, either by the shipowner or by the charterer, to carry the goods of a number of persons under different bills of lading.

General Synod. *See* SYNOD.

General tail. *See* TAIL GENERAL.

General verdict. A verdict which, in a civil suit, is absolutely for the plaintiff or for the defendant, or, in a criminal case, is a verdict of guilty or not guilty; opposed in either case to a special verdict, in which the facts are stated, and the inference of law left to be determined by the Court.
See SPECIAL VERDICT.

General words. These used generally to be added in conveyance, to convey the easements and rights subsisting in the grantor. They are now implied by the Law of Property Act 1925, s 62.

Generalia specialibus non derogant. Generalities do not derogate from particular provisions.

Generalia verba sunt generaliter intelligenda. General words are to be understood generally.

Genocide. Acts committed with the intention of destroying, wholly or in part, a national, ethical, racial or religious group. A Convention on the Prevention and Punishment of the Crime of Genocide (approved by the General Assembly of the United Nations) was entered into by the United Kingdom and brought into force by the Genocide Act 1969.

Gentleman Usher of the Black Rod.
See BLACK ROD.

Gift. A conveyance or transfer which passes either land or goods, gratuitously, ie not in fulfilment of an obligation under a contract or on sale. Gifts may be between living persons, or *inter vivos*, or testamentary, occurring by the execution of the will of a deceased. As to things immovable, 'gift' was once said to be applicable only to lands and tenements given in tail. This limitation of the word is, however, quite obsolete. Blackstone distinguishes a *gift* from a *grant* in that a gift is always gratuitous, without binding consideration, and therefore void in certain cases, whereas a grant is made on some consideration or equivalent, though *grant* is better used to indicate a transfer of property (in particular, land) which is effected by a written instrument.
See GRANT. *See also* DONATIO MORTIS CAUSA.

Gift over. Either a future interest in property, which falls into possession when a preceding interest comes to an end, or a contingent interest which vests in interest upon the occurance of an event.

Gild. A voluntary association or fraternity.
See GUILD.

Gilt edged. United Kingdom Government stocks.

Gipsies. An early definition under a statute of Henry VIII (1530) described 'Egyptians' as wandering impostors and jugglers, using no craft nor feat of merchandise, pretending to tell men's and women's fortunes, and by craft and subtlety defrauding the people of their money.

This description would probably be most offensive to a true Romany, who would claim to be strictly honest and the preserver of various old country crafts. Nevertheless the colloquial meaning of gipsies is that of 'persons without fixed abode who lead a nomadic life, dwelling in tents or other shelters, or in caravans or other vehicles' (*Mills v Cooper* [1967] 2 All ER 100).

By the Caravan Sites Act 1968, s 16, 'gipsies' means persons of nomadic habit of life, whatever their race or origin, but does not include members of an organised group of travelling showmen, or of persons engaged in travelling circuses.

Glanville. The author of a book, written about 1181, entitled *Tractatus de legibus et consuetudinibus regni Angliae*, probably the first work of the kind in England.

Gold. Where English law is the proper law of a contract under which a debt is payable, any reference in the contract to gold or gold coin will *prima facie* be construed as an indication of the means by which the amount of the debt is to be measured, and not as a requirement to make actual payment in gold. The word 'gold' generally means gold coin or gold bullion.

As to hallmarking of gold and silver, see Hallmarking Act 1973.
See ASSAY; CARAT; HALLMARK.

Good behaviour. Under the Magistrates' Courts Act 1980, ss 115, 116, magistrates have power to order any person to enter into a recognisance, with or without sureties, to keep the peace or to be of good behaviour. Such a person, if failing to comply with the order, may be committed to prison.

Good consideration. A consideration founded on relationship or natural love and affection. It is not a *valuable* consideration, and will not 'sustain a promise', ie whereas in certain cases a 'consideration' is necessary to give legal validity to a promise, so that an action may be brought for breach of the same, a merely 'good' consideration will not be sufficient for this purpose.

See CONSIDERATION; CONTRACT.

Good faith. A thing is deemed to be done in good faith where it is, in fact, done honestly, whether it is done negligently or not (see Bills of Exchange Act 1882, s 90).

See BONA FIDES.

Good leasehold title. Under the Land Registration Act 1925 leaseholds may sometimes be registered with a good leasehold title, which is intermediate between absolute and possessory title. The effect of first registration with a good leasehold title is the same as registration with an absolute title, except that such registration does not affect or prejudice the enforcement of any estate, right or interest affecting or in derogation of the title of the lessor to grant the lease (s 10).

See POSSESSORY TITLE; LEASE; REGISTERED LAND.

Good seamanship, rules of. *See* RULES OF GOOD SEAMANSHIP.

Goods and chattels. In the widest sense, this expression includes any kind of property which, regard being had either to the subject matter, or to the quantity of interest in it, is not freehold. But in practice, the expression is most frequently limited to things movable, especially things movable in possession.

See MOVABLES; PROPERTY; ESTATES.

Goodwill. The *goodwill* of a trade of business comprises every advantage which has been acquired by carrying on the business, whether connected with the premises in which the business has been carried on, or with the name of the firm by whom it has been conducted. 'Probability that the old customers will resort to the old place' (Lord Eldon in *Cruttwell v Lye* (1810) 17 Ves 346).

Government. This word is most frequently used to denote the principal executive officer or officers of a State or territory. Thus, in England, 'the government', generally is understood to mean the Ministers of the Crown for the time being. But sometimes the word is used differently so as to indicate the supreme legislative power in a State, or the Legislature in a dependent, or semi-independent territory. The word is also used to indicate the art or science of government.

Grace, days of. *See* DAYS OF GRACE.

Grant (Lat *Concessio*). **1** The transfer of property by an instrument in writing without the delivery or the possession of any subject matter thereof. This may happen: (i) where there is no subject matter capable of delivery, eg in the case of an advowson, patent right, or title of honour (*see* ADVOWSON; PATENT); (ii) where the subject matter is not capable of *immediate* delivery, in the case of a reversion or remainder (*see* REVERSION; REMAINDER); (iii) where, by reason of the subject matter of the property being in the custody of another, or for any other cause, it is impracticable or undesirable to transfer the immediate possession.

The person making the grant is called the *grantor*; the person to whom it is made the *grantee*. Where the grantor transfers his whole interest in any subject-matter, the grant is generally called an *assignment*.

A grant has always been the regular method of transferring incorporeal hereditaments; eg an advowson, etc, and estates in expectancy, because no 'livery', ie, physical delivery, could be made of such estates. For this reason they were said to *lie in grant*; while corporeal hereditaments in possession were formerly said to *lie in livery*. By the Law of Property Act 1925, s 59 the word 'grant' is not to imply any covenant in law except where otherwise provided by statute. Nor is the word 'grant' necessary to convey land or to create any interest in it. Nevertheless all lands and all interests lie 'in grant' and are no longer capable of being conveyed by livery (see ibid, s 51).

See LAND LAW; INCORPOREAL HEREDITAMENTS.

2 The word *grant* is also frequently used in reference to public money devoted by Parliament for special purposes. *May.*

Gratuitous. Made without consideration or equivalent.

See GIFT; CONSIDERATION.

Gravamen. 1 The *gravamen* of a charge or accusation is that part of it which weighs most heavily against the accused.

2 The word is applied specially to grievances alleged by the clergy and made by them a subject of complaint to the archbishop and bishops in Convocation.

Gray's Inn. One of the Inns of Court.

See INNS OF COURT.

Great Britain. England, Scotland, and Wales: Union with Scotland Act 1706, preamble, art 1; Interpretation Act 1978, s 22(1).

G

Great charter. *See* MAGNA CARTA.

Great Seal. A seal by virtue of which a great part of the royal authority is exercised. The office of the Lord Chancellor, or Lord Keeper, is created by the delivery of the Great Seal into his custody. By art 24 of the Union between England and Scotland it was provided that there should be one Great Seal for Great Britain, for sealing writs to summon Parliaments, for sealing treaties with foreign states, and all Acts of State which concern the United Kingdom.

See ACT OF STATE.

Green. A town or village green is land which has been allotted for the exercise or recreation of the inhabitants of any locality or on which such inhabitants have a customary right to indulge in lawful sports or pastimes (see Commons Registration Act 1965, s 22).

Green Belt land means (i) any land which for the time being is the subject of an express declaration made in the manner provided by the Green Belt (London and Home Counties) Act 1938; and (ii) any land acquired by a local authority under the powers conferred by s 3 of the Act: Green Belt (London and Home Counties) Act 1938, s 2(1).

Except with the consent of the Secretary of State or a local authority no building must be erected on Green Belt land: ibid, s 10.

Nothing in the Act prevents Green Belt land from being used for purposes of recreation or agriculture or camping: ibid, s 27.

Green Book. Colloquial term for *The County Court Practice*, which set out the rules of civil procedure in the county courts, as distinct from the White Book, *The Supreme Court Practice*, which set out the rules of civil procedure in the High Court. Both have been superseded by the Civil Procedure Rules 1998 made under the Civil Procedure Act 1997, which are set out in the replacement to the Green Book, *The Civil Court Practice*.

Gregorian epoch. The time from which the Gregorian calendar or computation dates; ie, from the year 1582. So called after Pope Gregory XIII, who ordained that ten days in that year should be suppressed, in order to adjust the incorrect Julian calendar to the solar year. The Gregorian calendar was adopted by most countries in Europe, though not by England until the passing of the Calendar (New Style) Act 1750.

Gretna Green marriages. An expression formerly applied to marriages contracted in Scotland by parties who had gone there for the purpose of being married without the delay and formalities required by the law of England. They were usually celebrated at Gretna Green in Dumfriesshire, as being the nearest and most convenient place for the purpose. The Marriage (Scotland) Act 1939 provided that such irregular marriages by declaration *de presenti* or by promise *subsequente copula* are invalid. The Act provided that any two persons who desired to be married in Scotland might contract to do so in the office of an authorised registrar, or, if certain conditions were complied with, by a sheriff's licence.

Gross, right in. *See* RIGHT IN GROSS.

Ground game. *See* GAME.

Guarantee. In the strict sense, where one person contracts as surety on behalf of another an obligation to which the latter is also liable as the primary party. A promise to answer for the debt, default or miscarriage of another, which to be enforceable must be evidenced in writing under the Statute of Frauds 1677.

See FRAUD.

Guardian. One who has the charge or custody of any person or thing; the person who has the custody and education of such persons as are unable to manage their own affairs.

1 *Guardian and ward.* The disabilities of a minor and his legal incapacity to manage his own affairs render it necessary that, for the protection of his interests and for the management of his property, he should have a guardian of his person and property, to whom he stands in the relation of ward. A person may be the guardian of a minor in various ways:

(i) *By parental right.* A father or mother has by parental right the guardianship of the person of a minor up to the age of eighteen as his natural guardian in the wider sense of the term.

(ii) *By parental appointment.* Both the father and the mother have power to appoint persons to act as guardians of a minor after their respective deaths, if the child is then a minor. No special words are necessary in making the appointment, which may be made by deed or will.

(iii) *By appointment of the court.* The court may appoint a person as a guardian where (a) a child has no parent with parental responsibility for him; or (b) a residence order has been made in respect of the child in favour of a parent or guardian of his who has died while the order was in force: Children Act 1989, s 5. A person who has been appointed a guardian may disclaim his appointment: ibid, s 6(5). Any appointment may be brought to an end at any time by an order of the court: ibid, s 5(7).

2 *Guardian ad litem.* A guardian *ad litem* may be appointed by the court to represent a child in certain proceedings (eg on an application for a care order or a supervision order): Children Act 1989, s 41. A guardian ad litem is now known as a 'litigation friend' under the Civil Procedure Rules 1998.

See CARE AND SUPERVISION ORDER.

3 *Guardian of mental patient.* An application for guardianship of a patient may be made under the Mental Health Act 1983, s 17, on the grounds that such patient (i) is suffering from mental disorder, that is, mental illness or severe subnormality (or in the case of a patient under 21 years, psychopathic disorder or subnormality) and (ii) that it is necessary (because his condition warrants it) that he should be so received into guardianship. The person named a guardian in the guardianship application must either be a local social services authority, or a person acceptable to the local social services authority. Regulations as to guardianship, correspondence with patients, visits and medical examinations, leave of absence from hospital, etc, while under guardianship are all dealt with in ss 35 *et seq* of the Act.

Guardian's allowance. An allowance payable to a person in respect of a child if he is entitled to child benefit in respect of that child and (i) both parents are dead; or (ii) one parent is dead and the person claiming the allowance was unaware of the death of, and has made all reasonable efforts to discover the whereabouts of, the other parent; or (iii) one of the parents is dead and the other is in prison: Social Security Contributions and Benefits Act 1992, s 77(1),(2).

Guild. A voluntary association or fraternity, usually for some commercial purpose.

Guild church. Certain churches have been established in the City of London as guild churches, with the primary purpose of serving the non-resident daytime population of the City. Such churches are free from the normal jurisdiction and control of incumbent churchwardens and parochial church councils, and their freeholds vest in the Bishop of London. See more fully City of London (Guild Churches) Acts 1952 and 1960.

Guild hall. The place of meeting of a guild. *See* GUILD.

Guild merchant. A mercantile meeting of a guild. *See* GUILD.

Guildhall sittings. Sittings held in the Guildhall of the City of London for City of London causes.

Gypsies. *See* GIPSIES.

H

HL. House of Lords.

See HOUSE OF LORDS.

Habeas corpus. The most celebrated writ in English law, being the great remedy which that law has provided for the violation of personal liberty.

The most important type of *habeas corpus* is that of *habeas corpus ad subjiciendum*, which is the remedy used for deliverance from illegal confinement. This is directed to any person who detains another in custody, and commands him to produce the body, with the day and cause of his seizure and detention, *ad faciendum, subjiciendum et recipiendum*—to do, submit to, and receive whatsoever the Judge or Court awarding such writ shall direct. The writ existed at Common Law, though it has been improved by statute. By the Habeas Corpus Act 1862, no writ of *habeas corpus* may issue out of England, by authority of any Judge or Court there, into any colony or foreign dominion of the Crown, where Her Majesty has a lawfully established court with power to grant and issue such writ, and with power to ensure its due execution throughout such colony or dominion. It has been held that this statute does not extend to the Isle of Man.

There are also other kinds of *habeas corpus*.

1 *Ad respondendum*; which was to bring up a prisoner confined by the process of an inferior court to charge him with a fresh action in the court above.

2 *Ad satisfaciendum,* with a similar object when *judgment* in an inferior court had been obtained against the prisoner.

3 *Ad faciendum et recipiendum* (otherwise called a *habeas corpus cum causa*). This writ was applied for when, in an action in an inferior court, the defendant had been arrested; and it had for its object the removal of the proceedings and bringing up the body of the defendant to the court above, 'to do and receive what the King's court shall deliver in that behalf'.

4 *Ad prosequendum, testificandum, deliberandum*, etc, which was issued for bringing up a prisoner to bear testimony in any court, or to be tried in the proper jurisdiction.

But the present law of arrest for debt has lessened the importance of all these kinds except the last; and, with regard to the last, the occasions for its use have diminished now that, by various enactments, its objects can be attained by order of a Judge or of a Secretary of State.

Habendum. That clause of a deed which determines the estate or interest granted by the deed.

Habitual drunkard. A person who, not being a mentally disordered person within the meaning of the Mental Health Act 1983, is notwithstanding, by reason of habitual intemperate drinking of intoxicating liquor, at times dangerous to himself or to others, or incapable of managing himself or his affairs; or who so conducts himself that it would not be reasonable to expect a spouse of ordinary sensibilities to continue to cohabit with him. See Habitual Drunkards Act 1879, which establishes retreats, etc; and Matrimonial Proceedings (Magistrates' Courts) Act 1960, under which relief was made available to either husband or wife on the grounds of the habitual drunkenness of the other.

Hackney carriage. Any carriage for the conveyance of passengers which plies for hire within the limits of the Metropolitan Public Carriage Act 1869, and is not a stage carriage: Metropolitan Public Carriage Act 1869, s 4.

Hague Rules. Rules agreed on in September 1921 at a meeting of the International Law Association held at The Hague with the object of securing adoption by the countries represented of a set of rules relating to bills of lading so that the rights and liabilities of cargo owners and shipowners respectively might be subject to rules of general application.
See BILL OF LADING.

The Rules were revised and were embodied in the articles of an International Convention signed at Brussels in 1924. In relation to this country they have been replaced by the Hague–Visby Rules.
See HAGUE–VISBY RULES.

Hague–Visby Rules. Rules agreed on by a protocol signed at Brussels in February 1968 amending the International Convention agreed there in 1924. They replace the Hague Rules. The Carriage of Goods by Sea Act 1971 incorporates them into English law.
See HAGUE RULES.

Half-blood. The relationship between two persons who have only one *nearest* common ancestor, and not a pair of *nearest* ancestors.

Under the Administration of Estates Act 1925, which relates equally to real and personal estate, relatives of the whole blood take priority over relatives of the half-blood, ie the half-blood relatives take immediately after the whole blood relatives of the same degree.
See WHOLE BLOOD; DEGREE.

Hallmark. A stamp authorised to be impressed on gold or silver articles. The law as to hallmarking was revised by the Hallmarking Act 1973. Hallmarks must be stamped by assay offices.

Approved hallmarks for articles comprised of a single precious metal made in the United Kingdom are, for the respective assay offices: London, a leopard's head; Edinburgh, a castle; Birmingham, an anchor; Sheffield, a rose. For articles other than those made in the United Kingdom, the approved marks are: London, the sign of the constellation Leo; Edinburgh, St Andrew's Cross; Birmingham, an equilateral triangle; Sheffield, the sign of the constellation Libra. In addition, articles of gold made in the United Kingdom, must be marked with a crown, and those of silver with a lion passant (Edinburgh, a lion rampant) and those of platinum with an orb surmounted by a cross. All articles must also be marked with a standard of fineness.

See ASSAY; CARAT.

Ham. A house; also a village or little town.

Hamburg Rules. Rules contained in a Convention adopted at a United Nations conference on the carriage of goods by sea held in Hamburg in March 1978 which has not yet been ratified by the United Kingdom. The Rules will replace the Hague Rules.
See HAGUE RULES.

Hamlet. The diminutive of *ham*.
See HAM.

Handling. The modern expression for the offence formerly known as *receiving* stolen goods (see Theft Act 1968, s 22).

Hand-sale. A sale made by the shaking of hands.

Harbour. Any harbour, whether natural or artificial, and any port, haven, estuary, tidal or other river, or inland waterway navigated by sea-going ships, and includes a dock and a wharf (see Harbours Act 1964, s 57(1)).

Hare. A beast of warren. It is 'game' within the Game Act 1831, s 2. By the Hares Act 1848, s 1 owners and occupiers and persons authorised by them may kill hares without a game certificate. A close season for hares is imposed by the Hares Prevention Act 1892, which prevents them from being *sold* from March to July (see also Ground Game Act 1880, and Ground Game (Amendment) Act 1906).

Hawker. Any person who travels with a horse or other beast bearing or drawing burden, and who went from place to place or to other men's houses carrying to sell or exposing for sale any goods, wares or merchandise, including any person who travels by any means of locomotion to any place in which he did not usually reside or carry on business, and there sells or exposes for sale any goods, etc, in or at any house, shop, room, booth, stall, etc. Hawkers no longer require excise licences.

Haybote, or **Hedgebote.** Necessary material to make and repair hedges, or to make rakes and forks, and suchlike instruments; or a permission, expressed or implied, to take such material.

Headlease. *See* UNDERLEASE.

Hearing. The trial of an action. In general, all cases, both civil and criminal, must be heard in open court. But in certain exceptional cases, where the administration of justice would be rendered impracticable by the

presence of the public, the Court may sit in camera, eg where it is necessary for the public safety, or in proceedings for an offence against morality or decency when evidence is given by children or young persons.
See SITTINGS IN CAMERA.

Hearsay evidence. Evidence of a fact not actually perceived by a witness with one of his own senses, but proved by him to have been stated by another person.

Formerly, in any civil proceedings, a statement other than one made by a person while giving evidence in those proceedings was admissible only by virtue of the Civil Evidence Act 1968 or other statutory provision or by agreement of the parties (see Civil Evidence Act 1968, s 1(1)).

However, by s 1 of the Civil Evidence Act 1995, hearsay evidence is generally admissible, though subject to particular rules concerning its admission and the weight to be attached to it.

In criminal proceedings voluntary confessions are admissible and so are the dying declarations of the victim where a person is charged with murder or manslaughter.
See VOLUNTARY CONFESSION.

Heave. A movement of land upwards in a vertical direction.

Heir. *See* DESCENT.

Heirloom. A *limb* or member of the inheritance, specifically, those chattels which devolved in the same way as did estates in land upon death. Thus by *heirlooms* are generally meant implements or ornaments of a household, or other personal chattels, which accrued to the heir with the house itself by custom; or else such chattels, eg furniture, pictures, etc, as are directed by will or settlement to follow the limitations thereby made of some family mansion or estate.
See DESCENT; REAL AND PERSONAL PROPERTY.

Held covered. A term used in marine insurance policies meaning that the insurers agree to the subject matter continuing to be insured on payment of an additional premium in circumstances where the assured is guilty of a breach of warranty or has changed the voyage of a ship or the period of insurance under a time policy has expired while she is still at sea.
See CONTINUANCE CLAUSE; PREMIUM; WARRANTY.

Heralds' College. The College of Arms, or Heralds' College, is an ancient royal corporation instituted by Richard III in 1483. At its head is the Earl Marshal, a hereditary title held by the Dukes of Norfolk. He is assisted by 13 officers of the College, as follows: Garter King-at-Arms, Clarenceux King-at-Arms, Norroy King-at-Arms; the Richmond, Windsor, Somerset, Lancaster, York and Chester Heralds; and four Poursuivants, or messengers, with the titles Rouge Drago, Rouge Croix, Bluemantle, and Portcullis.

The Heralds' College is still empowered to make grants of arms and to permit changes of name. Their books are good evidence of pedigrees. The Earl Marshal also presides over the Court of Chivalry (*see* COURT OF CHIVALRY) which exercises jurisdiction in questions of precedence and the use of armorial bearings.

Herbage. The fruit of the earth, produced by nature for the bite and food of cattle. But it is also used for a liberty that a man has to feed his cattle on another person's ground.

Herbagium anterius. The first crop of grass or hay, in opposition to *aftermath*, or second cutting.

High Court of Justice. *See* SUPREME COURT.

High seas. That part of the sea which is more than 12 miles distant from the coast outside territorial waters, ie offences committed on board a British ship on the high seas are punishable by English law as if committed on British soil, such a ship being in law part of the territory of the United Kingdom.
See TERRITORIAL WATERS.

High Steward. An expression used:
1 Of the Lord High Steward of the Royal Household.
   See COURT OF LORD HIGH STEWARD OF THE QUEEN'S HOUSEHOLD.
2 Of the Lord High Steward of the University of Oxford, an officer of the University appointed to preside at the trial of any scholar or privileged person of the University, or any indictment for treason, of which the Vice-Chancellor of the University may have claimed and been allowed cognisance. Before the office of the High Steward is called into action he must have been approved by the Lord High Chancellor of England.

High treason. *See* TREASON.

High-water mark. That part of the seashore which the waters usually reach when the tide is highest.

Highway. A public road which all the subjects of the realm have a right to use for the purpose of passing and repassing. Highways exist by prescription, by Act of Parliament, or by dedication to the public on the part of individuals. The law relating to the creation, maintenance, improvement, etc, of highways is consolidated in the Highways Act 1980. *See* DEDICATION OF WAY; PRESCRIPTION.

Highway Code. A code compiled by the Secretary of State for the Environment, containing directions for the guidance of persons using the roads (see Road Traffic Act 1988, s 38). Failure to observe a provision of the Code does not of itself render a person liable to criminal proceedings, but such failure may be relied on by any party to proceedings as tending to establish a liability.

Hijacking. Seizure of an aircraft in flight or of a ship.

A person on board an aircraft in flight who unlawfully, by the use of force or by threats of any kind, seizes it or exercises control of it commits the offence of hijacking, whatever his nationality, whatever the State in which the aircraft is registered, and whether the aircraft is in the United Kingdom or elsewhere: Aviation Security Act 1982, s 1(1). As to when an aircraft is 'in flight', see ibid, s 38(3)(a).

A person who unlawfully, by the use of force or threats of any kind, seizes a ship or exercises control of it, commits the offence of hijacking a ship, whatever his nationality and whether the ship is in the United Kingdom or elsewhere: Aviation and Maritime Security Act 1990, s 8(1). 'Ship' means any vessel (including hovercraft, submersible craft and other floating craft): ibid, s 17(1).

Hire. A sum of money paid to the shipowner by a charterer under a time charter-party for the use of the vessel. If the money is not paid by the specified date, the shipowner may withdraw the vessel from service.

Hire-purchase agreement. An agreement, other than a conditional sales agreement under which (i) goods are bailed in return for periodical payments by the person to whom they are bailed, and (ii) the property in the goods will pass to that person if the terms of that agreement are complied with and one or more of the following occurs: (a) the exercise of an option to purchase by that person, (b) the doing of any other specified act by any party to the agreement, (c) the happening of any other specified event (see Consumer Credit Act 1974, s 189(1)).

Hire-purchase system. Under this system the person who hires the goods becomes, on payment of the last instalment of the amount fixed, the owner of them. The hirer is given certain rights although he defaults in his payments (see Consumer Credit Act 1974, which controls the extension of credit to individuals, including 'consumer hire agreements').

Hiring. A contract which differs from borrowing only in that hiring is always for a price, stipend, or additional recompense; whereas borrowing is merely gratuitous. It is a bailment for reward whereby the possession of goods, with a transient property in them, is transferred for a particular time or use, on condition that the hirer is to restore the goods so hired as soon as the time has expired or use performed. It is of four kinds. The hiring (i) of a thing for use; (ii) of work and labour; (iii) of services to be performed on the thing delivered; (iv) of the carriage of goods. *See* BAILMENT.

Historic building. Any building which in the opinion of the Historic Buildings and Monuments Commission is of historic or architectural interest (see National Heritage Act 1983, s 33(8)). *See* HISTORIC BUILDINGS AND MONUMENTS COMMISSION.

Historic Buildings and Monuments Commission. A Commission whose duty (so far as practicable) is:

(i) to secure the preservation of ancient monuments and historic buildings situated in England;

(ii) to promote the preservation and enhancement of the character and appearance of conservation areas situated in England; and

(iii) to promote the public's enjoyment of, and advance their knowledge of, ancient monuments and historic buildings situated in England and their preservation (see National Heritage Act 1983, s 33).

See ANCIENT MONUMENT; HISTORIC BUILDING; CONSERVATION AREA.

Historic wreck. *See* WRECK.

Holder. A payee or indorsee in possession of a bill of exchange or a promissory note.

See BILL OF EXCHANGE; PROMISSORY NOTE.

Holder in due course. One who has taken a bill of exchange, cheque or note, complete and regular on the fact of it, and who became the holder of it before it was overdue and without notice of previous dishonour and who took it in good faith and for value without notice of any defect in the title of the person who negotiated it (see Bills of Exchange Act 1882, s 29).

See BILL OF EXCHANGE; NEMO DAT QUOD NON HABET.

Holding, in the Agricultural Holdings Act 1986, means the aggregate of the land (whether agricultural land or not) comprised in a contract of tenancy (see Agricultural Holdings Act 1986, s 1(1)).

Holding company. A company controlling a subsidiary company.

See SUBSIDIARY COMPANY.

Holding out. Inducing other persons to believe in the existence of an authority which does not exist in fact. The party so holding out may afterwards be estopped from denying the supposed authority. As to holding oneself out as a partner, see Partnership Act 1890, s 3.

See ESTOPPEL.

Holding over is where a person having come into possession of land under a lawful title, continues in possession after the title has expired; eg if a person takes a lease for a year, and after the year has expired continues to hold the premises without any fresh lease from the owner of the estate.

See DOUBLE RENT; DOUBLE VALUE.

Holograph. A deed or writing written entirely by the 'grantor's' own hand. On account of the difficulty with which the forgery of such a document can be accomplished it is held by Scots law to be valid without witnesses. So, a holograph will is a will written in the testator's own hand.

Holy orders. In the English Church are the orders of bishops (including archbishops), priests and deacons.

Homicide. The killing of a human being by a human being. It is usually divided into three kinds—*justifiable, excusable,* and *felonious.*

1 *Justifiable homicide* is of three kinds:
   (i) The putting a man to death pursuant to a legal sentence, as eg for treason.
   (ii) The killing, by an officer of justice, of a person who assaults or resists him, and cannot otherwise be taken into custody.
   (iii) The killing of persons for the dispersion of riots or rebellious assemblies, or the prevention of serious crimes, such as murder and rape.
2 *Excusable homicide* is of two sorts: either—
   (i) by misadventure.
   (ii) in self-defence.
   This kind of self-defence is to be distinguished from that included under the head of justifiable homicide, to hinder the perpetration of a capital crime, by the fact that, in the case now supposed, the person killing has himself to blame (though ever so slightly) for the circumstances which have led to the killing. There is now no practical difference between justifiable and excusable homicide.
3 *Criminal homicide.* This is any killing not included in the two previous categories and is divided into three kinds, *manslaughter, murder* and *infanticide.*
   See MANSLAUGHTER; MURDER; INFANTICIDE.

Honorarium. A gratuity given for professional services.

Honour, besides its general meaning is a word used more especially in the following contexts.
1 The word is also used in reference to the acceptance *for honour* of a bill of exchange.
2 It is also used generally in regard to bills of exchange. To honour a bill is to pay it.
   See BILL OF EXCHANGE.

Hostage-taking. The detention of a person by another, whatever his nationality, in order to compel a State, or international governmental organisation to do or abstain from doing any act and threatening to kill, injure or continue to detain him (see Taking of Hostages Act 1982, s 1(1)).

Hostel. A building in which is provided for persons:
   (i) residential accommodation other-wise than in separate and self-contained sets of premises, and
   (ii) either board or facilities for the preparation of food adequate to their

needs, or both: Housing Associations Act 1985, s 106(1).

Hostile witness. If a witness under examination in chief shows himself 'hostile' to the party who called him, he may by leave of the judge be cross-examined by the party who called him, as though he had been called by the opposite party (see Criminal Procedure Act 1865, s 3). *See* EXAMINATION.

Hostilities does not mean the existence of a state of war but means acts of hostility or operations of hostility (see *Britain SS Co Ltd v R* [1921] 1 AC 99 at 133 (per Lord Wrenbury)). Such acts or operations must be committed by persons acting as agents of an enemy government or of an organised rebellion, and not by private individuals acting entirely on their own initiative (see *Atlantic Mutual Insurance Co v King* [1919] 1 KB 307 at 310 (per Bailhache, J)).

Hotchpot. Literally, a pudding mixed with divers ingredients. But, by a metaphor, it means a commixture or putting together of lands of several tenures, for the equal division of them. The word is frequently applied with reference to settlements which give a power to a parent of appointing a fund among his or her children, in which it is provided that no child, taking a share of the fund under any appointment, is to be entitled to any share in the unappointed part without bringing his or her share into 'hotchpot' and accounting for it accordingly. The effect of such a clause would be to prevent a child who takes under an appointment from claiming his full share in the unappointed part, in addition to his appointed share (see also Administration of Estates Act 1925, s 47). *See* SETTLEMENT; POWER; LAND LAW.

Hotel. An establishment held out by the proprietor as offering food, drink and, if so required, sleeping accommodation, without special contract, to any traveller presenting himself who appears able and willing to pay a reasonable sum for the services and facilities provided and who is in a fit state to be received (see Hotel Proprietors Act 1956, s 1(3)). *See* INN.

Hours of darkness. The time between half an hour after sunset and half an hour before sunrise: Highways Act 1980, s 329(1).

House in multiple occupation. A house which is occupied by persons who do not form a single household: Housing Act 1985, s 345.

House of Commons. The lower House of Parliament, consisting of the representatives of the nation at large, exclusive of the peerage and the prelates. *May*. Although the House of Commons together with the House of Lords forms the High Court of Parliament, it is not strictly speaking a judicial body. The House has jurisdiction over persons for committing any breach of the privileges of the House or of any of its members.

House of Keys. *See* KEYS.

House of Lords. The upper House of the legislature, consisting of the Lords Spiritual and the Lords Temporal. The Lords Spiritual consist of the archbishops of Canterbury and York; of the bishops of London, Durham, and Winchester; and of twenty-one other bishops. The Lords Temporal are the hereditary peers of England, Scotland, Great Britain and the United Kingdom who have not disclaimed their peerages under the Peerages Act 1963; life peers created under the Life Peerages Act 1958; and Lords of Appeal in Ordinary created under the Appellate Jurisdiction Act 1876. A certain number of peers are elected, under the Act of Union with Scotland, to represent in the House of Lords the body of the Scottish nobility; but it was held in *Petition of the Earl of Antrim* [1967] 1 AC 691, that the right to elect Irish representative peers no longer exists. The aggregate number of the Lords Temporal is not fixed, and may be increased at will by the Crown. By the House of Lords Act 1999 hereditary peers were excluded from the House of Lords save for 90 who, under current standing orders of the House, were elected by the body of hereditary peers. The House of Lords is also the court of final appeal in all cases, assigning this business by constitutional convention to its Appellate Committee, made up of the Law Lords sitting in panels of five and occasionally seven, except from certain Commonwealth courts, appeals from which are heard by the Judicial Committee of the Privy Council (*see* JUDICIAL COMMITTEE OF THE PRIVY COUNCIL) as a court of final appeal. *May*. In addition to its appellate jurisdiction, the House of Lords has jurisdiction in impeachment and over peerage claims, and also over any breach of its privileges. *See* IMPEACHMENT; PRIVILEGE.

Housebote. Estovers, ie an allowance of necessary timber for the repair and support of a house or tenement, and for fuel. This

belongs, of common right, to a lessee for years or for life.
See ESTOVERS.

Housing action trust. A trust whose objects are:
(i) to secure the repair or improvement of housing accommodation held by the trust;
(ii) to secure proper management and use of that accommodation: Housing Act 1988, s 63(1).

Housing association. A society, body of trustees or company
(i) which is established for the purpose of providing, constructing, improving or managing the construction or improvement of housing accommodation, and
(ii) which does not trade for profit: Housing Act 1985, s 5(1).

Housing trust. A corporation or body which is required by the terms of its constituent instrument (i) to use the whole of its funds for the purpose of providing housing accommodation; or (ii) to devote the whole, or substantially the whole, of its funds for charitable purposes, and, in fact, uses them for the purpose of providing housing accommodation: Housing Act 1985, s 6.

Human Fertilisation and Embryology Authority. An authority responsible for keeping under review information about embryos and the provision of treatment services and activities, and for granting licences: Human Fertilisation and Embryology Act 1990, ss 5 to 10.

Human Rights Act 1998. An Act providing for the implementation by courts in the United Kingdom of those protocols of the European Convention on Human Rights to which the United Kingdom is a signatory.
See HUMAN RIGHTS, EUROPEAN CONVENTION ON.

Human Rights, European Commission of. A commission whose function is to receive from States or individuals petitions claiming to be victims of a violation of a right set out in the European Convention on Human Rights
See HUMAN RIGHTS, EUROPEAN CONVENTION ON.
The commission must attempt to effect a friendly settlement, it must draw up a report and send it to the Committee of Ministers of the Council of Europe and to the State concerned.

In certain circumstances the matter may be referred to the European Court of Human Rights.
See HUMAN RIGHTS, EUROPEAN COURT OF.

Human Rights, European Convention on. A convention signed at Rome on 4th November 1950.
Its principal provisions relate to (i) the right to life (art 2); (ii) the prohibition of torture, degrading treatment and punishment (art 3); (iii) the prohibition of slavery and forced labour (art 4); (iv) the right to liberty (art 5); (v) the right to a fair trial and a public hearing of the proceedings (art 6); (vi) the right to private life and correspondence (art 8); and (vii) freedom of thought, conscience, religion and association (art 9).
See HUMAN RIGHTS ACT 1998.

Human Rights, European Court of. The Court's function is to hear cases submitted to it by the Committee of Ministers of the Council of Europe concerning the interpretation of the European Convention on Human Rights.
See HUMAN RIGHTS, EUROPEAN CONVENTION ON.
The Court's judgment is final.

Hush-money. A bribe to hinder the giving of information.

Hypnotism. Includes mesmerism, and any similar act or process which produces or is intended to produce in any person any form of induced sleep or trance, in which the susceptibility of the mind of that person to suggestion or direction is increased or intended to be increased. Demonstrations of hypnotism at places of entertainment and other places are controlled by the Hypnotism Act 1952.

Hypoteca, hypothec, or **hypothek.** A security for a debt which remains in the possession of the debtor; differing thus from a *pledge*, which is handed over to the creditor:
1 Thus, a mortgage of land, where the mortgagee does not take possession, is in the nature of a *hypotheca*. 2 Bl.
2 So, to mortgage a ship for necessaries is called *hypothecation*. 2 Bl.
See MORTGAGE; SECURITY INTEREST.

Hypothecation. *See* HYPOTHECA, HYPOTHEC OR HYPOTHEK.

IATA. The International Air Transport Association.
See INTERNATIONAL AIR TRANSPORT ASSOCIATION.

ILU. The Institute of London Underwriters.
See INSTITUTE OF LONDON UNDERWRITERS.

IMO. The International Maritime Organisation.
See INTERNATIONAL MARITIME ORGANISATION.

IOU (I owe you). A written acknowledgment of a debt. It operates merely as evidence of a debt due by virtue of an antecedent contract. It does not require to be stamped.

Ibidem, ibid, id. In the same place or case.

Id certum, etc. *See* CERTUM, ETC.

Idem sonans (sounding alike). The Court will not set aside proceedings on account of the misspelling of names, provided that the variance is so slight as not to mislead, or the name as spelt is *idem sonans*, eg Lawrance for Lawrence.

Identity of person. A phrase applied especially to those cases in which the issue before the jury is whether a person is the same person as one previously convicted.

Ides. A division of time used by the Romans. In the Roman calendar the Ides of March, May, July and October were on the 15th of the month; of the remaining months on the 13th.

Idle and disorderly person. *See* VAGRANT.

Ignorantia eorum quae quis scire tenetur non excusat. Ignorance of those things which one ought to know is no excuse.

Ignorantia juris (or **legis**) **neminem excusat.** Ignorance of the law excuses no man.

Illegal. Contrary to law, generally in the sense of committing a criminal or regulatory offence.
See UNLAWFUL.

Illegal practices. Offences committed during the course of Parliamentary or local government elections. They include voting offences, failure to make returns and declarations of expenses, incurring unauthorised expenses, causing disturbances at meetings, etc. Persons may be prosecuted for illegal practices under the Representation of the People Act 1983, s 168.

Illegitimacy. *See* BASTARD.

Imbargo. A stop or stay placed on ships by a public authority.
See EMBARGO ON SHIPS.

Imbasing of money. Mixing the species with an alloy below the standard of sterling.

Immemorial usage. A practice which has existed from the time of legal memory.
See LEGAL MEMORY.

Immoral contracts. Those founded on immoral considerations (*contra bonos mores*) are void. *Ex turpi causa non oritur actio.*
See EX TURPI CAUSA NON ORITUR ACTIO.

Immovable. A thing which can be touched but which cannot be moved and includes a chattel real (*see* CHATTELS). The general rule as to the law governing immovables is that all rights over, or in relation to them, are governed by the law of the country where the immovable is situated (the *lex situs*).

Immunity. Exemption from some obligation or liability, eg from taxation, or from prosecution.

Impanelling a jury. The writing and entering in a parchment schedule, by the sheriff, or the names of a jury.
See PANEL, 1.

Imparl. To confer with.

Impeachment. A prosecution of an offender before the House of Lords by the Commons of Great Britain in Parliament (*see* HOUSE OF

LORDS). The articles of impeachment are a kind of indictment found by the House of Commons, and afterwards tried by the House of Lords.

It has always been settled law that a peer could be impeached for any crime.

As regards commoners, however, Blackstone lays it down that a commoner cannot be impeached before the Lords for any capital offence, but only for committing high misdemeanours. The contrary doctrine, however, was laid down when Chief Justice Scroggs, a commoner, was impeached of high treason. And when, on 26th June 1689, Sir Adam Blair and four other commoners were impeached of high treason, the Lords resolved that the impeachment should proceed.

This form of prosecution has rarely been used in modern times; the last memorable cases are those of Warren Hastings in 1788 and Lord Melville in 1806. *May.*

Impeachment of waste. A restraint from committing waste on lands and tenements. The phrase is intended to denote the ordinary legal liability incurred by a tenant for life or other limited interest, in committing waste on the property.
See WASTE; WITHOUT IMPEACHMENT OF WASTE; TENANT FOR LIFE.

Imperfect obligations. Moral duties not enforceable at law, eg charity, gratitude, or the like.
See PURPOSE TRUST.

Imperfect trust. An executory trust.
See EXECUTED AND EXECUTORY, 6.

Impersonation. *See* FALSE PERSONATION.

Impertinence. Irrelevancy in pleading or evidence, by the allegation of matters not pertinent to the question in issue. Any unnecessary or scandalous, frivolous or vexatious pleading may be struck out by order of the Court.

Implead. To sue, arrest or prosecute by course of law.

Implication. A legal inference of something not directly declared.

Implied. This term can only be properly used to mean 'established by indirect or circumstantial evidence' or, which comes to the same thing, 'presumed in certain circumstances to exist, in the absence of evidence to the contrary', especially with

reference to inward intentions or motives as inferred from overt acts.

Thus an *implied trust* has been defined as 'a trust which is founded in an unexpressed but presumable intention', as contrasted with a *constructive trust*, which is one raised by construction of a court of equity without reference to the presumed intention of any party; in this it differs both from an *implied* trust and from an *express* trust.

But the general use of the word 'implied' is wider. The phrase 'implied contract' is often applied to all those events which in law are treated as contracts, whether they arise from a presumed mutual consent or not, provided only that they are not express contracts.

Thus, the phrase is used to mean *sometimes* a genuine consensual contract not expressed in words, or in signs which usage has rendered equivalent to words; *sometimes* an event to which, although not a consensual contract, the law annexes most or all of the incidents of a contract as against any person or persons.

The implied contract is frequently spoken of as a *tacit* contract. It may be defined, in opposition to an express contract, as 'a contract not expressed in words, or in signs which usage had rendered equivalent to words', eg, if I order a suit from a tailor, without saying anything as to the price or quality. The tailor, in undertaking the order, tacitly promises me that the suit shall be reasonably fit for wear. I tacitly promise him to pay a reasonable price for it. In implied contracts of this class there is no agreement as to the precise terms and conditions, but there *is* an agreement, though of a general character.

Formerly, on the now discredited 'implied contract' theory of the law of unjust enrichment, it was said that an implied contract imposed by a fiction of the law of *quasi*-contract generated the defendant's liability to make restitution to a plaintiff to reverse an unjust enrichment. Thus, a person saves my goods on board a ship which is being wrecked, and claims from me 'salvage money' for doing so. This claim was said to arise '*quasi ex contractu*' (*as if* from a contract). It is totally independent of any consent on the part of the owner to pay for the saving of his goods. In implied contracts of this class there is no agreement at all; the supposed agreement being a pure fiction of law, adopted for the purposes of what is called 'substantial justice'. Resort to this fiction has recently been superseded by the development of substantive principles in the law of unjust enrichment.

See UNJUST ENRICHMENT.

The expression 'implied request' is used in a manner analogous to 'implied contract'. A request is said to be 'implied by law' sometimes when it has been, in fact, made, though not in express words: sometimes when it has never been made.

Implied malice. *See* MURDER.

Implied warranty. A lesser term of a contract (ie not a CONDITION) which is implied by law or by the behaviour of the parties.

See eg SALE OF GOODS; CONTRACT.

In marine insurance means a promissory warranty (*see* PROMISSORY WARRANTY) implied by law, eg that a vessel is seaworthy or that the adventure is a lawful one.

See WARRANTY OF LEGALITY.

Impossibility of performance. Impossibility does not generally discharge the liability under a contract, but in certain cases the promisor is excused from performing his promise if it is shown that performance is impossible without any default on his part. A promise which is clearly incapable of performance either in fact or in law at the time when it was made cannot form a binding contract, because there is no real consideration; and where the subject matter of the contract has without the knowledge of either party ceased to exist before the contract was made, the contract is void on the ground of mistake. Impossibility, as an excuse for non-performance, must as a general rule be a physical or legal impossibility and not merely an impossibility with reference to the ability and circumstances of the promisor (see Law Reform (Frustrated Contracts) Act 1943).

See FRUSTRATION.

Impossibilium nulla obligatio est.
An impossible consideration carries no obligation.

See CONSIDERATION.

Impost (Lat *imponere*, to lay on). Any tax or tribute imposed by authority; particularly a tax or duty on imported goods.

Impostor. One who impersonates another.

See FALSE PERSONATION.

Impotence. Physical inability of a man or a woman to perform the act of sexual intercourse. A marriage is void if at the time of its celebration either party is incurably impotent, and may be declared void by a decree in a suit of nullity of marriage.

See NULLITY OF MARRIAGE.

Impotentia excusat legem. Inability avoids the law.

Impound. To place in a pound goods or cattle distrained.

See POUND; DISTRESS.

Also, to retain in the custody of the law: which is ordered when a forged or otherwise suspicious document is produced at a trial, so that the document may be produced in case criminal proceedings should be subsequently taken.

Impressment. The arresting and retaining of seamen for the Queen's service.

Imprimatur. A licence to print or publish.

Imprisonment. *See* FALSE IMPRISONMENT; PRISON.

Impropriation. *See* ADVOWSON; APPROPRIATION.

In alieno solo. In another's ground.

In articulo mortis. In a dying state.

In auter (or *autre*) **droit** (in another's right). Eg, where an executor sues for a debt in right of his testator.

See EXECUTOR.

In camera. *See* CAMERA.

In capite. Tenants who held their land *immediately* of the King were said to hold it *in capite*, or *in chief*.

In theory, all land is held originally of the Crown. The immediate tenants of the Crown under the feudal system frequently granted portions of their lands to inferior persons, who then became tenants to them, as they were of the King; and it was in contradistinction to such inferior tenants that those who held immediately of the King were called tenants *in capite*.

See LAND LAW.

In custodia legis (in the custody of the law). An expression used with regard to goods which, on account of having been already seized by the sheriff under an execution, are exempt from distress for rent.

See DISTRESS.

In esse. In actual existence, as opposed to a thing *in posse*, which may come into existence, but has not. Thus, a child, before he is born, is said to be *in posse*; but after he is born, and for many purposes after he is conceived, he is said to be *in esse*, or in actual being.

In extenso. In full; a copy of a document made *verbatim*.

In extremis. On the point of death.

In gross. That which belongs to a person individually and not in right of his being an owner of an estate in any manor, lands, etc. The phrase, applied to an incorporeal interest in land, means that the incorporeal interest in question is not appendant or appurtenant to any corporeal thing, but is enjoyed by its owner as an independent subject of property. *See* APPENDANT; APPURTENANCES; RIGHT IN GROSS.

In invitum. Against a person's will.

In jure, non remota causa sed proxima spectatur. In law the immediate, not the remote, cause of an event is regarded. *See* CAUSATION.

In limine (on the threshold). An objection *in limine* is a preliminary objection.

In loco parentis. In the place of a parent.

In odium spoliatoris omnia prae-sumuntur. Every presumption is made against a wrongdoer.

In pais. Done without legal proceedings. *See* ESTOPPEL.

In pari causa possessor potior haberi debet. Other things being equal the possessor is in the stronger position.

In pari delicto melior est conditio defendentis (or **possidentis**). Where both parties are equally in the wrong, the position of the defendant (or possessor) is the more favourable, on the principle that where the parties are equally in the wrong, the law leaves the situation as it is and will not act upon the plaintiff's claim.

In pari materia. In an analogous case.

In personam. A proceeding *in personam* is one in which relief is sought against, or punishment sought to be inflicted on, a specific person.

Rights *in personam* are rights enforceable against a person, and attach to that person rather to any particular property; rights which are enforceable against the present possessor or owner of a specific property, are called rights *in rem*.

In re (in the matter of). These words used at the beginning of a lawyer's letter indicate the subject of the letter. In headings to legal reports, they are applied especially (though by no means exclusively) to estates or companies which are being wound up, or to the owners of such estates.

In rem. A proceeding *in rem* is one in which relief is not sought against, or punishment sought to be inflicted on, any person. Actions *in rem* are generally instituted to try claims to some property or title or status; eg where it is sought to condemn a ship in the Admiralty Court, or to recover land.

Rights *in rem* are rights which attach to specific property, and may continue do so do despite a change in the ownership of the specific property. Thus, a legal easement of right of way over a piece of land is good despite the sale of that property to a new owner. *See* IN PERSONAM.

In terrorem (for the purpose of intimidation). A condition in a grant of property or a term of a contract made *in terrorem* will not be enforced by the law. *See* CONDITION.

In transitu (in passage from one place to another). Generally it is used of goods in their passage from the seller to the buyer. *See* STOPPAGE IN TRANSIT.

Inadequacy of consideration does not affect the validity of a contract. *See* CONSIDERATION.

Inalienable. Not transferable.

Incest. Sexual intercourse between a man and his grand-daughter, daughter, sister or mother; or between a woman of the age of 16 or over and her grandfather, father, brother, or son, by her consent (see Sexual Offences Act 1956, ss 10, 11).

Inchoate. Begun but not completed, eg the expression is used of bills of exchange by the Bills of Exchange Act 1882, s 20 (marginal note), and to describe attempts to commit crimes. *See* BILL OF EXCHANGE; CRIMINAL LAW.

Incident. An expression typically used in land law, to describe a right or obligation or power appertaining to or following upon another, larger, right, such as an estate in land, and passing with title to the land by a general grant of it.

In feudal land law, for example, one incident of an estate in fee simple was that the lord by which the land was held had the right of wardship, the right to take control of the land if the tenant in possession died leaving a minor heir. Or, today, rent may be made incident to a reversion (*see* REVERSION); and, when so incident, it passes by a general grant of the reversion.

Incitement. To incite another person to commit a crime. If a crime is actually committed, the person inciting becomes an accessory before the fact.
See ACCESSORY.

Inclosure. 1 The extinction of commonable rights in fields and waste lands. For restrictions on inclosure of commons, *see* Law of Property Act 1925, s 194.
2 Land inclosed.

Income Tax. A tax of so much in the pound on income. It is levied under various Schedules in respect of interest on government securities and other profits arising from public revenue dividends; professional or trade earnings or profits and from interest and other annual profits or gains; official and other salaries. The law relating to income tax has been consolidated in the Income and Corporation Taxes Act 1988.
See TAXATION.

Incoming partner. A partner joining an existing partnership.
   A person who is admitted as a partner into an existing firm does not thereby become liable to the creditors of the firm for anything done before he became a partner: Partnership Act 1890, s 17(1).

Incorporate. 1 To declare in writing in a document that another document shall be taken as part of the document, as if it were set out at length in it.
2 To establish as a corporation by grant from the Crown or Act of Parliament.

Incorporeal chattels. Personal rights and interests which are not of a tangible nature, eg annuities, stocks and shares, patents and copyrights. A rather rare usage of 'chattels' to mean 'personal property' in its entire extension; 'chattels' is normally restricted to tangible objects, such as chairs, books, etc, and 'incorporeal chattels' referred to as 'intangible personal property'.
See REAL AND PERSONAL PROPERTY.

Incorporeal hereditament. Intangible rights or interests in land, thus any possession or subject of property which, before 1926, was capable of being transmitted to heirs, and is not the object of the bodily senses. It is, in general, a right annexed to, or issuing out of, or exercisable within, a corporeal hereditament; eg a right of common of pasture, a right of way over land, or an annuity payable out of land. The provisions of Part I of the Law of Property Act 1925 relating to freehold land apply also to incorporeal hereditaments (see s 201 of the Act).
See LAND LAW.

Incumbent. A clergyman in possession of an ecclesiastical benefice.
See BENEFICE.

Incumber. To charge with an incumbrance.
See INCUMBRANCE.

Incumbrance. A charge or mortgage on real or personal estate.
See CHARGE; MORTGAGE.

Incumbrancer. A person entitled to enforce a charge or mortgage on real or personal estate.
See CHARGE; MORTGAGE.

Indecent assault. An assault accompanied by circumstances of indecency. It is an offence to commit such an assault on a woman, or on a man, by the Sexual Offences Act 1956, ss 14, 15. Consent, which would prevent an indecent act from being an assault, cannot be given by persons under 16.

Indecent conduct. Acts of gross indecency with or towards children under the age of 14, or inciting children to such acts.

Indecent exposure is an indictable offence at Common Law, and an offender is also punishable as a rogue and vagabond under the Vagrancy Act 1824, s 4.

Indecent prints or books. It is an offence under the Obscene Publications Acts 1959 and 1964 to publish any obscene article (containing or embodying matter to be read or looked at or both) the effect of which is such as to tend to deprave or corrupt.
See OBSCENITY.

Indefeasible. That which cannot be made void upon the happening of some event or by the exercise of a power. Typically used of interests in land or under a trust.
See DEFEASANCE.

Indefinite payment. Where a debtor owes several debts to the same creditor, and makes a payment without specifying to which of the debts the payment is to be applied.

Indemnification aliunde. An indemnity received by an insured from a third party before or after payment by the insurers of the sum insured having the effect of diminishing or extinguishing the loss.

Indemnity. Compensation for a wrong done, or trouble, expense, or loss incurred. An undertaking, usually by deed, to indemnify another.

Indemnity Act. An Act of Parliament formerly passed every year to relieve from forfeiture persons who had accepted office without taking certain oaths then required by law. Rendered unnecessary by the Promissory Oaths Act 1868. Also any Act for the pardon of past offences against the law, eg the Indemnity Act 1920, which restricted the taking of legal proceedings in respect of certain acts done during the First World War.

Indenture. A deed made by more than one party; so called because there ought regularly to be as many copies of it as there are parties, and historically such copies were engrossed on one sheet of parchment and separated by making indented cuts. By the Law of Property Act 1925, s 56(2), a deed purporting to be an indenture has the effect of an indenture, though not actually indented. By s 57 any deed, whether or not being an indenture, may be described as a deed simply or as a conveyance, mortgage, or otherwise according to the nature of the transaction. *See* DEED.

Independent contractor. *See* MASTER AND SERVANT.

Indictable offence. A criminal offence which is triable by indictment if committed by an adult.

Indictment. A written accusation that one or more persons have committed a certain crime.
See CRIMINAL PROCEDURE.

Indirect evidence. The same as circumstantial evidence.
See CIRCUMSTANTIAL EVIDENCE; EVIDENCE.

Indorsee. *See* INDORSEMENT.

Indorsement. A writing on the back of a document. Thus, one speaks of an indorsement on a deed, on a bill of exchange, on a writ, etc.

An *indorsement in blank* is where a person, to whom a bill or note is payable, writes his name on the back of it. The effect of such an indorsement is that the right to sue on the bill will be transferred to any person to whom the bill is delivered, ie to any bearer of it.
See BILL OF EXCHANGE.

A *special* indorsement is an indorsement directing payment of the bill to a specified person or his order; such person is called the *indorsee*. In this case the bill or note, in order to become transferable, must be again indorsed by the indorsee. For the requisites of a valid indorsement, see Bills of Exchange Act 1882, s 32.
See SANS RECOURS.

Indorsement of address. Formerly, by RSC 1965, Ord 6, r 5, it is provided that the solicitor of a plaintiff suing by a solicitor must indorse upon every writ of summons the address of the plaintiff, and also his own name or firm and place of business within the jurisdiction which must be an *address for service*. For the initiation of proceedings, see now Civil Procedure Rules 1998, Part 7.

Indorsement of claim. Formerly, by RSC 1965, Ord 6, r 2, every writ of summons in the High Court must be indorsed with a statement of claim or with a concise statement of the nature of the claim made, or of the relief or remedy required; such indorsement must be made on the writ before it is issued. For the initiation of proceedings, see now Civil Procedure Rules 1998, Part 7.

Indorsement of service. Formerly, by RSC 1965, Ord 10, r 1, the date of service and other particulars must be indorsed on every writ within three days of such service. For the initiation of proceedings, see now Civil Procedure Rules 1998, Part 7.

Indorser. A person who indorses any document.
See INDORSEMENT.

Indowment. *See* ENDOWMENT.

Inducement. The motive or incitement to any act.

Induction. A ceremony performed after a clergyman has been instituted to a benefice, by a mandate from the bishop to the archdeacon. It is done by giving the clergyman corporal possession of the church. This is the investiture of the temporal part of the benefice, as *institution* is of the spiritual.

Industriam, per. A phrase applied to the reclaiming of animals *ferae natura*, and making them tame by art, industry, and education; or else by confining them so that they cannot escape and use their natural liberty.

See ANIMALS.

Inevitable accident. An accident which cannot be avoided by the use of ordinary care, caution and skill. Where such inevitable accident is due, directly and exclusively and without human intervention, to natural causes against which no human foresight could provide, it is termed an Act of God. Inevitable accident is a defence to an action of negligence.

See ACT OF GOD.

Infamous conduct. Dishonourable or disgraceful conduct in a medical practitioner or dentist, which may be dealt with by the General Medical Council (*see* GENERAL MEDICAL COUNCIL) under the Medical Act 1983, s 36 and by the Professional Conduct Committee of the General Dental Council under the Dentists Act 1984, s 27.

Infant. Formerly, a person who was under the age of 21; an age at which persons were considered competent for all that the law required them to do, and which was, therefore, designated as *full age*. The age of majority was reduced to 18 (with some exceptions) by the Family Law Reform Act 1969, which also provides that any person not of full age may be described as a *minor* instead of an infant.

See GUARDIAN.

Infanticide. The Infanticide Act 1938, s 1 provides that where a woman by any wilful act or omission causes the death of her child, being a child under the age of twelve months, the balance of her mind being disturbed at the time by the after-effects of the child's birth, etc, her offence is to amount to infanticide and not to murder. A woman convicted of infanticide may be punished as if she had been guilty of manslaughter.

See MANSLAUGHTER.

Inferior courts. Derived their title of inferior courts because they are, in the great majority of cases, subject to the control and supervision of the Queen's Bench Division as a superior court. This means that they can be stopped from exceeding their jurisdiction by an order of prohibition.

See PROHIBITION.

Information. A proceeding on behalf of the Crown against a subject otherwise than by indictment.

Informations are of various kinds:

1 A criminal information in the Queen's Bench Division. This may be by the Attorney-General *ex officio*, or by a private prosecutor in the name of the Crown. But in the latter case the information cannot be filed except by the express direction of the Court itself.

2 A statement by which a magistrate is informed of the offence for which a summons or warrant is required. See generally the Magistrates' Courts Act 1980.

See CRIMINAL PROCEDURE.

Infortunium. Misadventure or mischance.

Infringement. A violation of another person's right; a word used principally with reference to the violation of another's patent or copyright.

See PATENT; COPYRIGHT; INTELLECTUAL PROPERTY LAW.

Ingress, egress and **regress.** Free entry into, going forth from, and returning to a place.

Inheritance. A perpetuity in lands or tenements to a man and his heirs. The word is mostly confined to the title to lands and tenements by *descent*.

See ESTATE; DESCENT.

Inheritance tax. Despite being called an 'inheritance tax', the tax brought in by the Finance Act 1986, Part v is not in truth an inheritance tax, but a DEATH DUTY. Under a true inheritance tax, the deceased's estate is not charged with a tax; rather, those who inherit from the estate are required to pay a tax on what they receive, eg by bringing such inheritances into their taxable income.

Inhibition. With regard to registered land an inhibition is an entry on the register prohibiting for a time or until the occurrence of an event named in it, or generally until further order, any or some specified dealing with the land (see the Land Registration Act 1925, ss 57, 61).

See LAND LAW.

Injunction. A writ issuing, prior to the Judicature Acts, only out of Chancery, in the nature of a prohibition or command, by

which the party enjoined was commanded to do some act, such as perform his or her contract, or not to do, or to cease from doing, some act, such act not amounting to a crime but rather a breach of an obligation of civil law. Injunctions may now be granted by all Divisions of the High Court and by the Court of Appeal. They are either (i) *interlocutory*, ie provisional or temporary until the hearing of the cause, or (ii) *perpetual*.
See MAREVA INJUNCTION.

Injuria. An actional wrong.

Injuria non excusat injuriam. An injury received is no excuse for doing an injury.

Injurious affection. A physical interference with the public or private property rights of others, by the construction of works on adjoining or nearby land. Compensation for injurious affection is awardable under the Compulsory Purchase Act 1963 and the Land Compensation Act 1973.

Injury. A violation of another person's right; or a violation of legal duty to the prejudice of another.

Inland Revenue. The revenue of the United Kingdom collected or imposed as stamp duties and taxes, and placed under the care and management of the Commissioners of Inland Revenue. After departmental reorganisation, now part of Her Majesty's Revenue & Customs.

Inn. An inn at Common Law is a house, the owner of which holds out that he will receive all travellers who are willing to pay a price adequate to the sort of accommodation provided, and who come in a condition in which they are fit to be received. The innkeeper is bound to accommodate and entertain all properly conducted persons provided there is room in the house. A similar definition has been applied to the word 'hotel' by the Hotel Proprietors Act 1956, s 1(1), which provides that a hotel within the meaning of the Act is deemed to be an inn. The rights and obligations of innkeepers are defined in the Act, eg as regards property belonging to guests, etc.
See HOTEL.
    An innkeeper may dispose of goods left with him, if unclaimed and unpaid for, after six weeks (see Innkeepers Act 1878, s 1).

Inner Temple. One of the Inns of Court.
See INNS OF COURT.

Innings. Lands recovered from the sea in Romney Marsh by draining. When they are rendered profitable, they are termed *gainage lands*.

Innkeepers. *See* INN.

Innovation. *See* NOVATION.

Inns of Chancery were Clifford's Inn, Clement's Inn, New Inn, Staple Inn, Barnard's Inn, Furnival's Inn, the Strand Inn, Lyon's Inn, and Thavie's Inn. There was also Serjeants' Inn, which consisted of serjeants only. The Inns of Chancery and the Inns of Court were originally two sorts of collegiate houses in the same juridical university, the Inns of Chancery being those in which the younger students of the law were usually placed. The Inns of Chancery have now sunk into insignificance, and an admission to them is no longer of any avail to a student in his progress to the Bar.
See INNS OF COURT.

Inns of Court are Lincoln's Inn, the Inner Temple, the Middle Temple, and Gray's Inn. They enjoy exclusive privilege of conferring the rank or degree of barrister, the possession of which constitutes an indispensable qualification for practising as counsel. The Inns of Court are governed by officers called 'benchers', to whom application is made by students wishing to be called to the Bar. The benchers have also authority to deprive a bencher or a barrister of his *status*, which proceedings are called respectively 'disbenching' and 'disbarring'. An appeal from decisions of the benchers lies to the judges in their capacity of visitors (*see* VISITOR). Full information as to the regulations, examinations, fees, etc. for call to the Bar can be obtained by application to the treasurer of any of the Inns.

Innuendo (from *innuo*, to beck or nod with his head) is a word the office of which is only to declare and ascertain the person or thing which was named or left doubtful before; as to say, he (*innuendo*, the plaintiff) is a thief. The word innuendo is most frequently applied to signify, in an action for libel, the averment of a particular meaning in a passage *prima facie* innocent, which, if proved, would establish its libellous character.
See LIBEL.

Inofficious testament. A will made contrary to the natural duty of the testator and without proper regard to the claims of his relatives.

Input tax, in relation to a taxable person, means
  (i) tax on the supply to him of any goods or services; and
  (ii) tax paid or payable by him on the importation of any goods,
being goods or services used for the purpose of any business carried on by him: Value Added Tax Act 1983, s 14(3).

Inquest. An inquisition or inquiry.
  1 A coroner's inquest is an inquiry into the manner of the death of anyone who has been killed, or has died suddenly, or in prison. It must be held before a jury which consists of not less than seven nor more than eleven jurors (see Coroners Act 1988, s 8(2)). Under the Coroners Act 1988, s 8(3), a coroner however, must hold an inquest with a jury in certain cases.
  2 Similarly, coroners have jurisdiction, under the Coroners Act 1988, s 30 to hold inquests on treasure trove.
  See TREASURE TROVE.

Inquiry, Court of. 1 A Court directed under military law to inquire into the conduct of officers, loss of materials, etc, with a view to further proceedings by court-martial or otherwise.
  See COURT-MARTIAL.
  2 Also a court for hearing the complaints of private soldiers.

Inquisitors. Sheriffs, coroners, or the like, who have power to inquire in certain cases.

Insanity. *See* MENTAL DISORDER.

Insider dealing. The taking advantage by a person of knowledge of the affairs of a company enabling him eg to buy or sell its shares at a profit.
  There is no civil liability in respect of insider dealing to the detriment of another person (*Percival v Wright* [1902] 2 Ch 421).
  But, in general, a person who is knowingly connected with a company must not deal on a recognised stock exchange in securities of that company if he has information which (i) he holds by virtue of being connected with the company; (ii) it would be reasonable to expect a person so connected not to disclose except for the proper performance of the functions attaching to the position of which he is so connected; and (iii) he knows is unpublished price sensitive information in relation to those securities (see Company Securities (Insider Dealing) Act 1985, s 1(1)).

If he does so deal, he is guilty of a criminal offence (see Company Securities (Insider Dealing) Act 1985, s 8).
  See STOCK EXCHANGE; SECURITIES.

Insolvency. Inability to pay debts.
  The Act relating to insolvent debtors is now the Insolvency Act 1986.

Insolvency practitioner. A person acting in relation to a company as its liquidator, provisional liquidator, administrator or administrative receiver or as supervisor of a voluntary arrangement approved by the company under Part I of the Insolvency Act 1986 (see Insolvency Act 1986, s 388(1)).
  A person acts as an insolvency practitioner in relation to an individual by acting eg as his trustee in bankruptcy or as trustee under a deed of arrangement (see ibid, s 388(2)).
  Acting without qualification is an offence (see ibid, s 389). For the required qualification see ibid, ss 390–398.

Insolvent debtor. *See* INSOLVENCY.

Inspection of documents. The right of a party in an action or suit to inspect and take copies of documents material to his case, which may be in the possession of the opposite party. Either party is, as a rule, entitled (after notice) to inspect documents referred to in the pleadings or affidavits of the other. With regard to other documents, the party desiring to inspect takes out a summons requiring his opponent to state what documents he has in his possession, and to make an affidavit in a prescribed form for that purpose.

Installation. The ceremony of inducting or investing with any commission, office, or rank, eg the installation of a bishop, of a dean, of a knight.

Instalment. 1 The ceremony by which possession is given of an ecclesiastical dignity.
  2 A sum of money less than the whole sum due, paid by a debtor in partial payment of the debt, eg the periodic repayments of a mortgage loan under a mortgage agreement.
  3 A sum of money paid, eg monthly, under a conditional sale agreement or a hire-purchase agreement.
  See CONDITIONAL SALE AGREEMENT; HIRE-PURCHASE AGREEMENT.

Instanter. Immediately, without delay.

Institute of London Underwriters. An Institute set up in 1889 to devise clauses known as the Institute Clauses to meet the constantly changing marine insurance requirements of modern commerce.

Institutes. 1 Justinian's Institutes. An elementary treatise on Roman law, written by command of the Emperor Justinian and published in AD 533.

See CORPUS JURIS CIVILIS.

2 Sir Edward Coke's Institutes. This work was published by Sir Edward Coke in 1628. They have little of the institutional method to warrant such a title. The first volume is an extensive comment on a treatise of tenures, compiled by Judge Littleton in the reign of Edward IV. The second volume is a comment on many old Acts of Parliament without any systematic order; the third, a more methodical treatise of the pleas of the Crown; and the fourth an account of the several types of courts.

See COKE, SIR EDWARD.

Institution. The ceremony by which a clergyman presented to a living is invested with the spiritual part of his benefice. Before institution, the clergyman must renew the declaration of assent to the Book of Common Prayer, as required by the Clerical Subscription Act 1865. He must also subscribe the declaration against simony (*see* SIMONY), and must take the oath of allegiance to the Queen before the archbishop or bishop, or their commissary, and he must also take the oath of canonical obedience to the bishop. Prior notice of institution must be given to the churchwardens under the Benefices Act 1898, s 2.

Instruct. To convey information, eg by a client to a solicitor, or by a solicitor to counsel; to authorise one to appear as advocate.

Instrument. A deed, will, or other formal legal document in writing.

Insufficiency. Formerly, where interrogatories were to be answered by affidavit, and the party interrogated answered insufficiently, the party interrogating might apply to the Court or a Judge, by motion or summons, for an order requiring him to answer further.

See INTERROGATORIES.

Insurable interest. A term to describe the legal or equitable relation in which the insured stands to the subject matter insured in consequence of which he may benefit by its safety or be prejudiced by its loss (see generally Marine Insurance Act, 1906, ss 5–14, and Life Assurance Act 1774, s 1).

Insurance, or **assurance,** is a contract by which one party, in consideration of a premium, engages to pay money on a given event, eg death, or indemnify another against a contingent loss. The party who pays the premium is called the insured or assured; the party promising to pay is known as the *insurer* or *underwriter* and the instrument is called a policy of insurance.

Insurances are mainly of six kinds:

1 Marine insurances, which are insurances of ship, goods, and freight, against the perils of the sea, and other dangers mentioned.

2 Fire insurances, which are insurances of a house or other property, against loss by fire. Losses to property by theft, flood, etc, are of the same type.

3 Life insurances, which are engagements to pay to the personal representatives (*see* PERSONAL REPRESENTATIVE) of the assured, or to a named third party nominated by him, often called a 'beneficiary', within a limited period from the date of his death, a specified sum of money, or to pay any such sum to the assured or his personal representatives, within a limited period of the death of some other person specified in the policy of assurance, or to pay to the assured on his attaining a certain age or to his representatives if he dies earlier (endowment policy). Though a life policy is not a contract of indemnity (as fire and marine policies are), a person can only insure a life in which he or she has an interest, viz, his or her own, his or her debtors', trustees', or spouse's.

See INSURABLE INTEREST.

4 Accident insurances, which are those against personal injuries caused by accidents of all kinds whether to the insured himself or to an employee.

5 Motor insurances which are insurances against liability in respect of accidents on the road caused by a motor vehicle and also against loss of or damage to the vehicle belonging to the insured. Compulsory insurance against liability to a third party is required under the Road Traffic Act 1988, Part VI.

6 Public liability insurances which are insurances against liability to members of the public, eg in the case of a collapse of a football stand.

Insurance agent. An agent appointed by the insurers eg to negotiate the terms of the proposal by the insured and to induce him to make a proposal which the insurers are willing to accept (see *Bawden v London, Edinburgh and Glasgow Assurance Co* [1982] 2 QB 534 at 539, CA (per Lord Esher MR)).

Insurance broker. A person acting as an intermediary between the insured and the insurer with a view to the effecting of an insurance policy. The broker is the agent of the insured and not of the insurers. To use the title 'insurance broker' he must be registered under the Insurance Brokers (Registration) Act 1977.

Intangibles, intangible property. *See* TANGIBLE PROPERTY.

Intellectual property. Any patent, trademark, copyright, design right, registered design, technical or commercial information, or other intellectual property: Supreme Court Act 1981, s 72.

Intellectual property law. Broadly framed, intellectual property law comprises the law of patents, industrial designs, trade marks and the law of passing off, the law of copyright, and confidential information. Minus copyright, this area of law is sometimes called 'industrial property'. In general, it concerns more or less exclusive rights, ie monopolies, which are regarded as providing a just framework for the exploitation of certain intangible goods in the market place, such as inventions, designs, literary or artistic works, the goodwill associated with a name, and so on. Although by various means the common law and equity provided some protections in respect of these (eg the action for passing off), the protection of trade marks, designs, patents, and copyright is generally now by way of statutory regimes.

The three central areas of intellectual property law are the law of trade marks, the law of copyright, and the law of patents. Trade marks are means by which goods or services in the market place are distinguished from others and so are a prime determinant in allowing for the formation and exploitation of goodwill, ie the likelihood that customers will choose to patronise one business over its competitors. By association with a successful product or products, the exclusive right to use a trade mark may itself become an asset of huge value. Trade marks can be seen to have two general functions associated with

their association with a product, the 'origin' function, and the 'communication' function. The 'origin' function is their use as a means of indicating the origin of the product involved, therefore allowing consumers who purchase by the trade mark to assume a product of more or less the same quality. More recently, given the nature of modern advertising, the 'communication' function has been stressed: the trade mark is invested in and presented as a symbol of more than a product's origin, but as an image its merits or qualities, in particular its superiorities vis-à-vis competing products. Clearly, on the latter function, the aesthetic and cultural properties and associations of the trade mark itself are important, as important as its function in merely distinguishing its owner's products from those of competitors, and trade mark law has to some extent been reshaped, both by Parliament and by the courts, in light of these two functions, which clearly do not indicate equivalent regimes of legal protection for trade marks. The best protection for trade marks is acquired upon registration of the trade mark in a public register.

The law of copyright provides creators of aesthetic, cultural, or informational products, with a monopoly on the right to make copies of these products. Historically, for obvious reasons, literary works, 'artistic' works (ie paintings, drawings, and sculptures), and musical compositions were the products protected, but the protection of this area of law has extended to cover films, videos, sound recordings and, more recently, computer programs. Perhaps the most fundamental, though very problematic, distinction in the law of copyright is that between 'expression' and 'idea'. Copyright protects the expression of ideas, not the ideas themselves. The distinction works most well in the case of literary works or pictorial art. Thus copyright protects an historian's book on the Second World War, but does not provide him or her with any monopoly on telling about and interpreting the events of the second world war. Similarly, Picasso's *Guernica* is copyright, but not the event it depicts. The distinction becomes much more problematical in the case of musical works, where the 'expression' and the 'idea' are much less distinguishable, and in the case of utilitarian or functional products, such as computer programs whose chief function is to direct the operations of a computer. Copyright 'subsists' in the created work upon its creation, ie the creator (or his or her employer where the work is created under a contract to do so) has copyright from the instant the work comes into being. Registration is not required.

By contrast with copyright, the law of patents provides a monopoly in the use of ideas themselves, in that an inventor may patent a novel and useful invention: for making the invention patent, ie open to all by disclosing the invention in the process of securing the patent, the inventor obtains the exclusive right to work the invention. For several reasons the justification of the law of patents is one of the most contentious areas of dispute in law and legal theory. The technological innovations which patents represent are now typically the result of scientific research, and the award of a patent only to the first inventor (or rather, the first inventor to file for the patent before the invention is published, ie put into the public realm) creates a 'winner takes all' incentive in industrial innovation. Secondly, there is no necessary connection between the effort expended in coming to an invention and the value of the patent that protects it, so that patents can appear to generate huge windfalls out of proportion to any preceding investment. On the other hand, patents may be defended as necessary incentives for the expenditure of money into research and innovation. Patents are granted for a limited time (generally 20 years from date of application), and there is a mass of law governing the scope of the patent monopoly intended to ensure that the monopoly is only so broad as to cover embodiments of the invention but nothing beyond.

The law of intellectual property concerns not only the rules concerning how monopoly rights are acquired, but the scope of such right, ie in which circumstances they are infringed, and much of the law concerns the licensing of such exclusive rights, and the problems to which licensing may give rise.
See COPYRIGHT; TRADE MARKS; PASSING OFF; PATENTS; DESIGN RIGHT.

Intendment. The understanding, intention, and true meaning of a document.

Thus, intendment of law is the intention and true meaning of law.

See INTENTION, 1.

Intention. 1 In reference to the construction of wills and other documents:

The *intention* of a document is the sense and meaning of it as gathered from the words used in it. Parol evidence (*see* PAROL EVIDENCE) is not ordinarily admissible to explain it; the main exceptions to the rule being in the case of a latent ambiguity (*see* AMBIGUITY), and in the case of a word or expression having acquired by local custom a sense different from the ordinary sense (*see* CUSTOM).

2 In reference to civil and criminal responsibility.

Where a person contemplates any result as not unlikely to follow from a deliberate act of his own, he may be said to *intend* that result, whether he desires it or not. Thus, if a man should, for a wager, discharge a gun into a crowd, and any person should be killed, he would be deemed guilty of *intending* the death of such person; for every man is presumed to *intend* the natural consequence of his own actions.

Intention is often confused with motive, eg when one speaks of a man's 'good intentions'.

Inter alia. Amongst other things.

Inter vivos. Between living persons; from one living person to another, eg in the case of a gift. Contrasted with a testamentary gift, one made in a will, or a *donatio mortis causa*, a gift made in anticipation of death.
See DONATIO MORTIS CAUSA; WILL.

Intercommoning is where the commons of two manors lie together, and the inhabitants of both have, time out of mind, grazed their cattle in each.
See COMMON, RIGHT OF.

Interdiction. An ecclesiastical censure prohibiting the administration of divine service.

Interest. 1 The compendious term to describe any right or title to, or estate in, any real or personal property.

2 The income of a fund invested; or the annual profit on a loan of money.

3 Or interests. The possibility or actuality of a personal advantage or disadvantage in the circumstances. For example, a fiduciary or a trustee must not allow his or her interests to come into conflict with his duty to serve the interests of his principal or beneficiary.

Similarly, an interest derivable from his judgment disqualifies a judge by virtue of the rule '*Nemo debet judex esse in causa sua propria*' (*see* NEMO DEBET JUDEX ESSE IN CAUSA SUA PROPRIA), eg where a judge is a shareholder in a company which is plaintiff in an action.

Interest does not now exclude a witness from giving evidence (see the Evidence Act 1843, s 1).

Interest in land. The general term to describe any right in land itself, from an ownership interest to an incorporeal hereditament of the least kind. The term is especially used to contrast a personal right against an owner of land to enter into, occupy, or use the land in a particular way, which arises from the owner's granting permission, or a 'licence', to do so. Such a right is personal against the owner, and is not an interest in the land itself as would bind a subsequent owner.
See LAND LAW; INCORPOREAL HEREDITAMENT.

Interest in possession. An interest in property entitling the owner to immediate possession or occupation; as opposed to a future interest, a present interest in property entitling the owner to take possession at some future date.
See FUTURE ESTATE, FUTURE INTEREST.

Interest in succession. *See* SUCCESSIVE INTERESTS.

Interest reipublicae ut sit finis litium. It is the State's interest that there should be an end of lawsuits.

Interest suit. An action in the Chancery Division to determine which party is entitled to a grant of letters of administration of the estate of a deceased person.
See ADMINISTRATOR.

Interference with goods. At common law there developed four different actions to remedy interference with an individual's right to possess goods (both owners and BAILEES had such rights to possess, and so could maintain these actions): TRESPASS TO GOODS, TROVER/ CONVERSION, and REPLEVIN. The former two entitled the plaintiff only to money damages equivalent to the value of the property, whereas under detinue and replevin the return of the goods *in specie* could be sought. Both trespass to goods and replevin were actions against a defendant who took goods out of the possession of the plaintiff, while trover/conversion could be maintained against anyone who came into the possession of the plaintiff's goods by any means and wrongfully withheld them. An action in detinue lay against one who came into possession of the plaintiff's goods lawfully, but wrongfully withheld them. Claims in respect of the tort of interference with goods are now governed by the Torts (Interference With Goods) Act 1977; while the general remedy is damages, recovery in specie is provided in certain cases by ss 3,4, ibid.

Interim dividend. A dividend declared at any time between two annual general meetings of a company as distinct from the final dividend (see *Re Jowitt, Jowitt v Keeling* [1922] 2 Ch 442).
See DIVIDEND; FINAL DIVIDEND.

Interim/interlocutory. Intermediate, with special reference to a suit or action, ie not final, eg an order given during the process of litigation before final judgment. Any former distinction between the terms 'interim' and 'interlocutory' in English civil procedure is now obsolete by virtue of the CIVIL PROCEDURE RULES under which only the term 'interim' is used.

Interim/interlocutory decree or order. An order to take effect provisionally, or until further directions. Formerly the expression 'interim' was used especially with reference to orders given pending an appeal. A decree or order which does not conclude a case, eg an order for inspection of documents.
See INSPECTION OF DOCUMENTS.

Interim/interlocutory injunction. An injunction granted for the purpose of keeping matters *in statu quo* until a decision is given on the merits of the case.
See INJUNCTION.

Interim/interlocutory judgment. A judgment in an action at law, given on some defence, proceeding, or default, which is only intermediate and does not finally determine or complete the action. The phrase is most frequently applied to those judgments whereby the *right* of the plaintiff to recover in the action is established, but the amount of damages sustained by him is not ascertained.

Interlineation. Writing between the lines in a deed, will, or other document. A deed may be avoided by interlineation, unless a memorandum is made of it at the time of the execution or attestation.

International Air Transport Association. An association of air transport service operators whose aim is to secure uniformity in air traffic documents and conditions applicable to transport by air.

International law (Lat *Jus inter gentes*). International law is divided into two branches:

1 Public international law, which comprises the rights and duties of sovereign States towards each other.

See PUBLIC INTERNATIONAL LAW.

2 Private international law, which comprises the rights and duties of the private individuals of different States towards each other, and is mainly involved with questions as to the particular law governing their transactions. This is also called the 'conflict of laws'.

See CONFLICT OF LAWS.

International Maritime Organisation. An organisation (formerly known as The Intergovernmental Maritime Consultative Organisation) established under a Convention which came into force in 1958. Its purposes are (i) to provide machinery for co-operation between governments as regards governmental regulation and practices relating to technical matters affecting shipping engaged in international trade; (ii) to encourage the general adoption of the highest practicable standards in matters concerning maritime safety and efficiency of navigation; (iii) to consider unfair restrictive practices by shipping concerns (see Convention for the Establishment of the Intergovernmental Maritime Consultative Organisation 1958 (TS 54 (1958)).

International Sales, Uniform Laws on.

See UNIFORM LAWS ON INTERNATIONAL SALES ACT 1967.

International will. A will made in accordance with the Annex to the Convention providing a Uniform Law on the Form of an International Will (1973), as set out in the Administration of Justice Act 1982: Administration of Justice Act 1982, s 27(3).

Interpleader. A proceeding for relief from adverse claims. It sometimes happens that a person finds himself exposed to the adverse claims of two opposite parties, each requiring him to pay a certain sum of money or to deliver certain goods, and that he is unable to comply safely with the demand of either, because a reasonable doubt exists as to which of them is the rightful claimant. Interpleader, in such cases, can be of two types: (i) *Stakeholder's interpleader*, where the person seeking relief is under a liability for any debt, money, goods, or chattels for or in respect of which he is, or expects to be, sued by two or more parties making adverse claims (*see* STAKEHOLDER); or (ii) *Sheriff's interpleader*, where the applicant is a sheriff or other officer charged with the execution of process etc, and a claim is made to goods, etc, by a person other than the person to whom the process is issued (*see* SHERIFF).

Interpretation clause. A clause frequently inserted in Acts of Parliament, declaring the sense in which certain words used in them are to be understood.

Interregnum. In kingdoms where the monarch is elected, the time during which the throne is vacant is called an interregnum. Where sovereignty is hereditary, no interregnum can occur.

Interrogatories. Formerly, questions in writing administered by a plaintiff to a defendant, or by a defendant to a plaintiff, on points material to the suit or action.

See DISCOVERY; DISCLOSURE.

Intervener. A person who intervenes in a suit, either on his own behalf or on behalf of the public.

Intestate, intestacy. Without making a will, or without fully disposing of property by will. As regards property not left by will there is an 'intestacy'. Administration of the estates of persons dying intestate is governed by the provisions of the Administration of Estates Act 1925.

See ADMINISTRATION.

Intimidation. The using of violence, threats, etc, to compel a person to do or abstain from doing that which he has a legal right to do or abstain from doing. Such intimidation is an offence under the Conspiracy and Protection of Property Act 1875, s 77; and it is an offence under the Sexual Offences Act 1956, s 2 to procure a woman to have unlawful intercourse by threats or intimidation.

Intoxication. *See* DRUNKENNESS.

Intra vires (within its powers). The converse of *ultra vires*.

See ULTRA VIRES.

Inuendo. *See* INNUENDO.

Inure. To take effect.

See ENURE.

Invention includes any new process or technique and must be construed without regard to whether or not a patent has been or could be granted: Development of Inventions Act 1967, s 15(2).

See PATENT; INTELLECTUAL PROPERTY.

Inventory. 1 A description or list made by an executor or administrator of all the goods and chattels of the deceased, which he is bound to deliver to the court if and when lawfully required to do so (see Administration of Estates Act 1925, s 25).

See ADMINISTRATOR; EXECUTOR.

2 Any account of goods sold, or exhibited for the purpose of sale.

Investiture. A ceremonial introduction to some office or dignity.

See INDUCTION; INSTITUTION; LAY INVESTITURE OF BISHOPS.

Investment business. The business of engaging in dealing in, or arranging deals in, or managing investments, or giving investment advice: Financial Services Act 1986, s 1(2).

Invitation to treat. An invitation to bargain, or deal; an expression of willingness to receive a contractual offer. Such an invitation does not amount to a contractual offer itself. Advertisements are typically held to be invitations to treat, not contractual offers.

See CONTRACT LAW.

Invoice. A list of goods which have been sold by one person to another, stating the particulars and prices. The invoice is sent by the seller to the buyer, either with the goods or separately by post.

Ipse dixit. He himself said; words used to denote an assertion resting only on the authority of an individual.

Ipso facto. By the very act. So, when it is enacted that any proceeding shall be *ipso facto* void, it means that such a proceeding is to have not even *prima facie* validity, but may be treated as void for all purposes *ab initio* (see VOID AND VOIDABLE).

Irregularity. A departure from a rule, or a neglect of legal formalities. In practice, the term is most frequently (though not exclusively) applied to such a departure, neglect, or informality as does not affect the validity of the act done. Thus, an *irregular distress* is not now vitiated, so as to make the distrainer a trespasser *ab initio*, and so to render all his proceedings illegal from the beginning. But where distress is made for rent justly due, a subsequent irregularity will do no more than give an action for damages to the party aggrieved, and not even that, if tender of amends is made before an action is brought (see Distress for Rent Act 1737, s 19). As to irregularity in proceedings, see RSC 1965, Ord 2, r 2.

See AB INITIO; DISTRESS.

Irrepleviable, or **irreplevisable.** That which cannot be replevied or set at large on sureties.

See REPLEVIN.

Irrevocable. That which cannot be revoked. Powers of appointment are sometimes executed so as to be irrevocable. A will is never irrevocable.

See POWER; TRUST.

Issue. 1 The children of a man and his wife.

2 Descendants generally (see Wills Act 1837, s 33).

3 The profits of lands and tenements.

4 The point or matter issuing out of the allegations and pleas of the plaintiff and defendant in a cause, on which the parties join, and put their cause on trial.

5 The putting out of banknotes and other paper money for public circulation.

See BANK-NOTE.

Issue at a discount. An issue of shares or of debentures at less than their nominal value eg an issue of shares with a nominal value of £1 at a price of 75p.

Shares must not be issued at a discount (see Companies Act 1985, s 100(1)). Because they do not form part of the capital of the company, debentures may be issued at a discount (see *Re Regent's Canal Ironworks Co* (1876) 3 Ch D 43).

See SHARE; DEBENTURE.

Issue at a premium. An issue of shares at more than their nominal value, eg an issue of shares with a nominal value of £1 at a price of £1.25.

Issued share capital. The nominal value of the shares of a company actually issued.

J

JP. Justice of the peace.
See JUSTICE OF THE PEACE.

Jetsam. Goods thrown overboard by a ship in danger, to lighten her, the vessel subsequently sinking.
See JETTISON; WRECK.

Jettison. The act of throwing goods overboard for the purpose of lightening a ship in danger of wreck. Such goods are called jetsam.
See JETSAM.

Joinder of causes of action. Joining in one action several causes of action. A plaintiff or claimant may, in certain circumstances, claim in one action relief against the same defendant in respect of more than one cause of action.
See ACTION; CAUSE OF ACTION.

Joinder of parties. Two or more persons may be joined together in one action, either as plaintiffs (or claimants) or as defendants.

Joint account clause. Where two or more persons advance money and take a mortgage to themselves jointly, the rule in equity is that they are tenants in common, and, therefore, the survivor is a trustee for the personal representatives of the deceased mortgagee. (*See* COMMON, TENANCY IN). To avoid this it became usual, where trustees lend money on mortgage, to insert what is known as a joint account clause in the mortgage deed declaring that on the death of one of the mortgagees the receipt of the survivor shall be a sufficient discharge for the money, and that the survivor shall be able to re-convey the land without the concurrence of the personal representatives of the deceased trustee. The Law of Property Act 1925, s 111, provides that where the sum advanced on mortgage is expressly stated to be lent on a joint account or the mortgage is made to the mortgagees jointly, the money lent shall be deemed to belong to the mortgagees on a joint account, and the survivor shall be able to give a complete discharge for the money.
See MORTGAGE; LAND LAW.

Joint and several liability. When two or more persons declare themselves jointly and severally bound, this means that they render themselves liable to a joint action against all, as well as to a separate action against each, in case the conditions of the bond or agreement are not complied with. This means that each may be sued for the entire amount of a claim. The party to whom they are so jointly and severally bound is called a joint and several creditor. Where two or more persons whose negligence has together caused a person injury, they are generally jointly and severally liable to such person. An individual who, as one jointly and severally liable, has paid the entirety of the claim, may bring an action for contribution from the others jointly and severally liable.
See CONTRIBUTION.

Joint enterprise. In criminal law, the willing participation together of two or more persons in a criminal act.

Joint stock bank. The name given to banking companies other than the Bank of England.

Joint tenancy. Where an estate is acquired by two or more persons in the same land, by the same title, not being a title by descent, and at the same period; and (if created by a written instrument) without any words importing that the parties are to take in distinct shares. The principal feature of this tenancy is that on the death of one of the parties his share accrues to the others by survivorship. Joint tenants are said to be seised *per my et per tout*. In joint tenancy there are four unities, viz, of possession, interest, title, and time. By the Law of Property Act 1925, s 36, it is provided that where a legal estate (not being settled land) is beneficially limited to or held in trust for any persons as joint tenants, it shall be held on trust for sale, but not so as to sever their joint tenancy in equity. And see Part IV of Sch 1 to that Act.

A joint tenancy is distinguished from a tenancy in common.

See COMMON, TENANCY IN; SEVERANCE, 2; LAND LAW; PROPERTY.

The phrase is also applied to the holding of personal property under the like conditions.

Joint venture. In civil law, the participation of two or more persons in a commercial endeavour for their mutual advantage, such association not amounting to a partnership between them.

Journals of the Houses of Parliament. The daily records of the proceedings of the Houses. They are evidence in courts of law of the proceedings in Parliament, but are not conclusive of facts alleged by either House unless they are within their immediate jurisdiction.

Judge. One invested with authority to decide questions in dispute between parties, and to award the proper punishment to offenders.

The judges of the High Court of Justice are the Lord Chancellor, the Lord Chief Justice, the President of the Family Division, and a number of puisne judges, who are attached to the several Divisions by the Lord Chancellor. (*See* DIVISIONS OF THE HIGH COURT). They are appointed by the Crown by letters patent. A Judge holds his office during good behaviour (*see* QUAMDIU BENE SE GESSERIT), subject to a power of removal by the Crown. No High Court Judge may sit in the House of Commons.

The Crown may also from time to time appoint *circuit* Judges to serve in the Crown Court and the County Courts and to carry out such other judicial functions as may be conferred on them under the Courts Act 1971 or any other enactment. Deputy circuit Judges may also be appointed.

By virtue of his office every circuit Judge is capable of sitting as a judge for any County Court district in England and Wales. In practice, they are assigned to different districts by the Lord Chancellor.

See CIRCUIT; COUNTY COURT; CROWN COURT.

No action lies against a judge for anything said or done in his judicial capacity, but if he acts without jurisdiction, he may be made answerable for the consequences.

See INTEREST, 3.

Judge-Advocate-General. An officer appointed to advise the Crown in reference to courts-martial and other matters of military law except the preparation of prosecutions which are dealt with by departmental staffs. *See* COURT-MARTIAL.

Judge's order. An order made on summons by a Judge in chambers. *See* CHAMBERS; SUMMONS.

Judgment. The sentence or order of the court in a civil or criminal proceeding.

See DEFAULT JUDGMENT; FINAL JUDGMENT; INTERIM/INTERLOCUTORY JUDGMENT.

Judgment creditor. A creditor by virtue of a judgment, eg a plaintiff (or claimant) who has successfully sued a defendant and received an award of damages is a judgment creditor of the defendant, who is a judgment debtor; ie a party entitled to enforce execution under a judgment.

Judgment debt. A debt due under a judgment.

Judgment debtor. A person against whom a judgment ordering him to pay a sum of money stands unsatisfied, and who is liable therefore to have his property taken in execution under the judgment.

Judgment summons. A summons issued on the application of a person entitled to enforce a judgment or order under the Debtors Act 1869, s 5 requiring a person, or where two or more persons are liable under the judgment or order, requiring any one or more of them, to appear and be examined on oath as to his or their means (see County Courts Act 1984, s 147(1)).

Judicature Acts 1973–75. These Acts ended the centuries-old division between the courts of common law and the court of equity, establishing one High Court, the judges of which are empowered and required to apply both the common law and equitable doctrine. Where the two conflict, the rules of equity are to prevail. *See* EQUITY; COMMON LAW; SUPREME COURT.

Judicial act. An act by a judicial officer which is not merely ministerial. By numerous statutes summary power is given to justices of the peace (*see* JUSTICE OF THE PEACE) and it is declared that certain acts shall only be valid if done by two magistrates. If such acts are merely ministerial, it is not required that the two magistrates should be together at the time of doing the act; if it is judicial, they must.

Judicial Committee of the Privy Council.
A council consisting of the Lord President of the Council, the Lord Chancellor, former Lords President, the Lords of Appeal in Ordinary, and such other members of the Privy Council as shall from time to time hold or have held high judicial office (see Judicial Committee Act 1833, as extended by Appellate Jurisdiction Acts of 1876 and 1887).

The jurisdiction of the Judicial Committee extends principally to appeals from certain parts of the Commonwealth, and some Admiralty and ecclesiastical appeals.

Judicial notice. A judge is entitled to take judicial notice, ie accept as being the case, those facts about the world, such as the course of nature, the rules of the road, the normal period of gestation, and so on, which are generally incontrovertible. By taking judicial notice of such facts, the judge accepts their truth without formal proof by the presentation of evidence in court.

Judicial review. A procedure used for certain forms of relief:

(i)   an order of *mandamus*, prohibition or *certiorari*;

(ii) an injunction to restrain persons from acting in offices in which they are not entitled to act (see Supreme Court Act 1981, s 31).

See ADMINISTRATIVE LAW.

Judicial separation. A order of separation of man and wife by the High Court or the County Court, which has the effect, so long as it lasts, of making the wife a single woman for all legal purposes, except that she cannot marry again; and similarly the husband, though separated from his wife, is not by a judicial separation empowered to marry again.

Judicial trustee. A trustee appointed by, and to act under the control of, the Court.
See Judicial Trustees Act 1896, and rules made under it.

Junior barrister. A barrister under the rank of Queen's Counsel. Also, the junior of two counsel employed on the same side in any judicial proceeding.
See QUEEN'S COUNSEL.

Jurat. 1 A short statement at the foot of an affidavit, of *when*, *where*, and *before whom* it was sworn.

2 An officer of the Court in the island of Jersey. In civil matters, at least two jurats sit with the presiding judge and are the sole finders of fact and assessors of any damages.

Juris et de jure (of law and from law). A presumption which may not be rebutted is so called.
See PRESUMPTION.

Jurisdiction. A dignity which a man has by a power to do justice in causes of complaint made before him (*Termes de la Ley*).

The authority which a court has to decide matters that are litigated before it or to take cognisance of matters presented in a formal way for its decision. The limits of this authority are imposed by the statute, charter or commission under which the Court is constituted, and may be extended or restricted by similar means. If no restriction or limit is imposed, the jurisdiction is said to be unlimited.

Jurisprudence. 1 The science of law, that is, the general theory or philosophy of law, the legal system, and the nature of legal rights and obligations. Historically, the two most prominent theories of law are the theories of *natural law* and *positivism*. Natural law theory, whose roots lie in antiquity, emphasises the connection of law and legal obligation with morality and moral obligation, and strictly speaking, holds that there is an essential connection between them such that legal obligation is a species of moral obligation. The most stringent version of this view holds that *lex injusta non est lex*, ie that a morally unjust 'law' does not have the status of law. Positivists, by contrast, emphasise the social, political, and historical character of law; positivism thus holds that the law is a particular kind of social/political institution having certain kinds of social/political functions, the most obvious of which is the rule-governed guidance of behaviour of the subjects of the legal system. Thus positivists regard the law's connection with morality as a secondary, perhaps a wholly inessential aspect of the nature of law, and hold that whether a legal system's laws are moral or immoral does not determine whether or not it counts as a legal system. There are myriad variants of these two positions, and some theories of law aim to escape the framework of this dichotomy entirely.

2 Sometimes used to describe a body of law, eg 'property jurisprudence'.

Juror. A member of a jury.
See JURY.

Jury. A body of persons sworn to inquire of a matter of fact and to declare the truth on such evidence as is before them.

Every person is qualified to serve as a juror and is liable to attend for jury service when summoned if (i) he is registered as a parliamentary or local government elector and is not less than 18 nor more than 70 years of age; and (ii) has been ordinarily resident in the United Kingdom, the Channel Islands or the Isle of Man for at least 5 years since attaining the age of 13: Juries Act 1974, s 1.

Some persons are ineligible to serve on juries, eg judges and justices of the peace, barristers, and solicitors (whether or not in actual practice as such), clergymen, mentally disordered persons: ibid, s 1, Sch 1.

The Lord Chancellor is responsible for the summoning of jurors for service: ibid, s 2. The arrangements to be made by him include the preparation of panels of jurors and the court sittings for which they are prepared: ibid, s 3.

The court may excuse a person from jury service: ibid, s 4. It may also defer his attendance: ibid, s 5.

The jury are selected by ballot in open court: ibid, s 11. An accused has a right to challenge the composition of the jury: ibid s 12.
See CHALLENGE.

The court may accept a majority verdict of the jury: ibid, s 17.
See MAJORITY VERDICT.

A person who serves on a jury is entitled to be paid in respect of (i) travelling and subsistence, and (ii) financial loss in consequence of his attendance: ibid, s 19. Regulations specifying the amount of such allowances are made under powers given by the Act: ibid, s 19.

In criminal cases trial by jury is required where a person is charged on indictment.

Civil juries are rare. There is a right to trial by jury in actions of libel, slander, malicious prosecution, or false imprisonment, and those where fraud is alleged against the party applying for a jury: Supreme Court Act 1981, s 69.

Jus accrescendi. The right of survivorship between joint tenants.
See JOINT TENANCY.

Jus ad rem. An inchoate and imperfect right; eg such as a clergyman presented to a living acquires, before induction, by presentation and institution.
See INDUCTION; PRESENTATION; INSTITUTION.

Jus ad rem is merely an abridged expression for *jus ad rem acquirendam*; and it denotes a right to the acquisition of a thing.

Jus civile. The Civil Law. Defined by Justinian as the law which each State has established for itself; but the term is now almost exclusively attached to Roman civil law.
See CORPUS JURIS CIVILIS.

Jus disponendi. The right of disposing of property.

Jus ex injuria non oritur. No right can arise in favour of a person out of an injury committed by him.

Jus gentium. The law of nations, which is thus described in the opening passages of Justinian's Institutes (*see* INSTITUTES, 1): 'Quod vero naturalis ratio inter omnes homines constituit, id apud omnes populos peraeque custoditur, vacaturque jus gentium, quasi quo jure omnes gentes utuntur' (that law which natural reason has established among men is maintained equally by all nations, and is called the law of nations, as being the law which all nations adopt).

Jus in personam. A right prevailing against a person or persons, as opposed to a right *in rem*, which avails against all the world.

Jus in re. Full and complete right, accompanied by corporal possession.

Jus in rem. A right availing against all the world. Thus, the phrase denotes the *compass* and not the *subject* of the right.

Jus patronatus. 1 The right of patronage or presentation to a benefice.
2 A commission from the bishop awarded when two rival presentations are made to him on the same vacancy of a living. This commission is directed to the bishop's chancellor, and others of a competent learning, who are to summon a jury of six clergymen and six laymen to inquire who is the rightful patron.

Jus tertii. The right of a third party. If A, who *prima facie* is liable to restore property to B, alleges that C has a title paramount to B's, and so B should not succeed in an action against A because B does not have the *best* title, A is said to set up the *jus tertii*. Setting up the *jus tertii* is generally not effective in the common law of property.
See PROPERTY, 3.

Justice of the peace. A magistrate; a person appointed for a commission area by the Lord Chancellor: Justices of the Peace Act 1979, s 6(1).

The Lord Chancellor has power to remove him: ibid, s 6(1).

In general a person cannot be appointed for a commission area unless he resides in or within 15 miles of that area: ibid, s 7(1).

He is entitled to travelling, subsistence and financial loss allowances: ibid, s 12.

Every magistrates' courts committee must make and administer schemes providing for courses of instruction for justices of the peace of their area: ibid, s 63.

See COMMISSION AREA.

Justices. Officers deputed by the Crown to administer justice, and do right by way of judgment. The puisne judges of the High Court are called 'Justices of the High Court' (see Supreme Court Act 1981, s 4(2)), but the word is usually applied to justices of the peace.

See JUSTICE OF THE PEACE.

Justices' clerk. A clerk to the justice for a petty sessional area: Justices of the Peace Act 1979, s 70(1).

Justiciary, High Court of (*Scotland*). The highest criminal court in Scotland, consisting of the Lord Justice-General, the Lord Justice-Clerk and other judges of the Court of Session.

Justifiable homicide. *See* HOMICIDE.

Justification. The showing of a sufficient reason, by a defendant, why he did what he is called on to answer, particularly in an action of libel, eg damages cannot be recovered for the publication of a defamatory statement if the defendant pleads and proves that it is true.

In a criminal prosecution for libel the truth of a matter is no defence unless the accused proves also that its publication was for the public benefit, or in an action of assault showing the violence to have been necessary.

By the Defamation Act 1952, s 5 it is provided that in an action for libel or slander in respect of words containing two or more distinct charges against the plaintiff, a defence of justification shall not fail by reason only that the truth of every charge is not proved, if the words not proved to be true do not materially injure the plaintiff's reputation, having regard to the truth of the remaining charges.

Justinian. *See* INSTITUTES.

Juvenile Courts. Renamed as 'Youth Courts' by the Criminal Justice Act 1991, s 70(1).

See YOUTH COURTS.

J

K

KB. King's Bench.

KBD. King's (now Queen's) Bench Division.
See QUEEN'S BENCH DIVISION.

KC. King's (now Queen's) Counsel.
See QUEEN'S COUNSEL.

Keeper of Public Records. *See* RECORD OFFICE.

Keeper of the Great Seal. Since the Lord Keeper Act 1562, the Lord Chancellor.
See GREAT SEAL.

Keeper of the Privy Seal. Now called the Lord Privy Seal.
See LORD PRIVY SEAL.

Keeping term, by a law student consists in eating a sufficient number of dinners in hall to make the term count for the purpose of being called to the Bar.
See BARRISTER; INNS OF COURT.

Keeping the peace. Avoiding a breach of the peace; or persuading or compelling others to refrain from breaking the peace.

Magistrates have power to bind over any person to keep the peace or be of good behaviour. (*See* BIND OVER) The person concerned enters into a recognisance. (*See* RECOGNISANCE), with or without sureties, and for failure to comply with the order he may be committed to prison (see Magistrates' Courts Act 1980, s 115; also s 116, dealing with discharge from recognisances).

Kerb-crawling. Soliciting a woman for the purpose of prostitution from a motor vehicle while it is in a street or public place, persistently or in such circumstances as to be likely to cause annoyance to her or nuisance to other persons in the neighbourhood: Sexual Offences Act 1985, s 1.

Keys. In the Isle of Man, the 24 chief commoners, who form the Legislature.

Kidnapping. The forcible abduction or taking away of a man, woman, or child from their own country, and sending them into another. As to children, see Offences against the Person Act 1861, s 56, which makes child-stealing an offence.

Abduction of a woman by force for the sake of her property is an offence under the Sexual Offences Act 1956, s 17, and other cases of abduction are dealt with by ss 19–21.

The civil aspects of international child abduction are dealt with by the Child Abduction and Custody Act 1985.

Kin. Legal relationship.

Kindred and affinity. *See* AFFINITY.

King. The King or Queen is the person in whom the supreme executive power of this kingdom is vested. In domestic affairs the Sovereign is a constituent part of the supreme legislative power, who once, in theory, could negative all new laws (although to do so would be a breach of probably the most important constitutional convention—*see* CONSTITUTIONAL LAW) and is bound by no statute unless specially named in it. The Sovereign is also considered as the commander-in-chief of the kingdom, and as such may raise armies, fleets, etc. The Sovereign is also the fountain of justice and general conservator of the peace, and may erect courts, prosecute offenders, pardon crimes, etc. The Sovereign is also head of the Church of England and as such appoints bishops, etc, and hears appeals in ecclesiastical causes.
See CIVIL LIST; QUEEN.

As the statutes of the realm and the older law cases and other records are often referred to as being of such a year of such a reign, a list is appended of the Kings and Queens of England, with the dates of their accessions and deaths, from 1066 to the present time.

Table 2

King or Queen	Accession	Reigned until
William I (the Conqueror)	1066	1087
William II (William Rufus, son of William I)	1087	1100
Henry I (youngest son of William I)	1100	1135
Stephen	1135	1154
Henry II	1154	1189
Richard I (otherwise called Richard Coeur de Lion)	1189	1199
John	1199	1216
Henry III	1216	1272
Edward I	1272	1307
Edward II	1307	1327
Edward III	1327	1377
Richard II	1377	1399
Henry IV	1399	1413
Henry V	1413	1422
Henry VI	1422	1461
Edward IV	1461	1483
Edward V	1483	1483
Richard III	1483	1485
Henry VII	1485	1509
Henry VIII	1509	1547
Edward VI	1547	1553
Mary (married in 1554 to Philip of Spain; hence the subsequent statutes of her reign are referred to as those of Philip and Mary)	1553	1558

King or Queen	Accession	Reigned until
Elizabeth I	1558	1603
James I	1603	1625
Charles I	1625	1649
Commonwealth declared	1649	
Oliver Cromwell, Protector	1653	1658
Richard Cromwell, Protector	1658	1659
Charles II*	1660	1685
James II	1685	1688
William III and Mary	1689	1702
Anne	1702	1714
George I	1714	1727
George II	1727	1760
George III	1760	1820
George IV	1820	1830
William IV	1830	1837
Victoria	1837	1901
Edward VII	1901	1910
George V	1910	1936
Edward VIII	1936	1936
George VI	1936	1952
Elizabeth II	1952	

* The statutes of the reign of Charles II are dated as if from 1649, when his father was beheaded, on the assumption that, as heir to the Crown, he began to reign immediately on his father's death. Thus, the Tenures Abolition Act 1660 is known by the regnal year and chapter number 12 Car 2, c 24; the Act of Uniformity, 1662 as 14 Car 2, c 4; etc.

King can do no wrong. *See* QUEEN CAN DO NO WRONG.

King's Bench. *See* COURT OF KING'S (OR QUEEN'S) BENCH; QUEEN'S BENCH DIVISION.

Kings-at-Arms. The principal heralds. There are three existing in England: Garter, Clarenceux, and Norroy. *Lyon* King-at-Arms is the chief in Scotland, and *Ulster* in Ireland.
See HERALDS' COLLEGE; LYON KING AT ARMS.

Kleptomania. A species of mental disorder in the form of an irresistible mania for thieving.

Knacker. A person whose trade or business it is to kill cattle not killed for the purpose of the flesh being used as butcher's meat: Protection of Animals Act 1911, s 15.

Knacker's yard. Any premises used in connection with the business of slaughtering, flaying or cutting up animals the flesh of which is not intended for human consumption (see Food Act 1984, s 132(1)).

Knight. A commoner of rank, originally one who bore arms, who for his martial powers was raised above the ordinary rank of gentleman. The following are different degrees of knights:

1 Knight of the Order of St George, or of the Garter: first instituted by Edward III, probably about 1345.

2 Knight Banneret. A knight formerly created on the field of battle by the ceremony

of cutting off the points of his *pennon* (triangular or swallow-tailed flag carried on the lance), thus converting it into a banner.

3 Knight of the Order of the Bath. So called from the ceremony, formerly observed, of bathing the knight before their creation.

4 Knight Bachelor; the most ancient, though the lowest title of dignity. King Alfred is said to have conferred this Order on his son Ethelstan.

5 Knight of the Order of St Michael and St George: an Order instituted on 27th April 1818, for the reward of public service in the Ionian Islands and Malta, and now conferred on persons for distinguished service in any part of the British Commonwealth.

6 Knight of the Thistle: an Order instituted by King Achias, of Scotland, and re-established by Queen Anne on 31st December 1703.

7 Knight of the Royal Victorian Order: instituted by Queen Victoria, 21st April 1896.

8 Knight of the Most Excellent Order of the British Empire: instituted in June 1917, and extended December 1918.

Knight of the Bath. *See* KNIGHT, 3.

Knight of the Chamber. A knight bachelor, so made in time of peace.
See KNIGHT, 4.

Knighthood. The dignity of a knight.
See KNIGHT.

Knock-out. An agreement among prospective bidders at an auction sale that certain of them shall refrain from bidding, so that the actual bidder may get the goods at a price lower than he might otherwise have done. By the Auctions (Bidding Agreements) Act 1927, such an arrangement is made illegal in certain circumstances.

'Knock for knock' agreement. A term used in motor insurance denoting an agreement between insurance companies whereby in the event of a collision between two cars 'each insurance company pays its own insured without questioning that which the insured is entitled to receive under the particular policy' (*Morley v Moore* [1936] 2 KB 359 at 361 (per Sir Boyd Merriman, P)).

Knot (nautical term). A division of the log-line equal to 1/120th part of a mile. The knots are counted per half minute. Thus, if a ship is going at 10 miles per hour it is said to be travelling at 10 knots.

Know-how. Any industrial information and techniques likely to assist in the manufacture or processing of goods or materials, or in the working of a mine, oil well, etc, or in the carrying out of any agricultural, forestry or fishing operations: Income and Corporation Taxes Act 1988, s 533(7).

K

L

LCJ. *See* LORD CHIEF JUSTICE OF ENGLAND.

LJ. *See* LORDS JUSTICES OF APPEAL.

LLP. *See* LIMITED LIABILITY PARTNERSHIP.

LS. *See* LOCUS SIGILLI.

La Reyne le veult. 'The Queen wills it so to be.' The form of words by which the Queen assents to a public bill which has passed through both Houses of Parliament. The form of assent to a private bill (*see* PRIVATE BILL) is in the words 'soit fait comme il est désiré', and to a money bill (*see* MONEY BILL) or grant of supply 'La Reyne remercie ses bons sujets, accepte leur bénévolence, et ainsi le veult.' The royal assent was normally given by Commissioners under powers granted in the reign of Henry VIII. The last time it was given in person was by Queen Victoria in 1854.

An alternative mode of signifying the royal assent was prescribed by the Royal Assent Act 1967, which makes it unnecessary for the Commons to attend the Lords, the royal assent being duly given by the Queen signing letters patent under the Great Seal.
See LETTERS PATENT; GREAT SEAL.

La Reyne s'avisera. 'The Queen will consider.' The form by which the Queen would refuse the royal assent to a bill passed by both Houses of Parliament. Such power has not been exercised since 1707, when Queen Anne refused her assent to a bill for settling the militia in Scotland.

Laches. Slackness or negligence. In general, it means neglect in a person to assert his rights, or long and unreasonable acquiescence in the assertion of adverse rights. This neglect or acquiescence will often have the effect of barring a person from the remedy which he might have had if he had resorted to it in proper time. Thus, under the Limitation Act 1980, the time is specified within which various classes of actions respectively mentioned in it may be brought. Independently of this statute, a court of equity will often refuse relief to a plaintiff who has been guilty of unreasonable delay in seeking it.
See LIMITATION, STATUTES OF.

Lacuna (Lat *a ditch*). A blank in writing.

Lady Day. 1 The 25th March, so called because it is the Feast of the Annunciation of the Blessed Virgin Mary. A quarter-day for the payment of rent.
See QUARTER-DAYS.

2 Sometimes also, eg, in Ireland, the 15th August, from the Catholic festival of the Assumption of the Blessed Virgin.

Lagan or **Lagon.** *See* LIGAN.

Lame duck. A defaulter, especially on the Stock Exchange.

Lammas Day. 1st August. On that day the tenants who held land of York Cathedral were bound by their tenure to bring a live lamb into the church at high mass.

Lammas lands. Lands over which there is right of pasturage, from about Lammas or reaping time until sowing time, by persons other than the owner of the land.

Land. Generally not only arable ground, meadow, pasture, woods, moors, waters, etc, but also messuages (*see* MESSUAGE) and houses; including everything of a permanent and substantial nature. Thus, an action to recover possession of a pool must be brought for so much land covered with water, etc. The word 'land' is used in a wide sense in the Law of Property Act 1925. It includes 'land of any tenure, and mines and minerals, whether or not held apart from the surface, buildings or parts of buildings (whether the division is horizontal, vertical or made in any other way) and other corporeal hereditaments (*see* CORPOREAL HEREDITAMENTS); also a manor an advowson (*see* ADVOWSON), and a rent (*see* RENT) and other incorporeal hereditaments and an easement (*see* EASEMENT), right, privilege, or benefit in, over, or derived from land; but not an undivided share in land' (see s 205(1)(ix)).

See REAL AND PERSONAL PROPERTY; PROPERTY; LAND LAW.

Land certificate. *See* CERTIFICATE, LAND.

Land charges. In general, interests in land lesser than ownership interests. The term is comprehensive, and includes a number of different rights and interests affecting land. They comprise, *inter alia*, restrictive covenants (*see* RESTRICTIVE COVENANTS), estate contracts (*see* ESTATE CONTRACT), general equitable charges (*see* GENERAL EQUITABLE CHARGE), and equitable easements (*see* EASEMENT).

The Land Charges Act 1972 consolidated previous legislation on the subject, dealing with the registration in the land charges register of various charges over unregistered land, that is, the land which is recorded in deeds. A holder of a land charge in the land of another could protect his interest by registering the charge against the name of that other. The registration of land charges in this way has waned in significance following the spread of land registration. The Local Land Charges Act 1975 repealed earlier legislation relating to local land charges.

See LAND LAW; LAND REGISTRATION.

Land compensation. *See* COMPULSORY PURCHASE.

Land law. The law governing property in land, in particular the various kinds of interest in land, and the means by which such interests are created and transferred. While 'land law' can be regarded as covering all manner of laws and legal regimes which affect land, eg the law of town and country planning, environmental law, the law of nuisance, etc, it is traditionally regarded as confined to the private law of land ownership.

Perhaps more than any other area of law, land law is profoundly a matter of its long history which colours the law to the present day. Following the Conquest, a new theory of land ownership was applied universally in England, whereby all land was 'held' of the Crown, giving rise to a system of *tenures*, or modes of holding land, and a coordinate system of *estates*, which indicated the extent in time of an individual's ownership

right to the land. Land not held under this feudal tenurial system is known as *allodial* land, and while allodial land persisted on the Continent, the universal application of the feudal tenurial system entailed that no English land is allodial. Thus the roots of present day land law lie in the feudal system. Under this system, the fruits of the predominantly agricultural economy were distributed primarily not by contract, but by rights of various kinds in productive land. The theory of this system holds that all land is held of the King or of the Crown (*nb*, 'held of', not 'owned by'), who grants holdings in the kingdom to his noble lords in return for rent service. These holdings are known as tenures, and the grantees of the land, tenants. There were different kinds of tenures characterised by the form of rent service required, the most prominent being knight service, the obligation to provide knights for the king's army, grand and petty serjeantry, the obligation to provide personal service to the king, frankalmoign, a spiritual tenure by which a religious house would perform spiritual duties, and socage, the obligation to provide agricultural goods. The nobles would in turn grant the land granted to them by the king to others in smaller parcels, likewise receiving rent service in return.

This process continued until a grant to a person who actually took possession of the land to work it (generally, originally, via the serfs who were attached to it). This feudal system of tenures waned in importance over time as different kinds of service were commuted to money payments, and these payments fell in value due to inflation. Eventually, the tenant in possession came to be regarded as the true owner, who, unless the feudal chain of grants could be proved, held directly of the Crown. By the property legislation of 1925 all tenures (save for certain ceremonial tenures) have been commuted to 'free and common' socage, which indicates that no rent service of any kind is due.

While this system of tenures remains as a part of land law only theoretically, the system of estates developed at the same time remains important. An estate is 'time in the land', and the duration of freehold estates, or estates of free men, were measured by the length of a life, or the continuing existence of one's family line (*see* ESTATE). The largest estate was the fee simple absolute (or unconditional), and this lasted essentially forever. The estate would only come to an end if a person died in possession intestate having no general heirs. This estate is equivalent to full ownership, and can be sold or given away in its entirety.

An entirely different system of land ownership developed for certain non-freehold titles held of local lords; this system was known as copyhold, for the reason that title was evidenced by taking copies of the manorial rolls which recorded the title. By the early 20th century, no major differences lay between freehold and copyhold ownership, though the procedures for conveyancing were different. Copyhold was abolished in 1925, whereupon all copyholds were converted into freeholds.

From the actions used to enforce rights in freehold land comes the distinction between real and personal property. Certain actions were called 'real' actions because, if one was successful, one obtained the real thing one was suing for, ie the land itself. Such actions were not available for the pressing of claims to leasehold land, ie land granted not so as to give rise to a freehold estate held by tenure, but granted for a certain time for a money rent, and so leasehold interests in land were originally classified as personal, not real, property.

Possession has a special relationship with title in English land law. Title, or the right to possess property, is obtained by possession. A person is said to be 'seised', ie possessed, of an estate in land, and this fact of possession generates the title to the land, not only the right to (continue in) possession, but the right to grant the land in its entirety to others or grant lesser interests in it to others. Thus possession is said to be the root of title. Where there is a dispute over ownership to land, the person having the *better* title wins, and the better title is the title deriving from the *earlier* possession. Thus any person in possession of land has a title to it (so long as his or her possession is more than a transient trespass), but his or her title may be defeated by one who can show prior possession, and the court will declare the party with the better title by prior possession to have the right to possess the property, and the court will give its assistance to the party with better title to take possession if necessary. Where one is granted land by another, the strength of one's own title is dependant upon the strength of one's grantor's, which is determined by the length of the grantor's own possession, and that of the chain of grantees to whose possession his own can be traced. Where land is possessed by a person to the exclusion of one with a better title, that possessor, called an adverse possessor or squatter, may obtain a title which cannot be challenged by the absent owner, in general if the absent owner does not bring an action to evict the adverse possessor within 12 years of his right to do so. (See Limitation Act 1980.)

The most important feature of property in land is the myriad sorts of different interests which may exist in the same piece of land. These can roughly be divided into ownership interests and lesser interests. Ownership interests in the same piece of land can be fractionated amongst people or in time. Thus, one can have co-ownership of land, the most two common kinds of which are the JOINT TENANCY and TENANCY IN COMMON. The main difference between the two is that with the former, upon the death of a joint tenant his or her interest disappears, so the surviving joint tenant(s) now own the property; the last surviving joint owner becomes a sole owner of the property. In general, any interest in land may be co-owned. The ownership of land can be split over time, most simply by the grant of a life estate. If X grants A a life estate in Blackacre (Blackacre is the standard imaginary piece of land discussed in English law), then A has an interest in possession in Blackacre which will last for his or her life, and X will have a future interest in Blackacre in reversion, ie the right to the estate will return to X (or his successor in title) upon the death of A. X might grant Blackacre to A for life and then to B in remainder, in which case B will have a future interest in Blackacre which will entitle him to possession upon A's death. In these examples A is a life tenant, X the reversioner, and B the remainderman. While originally the common law was somewhat restrictive in the extent to which it would allow a grantor to tailor his grant so as to fraction ownership interests in the land in time, EQUITY and statute enlarged the grantor's facilities for doing so, and very complicated grants of land could be created, by which present estates (those in possession) and future estates could be limited, and made conditional upon different events occurring.

Complicated settlements of land, involving the use of trusts, could be created which tied up land to the extended family, from one generation to the next. The property legislation of 1925 attempted to address this situation, to free up land from family settlements and to simplify the process of conveyancing. The most important aspects of the scheme were to alter the rules of intestate succession so that all property, both real and personal, devolved in the same way upon death, and secondly, to convert almost all legal co-ownership interests into equitable interests, in particular all conditional and future interests, and allow for their attachment to the purchase money received from the sale of land, not to the land itself. In this way, the buyer of land could take the property free of a complicated set of family interests in the property by purchasing from legal owners acting as trustees for that set of interests. (*See* TRUST.)

Lesser interests can be defined as interests in land less than ownership, in particular mortgages or charges, ie security interests in land; easements, eg a right of way across the land of another; restrictive covenants, eg a right that another not run an industrial business on his land; and profits, eg the right to cut and take wood from another's land. The main aspect of the property legislation of 1925 dealing with these lesser interests was to expand the registration of land charges, so that these interests could be found out on sale of the land by searching the register, and introducing the system of Land Registration, whereby title to land was recorded in a register, which would also contain entries recording lesser interests.

The law of landlord and tenant, ie of leasehold interests, has become almost a full branch of law in its own right, first because of the importance of this method of landholding for residential, commercial, and agricultural, purposes, but also because of the large amount of legislation governing the rights of landlords and tenants that has been introduced.

See CONDITIONS PRECEDENT AND SUBSEQUENT; ESTATES; FREEHOLD; TENURE; TERM OF YEARS; LEASE; MORTGAGE; CHARGE; EASEMENT; PROFIT À PRENDRE; LAND REGISTRATION; LAND CHARGES; DESCENT; SUCCESSION; PROPERTY; REAL AND PERSONAL PROPERTY.

Land registration. A statutory system of registration of title to land, now under the Land Registration Act 2002, which consolidated and replaced the Land Registration Acts, 1925 to 1997.

It replaced the previous system of deeds-based conveyancing, under which good title to land was proved on the basis of rightful possession, which turned upon an owner's possession of deeds establishing a series of transfers of possession back to a date which barred adverse claims by operation of the statutes of limitations (*See* CONVEYANCE; ABSTRACT OF TITLE; ROOT OF TITLE).

Under land registration, this deed-based system was replaced by the registration of purchasers of land as owners on the ownership register, such registration henceforth being conclusive proof of ownership. Thus, nowadays title to land does not pass until the new owner is registered, and consequently, the owner of or title holder to land is now styled the 'registered proprietor'. Conceptually, three principles are said to underlie land registration. The 'mirror principle' is that the register mirrors, or represents, all the interests currently held in a piece of land. Therefore there should be no hidden property interests, such as an EASEMENT or RESTRICTIVE COVENANT, which could be undiscoverable to a prospective purchaser of the land. The 'curtain principle' seeks to remove from the ownership register what might be called the 'internal' relations of co-owners. Prior to the 20th century, much land was held under complicated ownership arrangements and trusts, which made the purchase of land complex, in that a purchaser had to be sure that he dealt with each individual having an interest in the property. Under the registered system, the prospective purchaser is not to concern himself with any complicated ownership structure, which is to be organized under a TRUST. The trust acts as a curtain behind which the prospective purchaser need not look; so long as the purchaser pays the registered proprietors, who are limited in number to four, he takes the property free of the interests of the beneficial co-owners under the trust, and it is up to the registered proprietors, as trustees for any others with ownership interests in the property, to properly distribute the purchase money to those others so that each receives his proper share. Finally, the 'guaranty' principle is that the state guarantees the truth of the register. Thus, should, for any reason, a person incur a loss because of some inaccuracy in the register, the state should compensate that person. The central register is divided into three sections, the 'property register', which describes the property, the 'proprietorship register', which registers the owner(s), and the 'charges register', which registers the interests of non-owners in the property, such as a MORTGAGEE. It is important to note that, while all land in England and Wales is now capable of being registered, titles to land are not automatically transferred to the register, nor are persons holding title by deeds required to register them. Rather, the requirement to register is triggered when land is transferred. Therefore, land that has not been transferred since before 1925 (or later dates in parts of England and Wales) will not have been registered, and proof of title will still reside in the deeds held by the owner. Only when such land is next transferred will its registration be required. Because of this, upon that next transfer, proof of title will need to be made under the old deeds-based conveyancing technique by way of ABSTRACT OF TITLE.

See REGISTERED LAND.

Landlord. A person of whom lands and tenements are leased; a lessor; who has a right to distrain for rent in arrears, etc, the *tenant* being the person in possession of the lands by the lease.

See DISTRESS.

Lands Tribunal. A tribunal with powers to determine questions relating to the compulsory acquisition of land, valuation, etc. Constituted under the Lands Tribunals Act 1949.

See COMPULSORY PURCHASE ORDER.

Lapse. 1 A type of forfeiture whereby the right of presentation to a benefice accrues to the Ordinary (*see* ORDINARY, 2), by neglect of the patron (*see* PATRON) to present; to the archbishop, by neglect of the Ordinary; and to the Crown, by neglect of the archbishop. It is in the nature of a spiritual escheat.

2 The failure of a testamentary disposition in favour of any person, by reason of the death of the intended beneficiary in the lifetime of the testator.

In two cases, however, of the intended beneficiary dying in the testator's lifetime, there is no lapse. The first case is that of a devise of real estate to any person for an *estate tail* (*see* ESTATE), where any issue who would inherit under such entail are living at the testator's death. The second case is that of a devise or bequest to a *child* or *other issue* of the testator, leaving issue, any of whom are living at the testator's death (see Wills Act 1837, ss 32, 33).

Lapse of insurance policy occurs when it is not renewed at or before the expiration of the current period of insurance or of the days of grace, if any. The insured cannot enforce it in respect of any claim arising afterwards (see *Webb and Hughes v Bracey* [1964] 1 Lloyd's Rep 465).

See DAYS OF GRACE.

Larboard. A nautical term meaning 'port' as distinct from 'starboard'.

Larceny. The unlawful taking and carrying away of things personal, with intent to deprive the rightful owner of them. The taking had to be *animo furandi* (with the intention of stealing), in order to constitute larceny. There also had to be 'asportation', ie a 'carrying away'; but for this purpose the smallest removal was sufficient. Such an act is now 'theft' under the Theft Act 1968.

See BURGLARY; EMBEZZLEMENT; FRAUDULENT CONVERSION; ROBBERY; THEFT.

Last resort. A court from which there is no appeal.

Lasting power of attorney. *See* ENDURING POWER OF ATTORNEY.

Latent ambiguity. *See* AMBIGUITY; INTENTION, 1.

Laudibus Legum Angliae. The treatise *De Laudibus Legum Angliæ* was a panegyric on the laws of England written by Sir John Fortescue in the reign of Henry VI.

Law, in the sense of 'a law', has been variously defined; by Blackstone as a rule of action prescribed or dictated by a superior, which an inferior was bound to obey; by Austin, as being a *command* to *a course of conduct*; a *command* being the expression of a wish or desire conceived by a rational being that another rational being should do or forbear, coupled with the expression of an intention in the former to inflict some evil on the latter, in case he did not comply. But besides laws properly so called, Austin alluded to laws improper, imposed by public opinion; also laws metaphorical or figurative, eg the laws regulating the movements of inanimate bodies, or the growth or decay of vegetables; or that uniformity in the sequence of things or events which often goes by the name of *law*. However, these definitions probably rely to much on a simplistic positivist understanding of law (*see* JURISPRUDENCE). A better view is that a law is a rule which forms part of a system of laws, which system performs the function of guiding the behaviour of those subject to the authorities, either persons or institutions, that constitute an effective political settlement.

Law was sometimes opposed to equity (*see* EQUITY), where law means the common law; now, however, by the Supreme Court Act 1981, s 49, full effect is given to all equitable rights in all branches of the Supreme Court and in inferior courts.

Law Commission. A commission whose duty is to keep under review all the law with a view to its systematic development and reform, including in particular the codification of the law, the elimination of anomalies, the repeal of obsolete and unnecessary enactments, the reduction of the number of separate enactments, and generally the simplification and modernisation of the law: Law Commissions Act 1965, s 3(1).

Law List. An annual publication of a quasi-official character containing a list of barristers, solicitors, and other legal practitioners. It is *prima facie* evidence that the persons named in it as solicitors or certified conveyancers are such (see Solicitors Act 1974).

Law Lords. Peers who hold or have held high judicial office, ie a puisne judgeship of the High Court or higher office.

Law martial. Martial law.
See MARTIAL LAW.

Law merchant (*Lex mercatoria*). The general body of European usage in matters relative to commerce, comprising rules relative to bills of exchange, partnership, and other mercantile matters, incorporated into the law of England.
See BILL OF EXCHANGE; PARTNERSHIP.

Law of nations (Lat *Jus gentium*).
See INTERNATIONAL LAW; JUS GENTIUM.

Law Officers of the Crown. The Attorney-General and the Solicitor-General, the Attorney-General for Northern Ireland, and, in Scotland, the Lord Advocate.
See ATTORNEY-GENERAL; SOLICITOR-GENERAL; LORD ADVOCATE.

Law Reports. The authorised reports of decided cases commencing from 1866 inclusive.

They are published under the direction of the Incorporated Council of Law Reporting.
See REPORTS.

Law Society. A society of solicitors, whose function is to carry out the Acts of Parliament and orders of court with reference to the examinations of trainee solicitors, formerly called articled clerks; to provide for legal education; to keep an alphabetical roll of solicitors; to issue certificates to persons duly admitted and enrolled; also to exercise a general control over the conduct of solicitors in practice, and to deal with cases of misconduct. Disciplinary powers are conferred on a separate disciplinary committee (see generally Solicitors Act 1974).

Law spiritual. The ecclesiastical law, according to which the ordinary, and other ecclesiastical judges, do proceed in causes within their cognisance. *Cowel.*
See ORDINARY, 2.

Lawful merchandise. Goods which can be loaded without breach of the law in force at the port of loading and which can be lawfully carried and discharged at the port to which the charterer has ordered the vessel to proceed (see *Leolga Compania de Navigacion v John Glynn & Son Ltd* [1953] 2 All ER 327).

Laws of Oleron. *See* OLERON, LAWS OF.

Lay. A word opposed to *professional*. It is often used in opposition to *clerical*.

Lay corporations. Corporations not composed wholly of spiritual persons, nor subject to the jurisdiction of the ecclesiastical courts. Lay corporations are either *civil* or *eleemosynary*. Eleemosynary corporations are such as are constituted for the perpetual distribution of the free alms or bounty of their founder to such purpose as he had directed. All other lay corporations are civil corporations.
See CORPORATION.

Lay days. The days ordinarily allowed to the charterer of a vessel for the loading and unloading of the cargo.
See DEMURRAGE.

Lay investiture of bishops. The formal act whereby the Crown invested a bishop with the temporalities of his office.

Le Roy le veult. 'The King wills it so to be.' The form of words by which a King assented to a public bill which had passed through both Houses of Parliament.
See LA REYNE LE VEULT.

Le Roy s'avisera. 'The King will consider.' The
form in which a King could refuse the royal
assent to a bill passed by both Houses of
Parliament.
See LA REYNE S'AVISERA.

Leader. The leading counsel in a case as
opposed to a *junior*.

Leading cases. Cases which have had the most
influence in settling the law.

Leading marks. Signs placed on crates for
the purpose of easily identifying the goods
contained in them.

Leading questions. Questions which suggest
the answer which is expected: as 'Did you not
see this?' or 'Did you not hear that?'
Such questions are not allowed except in
cross-examination.
See EXAMINATION; HOSTILE WITNESS.

Leap Year. *See* BISSEXTILE.

Lease. A grant of land, giving possession of
the land, but not a grant of a freehold estate.
Also called a demise or letting of lands or
tenements. The grantor is called the *lessor*,
the grantee the *lessee*. Leases may be granted
for a term of years (ie a defined period) or
for life, or at will (ie for no certain time, but
merely until the lessor demands the giving up
of the land), and usually a rent is demanded.
The interest created by the lease must be
less than the lessor has in the premises, or
it is not a *lease* but an *assignment*. By the
Law of Property Act 1925, ss 53, 54 all leases
except those not exceeding three years and
with a rent of not less than two-thirds of the
improved annual value must be by deed.
See TERM OF YEARS.

Leasehold. Any interest in land less than
freehold. But, in practice, the word is
generally applied to an estate for a fixed term
of years.

Leasehold enfranchisement. Under the
Leasehold Reform Acts, tenants of houses
with long leases have a right to acquire a
new long lease, or the freehold. Under the
Leasehold Reform, Housing and Urban
Development Act 1993, tenants of flats
with long leases have a right to 'collective
enfranchisement', under which the nominee
of a sufficient percentage of the tenants of a
block of flats may acquire the freehold.

Leasehold Valuation Tribunal. A tribunal
dealing with disputes concerning residential
leasehold property, in particular disputes

over valuation of property when a tenant
or tenants pursue rights of LEASEHOLD
ENFRANCHISEMENT. Appeals lie to the Lands
Tribunal.
See LANDS TRIBUNAL.

Leave. Permission, as in 'leave to appeal'.

Legacy. A bequest or gift of goods and chattels
by will.
A legacy may be either specific,
demonstrative, or general.
1 A *specific legacy* is a bequest of a specific
part of the testator's personal estate.
2 A *demonstrative legacy* is a gift by will of a
certain sum directed to be paid out of a
specific fund.
3 A *general legacy* is one payable out of the
general assets of the testator.
See ADEMPTION OF A LEGACY.

Legal aid consists of advice, assistance and
representation provided under the Legal Aid
Act 1988.
The purpose of the Act is to establish
a framework for the provision of advice,
assistance and representation which is
publicly funded with a view to helping
persons who might otherwise be unable to
obtain advice, assistance or representation on
account of their means: Legal Aid Act 1988,
s 1, Access to Justice Act 1999.
The Act's principal provisions concern
(i) the Legal Aid Board (ss 3–7); (ii) advice
and assistance (ss 8–13); (iii) civil legal
aid (ss 14–18); (iv) representation in care
proceedings (ss 27, 28); and (v) representation
in contempt proceedings (s 29).
See LEGAL AID BOARD.

Legal Aid Board. A board set up by the
Legal Aid Act 1988 to secure that advice,
assistance and representation are available in
accordance with the Act, and to administer
the Act: Legal Aid Act 1988, s 1(1), (2).
Replaced by the Legal Services Commission
under the Access to Justice Act 1999.

Legal assets. Assets of a person available in a
court of law to satisfy the claims of creditors.
See ASSET.

**Legal Education and Conduct, Advisory
Committee on.** *See* ADVISORY COMMITTEE ON
LEGAL EDUCATION AND CONDUCT.

Legal estate. An estate in land, fully recognised
as such in a court of Common Law, has
been hitherto called the 'legal estate'.
For the different estates and interests in
land (subsisting or created at law) which

are by the Law of Property Act 1925 authorised to subsist or to be created at law and which are referred to in that Act as legal estates.
See ESTATE; EQUITABLE ESTATE.

Legal memory. The time of 'legal memory' runs back to the commencement of the reign of Richard I, ie 1189.

Legal Services Commission. *See* LEGAL AID BOARD.

Legal Services Ombudsman. An official appointed by the Lord Chancellor for the purpose of investigating complaints made to a professional body with respect to a barrister or solicitor: Courts and Legal Services Act 1990, ss 21, 22. (As to 'professional body', see ibid, s 22(11)).

Legal tender. A tender in payment of a debt which will be held valid and sufficient. Gold coin was always a legal tender, so far as a debt admits of being paid in gold, and still is so. The following are also legal tender: (i) coins of cupro-nickel or silver of denominations of more than ten new pence, for payment of any amount not exceeding £10; (ii) coins of cupro-nickel or silver of denominations of not more than ten new pence, for payment of any amount not exceeding £5; (iii) coins of bronze, for payment of any amount not exceeding twenty pence (see Coinage Act 1971, s 2).
See MONEY.

Legally assisted person. A person who receives, under the Legal Aid Act 1988, advice, assistance or representation: Legal Aid Act 1988, s 2(11).
See REPRESENTATION.

Legatee. A person who receives a legacy.
See LEGACY.

Legitimacy of child. A child born in wedlock.
The child of a void marriage, whenever born, is treated as the legitimate child of his parents if at the time of the insemination resulting in the birth or, where there was no such insemination, the child's conception (or at the time of the celebration of the marriage if later) both or either of the parents believed that the marriage was valid: Legitimacy Act 1976, s 1(1).
But s 1 only applies where the father of the child was domiciled in England or Wales at the time of the birth, or if he died before the birth, was so domiciled immediately before his death: ibid, s 1(2).

Legitimacy or **legitimation declaration.**
Any person may apply to the court for a declaration that he is the legitimate child of his parents: Family Law Act 1986, s 56(1).
He may also apply for one (or, in the alternative, the other) of the following declarations:
(i) a declaration that he has become a legitimated person;
(ii) a declaration that he has not become a legitimated person: ibid, s 56(2).
Any declaration is binding on Her Majesty and all other persons: ibid, s 58(2).

Legitimation of person. Where the parents of an illegitimate person marry one another, the marriage (if the father of the illegitimate person is at the date of the marriage domiciled in England or Wales) renders that person, if living, legitimate from the date of marriage: Legitimacy Act 1976, s 2.
A legitimated person is entitled to take any interest in property as if he had been born legitimate: ibid, s 5(3).

Leonina societas. A partnership in which one partner has all the loss, and another all the gain. It is so called, because the lucky partner has the 'lion's share' of the profits.

Lessee. A person to whom a lease is granted.
See LEASE.

Lessor. A person by whom a lease is granted.

Lethal weapon. A weapon capable of killing, eg a firearm.
See OFFENSIVE WEAPON.

Letter of credit. A letter written by one person (usually a merchant or bank) to another, requesting him to advance money, or entrust goods to the bearer, or to a particular person by name, and for which the writer's credit is pledged. It may be either *general*, addressed to all merchants or other persons, or *special*, addressed to a particular person by name. It is not negotiable.

Letters of administration. *See* ADMINISTRATION; ADMINISTRATOR.

Letters of request. 1 Letters whereby a bishop, within whose jurisdiction an ecclesiastical cause has arisen, and who wishes to waive such jurisdiction, requests the Dean of the Arches to take cognisance of the matter. The acceptance of such letters on the part of the Dean of Arches is not optional.
See DEAN OF THE ARCHES.

L

2 A letter addressed to the judicial authorities of a foreign country for the evidence of a witness to be taken there instead of in this country.

Letters of safe conduct. *See* SAFE CONDUCT.

Letters patent (Lat *Literæ patentes*). Writings sealed with the Great Seal of England, whereby a man is authorised to do or to enjoy anything which otherwise of himself he could not. They are so termed by reason of their form, because they are open (*patentes*) with the seal affixed, ready to be shown for confirmation of the authority given by them. *See* PATENT; GREAT SEAL.

Levant and couchant (Lat *Levantes et cubantes*).
1 When land to which a right of common pasture is annexed can maintain a certain number of cattle during the winter by its produce, or requires a certain number of cattle to plough and manure it, those cattle are said to be levant and couchant on the land.
See COMMON, RIGHTS OF.
2 If cattle escape from A's land into B's land by default of B (eg for failing to keep a sufficient fence) they cannot be distrained for rent by B's landlord until they have been levant and couchant on the land, ie until they have been at least one night there. If they escape by default of A, they may be distrained immediately.
See DISTRESS.

Lex domicilii. The law of the place of a person's domicile.
See DOMICILE.

Lex fori. The law of the *forum*, ie the law of the place in which a case is tried.
See FORUM; LEX LOCI CONTRACTUS.

Lex injusta non est lex. An unjust law is not law.
See JURISPRUDENCE; NATURAL LAW.

Lex loci actus. The law of the place where a legal act takes place, eg if X, a British subject domiciled in England, makes a will in Scotland, the *lex loci actus* is the law of Scotland.

Lex loci contractus. The law of the place in which a contract was made, eg if an action were brought in England on a contract made in France, the law of England would, as regards such action, be the *lex fori*, and the law of France the *lex loci contractus*.
See LEX FORI.

Lex loci rei sitæ, or **lex situs.** The law of the place in which a thing in question happens to be. Thus, it is said that the descent of immovable property is regulated according to the *lex loci rei sitæ*; ie according to the law of the place where it is situated.

Lex loci solutionis. The law of the place where a contract is to be performed, eg if X contracts in London to deliver goods to A in Italy, the *lex loci solutionis* is the law of Italy.

Lex non scripta. The unwritten or Common Law which includes general and particular customs.
See COMMON LAW; CUSTOM.

Lex posterior derogat priori. The latter law abrogates the earlier one.

Lex scripta. The written (or statute) law.
See STATUTE.

Liability. Generally, subject to a disadvantage at law, eg subject to being under an obligation or to punishment. One who commits a crime is liable to punishment; one who tortiously causes another injury is liable to an order to pay damages in compensation.

Libel (Lat *Libellus*). A little book.
1 An obscene, blasphemous, or seditious publication, whether by printing, writing, signs, or pictures.
See OBSCENITY.
2 A defamatory publication.
See DEFAMATION.

Liberties, or franchises. 1 At Common Law, a franchise is a royal privilege or branch of the Crown's Prerogative (*see* PREROGATIVE), subsisting in the hands of a subject, either by GRANT or by PRESCRIPTION. Liberties or franchises are of two classes—(i) those which originally formed part of the Crown's prerogative; eg the franchises of waifs, estrays, wrecks, royal fish, forests, etc; (ii) those which can only be created by granting them to a subject; such as fairs, markets, tolls, etc.
2 Franchise also means the locality subject to a franchise.
3 In ancient times, among other franchises usually granted by the Crown to a new borough on its incorporation, was the right of sending burgesses to Parliament; and hence franchise came to mean the right to elect members of Parliament, whether in boroughs or counties.

Library, British. *See* BRITISH LIBRARY.

Licence. 1 A permission to do some act which, without such permission, could not lawfully be done.

2 In real property law, an authority to do an act which would otherwise be a trespass. A licence to enter or occupy land passes no interest (*see* INTEREST IN LAND), and, therefore, if A grants to B the right to fasten boats to moorings in a river, this does not amount to a demise (*see* DEMISE), nor does it give the licensee an exclusive right to the use of the moorings.

Licence to marry. *See* MARRIAGE LICENCE.

Licensed conveyancer. A person who holds a licence from the Council for Licensed Conveyancers entitling him to provide conveyance services in accordance with the licence (see Administration of Justice Act 1985, s 11(2)).

Licensee. A person who enters premises with the permission of the occupier, granted either GRATUITOUSly or for CONSIDERATION.

Licensing Acts. 1 Acts of Parliament for the restraint of printing, except by licence; or any Act of Parliament passed for the purpose of requiring a licence for doing any act whatever.

2 The Acts regulating the sale of intoxicating liquor, now principally the Licensing Acts 1964 to 1967.

Lie. An action is said to *lie*, if particular set of facts, ie the circumstances, constitute a cause of action and thus the basis of a legal claim that can be pursued in the courts.

Lien. 1 As applied to personalty (*see* PERSONALTY), a lien is the right of an agent or a bailee to retain the possession of a chattel entrusted to him until his claim upon it is satisfied.
See BAILMENT; GENERAL LIEN; MARITIME LIEN; PARTICULAR LIEN.

2 As applied to realty, a *vendor's lien* for unpaid purchase-money is his right to enforce his claim on the land sold; a right which is recognised in a court of equity, subject to the doctrines of that court for the protection of *bona fide* purchasers for valuable consideration without notice.
See VENDOR'S LIEN.

3 As applied to the sale of goods, the unpaid seller has a lien under the Sale of Goods Act 1979, ss 41–43.
See UNPAID SELLER.

Lien clause. A clause in a charter-party or bill of lading giving a shipowner the right to retain the cargo until all sums due to him eg in respect of freight (*see* FREIGHT), dead freight (*see* DEAD FREIGHT) and demurrage (*see* DEMURRAGE) have been paid.

Lieutenant. *See* LORD LIEUTENANT.

Life annuity. *See* ANNUITY.

Life assurance. A transaction whereby in consideration of a single or periodical payment of premium a sum of money is secured to be paid on the death of the person whose life is assured or on his reaching a specified age.
See INSURANCE.

Life estate. *See* ESTATE.

Life, lives, in being. *See* PERPETUITY.

Life peerage. Letters patent, conferring the dignity of baron for life only, formerly did not enable the grantee to sit and vote in the House of Lords. A new class of life peers, having such rights and ranking as barons, was created by the Life Peerages Act 1958.
See LORDS OF APPEAL IN ORDINARY.

Life prisoner. A person serving one or more sentences of life imprisonment: Criminal Justice Act 1991, s 34(7). If recommended to do so by the Parole Board, the Secretary of State may, after consultation with the Lord Chief Justice and the trial Judge, order his release on licence: ibid, s 35(2).
See PAROLE BOARD.

Lifting the veil is where the Court ignores the principle of corporate personality (*see* CORPORATE PERSONALITY, PRINCIPLE OF) and looks at the economic reality of the situation eg where (i) the membership of the company falls below 2, as required by the Companies Act 1985, s 1(1); (ii) an officer of the company signs a bill of exchange on behalf of the company without any mention of the company's name on it contrary to the Companies Act 1985, s 349(4); (iii) there has been fraudulent trading (*see* FRAUDULENT TRADING); (iv) the company is a 'sham'; (v) it is believed in time of war that the company is controlled by alien enemies (see *Daimler Co Ltd v Continental Tyre & Rubber Co Ltd* [1916] 2 AC 307, HL).
See COMPANY LAW.

Ligan. Goods sunk in the sea but tied to a buoy in order to be found later.
See JETTISON.

L

Light dues. Dues payable in respect of the services provided by lighthouses, buoys, and beacons.

Lights. The right which a man has to have the access of the sun's rays to his windows free from any obstruction on the part of his neighbours. It is a type of easement (*see* EASEMENT). This is sometimes spoken of as 'the right to light and air'; sometimes as 'ancient lights', because the possessor must have enjoyed them for a certain time before the right is indefeasible (*see* INDEFEASIBLE). This period under the Prescription Act 1832 is 20 years.

Like cases are to be treated alike. The general principle underlying the doctrine of precedent.
See PRECEDENTS, 1.

Limitation, statutes of. A statute of limitation is one which provides that no Court shall entertain proceedings for the enforcement of certain rights if such proceedings were set on foot after the lapse of a definite period of time, reckoned as a rule from the date of the violation of the right. Various statutes have been passed with this object; they were consolidated with amendments by the Limitation Act 1980. The Act provides, inter alia, that actions founded on simple contract and tort should not be brought after the expiration of 6 years from the date on which the cause of action accrued; that an action on a specialty (*see* SPECIALTY) may not be brought after the expiration of 12 years; that, in general, no action may be brought to recover land after the expiration of 12 years from the date when the right of action accrued.

Limitation of actions. *See* LIMITATION, STATUTES OF.

Limitation of estates. The 'limitation' of an estate is the marking out, in a deed or other instrument in writing, of the estate or interest which a person is intended to hold in any property comprised in it.

Limitation of liability. The limitation of liability of members of a company according to their shareholdings.
See COMPANY; COMPANY LAW.

Limited administration. An administration of certain specific effects of a deceased person, the rest being committed to others.
See ADMINISTRATION.

Limited company. A company in which the liability of each shareholder is limited by the number of shares which he has taken or by guarantee, so that he cannot be called on to contribute beyond the amount of his shares or guarantee (*see*, generally, the Companies Act 1985).
See COMPANY; COMPANY LAW.

Limited executor. An executor of a deceased person for certain limited purposes, or for a certain limited time.
See EXECUTOR.

Limited liability. *See* LIMITED COMPANY; COMPANY LAW.

Limited liability partnership. A form of business organisation very close to that of the company, including the attributes of legal personality and limited liability, created under the Limited Liability Partnerships Act 2000.
See PARTNERSHIP; LIMITED COMPANY; COMPANY LAW.

Limited owner. A tenant for life, in tail or by curtesy, or other person not having a fee simple in his absolute disposition (see Settled Land Act 1925, s 20).
See SETTLED LAND.

Limited partner. A member of a limited partnership who at the time of entering into it contributes to it a sum or sums as capital or property valued at a stated amount, and who is not liable for the debts or obligations of the firm beyond the amount so contributed: Limited Partnerships Act 1907, s 4(2).
See LIMITED PARTNERSHIP.

Limited partnership. A partnership consisting of one or more persons called 'general partners', who are liable for all the debts and obligations of the firm, and one or more persons called 'limited partners' who at the time of entering into the partnership contribute a stated amount of capital, and are not liable for the obligations of the firm beyond that amount (see Limited Partnerships Act 1907).
See PARTNERSHIP.

Lincoln's Inn. One of the Inns of Court.
See INNS OF COURT.

Lineal consanguinity. The relationship between direct ascendants and descendants; as between father and son, grandfather and grandson, etc.
See DESCENT.

Lineal descendant. *See* DIRECT DESCENDANT; DESCENT.

Liquidated damages. An ascertained amount, expressed in pounds and pence, which an injured party has sustained, or is taken to have sustained. A term in a contract may specify an amount of liquidated damages for a breach of which the breaching party is bound to pay; the purpose of such a clause is to avoid the necessity of proving the extent of loss, and thus damages, at trial. The term is used in contradistinction to a penalty. Terms in contracts imposing penalties for breach are not generally enforceable at law.
See CONTRACT LAW.

Liquidation. The winding up of a company.
See LIQUIDATOR.

Liquidation committee. A committee appointed by the creditors and members of a company in liquidation to exercise the functions conferred on the committee by the Insolvency Act 1986 (see Insolvency Act 1986, ss 101, 141).

Liquidator. An officer appointed to conduct the winding-up of a company; to bring and defend actions and suits in its name, and to do all necessary acts on behalf of the company. He may be appointed either by resolution of the shareholders in a voluntary winding-up, or by the Court in a compulsory winding-up (see Insolvency Act 1986, ss 91, 135–140).
See OFFICIAL LIQUIDATOR.

Lis mota. A lawsuit put in motion.

Lis pendens. A pending suit. An expression used especially of pending suits relating to land, as affecting the title to the land in question. By the Land Charges Act 1972, s 5 a pending action may be registered in the register of pending actions.

Listed building. A building which is included in a list compiled or approved by the Secretary of State under the Planning (Listed Buildings and Conservation Areas) Act 1990, s 1: Planning (Listed Buildings and Conservation Areas) Act 1990, s 1(5).
Works affecting such buildings are restricted: ibid, ss 7–22.

Listed securities in relation to a company, means any securities of the company listed on a recognised stock exchange (see Company Securities (Insider Dealing) Act 1985, s 12(b)).

See STOCK EXCHANGE; SECURITIES.

Lite pendente. While a suit is pending.
See LIS PENDENS.

Literary work. Any work, other than a dramatic or musical work, which is written, spoken or sung and includes a table or compilation and a computer program: Copyright, Designs and Patents Act 1988, s 3(1).
See MUSICAL WORK.

Litigant. A party to litigation.

Litigant in person. A party to litigation who represents himself.

Litigation. The prosecution and determination of a legal dispute through the courts.
See ALTERNATIVE DISPUTE RESOLUTION.

Litigation friend. *See* GUARDIAN AD LITEM.

Litigious. A church is said to be *litigious* when two rival presentations are offered to the bishop on the same avoidance of the living.
See AVOIDANCE; JUS PATRONATUS.

Littleton. A judge in the reign of Edward IV, who wrote a treatise of tenures on which Chief Justice Coke has written an extensive comment.

Livery (Lat *Liberatura*). The members of a company of the City of London chosen out of the freemen.
See LIVERYMAN.

Livery of seisin. Delivery of possession of land. The ancient common law means by which an ENFEOFFMENT was effected. It consisted of a ceremonial transfer of the land from grantor to grantee, which took place upon the land to be granted, the grantor handing a twig or clod of earth from the land to the grantee before witnesses, the delivery of the piece of the land standing for the whole.
See FEOFFMENT.

Liveryman. A member of a company in the City of London, chosen out of the freemen, to assist the master and wardens in the government of the company.

Lloyd's. An association in the City of London regulated by Lloyd's Act 1982. Its members are (i) underwriters who undertake liability on contracts of insurance; and (ii) brokers who act as intermediaries between underwriters and persons wishing to effect insurances with them.

Lloyd's agents. Agents appointed by the Corporation of Lloyd's in all the principal ports of the world, their duty being to forward accounts of all arrivals and departures of vessels at their ports, reports of losses and casualties and information relating to shipping and insurance.

Load lines. Lines on each side of a ship indicating the various maximum depths to which she may be loaded (see Merchant Shipping (Load Lines) Act 1967, s 2(d)). The line is often known as the 'Plimsoll line' because Samuel Plimsoll (1824–98), MP, suggested the idea of having them.

Loan societies. Those established for advancing money on loan to the industrial classes (see Loan Societies Act 1840).

Local allegiance. Such as is due from an alien or stranger born so long as he continues within the Sovereign's dominions and protection and in certain circumstances even after he has left.

Local and personal Acts. This expression is applied to the second category of Acts of Parliament as classified for publication. These Acts when passed are to be judicially noticed as public Acts (see Interpretation Act 1978, s 3).

Local authority. Local authorities were reorganised by the Local Government Act 1972. The expression now means a county council, a district council, a London borough council or a parish or community council (see ibid, s 270(1)).

Local courts. Courts whose jurisdiction is confined to certain districts, eg the County Courts, Magistrates' Courts, etc.

Local Government Commission. A commission responsible for conducting a review in areas specified by the Secretary of State and recommending to him structural, boundary or electoral changes in them: Local Government Act 1992, ss 12–14.

Local lighthouse authority. A person or body of persons having, by law or usage, authority over local lighthouses, buoys or beacons (see Merchant Shipping Act 1894, s 634(1)).

Lock-out. A closing of a place of employment, or the suspension of work, or the refusal of an employer to continue to employ any number of persons employed by him in consequence of a dispute, done with a view to compelling those persons, or to aid another employer in compelling persons employed by him to accept terms or conditions of or affecting employment: Employment Protection

(Consolidation) Act 1978, s 151, Sch 13, para 24(1).

There is no lock-out where an employer dismisses them because he has no work for them (see *Re Richardsons and M Samuel & Co* [1898] 1 QB 261, CA).

Locum tenens. A deputy or substitute.

Locus in quo. The place in which anything is alleged to be done.

Locus poenitentiæ. A place or chance of repentance. A phrase generally applied to a power of drawing back from a fraudulent transaction before anything has been done to confirm it in law or give it effect.

Locus regit actum. The place governs the act, ie, the act is governed by the law of the place where it is done.

Locus sigilli. The place of the seal. The initials (LS) are also used in a copy of a document, to indicate the place where the seal was in the original document.

Locus standi (a place of standing). A right of appearance in a court of justice, or before Parliament, on any given question. In other words, it means a right *to be heard*, as opposed to a right *to succeed on the merits*. In general, it refers to the right to be a party to legal proceedings, and generally only those who personally have a legal claim, or are themselves defendants to a claim, in rough terms, those who have a direct, legal, 'stake' in the dispute, have *locus standi* in any proceeding.

Lodger. A tenant having exclusive possession of a part of a house, the general control over which remains in the landlord or his agent. A lodger's goods are protected against distress by the superior landlord by the Law of Distress Amendment Act 1908.
See DISTRESS.

Log. A float attached to a line wound on a reel for gauging the speed of a ship.

Log book. A book with a permanent record made of all events occurring during a ship's voyage including her rate of progress shown by the ship's log.
See LOG; OFFICIAL LOG BOOK.

Loitering. Travelling indolently, with frequent pauses, lingering (see *Williamson v Wright* [1924] SC (J) 57). Loitering or soliciting for purposes of prostitution is an offence under the Street Offences Act 1959.

London cab. A vehicle which is a hackney carriage within the meaning of the Metropolitan Public Carriage Act 1869: Local Government (Miscellaneous Provisions) Act 1976, s 80(1).
See HACKNEY CARRIAGE.

London commission area means (i) the 'inner London area' consisting of the inner London boroughs; and (ii) the 'outer London areas' which are:
(a) 'north-east London area', consisting of the London boroughs of Barking, Havering, Newham, and Waltham Forest;
(b) 'south-east London area', consisting of the London boroughs of Bexley, Bromley, and Croydon;
(c) 'south-west London area', consisting of the London boroughs of Kingston upon Thames, Merton, Richmond upon Thames, and Sutton; and
(d) 'Middlesex area' consisting of the London Boroughs of Barnet, Brent, Ealing, Enfield, Haringey, Hillingdon, and Hounslow: Justices of the Peace Act 1979, s 2(1).

London Gazette. *See* GAZETTE.

London Salvage Corps. A corps founded by insurance companies insuring property within Greater London and charged with the duty of attending at fires and saving insured property. It is the duty of the London Fire Brigade to afford the necessary assistance to the Corps (see Metropolitan Fire Brigade Act 1865, s 29).

Long-term prisoner. One serving a sentence of imprisonment for a term of 4 years or more: Criminal Justice Act 1991, s 33(5). As soon as he has served two-thirds of his sentence, he must be released on licence: ibid s 33(1). After he has served one-half of his sentence, the Secretary of State may if recommended to do so by the Parole Board, release him on licence: ibid, s 35(1).
See PAROLE BOARD.

Long Vacation. The Long Vacation, during which there are no regular sittings of the Supreme Court, in particular for trials, begins on 1st August, and ends on 30th September.

Longs. Government stock which is long-dated, ie stock which is not redeemable for 15 years.

Lord Advocate. The principal Crown lawyer in Scotland.
See ATTORNEY-GENERAL.

Lord Cairn's Act. The Chancery Amendment Act 1858. Section 2 of this Act empowered the Court of Chancery to award damages, formerly a remedy available only to judges of the common law courts, in lieu of or in addition to the award of an injunction.
See EQUITY.

Lord Campbell's Acts. 1 The Libel Act 1843 for amending the law respecting defamatory words and libel, by allowing a defendant in pleading to an *indictment* or *information* for criminal libel to allege the truth of the matters charged and that their publication was for the public benefit.
2 The Fatal Accidents Act 1846 for enabling the executors or administrators of persons killed by negligence to bring actions for the benefit of the wife, husband, parent or children of the deceased, against the party guilty of negligence.
3 The Obscene Publications Act 1857 authorising magistrates to issue warrants for the seizure of obscene books, papers, writings, or representations kept in a place for the purpose of being sold, distributed, lent on hire, or otherwise published for gain. Repealed and replaced by the Obscene Publications Acts 1959 and 1964.

Lord Chamberlain. *See* CHAMBERLAIN.

Lord Chancellor. *See* CHANCELLOR.

Lord Chief Justice of England. The presiding judge of the Queen's Bench Division, and, in the absence of the Lord Chancellor, President of the High Court. He is also an *ex-officio* judge of the Court of Appeal.

Lord High Steward. *See* HIGH STEWARD.

Lord Justice. *See* LORDS JUSTICES OF APPEAL.

Lord Justice-Clerk (*Scotland*). A judge of the High Court of Justiciary; also senior judge of the second division of the Court of Session.
See COURT OF SESSION.

Lord Justice-General. *See* LORD PRESIDENT.

Lord Keeper. *See* KEEPER OF THE GREAT SEAL.

Lord Lieutenant. One of the principal honorary officers of a county, originally appointed for the purpose of mustering the inhabitants for the defence of the country. See, further, Lieutenancies Act 1997.

Lord Mayor's Court. *See* MAYOR'S AND CITY OF LONDON COURT.

Lord President (*Scotland*). The president of the first division of the Court of Session, the office being united with that of Lord Justice-General in the criminal courts.

See COURT OF SESSION.

Lord Privy Seal. Usually one of the members of the Cabinet, through whose hands all charters, etc, passed before they came to the Great Seal. The Great Seal Act 1884, s 3, provided that it should not be necessary in future that any instrument passed under the Privy Seal. The Lord Privy Seal has really no duties as such.

See GREAT SEAL.

Lord Treasurer. Otherwise called the Lord High Treasurer of England. A high officer of State, who had the charge and government of the King's wealth contained in the Exchequer. The office of Lord Treasurer has now for a long time been entrusted to commissioners, who are called the Lords Commissioners of the Treasury. The chief of the Commissioners is called the First Lord, and the Chancellor of the Exchequer is the second, and there are five others, who usually act as 'Whips' for the political party in power.

Lord Warden of the Cinque Ports. The principal officer of the Cinque Ports having the custody of them, and formerly having a civil jurisdiction in them.

See CINQUE PORTS.

Lords Commissioners. When a high public office in the State, formerly executed by an individual, is put into commission, the persons charged with the commission are called Lords Commissioners, or sometimes Lords or Commissioners simply. At the present time the places of the Lord Treasurer (*see* LORD TREASURER) and Lord High Admiral of former times are taken by the Lords Commissioners of the Treasury, and the Lords Commissioners of the Admiralty; and whenever the Great Seal (*see* GREAT SEAL) is put into commission, the persons charged with it are called Commissioners or Lords Commissioners of the Great Seal.

Lords, House of. *See* HOUSE OF LORDS.

Lords Justices of Appeal. The ordinary Judges of the Court of Appeal.

Lords of Appeal in Ordinary. Persons having held high judicial office for two years or practised at the bar for not less than fifteen years, to aid the House of Lords by serving on its Appellate Committee (the committee of the House of Lords to which its function as the highest court of appeal is assigned by constitutional convention) and the Judicial Committee of the Privy Council in hearing appeals. Also called the Law Lords, they rank as barons for life, but sit and vote in the House of Lords during the time of their office only (see the Appellate Jurisdiction Acts 1876 to 1947).

At least two are normally appointed from the Scottish Bench or Bar.

Lords Spiritual. Those bishops who have seats in the House of Lords; being the Archbishops of Canterbury and York, the Bishops of London, Durham, and Winchester, and 21 other bishops.

See HOUSE OF LORDS.

Lords Temporal. The peers of the realm who have seats in the House of Lords, other than the bishops.

See HOUSE OF LORDS.

Loss. Generally, any disadvantage that may be compensated by an award of damages, ie money compensation. It can include, in particular in respect of profits lost due to a breach of contract, a loss by not getting what one might get, as well as a loss by parting with or destruction of what one has.

Loss of amenity. In the assessment of damages for personal injury, loss of amenity refers to loss of capability or loss of enjoyment of life occasioned by the injury.

Loss, total. *See* TOTAL LOSS.

Lottery. A game of chance, or a distribution of money or prizes by chance, without the application of choice or skill. Illegal unless falling within the provisions of the Betting, Gaming and Lotteries Act 1963 and the Lotteries Act 1975, which permit certain lotteries for sporting or other purposes, and the National Lottery etc Act 1993.

Lucid interval. A period of sanity which intervenes between two attacks of insanity. Acts done during such an interval are valid.

Lugano Convention. An international convention on jurisdiction and the enforcement of judgments in civil and commercial matters opened for signature at Lugano on 16th September 1988.

It has been brought into force by the Civil Jurisdiction and Judgments Act 1991.

Lump sum freight. Freight paid as a lump sum for the use of a ship, irrespective of the amount of cargo loaded.

Lying by. Neglecting to assert rights, or allowing persons to deal with land or other property as if one had no interest in it; eg when a mortgagee allows his mortgagor to retain the title deeds and raise money on a fresh mortgage of the land, without notice to the new mortgagee of the prior mortgage. *See* LACHES.

Lynch law. The execution of summary justice by a mob without reference to the process of ordinary law.

Lyon King at Arms. An officer who takes his title from the armorial bearing of the Scottish king, the lion rampant.
See KINGS-AT-ARMS.

Lyon's Inn. *See* INNS OF CHANCERY.

Lyttleton. *See* LITTLETON.

L

MEP. Member of the European Parliament.
See EUROPEAN PARLIAMENT.

MOH. Medical Officer of Health.
See MEDICAL OFFICER OF HEALTH.

MP. Member of Parliament.
See HOUSE OF COMMONS.

MR. Master of the Rolls.
See MASTER OF THE ROLLS.

Maastricht Treaty. Familiar name for the Treaty of European Union of 1992, signed at Maastricht on 7th February, 1992.
See EUROPEAN UNION.

Magistrate. A person entrusted with the commission of the peace for any county, city, or other jurisdiction.
See JUSTICE OF THE PEACE; STIPENDIARY MAGISTRATE.

Magistrates' court. Any justice or justices of the peace acting under any enactment or by virtue of his or their commission or under the Common Law: Magistrates' Courts Act 1980, s 148.
Such a court has both criminal and civil jurisdiction: ibid, Part I and Part II respectively.

Magistrates' Courts Committees. Committees with functions in relation to (i) justices' clerks; (ii) the division into petty sessional divisions of non-metropolitan counties, metropolitan districts and outer London boroughs; and (iii) the provision of courses of instruction for justices: Justices of the Peace Act 1979, s 19(1).
As to their constitution, see s 20.

Magna Carta. A charter granted by King John in 1215, at Runnymede, and confirmed in Parliament in 1225, and again by the *Confirmation Chartarum* in 1297.
See CONFIRMATIO CHARTARUM.

This Great Charter is based substantially on the Saxon common law and contains 38 chapters on various subjects, especially with reference to landed estates and their tenures. Many of its provisions are now repealed.

Mail. Every conveyance by which postal packets are carried, whether it is a ship, aircraft, vehicle, horse, or any other conveyance; also a person employed in conveying or delivering postal packets.

Maim. At common law, to injure a person so as to deprive him of the use of part of his body, the loss of which makes him less capable of fighting or of defending himself.

'Main objects' rule. A rule that where the 'objects' clause of a company's memorandum of association sets out the company's main object, and also lists other objects, those other objects are to be construed as being merely incidental to the main object (see *Stephens v Mysore Reefs (Kangundy) Mining Co Ltd* [1902] 1 Ch 745). The rule can be excluded by making all the objects of the company independent objects (see *Cotman v Brougham* [1918] AC 514). If a company's 'main object' has gone, the company may be wound up (see *Re Amalgamated Syndicate* [1897] 2 Ch 600).
See OBJECTS CLAUSE.

Maintainors. Persons guilty of *maintaining* a lawsuit.
See MAINTENANCE, 1.

Maintenance. 1 An officious intermeddling in a suit which in no way belonged to one, by maintaining or assisting either party, with money or otherwise, to prosecute or defend it.
2 Providing children, or other persons in a position of dependence, with food, clothing, and other necessaries.

Maintenance, power of. A power, provided in a deed or will in which property is conveyed or bequeathed on trust, empowering the trustee or trustees to spend the income of the trust property in the maintenance and education of the children who are to participate in the property when they come of age. The present provisions as to the maintenance and education of children are contained in the Trustee Act 1925, s 31.
See TRUST.

Majora regalia. The Queen's dignity, power, and royal prerogative; as opposed to her *revenue*, which is comprised in the *minora regalia*.
See PREROGATIVE.

Majority. Full age. Reduced to 18 from 21 by the Family Law Reform Act 1969.

Majority verdict. The verdict given by a majority of the members of a jury. In the Crown Court or the High Court their verdict need not be unanimous if (i) in a case where there are not less than eleven jurors, ten agree on the verdict; (ii) in a case where there are ten jurors, nine agree on the verdict: Juries Act 1974, s 17(1). In civil proceedings the court may accept a majority verdict with the consent of the parties: ibid s 17(5).
See VERDICT.

Maker, of a promissory note, is the person who signs it. By doing so, he engages to pay it according to its tenor (see Bills of Exchange Act 1882, s 88).
See PROMISSORY NOTE.

Making off without payment. A form of theft under the Theft Act 1968. It is committed by a person who receives goods or services, knowing that payment for them is required or expected, and dishonestly makes off without paying and with the intent to avoid doing so.

Mal. A prefix meaning bad, wrong, fraudulent.

Mala fides. Bad faith.

Mala grammatica non vitiat chartam. Bad grammar does not vitiate a deed.

Mala in se. Acts which are wrong in themselves, eg murder, whether prohibited by POSITIVE LAW or not, as distinguished from *mala prohibita*, which are wrong by reason of being expressly prohibited by POSITIVE LAW, eg playing at unlawful games.

Mala prohibita. *See* MALA IN SE.

Malfeasance. The commission of some act which is in itself unlawful, as opposed to *non-feasance*, which is the omission of an act which a man is bound by law to do; and to *misfeasance*, which is the improper performance of some lawful act.

Malice. 1 The wicked and mischievous purpose which is of the essence of the crime of murder. Also called 'malice aforethought', 'malice and forethought', 'malice prepense'. It exists where anyone contemplates the death of any person or persons as a probable consequence of an act done by himself without lawful justification or excuse, or of some unlawful omission, and is implied where he does any act, the natural or probable consequence of which is to cause the death of a person.
2 As regards malicious injuries to persons or property, especially the latter, a 'malicious act' has been defined as a wrongful act, intentionally done without just cause or excuse (see *Bromage v Prosser* (1825) 4 B & C 247 at 255). Under the Malicious Damage Act 1861 it must be understood in a more restricted sense than the malice which is of the essence of murder. An act lawful in itself is not converted by malice into an actionable wrong (see *Allen v Flood* [1898] AC 1).

Malicious communication. A letter or other article sent or delivered to another person for the purpose of causing distress or anxiety: Malicious Communications Act 1988, s 1.

Malicious damage. *See* CRIMINAL DAMAGE.

Malicious falsehood. A form of the tort of defamation, whereby a false and malicious statement is made about a person's business or commercial interests, thereby harming those interests.
See SLANDER OF TITLE.

Malicious prosecution. A prosecution undertaken against a person without reasonable or probable cause. In an action for malicious prosecution, the burden lies on the plaintiff to show that no probable cause existed.

Malingering. Falsely pretending to be suffering from sickness or disability. Used principally of members of the Forces so doing to escape duty. Punishable under the Naval Discipline Act 1957, s 27 and under the Army Act 1955, s 42 and the Air Force Act 1955, s 42.

Malitia supplet aetatem. Malice supplies the want of age.
See DOLI CAPAX.

M

Malus animus. With evil intent.

Malversation. Misbehaviour in an office, commission, or employment.

Manager. *See* RECEIVER.

Managing director. One of the directors of a company appointed to deal with the day to day management. The duration of his appointment, his remuneration and powers are defined by the directors. He is usually appointed under a service contract.

Mandamus. The order in lieu of the prerogative writ of *mandamus*. This is, in its form, a command issuing in the Queen's name, and directed to any person, corporation, or inferior court, requiring them to do some particular thing which appertains to their office and duty. In its application, it may be considered as confined to cases where relief is required in respect of the infringement of some *public* right or duty, and where no effective relief can be obtained in the ordinary course of an action.
See ADMINISTRATIVE LAW.

Mandate. 1 A command of the Queen, or her justices, to have anything done for the despatch of justice.
2 A direction or request, which may be provided for by a contract, but which is itself complied with for no (further) consideration. Thus a cheque is a mandate by the drawer to his banker (the drawee) to pay the amount to the payee. The issuer of a mandate may be called the mandator, and the person to whom the direction is addressed, the mandatory.

Mandated territory. The method adopted at the end of the First World War (1914–1918) for dealing with the colonies and territories of Germany and Turkey, which it was decided to detach from them, was known as the mandate system, and was embodied in Article 22 of the Covenant of the League of Nations. Under this system, those territories were not in the ownership of any State, but were entrusted to certain States called 'Mandatory States' to administer on behalf of the League on the conditions laid down in written agreements, called 'mandates', between the League and each mandatory. This system was a novelty in international law. It has been replaced by trusteeship under the United Nations.

Mandatory or Mandatary. 1 A person to whom a charge or commandment is given.
2 A person that obtains a benefice by *mandamus*.

Manifest. A document signed by the master of a ship giving a description of the ship, of the goods loaded on her, etc.

Mansion or Mansion-house. Under the Settled Land Act 1925 the principal mansion-house (unless it is usually occupied as a farm house, or its park, etc, does not exceed 25 acres in extent) may not be sold, exchanged, or leased by a tenant for life without the consent of the trustees of the settlement or an order of the Chancery Division. In regard to a settlement made or coming into operation after 1925 this restriction will only apply if the settlement expressly so provides (see Settled Land Act 1925, s 65).
See SETTLEMENT.

Manslaughter. The unlawful killing of another without malice express or implied: which may be either voluntarily or involuntarily, but in the commission of some unlawful or negligent act.
See MALICE, 1.
    The absence of such malice as would constitute the act one of murder may be inferred under the following circumstances:
1 Where the person charged was provoked to lose his self-control, whether by things done or by things said or by both together (see Homicide Act 1957, s 3).
2 Where there is time to consider the probable consequences of an unlawful act wilfully done, and yet the death of any person is by no means a natural or probable consequence of such unlawful act; eg if two parties fight without deadly weapons; or where there is a high degree of negligence, provided that the negligence in question is not such as to indicate a wanton and palpable disregard of human life, in which case it will amount to murder. This definition would imply that the difference between murder and manslaughter is often one of degree which is, in fact, the case.
See MURDER.
3 Persons suffering from diminished responsibility, ie mental abnormality of mind, must not be convicted of murder but of manslaughter (see Homicide Act 1957, s 2).

Man-traps, to catch trespassers, are unlawful except in a dwelling-house for defence between sunset and sunrise (see Offences against the Person Act 1861, s 31).

Marches. Boundaries or frontiers.

The boundaries and limits between England and Wales, or between England and Scotland; or generally the borders of the possessions of the Crown.

Mare Clausum. A celebrated treatise by Selden (1584–1654) written in answer to the treatise called *Mare Liberum*.

See MARE LIBERUM.

Mare Liberum. A famous treatise by Grotius (1583–1645) to prove that all nations have an equal right to use the sea.

Mareva injunction. An injunction (which takes its name from *Mareva Compania Naviera SA v International Bulkcarriers SA* [1980] 1 All ER 213 n, CA) which may be granted to restrain a defendant from transferring abroad any of his assets which are within the jurisdiction. Mareva injunctions are now called 'freezing orders' after the usage in the Civil Procedure Rules 1998.

Margin of appreciation. Doctrine of the European Court of Human Rights under which member states have a degree of flexibility in implementing the European Convention of Human Rights in their individual jurisdictions so as to reflect the mores of the particular national community.

Marine adventure occurs where '(*a*) any ship, goods or other movables are exposed to maritime perils; (*b*) the earning or acquisition of any freight, passage money, commission, profit or other pecuniary benefit, or the security for any advances, loan or disbursements is endangered by the exposure of a ship, goods or other movables to maritime perils; (*c*) any liability to a third party may be incurred by the owner of, or other person interested in or responsible for insurable property by reason of maritime perils' (see Marine Insurance Act 1906, s 3(2)).

See MARITIME PERILS.

Marine insurance. A contract whereby the insurer undertakes to indemnify the assured in manner and to the extent thereby agreed, against marine losses, that is to say, the losses incident to marine adventure (see Marine Insurance Act 1906, s 1).

See MARINE ADVENTURE.

Marital. Pertaining to a husband, or of the nature of marriage.

Maritime law. The law relating to harbours, ships, and seamen.

Maritime lien. A claim which attaches to the *res*, ie the ship, cargo, or freight. It arises either *ex delicto*, eg in respect of compensation for damage by collision, or *ex contractu*, in respect of services rendered to the *res*.

See LIEN.

Maritime perils means 'the perils consequent on, or incidental to, the navigation of the sea, that is to say, perils of the sea, fire, war perils, pirates, rovers, thieves, captures, seizures, restraints and detainments of princes and peoples, jettisons, barratry and any other perils of the like kind or which may be designated by the policy' (see Marine Insurance Act 1906, s 3(2)).

Market. A place of commerce or of buying and selling; or the liberty to set up such a place, which any person or body corporate may have by Act of Parliament, grant, or prescription.

Market maker. A person (whether an individual, partnership or company) who
(i) holds himself out at all normal times in compliance with the rules of a recognised stock exchange as willing to buy and sell securities at prices specified by him; and
(ii) is recognised as doing so by that recognised stock exchange (see Company Securities (Insider Dealing) Act 1985, s 3(1)).

Market overt. Open market. An expression applied to the open sale of goods as opposed to a clandestine or irregular sale. Market overt, in the country, is held only on the special days provided for particular towns; but in the City of London every day, except Sunday, is market-day. Also in the country the market-place is the only market overt; but in the City of London every shop in which goods are exposed publicly for sale is market overt for the sale by the occupier of such things as he professes to trade in (see Sale of Goods Act 1979, s 22).

Formerly, the effect of a sale in market overt was that it would, in general, give the buyer a good title to the goods which he had bought, though the seller had no property in them; to this rule, however, there were some exceptions; eg if the goods were Crown property. This rule was abolished by the Sale of Goods (Amendment) Act 1994.

Market towns. Towns entitled to hold markets. *See* MARKET.

Marksman. A person who cannot write, and therefore, instead of signing his name, makes his mark, generally a cross. In practice, it is desirable that the mark should be attested by a witness.

Marquis, or **Marquess.** A title of honour next before an earl (*see* EARL), and next after a duke (*see* DUKE). It originated in the time of Richard II, when it was applied to those lords who had the charge and custody of *marches* or limits (*see* MARCHES), and who before that time were called *marchers* or *lords marchers*.

Marriage. The ceremony or process by which the legal relationship of husband and wife is constituted.

The law of marriage is consolidated in the Marriage Acts 1949 to 1970. The Act of 1949 is divided into six parts. Part I sets out the various restrictions on marriage, eg the prohibited degrees of kindred and affinity (*see* AFFINITY), age, and the hours in which marriage may be solemnised. Part II regulates marriage according to the rites of the Church of England, whether after the publication of banns of matrimony, or on the authority of a special licence, a common licence, or the certificate of a superintendent registrar (*see* MARRIAGE LICENCE). Part III makes provision for marriage under a superintendent registrar's certificate, eg, marriages in a register office, Quaker marriages, Jewish marriages, etc. Part IV deals with the registration of marriages, Part V with marriage in naval, military and air force chapels, and Part VI with miscellaneous and general matters.

Marriage articles. Heads of an agreement for a marriage settlement.
See MARRIAGE SETTLEMENT.

Marriage brokage contracts. Agreements whereby a party engages to give another a remuneration if he will negotiate a marriage for him. Such agreements are void, as tending to introduce marriage not based on mutual affection, and, therefore, contrary to public policy.

Marriage by certificate. A person may be married by superintendent registrar's certificate without licence. In order to obtain this certificate, notice in the prescribed form must be given to the superintendent registrar of the district or districts in which both parties have dwelt for not less than 7 days. After 21 days the certificate is issued (see Marriage Act 1949, ss 27, 31).
See MARRIAGE LICENCE.

Marriage licence.
1 A common licence, granted by the Ordinary or his surrogate.
  See ORDINARY, 2; SURROGATE.
2 A special licence from the Archbishop of Canterbury or any other person by virtue of the Ecclesiastical Licences Act 1533.
3 A licence from the superintendent registrar of the district.
  A licence obtained in either of the forms 1 or 2 will enable the parties to marry without banns, according to the forms of the Church of England; and a licence obtained in form 3 will enable the parties to marry in any other lawful manner (see Marriage Act 1949).
  See BANNS.

Marriage settlement. A settlement of property between an intended husband and wife, made in consideration of their marriage.

Marrow. Author of a famous book, written in the reign of Henry VII, on the office of a justice of the peace.

Marshal. An official of the Admiralty Court, having duties very similar to a sheriff at Common Law.
See SHERIFF.

Marshalling of assets. An adjustment of the assets of a deceased person so as to pay as many claims on his estate as possible. Thus, if A has a claim on funds X and Y, and B only on X; and A goes against X and thus disappoints B of his fund, B under this doctrine may go against Y fund to the extent that A had drawn on X funds.

Martial Courts. *See* COURT-MARTIAL.

Martial law. A state of war in which a military commander is in full control. It is not law in the ordinary sense.

Martinmas. The 11th of November, the feast of St Martin of Tours. In Scotland, a quarter day.

Master. Unless the context otherwise requires, includes every person (except a pilot) having command or charge of any ship (see Merchant Shipping Act 1894, s 742).
See MASTERS IN CHANCERY; MASTERS OF THE SUPREME COURT.

Master and servant. Relationship between contracting parties, now more generally called 'employer and employee', where the former rewards the latter for work in the former's control. The servant or employer is to be distinguished from the 'independent contractor', a person who controls his own work but offers his services to others, eg a plumber hired to instal pipes. *See* SERVANT.

Master of the Chancery Division. *See* MASTERS IN CHANCERY.

Master of the Court of Protection. The Court of Protection is an office of the Supreme Court, whose task is the protection and management of the property of mentally disordered persons. The Master is appointed by the Lord Chancellor under the Mental Health Act 1983, s 93(2).

Master of the Faculties. An officer under the Archbishop of Canterbury, appointed to grant licences, dispensations, etc. *See* FACULTY.

Master of the Rolls was one of the Judges of the Court of Chancery, and keeper of the rolls of all patents and grants which pass the Great Seal, and of all records of the Court of Chancery. He was formerly one of the Masters in Chancery, and his earliest judicial attendances seem to have been merely as assessor to the Chancellor, with the other Masters. His character as an independent Judge was fully established in the reign of George II. The title now names the president of the Civil Division of the Court of Appeal (see Supreme Court Act 1981, s 3(2)), thus the most senior judge of civil law matters except for the LAW LORDS.

Masters in Chancery. Originally Masters of the High Court of Chancery, who assisted the Lord Chancellor. Their office was abolished in 1852, and their duties relegated to the Chief Clerks. Since 1897 the officials previously called Chief Clerks have been called Masters, and they are now officers of the Chancery Division of the High Court of Justice. Masters of the Chancery Division are attached to the chambers of the judges of that Division. They hear summonses and dispose of less important matters, and prepare others for judges. They also take accounts and institute inquiries under a judgment or an order of the court.

Masters of the Courts of Common Law. *See* MASTERS OF THE SUPREME COURT.

Masters of the Supreme Court. The most important officers of the courts of common law following the first appointments to the office in 1837, they became, under the JUDICATURE ACTS officers of the Supreme Court, and may, with certain exceptions, transact all such business as may be done by a judge in chambers.

Mate. The deputy of the master in a merchant ship. There are sometimes one, sometimes two, three, or four.

Matricide. The killing of one's mother.

Matrimonial causes. Causes respecting the rights of marriage, now assigned to the Family Division by the Supreme Court Act 1981, s 61, Sch 1, para 3. The chief are either for—

(i) Judicial separation.
　See JUDICIAL SEPARATION.
(ii) Dissolution of marriage.
　See DIVORCE.
(iii) Nullity of marriage.
　See NULLITY OF MARRIAGE.
(See the Matrimonial Causes Act 1973.)

Matrimonial (or **civil partnership**) **home.** The domicile where a husband and wife, or civil partners, together live. The Family Law Act 1996 Part IV as amended gives to a spouse or civil partner who has no property rights in the home certain protections, ie (i) if in occupation, a right not to be evicted or excluded from the dwelling-house or any part of it by the other spouse or civil partner, except by court order; (ii) if not in occupation, a right, by court order, to enter and occupy the dwelling-house.

Matter. 1 *Matter in deed* is a truth to be proved by some deed or 'specialty', ie, writing under seal.
　See DEED.
2 *Matter in pais*, strictly speaking a thing done in the country, is a matter to be proved by witnesses, and tried by a jury of the country. This is otherwise called *nude matter*. The expression, however, is also used so as to include *matter in deed*.
　See ESTOPPEL.
3 *Matter of record* is a matter which may be proved by some record, as having been done in some court of record.
　See COURT OF RECORD.

M

Maturity. A bill of exchange or note is said to be at *maturity* when the time arrives at which it is payable.

See BILL OF EXCHANGE.

Mayor. The Queen, on a petition presented to her by the council of a district praying for the grant of a charter, may confer on that district the status of a borough, and thereupon the chairman and vice-chairman of the council will be entitled to the style of mayor and deputy mayor of the borough (see Local Government Act 1972, s 245(1)).

The council of a parish or community which is not grouped with any other parish or community may resolve that the parish or community has the status of a town, and thereupon the chairman and vice-chairman of the council respectively are entitled to the style of town mayor and deputy town mayor (see ibid, s 245(6)).

Greater London now has an elected mayor. See Greater London Authority Act 1999.

Mayor's and City of London Court. An amalgamation of two former courts, the Mayor's Court of London and the City of London Court. It was abolished by the Courts Act 1971 and the City of London became a County Court district. Nevertheless the County Court for the district of the City continues to be known as the Mayor's and City of London Court, and the judge assigned to it as the judge of the Mayor's and City of London Court.

McKenzie friend. A litigant in person is entitled to have another person, called a 'McKenzie friend' (from *McKenzie v McKenzie* [1971] P 33), sit beside him and offer quiet assistance and advice, although that person has no LOCUS STANDI in the dispute nor any right of audience as a qualified advocate.

See LITIGANT IN PERSON.

Measure. An enactment of the General Synod of the Church of England, with the effect of a statute.

See SYNOD.

Measure of damages. The rule by which the *amount* of damages in any given case is to be determined.

Medical Council. *See* GENERAL MEDICAL COUNCIL.

Medical jurisprudence. *See* FORENSIC MEDICINE.

Medical Officer of Health. An officer appointed by a local authority to supervise matters relating to public health.

Medium. A person who professes to communicate with spirits, or through whom persons in the next world communicate with those remaining in this; a spiritualist, a clairvoyant. Persons fraudulently purporting to act as spiritualistic mediums or to exercise powers of telepathy, etc, are punishable under the Fraudulent Mediums Act 1951.

Mediums. Government stock which has a life of 5 to 15 years.

Meeting. A gathering or assembly of persons, convened for the conducting of business, eg of a company, or relating to the affairs of a bankrupt.

Provisions as to meetings of companies are contained in the Companies Act 1985, ss 366 et seq. Such meetings include (i) *annual general meeting*, which must be held each year and at an interval of not more than 15 months after the preceding annual general meeting; (ii) *extraordinary general meeting*, which may be convened on the requisition of members holding not less than one-tenth of the paid-up capital of the company.

Melior est conditio possidentis et rei quam actoris. The position of the defendant in possession is better than that of the plaintiff.

Members' voluntary winding up. A winding up in the case of which a declaration of solvency has been made in accordance with the Insolvency Act 1986, s 89 (see Insolvency Act 1986, s 90).

See DECLARATION OF SOLVENCY.

Memorandum of association. A document to be subscribed by two or more persons for a lawful purpose, by subscribing which, and otherwise complying with the requirements of the Companies Act in respect of registration, they may form themselves into an incorporated company, with or without limited liability. It states the company's name, particulars of capital, objects, etc. Its objects cannot be varied even by the whole body of shareholders except under the special provisions of the Companies Act 1985, ss 4, 5, 6.

Memorial. A document containing particulars of a deed, etc, for the purposes of registration.

Memory, time of legal. *See* LEGAL MEMORY.

Menaces. *See* BLACKMAIL.

Mens rea. A guilty mind or intent; usually one of the essentials of a crime.
See MALICE; MISTAKE.

Mental disorder. Mental illness, arrested or incomplete development of mind, psychopathic disorder and any other disorder or disability of mind: Mental Health Act 1983, s 1(2).
See PSYCHOPATHIC DISORDER.

Mental impairment. A state of arrested or incomplete development of mind (not amounting to severe mental impairment) which includes significant impairment of intelligence and social functioning and is associated with abnormally aggressive or seriously irresponsible conduct on the part of the person concerned (see Mental Health Act 1983, s 1(2)).

Mercantile Courts. Courts outside London which hear High Court commercial claims that are more conveniently dealt with locally than in the High Court in London. They are situated in Birmingham, Bristol, Leeds, Liverpool, Manchester, and Newcastle.

Merchant Navy Reserve. A body of persons established and maintained by the Secretary of State whose members may be required by him to serve in ships belonging to or employed in the service of Her Majesty: Merchant Shipping Act 1988, s 28(1).

Merchantable quality of goods. Where the goods are as fit for the purposes for which goods of that kind are commonly bought as it is reasonable to expect having regard to any description applied to them, the price (if relevant) and all the other relevant circumstances: Sale of Goods Act 1979, s 14(6).

Mere right. A right of property without possession.

Merger. The sinking or drowning of a less estate in a greater, by reason that they both coincide and meet in one and the same person. Thus, if there is a tenant for years, and the reversion in fee simple descends to or is purchased by him, the term of years may be *merged* in the inheritance and cease to exist.

The Law of Property Act 1925, s 185 provides that there is no merger by operation of law only of any estate the beneficial interest in which would not be deemed to be merged or extinguished in equity.
See LAND LAW.

Merits. The substantial question in issue in an action or other proceeding.

Merton, Statute of. A statute of Henry III (1235), so called because it was passed at Merton, in Surrey.

Mesne. Middle, intermediate.
Mesne profits are profits of land taken by a tenant in wrongful possession, from the time that the wrongful possession commenced to the time of the trial of an action of ejectment brought against him.

Messuage. A house comprising the outbuildings, the orchard, and curtilage or courtyard and, according to the better opinion, the garden also.

Metric system. A decimal subdivision of weights and measures. See Sch 1 to the Weights and Measures Act 1985. The metric system is gradually being introduced into the United Kingdom. As to coinage, see the Decimal Currency Acts 1967 and 1969 and the Coinage Act 1971.

Metropolitan county. *See* COUNTY.

Michaelmas Day. *See* QUARTER DAYS.

Michaelmas sittings. *See* SITTINGS.

Michaelmas term. *See* SITTINGS.

Middle Temple. One of the Inns of Court.
See INNS OF COURT.

Middlesex Registry. A registry established in the reign of Queen Anne (1708) for the registration of deeds and wills affecting lands in the county of Middlesex. It was transferred to the Land Registry in 1891. The register is now closed for all purposes and accordingly no search may be made by the Chief Land Registrar or his officers or otherwise, and the Law of Property Act 1925, s 197 (making registration actual notice) has ceased to have effect as respects the register (see Middlesex Deeds Act 1940, s 1(1)).

Midsummer Day. *See* QUARTER DAYS.

Midwife. A woman who assists others at childbirth.

Midwives must be registered in a register kept by the Central Council for Nursing, Midwifery and Health Visiting: Nurses, Midwives and Health Visitors Act 1979, s 10. Local training committees are responsible for the training of midwives: ibid, s 9.

It is an offence to make a false claim that one is professionally qualified as a midwife: ibid, s 14.

M

Military courts. 1 Courts-martial, having jurisdiction to try and to punish offences committed against naval, military and air force law.

See COURT-MARTIAL.

2 The courts which, under the name of courts-martial, are used for dealing with offenders where a state of war actually exists.

See MARTIAL LAW.

Military will. A will made by a soldier on active service, without those forms which in ordinary cases are required by statute (see Wills Act 1837, s 11; see also Wills (Soldiers and Sailors) Act 1918).

Minister. 1 The holder of an office in the Government. He may be in the Cabinet, eg the Prime Minister, the Secretary of State for Foreign Affairs, etc, or not in the Cabinet, eg the Solicitor-General.

2 A clergyman. The term is generally used for non-conformist clergy.

See NONCONFORMISTS.

3 A foreign envoy, or minister plenipotentiary.

See PLENIPOTENTIARY.

Minor. A person under the age of 18 (see Family Law Reform Act 1969).

See GUARDIAN; INFANT.

Minor canons. Officers of a cathedral appointed to conduct the cathedral services. Their appointment is vested in the Chapter.

See CATHEDRAL; CHAPTER.

Minor interests. A term introduced under the REGISTERED LAND regime; major interests are those such as legal freehold or leasehold titles to land, whose registration forms the basis of the system; minor interests are lesser interests in land that may be protected by being registered against the title to the land to which the minor interest relates. The expression is defined by the Land Registration Act 1925, s 3 as 'the interests not capable of being disposed of or created by registered dispositions and capable of being overridden (whether or not a purchaser has notice thereof) by the proprietors unless protected as provided by this Act, and all rights and interests which are not registered or protected on the register and are not overriding interests, and include—

(i) in the case of land held on trust for sale, all interests and powers which are under the Law of Property Act 1925 capable of being overridden by the trustees for sale, whether or not such interests and powers are so protected; and

(ii) in the case of settled land, all interests and powers which are under the Settled Land Act 1925, and the Law of Property Act 1925, or either of them, capable of being overridden by the tenant for life or statutory owner, whether or not such interests and powers are so protected as aforesaid.'

See LAND LAW.

Minora regalia. The Queen's revenue, as opposed to her dignity and regal power.

Mint. The place where money is coined, now in Wales.

Minutes. 1 The record kept of a meeting.

2 *Of an order or judgment.* An outline of the order or judgment, drawn by one party and agreed to by the other party. Afterwards embodied in a formal order or judgment of the Court.

Mirror of Justice. Generally spoken of as the Mirror, or Mirrour. A work generally ascribed to the reign of Edward II. It is stated to have been written by Andrew Horne.

Misadventure. An unfortunate mischance arising out of a lawful act. It is a word generally used with reference to accidental homicide.

See CORONER'S VERDICT.

Miscarriage. 1 A failure of justice.

2 Abortion.

See ABORTION.

Mischief. The problem or situation to which a statute is addressed; thus to attend to the mischief of a statute is to attend to its object or purpose.

Misdemeanour. The lesser of the two categories of criminal offence at common law. An offence less than a felony.

See FELONY; CRIMINAL PROCEDURE.

Misdescription. A description of the subject matter of a contract which is incorrect or misleading in a material particular. Where substantial, the misdescription renders the contract voidable at the option of the party who is misled.

Misdirection. A wrongful direction of a Judge to a jury on a matter of law.

See NEW TRIALS.

Misfeasance. *See* MALFEASANCE.

Misprision (from the French *Mépris*). Contempt, neglect, or oversight.

Misprision of treason is a neglect or light account shown of treason by not revealing it to a judge or justice of the peace.

See TREASON.

Misrepresentation, ie *suggestio falsi*, either by words or by conduct. To found an action for tort the misrepresentation must be a false statement of fact, and not a mere broken promise. The statement must also be wilfully false: mere negligence in the making of false statements is not actionable (see *Derry v Peek* (1889) 14 App Cas 337).

See SUGGESTIO FALSI.

Innocent misrepresentation, ie when the statement is not known to be false, is a ground for relief against a contract if such statement furnished a material inducement to the plaintiff to enter into that contract (see generally Misrepresentation Act 1967).

See DECEIT; FRAUD.

Mistake. 1 In criminal law except in the case where proof of *mens rea* is unnecessary, *bona fide* mistake or ignorance as to matters of fact is available as a defence. Ignorance of law cannot be set up as a defence even by a foreigner, although it may be a ground for the mitigation of sentence. In cases where a particular intent or state of mind is of the essence of an offence, a mistaken but *bona fide* belief by a defendant that he had a right to do a particular act may be a complete defence as showing that he had no criminal intent.

2 In civil cases at Common Law, mistake was admitted as a foundation of relief in three cases only: (i) in actions 'for money had and received' to recover money paid under a mistake of fact (*see* UNJUST ENRICHMENT); (ii) in actions of deceit to recover damages in respect of a mistake induced by fraudulent misrepresentation (*see* MISREPRESENTATION); and (iii) as a defence in actions of contract where the mistake of fact was of such a nature as to preclude the formation of any contract in law, eg where there was a mutual mistake as to the subject matter of the contract, and therefore, no consensus *ad idem* by

the parties, or where the mistake was made as to the identity of one of the parties where such identity was an inducement to the other to enter into the contract, or where the mistake related to the nature of the contract under such circumstances as would, if the contract were embodied in a deed, justify a plea of *non est factum*.

See NON EST FACTUM.

3 In equity, mistake gives relief in a much wider range of cases than at Common Law, though it must be borne in mind that 'mistake', as a legal term on which a right to relief may be founded, has a much narrower meaning than as a popular expression. The relationship between the parties to a transaction may impose a duty on one party to inform the mind of the other party of all the material facts, and if, in such a case, the party owing such duty enters into a transaction with the party to whom the duty is owed, without informing him of all the material facts, the latter is entitled to relief on the ground of breach of duty.

Clearly proved and obvious mistakes in written instruments, etc, will also be relieved against by the Court. The rectification (*see* RECTIFICATION), setting aside, etc, of written instruments is part of the business assigned to the Chancery Division of the High Court.

Mitigation. Abatement of anything penal, or of damages.

An address in mitigation is a speech made by the defendant or his counsel to the Judge after verdict or plea of guilty, and which may be followed by a speech in *aggravation* from the opposing counsel.

As to damages, a plaintiff or claimant making a claim for damages for breach of contract cannot recover damages for any losses he might have avoided by reasonable efforts, ie for any losses he might have mitigated.

Mixed fund. A fund consisting of the proceeds of both real and personal property.

See REAL AND PERSONAL PROPERTY.

Mixed government. A form of government which combines the three usual forms of government, viz, monarchy, aristocracy, and democracy. The British Government is an instance.

Mixed property. 1 Property which, though falling under the definition of things real,

is attended with some of the legal qualities of things personal, eg *emblements*.
See EMBLEMENTS.

2 Property which, though falling under the definition of things personal, is attended with some of the legal qualities of things real, eg heirlooms.
See HEIRLOOM.

Mixed questions of law and fact. Cases in which a jury finds the facts and the Court decides, by the aid of established rules of law, what is the legal result of those facts.

M'Naghten rules. Rules which the courts apply to determine whether the evidence shows that a person is not guilty by reason of insanity. *R v M'Naghten* (1843) 10 CL & Fin 200.

Mobilia sequuntur personam. Movables follow the person.
See MOVABLES.

Moiety. One-half.

Money. A store of value and a medium of exchange which exists in units, or is denominated in units, which are units of account.

Money, payment of, into Court. *See* PAYMENT OF MONEY INTO COURT.

Money bill. A bill for granting aids and supplies to the Crown. It is defined in the Parliament Act 1911 as a public bill which in the opinion of the Speaker of the House of Commons contains only provisions dealing with finance and taxation.
See SPEAKERS OF THE HOUSES OF PARLIAMENT.

Money had and received. Common law formulation of a claim for restitution, eg where A paid money to B under the mistaken belief that it was due under a contract, A was entitled to recover a like sum from B under the 'action for money had and received to the plaintiff's use'.
See MISTAKE; RESTITUTION; UNJUST ENRICHMENT.

Money laundering. The process of making assets which are the proceeds of fraud or crime appear to have a legitimate source, eg by representing them to be the profits of a cash business, or via a series of sophisticated transfers between local and foreign companies so that their origin is obscure.

Money paid. Common law formulation of a claim for restitution, eg where A paid C in such a way that B was benefited, eg where A's paying C discharged B's debt, A would be

entitled to recover a like sum from B under the action for 'money paid'.
See RESTITUTION; UNJUST ENRICHMENT.

Monopolies and Mergers Commission.
A commission whose duty it is to investigate and report on any question referred to it with respect to (i) the existence of a monopoly situation; (ii) a newspaper merger; or (iii) the creation of a merger situation: Fair Trading Act 1973, s 5(1). A monopoly reference may be made to the Commission by the Director General of Fair Trading (ibid, s 50) or by the Secretary of State or by him and any Minister acting jointly (ibid, s 51). Such a reference may be limited to the facts (ibid, s 48), or not so limited (ibid, s 49). If the reference was made to the Director General of Fair Trading, the Commission must make a report to the Secretary of State: ibid, s 54(1). If the reference was made by a Minister, the report must be made to that Minister: ibid, s 54(1). The report must be laid before Parliament (ibid, s 83). It may be published in such manner as appears to the Minister to be appropriate (ibid, s 83).
See MONOPOLY SITUATION; INTELLECTUAL PROPERTY LAW.

Monopoly. A licence or privilege allowed by the Sovereign for the buying and selling, making, working, or using of anything to be enjoyed exclusively by the grantee. Monopolies were, by the Statute of Monopolies 1623, declared to be illegal and void, subject to certain exceptions specified in it, including patents in favour of the authors of new inventions.

The question whether a monopoly situation exists may be referred to the Monopolies and Mergers Commission.
See MONOPOLIES AND MERGERS COMMISSION; PATENT; INTELLECTUAL PROPERTY.

Monopoly situation. A situation existing in the supply of goods or services: Fair Trading Act 1973, ss 6 and 7. It exists in the case of the supply of goods where, eg at least one-quarter of all the goods of any description are supplied in the United Kingdom by one person: ibid, s 6(1)(a). It exists in the case of the supply of services where, eg at least one-quarter of that supply is made by one person: ibid, s 7(1)(a).
See MONOPOLIES AND MERGERS COMMISSION.

Month. A space of time containing by the week 28 days, and by the calendar 28, 30, or 31 days. At Common Law the meaning of the term 'month' is 28 days, otherwise called a *lunar month*. But, in ecclesiastical and commercial matters, a month is interpreted to mean a calendar month; also, by the Interpretation Act 1978, in an Act of Parliament it is to mean a calendar month. Also by the Law of Property Act 1925, s 61 the word 'month' in all deeds, contracts, wills, orders, and other instruments executed, made, or coming into operation after 1925, means a calendar month, unless the context otherwise requires.

Montreal Convention. An international convention signed on 23rd September 1971, concerning acts of violence against a person which might destroy or endanger the safety of aircraft or air navigation facilities. It was supplemented by a protocol signed on 24th February 1988 concerning acts at an airport serving international civil aviation. (See Aviation and Maritime Security Act 1990).

Monuments. *See* ANCIENT MONUMENTS.

Moot. An exercise, or arguing of cases, which was practised by students in the Inns of Court, to enable them to defend their clients. Hence, a *moot point* signifies a point open to argument and discussion.
See INNS OF COURT.

Moral hazard. A term describing facts which suggest that the proposed insured, by reason of his previous experience in matters relevant to the insurance, is not a person whose proposal can be accepted in the ordinary course of business and without special consideration, eg (i) where other insurers have refused to grant an insurance similar to the insurance proposed (see *Glicksman v Lancashire and General Assurance Co Ltd* [1927] AC 139, HL); (ii) where a proposer for a burglary policy has a criminal record (see *Schoolman v Hall* [1951] 1 Lloyd's Rep 139, CA).

Moral rights, in relation to copyright consist of (i) a right of the author of a copyright literary, dramatic, musical or artistic work, and of the director of a copyright film, to be identified as such when the work is performed in public or broadcast or when the film is shown in public or broadcast (Copyright, Designs and Patents Act 1988, s 77); (ii) the right of the author of such works to object to derogatory treatment of them (ibid, s 80). ('Derogatory treatment' means distortion or mutilation of the work prejudicial to the honour or reputation of the author or director (ibid, s 80(2)(b)). The moral rights continue to subsist as long as copyright subsists in the work (ibid, s 86(1)); and (iii) the right of a person not to have a literary, dramatic, musical work or artistic work falsely attributed to him as author, and not to have a film falsely attributed to him as director (ibid, s 84). (The right as to false attribution continues to subsist until 20 years after a person's death: ibid, s 86(1).)
See COPYRIGHT.

More or less. These words, appended to measurements in a conveyance of land, import a vagueness, within certain small limits, in the measurements of the land referred to: if there is a considerable deficiency, the purchaser will be entitled to an abatement of the price.

Morganatic marriage. The marriage which a prince or nobleman contracts with a woman of ordinary birth, on the express condition that the ordinary civil effects will not result from it, and that the wife and children shall be content with certain specified advantages. The restrictions relate only to the rank of the parties and succession to property, and do not affect the nature or validity of the marriage.

Mortgage (Lat *Mortuum vadium*, ie dead pledge). A conveyance, assignment, or demise of real or personal estate as security for the repayment of money borrowed.

If the conveyance, assignment, or demise is of land or any estate in it, the transaction is called a mortgage, notwithstanding that the creditor enters into possession. But the transfer of the possession of a movable chattel to secure the repayment of a debt is called not a *mortgage*, but a *pledge*. Mortgages are either (i) legal, including statutory; or (ii) equitable.

The term 'mortgage' is applied: (i) to the mortgage transaction; (ii) to the mortgage deed; and (iii) to the rights conferred by it on the mortgagee. By the Law of Property Act 1925, s 85, a mortgage of an estate in fee simple is only capable of being effected at law either by a demise for a term of years absolute, subject to a provision for cesser on redemption, or by a charge by deed expressed to be by way of legal mortgage. Any purported conveyance of an estate in fee simple by way of mortgage made after 1925 will operate as a demise to the mortgagee, in the case of a first mortgage, for a term

M

of 3,000 years; and in the case of a second or subsequent mortgage for a term one day longer than the term vested in the first or other mortgagee.

See CHARGE BY WAY OF LEGAL MORTGAGE.

Under s 86 a legal mortgage of leaseholds can now only be made by a sub-demise for a term of years absolute, less by one day than the term vested in the mortgagor, or by a charge by deed expressed to be by way of legal mortgage. The right to create equitable charges by deposit of documents or otherwise is, however, preserved.

Mortgagee. The creditor in whose favour a mortgage is created.

See MORTGAGE.

Mortgagor. The debtor who creates a mortgage.

See MORTGAGE.

Mortis causa donatio. *See* DONATIO MORTIS CAUSA.

Mortuary. A place for the temporary reception of the dead.

Motion. An application made to a Court or Judge *viva voce* in open court. Its object is to obtain an order or rule, directing some act to be done in favour of the applicant.

A motion must, in general, be preceded by notice to any party intended to be affected by it. Sometimes, however, it may be made *ex parte*.

See EX PARTE, 1.

Motor Insurers Bureau. A company, whose members are motor insurers, formed in 1946. In 1972 the Secretary of State for the Environment and the Motor Insurers Bureau entered into agreements to secure compensation for the victims of road accidents in cases where, notwithstanding the provisions of the Road Traffic Act 1972, they were deprived of compensation through the drivers of the vehicles being uninsured or untraced.

Movables. Goods, furniture etc, which may be moved from place to place.

Multiple occupation, house in. *See* HOUSE IN MULTIPLE OCCUPATION.

Multiplicity of suits or **actions.** Where several different suits or actions are brought on the same issue. See Supreme Court Act 1981, s 49.

See CONSOLIDATION ORDER.

Municipal corporation. The corporation of a borough, consisting of a mayor, aldermen and burgesses. By the Local Government Act 1972, s 1(1) the municipal corporation of every borough outside Greater London ceased to exist on 1st April 1974 (see ibid, s 20(6) as to Wales). Their functions were transferred from the former borough councils to county or district councils. London borough councils were retained.

Municipal law. The law of a municipality. The expression is, however, generally used to denote the law of a particular State as opposed to the law of nations or international law.

See INTERNATIONAL LAW; PUBLIC INTERNATIONAL LAW.

Murder. Unlawful homicide committed with 'malice aforethought', express or implied. Express malice exists where the person killing does so with the *intention* of causing death or grievous bodily harm. Implied malice exists where the person killing does not actually intend to kill or do grievous bodily harm, yet intentionally does an act which to his knowledge is likely to cause such death, etc.

The death penalty for murder was abolished for a trial period by the Murder (Abolition of Death Penalty) Act 1965, the Act finally being made permanent by affirmative resolutions of both Houses of Parliament in December 1969.

All murders are now punishable with imprisonment for life.

See HOMICIDE; MANSLAUGHTER; PROVOCATION; SUICIDE.

Mushrooms. By the Theft Act 1968, s 4(3) the picking of mushrooms growing wild on another person's land is not stealing, unless picked for sale. Wild flowers and fruit (as, eg blackberries) are included in the subsection. 'Mushroom' includes any fungus.

Musical work. A work consisting of music, exclusive of any words or action intended to be sung, spoken or performed with music: Copyright, Designs and Patents Act 1988, s 3(1).

Mutatis mutandis. With the necessary changes.

Mute. Speechless, a person who refuses to speak. The Court may order the proper officer to enter a plea of 'not guilty' on behalf of the prisoner standing mute (see the Criminal Law Act 1967, s 6(1)(c)).

Mutiny. A combination between two or more persons subject to service law to overthrow or resist lawful authority in Her Majesty's forces, etc. For the full statutory definition see

M

Army Act 1955, s 31, Air Force Act 1955, s 31, and Naval Discipline Act 1957, s 8.

Mutual debts. Debts due on both sides, as between two persons.

See SET-OFF.

Mutual promises. Concurrent considerations which support one another, unless one or the other is void. In that case, as there is no consideration on one side, no contract can arise. *See* CONSIDERATION.

Mutual wills. Wills made by two persons who leave their estate reciprocally to the survivor.

Mutuality. Reciprocity of obligation, two persons being mutually bound.

Mystery. An art, trade, or occupation involving the practice of a particular skill, which formerly was learned by apprenticeship to a master. Medieval guilds were typically formed by the association of masters of a particular art or mystery.

M

NRA. The National Rivers Authority.
See NATIONAL RIVERS AUTHORITY.

Name. Either christian or surname. A person
may change his or her surname and christian
name, but the latter strictly only by Act of
Parliament or on confirmation by a bishop
or by addition or adoption. See the review of
the law in *Re Parrott* [1946] Ch 183. See also
Business Names Act 1985 in relation to the
names of companies.

Name and arms clause. A clause sometimes
inserted in a settlement or a will which
directs a person to assume the name and arms
of the settlor or testator or else to forfeit the
benefits which would otherwise be conferred
on him. Many such clauses have been held to
be void for uncertainty.
See TRUST.

'Names'. The members of a syndicate of
underwriters who do not take any active
part in the business, but authorise one of the
members to do so, and to underwrite policies
in their names (see *Thompson v Adams* (1889)
23 QBD 361 at 362 (per Mathew J)).
See SYNDICATE; UNDERWRITER.

National Audit Office. An office consisting
of the Comptroller and Auditor General
and his staff: National Audit Act 1983, s 3,
Sch 2.
See COMPTROLLER AND AUDITOR GENERAL.

National Debt. The debt due by the nation
to individual creditors, whether our own
people or foreigners. The National Debt is in
part *funded* and in part *unfunded*; the former
being that which is secured to the national
creditor on the public funds; the latter, that
which is not so provided for. The unfunded
debt is comparatively of small amount, and
is generally secured by Exchequer bills and
bonds.
See CONSOLIDATED FUND.

National Health Service. The health service
first established under the National Health
Service Act 1946. The service was at first
free, but charges have been imposed from
time to time under various amending Acts.
The service was reorganised by the National
Health Service Act 1977.

National Health Service trusts. Trusts
established:
(i) to assume responsibility for the
ownership and management of hospitals
or other establishments or facilities which
were previously managed or provided
by Regional District or Special Health
Authorities; or
(ii) to provide and manage hospitals or other
establishments or facilities: National
Health Service and Community Care Act
1990, s 5(1).

National Insurance. A system of insurance to
which every person contributes a weekly
amount (part being paid by employers) with
corresponding benefits in the case of sickness,
unemployment, retirement, etc (see Social
Security Contributions and Benefits Act 1992).

National Parks. Extensive tracts of country
as to which it appears to the Countryside
Commission that by reason of:
(i) their natural beauty and
(ii) the opportunities they afford for open-air
recreation, having regard both to their
character and to their position in relation
to centres of population,
it is essentially desirable that they should be
designated as National Parks for the purpose
of preserving and enhancing their natural
beauty and promoting their enjoyment by
the public: National Parks and Access to the
Countryside Act 1949, s 1.

National Rivers Authority. An authority
responsible for flood defence under the Water

Resources Act 1991 and the Land Drainage Act 1991.

National Trust. The National Trust for Places of Historic Interest or Natural Beauty, established under the National Trust Acts 1907 to 1971, for the general purposes of promoting the permanent preservation of lands and tenements of beauty or historic interest, their natural features, animal and plant life, etc.

Nations, law of. See JUS GENTIUM; LAW OF NATIONS.

Natural affection. Often used in deeds for the motive or consideration for a gift arising from relationship. In many cases this consideration is not sufficient to 'sustain a promise', ie to give an action to the promisee against the promisor for its non-fulfilment.
See CONSIDERATION.

Natural allegiance. The perpetual allegiance due from natural-born subjects, as distinguished from *local* allegiance, which is temporary only.
See ALLEGIANCE.

Natural child. The child of one's body, whether legitimate or illegitimate. The word, however, in popular language, is usually applied only to an illegitimate child.

Natural justice. See ADMINISTRATIVE LAW.

Natural law. The law as determined by man's human, spiritual and, specially, moral nature, as opposed to the *positive law*; hence a theory of law which emphasises the connection of law to morality.
See JURISPRUDENCE; POSITIVE LAW.

Natural persons. Persons in the ordinary sense of the word, as opposed to *artificial* persons or corporations.
See PERSON.

Natural-born subjects included by the Common Law:

1 All English, Scottish, Irish or Welsh persons born within the United Kingdom, or in the Commonwealth and dependencies, except such as were born of alien enemies in time of war.
See ALIEN ENEMY.
2 The children of the Sovereign, wherever born.
3 The children of this country's ambassadors born abroad.

The law relating to British nationality is now contained in the British Nationality Act 1981 and the Immigration Act 1971.

See ALIEN; BRITISH SUBJECT.

Naturalisation. The giving to a foreigner the status of a natural-born citizen. This may be done by a certificate of the Secretary of State, on his taking the oath of allegiance. For conditions of such naturalisation see the British Nationality Act 1981, s 6 and Sch 1.
See ALIEN; ALLEGIANCE.

Nature Conservancy Council for England. A council whose functions are the establishment and maintenance of nature reserves and the provision of advice on conservation policies: Environmental Protection Act 1990, s 128.
See NATURE RESERVE.

Nature Conservancy Council for Scotland. A council whose functions are the establishment and maintenance of nature reserves and the provision of advice on conservation policies: Environmental Protection Act 1990, s 128.
See NATURE RESERVE.

Nature reserve. Land managed for the purpose of:
(i) providing special opportunities for the study of and research into matters relating to the fauna and flora and the physical conditions in which they live, and for the study of geological and physiographical features of special interest in the area; or
(ii) preserving flora, fauna or geological or physiographical features of special interest in the area,
or for both those purposes: National Parks and Access to the Countryside Act 1949, s 15.

Nautical assessors. Assessors sitting in the High Court or Court of Appeal to assist the Judges concerned.

They are usually Elder Brethren of Trinity House (see TRINITY HOUSE). They only advise the Court on matters of nautical skill on which information is desired, and it is the duty of the Court, having received that information, to exercise its own judgment and decide the case before it on its own responsibility (see *The Australia* [1927] AC 145, HL).

Nautical mile. A mile of 1,852 metres: Territorial Sea Act 1987, s 1(7).

Naval Discipline Act. The method of ordering seamen in the royal fleet, and keeping up a regular discipline there, was first directed by certain express rules, articles and orders, enacted by the authority of Parliament soon after the Restoration. The Act at present in force is the Naval Discipline Act 1957, as amended by the Armed Forces Act 1971.

Ne exeat regno (that he leave not the kingdom). A prerogative writ whereby a person is prohibited from leaving the realm, even though his usual residence is in foreign parts. The writ is directed to the sheriff of the county in which the defendant is resident, commanding him to take bail from the defendant not to quit England without leave of the Court. It is granted on motion, supported by affidavit showing that a sum of money is due from the defendant to the plaintiff, or will be due on taking accounts between them, and that the defendant intends to abscond.

The writ is now applied in civil matters only, and is almost superseded by orders under the Debtors Act 1869, s 6.

Nec vi, nec clam, nec precario. Neither by force, stealth, nor permission. A right, such as an easement of way, cannot be acquired by long user (ie by prescription), if the use was attended with force, or was concealed, or was with the permission of the title holder against whom the right is sought.
See PRESCRIPTION.

Necessaries. Goods suitable in life of a minor or other person concerned and to his actual requirements at the time of sale and delivery: Sale of Goods Act 1979, s 3(3). Where necessaries are sold and delivered to a minor or to a person who by reason of mental incapacity or drunkenness is incompetent to contract, he must pay a reasonable price for them: ibid, s 3(2).

Necessity. A constraint on the will, whereby a person is urged to do that of which his judgment disapproves, and is thereby excused from responsibility which might be otherwise incurred. It includes:
1 The obligation of civil subjection.
2 In certain cases also *duress per minas*, which impels a person to act in a given way from fear of death or personal injury.
See DURESS.
3 Where a man is constrained to choose the lesser of two evils.
4 Agent of.
See AGENT OF NECESSITY.

Negligence. The tortious failing to take adequate care so as to cause injury or loss to another, and which exposes the negligent party to an action for damages. In order to establish liability for negligence, it must be shown that the defendant owed a duty of care to the plaintiff (claimant), that the defendant fell below the standard of care appropriate to the circumstances in which the duty was owed, and that the plaintiff's injury or loss was caused by the defendant's breach of the standard of care, ie the injury was not too 'remote' in terms of CAUSATION.
See TORT; CONTRIBUTORY NEGLIGENCE.

Negligent escape is where a prisoner escapes without a prison officer's knowledge or consent. It is thus opposed to a *voluntary* escape, which is an escape by consent or connivance of the officer.
See ESCAPE.

Negotiable. Subject to a 'bona fide purchase rule', ie a person who gives good value in exchange for a negotiable property, such as a negotiable instrument or money, without notice of any defect in the title of the transferor (eg that it was acquired by theft or fraud), gets good title to the property. An exception to the 'nemo dat' principle.
See BONA FIDE PURCHASER; NEMO DAT QUOD NON HABET; NEGOTIABLE INSTRUMENTS.

Negotiable instruments. Instruments purporting to represent so much money, in which the property passes by mere delivery, eg bills of exchange, promissory notes, etc (see Bills of Exchange Act 1882, ss 31, 32). Such instruments constitute an exception to the general rule that a man cannot give a better title than he has himself.
See BILL OF EXCHANGE; PROMISSORY NOTE.

Negotiate. To transfer for value a negotiable instrument.
See NEGOTIABLE; NEGOTIABLE INSTRUMENTS.

Negotiorum gestor. A person who does an act to his own inconvenience for the advantage of another, but without the authority of the latter, or any promise to indemnify him for his trouble. The *negotiorum gestor* was entitled, by Roman law, to recover compensation for his trouble; and this is so in English law in cases of salvage, and in some other cases.
See SALVAGE; UNJUST ENRICHMENT.

Nemine contradicente (abbrev *nem con*). No one contradicting; ie unanimously; a phrase used with special reference to votes and resolutions of the House of Commons; *nemine dissentiente* being the corresponding expression as to unanimous votes of the House of Lords.

Nemo agit in se ipsum. No one brings legal proceedings against himself.

Nemo dat quod non habet. No one can give that which he has not (ie no one can give a better title than he has).
See NEGOTIABLE INSTRUMENTS; BONA FIDE PURCHASER; PROPERTY.

Nemo de domo sua extrahi debet. No one can be forcibly taken from his own house.

Nemo debet bis vexari pro eadem causa. No one should be vexed twice for the same cause.

Nemo debet judex esse in causa sua propria. No one ought to be a Judge in his own cause.
See INTEREST, 3.

Nemo potest esse simul actor et judex. No one can be at the same time suitor and Judge.

Nemo tenetur ad impossibilia. No one can be held to an impossible contract.

Nemo tenetur se ipsum accusare. No one is compelled to accuse himself.

New Inn. One of the Inns of Chancery.
See INNS OF CHANCERY.

New style. *See* OLD STYLE.

New town site. A site in an area designated by the Secretary of State which he considers expedient in the national interest for the development as such a town: New Towns Act 1981, s 1.

The Act controls the building of such towns. Examples of new towns are Crawley, Harlow, and Milton Keynes.

New trials have been granted in civil cases on the following amongst other grounds:

1 That the Judge misdirected the jury on a point of law.
2 That he admitted or rejected evidence improperly.
3 That he improperly discharged the jury.
4 That he refused to amend the record when an amendment ought to have been made.
5 That the defendant did not receive due notice of trial.
6 That the successful party misbehaved.
7 That the jury, or any of them, have misbehaved, eg by drawing lots for the verdict.
8 That the damages are excessive.
9 That the damages are too slight.
10 That the verdict has been obtained by a surprise.

11 That the witnesses for the successful party are manifestly shown to have committed perjury.
12 That the verdict was against the weight of evidence.
13 That new and material facts have come to light since the trial.
14 Default or misconduct of officer of court.
15 Absence of counsel or solicitor.
16 That one of several issues was wrongly decided.
17 Where there has been a previous new trial.

A new trial is not to be ordered on the ground of misdirection, or of the improper admission or rejection of evidence, or because the verdict of the jury was not taken on a question which the Judge at the trial was not asked to leave to them, unless in the opinion of the Court of Appeal some substantial wrong or miscarriage has been thereby occasioned.

A new trial is not the same thing as a *venire de novo*, which is a much more ancient proceeding and is applicable where the proceedings in the lower court were a nullity.

For the Court of Appeal's power to order a new trial in criminal cases, see Criminal Appeal Act 1968, ss 7, 8.

Next friend. A term previously given to an adult under whose protection an infant institutes an action or other legal proceeding, and who is responsible for the conduct and the costs of it.
See INFANT; LITIGATION FRIEND.

Mentally disordered persons also sue by their guardian or next friend, and defend by their guardian *ad litem*.
See GUARDIAN.

In accordance with the Civil Procedure Rules 1998, a next friend or guardian *ad litem* is now referred to as a litigation friend.

Next of kin. 1 An expression generally used for the persons who, by reason of kindred were on the death of a person intestate, before 1926, entitled to his personal estate and effects under the Statute of Distributions. For the rules of succession on intestacy, see Administration of Estates Act 1925.
See AFFINITY.

2 Those who are, lineally or collaterally, related in the nearest degree to a given person.

Next presentation. The right to present to a living on the next vacancy. The purchase of

N

the next presentation to a vacant benefice is illegal and void; so is the purchase by a clergyman, either in his own name or in another's, of the next presentation, simply with the view of presenting himself to the living, though the benefice is not vacant at the time of purchase. And see further restrictions under Benefices Act 1898 and Patronage (Benefices) Measure 1986.
See SIMONY.

Night. Night was at one time accounted to be the time from sunset to sunrise.

By the Night Poaching Act 1828, s 15 night is to be considered to commence at the expiration of one hour after sunset, and to conclude at the beginning of the last hour before sunrise.

In the Customs and Excise Management Act 1979, s 1(1) it is defined as the period between 11 pm and 5 am.

No case to answer. Following the presentation of the case for the prosecution, the defendant, in the absence of the jury, may make submissions contending that the prosecution failed to present even a *prima facie* case for the defendant's guilt, and as such, there is no case for the defendant to answer. If the submission is accepted, the verdict of not guilty is entered.

'No claim' bonus. A reduction from the renewal premium in accordance with a specified scale allowed by motor insurers where no claim has been made under the policy.

Nobility. The rank or dignity of peerage comprising—(i) Dukes. (ii) Marquesses. (iii) Earls. (iv) Viscounts. (v) Barons. (vi) Life peers, who rank as barons.

Nolens volens. Whether willing or unwilling.

Nolo contendere. I do not wish to dispute/ discuss (the accusation). An implied admission of guilt.

Nominal damages. A trifling sum recovered by verdict in a case where, although the action is maintainable, it is nevertheless the opinion of the Court that the plaintiff has not suffered substantial damage.

Nominal partner. *See* OSTENSIBLE PARTNER.

Nominal share capital. The nominal value of the shares which a company is authorised by its memorandum of association to issue.

Nominatim. By name. Often opposed to *in virtute officii*, in virtue of an office.

Nomination. 1 Of candidates at an election (see Representation of the People Act 1983, and Part III of the Local Government Act 1972).
2 By a member of a Friendly Society, of a person to whom his interest is to go at his death (see Friendly Societies Act 1992).

Nomination to a living. A power that a person has by virtue of a manor, or otherwise, to appoint a clerk to a patron of a benefice, to be by him presented to the Ordinary.
See ORDINARY, 2.

Also called an advowson.
See ADVOWSON.

Nominee shareholder. A person who is registered as the owner of shares in a company but who, in fact, holds them on behalf of and to the order of another person.
See BARE TRUST; TRUST.

Non compos mentis. Not of sound mind. A phrase sometimes used of mentally disordered persons, and less frequently of persons suffering from temporary loss of memory or drunkenness.

Non constat (it is not evident). This phrase is often used as meaning that an alleged inference is not deducible from given premises.
See NON SEQUITUR.

Non dat qui non habet. He cannot give who has not.

Non est factum. The plea in an action on a deed or other contract denying the *fact* of its having been executed.

Non sequitur (it does not follow). An expression used in argument to indicate that the premises do not warrant the inference drawn from them.

Non-access. *See* ACCESS.

Non-cumulative preference shares. Where preference shares are non-cumulative, and the dividend has not been paid on them in a particular year, the deficiency is not made up out of the profits of subsequent years.
See PREFERENCE SHARES; CUMULATIVE PREFERENCE SHARES.

Non-feasance. Failure to act; usually failure to carry out an obligation, for the consequences of which one might be liable.
See MALFEASANCE.

Non-metropolitan county. *See* COUNTY.

Non-negotiable, not negotiable. If a cheque is crossed with these words, the person taking it has not and is not capable of giving a better title to the cheque than that which the person from whom he took it had (see Bills of Exchange Act 1882, s 8).

See CHEQUE; BILL OF EXCHANGE; NEGOTIABLE INSTRUMENTS.

Non-trading partnership. A partnership not engaged in the buying and selling of goods: *Higgins v Beauchamp* [1914–1915] All ER Rep 937.

Nonage. The absence of full age, which is for most purposes 18 years.

Nonconformists. Dissenters from the Church of England; a word used more especially of the Protestant bodies who have seceded from the Church of England.

Northstead, Manor of. A manor, the stewardship of which is treated as an office of profit under the Crown, and, therefore, disqualifies the holder from membership of the House of Commons. A member wishing to retire from the House may therefore apply for this stewardship, or for that of the Chiltern Hundreds (see House of Commons Disqualification Act 1975, s 4).

See CHILTERN HUNDREDS.

Noscitur a sociis. The meaning of a doubtful word may be ascertained by reference to the meaning of words associated with it.

Not proven. A verdict of a jury in a Scottish criminal trial, to the effect that the guilt of the accused is not made out, though his innocence is not clear. The legal effect of such a verdict is the same as that of a verdict of Not Guilty.

Notary, or **Notary public** (Lat *Registrarius, Actuarius, Notarius*). One who attests deeds or writings to make them authentic in another country. He is generally a solicitor.

It is the office of a notary, among other things, at the request of the holder of a bill of exchange of which acceptance or payment is refused, to *note* and *protest* it.

See BILL OF EXCHANGE; NOTING A BILL; PROTEST.

Note of hand. A promissory note.

See PROMISSORY NOTE.

Notice. A word which sometimes means knowledge, either actual, or imputed by construction of law; sometimes a formal notification of some fact, or some intention of the party giving the notice; sometimes the expression of a demand or requisition. See the following entries.

See CONSTRUCTIVE NOTICE.

Notice of dishonour. A notice that a bill of exchange has been dishonoured, ie not accepted by the drawee. This notice the holder of a dishonoured bill is bound to give promptly to those to whom, as drawers (*see* DRAWER), or indorsers (*see* INDORSER), he wishes to have recourse for payment of the bill. The rules as to notice of dishonour are contained in the Bill of Exchange Act 1882, s 49.

See BILL OF EXCHANGE; DISHONOUR.

Notice of motion. *See* MOTION.

Notice of title. Where an intending mortgagee or purchaser has knowledge, by himself or his agent, of some right or title in the property adverse to that of his mortgagor or vendor. Thus, one speaks of a *bona fide* purchaser for valuable consideration *without notice*; meaning that the purchaser of the property has paid the price to those who, he believes, have the right to sell.

'Notice' does not of necessity imply actual knowledge. For whatever is sufficient to put a man of ordinary prudence on inquiry is constructive notice of everything to which that inquiry might have led, eg negligence in investigating a title will not exempt a purchaser from responsibility for knowledge of facts stated in the deeds which are necessary to establish the title.

In reference to real property, the doctrine of notice is mainly important as between a prior owner or incumbrancer of an *equitable* interest in the land, and a subsequent purchaser of the *legal* estate. The subsequent purchaser will have priority if, when he advances his money, he has no notice of the equitable incumbrance; but not otherwise.

As between incumbrancers on a fund in the hands of trustees, it is notice to the trustees which regulates the respective priorities of the incumbrancers; so that a prior incumbrancer neglecting to give notice of his claim will be postponed to a subsequent incumbrancer who gives notice. The Law of Property Act 1925, s 199, provides that a purchaser is not to be prejudicially affected by notice of rights capable of being registered under the Land Charges Act 1925, but not, in fact,

registered (see also Law of Property Act 1925, s 44(5), (8)).
See BONA FIDE PURCHASER.

Notice to quit. A notice often required to be given by landlord to tenant, or by tenant to landlord, before the tenancy can be terminated. In cases of a tenancy from year to year, the notice required is generally a six months' notice. The length of notice may vary according to special agreement between the parties or by local custom, or by statute: eg under the Agricultural Holdings Act 1986, s 25, which requires written notice of not less than one year in cases where the Act applies (see also Landlord and Tenant Act 1954, s 69).

Notice to third party. *See* THIRD PARTY.

Noting a bill. When a bill of exchange is not duly paid on presentation the holder applies to a notary public (*see* NOTARY), who again presents the bill; if not paid, he makes a memorandum of the non-payment, which is called *noting the bill*. Such a memorandum by the officer consists of his initials, the month, day and year, and his charges for minuting; and is considered as the preparatory step to a protest (see Bills of Exchange Acts 1882 to 1917).
See PROTEST, 3.

Nova statuta (new statutes). A name sometimes given to the statutes passed since the beginning of the reign of Edward III.

Novation. The substitution of a new obligation for an old one, or of a new debtor for an old one, with the consent of the creditor. Essentially a mutual agreement to terminate one contract and replace it with another.

Novels (Lat *Novellæ Constitutiones*).
The Constitutions of the Emperor Justinian, published after the completion of the Code.
See CORPUS JURIS CIVILIS.

Novus actus interveniens. A new act intervening. If the chain of causation between a person's act and the damage done is broken by the intervening act of a third person, he will not be liable for the damage unless it could be foreseen that it would necessarily follow from his original act.

Nude contract, or **Nudum pactum.**
A bare promise of a thing without any 'consideration' or equivalent.
See CONSIDERATION.

Nuisance. That which unlawfully annoys or damages another. Nuisances are of two kinds:

(i) public or common nuisances, which affect the public and are an annoyance to all, or at least to an indefinite number, of the Queen's subjects and typically amount to the interference with the exercise of the Queen's subjects of a common right, eg the obstruction of a highway preventing people from exercising their right to pass along it; the remedy is usually by indictment;
(ii) private nuisances, a species of tort, which cause special damage to particular persons, or a limited and *definite* number of persons, and do not amount to trespasses, eg where one man so uses his own property as to injure another; typical examples of nuisances are the creation of excessive noise, smells, smoke, and so on, which materially affect one's neighbours in their enjoyment of their land in the normal way: the remedy in this case is usually by action for an injunction and damages.
See TORT.

Nullity of marriage. A matrimonial suit instituted for the purpose of obtaining a decree declaring a supposed marriage null and void, eg on the ground that one of the parties is impotent in which case the marriage is voidable, or on the ground that it is a bigamous marriage in which case it is void.
   See Matrimonial Causes Act 1973, ss 11 and 12, which respectively set out fully the grounds on which a marriage is either void, or voidable.

Nullius filius (the son of no man).
An expression sometimes applied to a bastard.
See BASTARD.

Nullum crimen sine lege. No crime without law, ie no prosecution for an act unless, before its commission, there existed a law making it an offence. One aspect of the RULE OF LAW principle.

Nullum tempus occurrit regi. Time does not run against the Crown. As regards the criminal law, this expresses the principle that there is no limitation period for the prosecution of a crime. In the case of non-criminal law, this rule expressed the particular position of the Crown as litigant, and is modified by the Limitation Act 1980, s 37 of which applies the Act (with some exceptions) to the Crown and the Duke of Cornwall.

Nunc pro tunc. Now for, or to, then; meaning that a judgment is entered, or document enrolled, so as to have the same legal force and effect as if it had been entered or enrolled on an earlier day.

Nuncupative will. A will declared by a testator before a sufficient number of witnesses and afterwards reduced into writing. Nuncupative wills are not allowed, except in the case of soldiers and sailors on active service (see Wills (Soldiers and Sailors) Act 1918).

See MILITARY WILL.

N

O

OECD. *See* ORGANISATION FOR ECONOMIC CO-OPERATION AND DEVELOPMENT.

O.n.o. 'Or near offer'.

O yes. *See* OYEZ.

Oath. An oath is required by law for many purposes. The Oaths Act 1888, in certain circumstances, allows an affirmation instead of an oath to be made in all places and for all purposes where an oath is required by law. *See* AFFIRMATION.

Oath of allegiance. An oath to bear true allegiance to the Sovereign, required from most officers of the Crown, and for persons granted a certificate of naturalisation. *See* ALLEGIANCE; NATURALISATION.

Obiter dictum. A dictum, ie statement, of a Judge on a point not directly relevant to deciding the case before him. *See* RATIO DECIDENDI.

Objects clause. A clause in the memorandum of association setting out the objects of the company. *See* MEMORANDUM OF ASSOCIATION.

    The memorandum of every company must state the objects of the company (see Companies Act 1985, s 2(1)(c)). The company has power to alter the objects clause by special resolution (see ibid, s 4).

Objects of a power, objects of a trust. Where property is settled on trust and a power under the terms of the trust is given to any person or persons to appoint property among a limited class, the members of the class are called the *objects of the power*. Thus, if a parent has a power to appoint a fund among his children, the children are called the objects of the power. Similarly, those persons who are entitled to receive property under the terms of the trust are called the *objects of the trust*. *See* POWER; TRUST.

Obligation. 1 Legal or moral duty as opposed to physical compulsion. Legal obligations may exist by virtue of law, eg the obligation to take care so as not to negligently injure others, or may be voluntarily undertaken, as with contractual obligations.
2 A bond containing a penalty, with a condition annexed, for the payment of money, performance of covenants, or the like. *See* BOND.

Obligor. The person bound by an obligation to another person called the *obligee*, who is entitled to the benefit of the bond or obligation. *See* BOND.

Obscenity. For the purposes of the Obscene Publications Act 1959 and 1964 an article (book, record, film, picture, etc) is deemed to be obscene if its effect is such as to tend to deprave or corrupt persons who are likely to read, see, or hear the matter contained or embodied in it. Publication of any such article is an offence, punishable with a fine or imprisonment or both; such publication includes distributing, circulating, letting on hire, etc, or showing it, playing it, etc.

    In proceedings under the Act there is a defence that publication of the article in question is justified as being for the public good on the ground that it is in the interests of science, literature, art, or learning, or of other objects of general concern (see ibid, s 4).

Obstruction. A hindering, eg (i) of a police constable in the execution of his duty (see Police Act 1964, s 51(3)); (ii) of the free passage along a highway (see Highways Act 1980, s 137(1)).

Occupancy. The taking possession of those things which before belonged to nobody.

Occupier. The person residing or having the right to reside in or on any house, land or place.

Occupier's liability. The liability of occupiers to third parties entering their premises, eg for injuries suffered due to accidents caused by the premises' disrepair; see Occupiers' Liability Act 1957 and Occupiers' Liability Act 1984.

Offence. An act or omission punishable under the criminal law (see *Horsfield v Brown* [1932] KB 355 at 367, per Macnaghten J).
See CRIMINAL LAW.

Offensive trade. The trade of a blood boiler, blood drier, bone boiler, fat extractor, fat melter, fellmonger, glue maker, gut scraper, rag or bone dealer, size dealer, soap boiler, tallow melter, or tripe boiler: Public Health Act 1936, s 107(1).

Such trades are restricted in urban areas: ibid, s 107.

Offensive weapon. Any article made or adapted for use for causing injury to the person, or intended by the person having it with him for such use by him. It is an offence under the Prevention of Crime Act 1953 to carry such a weapon without lawful authority or reasonable excuse. A similar definition is to be found in the Theft Act 1968, s 10.

Offer. An expression of readiness to do something (eg to purchase or sell), which, if followed by the unconditional acceptance of another person, results in a contract.
See CONTRACT LAW.

As to the offer of shares or debentures in a company, see Companies Act 1985, s 45.
See SHARE; DEBENTURE, 2.

Offer to settle, offer of settlement. An offer made by one party to a legal proceeding to another to settle the case on particular terms. The offer is made by way of notice to the other side and, if accepted, concludes the legal proceeding. If the offer is not accepted, the court may take into consideration the offer in its award of costs. See Civil Procedure Rules 1998, Part 36.

Off-going crop. *See* AWAY-GOING CROP.

Office. A type of incorporeal hereditament, consisting in the right to exercise a public or private employment. But, in the more limited sense, it is a right which entitles a person to act in the affairs of others without their appointment or permission.
See INCORPOREAL HEREDITAMENT.

Office copy. A copy, made under the sanction of a public office, of any deed, record, or other instrument in writing deposited in it.

Office of profit. A paid office under the Crown. Certain offices still carry disqualification from sitting in the Commons (see ss 1, 4 of, and Sch 1 to, the House of Commons Disqualification Act 1975).
See CHILTERN HUNDREDS; NORTHSTEAD, MANOR OF.

Official custodian for charities. An officer appointed under the Charities Act 1960, s 3 to act as a trustee for charities in the cases provided for by the Act.

Official liquidator. The Official Receiver, or one of them nominated by the Secretary of State for Trade and Industry, in case of an order for the compulsory winding up of a company, is to bring and defend suits and actions in the name of the company, and generally to do all things necessary for the winding up of the affairs of the company, until he or any other person on the application of the creditors or contributories is appointed by the Court as liquidator. If he is appointed he is then called Official Receiver and Liquidator (see Insolvency Act 1986, s 136).
See LIQUIDATOR.

Official log book. A log book in a form approved by the Secretary of State to be kept in every ship registered in the United Kingdom (see Merchant Shipping Act 1970, s 68(1)).
See LOG BOOK.

Official Petitioner. An officer whose duty it is to discharge, in relation to cases in which a criminal bankruptcy order is made, the functions assigned to him under the Insolvency Act 1986 (see Insolvency Act 1986, s 1(1)). The Director of Public Prosecutions is the Official Petitioner (see ibid, s 1(1)).
See DIRECTOR OF PUBLIC PROSECUTIONS.
As to such functions, see ibid, s 1(2).
See CRIMINAL BANKRUPTCY ORDER.

Official receivers. Officials appointed by the Secretary of State, who act as interim receivers and managers of bankrupts' estates (see Insolvency Act 1986, ss 399–401).

Official Referees' business. Any cause or matter commenced in the Chancery Division or Queen's Bench Division
(i) which involves a prolonged examination of documents or accounts, or a technical, scientific or local investigation; or

(ii) which it is desirable in the interests of one or more of the parties on grounds of expedition, economy or convenience or otherwise to be dealt with as such business: RSC 1965, Ord 36, r 1.

Official secrets. Espionage, and the unauthorised obtaining or disclosure of official information, are offences under the Official Secrets Acts 1911 to 1989. The Acts have been extended by the European Communities Act 1972 to cover the communication of atomic secrets to unauthorised persons (see ibid, s 11(2)). The Official Secrets Act 1989 prohibits disclosure of any information by a person who is or has been a member of the security and intelligence services.

Official Solicitor. An officer of the Supreme Court who acts for persons suffering under disability, etc (see Supreme Court Act 1981, s 90).

Offshore. A term used by tax, trusts, and private banking lawyers to describe foreign jurisdictions, the employment of the financial services industries of which can result in advantages for 'onshore' residents, ie residents in the home jurisdiction, in terms of tax, estate planning for death, etc.

Old Bailey. *See* CENTRAL CRIMINAL COURT.

Old style. The mode of reckoning time which prevailed until 1752. This method (based on the Julian calendar, so-called from its introduction into the Roman Empire by Julius Caesar) differed from the *New Style* at present in use in the following particulars:

1 The year commenced on the 25th March, instead of, as now, on the 1st January.
2 The reckoning of days was based on the assumption that every fourth year was a leap-year, no exception being admitted; instead of, as now, 97 leap-years in 400 years.
3 The rules for determining the feast of Easter were far less elaborate than at present.
The New Style was introduced by the Calendar (New Style) Act 1750. A similar calendar, the Gregorian, introduced by Pope Gregory XIII, had prevailed in the Roman Catholic countries of the Continent since 1582.

Oleron, Laws of. A code of maritime laws compiled in the 12th century by Richard I at the isle of Oleron in the bay of Aquitaine, on the coast of France, then part of the possessions of the Crown of England.

Ombudsman. *See* COMMISSIONERS FOR LOCAL ADMINISTRATION; LEGAL SERVICES OMBUDSMAN.

Omnia præsumuntur contra spoliatorem. All things are presumed against a wrongdoer.

Omnia præsumuntur solemniter (or **rite**) **esse acta.** All things are presumed to have been done rightly.

Onus probandi. The burden of proof. *See* BURDEN OF PROOF.

Open contract. A contract of which not all the terms are expressly mentioned. The expression is used especially of a contract for sale of land in which there is no express condition as to title and in which the law makes certain presumptions.

Open court. A court to which the public have access as of right.

Open policy. An *open policy* is one in which the value of the subject insured is not fixed or agreed on in the policy, but is left to be estimated in case of loss. An *open policy* is opposed to a *valued policy*, in which the value of the subject insured is fixed for the purpose of the insurance, and expressed on the face of the policy. An *open policy* is often called an *unvalued policy*. *See* INSURANCE.

Open verdict. *See* CORONER'S VERDICT.

Opening accounts. The commencement of dealings in account. When an account has been settled and its correctness is afterwards impugned, it is said to be re-opened. *See* ACCOUNT.

Operation of law. When a legal right, duty, or liability comes into existence not by an individual's exercise of a legal power, it comes into existence by operation of law. Thus, when a party agrees a contract and in consequence has contractual rights and duties he or she did not have before, these rights and duties arise in virtue of his or her exercise of a power to make contracts, so these rights and obligations do not arise by operation of law. Where, however, A tortiously injures B, A is now legally liable to compensate B, and this liability arises by operation of law; A has not exercised any legal right or power to make himself liable to B by tortiously injuring B; A has no such legal right or power, indeed, A is under a legal duty not to injure B tortiously.

Operative part of a deed is that part whereby the object of the deed is effected, as opposed to the recitals, etc.
See RECITAL.

Opinio juris. *See* PUBLIC INTERNATIONAL LAW.

Option. 1 The word is used on the Stock Exchange to express a right to take or sell stock on a future day
See TIME BARGAIN.

2 An option of purchase in a lease is the right given to the lessee to purchase, during the term, the reversion.
See REVERSION.

As to options to purchase land, and registration thereof, see ss 2, 3 of Land Charges Act 1972. As to the powers of a tenant for life to grant options, see Settled Land Act 1925, s 51.

Order. Any command of a superior to an inferior may be so called. But the word is frequently applied to those acts of courts of justice which follow the rendering of a decision, either where the decision does not dispose of the merits of the case before them, eg in interlocutory proceedings, or where it does, in which case the order will normally be one which provides a successful plaintiff with a remedy, eg an order to the defendant to pay damages.
See INTERIM/INTERLOCUTORY DECREE OR ORDER.

Some Statutory Instruments are called Orders.
See STATUTORY INSTRUMENT.

Order, payable to. A bill of exchange or promissory note payable to order is a bill or note payable to a given person, or as he shall direct by any indorsement he may make on it. Until he has so indorsed it, no one else can maintain an action on it; and in this respect it differs from a bill or note *payable to bearer*.
See BILL OF EXCHANGE; PROMISSORY NOTE.

Order in Council. An Order made by Her Majesty in Council, 'by and with the advice of Her Privy Council'. An Order in Council is normally signed by the Clerk of Her Majesty's Privy Council.

Thus the Queen, in the exercise of the Royal Prerogative may make decrees, eg coinage proclamations, etc. But she cannot, by an Order in Council, not made in exercise of a statutory power, make decrees

which alter the Common Law or the statute law of the realm (see *The Zamora* [1916] 2 AC 90).
See PREROGATIVE.

Order of discharge. An order obtainable by a bankrupt; made by a court of bankruptcy, which has the effect of releasing the bankrupt from his debts, except such as have been incurred by fraud and certain other debts (see Insolvency Act 1986, ss 280, 281).

Ordinary. 1 In the Civil Law, an *ordinary* signifies any judge who has authority to take cognisance of causes in his own right, and not by deputation.

2 In the Common Law, it refers to the person who has exempt and immediate jurisdiction in ecclesiastical causes, who is generally the bishop of the diocese.

Ordinary resolution. A resolution passed by a majority of the shareholders in a company (see *Bushell v Faith* [1970] 1 All ER 53 at 56, HL (per Lord Upjohn)).

Ordinary share. A share entitling its holder to a dividend, if any, after the payment of the fixed dividend in respect of the preference shares. Ordinary shares, also called common shares, are generally those shares which entitle the holder to vote in the election of the board of directors, and are the shares whose dividends rise and fall with the profits of the company.
See DIVIDEND; PREFERENCE SHARES.

Ordination. The admission by the bishop of any person to the order of priest or deacon.

Ordnance Survey. A survey of Great Britain and the Isle of Man, first authorised by the Ordnance Survey Act 1841, and which is subject to continual revision and improvement.

Organisation for Economic Co-operation and Development. An organisation established by a Convention signed in Paris in December 1960 between the United Kingdom and various foreign powers. A support fund, to assist members who are in balance of payments difficulties, became available to United Kingdom participation by the OECD Support Fund Act 1975.

Original and derivative estates. An original estate is contrasted with a derivative estate; the latter is a particular interest carved out of a larger estate.
See ESTATE.

Originating summons. Formerly a summons whereby proceedings are commenced in the Chancery Division, and in some cases in the Queen's Bench Division, without the issue of a writ. Such summonses are used in a variety of matters, eg to determine particular questions arising in the administration of a trust, where a general administration is not required. Except for certain proceedings, the use of the originating summons has been abolished by the Civil Procedure Rules 1998 and replaced by what is known as a Part 8 claim, which like most other proceedings is initiated with the filing of a claim form.

Ostensible or **nominal partner.** A person who allows his credit to be pledged as a partner; eg where a person's name appears in a firm, or where he interferes in the management of the business, so as to produce in strangers a reasonable belief that he is a partner. The person so acting is answerable as a partner to all who deal with the firm without having notice at the time that he is unconnected with it.
See FIRM; PARTNERSHIP.

Ostium ecclesiæ. The door of the church.

Ouster. The dispossession of a lawful tenant, whether of freehold or chattels real, giving a remedy at law, in order to gain possession, with damages for the injury sustained.
See LAND LAW.

Ouster clause. A statutory provision which ousts the jurisdiction of the courts, eg one providing that the decisions of an administrative tribunal are not subject to review by the courts.

Out of court. A colloquial phrase often applied to a party to litigation, which may be otherwise expressed by saying that 'he has not a leg to stand on'. Thus, when the principal witness, who is expected to prove a party's case, breaks down, it is often said, 'that puts him *out of court*'.

Outer Bar. A phrase applied to the junior barristers who plead 'ouster' or outside the bar, as opposed to Queen's Counsel, who are admitted to plead within the bar.
See JUNIOR BARRISTER; QUEEN'S COUNSEL.

Outgoings. A term often found in connection with the sale of land. The liability to outgoings, eg rates and taxes, is co-terminous with the right to receive the rents and profits of the land, and, therefore, where a time for completion is fixed by the contract for sale,

as from which the purchaser is to be let into possession, or into receipt of the rents and profits, it is presumed that the vendor is liable to outgoings up to that date only.
See COMPLETION.

Where no time for completion is fixed, then, in the absence of express stipulation, the outgoings must be borne by the vendor up to the time when the purchaser could prudently have taken possession of the premises sold. Usually, however, the conditions of sale provide that, on completion, all rents, profits, rates, taxes and other outgoings are to be apportioned, if necessary, as from the date fixed for completion; so that where apportioned outgoings have been paid in advance by the vendor, as rates and taxes often are, he will require to be repaid the proportion due to be paid by the purchaser. As to apportioned outgoings not paid in advance, eg ground rent, the purchaser is allowed to deduct from the purchase money the proportion payable by the vendor.

Outlaw, outlawry. Formerly, a fugitive criminal offender could be made an 'outlaw'. The condition of 'outlawry' was that a person did not have the protection of law, either in his property or his person, and thus his killing would not constitute murder.

Outworker. A person to whom articles or materials are given out to be made up, cleaned, washed, altered, ornamented, finished or repaired, or adapted for sale in his own home or on other premises not under the control or management of the person who gave out the materials or articles.

Over. In conveyancing, a gift or limitation *over* means one which is to come into existence on the determination of a particular estate. Thus in a gift of Blackacre (*see* BLACKACRE) to A for life, but if he marries, then to B for life, the gift to B is a gift over.
See ESTATE; LIMITATION.

Overdue bill or note. A bill of exchange or promissory note is said to be *overdue* so long as it remains unpaid after the time for payment is past.
See BILL OF EXCHANGE; PROMISSORY NOTE.

Over-insurance. Where the whole amount insured in different policies is greater than the whole value of the interest at risk.

Over-reaching. In certain cases where trust property is disposed of, the interests of the beneficiary in the trust are said to be 'over-reached', which means that the purchaser of trust assets from the trustee takes good beneficial legal title free and clear of any equitable interest in the assets, while the beneficiaries' interest becomes attached to the purchase money in the hands of the trustee.

Over-reaching clause. In a resettlement this is a clause which keeps alive the powers in the original settlement annexed to the estates of the tenants for life; the object being to enable such powers to be exercised so as to over-reach the trust of the resettlement in the same manner as if the trust of the latter had been contained in the original settlement.

Over-rule. Where a court, in making its decision in the case before it, finds it necessary to hold that a previous decision of a court, which would otherwise have the force of precedent, is no longer to be followed, it 'over-rules' that case, which no longer stands as good law.

Overt (Fr *Ouvert*). Open: thus, an overt act is an open act, as opposed to an intention conceived in the mind, which can be judged only by overt acts.
See MARKET OVERT; POUND.

Ownership. The right to the exclusive enjoyment of things which can be owned, ie things which can be property. It may be *absolute*, in which case the owner may freely use or dispose of his property, or *restricted*, as in the case of co-ownership, where the general rule is that co-owners must act unanimously in the exercise of any powers incident to ownership, such as the power to give the property away. *Beneficial* ownership is the right of enjoyment of property; the legal owner of property has the beneficial ownership where there are no trust or equitable obligations binding the property; where the property is subject to a trust, the beneficiaries of the trust who have the equitable title enjoy the beneficial ownership, for the legal owner must act towards the property so as to benefit them.

Ownership is the largest interest in property, its unlimited and undefined scope deriving from the right to exclude others. There are however myriad other sorts of lesser interests in property, in particular land, such as security interests, easements over land, and so on. The chief distinguishing feature is that these interests can more or less be precisely defined. Thus an easement is a right of way across the land of another.
See PROPERTY.

Oyez (hear ye). Now generally pronounced O yes. It is used by criers in courts and elsewhere when they make a proclamation.

O

P

PAYE. *See* PAY-AS-YOU-EARN.

PC. Privy Council; Privy Councillor.
See PRIVY COUNCIL.

PP. *See* PER PROCURATIONEM.

Pact. A promise or contract.

Pacta sunt servanda. Agreements must be kept. Principle of international law by which treaties are regarded as binding.

Pairing off. A kind of system of negative proxies, by which a person whose opinions would lead him to vote on one side of a question agrees with a person on the opposite side that they shall both be absent at the same time, so that a vote is neutralised on each side. This practice has been resorted to for many years in the House of Commons. Generally, members of opposite parties pair with each other, not only on particular questions, but for a period. *May.*

Pandects. A name given to the Digest of Roman Law, compiled by order of the Emperor Justinian.
See CORPUS JURIS CIVILIS.

Panel. 1 A schedule or roll of parchment containing the names of jurors which the sheriff has returned to serve on any trial.
See JURY.
2 Any list of persons for official purposes.

Panel on Take-overs and Mergers. *See* CITY CODE ON TAKE-OVERS AND MERGERS.

Paper blockade. When a blockade is proclaimed in time of war, and the naval force on watch is not sufficient to repel attempts to enter or get out, the blockade is called a paper blockade as opposed to a *good* or *effective* blockade.
See BLOCKADE.

Parage. Equity of name, blood or dignity; also of lands to be partitioned. Hence comes the word *disparagement*, which signifies inequality.
See DISPARAGEMENT.

Paramount title. Superior title.
See TITLE.

Parcel (Lat *Particula*). A small piece of land.
A description of *parcels*, in a deed, is a description of lands with reference to their boundaries and local extent.
A *bill of parcels* is an account of the items composing a parcel or package of goods transmitted with them to a purchaser.

Parcenor. *See* COPARCENARY, ESTATE OF.

Pardon is either (i) by the Sovereign in virtue of the prerogative, or (ii) by Act of Parliament.
See PREROGATIVE.
1 Must be pleaded specially and at a proper time; it cannot, however, be pleaded in bar of an impeachment by the Commons.
See IMPEACHMENT.
2 Need not be pleaded, but the Court is bound to take notice of it.

Parens Patriæ (parent of his country). A title sometimes applied to the Queen (or King).

Parental responsibility. All the rights, duties, powers, responsibilities and authority which by law a parent of a child has in relation to the child and his property: Children Act 1989, s 3(1). As to who has parental responsibility, see ibid, s 2.

Pari passu. On an equal footing, or proportionately. A phrase used especially of the creditors of an insolvent estate, who (with certain exceptions) are entitled to payment of their debts in shares proportionate to their respective claims.
See PREFERENTIAL DEBTS.

Parish. 1 A circuit of ground committed to the charge of a parson or vicar, or other minister having the cure of souls in it.

2 A division of a district for the purposes of the Local Government Act 1972.

Parish councils. Established in 1894 for rural parishes with populations of 300 and above. Their principal duties are now set out in the Parish Council Act 1957, as amended by the Local Government Act 1972. Under the latter Act, which created new structures for local government in England and Wales, parish councils retain their former functions, having powers, eg, relating to footpaths and bridleways, off-street parking, footway lighting, open spaces, etc. Each parish council consists of a chairman and parish councillors, the number of which (not less than five) is fixed from time to time by the district council.

Parish meeting. A meeting of the local government electors of a parish. Such a meeting must be held once a year, or at least twice a year where there is no parish council (see Local Government Act 1972, ss 9–17).

Park. A piece of ground enclosed, and stored with beasts of chase, which a man might have by prescription, or the King's grant. Now used either of national parks, being large tracts of country, or small areas set aside for recreation, or the land attached to a mansion. *See* NATIONAL PARKS.

Parliament. A solemn conference of all the estates of the kingdom, summoned together by the authority of the Crown, to consider the affairs of the realm. The constituent parts of the Parliament are the Sovereign and the three estates of the realm, ie, the Lords Spiritual and Lords Temporal, who sit together with the Sovereign, in one House, and the Commons, who sit by themselves, in another. *May.*
See ESTATES OF THE REALM; HOUSE OF COMMONS; HOUSE OF LORDS; LORDS SPIRITUAL; LORDS TEMPORAL.

Parliamentary agents. Agents (generally solicitors) who, in Parliament, promote or oppose the passing of private bills, and conduct other proceedings for pecuniary reward. No member or officer of the House may act as an agent. *May.*
See PRIVATE BILLS.

Parliamentary committee. A committee appointed by either House for making inquiries, eg in the case of private bills.
See PRIVATE BILLS.

Parliamentary copyright. Copyright in a work made by the House of Commons or the House of Lords: Copyright, Designs and Patents Act 1988, s 165. Such a copyright exists in Parliamentary bills: ibid, s 166.
See COPYRIGHT.

Parliamentary sovereignty.
See CONSTITUTIONAL LAW.

Parol. Anything done by word of mouth.

Parol agreement. An agreement by word of mouth. Sometimes, however, the phrase is used to include writings not under seal; since at Common Law, prior to the Statute of Frauds, there was no difference between an agreement by word of mouth and one in writing without seal.
See CONTRACT LAW.

Parol evidence, otherwise called *oral evidence*, is evidence given *viva voce* by witnesses, as opposed to that given by affidavit. As a general rule, parol evidence cannot be given to contradict, alter, or vary a written instrument.

Parole Board. A Board advising the Secretary of State as to the release on licence of prison inmates (see Criminal Justice Act 1991, s 32).

Parricide. A person who kills his father; or the crime of killing a father.

Parson (*Persona ecclesiæ*). The rector or incumbent of a parochial church, who has full possession of all the rights of it. He is called parson, *persona*, because by his person the church, which is an invisible body, is represented; and he is himself a body corporate (*see* CORPORATION) in order to protect and defend the rights of the church, which he personates, by a perpetual succession. There are four requisites to his appointment: holy orders, presentation, institution, and induction.
See HOLY ORDERS; PRESENTATION; INSTITUTION; INDUCTION.

Parsonage. A certain portion of lands and offerings, established by law, for the maintenance of the minister who has the cure of souls. The word is generally used for the *house* set apart for the residence of the minister.

Part 8 Claim. *See* ORIGINATING SUMMONS.

Part 36 Offer. An offer to settle a case before trial.
See OFFER TO SETTLE.

Part owners. Persons who have a share in anything, especially those who have an interest in a ship (see Merchant Shipping Act 1894, s 5).

Part performance, Where a contract was otherwise unenforceable because it was not evidenced in writing, equity would intervene to bar a defendant's pleading the absence of writing as a defence to an action on the contract where the defendant had benefited from any substantial performance of the contract. Abolished by the Law of Property (Miscellaneous Provisions) Act 1989.
See CONTRACT; EQUITY.

Partial loss, in marine insurance, otherwise called an *average* loss, is one in which the damage done to the thing insured is not so complete as to amount to a *total loss*, either actual or constructive (see Marine Insurance Act 1906, s 56(1)). For the measure of indemnity in the event of a partial loss, see ibid, ss 69–71.
See TOTAL LOSS.

Particular average. *See* AVERAGE, 4.

Particular average loss. In marine insurance, a partial loss of the subject-matter, caused by a peril insured against, and which is not a general average loss (see Marine Insurance Act 1906, s 64(1)).
See GENERAL AVERAGE LOSS; PERIL INSURED AGAINST.

Particular estate. An estate in land which precedes an estate in remainder or reversion, so called because it is a *particula*, or small part, of the inheritance, eg a life estate.
See ESTATE; REMAINDER; REVERSION; CONTINGENT REMAINDER.

Particular lien, as opposed to a *general lien*, is a lien on a particular article for the price due or the labour bestowed on the article.
See GENERAL LIEN; LIEN; SECURITY INTEREST.

Particular tenant. The tenant of a particular estate.
See PARTICULAR ESTATE.

Particulars of claim. A plaintiff (claimant) is required to give the particulars of a claim, ie the facts upon which he relies so as to ground a claim in law, so as to let the defendant know the case he has to meet, in the claim form, or a summary statement followed by particulars, generally within 14 days. *See further* the Civil Procedure Rules, Parts 7, 8, and 16.

Particulars of sale. The particulars of the property which is to be sold, and the terms and conditions on which the sale is to take place.

Parties. 1 Persons who voluntarily take part in anything, in person or by attorney; eg the parties to a deed.
See ATTORNEY.
2 Persons required to take part in any proceedings, and bound by them, whether they do so or not; eg the defendants in a suit or action. *See further* the Civil Procedure Rules 1998.

Partition. A dividing of land held in joint tenancy or by tenancy in common, ie in one of the forms of co-ownership, between the co-owners, so that the estate in joint tenancy or tenancy in common is destroyed, and each party has henceforth an undivided share. This may be done by agreement, by deed of partition, or compulsorily by an action in the Chancery Division.
See JOINT TENANCY; COMMON, TENANCY IN.

Under the Supreme Court Act 1981, s 61(1), Sch 1 the partition of real estates is assigned to the Chancery Division of the High Court.

Partner, general. *See* GENERAL PARTNER.

Partner, incoming. *See* INCOMING PARTNER.

Partner, limited. *See* LIMITED PARTNER.

Partner, outgoing. *See* RETIRING PARTNER.

Partner, retiring. *See* RETIRING PARTNER.

Partner, sleeping. *See* SLEEPING PARTNER.

Partner's lien. A right vested in a partner to hold the whole or part of the partnership assets until certain payments are made to him. (*See* Partnership Act 1890, s 41(a).)

Partners, continuing. *See* CONTINUING PARTNERS.

Partnership, as defined by the Partnership Act 1890, s 1 is as follows: Partnership is the relation which subsists between persons carrying on a business in common with a view of profit.

In contrast to a company, which is a corporate body having its own legal personality (*see* COMPANY LAW), a partnership has no legal personality; vis-à-vis dealings with third parties, partners are essentially agents for each other, so that each partner is liable for the acts of each other undertaken in the course of the business of the partnership; partners are also fiduciaries in respect of each other, in that they must act so as to serve the interests of the partnership as a whole in the course of business of the partnership, not to benefit their own individual interests.

The law on the subject was codified by the Act of 1890.

See AGENT; FIDUCIARY; LIMITED LIABILITY PARTNERSHIP.

Partnership, dissolution of. The bringing of a partnership to an end.

A partnership may be dissolved (i) by the expiration of the period for which it is to last or by notice of dissolution; (ii) by the death or bankruptcy of a partner or a charge on his share; (iii) under a clause in the partnership agreement giving a right to claim dissolution if a specified event occurs; (iv) by illegality; (v) by an order of the Court; (vi) by an order of an arbitrator.

Partnership, limited. *See* LIMITED PARTNERSHIP.

Partnership, limited liability. *See* LIMITED LIABILITY PARTNERSHIP.

Partnership articles. The contract between partners setting out the details of the relationship between them.

Partnership at will. A partnership containing no fixed term for its duration.

Where no fixed term has been agreed on, any partner may determine the partnership on giving notice of his intention to do so to all the other partners: Partnership Act 1890, s 26(1).

Partnership property. All property and rights and interests in property originally brought into the partnership stock or acquired, whether by purchase or otherwise, on account of the firm, or for the purposes and in the course of the partnership business: Partnership Act 1890, s 20(1).

Party and party, costs as between. *See* COSTS.

Party-wall. A wall adjoining lands or houses belonging to two different owners. The common user of such a wall by the adjoining owners is *prima facie* evidence that it belongs to them in equal moieties as tenants in common. By the Law of Property Act 1925, s 38 and Sch 1, Part V, it is enacted that a wall which under the old law would have been held by tenants in common is to be regarded as severed vertically as between the respective owners, and that the owners of each part shall have such rights to support and user over the other part as he would have had as tenant in common under the old law. *Hill & Redman.*

Passage money. Fare paid to a shipowner by a passenger in respect of his being carried by sea.

Passing off. A civil wrong, originating in common law as a variation of TRESPASS ON THE CASE. Passing off is selling goods or carrying on business in a manner calculated to mislead the public into believing that the goods, business, etc, are those of another person. Passing off is typically accomplished by packaging one's goods so that they are 'confusingly similar' in appearance to the goods of a competitor. The plaintiff can be awarded both an injunction against the defendant from further sale of the confusingly similar articles, and damages measured by the past loss of custom deriving from the defendant's passing off. The current law of trade marks now deals with many situations which might formerly have been the province of the law of passing off.

See TRADE MARK.

Passive trust. A trust in which the trustee has no active duty to perform.

See BARE TRUST.

Passport. Strictly a licence to *pass* a *port* or *haven*; ie a licence for the safe passage of any person from one place to another.

Pasture. Any place where cattle may feed; also feeding for cattle.

See COMMON, RIGHTS OF.

Patent. A privilege granted to the first inventor of an invention.

Patents are the subject of the Patents Act 1977 (as amended by the Copyright, Designs and Patents Act 1988).

The Act relates principally to (i) patentability (*see* PATENTABLE INVENTION) (ss 1–6); (ii) the right to apply for a patent (ss 7–13); (iii) the application for a patent (ss 14–16); (iv) examination and search to see whether the application complies with requirements of the Act (ss 17–21); (v) the grant of a patent and its duration (ss 24, 25); (vi) registration (ss 32–34); (vii) licences of right and compulsory licences (ss 46–54); (viii) infringement (ss 60–71); (ix) revocation of patents (ss 72, 73); and (x) European, European Community and international protection of patents (ss 77–95).

A patent can be granted only if the invention is patentable: ibid, s 1 (*see* PATENTABLE INVENTION). Any person is allowed to apply for a patent: Patents Act 1977, s 7. An application must be made

P

in the prescribed form and must be filed at the Patent Office (*see* PATENT OFFICE): ibid, s 14(1). The application must then be published by the Registrar: ibid, s 16(1). He must then refer it to an examiner for preliminary examination and search: ibid, s 17. The term of a patent which is granted is 20 years: ibid, s 25. The Registrar must keep a register of patents: ibid, s 32.

An invention by an employee belongs to his employer if it was made in the course of the employee's normal duties: ibid, s 39(1). If it was not so made, it belongs to the employee: ibid, s 39(2).

The patentee may apply for an entry to be made in the register that licences under the patent are to be available as of right: ibid, s 46. After 3 years from the date of the grant of the patent a person may apply for a licence on the ground that eg it is not being commercially worked in the United Kingdom: ibid, ss 48–50.

A patent is infringed if (i) where the invention is a product, a person makes or disposes of it; or (ii) where the invention is a process, he uses it: ibid, s 60(1). A patentee may bring proceedings for infringement: ibid, ss 61–71.

A patent may be revoked: ibid, ss 72, 73.

A patentee may apply for a European patent (*see* EUROPEAN PATENT), a European patent (UK) (*see* EUROPEAN PATENT (UK)), and an international patent (*see* PATENT CO-OPERATION TREATY): ibid, ss 77–95. *See* INTELLECTUAL PROPERTY LAW.

Patent Co-operation Treaty. A treaty signed at Washington on 19th June 1970, giving the protection of a patent in all countries which are parties to it: Patents Act 1977, s 130(1).

Patent Office. An office established in 1853. Applications for patents are made to it. *See* PATENT.

Patentable invention. An invention which is (i) new; (ii) involves an inventive step, and (iii) is capable of industrial application: Patents Act 1977, s 1(1). An invention is 'new' if it does not form part of the state of the art: ibid, s 2(1). It involves an 'inventive step' if it is not obvious to a person skilled in the art: ibid, s 3. *See* PATENT.

Patentee. A person to whom a patent is granted.

Patricide. *See* PARRICIDE.

Patrimony. An hereditary estate. The legal endowment of a church or religious house was called ecclesiastical patrimony.

Patron. In the Canon and Common Law, is the person who has the gift of a benefice. *See* BENEFICE.

Pawn. The transfer of a chattel as security for a debt. *See* PLEDGE; SECURITY INTEREST.

Pawnbroker. One whose business it is to lend money, usually in small sums, on pawn or pledge.

Pawn-receipt. A receipt in respect of an article taken in pawn under a consumer credit agreement or a consumer hire agreement given to a person from whom it is received: Consumer Credit Act 1974, s 114(1). *See* CONSUMER CREDIT AGREEMENT; SECURITY INTEREST.

Pay-as-you-earn. The name popularly given to the system of tax collection under Schedule E to the Income and Corporation Taxes Act 1988, whereby the person chargeable has tax deducted by instalments from his salary by his employer, who is then accountable to the Commissioners of Inland Revenue for the payment of the sums so deducted. See Part V, Chapter V, and in particular s 203, of the Act of 1988.

Payee. A person to whom, or to whose order, a bill of exchange, cheque, or promissory note is expressed to be payable. *See* BILL OF EXCHANGE; CHEQUE; PROMISSORY NOTE.

Paymaster-General. A public officer whose duties consist in the payment of all the voted services for the Army and Navy, and all charges connected with naval and military expenditure. The Paymaster-General likewise makes payments for the civil services in England, and for some in Scotland. The office of Accountant-General was abolished in 1872 and its duties transferred to that of the Paymaster-General. By the Judicature Act 1925, s 133(6) the Paymaster-General was replaced by an Accountant-General as to the pay office of the Supreme Court. At the present day the personal duties of the holder of the office are nominal.

Payment of money into Court. Formerly, a defendant in an action for a debt or damages was entitled to pay money into Court in satisfaction of the cause of action, in order to save the expense of further proceedings.

The procedure for inducing early settlements has now been altered by the Civil Procedure Rules 1998, Part 36, and is now based on giving notice to the other side of an offer to settle, though where the offer to settle is made by a defendant and includes an offer to pay a certain amount in damages or otherwise, generally payment into court must be made as well.

As to lodgment of funds in Court in the Chancery Division by a life insurance company, a trustee, etc, see RSC 1965, Ord 92.

Payment without discount. In relation to hire due under a time charter-party this means that there is to be no discount for early payment (see *Compania Sud Americana de Vapores v Shipmair BV: The 'Teno'* [1977] 2 Lloyd's Rep 289 at 292 (per Parker J)). *See* HIRE.

Peace, Commission of. *See* COMMISSION OF THE PEACE.

Peace, Justices of. *See* JUSTICE OF THE PEACE.

Peace of the Queen. The peace and security, both for life and goods, which the Queen promises to all her subjects, or others taken under her protection.

Peculiar. A particular parish or church exempt from the jurisdiction of the Ordinary. *See* ORDINARY. All ecclesiastical causes arising within them are cognisable in the Court of Peculiars.

Peerage. The dignity of the lords or peers of the realm, whether hereditary peers or life peers under the Life Peerages Act 1958, although following the House of Lords Act 1999 most hereditary peers have been excluded from the upper house of Parliament. The House of Lords exercises an original jurisdiction in regard to matters of peerage. Since the time of Charles II all doubtful or contested claims to peerage have been referred to the Lords by the Crown. The procedure is by way of petition to the Crown. For an example see the *Ampthill Peerage Case* [1976] 2 All ER 411.

An hereditary peerage may be disclaimed for life by a person who succeeds to it: Peerage Act 1963, s 1. A disclaimer must be made within 12 months of his succeeding to the peerage: ibid, s 1(2). A disclaimer is irrevocable, but does not affect the devolution on his death: ibid, s 3(1). *See* HOUSE OF LORDS.

Peeress. A woman who has the dignity of peerage, either in her own right or by right of marriage. In the latter case she loses the dignity by a second marriage with a commoner.

Peers. Those who are the nobility of the realm and lords of Parliament, although following the House of Lords Act 1999 most hereditary peers have been excluded from the upper house of Parliament. *See* HOUSE OF LORDS.

Penal actions. *See* ACTION.

Penal bond. *See* BOND.

Penal laws. Laws imposing penalties or punishments for the doing of prohibited acts.

The question whether a given provision in an Act of Parliament is a penal one or not, is sometimes important, eg it is a rule that penal statutes must be construed *strictly* (ie narrowly), on the principle that a person should not be subject to a penalty unless he has committed an action which has been clearly prohibited.

Penal statutes. *See* PENAL LAWS.

Penalty. 1 Punishment; used of a pecuniary fine.

2 Money recoverable by virtue of a penal statute.

3 A sum named in a bond as the amount to be forfeited by the obligor in case he does not comply with the condition of the bond. Notwithstanding that a sum may be so named, still, in an action on the bond, a jury is directed to inquire what damages the plaintiff has sustained by breach of the condition; and the plaintiff cannot levy execution for a larger amount than the jury assess.

4 A sum agreed to be paid on the breach of an agreement, or some stipulation in it. *See* LIQUIDATED DAMAGES.

Pendente lite. While a suit is pending. Thus, letters of administration may be granted *pendente lite*, where a suit is commenced touching the validity of a will. *See* ADMINISTRATOR.

Pending action. *See* LIS PENDENS.

Pension. The payment of a sum of money; especially a periodical payment for past services.

Pensions Ombudsman. A commissioner whose duty it is to investigate and determine complaints by persons alleging that they

P

have sustained injustice in consequence of maladministration by the trustees or managers of an occupational personal pension scheme: Social Security Pensions Act 1975, s 59B.

Peppercorn rent. A rent of a peppercorn, that is, a nominal rent. Although of very little value, the payment of a peppercorn does count as the transfer of valuable consideration, and so a peppercorn rent is good consideration for the grant of a lease.
See CONSIDERATION.

Per autre vie. For another's life.
See PUR AUTRE VIE.

Per capita. *See* CAPITA, DISTRIBUTION PER.

Per curiam (by the court). An expression implying that such a decision was arrived at by the court, consisting of one or more judges, as the case might be.

Similarly, the word *per*, preceding the name of a Judge, signifies that a dictum which follows is quoted on the authority of the Judge.
See OBITER DICTUM.

Per incuriam. Through want of care. A case decided 'per incuriam' is one in which the judgment was rendered but where a relevant precedent or statute was not cited to the court by counsel. Such a judgment's precedential value is thereby severely weakened, if not extinguished, for the judgment cannot be regarded as a decision based on all relevant considerations.

Per infortunium. By mischance.

Per my et per tout. By half and by all. Used to describe the nature of a joint tenancy. In the case of an alienation of the joint tenants, each is entitled to an equal share (half in the case of two joint tenants) in the proceeds, but as regards occupation and the right arising upon survivorship, each is the holder of the whole.

Per procurationem. By means of procuration or agency. The phrase is often used, either in full or abbreviated into 'pp' where one person signs a receipt or other written document as agent for another. But the phrase is especially applied to the acceptance, etc, of a bill of exchange by one person as agent for another.

The words '*per procuration*', attached to a signature on a bill of exchange, are held to be an express intimation of a special and limited

authority; and a person who takes a bill so drawn, accepted, or indorsed, is bound to inquire into the extent of the authority (see Bills of Exchange Act 1882, ss 25, 26).
See BILL OF EXCHANGE.

Per se. Of itself, taken alone.

Per stirpes. *See* STIRPES, DISTRIBUTION PER.

Peremptory. A final and determinate act, without hope of renewing or altering.

Peremptory challenge. *See* CHALLENGE.

Perfect trust. An executed trust.

Performance. **1** The doing wholly or in part of a thing agreed to be done.
See SATISFACTION.

2 In relation to a performer's rights, means:
(i) a dramatic performance (which includes dance or mime);
(ii) a musical performance;
(iii) a reading or recitation of a literary work; or
(iv) a performance of a variety act or any similar presentation,
which is, or so far as it is, a live performance given by one or more individuals: Copyright, Designs and Patents Act 1988, s 180(2).
See PERFORMER'S RIGHTS.

Performance of dangerous nature includes all acrobatics and all performances as a contortionist: Children and Young Persons Act 1933, s 30(1).

No child under 12 must be trained to take part in such a performance except under a licence granted by a local authority: ibid, s 24(1).

Performer's rights, in relation to copyright, are infringed by a person who without his consent (i) makes otherwise than for his private and domestic use, a recording of a performer's performance; or (ii) broadcasts live such a performance: Copyright, Designs and Patents Act 1988, ss 184–185.
See COPYRIGHT; RECORDING; PERFORMANCE.

Peril insured against. A peril in respect of which the insured seeks and the insurers are willing to give protection.

Perils of the seas. Fortuitous accidents or casualties of the sea. It does not include the ordinary action of winds and waves (see Marine Insurance Act 1906, Sch, Rules for Construction of Policy, r 7).

Perjury. The swearing wilfully, absolutely, and falsely, in a judicial proceeding, in a matter material to the issue or cause in question. By many statutes, however, false oaths in certain cases, not of a judicial kind, are to be deemed to amount to perjury, and to be visited with the same penalties. The penalties of perjury also attach to wilful falsehood in an affirmation by a Quaker, Moravian, or Separatist, or any other witness, where such affirmation is in lieu of an oath, and would, if believed, have the same legal consequences (see Perjury Act 1911).

Permissive waste. *See* WASTE.

Permit. A licence or warrant for persons to pass with and sell goods, on having paid the duties of customs or excise for them.

Perpetual injunction. An injunction which is not merely temporary or provisional, and which cannot be dissolved except by appeal, or some proceeding in the nature of an appeal. An interim injunction granted on motion is sometimes made *perpetual* by the decree.
See INJUNCTION.

Perpetuating testimony. Proceedings in equity to enable a person to take evidence, otherwise in danger of being lost, where the facts likely to come into dispute cannot be immediately investigated by legal process eg where the person filing it has merely a future interest.
See EQUITY; FUTURE ESTATE, FUTURE INTEREST.

Perpetuity. The attempt, by deed, will, or other instrument, to control the devolution of an estate beyond the period allowed by law, is spoken of as an attempt to create a *perpetuity*, and the disposition so attempted to be made is void. The modern (post-17th century) common law rule required that interests in property given by *inter vivos* grant or trust, or by a will or testamentary trust, must vest in interest absolutely, ie the intended recipients must have the absolute right to an interest in the property (*see* VEST *et seq*), within a certain period from the time the grant or will or trust came into effect. Thus it prevented persons from controlling the distribution of their property long after they were dead by imposing restrictions upon it far into the future.

The rule was logically straightforward, but in practice was often very difficult to apply and it created various traps for inexperienced conveyancers and draughtsmen, both because of the way the time limit was calculated, and because of the way it took into account the possibility of events occurring which might make a gift fail. The time period of the rule was framed to allow testators to make gifts to their grandchildren that would not vest until the children reached the age of majority, which was 21 when the rule was devised. The rule was devised to make that possible, but also to make sure that this was the limit of what a testator could do to extend the time before his gifts actually vested; in consequence, the allowable time period was framed in a particular way, in reference to 'lives in being' plus a further period of 21 years. The way in which this limit worked is best explained by an example. If I leave property in my will to be divided equally between all my grandchildren who attain the age of 21, under the rule we calculate the time period within which the donees will become entitled to their shares of the property as follows: if I have any living grandchildren when I die their shares will vest when they each turn 21, and so, being alive at my death, they must turn 21 within 21 years following my death. But more children may be born to my living children. My own children who are alive at my death are lives in being for the purpose of the rule. (If I am a man and my wife is pregnant with my child, a child *en ventre sa mere*, as the expression goes, that child counts as a child living at my death, thus a life in being for the purpose of the rule.) The rule now works as follows: obviously, any child born to my children must be conceived before my children die; therefore, the last grandchild of mine which could possibly be born will be conceived no later than the death of my last living child; therefore that last grandchild will turn 21 (ignoring periods of gestation) no later than 21 years after the death of the last life in being. Thus a gift to any or all of my grandchildren who attain their age of majority, 21, must vest, if it vests at all (all of my grandchildren may, as it turns out, die before 21—that makes the gift fail, but not for perpetuity), within the period determined by the lifetime of the last surviving life in being plus 21 years. Thus the rule can be stated as follows: a gift is valid if the interests in the property of those who are intended to benefit must vest, if they vest at all, within 21 years following the death of the last surviving life in being.

The famous trap of the 'unborn widow' shows the complexities of applying the rule. Consider this testamentary gift: 'Blackacre to my son A for life, then to A's widow for life, then to A's eldest child then living absolutely.'

P

A is already alive, so is a life in being for the purpose of the rule. The problem is that A might marry someone who is not alive at the testator's death. After growing up and marrying A, she might outlive A (and anyone else alive at my death) by more that 21 years. So the gift to A's eldest son might vest more than 21 years after the death of the last life in being, so the gift is void from the outset.

The rule was modified by the Perpetuities and Accumulations Act 1964, which prevents gifts from failing for perpetuity at the outset of the gift because the gift might vest outside the perpetuity period. The Act takes a 'wait and see' approach, and in general any gifts which in fact vest within the perpetuity period (or a specified period of 80 years) will be good.

See WILL; ESTATE; TRUST; VEST.

Person. 1 A human being capable of rights, also called a *natural* person.
2 A corporation or legal person ie an *artificial* person (see the Interpretation Act 1978, s 5, Sch 1).

Personal action signifies:
1 An action which can be brought only by the person himself who is injured, and not by his representatives; such an action dies with the victim. An example is a victim of DEFAMATION.
2 An action which is not an action for the recovery of land.

Personal chattels. Things movable, as opposed to interests in land.
See CHATTELS.

Personal credit agreement. An agreement between an individual ('the debtor') and any other person ('the creditor') by which the creditor provides the debtor with credit of any amount: Consumer Credit Act 1974, s 8(1).
See CREDIT.

Personal injuries include any disease and any impairment of a person's physical or mental condition.

Personal pension scheme. A scheme or arrangement providing benefits, in the form of pensions or otherwise payable on death or retirement to employed earners who are members of the scheme: Social Security Act 1986, s 84(1).

Personal property. *See* REAL AND PERSONAL PROPERTY.

Personal representative. An executor or administrator, whose duty it is to settle the affairs and dispose of the property of a deceased person.
See ADMINISTRATOR; EXECUTOR.

Personal rights. 1 Rights of personal security, ie, those of life, limb, body, health, reputation and liberty.
2 Rights *in personam*.
See IN PERSONAM.

Personalty. Personal property. Personalty is either *pure* or *mixed*. Pure personalty is personalty unconnected with land; mixed personalty is a personal interest in land, or connected with it.
See PROPERTY; REAL AND PERSONAL PROPERTY; CHATTELS.

Personation. Pretending to be another person. Thus, a man who induces a married woman to have sexual intercourse with him by impersonating her husband is guilty of rape (see Sexual Offences Act 1956, s 1).

Personation in order to obtain admittance to a prohibited place is an offence under s 1(1)(*d*) of the Official Secrets Act 1920.
See OFFICIAL SECRETS.

Personation at a Parliamentary or local government election is an offence punishable with up to two years' imprisonment under the Representation of the People Act 1983, s 168. A person is deemed guilty of personation if he (i) votes in person or by post as some other person, whether as an elector or as proxy, and whether that other person is living or dead or is a fictitious person; or (ii) votes in person or by post as proxy either for a person whom he knows or supposes is dead or fictitious, or when he knows or supposes that his appointment proxy is no longer in force (ibid, s 60).

Perverse verdict. A verdict given by a jury who refuse to follow the direction of the Judge on a point of law, and/or one which is entirely against the evidence.
See VERDICT.

Petition. A general word for all kinds of supplications made by an inferior to a superior, especially one having jurisdiction and authority, eg petitions to the Queen, petitions to Parliament, etc. The subject has a right to petition the Sovereign, or Parliament, subject to certain restrictions.

A *petition in Chancery* is an application, addressed to a Judge, stating the matters on which it is founded, set out in the same manner as a bill, and concluding with a prayer for the specific order sought; or for such other order as the Judge thinks right.

The word 'petition' has been variously used in English legal proceedings, eg a *petition* for a receiving order in bankruptcy, a *petition* for a divorce (*see* DIVORCE). Petitions against the election of members of Parliament are tried by two Judges.

See ELECTION PETITION.

Petitioning creditor. A creditor who petitions that his debtor may be adjudicated bankrupt. The creditor's debt must be a liquidated one of not less than £750, and is one which the debtor appears either unable to pay or to have no reasonable prospect of being able to pay, and there is no outstanding application to set aside a statutory demand in respect of the debt (see Insolvency Act 1986, s 267).

See STATUTORY DEMAND.

Petty sessions. The sitting of two or more justices or a metropolitan or stipendiary magistrate for trying offences in a summary way under various Acts of Parliament empowering them to do so; for making orders, appeals, and other civil purposes.

Pew. An enclosed seat in a church. The right to sit in a particular pew in church arises either from prescription, the pew being appurtenant to a messuage, or from a faculty or grant from the Ordinary, who has the disposition of all pews which are not claimed by prescription.

See PRESCRIPTION; MESSUAGE; ORDINARY.

Photograph. A recording of light or other radiation on any medium on which an image is produced or from which an image may be by any means produced, and which is not part of a film: Copyright, Designs and Patents Act 1988, s 4(2). An artistic work includes a photograph: ibid, s 4(1).

See ARTISTIC WORK; FILM.

Picketing. The posting of persons outside a factory or place of business to molest or intimidate workmen.

By the Trade Union and Labour Relations (Consolidation) Act 1992, s 220 it is lawful for one or more persons in contemplation or furtherance of a trade dispute to attend at or near (i) the place where another person works or carries on business; or (ii) any other place where another person happens to be, not being a place where he resides, for the purpose only of peacefully obtaining or communicating information, or peacefully persuading any person to work or abstain from working.

See TRADE DISPUTE.

In *Hubbard v Pitt* [1975] 3 All ER 1, Lord Denning said: 'Picketing is not a nuisance in itself.... It does not become a nuisance unless it is associated with obstruction, violence, intimidation, molestation or threats.... Picketing is lawful so long as it is done merely to obtain or communicate information, or peacefully to persuade; and is not such as to submit any other person to any kind of constraint or restriction of his personal freedom.'

Pilot. A person who has the control of a ship, under the master; any person not belonging to a ship who has the conduct of her (see Merchant Shipping Act 1894, s 742).

Pin-money. A sum payable by a husband to a wife for her separate use, to be applied by her in attiring her person in a manner suitable to the rank of her husband, and in defraying other personal expenses.

Piracy. 1 The crime of piracy consists in committing those acts of robbery and depredation upon the high seas which, if committed upon land, would amount to a crime there.

Under the Piracy Acts, the following offences are also to be deemed piratical:
(i) the betrayal of his trust by a commander or other seafaring person (see Piracy Act 1698, s 8).
(ii) endeavouring to make a revolt on board ship (ibid).
(iii) trading with known pirates, or fitting out a vessel for a piratical purpose, etc (see Piracy Act 1721, s 1).

2 The infringement of a copyright.

See COPYRIGHT.

Pirates. 'Persons plundering indiscriminately for their own ends and not persons who are simply operating against the property of a particular State for a public end, the end of establishing a government, although that act may be illegal, although that act may be criminal, and although they may not be acting on behalf of a society which is politically organised.' (See *Bolivia Republic v Indemnity Mutual Marine Assurance Co Ltd* [1908–10] All ER Rep 264, CA (per Vaughan Williams, LJ).) The term 'pirates' includes passengers who mutiny and rioters who attack the ship from the shore (see Marine Insurance Act 1906, Sch, Rules for Construction of Policy, r 8).

Piscary. A liberty of fishing in another person's waters.
See COMMON, RIGHTS OF.

Pixing the coin. The ascertaining whether coin is of the proper standard. For this purpose, resort is had on stated occasions to an ancient mode of inquisition called the *trial of the pyx*, before a jury of members of the Goldsmith's Company. See now, as to coinage, Coinage Act 1971.

Plaint. Formerly, the written statement of an action in the County Court, which is entered by the registrar in a book kept for the purpose.

Planning permission. Permission to carry out development of land. Such permission must be sought from the local planning authority under the Town and Country Planning Act 1971.

Play means:
(i) any dramatic piece, whether involving improvisation or not, which is given wholly or in part by one or more persons actually present and performing and in which the whole or a major proportion of what is done by the person or persons performing, whether by way of speech, singing or acting, involves the playing of a role; and
(ii) any ballet given wholly or in part by one or more persons actually present and performing: Theatres Act 1968, s 18(1).

Plea. The formal reply to a charge brought against a criminal accused.

Pleading. 1 Drawing the written pleadings in a suit or action.
See PLEADINGS.
2 Advocating a client's cause *viva voce* in court.

Pleadings. Formal statements, made in writing or print, by the parties in an action or case, whose purpose is to lay out and make precise the point in issue between them. The principle pleadings are the statement of case (formerly the statement of claim) and the defence (formerly the statement of defence), though supplementary statements of reply, etc. may be made. The general rules of pleading are contained in the Civil Procedure Rules 1998.

Pledge. 1 The transfer of a chattel by a debtor to his creditor to secure the repayment of the debt.
2 The chattel so transferred.
3 A surety.

Plenary cause. A phrase used in ecclesiastical law of those causes in which the prescribed order of proceedings must be exactly adhered to; as opposed to summary. Plenary causes now comprise only suits for dilapidations and church sittings.
See DILAPIDATION.

Plene administravit. A plea by an executor or administrator to an action brought against him as representing the deceased, on the ground that he has already fully administered the estate of the deceased, and that the assets which have come into his hands have been exhausted in the payment of debts.

Plene administravit præter. A plea by an executor or administrator that he has fully administered the deceased's estate, with the exception of certain assets acknowledged to be still in his hands. If the plea is good, the plaintiff should enter judgment in respect of the assets acknowledged to be in the executor's hands and in respect of assets *in futuro* for the residue of his claim.

Plenipotentiary. A person who is fully empowered to do anything.

Plough bote. Wood to be employed in repairing instruments of husbandry.

Plough land or **carucate.** As much land as a team of oxen could plough in a season.

Plurality. The having two, three, or more benefices. The holder of them is called a *pluralist*. The holding of benefices in plurality is strictly regulated but not uncommon.

Poaching. The unlawful destruction of game, especially by night; also trespassing by night on land in pursuit of game (see Night Poaching Acts 1828 and 1844, and Poaching Prevention Act 1862). As to the offences of poaching deer and fish, see Theft Act 1968, Sch 1.

Police. A force for the due regulation and domestic order of the kingdom. Especially that part of it which is connected with the prevention and detection of crime.
See CONSTABLE.

P

Police Complaints Authority. An authority for the hearing of complaints against the police which are referred to it, where the complaint:
- (i) alleges that the conduct complained of resulted in the death of or serious injury to a person;
- (ii) is of a description specified in regulations made by the Secretary of State: Police and Criminal Evidence Act 1984, ss 83, 87.

Policy, arguments of. *See* PUBLIC POLICY.

Policy of assurance or Insurance. *See* INSURANCE.

Policyholders Protection Board. A body set up under the Policyholders Protection Act 1975, to indemnify policyholders who have been prejudiced by the inability of insurance companies to meet their liabilities.

Political asylum. *See* ASYLUM.

Poll. 1 A method of voting whereby each member of a company can vote for or against a resolution according to the number of shares which he has.
See RESOLUTION.

2 The process of giving and counting votes at an election.
See POLLING; POLLS.

Poll, deed. *See* DEED.

Polling. Counting heads; especially used of counting voters at an election.

Polls. Heads or individuals; also the place where polling takes place for the purpose of an election.

Polygamy. The having more wives than one. The Matrimonial Proceedings (Polygamous Marriages) Act 1972 empowers the Court to grant matrimonial relief and to make declarations concerning the validity of a marriage notwithstanding that the marriage in question was entered into under a law which permits polygamy.

Port. A place where persons and goods are allowed to pass into and out of the realm. The duty of appointing ports and sub-ports, and declaring their limits, is confided, by the Customs and Excise Management Act 1979, s 19 to the Commissioners of Customs and Excise.

Portion. A part of a person's estate which is given or left to a child or person to whom another stands *in loco parentis*. The word is specially applied to payments made to younger children out of the funds comprised in their parents' marriage settlement, and in pursuance of the trusts of it.
See ADVANCEMENT; SATISFACTION.

Positive law. The extant laws of a jurisdiction, as applied by its courts, irrespective of whether those laws are morally just, the law 'on the books', as it were. It is therefore sometimes referred to as the law 'properly so called', on the theory that every law is 'posited' or decreed or 'put forth' by some authority having the right to do so, thus refers to laws enacted by sovereign States, or by their authority, disobedience to which is, at the least, *malum prohibitum*, a proscribed wrong.
See MALA IN SE; MALA PROHIBITA; JURISPRUDENCE, 1.

Positivism, positivist. Positivism is the theory of law by which the positive law, regardless of whether the law is morally just or not, is the proper subject of legal philosophy, or jurisprudence. A positivist is one who endorses positivism.
See JURISPRUDENCE, 1.

Posse. A word signifying a possibility. A thing in *posse* means a thing which may be; as opposed to a thing in *esse*, or in being.

Possession. 1 When a man actually enters into lands and tenements. This is called actual possession.

2 When lands and tenements descend to a man, and he has not yet entered into them. This is called possession in law. Thus, there are estates in possession as opposed to estates in remainder or reversion. Into the former a man has a right to enter at once; of the latter the enjoyment is delayed.
See ESTATE; INTEREST IN POSSESSION; FUTURE ESTATE, FUTURE INTEREST.

3 The exercise of the right of ownership, whether rightfully or wrongfully. This has been defined as 'physical detention, coupled with the intention to use the thing detained as one's own'.
See OWNERSHIP.

4 As used in the Law of Property Act 1925, possession includes receipt of rents and profits or the right to receive the same, if any (see s 205(1)(xix)).

Possessory title. Under the Land Registration Act 1925 land may be registered with a possessory title, on the applicant or his nominee giving such evidence of title and serving such notices, if any, as may

P

for the time being be prescribed (s 4). The registration of a person as first registered proprietor of freehold land with a possessory title only, does not affect or prejudice the enforcement of any estate, right, or interest adverse to or in derogation of the title of the first proprietor and subsisting or capable of arising, at the time of registration of that proprietor; but, except as aforesaid, has the same effect as registration of a person with an absolute title (s 6). For the effect of registration of leaseholds with a possessory title, see s 11 of the Act.
See ABSOLUTE TITLE; LAND LAW; REGISTERED LAND.

Post. After. Occurring in a book it refers to a later page or line.

Post litem motam. After a suit has been in contemplation; or, 'after an issue has become, or appeared likely to become, a subject of judicial controversy'.

Post mortem (after death). Eg, a *post mortem* examination of a corpse, to ascertain the cause of death.

Post obit bond. A bond executed by a person on the receipt of money from another, whereby the borrower binds himself to pay to the lender a sum exceeding the sum so received, and the ordinary interest on it, on the death of a person on whose decease he (the borrower) expects to become entitled to some property.
See BOND.

Post-dating an instrument. The dating of an instrument as of a date after that on which it is executed. A bill of exchange, note or cheque may be post-dated (see Bills of Exchange Act 1882, s 13).
See BILLS OF EXCHANGE; PROMISSORY NOTE; CHEQUE.

Post-nuptial. After marriage; thus, a post-nuptial settlement is a settlement made after marriage, and, not being made in consideration of marriage, it is, in general, considered as *voluntary*, that is, as having been made on no valuable consideration.
See CONSIDERATION.

Potentia remota. A remote possibility, which cannot reasonably be expected to happen.

Pound (Lat *Parcus*). An enclosure for keeping cattle or other goods distrained. By the Distress for Rent Act 1737, s 10 any person distraining for rent may turn any part of the premises, on which a distress is taken, into a pound, *pro hac vice*, for the securing of such distress. A pound is either pound *overt*, that is, open overhead; or pound *covert*, that is, close.
See DISTRESS.

Poundbreach. The destruction of a pound, or any part, lock, or bolt of it, or the taking of cattle or other goods from the place where they are impounded (see the Distress for Rent Act 1689 and Pound-Breach Act 1843).
See POUND.

Poursuivant. The Queen's messenger. Those formerly attending the Kings in their wars were called *Poursuivants-at-Arms*.

There are four poursuivants in the Heralds' College called respectively *Rouge Croix, Bluemantle, Rouge Dragon, and Portcullis.*
See HERALDS' COLLEGE.

Power. A capacity at law to alter the rights, duties, or powers of oneself or others. Thus a person possessed of property has the power to transfer it by gift, thus altering the rights of the donee and his or her own, as each now stands in a different legal relationship to the property following the gift; a person has a power to give his property at death by will; and so on. The most common use of the term is in respect of powers of appointment, powers often given by will or under the terms of a trust to appoint, ie give real or personal property independently of the other terms of the will or trust and often in defeasance of other estates or interests otherwise given under the will or trust. The person entitled to exercise the power (who is called the *donee of the power*) may have no interest in the property in question, in which case the power is called a power *collateral*, or *in gross*; or he may himself have an interest in the property, and the power is then called a power *coupled with an interest*, or a power *appendant* or *appurtenant*, eg in case of a parent having a life interest in property, with power to appoint the property (either by deed or will) to his children after his death. The exercise of the power is called an *appointment*; and the persons taking the property under such an appointment are called *appointees*, and not grantees or assigns.

Powers may be *general*, giving a right to appoint as the donee may think fit, even to him or herself, or *special* only in favour of some or all of certain persons or classes of persons. Also they may be powers of *revocation*, eg in voluntary settlements, or of *revocation and new appointment*, eg in marriage settlements to enable shares of children to be rearranged. After 1925 powers of appointment, with certain exceptions, will operate only in equity (see Law of Property Act 1925, s 1(7)).

Power of attorney. An authority given by one person to another to act for him in his absence, eg to convey land, receive debts, sue, etc. The party so authorised to act is called the *attorney* of the party giving the authority. See the Powers of Attorney Act 1971, which provides that a power of attorney must be made by DEED. A form of general power of attorney is printed in Sch 1 to the Act. Some powers of attorney are not revoked by the mental incapacity of the donor and are known as enduring powers. *See* ENDURING POWER OF ATTORNEY.

Practice. The procedure in a court of justice, through the various stages of any matter, civil or criminal, pending in it.

The practice in the Supreme Court was formerly regulated by the Supreme Court Act 1981, and the Rules of the Supreme Court 1965, and amending rules, which may be found in the 'Supreme Court Practice'. The practice in the county courts was regulated by the County Courts Act 1984, and the County Court Rules 1981.

Both have been replaced save for minor reservations by the Civil Procedure Rules 1998 made under the Civil Procedure Act 1997.

Practice master. One of the Queen's Bench Masters, sitting by rotation for the purpose of answering queries as to points of practice. One such Master is on duty each week day throughout the year (except on bank holidays and days when the courts are closed) according to a rota arranged from time to time.

Practices, uncompetitive. *See* UNCOMPETITIVE PRACTICES.

Practitioner. A doctor, dentist, or veterinary surgeon (see Medicines Act 1968, s 132).

Præscription. *See* PRESCRIPTION.

Pratique. Permission for a disease-free ship to use a port.

Pray in aid. A phrase often used to mean 'claiming the benefit of an argument'. Especially in suits or actions in which there are several parties, the phrase is sometimes used by a counsel who claims the benefit, on behalf of his own client, of an argument already used on behalf of some other party in the suit or action.

Preamble of a statute. The recital at the beginning of some Acts of Parliament, to explain the minds of the makers of the Act, and the mischiefs they intend to remedy by it. *See* MISCHIEF.

In the case of private bills, if the Committee of either House, before whom the bill comes, finds the preamble 'not proven', the bill is lost. *See* PRIVATE BILLS.

Pre-audience. The priority of right of being heard in a court eg the Attorney- and Solicitor-General before Queen's Counsel, and Queen's Counsel before junior barristers, etc.

Prebend. A fixed portion of the rents and profits of a cathedral church set apart for the maintenance of the prebendaries.

Precatory words. Words in a will or settlement 'praying' or 'desiring' that a thing shall be done. In some cases such words have created a trust; and such a trust is sometimes called a *precatory trust*. *See* TRUST.

Precedent condition. *See* CONDITIONS PRECEDENT AND SUBSEQUENT.

Precedents. Examples which may be followed. The word is used principally, though by no means exclusively, to indicate one of the two following things:

1 A decision in a court of justice cited in support of any proposition for which it is desired to contend. A prior decision of the House of Lords is binding on all inferior courts, though no longer necessarily upon the House of Lords itself, and nothing except an Act of Parliament can alter it.
2 Drafts of deeds, wills, mortgages, pleadings, etc, which may serve as patterns for future draftsmen and conveyancers.

Precept. The demand for money made by a rating or council tax authority.

Precinct. Boundary. Hence it means—

1 A certain limited district round some important edifice, eg a cathedral.
2 The local district for which a high or petty constable is appointed. *See* CONSTABLE.

Pre-contract. A contract made before another contract; especially with reference to a contract of marriage, which, according to

P

ancient law, rendered void a subsequent marriage solemnised in violation of it.

Predecessor in title. A previous title-holder of property.

See SUCCESSOR IN TITLE.

Pre-emption. **1** A right of purchasing before another person. As to registration of rights of pre-emption, see Land Charges Act 1972, s 2(4)(iv); and as to releases of such rights, see Law of Property Act 1925, s 186 which provides that if not released, they remain in force as equitable interests only.

2 A right given to the owner from whom lands have been acquired by compulsory powers in case they should become *superfluous* for the undertaking for which they were acquired (see Lands Clauses Consolidation Act 1845, ss 127–129).

See COMPULSORY PURCHASE ORDER.

3 In international law it means the right of a belligerent compulsorily to purchase goods of a neutral at their commercial value to prevent their falling into the hands of the enemy.

Prefer. Often means to bring a matter before a court; eg when it is said that A preferred a charge of assault against B.

Preference, fraudulent. A term used in connection with payments, transfers, conveyances, etc, made by a company or person unable to pay his debts by way of preference to some of his creditors over others (see Insolvency Act 1986, s 239 (company) and s 340 (individual)). Where there has been a fraudulent preference, the Court may make such order as it thinks fit for restoring the position to what it would have been if the preference had not been given (see ibid, ss 239, 340).

Preference shares. In a company are shares entitling their holders to a preferential dividend; so that a holder of preference shares is entitled to have the whole of his dividend (or so much of it as represents the extent to which his shares are, by the constitution of the company, to be deemed preference shares) paid before any dividend is paid to the ordinary shareholders. Sometimes such shares have preference also in regard to capital in the event of winding up.

See SHARE.

Preferential debts. Payments that are made in preference to the right of others in bankruptcy, the winding up of companies,

or the administration of estates of persons dying insolvent. On a winding up one year's rates and taxes, sums due for value added tax for the last 6 months, four months' remuneration owed to an employee not exceeding a sum prescribed by order made by the Secretary of State in each case, and certain amounts under the Social Security Act 1975, are payable in priority to all other debts (see Insolvency Act 1986, s 386, Sch 6).

See PREFERENCE, FRAUDULENT.

Pre-incorporation contract. A contract purporting to be made by a company or by a person acting as its agent before the company has been incorporated.

Subject to any agreement to the contrary, such a contract has effect as one entered into by the person purporting to act for the company or as agent for it, and he is personally liable on the contract accordingly (see Companies Act 1985, s 36(4)).

Prejudice, without. Phrase often used in a solicitor's letter for the purpose of guarding himself as to anything contained in it being construed as an admission of liability.

Preliminary act. In actions for damage by collision between vessels a sealed document giving all particulars of the collision must be filed by the solicitor for each side before any pleadings are delivered. Such document is called a preliminary act (see RSC 1965, Ord 75, r 18).

Preliminary voyage. The voyage of a vessel from her present position to the port of loading declared in a charter-party.

Premier. *See* PRIME MINISTER.

Premises (Lat *Præmissa*). **1** The commencement of a deed, setting out the number and names of the parties, with their additions or titles, and the recital, if any, of such deeds and matters of fact as are necessary to explain the reasons on which the deed is founded; the consideration upon which it is made; and, if the deed is a disposition of property, the particulars of the property intended to be transferred by it; also the operative words, with the exceptions and reservations (if any).

See DEED; RECITAL; OPERATIVE PART OF A DEED.

2 Hence it has come to mean the lands granted; and hence any specified houses or lands.

3 Propositions antecedently supposed or proved.

Premium. 1 A reward.

2 The payment for the insurance of life or property.

3 A lump sum paid for the granting of a lease.
See FINE, 2.

4 A sum paid in excess of the nominal value of shares or stock.
See SHARE; STOCK.

Pre-nuptial agreement. *See* ANTE-NUPTIAL AGREEMENT.

Prepense. Aforethought. Thus, malice *prepense* is equivalent to malice aforethought.
See MALICE.

Prerogative. The special power, pre-eminence, or privilege which the Queen has, over and above other persons, in right of her Crown and independently of statute and the Courts.
See CONSTITUTIONAL LAW.

Prescribe to. To assert or claim anything by title or prescription.
See PRESCRIPTION.

Prescription. Prescription at Common Law, as defined by Blackstone, is where a person can show no other title to what he claims than that he, and those under whom he claims, have immemorially used and enjoyed it. The difference between prescription and custom is, that custom is a *local* usage, and not annexed to any *person*, whereas prescription is a *personal* usage. Prescription may, perhaps, in this sense be defined as the presumption of a grant arising from long usage.

This still applies to the acquisition of rights not included in the Prescription Act 1832, eg the right of support for buildings.

The Act of 1832 provides that a 30 years' enjoyment of rights of *common*, and other profits or benefits to be taken or enjoyed on any land, is no longer to be defeated by proof that the enjoyment commenced at a period subsequent to legal memory; and that a prescriptive claim of 60 years' enjoyment shall be absolute and indefeasible except by proof that such enjoyment took place under some deed, or written consent or agreement. In the case of *ways* and *watercourses*, the periods are 20 and 40 years respectively. In the case of *light*, the period is twenty years.
See LEGAL MEMORY.

The above is styled *positive* or *acquisitive prescription*, namely, that by which a title is acquired (as the *usucapio* of Roman law), and in English law properly applies to incorporeal hereditaments only. *Negative* prescription is that by which a right of challenge is lost (eg the prescription under the Statutes of Limitation), and this is applicable to corporeal rights; eg if an owner of land in the wrongful possession of another does not sue within 12 years from the time when such wrongful possession was obtained, he will usually lose his right to the property (see Limitation Act 1980, Highways Act 1980, and Law of Property Act 1925, s 12, which provides that nothing in Part I of the Act is to affect the operation of any Statute of Limitation relating to land or any law with reference to the acquisition of easements or rights over or in respect of land).
See EASEMENT; INCORPOREAL HEREDITAMENT.

Presentation. The act of a patron in offering his clerk to the bishop, to be instituted in a benefice of his gift. It includes collation, nomination, and any other manner of filling vacant benefices (see Pastoral Measure 1968).
See ADVOWSON; PRESENTMENT.

Presentative advowson. *See* ADVOWSON.

Presentee. A clerk presented by the patron of a living to the bishop.
See ADVOWSON; PRESENTATION.

Presentment. 1 Presentation to a benefice.
See PRESENTATION.

2 The presenting a bill of exchange to the drawee for acceptance, or to the acceptor for payment (see Bills of Exchange Act 1882, ss 39 *et seq*).
See ACCEPTANCE OF A BILL; BILL OF EXCHANGE.

Presents. A word in a deed meaning the deed itself, which is expressed by the phrase 'these presents'. It is especially used in a deed-poll, which cannot be described as 'This Indenture'. But see Law of Property Act 1925, s 57 which provides that any deed may be described as a deed simply, or as a conveyance, mortgage, lease, or otherwise according to the nature of the transaction intended to be effected.
See DEED; RECITAL; PREMISES; OPERATIVE PART OF A DEED.

President of the Council (Lord President of the Council). A high officer of the State, whose office is to attend on the Sovereign, and to propose business at the council table. He is a member of the Judicial Committee of the Privy Council, and of the Cabinet.
See JUDICIAL COMMITTEE OF THE PRIVY COUNCIL; CABINET.

P

Presumption. That which comes near, in greater or less degree, to the proof of a fact. It is called violent, probable, or light, according to the degree of its cogency. Presumptions are also divided into—(i) *præsumptiones juris et de jure*, otherwise called irrebuttable presumptions (often, but not necessarily, fictitious), which the law will not suffer to be rebutted by any counter-evidence; eg that an infant under ten years old is not responsible for his actions; (ii) *præsumptiones juris tantum*, which hold good in the absence of counter-evidence, but against which counter-evidence may be admitted; and (iii) *præsumptiones hominis*, which are not necessarily conclusive, though no proof to the contrary is adduced.

Presumption of death. The presumption that a person is dead where there is no direct evidence of the fact. This presumption takes place when a person has not been heard of for seven years; but the presumption is simply that he is dead, and not that he died at the end of the seven years, or any other specified time. So that if B, a legatee under A's will, has been last heard of six years before A's death, B's representatives will not, after A has been dead a year, be entitled to presume that B survived A, so as to claim the legacy.

Presumption of innocence. The presumption that a criminal accused is innocent until proven guilty beyond any reasonable doubt on evidence presented at a properly conducted trial.

Presumption of survivorship. The presumption that A survived B, or B survived A, when there is no evidence which died first, eg when both perish in the same shipwreck. The Common Law recognised no such presumption, and survivorship had to be proved. Under the Law of Property Act 1925, s 184 the presumption (subject to any order of the court) is that the younger survived.
See COMMORIENTES.

Presumptive evidence. A term especially used of evidence which, if believed, would not be necessarily conclusive as to the fact in issue, but from which, according to the ordinary course of human affairs, the existence of that fact might be presumed. In this sense it is synonymous with circumstantial evidence.
See CIRCUMSTANTIAL EVIDENCE.

Prevarication. The conduct of an advocate who betrayed the cause of his client, and by collusion assisted his opponent. Hence it means collusion between an informer and a defendant in a feigned prosecution; also any secret abuse committed in a public office or private commission.

To say that a witness *prevaricates* means that he gives quibbling and evasive answers to questions put to him.

Preventative justice. That portion of law which has reference to the direct prevention of offences. It generally consists in requiring those persons, whom there is probable ground to suspect of future misbehaviour, to give full assurance to the public that such offences as are apprehended shall not happen, by finding pledges or securities to keep the peace, or for their good behaviour.
See GOOD BEHAVIOUR; KEEPING THE PEACE.

Pricking for sheriffs. The custom with regard to the appointment of sheriffs is, that all the Judges, together with the other great officers, meet in Queen's Bench Division of the High Court on the morrow of St Martin (ie on 12th November), and then and there the Judges propose three persons for each county, to be reported (if approved of) to the King or Queen, who afterwards appoints one of them for sheriff. This appointment is made by marking each name with a prick of a pin, and is therefore called 'pricking for sheriffs'. This mode of appointment was continued by the Sheriffs Act 1887, which consolidated the law relating to sheriffs. The Sheriffs of London and Middlesex are now appointed by the Queen (see Local Government Act 1972, s 219).

Priest. A person in Holy Orders either in the Church of England or of Rome. Except by special dispensation, no person under 24 years of age can be ordained a priest.

Prima facie case. A litigating party is said to have a *prima facie* case when the evidence in his favour is sufficiently strong for his opponent to be called on to answer it. A *prima facie* case, then, is one which is established by sufficient evidence, and can be overthrown only by rebutting evidence adduced on the other side.
See REBUTTING EVIDENCE.

Prima facie evidence. A phrase sometimes used to denote evidence which establishes a *prima facie* case in favour of the party adducing it.
See PRIMA FACIE CASE.

Primæ impressionis (of first impression). A case of first impression is one as to which there is no precedent directly in point.
See PRECEDENTS.

Primage. A payment due to seamen for the loading of a ship.

Primary conveyances, as opposed to derivative conveyances, are conveyances which do *not* take effect by way of enlarging, confirming, altering, or otherwise affecting other conveyances; they are grants, gifts, leases, exchanges, partitions.
See DERIVATIVE CONVEYANCE.

Primary evidence. The best evidence, eg evidence which is not secondary, second-hand, or hearsay evidence.
See HEARSAY EVIDENCE; SECONDARY EVIDENCE; SECONDHAND EVIDENCE.

Primate. A title given to the archbishops of Canterbury and York, and of Dublin and Armagh.

Prime Minister, or **Premier.** A member of either one or other House of Parliament (by constitutional practice, now, of the House of Commons only) selected by the Queen as the person who is most likely to command a working majority in the House of Commons, to be head of Government.

Prince of Wales. The eldest son of the reigning Sovereign. Edward II, being born at Caernarvon, was the first English Prince of Wales. The heir apparent to the Crown is made Prince of Wales and Earl of Chester by special creation and investiture. He is also Duke of Cornwall by inheritance. The present Prince of Wales was invested at Caernarvon Castle in 1969.

Principal. 1 An heirloom.
    See HEIRLOOM.
  2 The amount of money which has been borrowed, as opposed to the interest payable thereon.
    See INTEREST, 2.
  3 The head of a college or other institution.
  4 A person who employs an agent.
  5 A person for whom another becomes surety.
  6 The general or compendious term for the person(s) to whom a fiduciary owes his fiduciary duties.
    See AGENT; FIDUCIARY; SURETY.

Priority. Any legal precedence or preference; eg when one says that certain debts are paid in *priority* to others; or that certain incumbrancers of an estate are allowed *priority* over others, ie are to be allowed to satisfy their claims out of the estate before the others can be admitted to any share in it, etc.
See PREFERENTIAL DEBTS.

Prison. A place of detention in safe custody, or for punishment after conviction.

Prison breach. *See* BREACH, 4.

Prison mutiny is where two or more prisoners, while on the premises of any prison, engage in conduct which is intended to further a common purpose of overthrowing lawful authority in that prison: Prison Security Act 1992, s 1(2).
See PRISON.

Private Act of Parliament. A local or personal Act affecting particular persons and private concerns.
See BILL, 2; LOCAL AND PERSONAL ACTS; PRIVATE BILLS.

Private bills. Bills brought into Parliament, on the petition of parties interested and on payment of fees. Such bills are brought in generally in the interest of individuals, counties, or other localities, and are distinguished from measures of public policy in which the whole community are interested. *May.*
See BILL, 4; LOCAL AND PERSONAL ACTS; PRIVATE ACT OF PARLIAMENT.

Private chapels. Chapels owned by noblemen and other privileged persons, and used by them and their families. They are thus opposed to *public chapels*, otherwise called *chapels of ease*, which are built for the accommodation of particular districts within a parish, in *ease* of the original parish church. As to the licensing of ministers at university, school, etc, chapels, see Extra-Parochial Ministry Measure 1967, s 2.

Private company. A company which is not a public company.
See PUBLIC COMPANY.

Private international law. An increasingly common name for that branch of law governing conflicts of law.
See CONFLICT OF LAWS.

Private law. The law governing the relations between individuals, not individuals and the state, except in so far as the state's rights are akin to those of private parties (ie as a tortfeasor, as a contracting party, as an owner of property, and as one able unjustly to enrich another or be unjustly enriched), thus the law of torts, contract, property, and unjust enrichment.

Privately fostered child. A child who is under 16 and is cared for, and provided with accommodation, by someone other than:
   (i) a parent of his;
   (ii) a person who is not a parent of his but who has parental responsibility for him; or
   (iii) a relative of his: Children Act 1989, s 66(1).

Privation. *See* DEPRIVATION.

Privies. *See* PRIVITY OF CONTRACT; PRIVITY OF ESTATE.

Privilege. That which is granted or allowed to any person, or any class of persons, either against or beyond the course of ordinary law.

Privilege, absolute. *See* ABSOLUTE PRIVILEGE.

Privilege, Crown. *See* PUBLIC INTEREST IMMUNITY.

Privilege, qualified. *See* QUALIFIED PRIVILEGE.

Privileged communication.
   1 A communication which, though *prima facie* libellous or slanderous, yet, by reason of the circumstances under which it is made, is protected either absolutely or in the absence of malice from being made the ground of proceedings for libel or slander, eg confidential communications without malice, etc.
      See DEFAMATION.
   2 A communication which is protected from disclosure in evidence in any civil or criminal proceeding; eg confidential communications between a party and his legal adviser in reference to the matter before the Court.

Privity. Knowledge of something being done; knowledge beforehand, and concurrence in it. See per Lord Denning, MR, in *The Eurysthenes* [1976] 3 All ER 243.

Privity of contract. The relation subsisting between the parties to the same contract. Thus if A, B, and C mutually contract, there is privity of contract between them. But if A contracts with B, and B makes an independent contract with C on that same subject matter, there is no privity of contract between A and C.
   Those not privy to a contract are normally neither liable under it nor entitled to bring

an action for any benefit under it. Now, however, by the Contract (Rights of Third Parties) Act 1999, third parties in certain circumstances may enforce a contract to obtain a benefit under it.
   See CONTRACT LAW.

Privity of estate. Between two persons is where their estates are so related to each other that they make only one estate in law, being *derived at the same time* out of the *same original seisin*. Thus if A, the owner of an estate, conveys it to B for a term of ten years, with remainder to C for his life, there is privity of estate between A and C. But if A conveys to B for his life, and B makes a lease for years to C, there is no privity between A and C.
   See ESTATE.

Privy. A partaker; one who has an interest in any action or thing. See the several entries immediately preceding this entry.

Privy Council. The principal council belonging to the Sovereign. Privy councillors are made on the Sovereign's nomination, without either patent or grant: and, on such nomination they become Privy Councillors, with the title of Right Honourable during the life of the Sovereign who has chosen them, but subject to removal at his or her discretion. The importance of the Privy Council has given way to that of the Cabinet.
   See JUDICIAL COMMITTEE OF THE PRIVY COUNCIL; CABINET.

Privy Purse. Her Majesty's Privy Purse is that portion of the public money voted to the Queen and her consort, which they may deal with as freely as any private individual may with his property. A certain sum per year is assigned by Parliament for this purpose. Salaries and expenses of Her Majesty's Household are payable under separate allowances, and these expenses, together with the Privy Purse, a further allowance for Royal bounty, alms, and special Services, and supplementary provision for expenses of the duties of the Royal Family, etc, are allowed in the Queen's Civil List by the Civil List Act 1972. The total sum may be altered from time to time under the provisions of the Civil List Act 1975.

Privy Seal and **Privy Signet.** The seal used for such grants from the Crown, or other things, as pass the Great Seal; first they pass the Privy Signet, then the Privy Seal, and lastly the Great Seal of England. The Privy Seal is also used in matters of small moment which never pass the Great Seal. The Privy Signet is one of the Sovereign's seals used for private letters and for grants which pass her hand by bill signed; it is always in the custody of the Queen's secretaries.

See LORD PRIVY SEAL; GREAT SEAL.

Prize Court. An international tribunal created by a special commission under the Great Seal in time of war to settle questions of capture, prize and booty (see Prize Acts 1864 to 1944; and see also Supreme Court Act 1981, s 27, declaring that the High Court is a Prize Court).

Prize of war. A ship or goods captured at sea or seized in port, by naval or air forces in time of war. When seized at sea, such goods are droits of the Crown; when seized in port they are droits of Admiralty. Prize differs from booty in that the former is taken by naval or air forces, the latter by land forces.

See BOOTY OF WAR.

If a ship, aircraft, or goods belonging to a British subject, after being taken as prize by the enemy, is, or are, retaken by any of Her Majesty's ships of war or aircraft, the prize must be restored to the owner on his paying *prize salvage*, one-eighth of the value of the prize as ascertained by the Prize Court, or such other sum, not exceeding one-eighth, as may be agreed.

Prize-fighting. In a public place is an affray, and an indictable offence on the part both of combatants and backers. *Mere presence* at a prize-fight, however, would seem not to be sufficient to render a person guilty of assault.

See AFFRAY; ASSAULT.

Pro forma. For form's sake.

Pro hac vice. For this occasion. An appointment *pro hac vice* is an appointment for a particular occasion as opposed to a permanent appointment.

Pro indiviso. For an undivided part; a phrase used in reference to lands the occupation of which is in joint tenancy or in common.

See COMMON, TENANCY IN; JOINT TENANCY.

Pro interesse suo. For his own interest. These words are used, especially of a party being admitted to intervene *for his own interest* in a suit instituted between other parties.

Pro rata. Proportionately.

Pro rata freight. Freight proportionate to the part of the voyage covered.

See FREIGHT.

Pro tanto. For so much, or so far as it will go; eg if a tenant for life creates a lease for 100 years, the lease is good *pro tanto*, ie for such an estate or interest as the tenant for life may lawfully convey.

Probate. The exhibiting and proving wills by executors in the High Court on which the original is deposited in the registry of the court, and a copy, called the *probate copy*, is made out under the seal of the court, and delivered to the executor, together with a certificate of its having been proved.

It may be either *in common form* or *in solemn form per testes*, where the will is disputed or irregular. For the procedure in regard to the granting of probate, see Part V of the Supreme Court Act 1981. Contentious business is dealt with in the Chancery Division of the High Court; non-contentious business has been assigned to the Family Division.

See SOLEMN FORM.

Probate, Divorce and Admiralty Division. A former division of the High Court of Justice. The High Court was reorganised by the Administration of Justice Act 1970. The Probate, Divorce and Admiralty Division was renamed the Family Division, to which the High Court's matrimonial and domestic business was assigned. Admiralty business was assigned to the Queen's Bench Division and contentious probate business was transferred to the Chancery Division.

Probate action. An action for the grant of probate of the will, or letters of administration of the estate of a deceased person or for the revocation of such a grant, or for a decree pronouncing for or against the validity of an alleged will, not being an action which is non-contentious or common form probate business: Administration of Justice Act 1985, s 49(2).

See PROBATE; ADMINISTRATOR.

Probate Court. A court established by the Court of Probate Act 1857, and to which was transferred the testamentary jurisdiction which up to that time had been exercised by the ecclesiastical courts. The Probate Court was merged in the Supreme Court of Judicature in 1873. Its jurisdiction is now exercised partly by the Chancery Division (contentious business) and partly by the Family Division (non-contentious business).

See CHANCERY DIVISION; FAMILY DIVISION.

Probation. In certain circumstances a Court, instead of sentencing an offender, may make a *probation order*, ie an order requiring him to be under the supervision of a probation officer for a period of from one to three years. Generally, as to probation and discharge from it, see Powers of Criminal Courts Act 1973, ss 2, 13.

Procedure. The steps taken in an action or other legal proceeding.

See PRACTICE; CIVIL PROCEDURE; CRIMINAL PROCEDURE.

Process. Formerly, the writ commanding the defendant's appearance in an action. This is sometimes called *original* process or *originating* process. From the time of the Judicature Acts 1873–75 until the Civil Procedure Act 1997 and the Civil Procedure Rules made thereunder, the process for the commencement of all actions in all Divisions of the High Court was either a writ of summons or an originating summons.

See SUMMONS, 4.

The Civil Procedure Rules 1998 provide, with some exceptions, that all cases are initiated by the filing of a claim form.

Proclamation. A notice publicly given to any thing of which the Queen thinks fit to advertise her subjects. The Queen cannot by a Proclamation create any offence which was not an offence before, unless Parliament confers on her the power to do so.

Proctor. 1 One who manages another person's affairs.

2 One chosen to represent a cathedral or collegiate church, or the clergy of a diocese, in the General Synod.

See SYNOD.

3 One who prosecutes or defends a suit for another.

4 An executive officer of the University.

Procuration. *See* PER PROCURATIONEM.

Procuration of women. The procuring of women for the purpose of illicit intercourse is an offence under the Sexual Offences Act 1956, ss 22, 23.

Procurator Fiscal (*Scotland*). An officer of the sheriff court whose duty it is to inquire into suspected offences in his area.

He also acts as public prosecutor.

Product liability. Liability where any damage is caused wholly or partly by a defect in a product. The persons liable are:

(i) any producer of the product;

(ii) any person who, by putting his name on the product or using a trade mark, has held himself out to be the producer;

(iii) any person who has imported the product into a Member State of the EC from outside the EC in order, in the course of any business of his, to supply it to another: Consumer Protection Act 1987 s 2(1), (2).

See DEFECT.

Professional indemnity insurance. A type of insurance effected by various persons eg solicitors, accountants, brokers, architects against their liability to pay damages to their clients by reason of their negligence in the performance of their professional duties.

Profits à prendre. Rights exercised by one person in the soil of another, accompanied with participation in the profits of the soil, eg rights of pasture, or digging sand. *Profits à prendre* differ from easements in that the former are rights of profit, and the latter are mere rights of convenience without profit.

See EASEMENT.

Prohibited steps order. An order that no step which could be taken by a parent in meeting his parental responsibility for a child, and which is of a kind specified in the order, shall be taken by any person without the consent of the Court: Children Act 1989, s 8(1).

Prohibition. An order to forbid an inferior court from proceeding in a cause there pending, suggesting that the cognisance of it does not belong to that court, ie it is outside its jurisdiction. Application is made to the Divisional Court (see Administration of Justice (Miscellaneous Provisions) Act 1938).

Prohibition differs from injunction, in that prohibition is directed to a court as well as to the opposite party, whereas an injunction is directed to the party alone.

See INJUNCTION; ADMINISTRATIVE LAW.

Prolixity. Unnecessary, superfluous, or impertinent statement. It renders an affidavit liable to be taken off the file, and in pleadings the offending party may be made to pay the costs.

Promise. A voluntary engagement by one person to another for the performance or non-p erformance of some particular thing. It differs from a contract, in that a contract involves the idea of mutuality, which a promise does not.

See CONTRACT; COVENANT.

Promissory note, otherwise called a *note of hand*, is defined by the Bills of Exchange Act 1882, s 83 as an unconditional promise in writing, made by one person to another, signed by the maker, engaging to pay on demand or at a fixed or determinable future time, a sum certain in money, to or to the order of a specified person or to bearer. The person who makes the note is called the maker, and the person to whom it is payable is called the payee. It differs from a bill of exchange, in that the maker stands in the place of drawer and acceptor.
See BILL OF EXCHANGE.

Promissory warranty in marine insurance means 'a warranty by which the assured undertakes that some particular thing shall or shall not be done or that some condition shall be fulfilled, or whereby he affirms or negatives the existence of a particular state of facts' (see Marine Insurance Act 1906, s 33(1)). A warranty may be express or implied (see ibid, s 33(2)). A promissory warranty 'is a condition which must be exactly complied with, whether it be material to the risk or not. If it be not so complied with, then, subject to any expressed provision in the policy, the insurer is discharged from liability as from the date of the breach of warranty, but without prejudice to any liability incurred by him before that date' (see ibid, s 33(3)).

Promoters. 1 Persons or corporations at whose instance private bills are introduced into and passed through Parliament. *May.*
See BILL, 2; PRIVATE BILLS.
2 Especially those who press forward bills for the taking of land for railways and other public purposes; who are then called *promoters of the undertaking.*
3 Persons who assist in establishing companies (see Companies Act 1985, s 67).

Promotion money. Money paid to the promoters of a company for their services in launching the concern.
See PROMOTERS, 3.

Promulgation of a law. The publication of a law already made.

Proper law, of a contract, trust, etc.
A phrase used in the law of CONFLICT OF LAWS to indicate which jurisdiction's law will govern a contract, trust, or some other legal arrangement. In certain case the parties will employ a choice of law clause expressing, eg that 'this contract will be governed by the law of England and Wales'.

Property. The significance of the concept of property in any legal system is difficult to understate, for it dictates how valuable parts of the world (other than humans, generally) can be made the subject matter of rights, rights which may be distributed by various modes, such as gift, contract, or the command of law. The nature of property at law can be elaborated along different lines: (i) the different kinds of things which can be the subject matter of property; (ii) the sorts of interests the law will recognise in things; (iii) the nature of title.

1 The subject matter of property consists of the different sorts of things which can be owned. The sorts of property in the law are traditionally divided into two classes, real property and personal property, which roughly corresponds to the civil law distinction between *immovables* and *movables,* the former term in each case referring to land, and the latter to things other than land, in particular tangible objects like furniture, books, clothing, etc. Tangible objects of this latter kind are called 'chattels' in English law. Unfortunately, the traditional division between real 'estate' and personal property in English law is hampered by the fact that leasehold interests, ie the right of a lessee or tenant in the land leased to him, was regarded as personal property rather than real property because originally a lessee out of possession could not get the assistance of the courts of common law in a 'real' action to be put in possession of the land, ie get the real thing . As a consequence, leasehold interests in land were treated as personal property; land being tangible, a kind of chattel, but nevertheless an interest in land, the odd hybrid 'chattels real' was used to designate leasehold interests. Following the reorganisation of property law by the property legislation of 1925, leasehold interests are now regarded as property in land as much as any other kind of right in land. The great development of types of property has occurred on the personal side, for it is into that category that new forms of intangible property, ie property with no physically possessible subject matter, has been placed. Thus

P

personal property can be divided into
the tangible, chattels, and the intangible.
The traditional terms for marking this
distinction are *choses* in possession,
and *choses* in action, the former being
things ownership of which is secured by
possession, thus material chattels, the latter
being abstract rights the value of which
lies in action, ie the legal process. Thus
debts are *choses* in action because one is
secured the value of a debt (being paid
the certain sum of money one is owed) by
the power to proceed at law against the
debtor. The same goes, eg for bank balances
(the debt one is owed by one's bank).
Certain abstract rights of this kind can
be reduced to 'documentary intangibles',
that is, the rights become embodied in
paper, and the title to these rights can
be transferred by the proper transfer of
the paper. An important class of these is
NEGOTIABLE INSTRUMENTS, which are subject
to particular rules of title (see below).
A different kind of personal property
entirely is the right to a monopoly
constituted by a patent or copyright, ie
intellectual property rights. While again
these are abstract, and may be enforced
by legal process, the monopoly itself
is not secured by legal process; rather,
violations of the monopoly are enjoined or
compensated, and in this way intellectual
property rights are more like rights in
tangible property than choses in action.

2 There can be many different kinds of
interest in property besides the ownership
of it. Ownership is in one sense the largest
kind of interest in property, for ownership
is the exclusive right to the property, and
thus an owner may generally (subject to
the limits of the criminal law, tort law,
public policy, and so on) do anything with
the property that the sort of property it is
admits. Thus one may build on land, farm
it, and so on, and one may use chattels,
modify them, and consume or destroy
them if one is the owner. But in general,
what distinguishes ownership from other
rights is two things: first, the owner's use
of property is unlimited in the sense that
it is undefined. There is no specified list
of things one might do with one's land or
goods. (Clearly, with respect to *choses* in
action like debts, the only 'use' one can
make of the right is to demand payment

from the debtor, so this point cannot be
fully general.) Lesser interests, such as
an easement, eg the right of way over
land, are more or less precisely specified.
Secondly, lesser interests arise as a result of
an owner's use of his powers of ownership
to create them. Thus an easement is created
by the grant of this lesser right by the
owner to another. While an owner may,
of course, transfer his title to another, by
doing so the owner *transfers* what he or she
already has—he or she does not by doing
so *create* a new interest in the property.
Land, in particular, may be the subject
of many lesser interests, in particular
EASEMENTS, PROFITS, and RESTRICTIVE
COVENANTS. SECURITY INTERESTS, such as
MORTGAGES of land and PLEDGES of chattels,
are a further kind of interest less than
ownership. Property can, of course, also be
co-owned, and in general lesser interests in
property can be co-owned in the same way
as full ownership may.

3 'Title' is a term which is substantially
equivalent to 'right in property', but is
generally used in framing the rules by
which a right to property is acquired,
transferred, or lost. Title to property, in
particular title to land, is, in English law,
closely wedded to possession. In general, a
possessor of land acquires a title to land by
the fact of possession, and so a wrongful
possessor of land, such as a squatter,
acquires a title to the land, though it will
be an inferior title to that of the rightful
possessor. By lapse of time, however, a
squatter may acquire a better title; by
the Limitation Act 1980, the title of an
owner who does not seek to repossess
his or her land from a squatter within a
certain period, usually twelve years, will be
extinguished. While the ownership of land
could formerly be transferred by livery,
ie delivery, a sort of ritual in which the
old owner put the new owner in physical
possession of the land, ownership of land is
now transferred by a document of transfer,
generically called a GRANT. The creation of
lesser interests in land, such as easements,
necessarily occurs by grant. However, in
a way somewhat parallel to the squatter's
acquisition of title to land, a person may
acquire a valid lesser interest in land in
certain cases by PRESCRIPTION. For example,
if a land owner uses a path over another's

land for a long period (eg for 20 years) he or she may acquire an easement over the land. Typically, however, rights in property are acquired by creation by the owner, as in the case of a security interest, or transfer. Different sorts of property are transferred in different ways: land, as we have seen, by a document of transfer, chattels by delivery or deed of gift, *choses* in action such as debts by written assignment with notice to the debtor, negotiable instruments typically by indorsement and delivery. The rules of title also determine how a right to property might be extinguished, an example being the case of land, above, already discussed. Title to chattels is, in general, very robust. If a person loses a chattel, his title is not lost as well. If a chattel is stolen, the thief acquires a thief's title, a title by the thief's new possession inferior to the good title of the person from whom he stole it, and in accordance with the maxim *nemo dat quod non habet* (one cannot give what one doesn't have), cannot give good title to a buyer from him, even if the buyer is innocent of knowledge that the property was stolen. There is an exception to the *nemo dat* rule in the case of negotiable instruments: a 'holder in due course', ie someone who gives good value for the indorsement and delivery of a negotiable instrument to him or herself takes a good title to the claim embodied in it even if there was a defect in the title of the transferor. (A similar rule operates in respect of the bona fide purchaser of a legal interest in property as regards equitable proprietary interests in the property; *see* EQUITY; BONA FIDE PURCHASER.) Formerly for many centuries, the owner of land could not give it by will; upon death, the land descended by inheritance, ie to heirs whose rights were determined by the general law; now all property may be given upon death by will, and in the absence of a will, is distributed by the rules of intestate succession, and where there is no one to take under these rules, the property goes as *bona vacantia* (goods without an owner) to the Crown.

See LAND LAW; ESTATE; REAL AND PERSONAL PROPERTY; NEGOTIABLE INTERESTS; WILL; SUCCESSION; INTERFERENCE WITH GOODS.

Property Acts 1925, Property Legislation of 1925. A major legislative reorganisation and reform of Property law, in particular of land law, comprised of six Acts of 1925, plus further supplementary provisions and amendments passed in 1926. The six Acts comprising the legislation were the Law of Property Act, The Land Registration Act, the Land Charges Act, the Settled Land Act, The Trustee Act, and the Administration of Estates Act.

Property in action. As opposed to property in immediate possession, is the right to recover any thing (if it should be refused) by suit or action at law.

See CHOSE.

Propounder. The person who, as executor under a will, or claiming administration with a will annexed, proposes it as genuine in the Family Division, or in the Chancery Division if it is contended.

See ADMINISTRATOR; EXECUTOR; PROBATE.

Proprietary estoppel. Where an owner of land allows another to act as if he has an interest in the owner's land, eg allowing that other to build a house on the owner's land in the mistaken belief that he or she owns it himself or herself, and the owner takes no steps to prevent that other, the owner will be estopped, ie stopped, from exercising his strict legal rights against that other, eg to evict that other from the land. Proprietary estoppel arose from the old equitable doctrine of 'encouragement and acquiescence', but has been enlarged in its scope beyond it. In general, the court may protect the expectations of the non-owner at its discretion, and may award the non-owner as much as a full ownership interest in the land if justice so demands.

See EQUITY; CONSTRUCTIVE TRUST.

Proprio vigore. By its own force.

Prorogation of Parliament. A putting off by the Crown of the sitting of Parliament, the effect of which is to put an end to the Session. It differs from an *adjournment*, in that an adjournment is effected by each House separately (though it may be at the instigation of the Crown); and after it all things continue as they were at the time of the adjournment; whereas after a *prorogation*, bills introduced and not passed are as if they had never been begun at all. *May.*

Prosecution. 1 The proceeding with, or following up, any matter in hand.

2 The proceeding with any suit or action at law. By a caprice of language, a person

P

instituting *civil* proceedings is said to prosecute *his action or suit*; but a person instituting *criminal* proceedings is said to prosecute *the party accused*.

3 The party by whom criminal proceedings are instituted; so it is said, such a course was adopted by the prosecution, etc.

Prosecutor. Any person who prosecutes any proceeding in a court of justice, whether civil or criminal; but the caprice of language has confined the term so as to denote, in general, a party who institutes criminal proceedings by way of indictment or information on behalf of the Crown, who is nominally the prosecutor in all criminal cases.

See PUBLIC PROSECUTOR.

Prospectus is defined by the Companies Act 1985, s 744 as 'any prospectus, notice, circular, advertisement, or other invitation, offering to the public for subscription or purchase any shares or debentures of a company.'

Prostitution. The indiscriminate consorting of a woman with men for hire. It is an offence under the Sexual Offences Act 1956, s 22 to procure a woman to become a common prostitute; and under ibid, ss 30, 31, for a man to live on the earnings of prostitution, or for a woman to exercise control over a prostitute. It is also an offence for a person to keep a brothel or to manage, or act or assist in the management of, a brothel. Loitering or soliciting in a street or public place for the purpose of prostitution is punishable under the Street Offences Act 1959, s 1.

See BROTHEL.

Protected coin. Any coin which:
  (i) is customarily used as money in any country; or
  (ii) is specified in an order made by the Treasury (see the Forgery and Counterfeiting Act 1981, s 27(1)).

Protected tenancy. *See* ASSURED TENANCY

Protection. 1 The benefit or safety which is secured to every subject by the law.

2 A special exemption or immunity given to a person by the Queen, by virtue of her Prerogative, against suits in law or other vexations, in respect of the party being engaged in the Queen's service. It is now rarely granted.

See PREROGATIVE.

3 The giving advantages in respect of duties to home over foreign goods.

Protective trust. Trusts giving a 'protected' interest for life or any less period to a beneficiary, to ensure that the interest shall not be lost to the beneficiary's creditors. On the happening of the beneficiary's bankruptcy, or upon his attempting to assign his interest to another and other similar events, the protected life interest 'determines', ie is extinguished, and the interest is henceforward held under a DISCRETIONARY TRUST whereby the trustees may, in their absolute discretion, apply the income of the fund, usually for the beneficiary and his or her spouse and children. A statutory form of such trusts is provided by the Trustee Act 1925, s 33.

Protectorate. 1 The period during which Cromwell was Protector.

2 A relation sometimes adopted by a strong country towards a weak one, whereby the former protects the latter from hostile invasion, and interferes more or less in its domestic concerns.

Protest. 1 A caution, by which a person declares that he does either not at all, or only conditionally, yield his consent to any act to which he might otherwise be deemed to have yielded an unconditional assent.

2 A formal declaration by the holder of a bill of exchange, or by a notary public at his request, that the bill of exchange has been refused acceptance or payment, and that the holder intends to recover all the expenses to which he may be put in consequence of it. In the case of a foreign bill, such a protest is essential to the right of the holder to recover from the drawer or indorser (see Bills of Exchange Act 1882, s 51).

See BILL OF EXCHANGE; NOTARY.

3 A document drawn up by a master of a ship and attested by a justice of the peace, consul, or notary public, stating the circumstances under which damage to the ship or cargo has occurred.

Protocol (Fr *Protocole*). 1 A Byzantine term applied to the first sheet pasted on a MS roll, stating by whom it was written, etc.

2 The first or original copy of anything.

3 The entry of any written instrument in the book of a notary or public officer, which, in case of the loss of the instrument, may be admitted as evidence of its contents.

See NOTARY.

4 A document serving as the preliminary to, or opening of, any diplomatic transaction.

Prove. **1** To establish by evidence.

2 To establish a debt due from an insolvent estate, and to receive a dividend on it.

3 To prove a will.

See PROBATE.

Province. **1** The circuit of an archbishop's jurisdiction. *Cowel.*

See ARCHBISHOP.

2 A colony or dependency.

See COLONIES.

3 An administrative division of the country used by the Ministry of Agriculture.

Provincial Courts. The ecclesiastical courts of the Archbishops of York and Canterbury.

See PROVINCE.

Provisional orders. Orders by a Government department authorising public undertakings under the authority of Acts of Parliament. Such orders are termed 'provisional' because they do not come into force until confirmed by a further Act of Parliament.

Proviso. A condition inserted into a deed, on the observance of which the validity of the deed depends.

Provocation. The goading of a person into losing his self-control. Where, on a charge of murder, there is evidence on which the jury can find that the person charged was provoked, *whether by things done or by things said or by both together*, to lose his self-control, the question whether the provocation was enough to make a reasonable man do as he did must be determined by the jury, according to their view of the effect that such words or actions would have upon a reasonable man (see Homicide Act 1957, s 3).

Provost Marshal. **1** An officer in the Queen's Navy having charge of prisoners at sea.

2 A military or air force officer in control of military or air force police and having charge of prisoners.

3 An officer appointed in time of martial law to arrest and punish offenders. Execution parties are placed under his orders.

See MARTIAL LAW.

Proxies. **1** Payments made to a bishop by a religious house, or by parish priests, for the charges of his visitation.

See VISITATION.

2 By a *proxy* is generally understood a person deputed to vote in the place or stead of the party so deputing him, eg in the House of Lords; at meetings of creditors of a bankrupt; at meetings of the shareholders of a company; and on various other occasions.

Psychopathic disorder. A persistent disorder or disability of mind (whether or not including significant impairment of intelligence) which results in abnormally aggressive or seriously irresponsible conduct on the part of the person concerned: Mental Health Act 1983, s 1(2).

Puberty. The age of 14 in men and 12 in women, at which they were deemed formerly capable of contracting marriage.

Public Act of Parliament. An Act to be judicially noticed, which is not the case with all Acts of Parliament, except the very few in which a declaration is inserted to the contrary (see Interpretation Act 1978, s 3).

See ACT OF PARLIAMENT; PRIVATE ACT OF PARLIAMENT.

Public assembly. An assembly of 20 or more persons in a public place which is wholly or partly open to the air (see Public Order Act 1986, s 16). A senior police officer may give directions imposing conditions on public assemblies (see ibid, s 14).

Public chapels. Chapels of ease designed for the benefit of particular districts within a parish. They are opposed to PRIVATE CHAPELS, which are erected for the use of persons of rank, to whom the privilege has been conceded by the proper authorities; also to *proprietary chapels*, which are the property of private persons, and are erected with a view to profit or otherwise.

Public charitable collection. A charitable appeal which is made (i) in any public place, or (ii) by means of visits from house to house: Charities Act 1992, s 65(1).

No such collection must be conducted except in accordance with a permit issued by a local authority or an order made by the Charity Commissioners: ibid, s 66.

See CHARITABLE APPEAL.

Public company. A company limited by shares or limited by guarantee and having a share capital, being a company:

(i) the memorandum of which states that the company is to be a public company; and

(ii) in relation to which the provisions of the Act as to the registration or re-registration of a company as a public company have

233

been complied with (see Companies Act 1985, s 1(3)).

Public interest immunity. The right of the Crown to withhold the disclosure and production of a document on the ground that its disclosure and production would be injurious to the public interest.

The right can be claimed or waived by the Crown and not by the person to whom the document relates. The claim must be made by the Minister of the Government Department concerned by his giving a certificate that it is not in the public interest to disclose or produce the document.

The Court may allow or reject the claim.

Public international law. The law, including the legal rights, duties, and powers, governing the behaviour of sovereign states to each other. One of the most challenging and important questions concerning public international law (PIL) is one that has been continually raised, but not so far conclusively answered to general satisfaction: does PIL actually exist? While no one doubts that there is a body of standards of behaviour to which states more or less generally adhere, these standards and the behaviour of states toward them are significantly different from those which make up the various systems of municipal law, ie the laws of any particular state such as the UK, and these differences tend, by and large, to suggest that PIL is 'law' in a lesser or deficient way. For example, in contrast with municipal legal systems, there is no authority over states which has the power to make new public international laws or modify old ones, such as an international legislature; despite the existence of the 'World Court', or International Court of Justice (established in 1945 under the auspices of the United Nations and its principal judicial organ which superseded the Permanent Court of International Justice, created under the auspices of the League of Nations in 1921), there is no judicial body with the authority to command attendance and resolve any dispute of PIL brought before it by an aggrieved party, and no general, authoritative means of enforcement of international law. These differences are not determinative, however. The strongest ground for the existence of international law is that the standards which are identified to comprise it are generally complied with, and that a state's failure to comply with these standards in particular

instances attracts the criticism that the state is acting illegally. Furthermore, the system of standards is approached with the same legal intellectual skills, and the consequent involvement of lawyers, as are the laws of a municipal legal system. Finally, given the political and diplomatic context, the absence of authorities such as a world legislature, a world court with authority to administer the law without the acquiescence of the parties to a dispute or violation, or a world enforcement authority, may, properly understood, reflect not a deficiency of PIL but rather the appropriate institutional character of law in this kind of setting, ie very little if any institutionalisation of authority. So, while because of this minimal institutionalisation of authority PIL may be more static, more uncertain, and less efficient than municipal law, this accords with the nature of the community of its subjects, a group of sovereign states which are, nonetheless, interdependent in many ways and likely to become more so. The most crucial factor may be the extent to which the institutions and practitioners of PIL can in theory and practice actually guide the behaviour of the subjects of PIL, the many sovereign states, in an authoritative way. To the extent that states determine their actions vis-à-vis other states not by regarding the rules of PIL as more or less peremptory requirements, but merely as (important) considerations to be taken into account, PIL does not have the authoritative force which is generally regarded as a necessary aspect of law of any kind. It remains a matter of judgment whether PIL generally has this authoritative force in the decision-making of states.

The sources of PIL are described in Article 38 of the Statute of the International Court of Justice as follows:

'Article 38.

1. The Court, whose function is to decide in accordance with international law such disputes as are submitted to it, shall apply:
   (a) international conventions [ie treaties between or amongst states], whether general or particular, establishing rules expressly recognised by the contesting States [ie the states who are parties before the Court];
   (b) international custom, as evidence of a general practice accepted as law;

(c) the general principles of law recognised by civilised nations;

(d) subject to the provisions of Article 59 [which states, 'The decision of the Court has no binding force except between the parties and in respect of the particular case'.], judicial decisions and the teachings of the most highly qualified publicists of the various nations [ie the writings of prominent PIL jurists], as subsidiary means for the determination of rules of law.

2. This provision shall not prejudice the power of the Court to decide a case *ex aequo et bono*, if the parties agree thereto.'

It is generally understood that the sources of PIL are listed here in order of importance, the actual treaty obligations of states being the most certain and important standards. The determination of international custom is not a precise matter, but a consistency of practice among a significant number of states over some period of time, coupled with *opinio juris*, ie the understanding by states that the custom is binding upon them as law, are taken to be the normal essential elements of a custom. The customary rules of PIL called the rules of *jus cogens* are regarded as so fundamental that they cannot be abrogated by treaty, and although there is little certainty as to which customary rules fall into this category, the general prohibition against armed force save in cases of defence, or the freedom of the high seas, may be examples.

Some of the most important substantive areas of public international law are the rules concerning the nature and recognition of subjects of international law, principally states; the extent of a state's jurisdiction, ie the contours of the principle that a state may not exercise its power in the territory of another state; the immunity of states and their representatives from legal process in other states; the use of force, war crimes, and the peaceful settlement of disputes; the law of treaties, both bilateral treaties and multilateral treaties or conventions; international human rights; and the law of the sea, outer space, and Antarctica.

Public law. 1 As opposed to private law, the law in which the state or a public authority is interested, generally as a party, as an aspect of its function of governance; thus criminal law, regulatory law

(eg the administration of environmental regulation regimes and the prosecution of environmental offences), planning law, administrative law, and constitutional law.

2 As a traditional subject of study for an English law degree, constitutional and administrative law, sometimes with the addition of human rights law particularly in reference to the European Convention on Human Rights.

Public lending right. A right conferred on authors to receive from time to time out of a Central Fund payments in respect of such of their books as are lent out to the public by local library authorities in the United Kingdom (see Public Lending Right Act 1979, s 1(1)). For the Central Fund, see ibid, s 2, and for the scheme of payment and its administration, see ibid, s 3.

Public liability insurance. A type of insurance protecting the insured against liabilities to third parties other than his employees arising out of the condition or management of his property or the conduct of his business.

Public meeting. Any number of persons may meet for any lawful purpose in any place with the consent of the owner of the place, but there is no 'right of public meeting' known to English law, and persons have only a right to pass and re-pass in the public streets, etc.

Newspaper reports of public meetings are protected by qualified privilege under s 7 of and the Schedule to the Defamation Act 1952. *See* QUALIFIED PRIVILEGE.

As to disturbance of public meetings, see the Public Meeting Act 1908 and Public Order Act 1936; also Representation of the People Act 1983, s 97, which makes it an illegal practice to cause a disturbance at election meetings.
See ILLEGAL PRACTICES.

Public mischief. Once an offence which tended to the prejudice of the community. See *R v Manley* [1933] 1 KB 529. But now no longer a crime: *Director of Public Prosecutions v Withers* [1974] 3 All ER 984, HL.

Public nuisance. *See* NUISANCE.

Public place. Under the Prevention of Crime Act 1953 (prohibiting the carrying of offensive weapons without lawful authority or reasonable excuse) includes any highway and any other premises or place to which at the material time the public have or are permitted to have access, whether on payment or otherwise. See also the statutory definitions, including the Criminal Justice Act 1972, s 33, and Prevention of Terrorism (Temporary Provisions) Act 1989, s 3(3).

Public policy. In one sense, 'public policy' is used in the phrase 'against public policy'; a court will refuse to recognise or enforce certain classes of act which are against public policy as injurious to the public welfare or the interests of the state. In a second sense, 'public policy', or just 'policy', arguments or considerations are those considerations of a general nature concerning the public welfare or the administration of justice to which a judge may have recourse in deciding a case where the law is unsettled.

Public procession. A procession in a public place (see Public Order Act 1986, s 16). Written notice must be given of any proposal to hold a public procession intended:
(i) to demonstrate support for or opposition to the views or actions of any person or body of persons,
(ii) to publicise a cause or campaign, or to mark or commemorate an event (see ibid, s 11(1)).

The notice must be delivered to a police station (see ibid, s 11(4)). A senior police officer may give directions imposing conditions on public processions (see ibid, s 12).

Public prosecutor. The Director of Public Prosecutions appointed under the Prosecution of Offences Act 1979, whose duty it is to undertake the prosecution in cases where the magnitude of the offence makes it desirable.

Public sewers. Sewers vested in a water authority: Public Health Act 1936, s 21(2).

Public stores. Stores under the care, superintendence or control of a Secretary of State or any public department or office or of any person in the service of Her Majesty: Public Stores Act 1875, s 3.

Public trustee. An official appointed pursuant to the Public Trustee Act 1906 as a corporation sole to deal with trusts where there is a difficulty in finding someone to serve as a trustee, thus in a sense, a trustee of last resort.

Publication. 1 The declaration by a testator that a given writing is intended to operate as his last will and testament. This was formerly necessary to give legal effect to a will. But, by the Wills Act 1837, s 13 no publication is

necessary beyond the execution attested by two witnesses as required by s 9 of that Act.
2 The communication of a defamatory statement to any person or persons other than the party of whom it is spoken.
See DEFAMATION.

Publici juris. Of public right.

Publish. *See* PUBLICATION.

Published edition, in the context of copyright in the typographical arrangement of a published edition, means a published edition of the whole or any part of one or more literary, dramatic, or musical works: Copyright, Designs and Patents Act 1988, s 8(1). Copyright does not subsist in the typographical arrangement of a published work if it reproduces the typographical arrangement of a previous edition: ibid, s 8(2).
See COPYRIGHT; LITERARY WORK; MUSICAL WORK.

Puffer. A person employed to bid up the price at a sale by auction on behalf of the owner of the land or goods sold. The employment of a puffer is illegal, unless a right to bid is reserved to the owner by the conditions or particulars of sale. See, as to land, Sale of Land by Auction Act 1867, and, as to goods, Sale of Goods Act 1979, s 58.

Puisne. Younger; thus, *mulier puisne* is the younger legitimate brother. So, the Judges of the High Court, other than those having a distinctive title, are called the *puisne* judges.
See DIVISIONS OF THE HIGH COURT.

Puisne mortgage. Any legal mortgage not being a mortgage protected by a deposit of documents relating to the legal estate affected. Such a mortgage is included in the list of land charges registrable under the Land Charges Act 1972. *See* s 2(4) Class C(i).
See MORTGAGE.

Pupil, pupillage. A person undertaking 12 months' supervision under a practicing barrister, called pupillage; a requirement for qualification to practice as a barrister in England and Wales.

Pur autre vie. For another's life; eg a tenant *pur autre vie* is a tenant whose estate is to last during another person's life.
See ESTATE.

Purchase, besides its ordinary meaning, has a more extensive technical meaning in reference to the law of real property. The meaning is twofold:

1 The word signifies any lawful mode of coming to an estate by the act of the *party* as opposed to the operation of law.
See OPERATION OF LAW.

2 Any mode, other than descent, of becoming seised of real estate.
See PURCHASER; BONA FIDE PURCHASER.

Purchaser. 1 One who acquires real or personal estate by gift or contract.

2 Under the Law of Property Act 1925 the word means a purchaser in good faith for valuable consideration, and includes a lessee, mortgagee, or other person who for valuable consideration acquires an interest in property, except that in Part I of that Act and elsewhere as expressly provided, the word only means a person who acquires an interest in or charge on property for money or money's worth; and in reference to a legal estate includes a chargee by way of legal mortgage. See s 205(1)(xxi).

Purging. Atoning for an offence eg *purging a contempt of Court* is atoning for a contempt. The party then ceases to be 'in contempt' ie, liable to the disabilities of a person who refuses to obey the orders of the court.
See CONTEMPT OF COURT.

Purpose trust. A trust to carry out a purpose, as opposed to a trust for the distribution of the trust property to persons. Public, or charitable, purpose trusts are allowed by law and enforced by the Attorney-General or the Charity Commissioners. Purpose trusts not of a charitable nature are generally void, save for a few exceptions, trusts 'of imperfect obligation', ie testamentary trusts for the maintenance of animals, for the upkeep of graves, or for the saying of private masses for the better repose of the testator's soul.

Purview. 1 That part of an Act of Parliament which begins with the words, *Be it enacted*.
See STATUTE.

2 The scope of an Act of Parliament.

Put An option which a party has of delivering shares at a certain time, in pursuance of a contract, the other party to the contract being bound to take the shares at the price and time specified in it.
See OPTION, 1.

Putative father. The man who is supposed to be the father of a bastard child.

Pyx. *See* PIXING THE COIN.

P

Q

QB. Queen's Bench.

QBD. Queen's Bench Division.
See QUEEN'S BENCH DIVISION.

QC. Queen's Counsel.
See QUEEN'S COUNSEL.

QV. (*Quod vide*, Latin for 'which see'). This abbreviation directs a reader to consult some passage referred to.

Qualification. That which makes a person eligible to do certain acts or to hold office.

Qualification share. A share which a director of a company must hold in order to be appointed or to continue as such.

Where a qualification is fixed, it must be disclosed in the prospectus (see Companies Act 1985, Sch 3, Part I, para 1(b)).
See PROSPECTUS.

Qualified acceptance in the case of a bill of exchange is an acceptance with some variation of the effect of the bill as drawn (see Bills of Exchange Act 1882, s 19).
See BILL OF EXCHANGE; ACCEPTANCE OF A BILL.

Qualified indorsement, on a bill of exchange or promissory note, is an indorsement which restrains, limits or enlarges the liability of the indorser, in a manner different from that which the law generally imports as his true liability, deducible from the nature of the instrument. A particular type of this indorsement is one whereby the indorser repudiates liability, which may be made by annexing in French the words *sans recours*, or in English 'without recourse to me', or other equivalent expression (see Bills of Exchange Act 1882, ss 16(1) and 35).
See BILL OF EXCHANGE; INDORSEMENT; PROMISSORY NOTE.

Qualified privilege. A defence to an action for defamation. A statement otherwise actionable, is the subject of qualified privilege, where it is made:

(i) by a person in the course of performing a duty (eg an employer giving a reference for an employee);

(ii) by a person protecting his own interest eg when defending his reputation;

(iii) in a newspaper report of proceedings of certain bodies and associations as specified in the Schedule to the Defamation Act 1952 (Defamation Act 1952, s 7);

(iv) in communications between a solicitor and his client.

The defence of qualified privilege can be defeated by proof of *malice* on the defendant's part, ie that the statement was made through an improper motive.
See DEFAMATION.

Qualified property. A limited right of ownership; eg:

1 Such right as a man has in animals, *feræ naturæ*, which he has reclaimed.
See FERÆ NATURÆ; INDUSTRIAM, PER; PROPERTY.

2 Such right as a bailee has in the chattel transferred to him by the bailment.
See BAILMENT.

Qualified title. Under the Land Registration Act 1925 land may be registered with a qualified title. Where an absolute title is applied for, and on examination of the title it appears that the title can be established only for a limited period, or only subject to certain reservations, the registrar may, on the application of the person applying to be registered, by an entry made in the register, except from the effect of registration any estate, right or interest (i) arising before a specified date, or (ii) arising under a specified instrument or otherwise particularly described in the register, and a title registered, subject to such excepted estate, right, or interest is called a 'qualified' title.

The registration of freehold land with a qualified title has the same effect as registration with an absolute title, except that registration with a qualified title does not affect or prejudice the enforcement of any estate, right, or interest appearing by the register to be excepted (s 7). For the effect of registration of leaseholds with a qualified title, see s 12 of the Act.

See ABSOLUTE TITLE; REGISTERED LAND.

Quamdiu bene se gesserit (as long as he shall behave himself well). These words imply that an office or privilege is to be held during good behaviour (as opposed to *durante bene placito*, during the pleasure of the grantor), and therefore is not to be lost otherwise than by the misconduct of the occupant; except, of course, by his death or voluntary resignation. Judges hold their office thus (see Supreme Court Act 1981, s 11(3)).

Quantum. How much. The 'quantum of damages' is the amount of damages claimed or awarded at trial. 'Issues of quantum' refer to disputes over facts which determine the extent of loss for which damages are awarded.

See DAMAGES.

Quantum meruit (how much he has deserved). An action on a *quantum meruit* is an action to pay the plaintiff for work and labour so much as his trouble is really worth.

See UNJUST ENRICHMENT.

Quantum valebat (as much as it was worth). A phrase applied to an action for payment for goods transferred for as much as they were worth, where no price had been previously agreed.

See UNJUST ENRICHMENT

Quarantine. Forty days. Forty days' probation for ships coming from infected countries, or such other time as may be directed by an Order in Council.

Quarter days are, in England, the four following days:

1 The 25th March, being the Feast of the Annunciation of the Blessed Virgin Mary, commonly called Lady Day.
   See LADY-DAY.

2 The 24th June, being the Feast of St John the Baptist, otherwise called Midsummer Day.

3 The 29th September, being the Feast of St Michael and All Angels, commonly called Michaelmas Day.

4 The 25th December, being the Feast of the Nativity of Christ, commonly called Christmas Day.

Quash (Lat *Cassum facere*). To make void or annul, eg when one says that an order of justices, or a conviction in an inferior court, is *quashed* by the judgment of a superior court.

Quasi-contract. An act or event from which, though not a consensual contract, an obligation arises *as if* from a contract (*quasi ex contractu*), eg an executor or administrator is bound to satisfy the liabilities of the deceased to the extent of his assets received, *as if* he had contracted to do so.

See UNJUST ENRICHMENT.

Quasi-entail. An estate *pur autre vie* granted to a man and the heirs of his body (see Law of Property Act 1925).

See PUR AUTRE VIE; ESTATE; LAND LAW.

Quasi-personalty. Things which are movables in point of law, though fixed to things real, either actually, as emblements (*see* EMBLEMENTS), etc, or fictitiously, as chattels real (*see* CHATTELS), leases for years, etc.

Quasi-realty. Things which are fixed in contemplation of law to realty, but are movable in themselves, eg heirlooms, title deeds, etc.

See HEIRLOOM; TITLE DEEDS.

Queen. 1 A Queen Regent, regnant, or sovereign, is one who holds the Crown in her own right.
   See KING.

2 A Queen Consort is the wife of a reigning King.

3 A Queen Dowager is the widow of a deceased King.

Queen can do no wrong. This maxim means that the Queen is not legally responsible for anything she may please to do, or for any forbearance or omission. Common law principle which held the Crown immune from actions in the Courts. It does not mean that everything done by the Government is just and lawful; but that whatever is exceptional in the conduct of public affairs is not to be imputed to the Queen.

The impediment to suing the Crown which this maxim implies was removed by the Crown Proceedings Act 1947.

Queen Consort. *See* QUEEN, 2.

Queen Dowager. *See* QUEEN, 3.

Q

Queen's Bench Division. The jurisdiction of the former Court of Queen's Bench was assigned in 1873 to the then newly-constituted Queen's Bench Division of the High Court of Justice. This Division is still one of three which together form the High Court, the others being the Chancery Division and the Family Division.

The Queen's Bench Division consists of the Lord Chief Justice, who is the president of it, and Puisne Judges, the numbers of which are laid down by Orders in Council made under the Supreme Court Act 1981, s 4(4). As to the assignment of business to the Queen's Bench Division, see Supreme Court Act 1981, s 61(1), Sch 1.
See PUISNE.

Queen's Coroner and Attorney. An officer of the Queen's Bench Division whose office is now merged in that of Master of the Crown Office, and is held by one of the Masters of the Supreme Court.

Queen's Counsel. A name given to barristers appointed by letters patent to be Her Majesty's counsel learned in the law. Their selection and removal rests, in practice, with the Lord Chancellor. A Queen's Counsel, in taking that rank, renounces the preparation of written pleadings and other chamber practices.

Queen's enemies. The armed forces of a State at war with the United Kingdom or if a chartered ship is a foreign ship, with the country to which the ship belongs (see *Russel v Niemann* (1864) 17 CBNS 163).

Queen's evidence. Evidence for the Crown. An accused person who 'turns Queen's evidence' is a person who confesses his guilt and proffers himself as a witness against his accomplices. His admission, however, in that capacity requires the sanction of the Court; and, unless his statements are corroborated in some material part by unimpeachable evidence, the jury must be warned by the Judge of the danger of convicting. If his evidence is unsatisfactory, he may still be convicted on his original confession or other evidence.
See ACCOMPLICE.

Queen's peace. *See* PEACE OF THE QUEEN.

Queen's Remembrancer. *See* REMEMBRANCERS.

Qui approbat non reprobat. He who accepts cannot reject.

Qui facit per alium facit per se. He who does a thing through another does it himself.

Qui prior est tempore potior est jure. He who is earlier in time is better in right. A maxim of the common law applying to the priority of interests in property.

Quia timet. Because he fears. A suit in equity for a *quia timet* injunction seeks an injunction to prevent a harm which the plaintiff fears the defendant will cause him.

Quicquid plantatur solo, solo cedit. Whatever is affixed to the soil, belongs to the soil.
See FIXTURES.

Quid pro quo. A compensation, or the giving of one thing of value for another thing of like value.
See CONSIDERATION.

Quiet enjoyment. A phrase applied specially to the undisturbed enjoyment, by a purchaser of landed property, of the estate or interest so purchased. A general covenant, by a vendor or lessor, for quiet enjoyment by the purchaser or lessee, extends only to secure the covenant against the acts of persons claiming under a *lawful* title, for the law will never adjudge that a lessor (or vendor) covenants against the wrongful acts of strangers, unless his covenant is express to that purpose.

The construction, however, is different where an individual is named, for there the covenantor is presumed to know the person against whose acts he is content to covenant, and may, therefore, be reasonably expected to stipulate against any disturbance from him, whether by lawful title or otherwise. See also s 76 of, and Sch 11 to, the Law of Property Act 1925, which deal with covenants for title. *Hill and Redman.*

Quietus. 1 Acquitted or discharged; a word used specially of the sheriffs and other accountants to the Exchequer, when they had given in their accounts.
See EXCHEQUER.
2 An acquittance or discharge.

Quittance. A release.

Quo animo (with what intention). A phrase once often used in criminal trials, where there is no question of certain overt acts having been committed by the accused, and the only question is with what intention (*quo animo*) they were done.
See FURANDI ANIMUS.

Quoad hoc (in respect of this matter). A term used in law reports to signify, *as to this matter* the law is so.

Quod approbo non reprobo. That which I accept I do not reject.

Quorum. 1 A word used in commissions of the peace, by which it is intended to indicate that some particular justices, or some or one of them are always to be included in the business to be done, so that no business can be done without their presence; the words being '*quorum aliquem vestrum*, A, B, C, D, etc, *unum esse volumus*'. The particular justices so named are called justices of the *quorum*.

2 The *minimum* number of persons necessarily present in order that business may be proceeded with, at any meeting for the dispatch of business, in the Houses of Parliament. *May.*

3 The *minimum* number of persons necessarily present for a meeting eg the annual general meeting of a company.

R

R. *Rex* or *regina,* as in the Queen's signature, Elizabeth R.

RSC. Rules of the Supreme Court made by a Rule Committee of judges and lawyers under the authority of the Supreme Court Act 1981. The rules were revised in 1965, and might be found in 'The Supreme Court Practice'; these rules have largely been superseded by the Civil Procedure Rules 1998, made under the Civil Procedure Act 1997.
See CIVIL PROCEDURE.

Rabbit. A beast of warren, also termed a 'coney'. Unlawfully taking or destroying rabbits by night is an offence under the Night Poaching Act 1828, s 1; similarly, it is an offence to trespass in pursuit of rabbits in the daytime under the Game Act 1831, ss 30–32. As to the right of a tenant to shoot rabbits on his farm, see Ground Game Act 1880. The destruction and control of rabbits are provided for under the Pests Act 1954.

Racial discrimination. *See* DISCRIMINATION.

Racial grounds. The grounds of colour, race, nationality, or ethnic or national origins (see Race Relations Act 1976, s 3(1)).

Racial group. A group of persons defined by reference to colour, race, nationality, or ethnic or national origin (see Race Relations Act 1976, s 3(1)).

Racial hatred. Hatred against a group of persons in Great Britain defined by reference to colour, race, nationality (including citizenship), or ethnic or national origins (see Public Order Act 1986, s 17). It is an offence to commit acts intended or likely to stir up racial hatred (see ibid, ss 18–22). It is also an offence to be in possession of racially inflammatory material (see ibid, s 23). Chanting at a football match words of a racialist nature including matter which is threatening, abusive, or insulting to a person by reason of his colour, race, nationality, or ethnic or national origin is an offence: Football (Offences) Act 1991, s 1.

Rack. Torture for the purpose of extorting a confession from an accused person.

Rack-rent. Rent of the full annual value of the tenement on which it is charged, or as near to it as possible.

Radio Authority. An authority whose function is to regulate the provision of sound broadcasting services which are provided from places in the United Kingdom by persons other than the BBC: Broadcasting Act 1990, s 84(1). It may grant licences for this purpose, and must do all that it can to ensure a diversity of national services each catering for different tastes and interests, and a range of diversity of local services: ibid, s 85(1), (2). It must draw up a general code for programmes: ibid, s 91(1).

Railway. A system of transport employing parallel rails which:
  (i) provide a support and guidance for vehicles carried on flanged wheels, and
  (ii) form a trackway which either is of a gauge of at least 350 mm or crosses a carriageway (whether or not on the same level),
  but does not include a tramway: Transport and Works Act 1992, s 67(1).

Ransom. The sum paid for the redeeming of a person taken prisoner. *TL; Cowel; 2 Bl.*

Rape. The ravishment of a woman without her consent by force, fear or fraud. It is an offence under the Sexual Offences Act 1956, s 1 punishable with imprisonment for life. Attempted rape is punishable with imprisonment for seven years. A man who induces a married woman to have sexual intercourse by impersonating her husband is guilty of rape (ibid, s 1(2)).
See PERSONATION.

Rate. A tax levied by local authorities on the occupation of hereditaments, irrespective of a person's income generally, and irrespective of whether the ratepayer was, in fact, deriving profits or gain from such occupation.

Rates are payable in respect of business premises only.

The tax in respect of domestic property is now the Council Tax.

See COUNCIL TAX.

The Act relating to rates with regard to business premises is the General Rate Act 1967.

Ratification. Confirmation, eg of a contract.

Ratio decidendi. The reasons or ground upon which a case is decided; a phrase often used in opposition to *obiter dictum.*

See OBITER DICTUM.

Ravishment. *See* ABDUCTION; RAPE.

Re. In the matter of.

See IN RE.

Reader. 1 The chaplain of the Temple.

See TEMPLES.

2 A lecturer.

Reading in. A phrase used to denote the reading of the Thirty-nine Articles of Religion, and repeating the Declaration of Assent prescribed by the Clerical Subscription Act 1865, which is required of every incumbent on the first Lord's Day on which he officiates in the church of his benefice, or such other Lord's Day as the Ordinary appoints and allows.

See ORDINARY.

Real, besides its ordinary meaning, has two special meanings:

(i) first, as being applicable to a thing in contradisctinction to a person:

(ii) secondly, as applicable to land, and especially freehold interests in it, as opposed to other rights and interests.

Real and personal property. Real property is not synonymous with property in land, nor is personal property synonymous with movable property. Thus, a title of honour, though annexed to the person of its owner, is real property, because in ancient times such titles were annexed to the ownership of various lands. On the other hand, shares in companies are personal property. A lease for years is also personal property, because in ancient times an ejected lessee could not recover his lease by a real action; but he could bring a personal action for damages against his landlord, who was bound to warrant him possession.

The code of succession on intestacy which was enacted by Part IV of the Administration of Estates Act 1925 applies alike to real and personal property.

See PROPERTY; LAND LAW.

Real evidence. Evidence provided by the production of material objects, as in exhibits produced in court, or eg by the court's inspection a location ('taking a VIEW').

Realise (a) security. Enforce a security right by selling or otherwise taking advantage of property securing a debt; where the security is not already in the possession of the creditor, this will first require exercising the right to take possession of the property.

See SECURITY.

Realty. Real estate; ie freehold interests in land; or, in a larger sense (so as to include chattels real), things substantial and immovable, and the rights and profits annexed to or issuing out of them.

See CHATTELS.

Reasonable and probable cause. A phrase used in connection with the defence to an action for false imprisonment, that the defendant had reasonable and probable cause for arresting the plaintiff. Also in an action for malicious prosecution the plaintiff must prove that there was no reasonable and probable cause for the prosecution.

The question of reasonable and probable cause when the facts are found is a question for the judge.

See FALSE IMPRISONMENT; MALICIOUS PROSECUTION.

Reassurance. *See* REINSURANCE.

Rebate. Discount; a deduction from a payment in consideration of its being made before it is due.

Rebellion. The taking up of arms traitorously against the Crown whether by subjects of the Queen or others when once subdued.

See TREASON.

Rebutting evidence. Evidence adduced to *rebut* a presumption of fact or law, ie to avoid its effect. But the word is also used in a wider sense to include any evidence adduced to destroy the effect of previous evidence, not only in explaining it away while admitting its truth, but also by direct denial, or by an attack on the character of the witness who has given it.

See PRESUMPTION.

Recaption. The retrieval, by taking possession, of one's own goods wrongfully detained by another.

See SELF-HELP.

Receipt. A written acknowledgment of the payment of money. A receipt for the purchase-money of land may be embodied in the purchase-deed (see Law of Property Act 1925, ss 67, 68).

Receiver. 1 One who receives stolen goods, knowing them to be stolen. The term 'receiving' has now been replaced by that of 'handling' stolen goods under the Theft Act 1968, s 22. By this section, a person is said to 'handle' stolen goods if (*otherwise* than in the course of stealing them) he dishonestly 'receives' them, or assists in their removal, disposal, etc.

2 An officer appointed to receive the rents and profits of property, and account for them to the Court, eg in actions for dissolution of partnership or for the administration of an estate. If there is a business to be carried on temporarily the receiver may also be appointed *manager*. A receiver may be appointed by an interlocutory order of the Court in all cases in which it appears to be just or convenient. As to the power of a mortgagee to appoint a receiver, see Law of Property Act 1925, s 101.

3 Under the Insolvency Act 1986, s 287 the Official Receiver may be appointed to act as interim receiver of the debtor's property.

4 Under the Mental Health Act 1983, s 99 a Judge may by order appoint a receiver for a mentally disordered person.

Receivers of wrecks. Officers appointed to summon as many men as may be necessary, to demand help from any ship near at hand, or to press into their service any vehicles, for the purpose of preserving or assisting any stranded or distressed vessel, or her cargo, or for the saving of human life (see Merchant Shipping Act 1894, ss 511–514).

See WRECK.

Recital. That part of a deed which recites the deeds, agreements, and other matters of fact, which may be necessary to explain the reasons on which it is founded.

Recitals are not essential to the validity of a deed, and are often dispensed with.

See DEED; PREMISES; OPERATIVE PART OF A DEED.

Recklessness. Acting recklessly is to act without reckoning the consequences; to act with understanding of the dangers the act involves, but wilfully or carelessly disregarding those dangers. Sometimes called 'advertent' negligence.

See INTENTION.

Recognisance. An obligation, which a person enters into before a court of record, or magistrate duly authorised, binding himself under a penalty to do some particular act; eg to appear before the Crown Court, to keep the peace, to pay a debt, or the like (see Powers of Criminal Courts Act 1973, 31); and as to recognisances given in Courts of summary jurisdiction, see Magistrates' Courts Act 1980, ss 115–120.

Recognisee. The person to whom another is bound in a recognisance.

See RECOGNISANCE.

Recognisor. A person bound in a recognisance.

See RECOGNISANCE.

Reconstruction occurs when a company transfers the whole of its undertaking and property to a new company under an arrangement by which the shareholders of the old company are entitled to receive shares or other similar interests in the new company.

Re-conversion. The restoration, in contemplation of equity, to its actual original quality of property which has been constructively converted.

See CONVERSION.

Re-conveyance. A deed by which, on the redemption of a mortgage, the legal estate in the mortgaged property is re-vested in the mortgagor. A receipt indorsed on a mortgage usually will operate as a re-conveyance, as is also the case in regard to mortgages to building societies (see Law of Property Act 1925, s 115, and Sch 3, Form No 2).

Record. An authentic testimony in writing preserved in the archives of a court of record.

Record, debt of. A sum of money which appears to be due by the evidence of a court of record, eg a judgment, etc.

See COURT OF RECORD.

Record Office. An office for the keeping of public records, under the direction of the Lord Chancellor. The actual charge of the

R

office is taken by the Keeper of Public Records appointed under s 2 of the Public Records Act of 1958.

Recordable offence. An offence which is recorded in national police records in accordance with regulations made by the Secretary of State: Police and Criminal Evidence Act 1984, s 118(1).

Recorder. The principal legal officer of a city or town to which the right to have such an officer has been granted.

Under the Courts Act 1971 the Crown may from time to time appoint qualified persons as recorders, to act as part-time judges of the Crown Court and to carry out other judicial functions. They must have been recommended by the Lord Chancellor and must be barristers or solicitors of at least ten years' standing. They must take the oath of allegiance and the judicial oath.

See OATH OF ALLEGIANCE.

By virtue of his office and with his consent a recorder is capable of sitting as a judge for any County Court district in England and Wales, and he may be requested to sit as a judge of the High Court.

Recording, in relation to a performance means a film or sound recording:

(i) made directly from the live performance;
(ii) made from a broadcast of the performance; or
(iii) made, directly or indirectly, from another recording of the performance: Copyright, Designs and Patents Act 1988, s 180(2).

See PERFORMANCE; FILM; SOUND RECORDING.

Recording rights, in relation to copyright, exist where there is a contract between a performer and another person giving him an exclusive recording contract to make recordings of a performance with a view to their commercial exploitation: Copyright, Designs and Patents Act 1988, ss 185–187. It is an offence to make, deal with or use an illicit recording: ibid, s 198. As to 'illicit recordings', see ibid, s 197.

See COPYRIGHT.

Recovery. A means by which a tenant in tail in possession could 'bar the entail' of a fee tail or entailed estate, so as to convert the estate into one in fee simple; thus, not only were the 'issue in tail', ie the succeeding generations in the direct line of the original grantee disinherited, but the estate would no longer terminate upon the extinction of the original grantee's direct line.

See ENTAIL; FINE; ESTATE; LAND LAW.

Recovery order. An order made where the Court has reason to believe that a child (i) has been unlawfully taken away; (ii) has run away; and (iii) is missing: Children Act 1989, s 50(1). The order (i) operates as a direction to any person who is in a position to do so to produce the child; (ii) authorises the removal of the child by an authorised person; (iii) requires a person who has information as to the child's whereabouts to disclose it; and (iv) authorises a constable to enter any premises specified in the order and search for the child: Children Act 1989, s 50.

Rectification. 1 The correction of an instrument in writing so as to express the true intention of the parties. Actions for this purpose are assigned to the Chancery Division (see Supreme Court Act 1981, s 61(1), Sch 1).

2 Rectification of the Land Register; see Land Registration Act 1925, s. 82.

Rector. 1 A person who has full possession of the rights of a parochial church. As opposed to a *vicar*, a rector is an incumbent of an unappropriated church. A rector (or parson) has for the most part the whole right to all the ecclesiastical dues in his parish, and the chancel is vested in him: whereas, a vicar has an appropriator over him, entitled to the best part of the profits, to whom the vicar is, as it were, a perpetual curate, with a standing salary. Where the appropriator is a layman, he is called lay impropriator, or lay rector.

See APPROPRIATION; VICAR.

2 In some of the colleges in Oxford, the head is called by the title of Rector.

Rectory. 1 A parish church, with its rights, glebes, and other profits.

2 The rector's mansion or parsonage-house.

See RECTOR; PARSONAGE.

Red ensign. A red flag with a Union Jack described in a canton in the upper corner next to the staff. It is the proper national colour for all ships or boats belonging to any British subject (see Merchant Shipping Act 1894, s 73(1)). By Admiralty warrant under that subsection certain yacht clubs are allowed to carry the red ensign with distinctive marks on the flag.

Reddendo singula singulis. A phrase indicating that different words in one part of a deed or other instrument are to be applied respectively to their appropriate objects in another part.

R

Reddendum. The clause in a lease whereby rent is reserved to the lessor. It usually specifies the periods at which the rent is to be paid or rendered. No special form of words is required.
See LEASE.

Redemption. 1 A ransom.
See RANSOM.
2 Especially, the buying back of a mortgaged estate by payment of the sum due on the mortgage.
See EQUITY OF REDEMPTION.
3 Redemption of rentcharge (see Law of Property Act 1925, s 191).
See RENT.

Reductio ad adsurdum. A method of proving the fallacy of an argument by showing that it leads to an absurd result.

Reduction into possession. The turning of a *chose in action* into a *chose in possession*; eg when a person takes money out of a bank at which he has a balance, or procures the payment of a debt due.
See CHOSE.

Reduction of capital. As to the cases in which a company may reduce its capital, see the Companies Act 1985, s 135. In all cases a special resolution must be passed, and in most cases an application to the Court is necessary. The words 'and reduced' may be ordered to be added to the name of the company.

Re-entry. The resuming or retaking of possession lately had.
A *proviso for re-entry* is a clause in a deed of grant or demise providing that the grantor or lessor may re-enter on breach of a condition by the grantee or lessee. A proviso for re-entry will be strictly construed, unless a decisive reason is shown for departing from it. The Schedule to the Law of Property (Amendment) Act 1926 provided that a fee simple subject to a right of entry or re-entry should be a fee simple absolute, ie it was not converted into an equitable interest. And see Law of Property Act 1925, s 146, and Landlord and Tenant Act 1927, s 18(2), which impose restrictions on the enforceability of rights of re-entry.
See FORFEITURE.

Re-examination. The examination of a witness by the counsel of the party on whose behalf he has given evidence, in reference to matters arising out of his cross-examination.

See EXAMINATION.

Re-exchange. The expense incurred by a bill of exchange being dishonoured in a foreign country where it is made payable and returned to that country in which it was drawn or endorsed. For this expense the drawer is liable.
See BILL OF EXCHANGE; DISHONOUR.

Referee. 1 A person to whose judgment a matter is referred, whether by consent of the parties or by compulsory reference under the Arbitration Act 1950.
2 Persons to whom are referred questions as to the *locus standi* of petitioners against private Parliamentary bills.
See PRIVATE BILLS.

Referee in case of need. The drawer or indorser of a bill of exchange may insert in it the name of a person to whom the holder may resort in case of need, ie in case the bill is dishonoured (see Bills of Exchange Act 1882, s 15).
See BILL OF EXCHANGE; DISHONOUR.

Reference. Referring a matter to an arbitrator, or to a master or other officer of a court of justice, for his decision on it.
See ARBITRATION.

Referendum. A mode of appealing from an elected body to the whole electorate. The Referendum Act 1975 provided for the holding of a referendum on whether the United Kingdom should remain a member of the European Community, the result showing a substantial majority in favour.

Refresher. A further or additional fee paid to counsel where a case is adjourned from one term or sittings to another, or where the hearing lasts over the first day and for more than five hours. It may be allowed on taxation.

Regal fishes. *See* FISH ROYAL.

Regalia. 1 The royal rights of the Queen comprising:
(i) Power of judicature.
(ii) Power of life and death.
(iii) Power of war and peace.
(iv) Ownerless goods.
See BONA VACANTIA.
(v) Assessments.
(vi) Minting of money.
2 Also the crown, sceptre with the cross, and other jewels and ornaments used at a coronation.

Regent. A person appointed to conduct the affairs of State in lieu of the reigning Sovereign, in his absence, disability, or minority (see Regency Acts 1937 to 1953).

Register. 1 The register of a parish church, in which baptisms, marriages, and burials are registered. Instituted by Thomas Cromwell, vicar-general of Henry VIII, 1538.
See REGISTRAR, 1.

2 A record of deeds and other documents relating to land, such as exists in Yorkshire, and in Scotland and Ireland (see Law of Property Act 1925, ss 11, 197 and Land Registration Act 1925, s 135).
See YORKSHIRE DEEDS REGISTRIES.

3 A record of titles to land.
See REGISTERED LAND.

4 And, generally, a register means an authentic catalogue of names or events, eg the register of companies under the Companies Act 1985, or a register of electors.
See ELECTION.

Register of patents. A book of patents kept at the Patent Office for public use (see Patents Act 1977, s 32).
See PATENT.

Registered design. *See* DESIGN RIGHT.

Registered land. Land or any estate or interest in land the title to which is registered under the Land Registration Act 1925, including any easement, right, privilege, or benefit which is appurtenant or appendant to it, and any mines and minerals within or under it: Land Registration Act 1925, s 3.

The system of registered land is governed by the Land Registration Acts 1925 to 1986. Land may be registered with:
(i) an absolute title (*see* ABSOLUTE TITLE);
(ii) a possessory title (*see* POSSESSORY TITLE); or
(iii) a qualified title (*see* QUALIFIED TITLE).

A register of title to freehold land must be kept by the Chief Land Registrar: Land Registration Act 1925, s 1.

There is power to make orders rendering registration compulsory in certain areas: ibid, s 120.
See LAND REGISTRATION; MINOR INTERESTS.

Registered office. An office of the company to which all communications and notices may be addressed.

A company must at all times have a registered office (see Companies Act 1985, s 287(1)).

Registered office clause. A clause in the memorandum of association stating whether the company's registered office is to be situate in England or Scotland, and thus fixing the nationality of the company.
See REGISTERED OFFICE.

Registered proprietor. The term used to describe the title holder of land under the land registration system. The owner, or title holder, is the person whose name is on the ownership register with respect to the land in question.
See LAND REGISTRATION; REGISTERED LAND.

Registrar. An officer appointed to register the decrees of a court of justice, or in any manner to keep a register of names and events. Of these may be mentioned:

1 The Registrar-General of Births, Deaths and Marriages in England, to whom, subject to such regulations as are made by a principal Secretary of State, the general management of the system of registering births, deaths and marriages is entrusted. He is now controlled by the Treasury.

2 The superintendent registrars of births, marriages and deaths.

3 The Registrar of Companies (an officer appointed by the Secretary of State), whose business it is to certify when a company is incorporated, etc.

4 The Registrars in Bankruptcy of the High Court, who are required to exercise such judicial powers as may be delegated to them from time to time by the judge of the court; and to perform various duties in connection with bankruptcy.

5 Chancery Registrars are officers of the Chancery Division whose duty it is to enter causes for trial, to attend in court and take minutes of decisions given, and afterwards draw them in proper form, and settle them in the presence of the different parties or their solicitors.

6 Registrars of the Family Division have power to transact all such business and to exercise all such authority and jurisdiction in respect of the same as a judge in chambers.

7 District Registrars.

8 The Registrar of a County Court, who is an officer appointed by the judge, subject to the approval of the Lord Chancellor. If the County Court is one having jurisdiction in bankruptcy, he will be a registrar in bankruptcy.

R

9 The Deputy-Registrar of a County Court, who is an officer appointed by the Registrar, subject to the approval of the Judge.

10 The Registrar of Friendly Societies; an officer whose duty it is to examine the rules of friendly societies, and, if he finds them conformable to law, to certify them as being so.

11 The Registrar of the Privy Council, whose duty it is to summon the members of the Judicial Committee when their attendance is required, and to transact other business relating to the Privy Council.

12 The Registrar-General of Shipping and Seamen.

Registration of title. *See* LAND REGISTRATION.

Registry. A place where a register is kept. *See* REGISTER.

Regius Professor. This title, when applied to a professor, or reader of lectures in the universities, indicates that his office was founded by the King. King Henry VIII was the founder of five professorships in the universities of Oxford and Cambridge, ie the professorships of Divinity, Greek, Hebrew, Law, and Physic.

Regulation. 1 As opposed to a statutory provision or law, a regulation is a rule made by Order In Council as authorised by statute.
2 In European Union law, a form of legislation.
See EUROPEAN COMMUNITY REGULATION.

Rehabilitation of Offenders Act 1974. An Act to rehabilitate offenders who have not been reconvicted of any serious offence for periods of years and to penalise the unauthorised disclosure of their previous convictions.

Where a question (eg in an insurance proposal form) seeking information with respect to a person's previous convictions is put to him, the question must be treated as not relating to spent convictions or any circumstances ancillary to spent convictions and the answer thereto may be framed accordingly (see Rehabilitation of Offenders Act 1974, s 4(2)(a)).
See SPENT CONVICTION.

Reinstatement. The replacement of insured property which is destroyed or the repair of it if it is damaged. Reinstatement can take place as a result of the action of the insurers or of the insured.

The insurers are entitled to reinstate the property under a clause of a policy to that effect or under the power given to them by the Fires Prevention (Metropolis) Act 1774 where the property is lost or damaged by fire.

The insured is under a liability to reinstate the property if (i) there is a contract between him and the insurers to that effect; or (ii) there is a statute to that effect as in the case of (a) property subject to a trust or settlement (see the Trustee Act 1925, s 20(4)); (b) mortgaged property (see Law of Property Act 1925, s 104(4)); and (c) ecclesiastical property (see Repair of Benefice Buildings Measure 1972, s 12, as amended by the Endowments and Glebe Measure 1976, s 47(4), Sch 8).

Reinsurance. A type of insurance the purpose of which is to indemnify the insurers taking the place of the original insured against the loss which they may themselves sustain in their capacity of insurers under the original policy. Reinsurance is of two kinds:
(i) *facultative reinsurance* ie reinsurance against the liability on a particular policy; and
(ii) *treaty reinsurance* ie reinsurance against liabilities on policies generally.

Relative. In relation to a child, 'relative' means a grandparent, brother, sister, uncle or aunt, whether of the full blood, of the half-blood, or by affinity (see Adoption Act 1976, s 72(1)).

Relator. A private person at whose instance the Attorney-General allows an information to be filed.

A relator action is one in which a person or body claiming to be entitled to restrain interference with a public right or to abate a public nuisance must bring such action in the name of the Attorney-General. The action is expressed to be brought by 'the Attorney-General *at the relation of X'*.

Relator action. *See* RELATOR.

Release (Lat *Relaxatio*). 1 A discharge or conveyance by a person who has a right or interest in lands, but not the possession, whereby he extinguishes his right for the benefit of the person in possession.
2 An instrument whereby a party beneficially entitled to any interest in property held on trust discharges his trustee from any further claim or liability in respect of it.
See TRUST.

Relief. 1 The specific assistance prayed for by a party who institutes an action in Chancery.

2 A tenant may apply to the Court for relief against the forfeiture of a lease on account of non-payment of rent or of other breach.

See FORFEITURE.

Relinquishment, deed of. Under the Clerical Disabilities Act 1870 any person admitted to holy orders, after having resigned his preferment, may execute and cause to be enrolled in Chancery a *deed of relinquishment*. By this means he divests himself of holy orders.

See HOLY ORDERS.

Rem. *See* IN REM; JUS IN REM.

Remainder. Where any estate or interest in land is granted out of a larger one, and an ulterior estate expectant on that which is so granted is at the same time conveyed away by the original owner. The first estate is called the *particular estate*, and the ulterior one the *remainder*, or the *estate in remainder*. Thus, if land is conveyed to A for life, and after his death to B , A's interest is called a *particular* estate, and B's a *remainder*. The word, though properly applied to estates in land, is also applicable to personalty. After 1925 remainders subsist only as equitable interests. See Part I of Law of Property Act 1925.

See CONTINGENT REMAINDER; REVERSION.

Remainderman. A person entitled to an estate in remainder.

See REMAINDER.

Remand. The recommittal of an accused person to prison, or his readmission to bail, on the adjournment of the hearing of a criminal charge in a magistrates' court. A remand may be granted for securing the attendance of witnesses, for making inquiries into the previous history of the accused, or other reasonable cause.

Remedial statutes. Such as supply some defect in the existing law, and redress some abuse or inconvenience with which it is found to be attended, without introducing any provision of a penal character.

Remedy. The means given by law for the recovery of a right, or of compensation for its infringement, to be distinguished from punishments or penalties, which are not remedies for the victim whose rights were violated, but harms or disadvantages levied in the name of the public upon those guilty of committing an OFFENCE. The law has remedies of various kinds, which can be distinguished in different ways. A first distinction is that between a *personal* and a *proprietary* remedy. A personal remedy is one which binds only the defendant against whom it is awarded, the most typical example being an award of DAMAGES, ie a money payment in compensation for an injury or loss. The defendant subject to an order to pay damages has an obligation to do so, but only he or she is bound. If he or she is bankrupt, or dies and his or her estate is insufficient to provide for the payment, the plaintiff will not recover. Impecunious defendants subject only to a remedy of damages are for this reason sometimes said to be 'judgment proof'. Proprietary remedies are orders in respect of specific property; thus, for example, a successful action establishing title to land will result in the award of a right to the immediate possession of the land, and an order for the eviction of a wrongful possessor if necessary. Certain remedies, in particular pecuniary remedies, may also be characterised on the basis of whether they are *compensatory, restitutionary*, or effect *disgorgement*. A compensatory remedy compensates a plaintiff for a loss or injury suffered; a restitutionary remedy is one which restores value received by the defendant to the plaintiff; a disgorgement remedy (which is sometimes included under the rubric 'restitutionary') is one which by which the defendant must provide value to the plaintiff measured not by the plaintiff's loss, nor by an amount of value received by the defendant from him or her, but by the value the defendant acquired in the course of some breach of the plaintiff's rights, as for example, where a fiduciary makes a profit from his or her principal in breach of the obligation of loyalty and good faith.

See UNJUST ENRICHMENT.

Generally, where a plaintiff has suffered a loss, an award will be compensatory. However, the law occasionally gives *exemplary* or *punitive* damages, damages which are more than compensatory, to make an example of or punish the defendant where his or her violation of the plaintiff's right has been particularly egregious, or perhaps as a means of effecting disgorgement so as to prevent the defendant profiting from his or her wrong.

Besides the foregoing remedies, the court may *enjoin* the parties in various ways, ie issue an injunction to a party to do something (a positive or mandatory injunction) or refrain from doing something (a negative injunction). An example of a negative injunction is the court's enjoining a defendant from continuing to commit a NUISANCE, eg by ordering him or her to cease industrial operations creating excessive noise. An example of a positive injunction is a court's order to a seller of land to convey the land to the buyer upon payment of the price. A positive injunction in this context is called an order for the SPECIFIC PERFORMANCE of the contract of sale. Injunctions originally developed in the Court of EQUITY, as did the Court's power to rescind or rectify documents, and a rescission or rectification of a document may similarly dispose of a dispute.

The court may also make declarations, ie the court may declare what the right of the parties are. While not a remedy, strictly speaking, declarations of this kind may serve to resolve a dispute, and in that respect may be considered a remedy.

See also ADMINISTRATIVE LAW.

Remembrancers. 1 The duty of the Queen's Remembrancer is to enter in his office all recognisances taken for debts due to the Crown, etc; to take bonds for such debts, and to make out process for breach of them; also to issue process against the collectors of customs and other public payments for their accounts. He is now an officer of the Supreme Court. Under the Supreme Court Act 1981, s 89(4) the Senior Master of the Supreme Court (Queen's Bench Division) is to hold and perform the duties of the Queen's Remembrancer.

2 The Remembrancer of the City of London is an ancient officer of the Corporation, whose original duties were mainly ceremonial, it being his office to see to the due observance of all presentations, public processions and other matters affecting the privileges of the Corporation. He performs the duty of Parliamentary solicitor to the Corporation. He attends the Houses of Parliament, and examines bills likely to affect the privileges of the City, and reports upon them to the Corporation. He also attends the Courts of Alderman and Common Council, and committees, when required.

Remission. Pardon of an offence.
See PARDON.

Remoteness. 1 Where an attempt is made by any instrument in writing to tie up, or to dictate the devolution of, property, or to keep the same in suspense without a beneficial owner, beyond the period allowed by law.
See PERPETUITY.

2 *Remoteness of damage.* This expression is used to denote a lack of direct connection between a wrong complained of and the injury alleged to have been sustained by it.
See CONTRACT LAW; TORTS, LAW OF.

Removal of actions. Actions may, in certain cases, be transferred from the High Court to the County Court, or vice versa. They may be transferred under various sections of the Civil Procedure Rules 1998.

Remuneration. Payment for services. Can include reasonable allowances in respect of expenses properly incurred in the pursuance of the duties of any office.

Render. To give up again; to restore.

Renewal of lease. A re-grant of an expiring lease for a further term. Leases may be surrendered in order to be renewed without a surrender of under-leases by virtue of the Law of Property Act 1925, s 150. For rules in regard to renewal of leases, see eg the Landlord and Tenant Act 1954, which provides security of tenure for certain tenants occupying residential premises under ground leases, and for occupying tenants of business premises.

Renouncing probate, is where a person appointed executor of a will refuses to accept the office.
See EXECUTOR; PROBATE.

Rent. The periodic payment, generally of money, by a tenant to his or her landlord in consideration of the former's right to possess the land. A rent includes a rent service or a rentcharge, or other rent, toll, duty, royalty or annual or periodical payment in money or money's worth, reserved or issuing out of or charged on land: Law of Property Act 1925, s 205(1)(xxiii).

Rentcharge. Any annual or other periodic sum charged or issuing out of land except (i) rent reserved by a lease or tenancy; or (ii) any sum payable by way of interest: Rentcharges Act 1977, s 1.

A rentcharge in possession issuing out of or charged on land being either perpetual or for a term of years is a legal estate: Law of Property Act 1925, s 1(2).

No rentcharge may be created after 22nd August 1977: Rentcharges Act 1977, s 2(1).

Renvoi. Doctrine in the conflict of laws where a court determines the law governing a matter by examining the law of a foreign jurisdiction, including that jurisdiction's choice of law rules.

See CONFLICT OF LAWS; CHOICE OF LAW PRINCIPLES

Repeal (Fr *Rappel*). A calling back. The revocation of one statute, or a part of it, by another (see Interpretation Act 1978, s 17).

Replevin. A redelivery to the owner of his cattle or goods distrained on any cause upon security that he will prosecute the action of replevin against the person who distrained. The 'replevisor' is the party who takes back his goods.

See INTERFERENCE WITH GOODS.

Reply. 1 The *reply* of a plaintiff is that statement in his pleading whereby he *replies* to the defence.

See PLEADINGS.

2 The speech of counsel for the plaintiff in a civil case, or for the prosecution in a criminal case, in answer in either case to the points raised by the defence, is generally called the *reply*.

Reports. 1 Histories of legal cases, with the arguments used by counsel and the reasons given for the decision of the Court.

2 The reports of Chief Justice Coke are especially styled The Reports, and are, in general, cited without the author's name, as 'Rep'.

See LAW REPORTS.

The following is a list of the principal Reports.

Table 3

Report	Abbreviation
Acton (Prize Cases)	Acton
Adam	Adam
Addams	Add
Adolphus & Ellis	Ad & El *or* A & E
Adolphus & Ellis New Series	Ad & El, NS (*or* QB for Queen's Bench.)
Alcock & Napier	Alc & N
Alcock's Registry Cases	Alc
Aleyn	Aleyn
All England	All ER
All England Reprint	All ER Rep

Report	Abbreviation
Ambler	Amb *or* Ambl
Anderson, Sir E	And
Andrews, George	Andr
Annaly	Ann
Anstruther	Anst
Appeal Cases	AC *or* App Cas
Arkley	Arkl
Armstrong, Macartney & Ogle	Arm Mac & O
Arnold	Arn
Arnold & Hodges	Arn & H
Aspinall's Maritime Law Cases	Asp MLC
Atkyns	Atk
Ball & Beatty	Ball & B *or* B & B
Bankruptcy and Companies Winding-up	B & CR
Barnardiston (Ch)	Barnard (Ch)
Barnardiston (KB)	Barnard (KB)
Barnes' Notes of Cases	Barnes
Barnewall & Adolphus	Barn & Ad *or* B & A
Barnewall & Cresswell	Barn & Cress *or* B & C
Barron & Arnold	Bar & Arn
Barron & Austin	Bar & Aust
Batty	Batt
Beatty	Beat
Beavan	Beav
Bell (Crown Cases)	Bell, CC
Bell (Scotch Appeals)	Bell, Sc App
Bell (Scotch Decisions)	Bell, Ct of Sess
Bellewe's Reports (published 1585)	Bellewe
Belt's Supplement to Vesey Sen	Belt's Sup
Benloe	Benl
Benlow	Ben
Best & Smith	B & S
Bingham	Bing
Bingham's New Cases	Bing NC
Blackham, Dundas & Osborne	B D & O
Blackstone, Henry	H Bl
Blackstone, Sir W	W Bl
Bligh	Bli
Bligh's New Series	Bli NS
Bluett's Notes of Cases	Blu
Bosanquet & Puller	Bos & P *or* B & P
Bosanquet & Puller's New Reports	Bos & PNR
Bridgman, Sir John	J Bridg
Bridgman, Sir Orlando	O Bridg
British & Colonial Prize Cases	Br & Col Pr Cas

Table 3 (continued)

Report	Abbreviation
Broderip & Bingham	Bro & B or B & B
Brooke's New Cases	Brooke, NC or BNC
Broun	Broun
Brown's Reports of Cases in Chancery	Bro CC
Brown's Reports of Cases in Parliament	Bro PC
Browne & Macnamara Railway Cases	Bro & Mac
Browning & Lushington	B & L
Brownlow & Goldesborough	B & G
Bruce's Reports	Bruce
Buck's Cases in Bankruptcy	Buck
Bulstrode	Bulstr
Bunbury	Bunb
Burrow's Reports	Burr
Burrow's Settlement Cases	Burr SC
Butterworths Company Law Cases	BCLC
Butterworths Medico-Legal Reports	BMLR
Butterworths Workmen's Compensation Cases	BWCC
Cababe & Ellis	Cab & El
Caldecott's Settlement Cases	Cald SC
Calthorp's Cases on the Customs of London	Calthorp
Campbell	Camp
Carpmael's Patent Cases	Carp PC
Carrington & Kirwan	Carr & K or C & K
Carrington & Marshman	Car & M or C & M
Carrington & Payne	Car & P or C & P
Carrow, Hamerton & Allen's New Sess Cases	CH & A or New Sess Cas
Carter	Cart
Carthew	Carth
Cary	Cary
Cases in Chancery	Ch Ca
Cases in Equity Abridged	Cas Eq Ab or Eq Cas Abr
Cases in the time of Finch	Cas temp Finch
Cases in the time of Lord Hardwicke	Cas temp Hardwicke
Cases in the time of Lord Talbot	Cas temp Talbot
Cases of Practice, King's Bench	Cas Pra KB
Chancery	Ch
Chancery Appeal Cases	Ch App
Chancery Division	Ch D
Chitty	Chit

Report	Abbreviation
Choice Cases in Chancery	Cho Ca Ch
Clark & Finnelly	Cl & Fin or C&F
Clayton	Clay
Cockburn & Rowe	C & R
Coke, Sir Edward	Co Rep or Rep
Colles	Colles
Collyer	Coll
Coltman's Registration Cases	Colt
Comberbach	Comb
Commercial Cases	Com Cas
Common Bench Reports	CB
Common Bench Reports, New Series	CB, NS
Common Law Reports	CLR
Common Market Law Reports	CMLR
Common Pleas Division	CPD
Comyns Digest	Com Dig
Connor & Lawson	Conn & Law, or C& L
Cooke	Cooke Pr Cas
Cooke & Alcock	C & A
Cooper, George	Coop G
Cooper's Cases in Chancery	Coop temp Brough
Corbett & Daniell	Corb & D
County Court Cases	CC Cas
Couper	Coup
Court of Session Cases	Court Sess Ca
Cowell's Indian Appeals (Law Rep vol ii)	LR, 2 Ind App
Cowper	Cowp
Cox (Chancery)	Cox
Cox (Criminal Law)	Cox's CC
Cox & Atkinson's Registration Appeals	Cox & Atk
Craig & Phillips	Cr & Ph
Craigie Stewart & Paton's Scotch Appeals	Cr St & P
Crawford & Dix	Cr & D
Cresswell's Insolvent Cases	Cress Insolv Cas
Criminal Appeal Reports	Cr App Rep
Criminal Appeal Reports (Sentencing)	Cr App Rep(S)
Cripps' Church Cases	Cripps' Church Cas
Croke, time of Charles I	Cro Car
Croke, time of Elizabeth	Cro Eliz
Croke, time of James I	Cro Jac
Crompton & Jervix	Cr & J or C & J
Crompton & Meeson	Cr & M
Crompton, Meeson & Roscoe	Cr M & R
Cunningham	Cunn
Curteis	Curt

Table 3 (continued)

Report	Abbreviation
Dalrymple, Sir Hew	Dalr
Daniell	Dan
Danson & Lloyd	D & L
Davies' Patent Cases	DPC
Davis, Sir John	Davis
Davison & Merivale	D & M
De Gex	De G
De Gex & Jones	De G & Jo or D & J
De Gex & Smale	De G & Sm
De Gex, Fisher & Jones	De G F & Jo or D F & J
De Gex, Jones & Smith	De G J & Sm or D J & S
De Gex, Macnaghten & Gordon	De G Mac & G or D M & G
Deacon	Deac
Deacon & Chitty	Deac & Chit
Deane's Reports completed by Swabey	Deane or Dea & Sw
Dearsly	Dears CC
Dearsly & Bell	Dearsl & B or D & B
Deas & Anderson	Deas & And
Delane	Delane
Denison	Den CC
Dickens	Dick
Dodson	Dods
Douglas' Election Cases	Doug El Cas
Douglas' King's Bench	Dougl KB
Dow	Dow
Dow & Clarke	Dow & Cl
Dowling & Lowndes	Dowl & L or D & L
Dowling & Ryland King's Bench	Dowl & Ry or D & R
Dowling & Ryland, Nisi Prius	D & R, NP
Dowling & Ryland's Magistrates' Cases	D & RMC
Dowling's Practice Reports	Dowl or DPC
Dowling's Practice Reports, New Series	Dowl, NS
Drewry	Drew
Drewry & Smale	Dr & Sm
Drinkwater	Drink
Drury	Dru
Drury & Walsh	Dru & Wal
Drury & Warren	Dru & War
Dunlop, Bell & Murray	Dunlop or Dunl B & M
Durie	Durie
Durnford & East's Term Reports	Durn & E or TR
Dyer	Dy
Eagle and Young's Collection of Tithe Cases	E & Y

Report	Abbreviation
East	East
Eden	Eden
Edgar	Edg
Edwards	Edw
Elchie	Elch
Ellis & Blackburn	Ell & Bl or E & B
Ellis & Ellis	Ell & E
Ellis, Blackburn & Ellis	Ell Bl & Ell or E B & E
Equity Cases Abridged	Eq Cas Abr
Equity Reports	Eq R
Espinasse	Esp
Estates Gazette	EG
Estates Gazette Law Reports	EGLR
Estates Gazette Planning Law Reports	PCR
European Court Reports	ECR
European Human Rights Reports	EHRR
Exchequer Division	Ex D
Exchequer Reports	Exch
Faculty Decisions	Fac Dec
Falconer	Falc
Falconer & Fitzherbert	Falc & F
Family Division	Fam
Family Law Reports	FLR
Ferguson	Ferg
Ferguson's Consistorial Reports	Ferg
Finch	Finch
Finch's Precedents	Finch Prec Ch
Finlason's Leading Cases	Finl LC
Fitzgibbons	Fitz-G
Flannagan & Kelly	Fl & K
Fleet Street Reports	FSR
Fonblanque	Fonb
Forbes	Forb
Forester's Cases in the time of Talbot	Cas temp Talbot
Forrest	Forr
Fortescue	Fort
Foster (Crown Law)	Fost CL
Foster & Finlayson	F & F
Fountainhall	Fount
Fox & Smith	Fox & S
Fox & Smith, Registration Cases	Fox & S, Reg
Fraser	Fras
Freeman (Chancery)	Freem (Ch)
Freeman (King's Bench)	Freem (KB)
Gale	Gale

R

Table 3 (continued)

Report	Abbreviation
Gale & Davidson	G & D
Gibson	Gibs
Giffard	Giff or Gif
Gilbert	Gilb (Ch)
Gilmour & Falconer	Gil & Fal
Glascock	Glasc
Glyn & Jameson	G & J
Godbolt	Godb
Gouldsborough	Gouldsb
Gow	Gow
Gwillim	Gwil
Haggard (Adm)	Hagg Adm
Haggard's Consistorial Reports	Hagg Cons
Haggard's Ecclesiastical Reports	Hagg Eccl
Hailes	Hail
Hall & Twells	Hall & Tw or H & Tw
Hanmer's Lord Kenyon's Notes	Ld Ken
Hansell	HBR
Harcarse	Harc
Hardres	Hardr
Hare	Hare or Ha
Harrison & Rutherford	Har & Ruth
Harrison & Wollaston	Har & W
Hayes	Hayes
Haynes & Jones	Haynes & Jo
Hemming & Miller	Hem & Mill or H & M
Hetley	Het
Hobart	Hob
Hodges	Hodg
Holt (LCJ)	Holt (KB)
Holt, Wm	Holt, Eq
Holt's Nisi Prius	Holt
Home	Home Ct of Sess
Hopwood & Coltman	Hop & C
Hopwood & Philbrick	Hop & Ph
Horn & Hurlstone	H & H
House of Lords' Cases	HL Cas
Housing Law Reports	HLR
Hovenden's Supplement to Vesey, Jnr	Hov Suppl
Howell's State Trials	How St Tr or State Tr
Hudson & Brooke	H & B
Hume	Hume
Hunt's Annuity Cases	Hunt
Hurlstone & Coltman	H & C
Hurlstone & Gordon	Included in Exch Reports
Hurlstone & Norman	H & N

Report	Abbreviation
Hurlstone & Walmssley	H & W
Hutton	Hutt
Immigration Appeals Reports	Imm AR
Industrial Cases Reports	ICR
Industrial Relations Law Reports	IRLR
International Court of Justice Reports	ICLR
Irish Chancery	Ir Ch
Irish Circuit Cases	Ir Cir Ca
Irish Common Law Reports	Ir CLR
Irish Equity Reports	Ir Eq R
Irish Jurist	Ir Jur
Irish Law Recorder	Ir L Rec
Irish Law Reports	Ir L Rep
Irish Reports	IR
Irish Reports Common Law	ICLR
Irish Reports, Equity	I Eq R
Jacob	Jac
Jacob & Walker	Jac & W or J & W
Jebb	Jebb CC
Jebb & Bourke	J & B
Jebb & Symes	J & S
Jenkins' Centuries (ie Hundreds) of Reports	Jenk Cent
Johnson	Johns or Jo
Johnson & Hemming	John & H or J & H
Jones	Jon Ex R
Jones & Carey	Jones & C
Jones & Latouche	Jo & Lat
Jones, Sir T	Jo or T Jo
Jones, Sir W	Jo or W Jo
Jurist Reports	Jur
Jurist Reports, New Series	Jur, NS
Jurist (Scottish)	Sc Jur
Justice of the Peace	JP
Kay	Kay
Kay & Johnson	Kay & J
Keane & Grant	K & G
Keble	Keb
Keen	Keen or Kee
Keilway	Keil
Kelynge	Kel W
Kenyon's Notes of Cases	Ld Ken or Keny
Knapp	Knapp
Knapp & Ombler	Knapp & O
Lane	Lane
Latch	Lat
Law Gazette Report	LS Gaz Rep
Law Journal	LJOS
Law Journal, New Series	LJ, NS, or LJ Rep, NS

Table 3 (continued)

Report	Abbreviation
Law Recorder (Ireland)	Ir L Rec
Law Reports	Law Rep *or* LR
Law Times Report	LTOS
Law Times, New Series	LT
Leach	Leach
Lee	Lee
Lee's Cases, in the time of Hardwicke	Lee *temp* Hard
Legal Observer	Leg Ob
Leigh & Cave	L & C
Leonard	Leon
Levinz	Lev
Lewin's Crown Cases	Lew CC
Ley	Ley
Lilly's 'Cases in Assize'	Lil
Littleton	Litt
Lloyd & Goold, in the time of Plunkett	L & G *temp* Plunk *or* Ll & G *t* Pl
Lloyd & Goold, in the time of Sugden	L & G *temp* Sug *or* Ll & G *t* Sugd
Lloyd & Welsby	L & Welsb
Lloyd's List Law Reports	Lloyd L Rep
Lloyd's Prize Cases	Lloyd Pr Cas
Lloyd's Reports	Lloyd's Rep
Local Government Reports	LGR
Lofft	Lofft
Longfield & Townshend	L & T
Lowndes & Maxwell	L & M
Lowndes, Maxwell & Pullock	LM & P
Luders	Luders
Lumley's Poor Law Cases	Lumley PLC
Lushington	Lush
Lutwyche	Lutw
Lutwyche's Registration Cases	Lutw Reg Cas
M'Cleland	M'Clel
M'Cleland & Younge	M'Clel & Y
Macfarlane	Macf
Maclaurin	Macl
Maclean & Robinson	Macl & R
Macnaghten & Gordon	Macn & Gor
Macpherson's Court of Session Cases	Macph (Ct of Sess)
Macpherson's Indian Appeals (in connection with the Law Reports [vol i])	Macph Ind Ap *or* LR, 1 Ind. App
Macqueen's	Macq Sc App
Macrea & Hertslet	Mac & H
Macrory's Patent Cases	Mac PC
Maddock	Madd

Report	Abbreviation
Maddock & Geldard	Madd & Gel *or* 6 Mad
Magistrate, The	Mag
Manning & Granger	Man & Gr *or* M & G
Manning & Ryland	M & R (KB)
Manning & Ryland's Magistrates' Cases	M & R (MC)
Manning, Granger & Scott (CB, 1st nine volumes)	CB (for Common Bench)
Manson's Reports	Mans
March's New Cases	Mar
Marriot	Marr
Marshall	Marsh
Maule & Selwyn	M & S
Medical Law Reports	MLR
Meeson & Welsby	Mees & Wels *or* M & W
Megone's Company Cases	Meg
Merivale	Mer
Milward	Milw
Modern Reports (Leach's)	Mod
Molloy	Moll
Montagu	Mont
Montagu & Aryton	Mont & Ayr *or* M & A
Montagu & Bligh	Mont & B *or* M & B
Montagu & Chitty	Mont & Chi *or* M & C
Montagu & M'Arthur	Mont & M'A
Montagu, Deacon & De Gex	Mont D & De G
Moody	Mood CC
Moody & Malkin	Mood & M *or* M & M
Moody & Robinson	Mood & Rob *or* M & R
Moore	Moore (CP)
Moore (see also the following names)	Moore (KB)
Moore & Payne	Moore & P *or* M & P
Moore & Scott	Moo & S *or* M & Scott
Moore's Indian Appeals	Moo Ind App
Moore's Privy Council Cases	Moo PCC
Moore's Privy Council Cases, New Series	Moo PCC, NS
Morrel, Bankruptcy Reports	Morr BR
Mosely	Mos
Murphy & Hurlstone	M & H
Murray's Reports	Murr
Mylne & Craig	My & Cr
Mylne & Keen	My & K
Nelson	Nels
Neville & Macnamara's Railway and Canal Cases	Nev & M
Neville & Manning	Nev & M (KB)
Neville & Manning (Magistrates Cases)	N & M (MC)
Neville & Perry	Nev & P (KB) *or* N & P (KB)
New County Court Cases	NCC Cas

R

Table 3 (continued)

Report	Abbreviation	Report	Abbreviation
New Law Journal Reports	NLJR	Revised Reports	RR
New Magistrates' Cases	NMC *or* New Mag Cas	Ridgway, Lapp & Shoales	RL & S
New Practice Cases	NPC *or* New Pract Cas	Ridgway's Cases in the time of Lord Hardwicke	Ridg *temp* Hard
New Reports	NR *or* New Rep		
New Sessions Cases	New Sess Cas	Ridgway's Parliamentary Reports	Ridg PC
Nisbet	Nisb		
Nolan (Magistrates' Cases)	Nolan	Road Traffic Reports	RTR
Northern Ireland Law Reports	NI	Robertson (Eccl Reports)	Rob Eccl
		Robertson (Scotch Appeals)	Rob Sc App
Notes of Cases	Notes of Cases	Robinson (Chr)	Ch Rob
Noy	Noy	Robinson, Geo (Scotch Appeals)	G Rob *or* Robin App
O'Malley & Hardcastle	O'Malley & H		
Owen	Owen	Robinson, W	Wm Rob
Palmer	Palm	Rolle, Sir H	Roll Rep, *or* Rolle
Parker	Park App	Rose	Rose
Paton's Scotch Appeals	Pat App	Ross' Leading Cases on Commercial Law	Ross, LC
Peake	Peake		
Peake's Additional Cases	Peake, Add Cas	Ross' Leading Cases on the Law of Scotland	Ross, LC
Peckwell	Peckw		
Peere Williams	P Wms	Russell	Russ
Perry & Davidson	Per & Dav	Russell & Mylne	Russ & Myl *or* R & M
Perry & Knapp	Per & Kn	Russell & Ryan	Russ & Ry
Personal Injuries and Quantum Reports	PIQR	Ryan & Moody	Ry & M
		Ryde's Rating Cases	RRC
Phillimore	Phil Eccl	Salkeld	Salk
Phillips	Phill *or* Phil EL Cas	Saunders	Saund
Pigot & Rodwell (Reg Cas)	Pig & Rod	Saunders & Cole (Bail Ct)	BCR
Pitcairn's Criminal Trials	Pitc	Sausse & Scully	Sau & Sc
Plowden	Plowd	Saville	Sav
Pollexfen	Pollexf	Sayer	Say
Popham	Poph	Scott	Scott
Power, Rodwell & Dew	PR & D	Scott's New Reports	Scott, NR
Precedents in Chancery	Prec Ch	Searle & Smith	Se & Sm
Price	Price	Select Cases in Chancery	Sel Ca Ch
Probate	P	Session Cases	SC *or* Sess Cas (KB)
Probate Division	PD	Shaw	Shaw
Property and Compensation Reports	P & CR	Shaw & Dunlop	S & D *or* Sh Just
		Shaw, Dunlop, Napier Bell	S, D, N & B *or* Sh Teind Ct
Queen's Bench Division	QBD		
Queen's Bench Reports	QB	Shaw & M'Clean's Scotch Appeals	Sh & M'C
Railway and Canal Cases	Rail Cas *or* Rail & Can Cas		
		Shaw's Scotch Appeals	Sh Sc App
Railway and Canal Traffic Cases	Ry & Can Tr Cas	Shoales & Lefroy	Sch & Lef *or* S & L
		Shower	Show
Rating Appeals	RA	Shower's Cases in Parliament	Show PC
Raymond, Lord	Ld Raym	Siderfin	Sid
Raymond, Sir T	Raym *or* T Raym	Simon's Tax cases	STC
Real Property and Conveyancing	Tudor LCRP	Simons	Sim
		Simons & Stuart	Sim & St *or* S & S
Real Property Cases	RP Cas	Simons, New Series	Sim, NS
Reports in Chancery	Ch Rep *or* Rep Ch	Skinner	Skin
Reports of Patent Cases	RPC	Smale & Giffard	Sm & Giff

Table 3 (continued)

Report	Abbreviation
Smith	Smith (KB)
Smith & Batty	Sm & Bat
Smith's (Lacey) Registration Cases	Smith, Reg Cas
Smith's Leading Cases	Smith, LC
Smythe	Smythe
Solicitors' Journal and Reporter	SJ or Sol Jo
Spinks	Spinks or Ecc & Ad
Spinks' Prize Cases	Spinks' Pr Cas
Stair	Stair Rep
Starkie	Stark
State Trials (ed Howell)	How St Tr or State Tr
Strange	Stra
Stuart, Milne & Peddie	Stu M & P
Style	Sty
Swabey	Swab
Swabey & Tristram	Sw & Tr
Swanston	Swanst
Swinton	Swint
Syme	Sym
Tamlyn	Taml
Taunton	Taunt
Tax Cases	Tax Cas
Taxation Reports	TR
Temple & Mew	T & M
Term Reports, by Durnford & East	Term Rep or T Rep
Thornton's Notes of Cases	Thorn or Notes of Cases
Times Law Reports	TLR
Tothill	Toth
Traffic Cases	Traff Cas
Tudor's Leading Cases: Mercantile and Maritime Law	Tudor LC Merc Law
Turner & Russell	Turn & Russ or T & R
Tyrwhitt	Tyr
Tyrwhitt & Granger	Tyr & Gr
Value Added Tax Tribunal Reports	VATTR
Vaughan	Vaugh
Ventris	Vent
Vernon	Vern
Vernon & Scriven	V & S or Vern & Scr
Vesey & Beames	V & B or Ves & B
Vesey junior	Ves jun or, after the first two vols, simply Ves
Vesey senior	Ves Sen
Wallis	Wall
Webster's Patent Cases	Webst Pat Cas

Report	Abbreviation
Weekly Law Reports	WLR
Weekly Notes	WN
Weekly Reporter	WR
Welsby, Hurlstone & Gordon	Exch (for Exchequer)
Welsh	Welsh Reg Cas
West (Chancery)	West (Ch) or West temp Hard
West (House of Lords)	West (HL)
White & Tudor's Leading Cases	Wh & Tud LC or LC Eq
Wightwick	Wight
Willes	Willes
Williams (Peere)	P Wms
Willmore, Wollaston & Davison	WW & D or Will Woll & Dav
Willmore, Wollaston & Hodges	WW & H or Will Woll & H
Wilmot's Opinions	Wilm
Wilson, George	Wils or G Wils
Wilson, John	Wils Ch or Wils Ex Eq
Wilson & Shaw's Scotch Appeals	Wils & S or W & S
Winch	Winch
Wolferston & Bristow	Wolf & B or W & B
Wolferston & Dew	Wolf & D or W & D
Wollaston's Practice Cases	WPC or Woll
Wood's Tithe Cases	Wood
Workmen's Compensation Cases (Minston–Stenhouse)	WCC
Year Books	YB
Yelverton	Yelv
Younge	Younge
Younge & Collyer (Chancery)	You & Coll CC or Y & CCC
Younge & Collyer (Exchequer, Equity)	You & Coll Ex Eq or Y & C Ex
Younge & Jervis	Y & J

Representation. 1 For the purposes of intestate succession to anyone, the children of a deceased relative are, within certain degrees, allowed to *represent* their parents: eg if a person dies leaving a brother A, and the children of a deceased brother B, the children of B are said to take by *representation*. See now Part IV of the Administration of Estates Act 1925.

2 The character borne by an executor or administrator.

See PERSONAL REPRESENTATIVE.

3 A statement.

See MISREPRESENTATION.

4 A system by which electors choose representatives in an assembly. Election law is principally contained in the Representation of the People Act 1983.

5 Representation of a legally assisted person for the purposes of proceedings includes:

(i) all such assistance as is usually given by a solicitor or counsel in the steps preliminary or incidental to any proceedings;

(ii) all such assistance as is usually given in civil proceedings in arriving at or giving effect to a compromise to avoid or bring to an end any proceedings; and

(iii) in the case of criminal proceedings, advice and assistance as to any appeal: Legal Aid Act 1988, s 2(3).

See LEGALLY ASSISTED PERSON.

Reprieve. The suspension of the execution of a criminal sentence.

Reprisal. A taking in return; ie taking the goods of a wrongdoer to make compensation for the wrong he has done, or as a pledge for amends being made.

Republication of will. The revival of a will revoked, either by re-execution or by a codicil adapted to the purpose.

Repudiation. A rejection or disclaimer; especially of a person's disclaiming a share in a transaction to which he might otherwise be bound by tacit acquiescence.

Repugnant. Inconsistent; generally used of a clause in a written instrument inconsistent with some other clause or with the general object of the instrument.

Reputation. 1 A person's good name.

2 That which generally has been and many men have said and thought.

Request, letters of. *See* LETTERS OF REQUEST.

Requisitions of title. Under the old system of deed-based conveyancing, written inquiries made by the solicitor of an intending purchaser of land, or of any estate or interest in it, and addressed to the vendor's solicitor, in respect of some apparent insufficiency in the abstract of title.

See ABSTRACT OF TITLE; LAND REGISTRATION.

Res gestae. The material facts of a case as opposed to mere hearsay. The phrase is generally used in reference to that which is apparently hearsay, and yet is, in fact, immediately relevant to the matter in question. Thus, proof may be received of the language used at seditious meetings, in order to show their objects and character.

Res integra. An affair not broached or meddled with; one on which no action had been taken, or deliberation had been made.

Res inter alios acta alteri nocere non debet. A matter litigated between two parties ought not to prejudice a third party. That is the general rule; but it must be taken with this important qualification, that though a decision, in a case between A and B, cannot directly prejudice C, yet if there is a legal point at issue in C's case identical with one which was in controversy between A and B, the Court will generally regard itself as bound by the prior decision, at least if the Court which pronounced it was the same, or one of equal or superior authority.

See PRECEDENT.

Res ipsa loquitur. The matter itself speaks; or, 'the thing speaks for itself'. A phrase used in actions for damage occasioned by negligence where no proof is required of negligence beyond the accident itself; where, for example, a barrel rolls out of a warehouse striking the plaintiff (claimant) and causing him or her injury, no further proof of negligence beyond those facts themselves are necessary for the plaintiff to make out a case; the defendant, to avoid a finding of liability on these facts, must adduce evidence showing why the injury was not due to negligence.

Res judicata. A matter which has been adjudicated on.

Res nullius. A thing which has no owner.

Rescission. A remedy by which a court holds that a written instrument, in particular a contract, is rescinded, ie has no legal effect, typically when the contract has been induced by misrepresentation.

Rescous or **rescue.** A resistance against lawful authority, in taking a person or thing out of the custody of the law; eg if a bailiff or other officer, on a writ, arrests a person and others by violence take him away, or procure his escape; this is a *rescous in fact*.

Reservation. A keeping back, eg when a person lets his land, *reserving* a rent. Sometimes it means an exception; eg when a person lets a house, and *reserves* to himself one room. And see Law of Property Act 1925, s 65, which provides that a reservation of a legal estate operates at law without any execution of the conveyance by the grantee of the legal estate out of which the reservation is made.

Reservation of title. *See* RETENTION OF TITLE.

Residence. A continuance of a spiritual person on his benefice. (*See* BENEFICE). Now used generally for any person's continuance in a place, and defined for various purposes by different Acts of Parliament, eg in the case of the Parliamentary franchise.

Residence order. An order settling the arrangements to be made as to the person with whom a child is to live: Children Act 1989, s 8(1).

Residuary devisee. A person entitled under a will to the *residue* of the testator's lands; ie to such as are not specifically devised by the testator's will. By the Wills Act 1837, s 25 it is provided that, unless a contrary intention appears by the will, such real estate or interest as is comprised, or intended to be comprised in any devise in such will contained, which fails or is void by reason of the death of the devisee in the lifetime of the testator, or by reason of the devise being contrary to law, or otherwise incapable of taking effect, is included in the residuary devise (if any) contained in the will.

Residuary estate. A term meaning:
1 A testator's property not specifically devised or bequeathed (see Administration of Estates Act 1925, s 33(4)).
2 Such part of the personal estate as is primarily liable to the payment of debts.
3 That which remains after the debts and legacies have been paid.

Residuary legatee. A person to whom the residue or a proportionate share in the residue of a testator's personal property is left, after debts, funeral expenses, and specific and pecuniary legacies have been satisfied.

Residue. The residue of the personal estate of a deceased person after payment of the debts and specific and pecuniary legacies.

Resignation. 1 The giving up of a benefice into the hands of the Ordinary.
See BENEFICE; ORDINARY.
2 The giving up of any office by letter or other instrument in writing delivered to the party lawfully authorised to receive it (see the Local Government Act 1972, s 84).

Resolution. Any matter resolved upon, especially at a public meeting.

1 *Resolutions of creditors*—These are resolutions passed at meetings of the creditors of a bankrupt. Resolutions thus passed are of three kinds:
  (i) An *ordinary resolution*, which is decided by a majority in value of the creditors present personally or by proxy at the meeting and voting on such resolution.
  (ii) A *special resolution*, which is decided by a majority in number and three-fourths in value of the creditors present personally or by proxy at the meeting and voting on such resolution.
  (iii) A resolution which is required for the approval of a debtor's composition or scheme (see the Insolvency Act 1986, Part VIII).
2 *Resolutions of companies*—An extraordinary resolution is defined to be a resolution passed by a majority of not less than three-quarters of the members of the company present in person or by proxy at a general meeting of which notice specifying the intention to propose the extraordinary resolution has been duly given (see Companies Act 1985, s 378(1)).
  A special resolution is defined as one which has been (i) passed in the manner required for an extraordinary resolution, and (ii) confirmed by a majority of such members as may be present at a subsequent meeting of which not less than 21 days' notice has been given (see Companies Act 1985, s 378(2)).
3 *Resolutions in Parliament*— In Parliament, every question, when agreed to, assumes the form of an *order*, or a *resolution* of the House. By its *orders*, the House directs its committees, its members, its officers, the order of its own proceedings and the acts of all persons whom they concern. By its *resolutions*, the House declares its own opinions and purposes.

Resolution for voluntary winding up. A resolution under any of the provisions of the Insolvency Act 1986, s 84(1), which provides that a company may be wound up voluntarily:
  (i) when the period (if any) fixed for the duration of the company by the articles expires, or the event (if any) occurs, on the occurrence of which the articles provide that the company is

to be dissolved, and the company in general meeting has passed a resolution requiring the company to be wound up voluntarily;

(ii) if the company resolves by special resolution to be wound up voluntarily;

(iii) if the company resolves by extraordinary resolution to the effect that it cannot by reason of its liabilities continue its business, and that it is advisable to wind up (see Insolvency Act 1986, s 84(2)).

Resort, court of last. A court from which there is no appeal.

Respite. Delay or forbearance.

Respondeat superior. Let the superior be held responsible. In pursuance of this maxim, a principal is liable for the act of his agent, and an employer for the act of his employee; provided that in each case the act of the agent or employee, whether specifically authorised or not, was within the scope of the duties imposed by the principal or employer.

Respondent. A party called on to *answer* a petition or an appeal.

Respondentia. A loan on the security of the goods in a vessel, or on the mere hazard of a voyage. Such a loan is insurable.
See BOTTOMRY.

Restitutio in integrum. The rescinding of a contract or contracts (eg on the ground of fraud) so as to restore the parties to their original position.

Restitution. 1 A kind of remedy whereby the plaintiff receives an award, eg in money, measured not by the plaintiff's loss but by the defendant's (unjust gain) or unjust enrichment.
See REMEDY; UNJUST ENRICHMENT.
2 The restoring of anything unlawfully taken from another person. It was used in the Common Law for the setting a person in possession of lands and tenements where he has been unlawfully dispossessed of them.

Restitution, law of. *See* UNJUST ENRICHMENT.

Restitution order. An order for the restitution of stolen property (see Theft Act 1968, s 28, as amended by Criminal Justice Act 1972).

Restraint of marriage. Conditions attached to a gift or bequest in *general* restraint of marriage are void on the grounds of public policy, but not so conditions against a second marriage, or if the restraint is *partial* only.

Restraint of trade. Contracts in general restraint of trade, ie unlimited as to time or area, are void. Contracts in partial restraint may, however, be upheld.

Restraint upon alienation. Conditions restricting the right of a grantee of a fee simple estate to alienate the property by way of gift or sale. Generally regarded as void at common law for being 'repugnant to', ie conceptually or logically inconsistent with, the grant of full ownership.
See LAND LAW.

Restrictive covenant. An interest in the land of another, first recognised in equity. An owner of one piece of land may hold a restrictive covenant over the land of another; such a covenant restricts the second owner in the use of his property. A typical restrictive covenant prevents the owner bound from using his land for industrial purposes. Such covenants were a means by which developers of land could maintain the amenities of a neighbourhood before the advent of public planning law.

Restrictive indorsement. An indorsement on a bill of exchange or promissory note which restricts the negotiability of the bill or note to a particular person, or a particular purpose; as 'pay to I.S. only', or 'pay John Holloway for my use'. It is to be distinguished from a *blank indorsement*, which consists merely of the signature of the indorser; from a *full indorsement*, which makes the bill or note payable to a given person or his order; and from a *qualified indorsement*, which qualifies the liability of the indorser (see Bills of Exchange Act 1882, s 35).
See BILL OF EXCHANGE; PROMISSORY NOTE; INDORSEMENT; QUALIFIED INDORSEMENT.

Rests. Periodic balancings of an account made for the purpose of converting interest into principal, and charging the party liable with compound interest.

Resulting trust. A trust whereby the beneficial interest in the trust property 'results' or jumps back to the settlor. Presumed intention resulting trusts are informal trusts where the beneficial interest results to the settlor on the basis of an evidentiary presumption, thus, eg where there is no evidence of X's intentions when X gratuitously transferred property to Y, Y will generally hold the property on bare trust for X (*see* BARE TRUST). Automatic resulting trusts arise on the failure of an intended gift on trust, thus, eg where X transfers property to Y on trust for A for life and then to A's children in equal shares, and A dies childless, following A's death Y will hold the property on bare trust for X (or X's successor in title).

See TRUST.

Retainer. 1 A counsel's retaining fee. Retainers in this sense are either general or special.

2 An authority given to a solicitor to proceed in an action. This may be given verbally; but a written retainer is always preferable. A retainer of this kind is either *general* or *special*. A solicitor has an implied authority from his client to accept service of process, but he cannot, in general, commence an action for him without a special retainer.

Retention of title. Under a term of a contract for the SALE OF GOODS, a seller may deliver the goods on credit (ie for a future payment of the price) to the buyer but *reserve* or *retain* the title to the goods though they go into the buyer's possession, such that the title will only pass to the buyer upon his payment of the purchase price; should the buyer fail to do so, the seller, retaining title, will have a right to re-take possession of the goods. Such a clause in these circumstances performs a similar function to one creating a SECURITY INTEREST in the goods.

See SECURITY INTEREST; SALE OF GOODS.

Retiring partner. A partner who leaves a partnership.

A partner who retires from a firm does not thereby cease to be liable for partnership debts or obligations incurred before his retirement: Partnership Act 1890, s 17(2). A retiring partner may be discharged from any existing liabilities by an agreement to that effect between himself and the members of the firm as newly constituted and the creditors: ibid, s 17(3).

Retour sans protet or **sans frais.** A request or direction by the drawer of a bill of exchange, that, in case the bill should be dishonoured by the drawee, it be returned without protest and without expense (*sans frais*). The effect of such a request is to prevent the drawer of the bill (and perhaps also the indorsers) from resisting payment of the bill on the ground that it has not been protested.

See BILL OF EXCHANGE; PROTEST.

Return. 1 The return of a writ by a sheriff or bailiff, or other party to whom a writ is directed, is a certificate made to the court of that which he has done with regard to the execution of the writ directed to him.

2 The return of a member to serve in Parliament for a given constituency. This is the return of the writ which directed the sheriff or other officer to proceed to the election.

See RETURNING OFFICER.

3 A certificate or report by commissioners on a matter on which they have been directed to inquire. The word is especially so used in reference to matters of statistic detail; eg 'the returns of the census', etc.

See CENSUS.

4 The return of goods replevied.

See REPLEVIN.

Returning officer. The officer to whom a writ is directed, requiring him to proceed to the election of a member to serve in Parliament or some other public body (see Representation of the People Act 1983, s. 27).

Returns clause. A clause used in marine insurance policies specifying the circumstances in which a return of premium will be made if the policy is cancelled or if the insured vessel is laid up.

See PREMIUM, 2.

Revenue. The yearly rent that accrues to every man from his lands and possessions. But it is applied especially to the general income received by the State in taxes, etc, and to the hereditary revenues of the Crown.

Reversal of judgment. The annulment of a judgment on appeal by the court to which the appeal is brought.

Reversion. 1 A reversion means properly the residue of an estate in land *left in the grantor* to commence in possession after the determination of some particular estate granted by him; eg, where X, the owner of Blackacre, grants Blackacre to A for life, X has the reversion, ie the right to take back the property upon A's death. Similarly, a landlord has the reversion in the estate in land he has leased for the land will return to him on the end of the lease.

2 But it is frequently, though improperly, used so as to include any future estate, whether in reversion or remainder.

See ESTATE; LAND LAW; REMAINDER.

Reversionary interest. An interest in real or personal property in remainder or reversion.

See REMAINDER; REVERSION.

Reversionary lease. 1 A lease to take effect *in futuro.* Such a lease must take effect within 21 years from the date of the instrument purporting to create it; otherwise it is void (see Law of Property Act 1925, s 149(3)).
2 A general lease to take effect after the expiration of a former lease.

Reversioner. A person entitled to an estate in reversion; but the word is used generally to mean any person entitled to any future estate in real or personal property, eg dealings with expectant non-reversioners, etc.

Reverter. Returning or reversion.

Revival of insurance policy occurs as a result of mutual consent of the insurers and the insured after a policy has lapsed.
See LAPSE OF INSURANCE POLICY.

Reviving. A word metaphorically applied to rents, debts and rights of action, meaning a renewal of them after they have been extinguished, eg debts barred by the Limitation Act 1980 are revived by acknowledgment in some cases.

Revocation. The reversal by any one of a thing done by himself, eg when it is provided in a marriage settlement or other instrument, that an appointment may be made 'with or without power of revocation', it is implied that the party making the appointment may, if he thinks fit, reserve the power of annulling what he has done.

A power granted or reserved in a deed or other instrument to revoke an appointment already made, and to make a fresh one, is called a *power of revocation and new appointment.* Any act or instrument which is capable of being annulled by its author is said to be *revocable.*

Some instruments are in their nature revocable, eg wills. Deeds under seal are not, in general, revocable, unless a power to revoke is expressly reserved.

A will may be revoked (i) by marriage (unless it is expressed to have been made in contemplation of marriage); (ii) by the execution of another will or codicil or by some writing of revocation executed as a will; (iii) by the burning, tearing or other destruction of the original will (*animo revocandi*) by the testator, or by some other person in his presence and by his direction (see Wills Act 1837, ss 19, 20). Where the whole property is disposed of during the testator's lifetime, the will ceases to have effect.

Revocation of probate. Where probate of a will, having been granted, is afterwards recalled by the Court on proof of a subsequent will, or other sufficient cause.
See PROBATE.

Rhodian law. An ancient code of maritime law used by the people of Rhodes, some of the principles of which have been adopted in our own shipping law.

Rider. 1 A clause proposed to be added to a motion before a meeting.
2 An addition to the verdict of a jury.

Right. A lawful title or claim to anything. Rights, along with duties (or obligations) and powers, are the basic elements which determine a person's legal position. *General* rights are those which apply to all persons, simply in virtue of their being full subjects of the law, eg the right to assemble, the right not to be assaulted. *Special* rights are those which arise by the exercise of powers, eg the rights of the parties under a contract having exercised their power to make a contract, or by operation of law on the occurrence of certain events, such as the right to bring a claim for damages against one who has negligently cause one loss or injury.
See IN PERSONAM; IN REM; POWER; and the entry which follows.

Right in gross. A right of ownership of an incorporeal property, such as a right of FISHERY, which is not held in virtue of owning an estate in land to which the right is connected. Thus a right *in gross* is one which does *not* belong to the party invested with it *as being the owner or occupier of specifically-determined land* (ie which is not *appendant* or *appurtenant* to another thing), but is annexed to, or inheres in, his person, that is, is his personally; being quite unconnected with anything corporeal, and existing as a separate subject of transfer; thus one speaks of a common *in gross,* an advowson *in gross,* etc.
See INCORPOREAL HEREDITAMENT; LAND LAW.

Right of action. The right to bring an action in any given case. But the phrase is frequently used in a more extended sense, as identical with *chose in action,* to mean all rights which are not rights of possession, and to include the large class of rights over things in the possession of others, which must be asserted by action in cases where the qualified or temporary possessor refuses to deliver them up.

Right of audience. The right of a person to appear before the court in any proceeding for the purposes of representing one of the parties.

Right of search. The right of a belligerent to examine and inspect the papers of a neutral vessel on the high seas, and the goods contained in her, to see whether she is neutral or an enemy, and to ascertain whether she has contraband of war or enemies' property on board.

See CONTRABAND.

Right of way. A right enjoyed by one person (either in his own character or as a member of the public) of passing over another's land, subject to such conditions and restrictions as are specified in the grant, or sanctioned by the custom, by virtue of which the right exists. Rights of way are susceptible of almost infinite variety; they may be limited both as to the intervals at which they may be used (as a way to church) and as to the actual extent of the user authorised (as a footway, bridleway or carriageway). As to public rights of way, and dedication of ways, see Highways Act 1980, ss 30–32.

Right to begin. The right to commence the argument on a trial, which belongs to that side on whom the burden of proof rests. The party beginning has also the right to reply to his opponent's case. The appellant begins all civil appeals.

See BURDEN OF PROOF.

Rights, Bill of. *See* BILL OF RIGHTS.

Rights issue. A right given to a shareholder to subscribe for further shares in the company usually at a price lower than the market price of the existing shares, the number usually being in proportion to the shareholder's present shareholding eg a right to subscribe for one new share for every five which he holds.

Ringing the changes. A trick by which a criminal, on receiving a piece of money in payment of an article, pretends that it is not good, and, changing it in such a manner as not to be seen by the buyer, returns to the latter a spurious coin. This is held to be an uttering of false money: *Frank's case* (1794) Leach 644. The phrase is also generally applied to fraudulent exchanges of coin, effected in the course of paying money or receiving money in payment.

Riot. Where 12 or more persons who are present together use or threaten unlawful violence for a common purpose and the conduct of them (taken together) is such as would cause a person of reasonable firmness present at the scene to fear for his personal safety, each of the persons using unlawful violence for the common purpose is guilty of riot (see Public Order Act 1986, s 1(1)). It is immaterial whether or not the 12 or more use or threaten violence simultaneously (see ibid, s 1(2)). The common purpose may be inferred from conduct (see ibid, s 1(3)). No person of reasonable firmness need actually be, or be likely to be, present at the scene (see ibid, s 1(4)). Riot may be committed in private as well as in public places (see ibid, s 1(5)). A person guilty of riot is liable on conviction on indictment to imprisonment for a term not exceeding 10 years or a fine or both (see ibid, s 1(6)).

Riparian. Relating to rivers or river banks.

Riparian proprietors. Proprietors of the banks of a river.

Riparian States. States whose jurisdictions are bounded by the banks of a river.

Road. Any highway and any other road to which the public has access, and bridges over which a road passes: Road Traffic Act 1988, s 192(1).

See HIGHWAY.

Robbery. A person is guilty of robbery if he steals, and immediately before or at the time of doing so, and in order to do so, he uses force on any person or puts or seeks to put any person in fear of being then and there subjected to force. A person guilty of robbery, or of an assault with intent to rob, is liable to imprisonment for life (see Theft Act 1968, s 8).

Rogue. An idle wandering beggar, vagrant or vagabond; a fraudster.

Roll. A schedule of paper or parchment, which may be turned or wound up.

Rolls of Parliament. The manuscript registers of the proceedings of Parliament.

Romalpa clause. A clause reserving the seller's title to goods not yet paid for by the buyer and purporting to enable the seller to trace and recover the proceeds of sub-sales in priority to other creditors of the buyer. Such a clause is named after *Aluminium Industrie*

R

Vaassen BV v Romalpa Aluminium Ltd [1976] 2 All ER 577, CA.
See RETENTION OF TITLE; SECURITY INTEREST.

Root of title. Under the old deeds-based system of conveyancing, it is the duty of a vendor in making title, on a sale of land, to show what has happened to the absolute ownership of the land for a sufficient number of years in the past, and to prove that it now resides in him. The number of years the law regarded as sufficient has been consecutively reduced by statute from 40, to 30, and finally to 15 years; Law of Property Act 1925, s 44 (1); Law of Property Act 1969, s 23. It is necessary, therefore, that the abstract of title should contain a 'good root of title', ie some document at least 15 years old that deals with the absolute ownership, both at law and in equity, and which contains nothing to cast doubt on the title of the party which disposed of the land under that deed. A good root of title must also deal with the legal and the equitable interest transferred in such a fashion that the property itself is adequately identified.
See ABSTRACT OF TITLE.

A mortgage deed or a purchase deed 15 years old is usually a good root of title, but a general devise in a will is not sufficient.

Royal Assent (Lat *Regius assensus*). The assent given by the Sovereign to a bill passed in both Houses of Parliament. The royal assent to a bill had formerly to be given either in person, or by commission by letters patent under the Great Seal, signed with the Sovereign's hand, and notified to both Houses assembled together in the upper House. The procedure has been modified by the Royal Assent Act 1967. A bill, on receiving the royal assent, becomes an Act of Parliament.
See LA REYNE LE VEULT; LA REYNE S'AVISERA.

Royal fish. *See* FISH ROYAL.

Royal grants. Grants by letters patent or letters close from the Crown. These are always matters of record.

Royal style and titles. These were made by Proclamation in 1953, and are: 'Elizabeth II, by the Grace of God of the United Kingdom of Great Britain and Northern Ireland and of Her other Realms and Territories Queen, Head of the Commonwealth, Defender of the Faith.'

Royalty. 1 The royal dignity and prerogatives.
See PREROGATIVE.

2 A *pro rata* payment to a grantor or lessor, on the working of the property leased, or otherwise on the profits of the grant or lease. The word is especially used in reference to mines, patents and copyrights.
See PATENT; COPYRIGHT.

Rubric. Directions and instructions contained in the Book of Common Prayer.
See BOOK OF COMMON PRAYER.

Rule. 1 A regulation for the government of a society, eg a club or trade union, agreed to by its members.
2 A rule of procedure made by a lawful judicial authority for some court or courts of justice, eg Rules of the Supreme Court 1965. See also Supreme Court Act 1981, s 84.
3 An order made by a superior court on motion in some matter over which it has summary jurisdiction.
4 A point of law settled by authority.

Rule against perpetuities. *See* PERPETUITY.

Rule of court. 1 An order made on motion, generally in open court, or else made generally to regulate the practice of the court.
2 A submission to arbitration, or the award of an arbitrator, is said to be made a *rule of court*, when the Court makes a rule that such submission or award is to be conclusive (see the Arbitration Act 1950, ss 1, 26).

Rule of law. The principle of rule by laws, not by men, ie that all men are equal before the law, and that acts of officials in carrying out government orders are valid only if within the law, and are invalid if not, as determined by the ordinary courts of law, ie that official position provides no authority to act contrary to law. The principle imposes certain requirements on the form of law and its administration so that subjects of the law can know 'where they stand' in relation to the law, and can have confidence that the law will be faithfully and impartially applied, eg laws should be clear, publicly promulgated, and reasonably stable, and tribunals should apply the law faithfully, procedure in courts should be fair, and judges should be unbiased and their independence from political influence assured.

Rules of good husbandry. Rules under which the occupier of an agricultural unit is deemed to be fulfilling his responsibilities under the

Agriculture Act 1947. They include properly mowing or grazing permanent pasture, the maintaining of crops and livestock free from disease, etc. See s 11 of the Act.

Rules of good seamanship. Rules determining whether a vessel has carried out her duties in relation to other vessels. The question of good seamanship is one of fact to be decided on a consideration of all the circumstances (see *SS Heranger (Owners) v SS Diamond (Owners)* [1939] AC 94, HL). Where a rule of good seamanship conflicts with a rule of the Collision Regulations 1989, the Regulations must be obeyed (see Collision Regulations 1989, reg 2(a)).

Running days. A term used in a charter-party denoting consecutive days including Sundays and holidays (see *Nielson & Co v Wait, James & Co* (1886) 16 QBD 67 at 72, CA (per Lord Esher, MR)).

Running down case. An action against the driver of one vehicle for running into another; or against a ship for damaging another by collision.

Running with the land. A covenant is said to *run with the land* when each successive owner of the land is entitled to the benefit of the covenant, or liable (as the case may be) to its obligation. As to such covenants, see the Law of Property Act 1925, s 80.
See RESTRICTIVE COVENANT.

Rural dean. An officer of the church, generally a parochial clergyman, appointed to act under the bishop or archdeacon (*see* BISHOP; ARCHDEACON); his proper duty being to inspect the conduct of the parochial clergy, to inquire into and report dilapidations (*see* DILAPIDATION) and to examine candidates for confirmation.

Rural deanery. The circuit of the jurisdiction of a rural dean. Every diocese is divided into archdeaconries, each archdeaconry into rural deaneries, and each rural deanery into parishes.
See RURAL DEAN.

R

S

S. Section (of an Act).

SI. Statutory instrument. *See* STATUTORY INSTRUMENT.

SP. *Sine prole*, without issue. *See* SINE PROLE.

Sacrilege. Stealing things dedicated to the offices of religion.

Safe conduct. A security given by the Sovereign, under the Great Seal of England, for enabling a foreigner of a nation at war with this country quietly to come into and pass out of the realm. *See* GREAT SEAL.

Safe port. A port to which a vessel can get laden as she is and at which she can lie and discharge, always afloat (see *Hall Bros SS Co Ltd v R & W Paul Ltd* (1914) 111 LT 811 at 812 (per Sankey J)). The port must be one from which she can safety return (see *Islander Shipping Enterprises SA v Empresa Maritima del Estado SA: The 'Khian Sea'* [1977] 2 Lloyd's Rep 439).

Sale. A transfer of property from one person to another in consideration of a price paid in money.

Sale of goods, contract for. A contract by which the seller transfers or agrees to transfer the property in goods to the buyer for a money consideration, called the price: Sale of Goods Act 1979, s 2(1). The contract may be absolute or conditional: ibid, s 2(3).

There are implied conditions that the seller has a good title to the goods (ibid, s 12); that they will comply with their description (ibid, s 13); and that, in a contract for sale by sample, the bulk will correspond with the sample in quality, the buyer will have a reasonable opportunity of comparing the bulk with the sample, and the goods will be free from any defect, rendering them unmerchantable, which would not be apparent on reasonable examination of the sample (ibid, s 15(2)).

There is an implied warranty that (i) the goods are free, and will remain free until the time when the property is to pass, from any charge or encumbrance not disclosed or known to the buyer before the contract is made; and (ii) the buyer will enjoy quiet possession of the goods except so far as it may be disturbed by the owner or other person entitled to the benefit of any charge or encumbrance so disclosed or known: ibid, s 12(2).

Where the seller sells goods in the course of a business, there are implied conditions that:
- (i) the goods are reasonably fit for the purpose for which they are supplied;
- (ii) they are of merchantable quality: ibid, s 14(2), (3).

As to the extent to which a seller may contract out of the above conditions and warranties, see ibid, s 55.

Salvage or **salvage money.** A reward payable by owners of ships and goods saved at sea from pirates, enemies, or the perils of the sea, to those who have saved them.

Claims for salvage may be made in the High Court or in County Courts having Admiralty jurisdiction.

Salvage charges in marine insurance mean the charges recoverable under maritime law by a salvor independently of contract (see Marine Insurance Act 1906, s 65(2)). They do not include the expenses of services in the nature of salvage rendered by the assured or his agents, or any person employed for hire by them, for the purpose of averting a peril insured against (see ibid, s 65(2)).

Salved vessel. A vessel to which salvage services are rendered. *See* SALVAGE.

Salving vessel. A vessel rendering salvage services. *See* SALVAGE.

Sample, sale by is where in the contract there is an express or implied term to that effect: Sale of Goods Act 1979, s 15(1). There is an implied condition that (i) the bulk will correspond with the sample in quality; (ii) the buyer will have a reasonable opportunity of comparing the bulk with the sample; and (iii) the goods will be free from any defect, rendering them unmerchantable, which would not be apparent on reasonable examination of the sample: ibid, s 15(2).

Sanction of a law. The provision for enforcing it.

Sans frais. Without incurring any expenses.

Sans nombre. Without stint. A term sometimes applied to the case of common for cattle *levant et couchant*. But a common *sans nombre* generally means a common of pasture without any limit to the number of beasts which may be turned on it to feed there; which can only happen if it is a common in gross.

See COMMON, RIGHTS OF; LEVANT AND COUCHANT; SURCHARGE OF COMMON.

Sans recours. Without recourse; meaning 'without recourse to me'. These words are appended to an indorsement on a bill of exchange or promissory note to qualify it, so as not to make the indorser responsible for any payment on it. This is the proper mode of indorsing a bill where an agent indorses on behalf of his principal.

See BILL OF EXCHANGE; QUALIFIED INDORSEMENT; PROMISSORY NOTE.

Satisfaction. 1 The acceptance by a party injured of a sum of money, or other thing, in bar of any action he might otherwise have had in respect of such injury. Payment of a sum of money will not operate as satisfaction of a larger sum owing; but payment in any other form, eg even by cheque or bill of exchange, will.

2 The making of a donation with the express or implied intention that it shall be taken as an extinguishment of some claim which the donee has on the donor. This generally happens under one of the two following states of circumstances: (i) when a father, or person *in loco parentis*, makes a double provision for a child, or person standing towards him in a filial relation, ie satisfaction of portions by legacies, or legacies by portions; (ii) when a debtor

confers, by will or otherwise, a pecuniary benefit on his creditor.

In the first case the question arises whether the later provision is in *satisfaction* of the former, or intended to be added to it. In the second, the question is whether the benefit conferred is intended *in satisfaction* of the debt, or whether the creditor is to be allowed to take advantage of it, and nevertheless claim independently against other assets of the debtor.

Satisfaction differs from *performance*, in that satisfaction implies the substitution of something different from that agreed to be given, while in cases of performance the thing agreed to be done is taken to be in truth wholly or in part performed.

Scandal. 1 A report or rumour, or action whereby a person is affronted in public.

2 An irrelevant and abusive statement introduced into the pleadings in an action. The Court or a Judge may order scandalous statements to be struck out of the pleadings, and out of affidavits.

Schedule. An appendix to an Act of Parliament or instrument in writing, for the purpose of facilitating reference in the Act or instrument itself.

Scheme of arrangement. An arrangement between a debtor and his creditors whereby it is agreed that the debts are to be paid or partly paid under an agreed scheme, instead of the debtor being adjudged bankrupt.

Scienter. Knowingly; a word applied especially to the clause in a declaration in certain classes of actions in which the plaintiff alleged that the defendant *knowingly* did or permitted that from whence arose the damage of which the plaintiff complained. In an action of deceit the *scienter* must be averred and proved. *Scienter* formerly had also to be proved in cases of injuries done by animals, except in the case of injury done by dogs to sheep, cattle, etc (see now Animals Act 1971).

Scilicet. 'That is to say'; or 'to wit'.

See VIDELICET.

Scold. A troublesome and angry woman, who, by brawling and wrangling amongst her neighbours, broke the public peace, increased discord, and became a public nuisance to the neighbourhood. Scolds were punished by means of the castigatory or cuckingstool.

See NUISANCE.

Scrip. Certificates of shares in a company. A scrip certificate is a certificate entitling the holder to apply for shares in a company, either absolutely or on the fulfilment of specified conditions.

Script. 1 A testamentary document of any kind, whether a will, codicil, draft of a will or codicil, or written instructions for them. *See* CODICIL.

2 In relation to the performance of a play, means the text of the play together with any stage or other directions for its performance: Theatres Act 1968, s 9(2). Scripts of new plays must be sent to the British Library: ibid, s 11. *See* PLAY; BRITISH LIBRARY.

Scrutiny. In regard to elections, the examination and checking of votes. Obtained by means of the presentation of an election petition. *See* ELECTION PETITION.

Seal. Wax impressed with a device, and attached as a mark of authenticity to letters and other instruments in writing. A contract under seal is called a *specialty contract* or *covenant.* It needs no valuable consideration to support it, as a contract not under seal does. *See* DEED; CONSIDERATION; CONTRACT.

Seaman, unless the context otherwise requires, includes every person employed or engaged in any capacity on board any ship (see Merchant Shipping Act 1894, s 742).

Search order. *See* ANTON PILLER ORDER.

Search, right of. *See* RIGHT OF SEARCH.

Search warrant. A warrant granted by a judge or magistrate to search a house, shop or other premises, eg a warrant may be granted by a justice under the Theft Act 1968, s 26 for the purpose of searching for stolen goods.

Searches. Usually made by purchasers to find out incumbrances. Such searches are made at the Land Registry (generally by obtaining an official certificate of search) for land charges, and at the office of local authorities for local land charges etc. *See* INCUMBRANCE; LAND CHARGES.

Seaworthy. Reasonably fit in all respects to encounter the ordinary perils of the sea.

1 *Marine insurance.* In a voyage policy there is an implied warranty that at the commencement of the voyage the ship shall be seaworthy for the purpose of the particular adventure insured (see Marine Insurance Act 1906, s 39(1)). (*See* IMPLIED WARRANTY). Where the voyage is to be performed in different stages during which the ship requires different kinds of or further preparation or equipment there is an implied warranty that at the commencement of each stage the ship is seaworthy in respect of such preparation or equipment for the purposes of that stage (see Marine Insurance Act 1906, s 39(3)).

In a time policy there is no implied warranty that the ship shall be seaworthy at any stage of the adventure, but where, with the privity of the assured, the ship is sent to sea in an unseaworthy state, the insurer is not liable for any loss attributable to unseaworthiness (see Marine Insurance Act 1906, s 39(5)).

2 *Carriage by sea.* In charter-parties and in bills of lading to which the Hague–Visby Rules do not apply the shipowner is under an absolute duty to supply a seaworthy ship. But in bills of lading to which the Hague–Visby Rules apply he is bound only before and at the beginning of the voyage to exercise due diligence to make the ship seaworthy (see Art III, r 1). *See* HAGUE–VISBY RULES.

Secondary action in relation to a trade dispute occurs when a person:

(i) induces another to break a contract of employment or to interfere with its performance, or

(ii) threatens that a contract of employment under which he or another is employed will be broken or its performance interfered with,

and the employer under the contract of employment is not a party to the dispute: Employment Act 1990, s 1(2). *See* TRADE DISPUTE.

Secondary evidence. Evidence not of the best and most direct character; which is admissible in certain cases where the circumstances are such as to excuse a party from giving the proper or primary proof, eg a copy of a deed is secondary evidence of its contents. Secondary evidence is admissible in many cases. There are no degrees of secondary evidence. The testimony of a witness is as sufficient secondary evidence of the contents of a written instrument as a copy of it would be although the latter would be more satisfactory. *See* PRIMARY EVIDENCE.

Secondary evidence must not be confused with secondhand evidence.

See SECONDHAND EVIDENCE.

Secondhand evidence. The same as *hearsay evidence*, the ordinary meaning of which is the oral or written statement of a person who is not produced in court, conveyed to the Court either by a witness or by the instrumentality of a document.

See HEARSAY EVIDENCE.

Secret trust. A trust created by a testator who leaves property by his will to a person who has agreed to hold the property on trust for another when he receives it under the distribution of the testator's estate. As such, the trust is a testamentary trust which does comply with the formality requirements of the Wills Act 1837, viz that any testamentary gift must be made in writing signed by the testator and attested by two witnesses, but EQUITY has enforced such trusts, either on the principle that it would be a fraud to allow the legatee to resile from his agreement and take the property for his own benefit, or on the basis that being made between the testator and the legatee while alive, the trust is INTER VIVOS, though 'constituted' at the testators death, and as such is not testamentary so need not comply with the Wills Act.

A half or semi-secret trust is one in which the trust obligation is made apparent in the will, but the particular OBJECT OF THE TRUST is not disclosed. Such trusts are likewise enforced by EQUITY, though the rules differ slightly, as do the possible rationales for doing so.

See TRUST.

Secure accommodation. Accommodation provided for the purpose of restricting liberty: Children Act 1989, s 25(1).

Secured creditor. A creditor who holds some special security for his debt, eg a mortgage or lien.

See SECURITY.

A secured creditor in the liquidation of a company may either give up his security, or give credit for its value and prove, ie claim in the liquidation proceedings, for his whole debt, or else realise his security, prove for the balance, and receive a dividend *pari passu* with the other creditors (see Insolvency Act 1986 and Rules made under it).

Securities in the Company Securities (Insider Dealing) Act 1985 means listed securities and, in the case of a company within the meaning of the Companies Act 1985 or a company registered under Chapter II of Part XXII of that Act or an unregistered company, the following securities (whether or not listed), that is to say, any shares, any debentures or any right to subscribe for, call for or make delivery of a share or debenture (see Company Securities (Insider Dealing) Act 1985, s 12(1)).

See LISTED SECURITIES.

Security, security Interest. A kind of interest, or right, in property owned by another. A security interest 'secures' the repayment of a debt by an owner of property, for if the debtor/owner fails to pay the debt according to the terms of the contract for repayment, the creditor with the security interest, called a 'secured creditor', can take action with respect to the secured property, typically by exercising a power to sell the property and take the proceeds of sale as repayment of the debt; taking this action is known as 'realising' the security. Originally at common law, all security interests were effected by way of possession. Thus, under a mortgage, the lender, the mortgagee, secured his loan by taking a conveyance of land from the borrower, the mortgagor. The lender thus became the legal owner of the property with the immediate right to its possession. Under the terms of the mortgage, the mortgagee had the obligation to re-convey the property to the mortgagor on repayment of the mortgage loan, but should the mortgagor fail to meet his repayment obligations, the mortgagee, having ownership and thus the immediate right to take possession of the land, could take possession of the land for his own use, or sell it. Similarly, chattels were pledged. A pledge is a form of BAILMENT, by which the pledgor, the borrower, gives possession of a chattel to his lender, the pledgee, as security for the repayment of his loan. On the pledgor's failure to meet his repayment obligations, the pledgee is entitled to sell the chattel. Many security interests no longer take effect by way of possession, as for example the modern mortgage, but by way of legal rights to sell the property of the lender upon his failure to meet his repayment obligations. Irrespective of how the security interest takes effect, a security interest is a proprietary interest or right in the property of the lender; thus it will (generally) bind third parties who take the property from the lender by way of sale or gift or otherwise, for the right attaches to the property itself. Where the more modern form of security interest is created, ie not by way of the creditor taking possession of the property, it is generally not obvious to third parties whether a particular item of property, whether land or a chattel, is the subject of a security interest, for it remains in the possession of the lender, and therefore Parliament has imposed various registration regimes (eg LAND REGISTRATION, Companies Act 1985, s 395) whereby the existence of security interests can be determined by a search of a public register.

Security for costs. A defendant may apply to the court for an order for security for costs to be given by the plaintiff, in circumstances where there is reason to believe that the plaintiff, if unsuccessful, could not be made to pay the costs of the action.

Security for good behaviour. *See* GOOD BEHAVIOUR.

Security for keeping the peace. *See* KEEPING THE PEACE.

Security of tenure. The right of a tenant to continue in possession of leasehold property. Under the common law such right was governed more or less entirely by the strict contract of the lease between the parties. However, Parliament has intervened extensively in this area to provide greater protection to tenants, eg the Agricultural Holdings Act 1986, the Landlord and Tenant Act 1954 Part II (business tenancies), the various Housing Acts (residential tenancies).

Security Service. A service whose function is the protection of national security, in particular, against threats from espionage, terrorism and sabotage, from the activities of agents of foreign powers and from actions intended to overthrow or undermine Parliamentary democracy by political, industrial or violent means: Security Service Act 1989, s 1(1).

Secus. Otherwise; not so.

Sedition. Attempts made, by meetings or speeches, or by publications, to disturb the tranquillity of the State, which do not amount to treason.

See TREASON.

See (Lat *Sedes*). The circuit of a bishop's jurisdiction; or his office or dignity as being bishop of a given diocese.

Seisin. Common law concept of possession of freehold land, under which, for example, the grant or transfer of title to land was conceived as the delivery of possession of the land (livery of seisin), and possession of land is itself regarded as a ground of title. *See* PROPERTY, 3; LIVERY OF SEISIN.

Select Committee. A committee appointed either by the House of Lords or the House of Commons to hear evidence on and consider some subject, and report back.

Self-defence. If a person, in order to defend himself or his family or property, uses force which is reasonable in the circumstances and unintentionally kills his assailant, the killing is excusable. In defending himself, in such a case, a person must retreat as far as he can before resorting to force, though a person defending his house apparently need not do so (*R v Hussey* (1924) 89 JP 28). He must demonstrate by his actions that he does not want to fight (*R v Julien* [1969] 2 All ER 856).

Self-help. Actions available to an individual to remedy a legal wrong without the assistance of the courts, eg the peaceable eviction of a trespasser from one's property without seeking an order for possession from the court. Self-help is often likely to lead to a breach of the peace, and for that reason certain kinds of self-help have been made unlawful or heavily restricted by statute.

Semble. It appears; an expression often used in law reports, to indicate that such was the opinion of the Court on a point not directly before it.

Sentence of a court. A definitive judgment pronounced in a civil or criminal proceeding. *See* DEFERMENT OF SENTENCE; SUSPENDED SENTENCE.

Separate maintenance. Maintenance provided by a husband for his wife on the understanding that she is to live separate from him.

Separation. The living apart or separately by a husband and wife often, though not necessarily, with the intention later to divorce. A deed of separation is a deed made between husband and wife, whereby each covenants not to molest the other, and the husband agrees to pay so much to trustees for her separate maintenance, the trustees covenanting to indemnify him against his wife's debts.

See SEPARATE MAINTENANCE.

Though the law allows provision to be made for a separation already determined on, it will not sanction any agreement to provide for the contingency of a future separation.

A *decree* for judicial separation may be granted under the Matrimonial Causes Act 1973, s 17. An *order* for separation (now known as a 'matrimonial order') may be obtained from justices under the Matrimonial Proceedings (Magistrates' Courts) Act 1960, s 2.

See DIVORCE.

Sequester. A term used in the Civil Law for renouncing. The word also means the setting apart of a man's property, or a portion of it, for the benefit of creditors.

See SEQUESTRATION.

Sequestration. 1 The order sent out by a bishop in execution of the writ of *sequestrari facias*, whereby the bishop directs the churchwardens to collect the profits of the defendant's benefice, and pay them to the plaintiff, until the full sum is raised.

See CHURCHWARDENS.

2 A writ directed by the court to commissioners, usually four in number, commanding them to enter the lands and take the rents and profits and seize the goods of the person against whom it is directed. This may be issued against a defendant who is in contempt by reason of neglect or refusal to appear or answer, or to obey a decree of the Court. This writ may be issued in whatever Division of the High Court the action may be brought (see RSC 1965, Ord 46).

Seriatim. Individually, separately and in order.

Serious arrestable offence. An offence specified in the Police and Criminal Evidence Act 1984, Schs I and II, and certain offences specified in the Drug Trafficking Offences Act 1986, s 38(1): Police and Criminal Evidence Act 1984, s 116(2).

See ARRESTABLE OFFENCE.

Serious Fraud Office. An office constituted under the Criminal Justice Act 1987. Its Director is appointed by the Attorney-General and is under his superintendence (see Criminal Justice Act 1987, s 1(2)). The Director may investigate any suspected offence which appears to him on reasonable

grounds to involve serious or complex fraud (see ibid, s 1(3)). He may, if he thinks fit, conduct any such investigation in conjunction with the police or with any other person who is, in his opinion, a proper person to be concerned in it.

Serjeant, or **Sergeant** (Lat Serviens):

1 *Sergeants at arms*, whose office is to attend the person of the Sovereign; to arrest traitors and persons of quality offending, and to attend the Lord High Steward of England sitting in judgment on any traitor. Two of them, by allowance of the Sovereign, attend on the two Houses of Parliament. Their duties are to execute the commands of the House in arresting offenders.

2 *The Common Serjeant*, a judicial officer in the City of London. He acts as a circuit judge by virtue of his office.

Servant. Servants are of several types: (i) menial servants: being persons retained by others to live within the walls of the house and to perform the work and business of the household; (ii) persons employed by others, to assist them in their particular trades or professions; (iii) apprentices, who are placed with a master to learn his trade.

See APPRENTICE.

1 A master may *maintain*, that is, abet and assist, his servant in any action at law against a third party: whereas, in general, to do this is an offence against the law.

See MAINTENANCE,

1. If a servant by his negligence does any damage to a third party, the master is liable for his negligence, provided the damage is done while the servant is acting in his master's employment.

Service (*Servitium*). **1** The duty which a servant owes to his master.

2 *Service of process*—The delivery of a writ, summons, notice, statement of case, etc, in any action or suit being instituted, or notice of any step or process in it, to the party to be affected thereby, or his solicitor, or other party having an interest in the subject-matter of the suit. An *address for service* is an address at which such notice may be served, so as to bind the party whom it is thereby intended to serve.

3 Of notices by landlord or tenant.

Servient tenement. A tenement subject to an easement or servitude.

See DOMINANT TENEMENT; EASEMENT.

Servitude. Non-possessory rights over the land of another, eg an easement or profit à prendre.
See PROFIT À PRENDRE; EASEMENT.

Session. 1 The sitting of Parliament from its meeting to its prorogation, of which there is, in general, only one in each year.
See PROROGATION OF PARLIAMENT.

2 The sitting of justices in court upon commission.

Session, Court of. *See* COURT OF SESSION.

Set-off. The merging (wholly or partially) of a claim of one person against another in a counterclaim by the latter against the former. Thus, a plea of set-off is a plea whereby a defendant acknowledges the justice of the plaintiff's demand, but sets up another demand of his own, to counter-balance that of the plaintiff, either in whole or in part.

Where a claim by a defendant to a sum of money is relied on as a defence to the whole or part of a claim made by the plaintiff, it may be included in the defence and set off against the plaintiff's claim, whether or not it is also added as a counterclaim.
See COUNTERCLAIM.

Sets of bills. Exemplars or parts of a bill of exchange made on separate pieces of paper; each part referring to the other parts and being separately numbered; the set or parts constitute one bill (see Bills of Exchange Act 1882, s 71).
See BILL OF EXCHANGE.

Settled estates. *See* SETTLEMENT; SETTLED LAND.

Settled land. Land limited by *way of succession*, that is, limited to a person other than the person for the time being entitled to the beneficial enjoyment of it; thus land which is held by A for life, and thereafter to B, is limited by way of succession and is settled land. A in this example is called a limited owner (see Settled Land Act 1925). A is also the tenant for life, and the Settled Land Act 1925 expanded the powers of the tenant for life of settled land to mortgage, lease, sell, or otherwise deal with it, the Act providing protections for those with future interests in the land.
See LIMITED OWNER.

Settlement. 1 A deed whereby property is *settled*, ie subjected to a string of limitations, ie a series of SUCCESSIVE INTERESTS. In this sense one speaks of *marriage settlements* and *family settlements*.
See MARRIAGE SETTLEMENT; STRICT SETTLEMENT.

2 Any trust, but particularly one providing for SUCCESSIVE INTERESTS.

3 The termination of a disputed matter by the adoption of terms agreeable to the parties to it.

4 A colony or plantation.
See COLONIES.

Settlement, Act of. *See* ACT OF SETTLEMENT.

Settlement days, on the Stock Exchange, are the days appointed for the settlement of accounts arising from purchases and sale of stock.

Settlor. A person who makes a settlement or trust of his land or personal property.
See SETTLEMENT; TRUST.

Sever. *See* SEVERANCE.

Several covenants. Covenants entered into with several persons in such a manner or in such circumstances that they are construed as separate. If the interest of several parties in a deed appears to be separate, the covenants will be construed as separate, unless the language expressly and unequivocally indicates a joint covenant.
See COVENANT.

Several fishery. A fishery of which the owner is also the owner of the soil, or derives his right from the owner of the soil. Generally an exclusive right.
See FISHERY.

Severalty, or several tenancy. The holding of lands by a person in his own right only, without any other person being joined or connected with him in point of interest during his estate in it. It is thus opposed to holding in joint tenancy or tenancy in common.
See COMMON, TENANCY IN; JOINT TENANCY.

Severance. 1 The singling or severing of two or more persons who are joined in one writ, action or suit, eg when two persons made defendants in a suit in respect of the same interest *sever* their defences, ie adopt independent defences.

2 The dissolution of a joint tenancy, so as to create a tenancy in common. By severing a joint tenancy so as to create a tenancy in common, the right of survivorship among the co-owners as joint tenants is destroyed.

Sex discrimination. *See* DISCRIMINATION.

Shack. *Common of shack* is the right of persons, occupying lands lying together in the same common field, to turn out their cattle after harvest to feed together in that field.

Shadow director. A person in accordance with whose directions or instructions the directors of a company are accustomed to act (see Companies Act 1985, s 741(2)). But a person is not deemed a shadow director by reason only that the directors act on advice given by him in a professional capacity (see ibid, s 741(2)).

Sham. An act done or a document executed with the intention of falsely representing the legal nature of a transaction between the parties.

Sham plea. A plea manifestly frivolous and absurd, pleaded for the purpose of vexation and delay. The Court or a Judge may order to be struck out or amended any matter in the pleadings which may tend to prejudice, embarrass, or delay the fair trial of the action. *See* IMPERTINENCE.

Share. A share or proportion of the capital of a company, entitling the holder to a share in the profits of the company. Shares may be of different classes, the principal among which are:

(i) *Preference shares*, the holders of which have preference over other classes as regards dividends and the repayment of capital. These may be either *non-cumulative* or *cumulative*, the latter entitling the holders to arrears of dividend, as well as to current dividends, in priority to other shareholders; they may also be *redeemable* at a future date. *See* DIVIDEND.

(ii) *Ordinary shares*, which carry no such special rights or privileges.

(iii) *Deferred shares*, the holders of which are entitled to any surplus after payment of dividends to the other classes of shareholders in accordance with the terms laid down in the memorandum and articles of association of the company. *See* MEMORANDUM OF ASSOCIATION; ARTICLES OF ASSOCIATION.

Share, forfeiture of. *See* FORFEITURE OF SHARE.

Share, founder's. *See* FOUNDER'S SHARE.

Share, surrender of. *See* SURRENDER OF SHARE.

Share certificate. A certificate specifying the number of shares held by a member of a company.

It is *prima facie* evidence of his title to the shares: Companies Act 1985, s 186.

Share dividend. A dividend paid by a company in the form of extra shares instead of in cash. *See* DIVIDEND.

Share warrant. A warrant stating that its bearer is entitled to the share specified in it (see the Companies Act 1985, s 188(1), (2)). The shares may be transferred by delivery of the warrant (see ibid, s 188(2)).

Shares, consolidation of. *See* CONSOLIDATION OF SHARES.

Shares, sub-division of. *See* SUB-DIVISION OF SHARES.

Shepway, Court of. A court held before the Lord Warden of the Cinque Ports. *See* CINQUE PORTS.

Sheriff, or **Shire-reeve.** The chief bailiff or officer of the *shire*; an officer of great antiquity in the kingdom. He is called in Latin *vice-comes*, as being the deputy of the earl, or *comes*, to whom the custody of the shire is said to have been committed at the first division of the kingdom into counties. But the earls gradually withdrew from the county administration, and now the sheriff is the chief officer of the Crown in the county, and performs all the Queen's business in it; the Crown committing the custody of the county to the sheriff, and to him alone.

For many centuries the bulk of the administrative work in the county was done by the justices and since 1888 by the county council. The sheriff's duties now are few; to superintend Parliamentary elections, to execute process, to attend the judges at the Crown Court, and to return the jury in criminal trials. Even those duties are carried out by deputies.

As to the present mode of appointing sheriffs, see Local Government Act 1972, s 219. *See* PRICKING FOR SHERIFFS.

Sheriff's officers. Bailiffs.

Ship. Under the Merchant Shipping Act 1894, s 742 the term includes 'every description of vessel used in navigation not propelled by oars'. By the Harbours Act 1964, s 57 it includes seaplanes and hover vehicles.

S

The ownership of every British ship is divided into 64 shares, all of which may belong to one person, or they may be divided amongst two or more persons. Not more than 64 persons can be registered as part owners, except that five persons may be regarded as joint owners of one share.

Shipbroker. One whose business it is to procure freights or charter-parties and to negotiate the sale of ships.

Shipper. A consignor of goods to be sent by sea.

Ship's husband. The general agent of the owners of a vessel in her use and employment. His duty is, in general, to exercise an impartial judgment in the employment of tradesmen and the appointment of officers; to see that the ship is properly repaired, equipped, and manned; to procure freights and charter-parties; to preserve the ship's papers (see SHIP'S PAPERS), make the necessary entries, adjust freight and averages (see AVERAGE), disburse and receive moneys, and keep and make up the accounts as between all parties interested.

Ship's papers. The papers or documents required for the manifestation of property in a ship or cargo.

They are of two kinds:
1 Those required by the law of a particular country, eg the certificate of registry, bills of lading, etc, required by English law.
2 Those required by the law of nations to be on board neutral ships, to vindicate their title to that character, eg the passport, muster-roll, etc.

Short bill. *See* ENTERING BILLS SHORT.

Short entry. *See* ENTERING BILLS SHORT.

Short title. Every Act of Parliament now contains a section or subsection giving a short title, ie, a title that can be conveniently and easily cited, to such Act. Many former statutes were given short titles by the Short Titles Act 1896.
See TITLE, 4.

Shorts. Government stock with a life of less than 5 years.

Show of hands. A method of voting in which the members of a company raise their hands to vote in favour of or against a resolution.
See RESOLUTION.

Each member present counts for one vote only, however many shares he may have.

Shrievalty. The sheriff's office.

See SHERIFF.

As used with reference to any given person, it means the period during which he was sheriff.

Sic utero tuo ut alienum non laedas. Use your own (property) so as not to harm your neighbour's. Common law maxim expressing the principle of the law of nuisance.
See NUISANCE.

Sight, bills payable at are equivalent to bills of exchange payable on demand (see Bills of Exchange Act 1882, s 10).
See BILL OF EXCHANGE.

Signature. An indication, by sign, mark, or generally by the writing of a name or initials, that a person intends to bind himself to the contents of a document.

Signet. 1 One of the Queen's seals with which her private letters are sealed.
2 Writers to the Signet in Scotland perform substantially the same functions as solicitors in England.

Sign-manual. The signature of the Sovereign.

Silk gown. A phrase used especially of the silk gowns worn by Queen's Counsel; hence 'to take silk' means to attain the rank of Queen's Counsel.
See QUEEN'S COUNSEL.

Silver. *See* HALLMARK; STERLING.

Simony. The corrupt presentation of, or the corrupt agreement to present, any person to an ecclesiastical benefice for money, gift, or reward. It is generally committed in one of the two following ways:
1 By the purchase of the next presentation to a living actually vacant.
2 By a clergyman purchasing, either in his own name or another's, the next presentation to a living, and afterwards presenting, or causing himself to be presented, to it. But the purchase by a clergyman of an entire advowson, or even of a limited interest in it, is not simony, though the purchaser afterwards present himself. See now the declaration contained in the Schedule to the Benefices Act 1898.
See BENEFICE; ADVOWSON.

Simple contract. A contract, express or implied, which is created by a verbal promise, or by a writing not under seal.
See CONTRACT; DEED.

Simple contract debt. A debt arising out of a simple contract.
See SIMPLE CONTRACT.

Simple trust. A trust which requires no act to be done by the trustee except conveyance or transfer to his *cestui que trust* on request by the latter.
See CESTUI QUE TRUST.

Sine die. Without a day; ie without any day appointed for the resumption of the business on hand, eg an adjournment *sine die* is an adjournment without appointing any day for meeting again.
See EAT INDE SINE DIE.

Sine prole. Without issue; frequently abbreviated into 'sp'.

Sinecure. Without cure of souls; a word used in former times of a rector who by custom was relieved from residence, and had no spiritual duties, these being performed by the vicar. By the Ecclesiastical Commissioners Act 1840 provision was made for the abolition of sinecure rectories.
See RECTOR; VICAR.

A sinecure office is generally understood to mean a nominal office, with no duties attaching to it.

Single entry. A system of book-keeping according to which each entry in the day-book, invoice-book, cash-book and bill-book is posted or entered *once* to some account in the ledger; whereas, in *double entry* each entry is posted to *two* different accounts.
See DOUBLE ENTRY.

Sinking fund. A fund for the reduction of the National Debt, regulated by various Acts of Parliament.
See NATIONAL DEBT.

Sittings. There are four sittings of the High Court in each year viz, the Michaelmas, Hilary, Easter, and Trinity sittings, following which there is the long vacation.

Sittings in camera. Sittings other than sittings in open court. This course is often adopted for the hearing of cases where a public hearing would defeat the ends of justice, or on the grounds of public decency, eg in the hearing of evidence as to impotence, etc, in nullity cases (*see* IMPOTENCE); (see Matrimonial Causes Act 1973, s 48(2)). The Court may also sit in camera where it is necessary for the public safety.
See CAMERA.

Skeleton argument. Written summary of submissions to be made to the court, provided in advance to the judge(s).

Skilled witness, also called an *expert* or *professional witness*, is a person called to give evidence in a matter relating to his own trade or profession, eg when a medical practitioner is called to give evidence on the effects of poison.

Slander. Defamatory language used of another. It is *oral*, not in writing or print (see Defamation Act 1952).
See DEFAMATION.

Slander of title. Form of tortious defamation in which a person's title to property is impugned.

Sleeping partner. A partner taking no active part in the administration of a firm. But as far as creditors are concerned, he is as much a partner and as responsible as such as if he took an equally active part in the administration with the partner or partners who ostensibly carry it on.

Slip. An unstamped memorandum of an intended marine insurance policy. Such a document, even where it is invalid as a legal contract, is admissible in evidence for certain collateral purposes (see Marine Insurance Act 1906, s 21). Non-disclosure of facts material to the risk, discovered subsequently to the execution of the 'slip', does not vitiate a policy afterwards executed.

Smuggling. The offence of importing or exporting prohibited goods, or importing or exporting goods not prohibited without paying the duties imposed on them by the laws of the customs and excise.

Socage. *See* LAND LAW.

Soit fait comme il est désiré. Let it be as it is desired.
See LA REYNE LE VEULT.

Sold note. *See* BOUGHT AND SOLD NOTES.

Sole. Not married, single.

Sole corporation. *See* CORPORATION.

Sole tenant (Lat *Solus tenens*). One who holds in severalty; ie in his own sole right, and not with another person.
See SEVERALTY.

Solemn form. There are two kinds of probate, ie probate in *common form*, and probate in *solemn form*.

S

Probate in common form is granted in the registry, without any formal procedure in court, on an *ex parte* application made by the executor.

Probate in solemn form is in the nature of a final decree pronounced in open court, all parties interested having been duly cited.

The difference between the effect of probate in common form and probate in solemn form is that probate in common form is revocable, whereas probate in solemn form is irrevocable as against all persons who have been cited to the proceedings, or who can be proved to have been privy to them except in the case where a will of subsequent date is discovered, in which case probate of an earlier will, though granted in solemn form, would be revoked.

See PROBATE.

Solicitation. Incitement or inducement to commit an offence.

The solicitation to the commission of an offence is an offence at Common Law, and punishable by fine and imprisonment, even though no offence is, in fact committed.

Soliciting. *See* STREET OFFENCES.

Solicitor. To become a solicitor a person must serve a period of traineeship, pass the necessary examinations conducted by the Law Society, and be admitted by the Master of the Rolls. A certificate to practise must be taken out annually.

See BARRISTER.

Solicitor-General. The second law officer of the Crown, next to the Attorney-General.

See ATTORNEY-GENERAL.

Sound recording means, in relation to copyright,

(i) a recording of sounds, from which the sounds may be reproduced, or

(ii) a recording of the whole or any part of a literary, dramatic or musical work, from which sounds reproducing the work or part may be reproduced,

regardless of the medium on which the recording is made or the method by which the sounds are produced or reproduced: Copyright, Designs and Patents Act 1988, s 7(1). Copyright does not subsist in a sound recording which is a copy taken from a previous sound recording: ibid, s 7(2).

See COPYRIGHT; LITERARY WORK; MUSICAL WORK.

Sounding in damages. This phrase is used of an action which is brought in point of form for damages.

Sovereign. *See* KING; QUEEN.

Speakers of the Houses of Parliament.

The Speaker is the officer who is, as it were, the common mouth of the rest; and as there are two Houses, so there are two Speakers.

The one, the Lord Speaker of the House of Peers, who is most commonly the Lord Chancellor, or Lord Keeper of the Great Seal of England. The other, being a member of the House of Commons, is called the Speaker of the House of Commons. The Speaker of the House of Commons holds office till the dissolution of the Parliament in which he was elected. It is the duty of the Speaker to preside over the debates of the House, and manage the formality of business. He also has special duties in regard to giving certificates under the provisions of the Parliament Act 1911.

See DISSOLUTION, 1.

The Speaker of the House of Commons may not give his opinion or argue any question in the House; but the Speaker of the House of Lords, if he is a Lord of Parliament (which is generally but not necessarily the case), may do so. In the House of Commons the Speaker never votes, except when the votes are equal; but in the House of Lords the Speaker has a vote with the rest of the House, but no casting vote, for should the votes be equal the non-contents prevail. *May.*

See CASTING VOTE.

Special acceptance of a bill of exchange.

The acceptance of a bill of exchange as payable at a specified place, and not elsewhere.

See ACCEPTANCE OF A BILL; BILL OF EXCHANGE.

Special administration. The administration of certain specific effects of a deceased person; otherwise called a *limited* administration.

See ADMINISTRATION; LIMITED ADMINISTRATION.

Special agent. An agent empowered to act as such in a particular matter, and not generally.

See GENERAL AGENT.

Special case. 1 A statement of facts agreed to on behalf of two or more parties, and submitted for the opinion of a court as to the law bearing upon the facts so stated.

2 A case stated by justices for the opinion of the High Court under the Magistrates' Courts Act 1980, s 111.

Special constables. *See* CONSTABLE, 6.

Special damages. Damage which in a particular case may be shown to have arisen to the plaintiff from the conduct of the defendant. In some cases, eg in cases of assault and false imprisonment, an action will lie without showing special damage; in others it is necessary to prove special damage in order to maintain the action.
See GENERAL DAMAGES.

Special jury. A jury consisting of persons who were of a certain station in society; namely, esquires or persons of higher degree, or bankers, or merchants, or persons who occupied a house or premises of a certain rateable value. Now abolished except in commercial cases in the City of London.
See JURY.

Special licence. *See* MARRIAGE LICENCE.

Special property. A limited or qualified right in any subject of property, eg a person who hires a horse to ride has a special property in it.

Special resolution. *See* RESOLUTION.

Special sessions. A sessions held by justices acting for a division of a county for the transaction of special business. A special sessions is generally held by virtue of a provision of an Act of Parliament.
Due notice of it is usually given to all the justices resident within the division for which it is held; and in some cases this is required by Act of Parliament. A special sessions is sometimes called a *special petty sessions*; and a special sessions held for the purpose of licensing public houses is sometimes called a *Brewster Sessions*.
See PETTY SESSIONS.

Special tail. *See* ESTATE.

Special trust. A trust imposing active duties on the trustee; otherwise called an *active trust*.
See TRUST.

Special verdict. 1 A verdict in which the jury state the facts of a case, as they find them to be proved, leaving it to the Court to draw the proper legal inferences therefrom. Special verdicts in criminal cases are very rare.

2 A verdict that the accused is not guilty by reason of insanity. (See Trial of Lunatics Act 1883, s 2.)
See VERDICT.

Specialty, or specialty debt. An obligation contracted by matter of record, or by bond or other instrument under seal.
See BOND; DEED.

Specialty contract. A contract under seal.
See CONTRACT; DEED; SEAL.

Specific devise. A devise of specific land.
See DEVISE; RESIDUARY DEVISEE.

Specific legacy. A legacy of a specific fund or of a specific chattel.
See LEGACY.

If the subject of such a legacy is sold or otherwise disposed of in the testator's lifetime, the legacy is adeemed.
See ADEMPTION OF A LEGACY.

Specific performance. A suit for specific performance is one in which a person with whom another has made a contract prays that the latter may be ordered specifically to perform it. The specific performance of a contract has in general been decreed in equity where the contract is not a positive contract of a personal nature (as to sing at a theatre), nor one for the non-performance of which damages would be a sufficient compensation (as to pay a liquidated sum of money); the grant of specific performance of the vendor's obligation under contract for the sale of land is, however, normally granted.

Specification. The particular description of an invention in respect of which a patent is sought (see Patents Act 1977, s 14).

Spent conviction. A term used to denote a previous conviction which is regarded as no longer of any effect by reason of the Rehabilitation of Offenders Act 1974 after the lapse of a specified time.
See REHABILITATION OF OFFENDERS ACT 1974.

Spiritual Lords. *See* LORDS SPIRITUAL.

Splitting a cause of action. The bringing of separate actions for the different parts of a claim; or otherwise bringing several actions where one would suffice. This is prohibited.

Stag. A person who subscribes for shares in a new issue of shares hoping to sell them quickly at a profit.

Stakeholder. A person with whom a stake is deposited pending the decision of a wager, etc.
See WAGER.

The term is also used in relation to a sum of money paid as a deposit on a contract for the purchase of property. Such sum is often paid to a person as a stakeholder as between the two parties, not as agent for the vendor.

Stallage. Money paid for pitching stalls in fairs or markets; or the right to do so.

Stamp duties. Taxes imposed on written instruments eg conveyances, etc; they are either *ad valorem* duties, or are fixed in amount.

See AD VALOREM.

Where a stamp is essential to the legal validity of a writing, that writing cannot be given in evidence in civil proceedings if it is unstamped, or is insufficiently stamped, except on complying with the conditions and the payment of the penalties specified in the Stamp Act 1891, ss 14, 15. But this rule does not apply to criminal proceedings.

Standard of proof. *See* BURDEN OF PROOF.

Standard time. *See* SUMMER TIME.

Standing orders. Orders framed by each House of Parliament for the permanent guidance and order of its proceedings. Such orders, if not vacated or repealed, endure from one Parliament to another, and are of equal force in all. They occasionally fall into desuetude, but by the law and custom of Parliament they are binding until their operation is concluded by another vote of the House on the same matter.

Stannaries. The mines and works where tin metal is worked.

See COURT OF STANNARIES OF CORNWALL AND DEVON.

Stannary courts. *See* COURT OF STANNARIES OF CORNWALL AND DEVON.

Staple Inn. One of the Inns of Chancery, between Holborn Bars and Southampton Buildings, Chancery Lane.

See INNS OF CHANCERY.

Starboard. *See* LARBOARD.

Stare decisis. Stand by what is decided. The principle that courts should abide by precedent.

See PRECEDENTS, 1.

Statement of affairs. A statement by a debtor in bankruptcy proceedings, listing his debtors, creditors, assets, etc (see Insolvency Act 1986, s 288).

Statement of case, statement of claim.

A statement of claim was the statement by the plaintiff, in an action brought in the High Court of Justice, of the ground of his complaint and of the relief or remedy to which he claimed to be entitled. 'Statement of case' is the term to be used both in the High Court and county courts following the introduction of the Civil Procedure Rules 1998.

Statement of defence. The statement, now called simply a 'defence' under the Civil Procedure Rules 1998, delivered by a defendant in answer to the plaintiff's statement of claim. The defendant may, in his statement of defence, adduce any facts on which he seeks to reply as supporting a right of set-off or counterclaim.

See STATEMENT OF CASE, STATEMENT OF CLAIM; SET-OFF; COUNTERCLAIM.

Stationery Office. A Government office controlling the printing of Acts of Parliament and other books and publications required by Parliament and Government departments to be printed.

Status. The condition of a person in the eye of the law.

Status quo. The state in which any thing is already. Thus, when it is said that, provisionally, matters are to remain *in statu quo*, it is meant that, for the present, matters are to remain as they are. Sometimes, however, the phrase is used retrospectively: and, if so, this will generally be indicated by the context; eg when, on a treaty of peace, matters are to *return* to the *status quo*, this means the *status quo ante bellum*, their state prior to the war.

Statute. An Act of Parliament made by the Queen in Parliament. It normally requires the consent of the Lords and Commons; but see the Parliament Act 1911, for the circumstances in which a bill may become law without the consent of the Lords.

A *statute*, in the original sense of the word, means the legislation of a session; the various Acts of Parliament passed in it being so many *chapters* of the entire statute. Thus, by the Statute of Gloucester, the Statute of Merton, etc, is meant a body of legislation comprising various chapters on different subjects. But in reference to modern legislation the word *statute* denotes a *chapter* of legislation, or what is otherwise called an *Act of Parliament*.

See DECLARATORY ACT; ENABLING STATUTE.

Statute of Westminster 1931. An Act defining the constitutional position of the older

Dominions and their relationship with the United Kingdom.

See DOMINION.

Statutory declaration. A declaration made before a magistrate or commissioner for oaths in the form prescribed by the Statutory Declarations Act 1835.

See COMMISSIONERS FOR OATHS.

Statutory demand. A demand served by a petitioning creditor on a debtor in the prescribed form requiring him to pay the debt or to secure or compound for it to the creditor's satisfaction (see Insolvency Act 1986, s 268(1)).

See PETITIONING CREDITOR.

Statutory instrument. The most important form of delegated legislation including all Orders in Council and all statutory rules and orders which have to be laid before Parliament.

Statutory trusts. It is enacted by the Administration of Estates Act 1925, s 47 that in the case of a person dying intestate, a certain part of his property is to be held by the personal representative upon which are called the 'statutory trusts'. Under the 'statutory trusts' for issue, the property must be divided equally among the children who are alive at the death of the intestate, as soon as they attain the age of 21 or marry. The share of any child who dies before the intestate goes to the issue of that child on the 'per stirpes' principle as soon as such issue attain 21 or marry (see also Law of Property Act 1925, s 35).

See STIRPES, DISTRIBUTION PER.

Stay of proceedings. The putting an end to the proceedings in an action by a summary order of the court. It differs from an injunction and from a prohibition as follows:

1 Staying proceedings is effected by the Court in which the action is brought, or by some other court on appeal from it.
2 An injunction to restrain proceedings is an order of an independent court restraining the plaintiff from proceeding in the action.
   See INJUNCTION.
3 A prohibition is an order of a superior court, prohibiting the court in which the action is brought from taking cognisance of it.
   See PROHIBITION.

Stealing. The dishonest appropriation of property belonging to another person with the intention of permanently depriving the other of it.

See THEFT.

Sterling. A word used to indicate that silver is of a standard of fineness of 925 parts to 1,000. Formerly also used of the currency, eg 'the pound sterling'. The former silver currency is now debased.

Stethe. A bank of a river.

Stevedore. A person who stows packages and goods in a ship's hold, and discharges cargoes.

Stipend. Any periodical payment for services; especially the income of an ecclesiastical living or curacy.

Stipendiary magistrate. A paid full-time magistrate appointed by Her Majesty under the Justices of the Peace Act 1979, s 13(1). Now called 'District Judges (Magistrates Courts)'.

Stirpes, distribution per. A division of property among families according to stocks of descent. So, for example, if X has three children, A, B, and C, there are three stocks of descent. If X dies leaving one living child, A, but both B and C have died leaving children of their own, B leaving D and E, and C leaving F, G, and H, a distribution *per stirpes* takes D, E, F, G and H into consideration as 'representatives' of the deceased person, B or C respectively, who, had they survived, would themselves have taken property along with A. A and B and C would each have received a third of X's estate had they all survived X, being kin of X 'in equal degree' (all children of X); A, still alive, will receive one third, and under a distribution *per stirpes* D and E will together take the third that would have gone to B, and F, G, and H will together take the third that would have gone to C. This form of distribution is in contrast to distribution *per capita*, whereby descendants of equal degree take equally regardless of stocks of descent. Under such a distribution, all grandchildren, if they were to inherit at all, would all inherit an equal amount, regardless of the stocks of descent, for all are kin of equal degree to the deceased. For the present rules of succession on intestacy applying alike to real, and personal property, see Administration of Estates Act 1925, Part IV.

Stock. 1 A race or family.
2 In reference to the investment of money, the term 'stock' implies those sums of

money contributed towards raising a fund whereby certain objects, e g of trade or commerce, may be effected. It is also employed to denote the moneys advanced to the Government, which constitute a part of the National Debt, on which a certain amount of interest is payable. (*See* NATIONAL DEBT). Since the introduction of the system of borrowing on interminable annuities, the meaning of the word 'stock' has gradually changed; and instead of signifying the security on which loans are advanced, it has for a long time signified the principal of the loans themselves. In this latter sense one speaks of the sale, purchase, and transfer of stock.

See STOCKBROKER; STOCK EXCHANGE.

Stock certificate. A certificate showing that the stockholder is the owner of a specified amount of stock.

Stock exchange. An association of stockbrokers and market makers in the city of London and elsewhere.

See STOCKBROKER.

The regulations of the Stock Exchange are, like the other usages of trade, recognised by courts of law as evidence of the course of dealing between the parties to a contract.

Stockbroker. A person who, for a commission, negotiates for other parties the buying and selling of stocks and shares, according to the rules of the Stock Exchange.

See STOCK EXCHANGE.

Stop notice. A notice requiring any person on whom it is duly served to refrain from taking, in respect of any securities mentioned in it, any steps eg the registration of any transfer of them, without first notifying the person by whom, or on whose behalf, the notice was served: Charging Act 1979, s 5(1).

Stop order. An order prohibiting the taking, in respect of any of the securities specified in it, of any steps eg the registration of any transfer of them: Charging Orders Act 1979, s 5(1).

Stoppage in transit. The right which an unpaid seller of goods has, on hearing that the buyer is insolvent, to stop and reclaim the goods while in transit and not yet delivered to the buyer. This right will not be affected by the mere fact that the seller has consigned the goods to the buyer under a bill of lading. But if the buyer has indorsed the bill of lading to a third party for valuable consideration, and without notice of the facts, such party's claim, as assignee of the property under the bill of lading, is paramount to the seller's right to stop in transit. The leading case on the subject of *stoppage in transit* is *Lickbarrow v Mason* (1787) 6 East 21. See Sale of Goods Act 1979, ss 44–46.

See BILL OF LADING.

Stowage. 1 A place where goods are stowed.
2 The money paid for such a place.
3 The act of stowing cargo in a vessel.
   The stowage of the cargo is primarily a duty of the shipowner and master, and nothing absolves them from this obligation short of express agreement with the charterer, or the unambiguous usage of the port.

Strand Inn. *See* INNS OF CHANCERY.

Stranger. One not a party or privy to any act or transaction.

See THIRD PARTY.

Stranger in blood. One who is no relation in blood. The term was used chiefly in reference to the different scales of the former legacy or succession duty.

Stray, otherwise **estray.** A beast gone astray, of which the owner is not known.

Street betting. An offence under the Betting, Gaming and Lotteries Act 1963.

Street offences. Various offences capable of being committed in streets are specified in the Metropolitan Police Act 1839, s 54 and the Town Police Clauses Act 1847, s 28. Such offences include sliding on ice or snow, ringing doorbells, making bonfires, blowing horns, etc. The Street Offences Act 1959 makes loitering or soliciting for the purpose of prostitution an offence punishable by a fine or imprisonment or both.

Street trading includes the hawking of newspapers, matches, flowers and other articles, playing, singing or performing for profit, shoe-blacking and other like occupations carried on in streets or other public places: Children and Young Persons Act 1933, s 30(1).

No child must engage or be employed in street trading: ibid, s 20(1).

Strict liability. Liability for a breach of duty irrespective of intent.

Strict settlement. 1 This phrase was formerly used to denote a settlement whereby land was limited to a parent for life, and after his death to his first and other sons or children in tail, with a trust imposed 'to preserve contingent remainders', ie a trust to preserve contingent interests in remainder. *See* ESTATE; CONTINGENT REMAINDER.

2 Generally, a settlement in which land is limited to, or is held in trust for, persons by way of succession, ie whose interest take one after another in succession, unless it is subject to 'an immediate binding trust for sale'. Its object is to keep lands in a particular family. Important alterations in the mode of creating strict settlements are contained in the Settled Land Act 1925. Under that Act a settlement of a legal estate in land *inter vivos* is to be effected (except as provided in the Act) by two deeds, ie a vesting deed declaring that the land is vested in the tenant for life or statutory owner for the legal estate the subject of the intended settlement, and a trust instrument declaring the trusts affecting the settled land.
See SETTLEMENT; SETTLED LAND; VESTING DEED; TRUST INSTRUMENT.

Strike. A cessation of work by a body of persons employed acting in combination, or a concerted refusal or a refusal under a common understanding of any number of persons employed to continue to work for an employer in consequence of a dispute done as a means of compelling their employer or any person or body of persons employed, or to aid other employees in compelling their employer or any person or body of persons employed, to accept or not to accept terms or conditions of or affecting employment: Employment Protection (Consolidation) Act 1978, s 151, Sch 13, para 24(1).

Striking off the roll. The removal of a solicitor of the Supreme Court from the roll of solicitors. It takes place either at the party's own request, or for misconduct.
See SOLICITOR.

Striking out pleadings. The Court or a Judge may at any stage of the proceedings order to be struck out or amended anything in the pleadings which is unnecessary, scandalous, or which tends to embarrass or delay the fair trial of the action.

Structured settlement. A settlement whereby a successful plaintiff suing for damages for personal injury is awarded a lump sum and also an index-linked annuity from the defendant's insurers. See Damages Act 1996.

Stuff gown. The gown of a member of the junior bar. Hence the phrase is used of junior barristers, as opposed to Queen's Counsel.
See SILK GOWN.

Sub judice. Before the court, but not yet decided; under judicial consideration. It is a contempt of court to publish articles about a matter which is *sub judice* that may have the affect of jeopardising a fair trial.
See CONTEMPT.

Sub modo. Under condition or restriction.

Sub silentio. In silence.

Sub-division of shares. The division of shares of a certain nominal value into a larger number of shares of a smaller nominal value eg the division of a £1 share into four 25p shares.

Sublease. A lease created by a lessee of land out of his leasehold interest. To create such a lease is to *sublease* or *sublet* the land, and the lessee creating the sublease is styled a *sublessor* and his lessee the *sublessee*.
See LEASE; UNDERLEASE.

Submission. A word especially used with reference to the submission of a matter in dispute to the judgment of an arbitrator or arbitrators.

Subornation of perjury. The offence of instructing or procuring another to commit perjury.
See PERJURY.

Subpoena (Lat *Sub poena*, under a penalty).
1 A writ directed to a person commanding him, under a penalty, to appear and give evidence. This is called a *subpoena ad testificandum*.
2 A writ directed to a person, requiring him not only to give evidence, but to bring with him such deeds or writings as the party who issues the *subpoena* may think material for his purpose. This is called a *subpoena duces tecum*, being a type of *subpoena ad testificandum*.

Subrogation. A means at law whereby one party steps into the shoes of another so as to take on the benefit of that other's rights, in particular the right to sue a defendant and receive the remedy that other would have been awarded. It is similar in result to the assignment of one party's rights to another, though subrogation can occur not only by agreement but by OPERATION OF LAW. A typical example of subrogation

S

occurs in the INDEMNITY insurance context: where an insurer pays the insured's claim to cover a loss caused by a tortfeasor, the insurer is subrogated to the insured's right to bring an action against the tortfeasor and recover damages in an amount calculated to compensate the insured's loss.

See UNJUST ENRICHMENT.

Subscriber. 1 A person who signs the original memorandum of association and the articles of association of a company.

See MEMORANDUM OF ASSOCIATION; ARTICLES OF ASSOCIATION.

2 A person who pays or agrees to pay a company in respect of shares or debentures offered to him by it.

See PROSPECTUS.

Subscribing witness. A person who puts his name to an instrument as attesting witness.

See ATTESTATION.

Subsequent condition. *See* CONDITIONS PRECEDENT AND SUBSEQUENT.

Subsidence. Movement of land in a vertical direction; includes in its popular sense 'settlement', which strictly speaking means movement in a lateral direction (see *David Allen & Sons Billposting Ltd v Drysdale* [1939] 4 All ER 113).

Subsidence, coal mining, damage by. Any damage to land or buildings caused by the withdrawal of support from land in connection with lawful coal mining operations: Coal Mining Subsidence Act 1991, s 1(1).

The Act imposes obligations on the British Coal Corporation to provide compensation for subsidence damage.

Subsidiary company. A company controlled by another company.

A company is a subsidiary of another company (ie the 'holding company') if that company:

(i) holds a majority of the voting rights in it, or

(ii) is a member of it and has the right to remove a majority of its board of directors, or

(iii) is a member of it and controls alone, pursuant to an agreement with other shareholders or members, a majority of the voting rights in it,

or if it is a subsidiary of a company which is itself a subsidiary of the holding company: Companies Act 1985, s 736(1).

Subsidy. 1 An aid, tax or tribute granted by Parliament to the Queen for the urgent occasions of the kingdom, to be levied of every subject on his property, at such rate as Parliament may think fit.

2 A type of customs duty payable on exports and imports of staple commodities.

3 A payment made out of taxation to producers of goods for the purpose of keeping down the price.

Substantial damages, given by the verdict of a jury, are damages which amount to a substantial sum, as opposed to merely nominal damages.

See NOMINAL DAMAGES.

Substituted service is where a writ or other process is served on some person other than the person on whom the service ought more properly to be effected, by reason of its being impossible to effect personal service.

See SERVICE.

Succession. Where a person succeeds to property previously enjoyed by another. It is either *singular* or *universal*.

Singular succession is where the purchaser, donee, or legatee of a specific chattel, or other specific property, succeeds to the right of the vendor, donor, or testator. Universal succession is the succession to an indefinite series of rights, eg the succession by the trustee of a bankrupt to the estate and effects of the bankrupt, or by an executor or administrator to the estate of the deceased.

For the present rules of succession on intestacy, or intestate succession, applying alike to real and personal estate, see Administration of Estates Act 1925, Part IV.

Successive interests. Ownership interests in the same property which take one after another in time, eg where property is given on trust to A for life (a life estate) and then to B (in fee simple). To be contrasted with concurrent interests, ie co-ownership interests where two or more persons have ownership interests in the same property at the same time. A disposition of property, nowadays always a disposition on trust, which contains successive interests, is called a 'settlement'.

See SETTLEMENT; CONCURRENT INTERESTS.

Successor in title. Any person who will or has become entitled to property after the owner in question, ie any person who *succeeds* to the title of the property.

Sue. To take legal proceedings claiming a civil right against anyone.

Sufferance. An estate at sufferance is where one comes into possession of land under a lawful title, and, after the title has come to an end, keeps it without any title at all, by the sufferance of the rightful owner. The party continuing in possession is called a *tenant at sufferance*.

See ESTATE.

Suffragan. A word signifying *deputy*.

A suffragan bishop is a titular bishop appointed to aid and assist the bishop of the diocese in his spiritual function.

Bishops are also called *suffragan* in respect of their relation to the archbishops of their province.

Suffrage. Vote, elective franchise; aid, assistance.

Suggestio falsi. A suggestion or insinuation of something false. Normally used in conjunction with *suppressio veri*.

See MISREPRESENTATION; SUPPRESSIO VERI.

Sui juris. A phrase used to denote a person who is under no disability affecting his legal power to make conveyances of his property, to bind himself by contracts, and to sue and be sued; as opposed to persons wholly or partially under disability, eg infants, mentally disordered persons, prisoners, etc.

Suicide. Self-killing, no longer a crime. In the case of a suicide pact between two persons, where one dies and the other survives, the survivor liable to a sentence of imprisonment (see the Suicide Act 1961, s 2).

Summary. Of legal proceedings, relatively simple, immediate, eg summary conviction, a conviction before magistrates without the intervention of a jury.

Summary jurisdiction. The power of a court to give judgment or make an order immediately. Specially, in criminal cases, the power of magistrates to hear or dispose of a case without sending it for trial at the Crown Court.

Summer Time. The time (being one hour in advance of Greenwich Mean Time). The Summer Time Act 1972 allows time to be advanced by one hour in summer, or by two hours if so directed by Order in Council.

Summing up. In a civil or criminal trial before a judge and jury, is the charge of the Judge to the jury, recapitulating in greater or less detail the statements of the witnesses and the contents of the documents (if any) adduced on either side, commenting on the manner in which they bear on the issue, and giving his direction on any matter of law which may arise on them.

Summons. A citation to appear before a Judge or magistrate. The word is used variously, as follows:

1 A citation summoning a person to appear before a stipendiary magistrate or bench of justices.

2 An application to a Judge at chambers, whether at law or in equity.

3 The writ of summons which formerly commenced an action.

See ORIGINATING SUMMONS; STATEMENT OF CASE, STATEMENT OF CLAIM.

Summons for directions. *See* DIRECTIONS, SUMMONS FOR.

Super visum corporis (on view of the body). A phrase applied to the view had by a coroner's jury of the body of the deceased concerning whose death they are appointed to inquire.

See CORONER.

Supercargo. A factor or agent who goes with a ship beyond the seas by order of the owner of the goods carried in her, and disposes of them to the best advantage.

Superior courts. Today the Court of Appeal, the High Court and the Courts-Martial Appeal Courts are superior courts; so, too, is the Crown Court, although it is in some respects subject to the supervisory jurisdiction of the High Court.

No matter is deemed to be beyond the jurisdiction of a superior court unless it is expressly shown to be so. The unreversed judgment of a superior court is conclusive as to all relevant matters decided by it.

See INFERIOR COURTS; SUPREME COURT.

Superstitious uses. A superstitious use has been defined as 'one which has for its object the propagation of the rites of a religion not tolerated by the law', eg a gift of money for saying prayers for the dead. Superstitious uses are opposed to charitable uses which are recognised by law.

See CHARITABLE TRUST.

Supervision order. An order putting a child under the supervision of a designated local authority or of a probation officer: Children Act 1989, s 31(1)(b).

Supplemental deed. Recitals are often used when the deed in which they occur is effectual only by virtue of its complying with the terms of some other deed, to show that the terms have been duly complied with. But lengthy recitals of a previous instrument may be avoided by expressing the deed to be 'supplemental' to the previous instrument. Such a supplemental deed has to be read in conjunction with the deed to which it is expressed to be made supplemental in order to see that the terms of the latter deed have been duly complied with.

See RECITAL.

Supply of Goods and Services Act 1982 sets out the terms to be implied in certain contracts for (i) the transfer of the property in goods; (ii) the hire of goods; and (iii) the supply of a service.

Support. The right of support is the right of a person to have his buildings or other landed property supported by his neighbour's house or land.

Every person is entitled to have his land in its natural state supported by the adjoining land of his neighbour, against whom an action will lie if, by digging on his own land, he removes that support. This right to lateral support from adjoining soil is not an easement, but is a right of property passing with the soil, eg if the owner of two adjoining properties conveys away one of them, the alienee, without any grant for that purpose, is entitled to the lateral support of the other property the very instant that the conveyance is executed, as much as he would be after the expiration of twenty years or of any longer period.

See EASEMENT.

But, where a person builds to the utmost extremity of his own land, and thereby increases the lateral pressure on the soil of his neighbour, if the latter digs his own ground, so as to remove some part of the soil, an action will not lie for the injury occasioned to the former, unless he has, by grant or prescription, acquired a right to the support of the house by the soil of his neighbour.

Suppressio veri. The suppression of truth; ie the suppression of some material fact.

See MISREPRESENTATION; SUGGESTIO FALSI.

Supra. Above. Often used to refer a reader to a previous part of a book.

Supreme Court presently consists of the Court of Appeal and the High Court, together with the Crown Court (see now Supreme Court Act 1981, s 1(1)).

The Court of Appeal consists of two Divisions, the Civil Division and the Criminal Division.

The High Court consists of three Divisions: the Queen's Bench Division, the Chancery Division, and the Family Division (see Supreme Court Act 1981, s 5).

The Crown Court was established by the Courts Act 1971. It is part of the Supreme Court, with jurisdiction throughout England and Wales, and is a superior court of record.

Under the Constitutional Reform Act 2005, Part 3, a new Supreme Court is to be established, which will serve as a final court of appeal assuming the present jurisdiction of the APPELLATE COMMITTEE OF THE HOUSE OF LORDS.

Surcharge and falsify. To *surcharge* is to show an omission of something for which credit ought to have been given; and to *falsify* is to prove an item to have been wrongly inserted.

See ACCOUNT.

Surcharge of common. When a commoner puts more beasts in a forest, or in pasture, than he has a right to do.

Surety. A person who contracts to be answerable for another in such a manner that the latter is primarily answerable, eg if money is advanced to A; and B, his friend, joins with him in giving a bond for its repayment; then B is surety for A.

Surety of good behaviour. *See* GOOD BEHAVIOUR; KEEPING THE PEACE.

Surplusage. A superfluity, or addition of something unnecessary, in any legal document.

Surrender (Lat *Sursum reditio*). The falling of a less estate into a greater.

1 *Surrender in deed*. This takes place by the yielding up of an estate for life or years to the person who has the immediate reversion or remainder. To constitute a valid express surrender, it is essential that it should be made to, and accepted by, the owner (in his own right) of the reversion or remainder.

See REVERSION; REMAINDER.

2 *Surrender by operation of law*. This phrase is properly applied to cases where the tenant for life or years has been a party to some act the validity of which he is by law afterwards estopped from disputing,

and which would not be valid if this particular estate continued to exist; eg when a lessee for years accepts a new lease from his lessor, he is estopped from saying that his lessor had not the power to make the new lease, so that the acceptance of the new lease amounts in law to a surrender of the former one. The effect of a surrender by operation of law is expressly reserved by the Law of Property Act 1925, s 54(2).

See ESTOPPEL.

Surrender of share. The yielding up of shares to the company by a member. The articles of association may give power to the directors to accept a surrender of shares. This relieves them of going through the formality of forfeiture if the member is willing to surrender the shares.

See FORFEITURE OF SHARE.

Surrogacy arrangement. An arrangement whereby a woman becomes a surrogate mother (see the Surrogacy Arrangements Act 1985, s 1(3)).

See SURROGATE MOTHER.

Negotiating surrogacy arrangements on a commercial basis is illegal (see the Surrogacy Arrangements Act 1985, ss 2, 4). Advertisements relating to surrogacy are also illegal (see ibid, s 3).

Surrogate. A person who is substituted or appointed in the place of another. The word is most commonly used of a person who is appointed by the bishop for granting marriage licences.

See MARRIAGE LICENCE.

Surrogate mother. A woman who carries a child in pursuance of an arrangement (i) made before she began to carry the child, and (ii) made with a view to any child carried in pursuance of it being handed over to, and the parental rights being exercised (so far as practicable) by, another person or other persons (see Surrogacy Arrangements Act 1985, s 1(2)).

Survivorship. A word used not merely of the *fact* of survivorship, but of the rights arising from it; ie of the right of the survivor or survivors of joint tenants to the estate held in joint tenancy, to the exclusion of the representatives of the deceased.

See JOINT TENANCY; PRESUMPTION OF SURVIVORSHIP.

Suspended sentence. By the Powers of Criminal Courts Act 1973, s 22, a Court which passes a sentence of imprisonment for not more than two years for an offence may order that the sentence is not to take effect unless, during a period specified in the order, the offender commits another offence punishable with imprisonment, in which case the original sentence may be revised.

Suspension. 1 A temporary stop or cessation of a person's right. Or, of his exercise of an office, eg of a clergyman by an ecclesiastical court.

2 A temporary revocation of any law by a proper authority.

Symbolic delivery. A delivery of a small thing in token of a transfer of something else.

Syndic. An agent or attorney who acts for a corporation or university. By the Supreme Court Act 1981, s 115(2) probate or administration is not to be granted to a syndic or nominee on behalf of a trust corporation.

See TRUST CORPORATION.

Syndicate. A group of underwriters associating themselves for business purposes, each syndicate being given a number. A list of the members of the syndicate is attached to the policy.

See 'NAMES'; LLOYD'S.

Syngraph. 1 The name given by the canon lawyers to deeds of which *both parts* (ie the copies corresponding to each party) were written on the same piece of parchment, with some word or letters of the alphabet written between them, through which the parchment was cut in such a manner as to leave half the word on one part and half on the other.

2 Hence, a deed or writing under the hand and seal of all the parties.

Synod. A meeting or assembly of ecclesiastical persons concerning religion, of which there were originally four kinds:

1 General, when bishops, etc, of all nations met together.

2 National, when those of one nation only came together.

3 Provincial, when those of one province met, being what was called the Convocation.

S

4 Diocesan, when those of only one diocese met.

Under the Synodical Government Measure 1969 the functions, authorities, right, and privileges of the Convocations of Canterbury and York were vested in the General Synod of the Church of England. This has had the effect of renaming and reconstituting the former Church Assembly.

S

T

Tables A to G. Tables set out in regulations made under the Company Act 1985 providing specimen regulations for the management of a company and forms of memoranda for different sorts of company.
See LIMITED COMPANY; MEMORANDUM OF ASSOCIATION; PRIVATE COMPANY; PUBLIC COMPANY; ARTICLES OF ASSOCIATION; COMPANY LIMITED BY GUARANTEE.

Tacking. A means whereby, when a third or subsequent mortgagee of land, by getting a conveyance to himself of the legal estate of the first mortgagee, was enabled to obtain for his own security, priority over the second mortgagee.
See MORTGAGE.

Tail. *See* ESTATE.

Tail female. Where a real estate was settled on A and the heirs female of his or her body. Under such words of limitation, females alone could succeed and would inherit together; nor could any female claim except through females. In practice, it never now occurs.
See ESTATE.

Tail general. Where an estate is limited to a man and the heirs of his body, without any restriction at all.
See ESTATE.

Tail male. Where an estate is limited to a man and the heirs male of his body; ie so far as regards the first generation, to males; and, so far as regards subsequent generations, to males claiming exclusively through males.
See ESTATE.

Tales. A supply of jurymen to make up a deficiency. If a sufficient number of jurors did not appear, or if by means of challenges or exemptions a sufficient number of unexceptionable ones did not remain, either party may pray a *tales*. The Judge who tries the cause can award a *tales de circumstantibus*; ie to command the sheriff to return so many other persons duly qualified as can be present, or cannot be found, to make up the number required, and to add their names to the former panel.
See JURY.

Tangible property. Property which may be touched and is the object of sensation, corporeal property; this kind of property is opposed to intangible rights or incorporeal property, eg bank balances, patents, copyrights, advowsons, rents, etc.

Taxation, law of. The law providing for and governing the state's gathering of revenue for public purposes created by Act of Parliament (as opposed to Crown revenues deriving from ancient feudal rights, etc), by imposing obligations upon persons for the payment of sums of money. Taxes are generally classified as direct or indirect; a direct tax is one which is imposed on the person who is intended to bear the burden of paying it; an indirect tax is imposed for convenience on some other person, who is expected in the course of things to pass on the cost of paying it to those who should bear its burden. Income taxes imposed on individuals or companies are examples of direct taxes, excise taxes and customs duties of indirect taxes.

Taxation of costs. *See* ASSESSMENT OF COSTS.

Taxing master. An officer appointed to tax costs, now called a 'costs judge'.
See ASSESSMENT OF COSTS.

Tellers. Members of Parliament appointed by the Speaker to count the numbers in a Parliamentary division. *May.*

Tempest. A severe storm (see *Oddy v Phoenix Assurance Co Ltd* [1966] 1 Lloyd's Rep 134 at 138 (per Veale J)).

Temples. Two of the Inns of Court.
See INNS OF COURT.

At the suppression of the order of Knights Templars their building was purchased by the professors of the Common Law, and converted into Inns of Court in 1340. They are called the Inner and Middle Temple. Essex House, built in 1185, was formerly a part of the house of the Templars, and was called the Outer Temple because it was situated outside Temple Bar.

Tenancy. The holding of land. All FREEHOLD owners of land under English law are tenants, in that the theory of land ownership holds that all land is held indirectly via a superior Lord to the Crown, or of the Crown directly. A LEASEHOLDer is a tenant of a freeholder from whom his or her land is leased, who is known as the landlord. Tenancy and tenant are now generally used only of leasehold tenants, save for the terms indicating the two modes of co-ownership (of any kind of property), viz TENANCY IN COMMON and JOINT TENANCY. Though strictly speaking the freeholder's status as tenant of the Crown remains the basis of land ownership, his holding is referred to as a TENURE, not a tenancy.

Tenancy, assured. *See* ASSURED TENANCY.

Tenancy, assured shorthold. *See* ASSURED SHORTHOLD TENANCY.

Tenancy, long. A tenancy granted for a term of years certain exceeding 21 years, whether or not subsequently extended by act of the parties or by any enactment: Rent Act 1977: Landlord and Tenant Act 1954, s 2(4).

Tenancy, protected. A tenancy under which a dwelling-house (which may be a house or part of a house) is let as a separate dwelling: Rent Act 1977, s 1.
See ASSURED TENANCY.

Tenancy, regulated. A tenancy which is a protected tenancy or a regulated one: Rent Act 1977, s 18(1).
See ASSURED TENANCY.

Tenancy, statutory. A tenancy arising after the termination of a protected tenancy of a dwelling-house: Rent Act 1977, s 2(1).
See ASSURED TENANCY.

Tenancy in common. *See* COMMON, TENANCY IN.

Tenant. 1 One who holds or possesses land or tenements by any right, whether for life, years, at will (*see* TENANT AT WILL) or at sufferance (*see* TENANT AT SUFFERANCE), custody or otherwise; all lands being considered as held of the Crown or in the past of some superior lord.
See TENURE.

2 Especially, a tenant under a lease from year to year, or other fixed period. *See* TERM OF YEARS; TENANCY.

3 The word is sometimes used in reference to interests in pure personalty eg of a tenant for life of a fund, etc.
See TRUST.

Tenant at sufferance. A person who, having been in lawful possession of land, wrongfully continues in possession after his title has come to an end, without the agreement or disagreement of the person then entitled.

Tenant at will. A person in possession of lands let to him to hold at the will of the lessor. Such a tenancy may arise under an express lease or by implication of law. It is implied wherever a person is in possession of land with the permission of the owner, provided that he is neither a freeholder nor the holder of a term of years absolute, and provided that he does not hold possession in his capacity as servant of the owner.

Tenant by sufferance. *See* TENANT AT SUFFERANCE.

Tenant for life. A person who holds an estate for life. Under the Settled Land Act 1925 a tenant is given wide and unfettered powers of dealing with land.
See ESTATE; SETTLEMENT.

Tenant for years. One who holds for a term of years.
See TERM OF YEARS.

Tenant from year to year. A tenancy from year to year is now fixed, by general usage, to signify a tenancy determinable at half a year's notice (or in an agricultural tenancy, one year's notice) on either side, ending with the current year of the tenancy. If the tenancy commences on one of the quarterly feast days the half-year may be computed from one of such feast days to another; otherwise, the half-year must consist of 182 days (see Agricultural Holdings Act 1986).
See QUARTER DAYS.

Tenant in tail. *See* ESTATE.

Tenant right. The right of a tenant on the termination of his tenancy to compensation for unexhausted improvements effected on his holding. Governed by the Agricultural

Holdings Act 1986. Also used to indicate the moneys so paid.

Tenantable repair. Such a state of repair in houses or buildings as renders them fit for the occupation of a tenant.

A tenant from year to year of a house is bound to keep it wind and water tight, to use it in a tenant-like manner, and to make fair and tenantable repairs, eg putting in windows or doors which have been broken by him, so as to prevent waste and decay of the premises. *Hill and Redman.*

See TENANT FROM YEAR TO YEAR.

Tenants in common. *See* COMMON, TENANCY IN.

Tender. 1 An offer of money or any other thing in satisfaction of a debt or liability.

See TENDER, PLEA OF.

2 Coin or paper money, which, so far as regards its nature and quality, a creditor may be compelled to accept in satisfaction of his debts, is called *legal tender*.

See LEGAL TENDER.

Tender, plea of. A plea by a defendant that he has been always ready to satisfy the plaintiff's claim, and now brings the sum demanded into court.

Tenor. 1 By the *tenor* of a deed, or other instrument in writing, is meant the matter contained in it, according to its true intent and meaning.

2 The word *tenor*, in reference to writs and records, means a copy or transcript, whereas *effect* signifies that the substance only is set out.

Tenths payable to the Pope, and, after the Reformation, to the Crown, until applied by Queen Anne for the purposes of Queen Anne's Bounty to make up the deficiencies of smaller benefices.

Tenure. A holding of land. While a LEASEHOLDer is known as a tenant, he or she is said to have a TENANCY, not a tenure. Specifically, a tenure was the specific mode of owning freehold land under the feudal system of land ownership. Under this system, all land was held of the King or the Crown, ultimately, under different modes of holding called tenures requiring 'rent-service' by the tenant of various kinds. (*See* LAND LAW.) All freehold land (save for several exceptions) is now held by the tenure of 'free and common socage', under which no rent-service of any kind is due.

Term of years. A lease of land. Although expressed in years, a lease can be of any duration. The significance of this phrase is that period for which the holder of a term of years, called a 'termor', holds the land is a fixed time, rather than measured by the duration of a life or by continuing inheritance.

See ESTATE.

For definition of 'term of years absolute' as used in the Law of Property Act 1925, see s 205(1)(xxvii) thereof.

Terminus a quo. The starting point.

Terminus ad quem. The terminating point.

Termor. A person who holds lands or tenements for a term of years or life.

Terms, to be under. A party in an action or other legal proceeding is said to be *under terms*, which an indulgence is granted to him by the Court in the exercise of its discretion, on condition of his observing certain things.

Territorial waters. The breadth of the territorial sea adjacent to the United Kingdom is for all purposes 12 nautical miles (see Territorial Sea Act 1987, s 1(1)(a)). Baselines from which the breadth of the territorial sea is to be measured are for all purposes those established by Order in Council (see ibid, s 1(1)(b)). Nautical miles means international nautical miles of 1,852 metres (see ibid, s 1(7)).

Terrorism. The use of violence for political ends, including any use of violence for the purpose of putting the public or any section of the public in fear (see Prevention of Terrorism (Temporary Provisions) Act 1989, s 20(1)).

Testament. The declaration of a person's last will as to that which he would have to be done after his death. Strictly speaking, a testament is a disposition of *personal* property only.

See WILL.

Testamentary guardian. A guardian appointed by will.

Testate. Having made a will.

Testator. A man who makes a will.

See WILL.

Testatrix. A woman who makes a will.

See WILL.

Testatum. The witnessing part of a deed, beginning 'Now this Deed witnesseth'.

Testes, proof of will per. A proof of a will by witnesses, in a more solemn form than usual, in cases where the validity of the will is disputed. It is by action in the Chancery Division or in some cases in the County Court.

See SOLEMN FORM.

Testimonium clause. The final clause in a deed or will, commencing 'In witness, etc'.

Testimony. Evidence.

See EVIDENCE; PERPETUATING TESTIMONY.

Theft. The basic definition of theft is given in the Theft Act 1968, s 1, which enacts that 'a person is guilty of theft if he dishonestly appropriates property belonging to another with the intention of permanently depriving the other of it', it being immaterial whether the appropriation is made with a view to gain or is made for the thief's own benefit.

Sections 2–6 of the Act then expand and explain this basic definition by stating what is meant by *dishonestly* (s 2); *appropriates* (s 3); *property* (s 4); *belonging to another* (s 5); and *with the intention of permanently depriving the other of it* (s 6).

This definition of theft incorporates those offences formerly known as EMBEZZLEMENT; FRAUDULENT CONVERSION; and LARCENY.

Other sections of the Theft Act define robbery, burglary, blackmail, etc.

See EMBEZZLEMENT; FRAUDULENT CONVERSION; LARCENY; APPROPRIATION; BURGLARY; BLACKMAIL; DISHONEST; PROPERTY; ROBBERY.

Things. The subject of property, which may be either *in action* or *in possession*. Things *in action* are not immediately available to the owner without the consent of another person, whose refusal will give a right of *action*. Things *in possession* may be used immediately without the concurrence of any other person.

See CHOSE.

Third party. One who is a stranger to a legal proceeding or transaction between two other persons. A third party may, by leave of the Court or a Judge, be introduced into an action by a defendant claiming an indemnity or other remedy over against him. A third party to a contract or conveyance may acquire a benefit in fact from the making of the contract or conveyance, eg where A buys dinner at a restaurant for both himself and B, who though he is fed is a third party to the contract between A and the restaurant, but third parties generally have no legal rights or obligations under conveyances or contracts.

See PRIVITY OF CONTRACT; CONTRACT LAW.

Third-party insurance. A policy of insurance which insures a person in respect of any liability which may be incurred by him in respect of damage or injury to any person not a party to the policy. Such insurance is compulsory in the case of users of motor vehicles (see Road Traffic Act 1988, Part VI).

'This day six months.' An expression used in Parliament to mean 'never'. Thus, a proposal to read a Bill 'this day six months' is a proposal to reject it, because Parliament would not be sitting six months hence. 'This day three months' has the same meaning. The term fixed in either case is one beyond the probable duration of the session. If, however, the session should last to the time so nominally specified, it seems that the Bill will appear amongst the orders of the day. *May.*

See BILL, 2.

Threat. Any menace of such a nature and extent as to unsettle the mind of the person on whom it operates, and to take away from his acts that free voluntary action which alone constitutes consent.

See BLACKMAIL.

'Through' bill of lading. A bill of lading issued to a shipper where the goods have to be carried for a portion of the journey by land on a conveyance belonging to some person other than the shipowner.

See BILL OF LADING.

Ticket of leave. A written licence to a prisoner serving a life sentence to be at large, on such conditions as the Home Secretary thinks fit. The present provisions as to release on licence will be found in the Criminal Justice Act 1967, s 61.

Tidal water means, unless the context otherwise requires, any part of the sea and any part of a river within the ebb and flow of the tide at ordinary spring tides, and not being a harbour (see Merchant Shipping Act 1894, s 742).

Timber. Wood fit for building or other such-like uses. Oak, ash, and elm are timber in all places; and, by the custom of some particular counties, in which other kinds of trees are generally used for building, they are also for that reason considered as timber.

For a tenant for life (unless he is unimpeachable for waste) to cut down timber trees, or to do any act whereby they may decay, is waste, timber being part of the inheritance. But even where a tenant for life is impeachable for waste, he has a statutory power to cut and sell timber which is ripe and fit for cutting, provided that he obtains the consent of the trustees or an order of the Court. In such a case, however, three-quarters of the net proceeds become capital money, and one-quarter becomes income (see Settled Land Act 1925, s 66).
See WASTE.

Time. *See* SUMMER TIME.

Time bargain. A contract for the sale of a certain amount of stock at a certain price on a future day, the seller not in general having such stock to sell at the time of the contract, but intending to purchase it before the time appointed for the execution of the contract.

Time immemorial. Time out of mind. These expressions denote time beyond legal memory; ie the time prior to the commencement of the reign of Richard I, ie 1189 (but see Prescription Act 1832).
See LEGAL MEMORY.

Time the essence of the contract. Where a contract specifies a time for its completion, or something to be done towards it, then, if time is of the essence of the contract, the non-performance by either party of the act in question by the time so specified will entitle the other party to regard the contract as broken.

Whether time is or is not of the essence of the contract must, in the absence of express words, be gathered from the general character of the contract and the surrounding circumstances.

By the Law of Property Act 1925, s 41, stipulations in a contract as to time, or otherwise, which according to rules of equity are not deemed to be or to have become of the essence of the contract, are also construed and have effect at law in accordance with the same rules.

Tipstaff. An officer who attends the court, his duty being to take charge of prisoners committed by the court for contempt.
See CONTEMPT OF COURT.

TIR Convention. The Customs Convention on the International Transport Under Cover of TIR Carnets (Geneva, 14th November 1975).

Title. 1 A title of honour; which is in addition to a person's name, implying that he has some honour, office, or dignity.

2 A title to orders; which is a certificate of preferment or provision required by the 33rd Canon, in order that a person may be admitted into holy orders; unless he is a fellow or chaplain in Oxford or Cambridge, or master of arts of five years' standing in either of the universities, and living there at his sole charges; or unless the bishop himself intends shortly to admit him to some benefice or curacy.
See HOLY ORDERS.

3 Title to lands or goods. This means either (i) a party's right to the enjoyment of them; or (ii) the means whereby such right has accrued, and by which it is evidenced; or, as it is defined by Blackstone, the means whereby an owner has the just possession of his property.

When one speaks of a person having a *good title* to his property, one means that the evidence of his right is cogent and conclusive, or nearly so; and when one speaks of a *bad title*, one means that the evidence is weak and insufficient.

A 30 years' title is, in general, sufficient in the case of sale of land, under the Law of Property Act 1925, s 44.
See PROPERTY; DOCUMENT OF TITLE.

4 The title of an Act of Parliament is its heading, and in modern times it has also a 'short title', more condensed than the heading, mentioned in the body of the Act as the name by which it is to be known (see Short Titles Act 1896).

5 The title of an affidavit consists of two parts: (i) the style of the court (or Division of the High Court) in which the affidavit is to be used; and (ii) the names of the parties to the action or other proceeding.

Title, covenants for. On dispositions of real estate the transferee is entitled to covenants for title. These were formerly express and varied according to the nature of the disposition, eg a vendor gave *limited* covenants extending to all acts committed by him or any one through whom he derived title otherwise than by purchase for value; a mortgagor gave *absolute* covenants, not confined to the above acts. They are now implied by the use of the proper words, eg beneficial owner, trustee, etc (see s 76 of, and Sch 2 to, Law of Property Act 1925, and Land Registration Act 1925, s 38(2)).

T

Title deeds. Deeds evidencing a person's right or title to lands. Before Land Registration, whereby title to land is recorded at HM Land Registry, title deeds provided the standard proof of title to land, and the grants of land by deed was the basic transaction in 'unregistered' conveyancing. All titles to land must be registered on their transfer by sale, and so unregistered will become even less prevalent than it is now.
See REGISTERED LAND; LAND LAW.

The possession of the title deeds of land yet unregistered is of importance, as the land cannot be sold without them. Thus, what is called an 'equitable mortgage' is generally effected by a deposit of title deeds. Moreover, any mortgagee who negligently allows his mortgagor to retain the title deeds, and to raise money on a second mortgage of the land by fraudulently concealing the first mortgage, will have his security postponed to that of the second mortgagee. For the present rules relating to the priority of mortgagees, see Law of Property Act 1925, s 97 et seq.
See EQUITABLE MORTGAGE.

Tokyo Convention. An international convention signed on 14th September 1963 concerning offences and certain other acts committed on board aircraft.

Toll. 1 A liberty to buy and sell within the precincts of a market.
2 A tribute or custom paid for passage.
3 A liberty to take, or to be free from such tribute. See also the following entries.

Toll thorough. Money paid for the passage of man or beast in or through highways, or over ferries, bridges, etc.

Toll traverse. A toll paid for passing over a private person's ground. It is thus opposed to *toll thorough*, which is paid for passing over a public highway.
See TOLL THOROUGH.

Tolled. To *toll* is to take away; thus, when a person's right of entry on lands was barred or taken away by lapse of time, or otherwise, it was said to be *tolled*.

Tomlin order. An order of the court staying proceedings in light of the parties agreeing terms for the resolution of the dispute, the terms of which are attached in a schedule to the order. Liberty is given to the parties to apply to the court only for the purpose of carrying out the agreed terms.

Tonnage. 1 A custom or impost paid to the King for goods carried out or brought in in ships, at a certain rate for every ton. It was at first granted for the defence of the realm, the safeguard of the seas, and the safe passage of goods.
2 The number of tons burden which a ship will carry, or the number of tons of water displaced by her.

Tonnage-rent. A royalty payable on every ton of mineral extracted.

Tontine. A type of loan in which the parties who invest receive life annuities, with benefit of survivorship; so called from Lorenzo Tonti, a Neapolitan, who lived in the 17th century. The nature of the plan is this: an annuity, after a certain rate of interest, is granted to a number of people, divided into classes according to their respective ages; so that the whole annual fund of each class is regularly divided among the survivors of that class; and, on the death of the last survivor, it reverts to the power by which the tontine was created.
See ANNUITY.

Tools are those implements which are commonly used by the hand of man in some labour necessary for his subsistence. The tools of a person's trade are, by the Insolvency Act 1986, s 283, excepted to a limited amount from the general property which on his bankruptcy passes to his creditors.

Tort. A wrong; so called because it is wrested (*tortum*), wrung, or crooked. The word 'tort' is especially used to signify a civil wrong independent of contract ie an actionable wrong not consisting exclusively in a breach of contract, the infringement of a purely equitable right, or a crime. An action for such a wrong is called an *action in tort*. Of this class are actions of libel, assault, trespass, etc.
See TORTS, LAW OF; WRONG.

Tortfeasor. A wrongdoer, a trespasser; one who commits a tort.

Tortious. Wrongful.

Torts, law of. The history of the law of torts in England has been largely a matter of the development of a general law of negligence, whereby any injury carelessly or negligently caused can be remedied via an action for damages, out of a prior law of torts which focussed upon the violation of particular rights, which were remedied by various forms of actions which named the particular 'trespass' that occurred. These can broadly be grouped into TRESPASS TO LAND, TRESPASS TO GOODS, and TRESPASS TO THE PERSON, all of which were versions of TRESPASS VIS ET ARMIS, trespass with force and arms. The modern law of negligence arose out of the creation of a new form of the action for trespass which did not require the plaintiff to plead an injury forcibly caused by the defendant, but pleaded rather the special facts of the case which showed that the defendant should be liable even though no such force was used, an action styled TRESPASS ON THE CASE. Early on the distinction between trespass *vis et armis* and trespass on the case appeared to turn on the difference between an action caused by the direct force of the defendant and one caused indirectly by him, for example by his having thrown a log into the road heedless of passers-by over which the plaintiff then tripped. However, later developments re-focussed the action on the case so as to make the defendant's fault, that is his negligence in causing the injury, indirect or not, the gravamen of the complaint. Further developments through the 19th century gave rise to the modern law of negligence.

The tort of negligence is the most general form of tort; any injury which is caused by the defendant's negligence may be the ground of an action. The notion of the defendant's *fault* is central. Three central concepts define the scope of liability for negligence: the duty of care; the standard of care; and causation/remoteness of damage. As a general proposition it may be said that all three are defined in terms of reasonableness or reasonable foreseeability. Thus a person owes a duty to take care to anyone who is the reasonably foreseeable victim of his failing to take care. The duty of care thus expressed is fully general; much of the law concerning duty of care concerns restriction upon the generality of this duty for reasons of public policy, eg the police owe no duty of care to the general public in their conduct of criminal investigations, so are not liable to a victim for injuries caused by a criminal whom they would have arrested sooner and prevented from committing the crime had they been diligent in their investigation. A person breaches the standard of care by acting in such a way, eg failing to take suitable precautions, such that it is reasonably foreseeable that an injury to a person may

result, and the defendant's careless act or omission must be the factual cause of the plaintiff's injury, and the injury must be not too remote, in general, a reasonably foreseeable injury flowing from the careless act or omission.

An important aspect of the law of negligence is that a person may be vicariously liable for the negligent acts of others over whom he is in charge or has some form of control, typically, an employer who is vicariously liable for the negligent act of his employees.

While the law of negligence provides a general remedy for most injury to life, limb and property, there remain in English law a number of torts which have not been assimilated into this general formulation because of their particular features. The law of NUISANCE provides a remedy in the form of an injunction or damages or both for the interference with an owner's enjoyment of his land, eg cases where a neighbour causes excessive noise or emits unreasonable amounts of smoke or sickening smells, etc. Where a person publishes a falsehood that harms another's reputation, ie makes a false statement which would lower that other's standing among right-thinking members of the community, he will be liable to pay damages for DEFAMATION (for libel if the statement is in a permanent form, eg published in a newspaper, for slander if the defamatory statement is made orally). Where the tortious violation is intentional, actions for assault, battery, false imprisonment, trespass to land and CONVERSION (*see also* INTERFERENCE WITH GOODS) may be brought.

Finally, Parliament has by statute created a number of specific statutory regimes which have modified or replaced areas of law formerly governed by the preceding common law rules, in particular, liability to consumers for defective products, the liability of occupiers of land for injuries caused on the premises, and employers' liability for accidents and injuries in the workplace.

Torture. A cruel and wanton infliction of pain on any living being.

The word is used especially in relation to the rack which was sometimes applied to extort confessions from criminals.

A public official or person acting in an official capacity, whatever his nationality, commits the offence of torture if in the United Kingdom or elsewhere he intentionally inflicts severe pain or suffering on another in the performance or purported performance of his duties: Criminal Justice Act 1988, s 134.

Total loss. The entire loss of an insured vessel, or of goods insured, so as to render the underwriters liable to the owner. *See* UNDERWRITER.

Total loss is either *actual* or *constructive*; actual, when the thing is actually destroyed, or so damaged that it cannot arrive in specie at the port of destination; constructive, when the injury, though short of actual loss, is yet so great as to make the subject of it useless to its owner.

When the subject of the insurance, though not wholly destroyed, is placed in such peril as to render the successful prosecution of the venture improbable, the insured may treat the case as a total loss, and demand the full sum insured. In such case, however, he must, within a reasonable time, give notice to the insurer of his intention, and of his abandonment to the insurer of all rights in the thing insured (see Marine Insurance Act 1906, s 61 et seq). *See* ABANDONMENT.

Totidem verbis. In so many words.

Toties quoties. As often as occasion shall require.

Town. A tithing or vill; any collection of houses larger than a village.

Town clerk. A person (usually a solicitor) formerly appointed by a local authority to manage their affairs under the repealed Local Government Act 1933.

Town Council. *See* MUNICIPAL CORPORATION.

Town or village green. Land which has been allotted by or under any Act for the exercise or recreation of the inhabitants of any locality or on which the inhabitants of any locality have a customary right to indulge in lawful sports and pastimes or on which they have indulged in such sports and pastimes as of right for not less than 20 years: Commons Registration Act 1965, s 22(1).

Town planning. Town and country planning is now governed by the Town and Country Planning Act 1971. The Act primarily imposes a control over all land by making it unlawful to develop land without planning permission, which must first be granted either by the local planning authority, eg the county council or by the Secretary of State.

Trade association. A body formed for the purpose of furthering the trade interests of its members: Fair Trading Act 1973, s 43(1).

Trade custom. *See* USAGE.

Trade description. Any description, statement, etc, as to number, quantity, gauge or weight of any goods, or as to their standard of quality or fitness, as to their country of origin or mode of manufacture, etc (see TRADE DESCRIPTIONS ACT 1968).

Trade Descriptions Act 1968 prohibits the misdescription of goods (ss 1 to 6), contains powers requiring the display of information (ss 7 to 10), creates offences (ss 18 to 23), sets out defences (ss 24, 25), and the duties of enforcement authorities.

Trade dispute. A dispute between employers and workers or between workers and workers, connected with one or more of the following: (i) terms and conditions of employment, or the physical conditions in which workers are required to work; (ii) engagement or non-engagement, or termination or suspension of employment or the duties of employment, of one or more workers; (iii) allocation of work or the duties of employment as between workers or groups of workers; (iv) matters of discipline; (v) the membership or non-membership of a trade union on the part of a worker; (vi) facilities for officials of trade unions; and (vii) machinery for negotiation or consultation, etc (see Trade Union and Labour Relations (Consolidation) Act 1992, s 244).

Trade fixtures. Those FIXTURES installed in a premises for the purposes of business, including machinery and utensils of a chattel nature, eg saltpans, vats, etc, for soap-boiling; engines for working collieries; also buildings of a temporary nature erected by the tenant for the purpose of carrying on his business.

Trade mark. By the Trade Marks Act 1994, s 1, a trade mark is defined as: 'a sign capable of being represented graphically which is capable of distinguishing goods or services of one undertaking from those of other undertakings. A trade mark may, in particular, consist of words (including personal names), designs, letters, numerals or the shape of goods or their packaging.'

T

By section 2(1) ibid, '[a] registered trade mark is a property right obtained by the registration of the trade mark under this Act and the proprietor of a registered trade mark has the rights and remedies provided by this Act.'

In general, marks, pictures, designs, and the overall packaging and presentation of goods may be used to distinguish the goods of one trader from another, and the use of these means is in the nature of a limited monopoly, for anyone using such marks, pictures, etc. in a way likely to confuse customers so as to attract custom from the original user will be liable to damages and an injunction for 'passing off' his or her goods for those of the other. (*See* PASSING OFF.) Trade Marks Acts, most recently the Trade Marks Act 1994, provide a statutory regime for the registration of trade marks and mechanisms of enforcement of rights to their use. Thus a registered trade mark is a personal property right (*see* REAL AND PERSONAL PROPERTY) in the nature of a monopoly, the general effect of which is to permit the owner or 'proprietor' exclusively to use the trade mark to distinguish his or her goods or services from others in the market place.
See INTELLECTUAL PROPERTY LAW.

Trade mark agent. An agent acting for others for the purpose of applying for or obtaining the registration of trade marks: Trade Marks Act 1994, s 82 *et seq*.

A 'registered trade mark' agent is a person whose name is entered in the register kept under s 83, ibid. It is an offence for an unregistered person to describe himself as registered: ibid, s 84.
See TRADE MARK.

Trade marks, register of. A register kept under the Trade Marks Act 1994, s 63.
See TRADE MARK.

Trade union. By the Trade Union and Labour Relations (Consolidation) Act 1992 a trade union means an organisation (whether permanent or temporary) which either (i) consists wholly or mainly of workers of one or more descriptions and is an organisation whose principal purposes include the regulation of relations between workers of that description or those descriptions and employers or employers' associations; or (ii) consists wholly or mainly of (a) constituent or affiliated organisations which fulfil the conditions specified in paragraph (i) above…or (b) representatives of such constituent or affiliated organisations. In either case it must be an organisation whose principal purposes include the regulation of relations between workers and employers or between workers and employers' associations, or include the regulation of relations between its constituent or affiliated organisations.

A somewhat simpler definition is contained in Sch 20 to the Social Security Act 1975; 'an association of employed earners'.

Trader. One engaged in commerce. Formerly there was a distinction between traders and non-traders under the bankruptcy laws, but this distinction has been abolished.

Trading certificate. A certificate issued by the Registrar of Companies enabling a public company to commence business (see Companies Act 1985, s 117).
See PUBLIC COMPANY.

Transcript. A copy. Used particularly of a copy of a judgment.
See PAYMASTER-GENERAL.

Transfer of cause, transfer of case. The removal of a cause from one court or judge to another by lawful authority.
See further Civil Procedure Rules 1998, Part 30.

Transfer of share. The conveyance of a member's share to another person. The shares of a member are transferable in the manner provided by the articles (see Companies Act 1985, s 182(1)(b)). The transfer is executed by the transferor and handed to the transferee with the share certificate. The transferee executes the transfer where this is necessary and sends it to the company for registration. The company then issues a new share certificate to the transferee.
See SHARE CERTIFICATE.

Transhipment occurs where goods are shipped in one vessel, then unloaded from her and reloaded on to another vessel.

Transire. A warrant from the custom-house to let goods pass.

Translation. 1 A version of a book or publication out of one language into another. Where the laws of copyright require a *translation* to be made of a foreign work for which copyright is claimed, this requirement is not satisfied by mere *adaptation*.
2 The removal of a bishop from one diocese to another.
See DIOCESE.

Transmission of share. The vesting of a member's shares in another person by operation of law ie on the death or bankruptcy of the member.

On the death of a member his shares vest in his personal representatives. On the bankruptcy of a member they vest in his trustee in bankruptcy.

Treason. A betraying, treachery, or breach of faith, especially against the Sovereign.

Treason is defined by the Treason Act 1351 as consisting in one or other of the following acts:

1 When a man compasses or imagines the death of our lord the King, of our lady his Queen, or of their eldest son and heir. These words include a Queen Regnant. *See* QUEEN, 1.

2 If a man do violate the King's companion, or the King's eldest daughter unmarried, or the wife of the King's eldest son and heir.

3 If a man do levy war against our lord the King in his realm.

4 If a man be adherent to the King's enemies in his realm, giving to them aid and comfort in the realm, or elsewhere.

5 If a man slay the chancellor, treasurer, or the King's justices of the one bench or the other, justices in eyre, or justices of assize, and all other justices assigned to hear and determine, being in their places doing their offices.

In addition to the treasons specified in the Treason Act 1351 it is treason to attempt to hinder the succession to the Crown of the person entitled thereto under the Act of Settlement (see Treason Act 1702, s 3).

The procedure in all trials for treason or misprision of treason is the same as in that for murder (see Treason Act 1945).

Treason felony, under the Treason Felony Act 1848, is the offence of compassing, devising, etc, to depose Her Majesty from the Crown; or to levy war in order to intimidate either House of Parliament, etc; or to stir up foreigners by any printing or writing to invade the kingdom. This offence is punishable with imprisonment for life. By the above statute the Government is enabled to treat as lesser offences many offences which might formerly have been treated as treason. *See* TREASON.

Treasure trove (Lat *Thesaurus inventus*). Money, coin, gold, silver, plate, or bullion found hidden in the earth or other private place, its owner being unknown. In such case the treasure belongs to the Crown, and any

person concealing it from the Crown is liable to fine and imprisonment.

Treasurer. *See* LORD TREASURER; TREASURY.

Treasury. The Lords Commissioners of the Treasury, being the department of State under whose control the royal revenue is administered. *See* LORD TREASURER.

Treating. Providing food, drink, or entertainment before, during, or after an election for corruptly influencing votes renders the person providing it liable to penalties, and a voter corruptly receiving it incapable of voting, and renders his vote void; it also may invalidate the election on petition (see Representation of the People Act 1983, s 114). *See* CORRUPT PRACTICES.

Treaty. 1 A negotiation.
2 A compact between nations.

Trespass (Lat *Transgressio*). 1 Generally, any transgression or offence against the law, ie any crime.

2 Any misfeasance or act of one person whereby another is injuriously treated or damnified and for which a civil remedy for the victim lies, ie any of a number of long-standing torts, eg trespass to the person, trespass to goods, trespass to land, trespass on the case.
See TRESPASS TO THE PERSON, etc; TORT.

3 The original term to describe lesser criminal offences, ie those which were not felonies, displaced by the term 'misdemeanour'.
See CRIMINAL PROCEDURE.

4 The specific tort of trespass to land.
See TRESPASS TO LAND.

Trespass de bonis asportatis. *See* TRESPASS TO GOODS.

Trespass quare clausum fregit. *See* TRESPASS TO LAND.

Trespass on the case. The origin of the tort of negligence; trespass on the case was distinguished from other sorts of trespass at first by requiring that the defendant caused the plaintiff's injury indirectly, thus by a chain of causation revealed by the circumstances or 'on the case'; later the distinction came to be that the gravamen of the action in trespass on the case or, simply, 'in case' was not the indirectness of the injury but the defendant's negligence in causing the injury to come about.
See TORT, LAW OF; TRESPASS VIS ET ARMIS; NEGLIGENCE.

T

Trespass to goods. The tort of directly interfering with a person's possession of his goods, ie his CHATTELS or CHOSES IN POSSESSION) either by taking them away, damaging, or coming into contact with them without the permission, or LICENCE, of their owner or rightful possessor. (cf CONVERSION). Originally a species of TRESPASS VIS ET ARMIS styled trespass *de bonis asportatis* (taking away goods).
See INTERFERENCE WITH GOODS.

Trespass to land. The tort of entering the land of another unlawfully, ie without the permission of the owner, or remaining on land entered upon with the permission of the owner but following the withdrawal of that permission and a reasonable time/opportunity to leave. Originally a species of TRESPASS VIS ET ARMIS styled trespass *quare clausum fregit* (inquire as to why the defendant 'broke' or entered the 'close' or enclosure of the plaintiff).

Trespass to the person. The compendious term for various tortious violations of a person's body, and a species of TRESPASS VIS ET ARMIS. The forms of the action crystallised around actions for assault, ie the immediate threat of forcible injury, battery, ie bodily contact causing injury, and false imprisonment, ie unlawful restriction of the plaintiff's bodily freedom.

Trespass vis et armis. Trespass 'with force and arms'. The general form of the action for trespass to goods, to land, and to the person. The plaintiff had to allege a forcible violation of rights by the use of arms to the grave injury of the plaintiff and in breach of the King's peace, although it appears that early on these aspects of the trespass could be asserted without subsequent proof, so that the defendant's having caused a particular sort of injury became the gravamen of the complaint rather than the flagrancy of the means by which he did it. While there were early on other forms of action available to remedy tortious violations of rights, an action for trespas *vis et armis* was advantageous in that it was tried by jury and the remedy was money damages.
See TRESPASS TO THE PERSON; TRESPASS TO GOODS; TRESPASS TO LAND; TORTS, LAW OF.

Trial. The examination of a cause, civil or criminal, before a Judge who has jurisdiction over it, according to the laws of the land.

Criminal trials generally take place before a Judge and Jury in the Crown Court or at the Central Criminal Court. Minor offences are, in general, dealt with summarily before magistrates.

Trial of the pyx. *See* PIXING THE COIN.

Tribunal. A body appointed to adjudicate or arbitrate on a disputed question or matter, as eg lands tribunal, rent tribunal (see Tribunals and Inquiries Act 1971).
See LANDS TRIBUNAL.

Trinity House. A company of masters of ships incorporated in the reign of Henry VIII, and charged by many successive Acts of Parliament with numerous duties relating to the sea, especially the appointment and licensing of pilots, and the superintendence of lighthouses, buoys, and beacons.
Trinity House is a self-elected body, and is composed of *Elder Brethren* and *Younger Brethren*. The Elder Brethren manage the affairs of the society, being for the most part elected from the Younger Brethren.

Trinity term. *See* SITTINGS.

Tripartite. Divided into three parts, having three corresponding copies; a deed to which there are three distinct parties.

Trover (From Fr *trouver*, to find.) One of the forms of action at law, by which an INTERFERENCE WITH GOODS could be remedied. It originated as a species of TRESPASS ON THE CASE, in which the plaintiff pleaded that the defendant, having 'found' the plaintiff's goods, thereafter converted them to his own use, and so the action was also known as 'trover and CONVERSION'. As the pleading of finding became a matter of mere form (ie the defendant was just as susceptible to the action if he took the plaintiff's goods intentionally, or was put into possession of them by the plaintiff under a bailment but then without permission used them for his own purposes and refused to re-deliver them) the action became known simply as 'conversion'. In this action the specific chattel could not be recovered, but only damages for its conversion, which generally approximated the value of the chattel.
See INTERFERENCE WITH GOODS.

Trust. A legal device by which the legal owner of property is required to exercise his rights and powers over the property for the benefit of another, called a beneficiary or *cestui que trust*, who is said to have the equitable title to the property in virtue of the fact that the beneficiary's interest in the property was enforced at EQUITY, not at common law. A trust is created by *self-declaration* when a legal owner of property declares that he holds the property on trust for a beneficiary or beneficiaries, or when a legal owner of property transfers property to another to hold on trust for a beneficiary or beneficiaries. In the latter case the trust is not established, or *constituted*, until the intended trustee acquires the legal title to the trust property. The original legal owner of the property who declares the trust is called the *settlor* and the legal owner of the property who holds it on trust is called the *trustee*. Where the trustee holds the legal title to the property to the order of the beneficiary, ie must do with the property as the beneficiary directs, including transferring the legal title to the property to the beneficiary absolutely, there is a *bare trust*. A trust may also arise by operation of law, whereby the law imposes a trust on property held by a legal owner; such a trust is called a constructive trust. The trust is a unique creation of English law involving a specific combination of property and obligations. With respect to property, the beneficiary's rights are *proprietary*, that is to say they bind the trust property itself; thus if the legal title to the property is transferred to a third party in breach of trust, the beneficiary may assert his equitable title to the property against the third party legal owner, except where the third party is a BONA FIDE PURCHASER for value of a legal interest in the trust property without notice that the property was transferred in breach of trust, eg if he buys the trust property from the trustee in good faith. The beneficiary's interest under the trust is also proprietary in the sense that the fate of his interest is tied to the fate of the property in cases of loss or theft. Where the trust property is lost or stolen through no fault of the trustee, the beneficiary's interest is similarly lost. Finally, if the trustee is made bankrupt, though he has legal title to the trust property, it does not form part of his estate in bankruptcy, but remains bound by the trust. As regards obligations, the trustee has the over-arching obligation to use his legal title to the trust property for the benefit of the beneficiary in accordance with the terms of the trust. He must distribute the trust property, ie pay its income and distribute its capital in accordance with the trust terms. (The equitable interests under a trust are often arranged so as to give one beneficiary or group of beneficiaries an interest in the income of the trust fund, who may be called the income beneficiaries, and others an interest in the capital, the capital beneficiaries.) The trustee is obliged to keep the trust accounts, ie the record of transactions with the trust property, must keep the trust property separate from his own and never mix the two, and must invest the trust property, generally to maintain the value of the trust property while ensuring a reasonable return. A trust has no separate legal personality in the way a corporate body does (*see* COMPANY LAW); in carrying out transactions with the trust property, the trustee contracts in his own name, but in so far as he does so in compliance with the terms of the trust, he is entitled to an indemnity from the trust fund for any liabilities or costs thus incurred.

In order to create a trust a settlor's declaration must meet the 'three certainties'; the intention to create the trust, eg as expressed in the words of a will, must be clear or certain; the subject matter of the trust, ie the property, must be certain, eg declaring a trust of 'the bulk of my estate' is too vague; and finally, the identity of the *objects* of the trust, ie, the beneficiaries of the trust, must be ascertainable.

The trustee is a fiduciary to the beneficiaries, and so must act in his dealings with the trust property only in the best interests of the beneficiaries, and in particular, never to favour his own interests. A trustee may not place himself in a position where his own interests conflict with those of his duty to serve the beneficiaries best interests, and in particular is not allowed any remuneration for his services not authorised by the terms of the trust, by court order, or by statute, and in particular is not entitled to retain any incidental profits or payments which may come his way in the course of administering the trust.

The court has always maintained a supervisory jurisdiction over trusts, and trustees are entitled and encouraged to apply to the court for directions or advice wherever there is doubt about the propriety of any course of conduct they propose to undertake in the conduct of the trust.
See EQUITY; DECLARATION OF TRUST; CONSTRUCTIVE TRUST; RESULTING TRUST; PURPOSE TRUST; TRUSTEE INVESTMENTS.

Trust corporation. The Public Trustee or a corporation either appointed by the Court in any particular case to be a trustee or entitled by rules made under the Public Trustee Act 1906, s 4(3) to act as custodian trustee (see Trustee Act 1925, s 68).

Trust instrument. The Settled Land Act 1925 provides that all settlements of land created *inter vivos* must be effected by two deeds, ie a vesting deed and a trust instrument, otherwise the settlement will not operate to transfer or create a legal estate (s 4(1)). The trust instrument sets out the terms of the trust on which the person who for the time being is entitled to the actual enjoyment of the land must hold the fee simple which has been transferred to him by the vesting deed (see s 4(3) and Sch 1, Form No 3).
See VESTING DEED.

Trustee. A person to whom an estate is conveyed, devised or bequeathed in trust for another, called the *cestui que trust* or beneficiary. As to the powers of trustees, see generally Trustee Act 1925; Trusts of Land and Appointment of Trustees Act 1996, and Trustee Act 2000.
See TRUSTEE INVESTMENTS.

Trustee, Public. *See* PUBLIC TRUSTEE; TRUST CORPORATION.

Trustee de son tort. A trustee by his own wrong. A person who without authority meddles in the administration of a trust. Such a person is liable for any breaches of trust as if he were properly installed as trustee.

Trustee investments. Formerly, by the Trustee Investments Act 1961, securities in which trustees were authorised by law to invest money. By that Act there were: (i) narrower-range investments not requiring expert investment advice, eg National Savings Certificates; (ii) narrower-range investments requiring that the trustee take expert investment advice, eg debentures issued by a company incorporated in the United Kingdom; and (iii) wider-range investments, eg any securities issued by a company incorporated in the United Kingdom. By the Trustee Act 2000 trustees are not restricted in their choice of investments by lists of this kind, but are bound by a general 'prudent investor' standard.
See TRUST.

Turbary (Lat *Turbagium*). The right to dig turf on another person's ground. And *common of turbary* is a liberty which some tenants have by prescription to dig on the lord's waste.
See COMMON, RIGHTS OF.

Turpis causa. An illegal or immoral consideration by which a contract is vitiated.

T

U

UN. United Nations.

Uberrima fides, uberrimae fidae. The most perfect frankness. This is essential to the validity of certain contracts between persons bearing a particular relationship to one another, eg guardian and ward, solicitor and client, insurer and insured.

Ubi jus, ibi remedium. Where there is a right, there is a remedy.

Ulpian. Domitius Ulpianus was one of the five great Roman jurists, on whose writings the compilations of Justinian are mainly founded. The greater part of his works were written in the reign of Caracalla. On the accession of Alexander Severus, in AD 222, he became the emperor's chief adviser.
See CORPUS JURIS CIVILIS.

Ultimatum. A final proposal in a negotiation in which it is intimated that, in case of its rejection, the negotiation must be broken off.

Ultra vires. Beyond their powers; a phrase applied especially to directors of companies exceeding their legal powers under the articles of association (*see* ARTICLES OF ASSOCIATION) or the Acts of Parliament by which they are governed; though it is equally applicable to excess of authority of any kind.

Umpire. 1 An arbitrator.
2 Especially a third person called in to decide when two arbitrators cannot agree (see Arbitration Act 1950).
See ARBITRATION.

Uncertainty. Where a deed or will is so obscure and confused that the Judge can make nothing of it, which sometimes occurs in wills made by testators without legal advice. Any disposition or conveyance to which it is impossible to give a meaning is said to be *void for uncertainty*; but the Judge will use every effort to give a meaning to the language used where it is possible to do so.

See TRUST.

Uncollected goods may be disposed of by a bailee provided that he has given notice to the bailor that he himself has power to impose an obligation for the bailor to collect the goods and that he intends to sell them: Torts (Interference with Goods) Act 1977, s 12, Sch.

Uncompetitive practices. Practices having the effect of preventing, restricting or distorting competition in connection with any commercial activities in the United Kingdom: Fair Trading Act 1973, s 137(2).

Unconscionable bargain. A bargain so one-sided and inequitable in its terms as to raise a presumption of fraud and oppression.

Undefended. 1 When a person sued in a civil cause or accused of a crime has no counsel to speak for him on his trial, and has to make his defence himself, he is sometimes said to be *undefended*, ie undefended by counsel.
2 An undefended cause is one in which a defendant makes default (i) in not acknowledging service; (ii) in not putting in his statement of defence; (iii) in not appearing at the trial, either personally or by counsel, after having received due notice of trial.

Underlease. A lease by a lessee for years, for a period less than the residue of the term, as opposed to an *assignment* by which the entire residue is conveyed. A lessee who grants a sublease or underlease, called an *underlessor* or *sublessor*, still remains liable as the *headlessee* on the covenants under the original lease (now often called the *headlease*), to the original lessor (head lessor), but the sub-lessee is not liable to the original lessor, whereas an *assignee* is so liable. As used in the Law of Property Act 1922 the term 'underlease', unless the context otherwise requires, includes a sub-term created out of a derivative leasehold interest. See s 190(4). And see the Law of Property Act 1925, s 146(5), whereby 'underlease' includes an agreement for an underlease where the underlessee has become entitled to have his underlease granted.

Under-sheriff. An officer who acts directly under the high sheriff, and performs all the duties of the sheriff's office except his functions as returning officer at Parliamentary elections. *See* RETURNING OFFICER. The high sheriff is civilly responsible for the acts or omissions of his under-sheriff. As to the appointment of under-sheriffs, see Local Government Act 1972, s 219.

See SHERIFF.

Undertaking. A promise; especially one given in the course of legal proceedings, which may be enforced by attachment or otherwise.

See ATTACHMENT.

Underwriter. A person who *underwrites* or subscribes his name to a policy of insurance, thereby undertaking to indemnify the assured against the losses referred to in the policy, to the extent mentioned in it. The word is used especially with reference to *marine insurance*.

Underwriters of shares in a company are persons who, for a commission, offer to take up any shares offered to but not taken up by the public.

See INSURANCE; LLOYD'S; UNDERWRITING AGREEMENT; UNDERWRITING COMMISSION.

Underwriting agreement. An agreement under which, before a company issues shares to the public, a person undertakes, in consideration of a commission, to take up the whole or a portion of such (if any) of the offered shares as may not be subscribed for by the public (see *Re Licensed Victuallers' Mutual Trading Association, ex parte Audain* (1889) 42 Ch D 1). A similar agreement may be made for underwriting debentures. Sometimes an underwriter enters into a sub-underwriting agreement with other persons in order to relieve him of some or all of his liability in exchange for a commission.

See UNDERWRITING COMMISSION.

Underwriting commission. A commission paid to a person who agrees to take up the whole or a portion of the shares or debentures of a company offered to the public but not subscribed for by them. For a company's entitlement to pay underwriting commission, see Companies Act 1985, s 97.

See UNDERWRITING AGREEMENT.

Undue influence. Any improper pressure put on a person to induce him to confer a benefit on the party exercising the pressure. A gift or will may be set aside by the Court where such pressure has been exercised.

In elections undue influence to induce persons to vote or refrain from voting by violence, restraint, threats, etc, renders the person using it guilty of an offence, and if by a candidate, disqualifies him from sitting in that Parliament for the constituency (see Representation of the People Act 1983, ss 115, 159).

See CORRUPT PRACTICES.

Unfair Contract Terms Act 1977. An Act which limits the extent to which civil liability for breach of contract or for negligence or other breach of duty can be avoided by means of contract terms and otherwise.

A person cannot by reference to any contract term or to a notice given to persons generally or to particular persons exclude or restrict his liability for death or personal injury resulting from negligence: Unfair Contract Terms Act 1977, s 2(1). In the case of other loss or damage, a person cannot so exclude or restrict his liability for negligence except in so far as the term or notice satisfies the requirement of reasonableness: ibid, s 2(2).

Where one of the parties to a contract deals as consumer or on the other's standard terms of business, the other cannot by reference to any contract term:
 (i) when himself in breach of contract, exclude or restrict any liability of his in respect of the breach; or
(ii) claim to be entitled
    (a) to render a contractual performance substantially different from that which was reasonably expected of him, or
    (b) in respect of the whole or any part of his contractual obligation, to render no performance at all,
except in so far as the contract term satisfies the requirement of reasonableness: ibid, ss 3(1), (2).

As to whether a contract term satisfies the requirement of reasonableness, see ibid, Sch 2.

Other sections of the Act concern the liability arising from the sale or supply of goods (ibid, ss 5 to 7), and varieties of exemption clauses (ibid, s 11).

See CONSUMER DEALING AS.

U

Uniform Laws on International Sales Act 1967 gives effect to international Conventions on (i) the application of the Uniform Law on the International Sale of Goods; and (ii) the application of the Uniform Law on the Formation of such contracts. Its principal provisions are (i) the sphere of application (Chapter I); (ii) general provisions (Chapter II); (iii) obligations of the seller (Chapter III); (iv) obligations of the buyer (Chapter IV); and (v) provisions common to the obligations of the seller and of the buyer (Chapter V).

Unilateral. One-sided; a word used especially of a bond or contract by which one party only is bound.
See BOND; UNILATERAL CONTRACT.

Unilateral contract. A contract in which one party's performance of the contract also constitutes his acceptance of the other party's contractual offer. Eg, where a person offers a reward of ten pounds for the return of his lost dog, a finder who returns the dog both accepts the offer, and so a contract between them is formed, *and* provides his performance under the contract, by doing so. Following the finder's return of the dog, the other party is contractually bound to pay the ten-pound reward.
See CONTRACT.

Union. The consolidation of two or more bodies or areas into one. This may (or might) be done:
1 In the past for the better administration of the Poor Laws. Under these laws, now repealed, any two or more parishes could be consolidated into one union under the government of a single board of guardians, to be elected by the owners and ratepayers of the component parishes. Each of such unions was to have a common workhouse, provided and maintained at the common expense. Such workhouse was frequently called 'the union workhouse', or, more briefly, 'the union'.
2 For ecclesiastical purposes, under the Acts for the union of benefices.
See BENEFICE.

United Kingdom unless the contrary intention appears, means Great Britain and Northern Ireland (see Interpretation Act 1978, s 5, Sch 1).
See GREAT BRITAIN.

Unity of possession. 1 The joint possession by one person of two rights by several titles.

See TITLE.
2 The holding of the same estate in undivided shares by two or more persons.
See COMMON, TENANCY IN.

Universal agent. A person appointed to do all the acts which the principal may lawfully do, and the power to do which he may lawfully delegate to another.
See AGENT.

Unjust enrichment. A cause of action developed at common law and equity whereby, roughly, a person who is unjustly enriched, either by receipt of value from the plaintiff in circumstances where he or she ought to return it, or by profiting from a wrong done to the plaintiff, is required to pay over the value of that enrichment to the plaintiff. The law of unjust enrichment, also sometimes called the law of restitution, was, until recently, confused in English law by operating via the implication to the defendant of a fictional promise or contract to pay or repay the value of the enrichment to the plaintiff, and much work yet needs to be done to reorganise and clarify the precise nature and scope of the law. The implied or fictional contract theory of unjust enrichment probably owed its origin to the importation of the Roman law term *quasi ex contractu*, roughly 'as if on a contract' to delimit the cause of action; because the defendant was held to be under an obligation to pay or repay value to the plaintiff as if he had a contractual obligation to do so, it was a short step to confining the circumstances where the cause of action could operate to circumstances where a real contract might actually have been made by the parties, and for a long time this hampered the provision of a satisfactory analysis of the law, which was generally taught as an adjunct to the law of contract under the rubric 'quasi-contract'. Partly because of this, there lingered a reliance upon the old common law form of action by which claims in respect of unjust enrichment could be brought to court, the action of assumpsit, and the particular counts of that action: MONEY HAD AND RECEIVED, MONEY PAID, QUANTUM MERUIT, and QUANTUM VALEBAT.
  Under the modern analysis of this area of law, the cases of unjust enrichment are divided into essentially two classes; (i) unjust enrichment by subtraction from the plaintiff, ie those cases in which value has flowed from the plaintiff to the defendant in

circumstances where it would be unjust for the defendant to retain the benefit; and (ii) unjust enrichment by wrongdoing, where a defendant profits by doing wrong to the defendant and where in justice the defendant ought to be stripped of the profit and it be transferred to the plaintiff.

The modern analysis is also devoted to explaining and making precise those 'unjust factors', ie facts of the case, which justify the claim that the defendant is *unjustly* enriched. A classic example of (i) is the case where A pays his gas bill a second time, forgetting that he had already paid it. The 'unjust factor' here is the plaintiff's mistake, ie it would be unjust for the defendant to retain the value of the second payment made by mistake. A classic example of (ii) is the case of the bribed fiduciary. A fiduciary is required to be loyal to and act in the best interests of his principal, and where he takes a bribe to act otherwise, the principal is entitled to bring an action against the false fiduciary for the value of the bribe, the obvious factor rendering it unjust for the fiduciary to retain the money being his breach of loyalty. Further examples of cases falling under class (i) are payments made by the plaintiff to the defendant under a void contract, and payments made to a public authority in response to a demand which is *ultra vires* the authority.

The typical remedy in these cases is clearly a restitutionary one, whereby the defendant is made to pay over the value of a gain he received but is not entitled to retain. However the modern analysis of unjust enrichment may also provide the rationale for certain other legal responses to events, for example certain cases of SUBROGATION; eg where an insurer under an INDEMNITY policy pays his insured upon the latter's being tortiously injured, the insurer is subrogated to the insured's rights to claim compensation from his tortfeasor; if subrogation did not occur in this circumstance, the insured might be doubly compensated for his injury, and so unjustly enriched.

Where a claim for restitution of value received is made, certain defences may be available to the innocent defendant, eg the gas company in the example above if it receives payment ignorant of the fact that it represents a second payment of the same amount owing. The most general defence is the defence of change of position. Where a defendant has innocently changed his position in reliance on the propriety of his receipt of value from the defendant, it may be unjust to demand that he make restitution of the entire amount received. For example, if a person receives a mistaken overpayment of interest by his bank which he thinks was correctly paid, and spends the windfall on a world cruise, an expenditure he would not have made but for the windfall he believed belonged to him, it would be unjust to require him to repay the entire amount of the overpayment, for that would put him in a worse financial position than he would have been in had he never received the payment at all, for he would not have spent for the world cruise at his previous level of wealth.

Unlawful. Unauthorised by law, or contrary to law. 'Unlawful' is less strong than 'illegal', which imports the idea of committing an offence.
See ILLEGAL.

Unlawful killing, death by. Death by murder, manslaughter, etc.
See CORONER'S VERDICT.

Unlimited company. A company not having any limit on the liability of its members (see Companies Act 1985, s 1(2)(c)).

Unpaid seller. A seller of goods is an unpaid seller (i) when the whole of the price has not been paid or tendered; (ii) when a bill of exchange or other negotiable instrument has been received as conditional payment, and the condition on which it was received has not been fulfilled by reason of the dishonour of the instrument or otherwise (see Sale of Goods Act 1979, s 38(1)).
An unpaid seller has:
(i)   a lien on the goods;
(ii) in case of the insolvency of the buyer a right of stopping the goods in transit;
      (*see* STOPPAGE IN TRANSIT).
(iii) a right of re-sale (see ibid, s 39(1)).

Unsound mind. *See* MENTAL DISORDER.

Unvalued policy. A policy in which the sum to be paid to the insured is not fixed, but is left to be ascertained after the loss has happened. The sum specified in the policy as the amount of insurance indicates the amount beyond which the liability of the insurers does not extend. For unvalued policies in marine insurance, see Marine Insurance Act 1906, s 28.

Unwritten law. *See* LEX NON SCRIPTA.

U

Usage may be either a general usage of trade or a particular usage prevailing only among particular classes or in particular localities. When a general usage has been affirmed by judicial decision, it becomes incorporated into the law merchant, and thenceforward evidence of any usage inconsistent with it is inadmissible (see *Goodwin v Roberts* (1875) LR 10 Exch 337 (Ex Ch) (per Cockburn CJ)). A particular usage must be proved by evidence in each case until it becomes so well known that the Courts take judicial notice of it. To constitute a valid usage it must be (i) notorious; (ii) certain; (iii) reasonable; and (iv) legal.

Usance. In reference to foreign bills of exchange, is the period, fixed by the usage or habit of dealing between the country where the bill is drawn and that where it is payable, for the payment of bills.
See BILL OF EXCHANGE.

Use. The forerunner of the trust, by which land could be conveyed to an owner, styled the 'feoffee to uses', who received the land 'to the use of', ie for the benefit of, the CESTUI QUE USE. The employment of the use as a means to transfer property to a grantee for the benefit of a third party was effectively abolished by the Statute of Uses 1535.
Over the course of the next century, the trust arose effectively taking its place.
See TRUST; FEOFFMENT.

Use and occupation. An action for use and occupation is an action brought by a landlord against a tenant for the profits of land.
This action is allowed by the Distress for Rent Act 1737, s 14 where there has been no demise by deed. It is also maintainable against a tenant holding over after a lease by deed has expired, in respect of such holding over. The measure of damages recoverable is the rent, where a rent has been agreed on; and where no rent has been agreed on, then such sum as the Court may find the occupation to be worth.
See HOLDING OVER.

User. The enjoyment of property.

Usher. A doorkeeper of a court.

Usque ad filum aquæ, or more fully, 'usque ad medium filum aquæ' (up to the middle thread of the water). A phrase used to express half the land covered by a stream; which, in the case of a stream not navigable, belongs to the proprietor of the adjoining bank.

Usucapion, or **usucaption.** The enjoying a thing by long continuance of time or title by prescription.
See PRESCRIPTION.

Usurpation. The using that which is not one's own. It is a word used especially in the Common Law to signify the *usurpation of an advowson* (*see* ADVOWSON); ie when a stranger, who is not the patron, presents a clergyman to the living, and the clergyman so presented is admitted and instituted.
See PRESENTATION; INSTITUTION.
So, an usurpation of a franchise is the use of a franchise by a person who has no right to it.
See FRANCHISE.

Usury. 1 The gain of anything in consideration of a loan beyond the principal or thing lent; otherwise called interest.
2 Especially any such gain above mentioned as is excessive. Laws against usury were repealed by the Usury Laws Repeal Act 1854.

Uterine brother (Lat *Uterinus frater*). A brother by the mother's side only.

Utmost good faith. *See* UBERRIMA FIDES, UBERRIMAE FIDEI.

Utter Bar. The outer or junior Bar, as opposed to Queen's Counsel.
See OUTER BAR; QUEEN'S COUNSEL.

Utter barristers. *See* OUTER BAR.

Uttering. To *utter* coins or documents (a phrase especially used in reference to false coin and forged documents) is to pass them off as genuine. But the word is not used in the Forgery and Counterfeiting Act 1981 which in s 15 refers to the 'passing or tendering as genuine' counterfeit notes and coins.
See FORGERY.

U

V. Versus.
See VERSUS.

VAT. *See* VALUE ADDED TAX.

V-C. Vice-Chancellor.
See VICE-CHANCELLOR.

Vacant possession. Where a tenant has virtually abandoned the premises which he held, eg where the tenant of a house locked it up and quitted it, the Court held that the landlord should treat it as a vacant possession.

The term is normally used to describe premises which are for sale or have been sold without being subject to any lease or underlease.

Vacant succession. Where, on the death of a Sovereign or other person of title, there is no one appointed by law to succeed. Or the phrase might be applied to an *hæreditas jacens*, where there was no one to succeed the deceased.

Vacantia bona. *See* BONA VACANTIA.

Vacation. The time between the end of one sittings and the beginning of another.
See SITTINGS.

By RSC 1965, Ord 64, r 1 the vacations to be observed in the courts and offices of the Supreme Court are: (i) The Long Vacation, from 1st August to 30th September; (ii) the Christmas Vacation, from 22nd December to 10th January; (iii) the Easter Vacation, from the Thursday before Easter Sunday to the second Monday after; (iv) and a vacation beginning on the Saturday before the Spring Holiday and ending on the Monday after. The days of the commencement and termination of each vacation are included in such vacation.

Vacation sittings. Sittings during the Long Vacation for the hearing of applications requiring immediate attention.
See VACATION.

Vagabond. One who wanders about and has no certain dwelling. By various statutes it is provided that certain acts shall constitute their perpetrator a rogue and vagabond (see Vagrancy Act 1824, s 4).
See VAGRANT.

Vagrant. A person belonging to one of the following classes: (i) idle and disorderly persons; (ii) rogues and vagabonds; (iii) incorrigible rogues. These several classes are defined by various Acts of Parliament (see principally Vagrancy Act 1824).

Valorem, ad. *See* AD VALOREM.

Valuable consideration. A consideration for a grant, contract or other act which the law deems an equivalent for it, must consist of money or money's worth. A Court will not, in general, enter into the question of the *adequacy* of a consideration which is *bona fide* intended as an equivalent. For the purposes of the Law of Property Act 1925 'valuable consideration' includes marriage, but does not include a nominal consideration in money. See s 205(1)(xxi).
See CONSIDERATION.

Value added tax. A tax charged on the supply of goods and services in the United Kingdom and on the importation of goods into the United Kingdom. (See now Value Added Tax Act 1983).

Value received. A phrase implying the existence of a valuable consideration.
See CONSIDERATION.

The phrase is especially used to indicate that a bill of exchange has been accepted for value and not by way of accommodation.
See BILL OF EXCHANGE; ACCOMMODATION BILL.

Vendee. A buyer to whom lands or goods are sold.

Vendor. A seller. In sales of lands the party selling is almost always spoken of as 'the vendor'; but in sales of goods he is quite as frequently spoken of as 'the seller'.

Vendor's covenants for title. *See* TITLE, COVENANTS FOR.

Vendor's lien. The hold which an unpaid vendor of land has over the land for the payment of the purchase-money. This lien exists against the purchaser and his heirs, and against persons claiming by a voluntary conveyance from the purchaser; also against purchasers under him, with notice that the purchase-money due from such purchaser has not been paid. Now, to remain enforceable against subsequent purchasers of land, it must be registered as a 'general equitable charge' under s 2(4)(iii) of the Land Charges Act 1972.

See LIEN.

As to the lien of an unpaid seller of goods see Sale of Goods Act 1979, ss 41–43.

See UNPAID SELLER.

Venison includes imported venison and means:
(i) any carcase of a deer, or
(ii) any edible part of the carcase of a deer, which has not been cooked or canned: Deer Act 1991, s 16.

Venue (Lat *Vicinetum*). The place of trial.

Verba accipienda sunt secundum subjectam materiam. Words are to be understood with reference to the subject matter.

Verba chartarum fortius accipiuntur contra proferentem. The words of a deed are construed more strongly against the grantor.

Verba ita sunt intelligenda ut res magis valeat quam pereat. Words are to be so construed that the thing may avail rather than perish.

Verdict. The answer given to the Court by the jury in any cause, civil or criminal, committed to their trial, and is either general or special: *general* when they give it in general terms, as guilty or not guilty; *special* when they find it at large according to the evidence given, and pray the direction of the Court as to what the law is on the facts so found. It is now possible for a jury to give a majority verdict (see Juries Act 1974).

See MAJORITY VERDICT.

Verge. Land at the side of a road which is part of the highway but not paved.

Versus. Against. Smith *versus* Jones is the action or case of Smith against Jones. Usually abbreviated to 'v'.

Vest (Lat *Vestire*). **1** To deliver to a person the full possession of land, and so to clothe him with the legal estate in it.

See INVESTITURE.

2 To become a vested interest.

See VESTED IN INTEREST.

Vested in interest. A phrase used to indicate a present fixed right of future enjoyment, eg reversions, vested remainders, and other future interests which do not depend on a period or uncertain event.

See REVERSION.

Vested in possession. A phrase used to indicate that an estate is an estate in possession, as opposed to an estate in reversion or remainder.

See REVERSION; REMAINDER.

Vesting assent. In relation to settled land, the instrument whereby a personal representative, after the death of a tenant for life or statutory owner, or the survivor of two or more tenants for life or statutory owners, vests settled land in a person entitled as tenant for life or statutory owner (see Settled Land Act 1925, s 117).

See SETTLED LAND.

Vesting declaration. A declaration made by the appointor in a deed of appointment of new trustees to the effect that the trust property is to vest in the persons who become or are the trustees. If the deed of appointment contains such a vesting declaration, the deed operates, without any conveyance or assignment, to vest in the persons named, as joint tenants and for the purposes of the trust, the estate, interest or right to which the declaration relates (see Trustee Act 1925, s 40).

See JOINT TENANCY.

Vesting deed. All settlements of land created *inter vivos* must be effected by two different deeds, namely, a vesting deed and a trust instrument (*see* TRUST INSTRUMENT); (see Settled Land Act 1925, s 4). The function of the vesting deed is to vest the legal fee simple in the person who for the time being is to have the actual enjoyment of the land, or, if he is a minor or otherwise incapable, then to vest it in some other person who is called a 'statutory owner'. For the contents of the vesting deed, see Settled Land Act 1925, s 5 and for specimen forms, see ibid, Sch 1, Forms Nos 1 and 2.

Vesting order. An order of the Chancery Division of the High Court, vesting the legal estate in property (generally land) in any person specified in the order. This can be done, eg under the Trustee Acts, when the trustees appointed are unwilling or unable to act in the execution of the trusts; or when for any reason it is desirable to appoint new trustees, and it is found impracticable or inconvenient to procure a conveyance to them in the ordinary way.

Vestry. 1 The place in a church where the priest's vestures are deposited.
2 An assembly of the minister, churchwardens and parishioners, so called because it is still very often usually held in the vestry of the church.
See CHURCHWARDENS.

Vetera statuta. Old statutes. This phrase is applied to the statutes from Magna Carta to the end of the reign of Edward II.
See MAGNA CARTA.

Veterinary practitioner. A person registered in the supplementary veterinary register kept under the Veterinary Surgeons Act 1966, s 8: Medicines Act 1968, s 132(1).

Veterinary surgeon. A person registered in the register of veterinary surgeons kept under the Veterinary Surgeons Act 1966, s 2: Medicines Act 1968, s 132(1).

Vexata quæstio. A question much discussed and not settled.

Vexatious action. An action brought merely for the sake of annoyance or oppression. The Court has an inherent power to stay such an action.

Vi et armis. With force and arms.
See TRESPASS VIS ET ARMIS.

Via regia. The Queen's highway or common way.

Viability. Capability of living after birth; possibility of continued existence.

Vicar, a substitute; one who performs the functions of another. The priest of every parish was called *rector*, unless the prædial tithes were impropriated, and then he was called vicar, *quasi vice fungens rectoris* (as if vicariously discharging the duty of a rector).

A vicar was originally the substitute of the appropriator in those parishes where the fruits of the living had been appropriated either by religious houses or by laymen. He took only the *small* tithes, and the chancel was not vested in him.
See APPROPRIATION; RECTOR.

Vicarage. The benefice, office or parsonage house of a vicar.
See PARSONAGE.

Vicarious liability. *See* TORTS, LAW OF.

Vice-Chancellor. 1 The Vice-Chancellor is the president of the Chancery Division.
2 A principal officer in the Universities of Oxford and Cambridge and other Universities.

Viceroy. A person in place of the Queen; hence a governor of a colony or dependency.
See COLONIES.

Vice-Warden of the Stannaries. The local Judge of the Stannary Courts.
See COURT OF STANNARIES OF CORNWALL AND DEVON.

Videlicet. Namely; often abbreviated to 'viz'.

Video recording. Any disc or magnetic tape containing information by the use of which the whole or a part of a video work may be produced (see Video Recordings Act 1984, s 1(3)).
See VIDEO WORK.

The Act regulates the supply of video recordings except in accordance with a classification by an authority designated by the Secretary of State, and creates a number of offences.

As to video recordings of testimony from child witnesses, see Criminal Justice Act 1988, s 32A.

Video work. Any series of visual images (with or without sound) (i) produced electronically by the use of information contained on any disc or magnetic tape, and (ii) shown as a moving picture (see Video Recordings Act 1984, s 1 (2)).

View. The act of viewing; a word especially applicable in speaking of a jury viewing any person or thing in controversy. In some cases, when the cause concerns lands or messuages, of which it is thought expedient that the jury should have a *view*, the officer of the Court will, on application, draw up a rule for one. Two persons will be appointed as *showers*, and six jurymen as *viewers*, and the sheriff will return their names to the associate for the purpose of being called at the trial. The Court or a Judge may make an order for the inspection of any property or thing being the subject of any cause or matter before him, or the Judge may inspect it himself.

V

Again, a coroner's inquisition into the death of a person is held *super visum corporis* (on view of the body).

Vinculo matrimonii. From the bond of marriage.

Vindictive damages. Damages given by way of punishing the defendant over and above the actual amount of injury suffered by the plaintiff.
See EXEMPLARY DAMAGES.

Violent disorder. Where three or more persons who are present together use or threaten unlawful violence and the conduct of them (taken together) is such as would cause a person of reasonable firmness present at the scene to fear for his personal safety, each of the persons using or threatening violence is guilty of violent disorder (see Public Order Act 1986, s 2(1)). It is immaterial whether or not the three or more use or threaten unlawful violence simultaneously (see ibid, s 2(2)). No person of reasonable firmness need actually be, or be likely to be, present at the scene (see ibid, s 2(3)). Violent disorder may be committed in private as well as in public places (see ibid, s 2(4)). A person guilty of violent disorder is liable on conviction on indictment to imprisonment for a term not exceeding five years or a fine or both, or on summary conviction to imprisonment for a term not exceeding six months or a fine not exceeding the statutory maximum or both (see ibid, s 2(5)).

Violent offence. An offence which leads, or is intended or likely to lead, to the death or physical injury of a person and an offence which is required to be charged as arson: Criminal Justice Act 1991, s 31 (1).
See ARSON.

Violent presumption. A presumption of such a nature as almost to amount to proof.
See PRESUMPTION.

Virtute officii. By virtue of his office.
See EX OFFICIO.

Vis major. Irresistible force; eg an interposition of human agency as is from its nature and power absolutely uncontrollable; eg the inroads of a hostile army, or forcible robberies, may relieve a person from liability under a contract.

Viscount. The degree of nobility next to an earl.
See EARL.

Visitation. The office of inquiring into and correcting the irregularities of corp-orations, universities, etc.
See VISITOR.

Visitor. 1 A person appointed to visit, inquire into, and correct irregularities arising in a society or corporation. The Ordinary is the visitor of ecclesiastical corporations; ie of corporations composed entirely of spiritual persons, ie bishops, etc. In the colleges of Oxford and Cambridge, the visitor is generally either the Crown, acting by the Lord Chancellor, or some bishop of the Church of England, or the chancellor or vice-chancellor of the university, or the head of a college *ex officio*. The errors and abuses of civil lay incorporations are inquired into and redressed by the Queen's Bench Division of the High Court.
2 An official visitor of mental patients. Such visitors are appointed by the Lord Chancellor under the Mental Health Act 1983, s 102 and are known as Lord Chancellor's Visitors. Their functions, set out in s 103 of the Act, are to visit patients for the purpose of investigating matters relating to the capacity of patients to administer their property and affairs, etc. Both medical and legal visitors are appointed.
3 Boards of visitors to prisons were established by the Courts Act 1971.

Viva voce. Orally.
See WITNESS.

Vivum vadium. *See* WELSH MORTGAGE.

Viz. *See* VIDELICET.

Void and voidable. A transaction is said to be *void* when it is a mere nullity and incapable of confirmation; whereas a *voidable* transaction is one which may be either avoided or confirmed by a matter arising *ex post facto*.
Thus, a transaction may be avoided on the ground of undue influence (*see* UNDUE INFLUENCE) or fraudulent misrepresentation.
See MISREPRESENTATION.

Void for uncertainty. *See* UNCERTAINTY.

Voir dire or **voire dire** (Lat *veritatem dicere*). A corruption of *vrai dire*. An examination of a witness on the *voir dire* is a series of questions by the Court and is usually in the nature of an examination as to his competency to give evidence, or some other collateral matter, and generally takes place prior to his examination-in-chief.

Volenti non fit injuria. No injury is done to a person who consents.

Voluntary confession. A confession of crime made by an accused person, without any promise of advantage held out to him as obtainable by the confession, or any harm threatened to him if he refuses to confess, the promise or threat being made by a person in authority. Such a confession is always admissible in evidence against the accused person.

Voluntary conveyance. A conveyance not founded on a valuable consideration. The Law of Property Act 1925, s 173 provides that every voluntary disposition of land made with intent to defraud a subsequent purchaser is void at the instance of that purchaser.
See VALUABLE CONSIDERATION.

Voluntary liquidation. *See* VOLUNTARY WINDING UP.

Voluntary settlement. A settlement made without valuable consideration.
See SETTLEMENT, 1; VALUABLE CONSIDERATION.

Voluntary waste. Waste committed on lands by the voluntary act of the tenant, as opposed to waste which is merely permissive.
See WASTE.

Voluntary winding up. A winding up in which a company and its members and creditors are left to settle their affairs without coming to the Court.

A voluntary winding up begins with the passing of a resolution that the company should be wound up.

See RESOLUTION FOR VOLUNTARY WINDING UP.

A voluntary winding up may be (i) a members' voluntary winding up if a 'declaration of solvency' has been made; and (ii) a creditors' voluntary winding up where no such declaration has been made (see Insolvency Act 1986, s 90).
See CREDITORS' VOLUNTARY WINDING UP; DECLARATION OF SOLVENCY; MEMBERS' VOLUNTARY WINDING UP.

Volunteer. The recipient of a gift; a donee.
See GIFT.

Vote. 1 The right of a shareholder in a company to express his decision for or against a proposed resolution.
See RESOLUTION.

In so far as the articles of the company do not make other provision, in the case of a company originally having a share capital, every member has one vote in respect of each share or each £10 of stock held by him, and in any other case, every member shall have one vote (see Companies Act 1985, s 370(1), (6)).

Voting may be by a show of hands (*see* SHOW OF HANDS) or on a poll (*see* POLL).

2 The right of a person to express his decision at a Parliamentary or local election.
See ELECTION.

Vouch (Lat *Vocare*). To answer for.

V

WS. Writer to the Signet.
See WRITER TO THE SIGNET.

Wager. A mutual contract for the future payment of money by A to B, or by B to A, according as some unknown fact or event, otherwise of no interest to the parties contracting, shall turn out. Wagers are void in law by the Gaming Act 1845, s 18. General provisions as to gaming are now contained in the Betting, Gaming and Lotteries Act 1963, as amended, and the Gaming Act 1968.

Wagering policies. Policies of insurance, in the subject-matter of which the assured has no interest; eg an insurance on the life of a stranger. They were rendered void by the Life Assurance Act 1774. As to marine insurance, see Marine Insurance (Gambling Policies) Act 1909.

Wages. Any money or salary paid or payable to any clerk or servant, labourer or workman. When an employer becomes bankrupt, a clerk or servant is entitled to be paid any sum owing to him, limited to a certain amount, in priority to the general creditors; and any labourer or workman is entitled to be paid any sum due not exceeding four months' wages, in priority to the general creditors.
See PREFERENTIAL DEBTS.

Wait and see. *See* PERPETUITY.

Waiver. The abandonment of a right by one party, so that afterwards he is estopped, ie stopped, from claiming it. Thus, it is said that a party waives a claim, or waives an objection, meaning that he does not put it forward. So, a person is said to *waive a tort* when he forgoes his right of treating a wrongful act as such; which he does, when he expressly, or by implication, adopts the act of the wrongdoer. Thus, if goods have been wrongfully taken and sold, and the owner thinks fit to receive the price or part of it,

he adopts the transaction, and cannot afterwards treat it as wrong.

Waiver clause. A clause in a marine insurance policy stating that measures taken by the assured or the underwriters with the object of saving, protecting or recovering the subject-matter insured are not to be considered as a waiver or acceptance of abandonment or otherwise to prejudice the rights of either party.
See ABANDONMENT.

War includes civil war unless the context makes it clear that a different meaning should be given to the word (see *Pesquerias y Secaderos de Bacolao de Espana SA v Beer* (1949) 82 Ll L Rep 501 at 514, HL (per Lord Morton)).

War risks. Risks arising from hostilities, rebellion, revolution and civil war, etc, including piracy. Such risks are insured by insurance companies, by mutual insurance associations, and by the Government under the Marine and Aviation (War Risks) Act 1952.

Ward (Lat *Custodia*) means *care* or *guard*, and is used variously to denote:
1 A portion of a city or town (see Local Government Act 1972, s 6);
2 And, generally, a minor under the protection or tutelage of a guardian.
See GUARDIAN.

Warden. A guardian; a person who has the custody of any person or things by his office; e g the Lord Warden of the Cinque Ports; the Warden of a college, etc.
See LORD WARDEN OF THE CINQUE PORTS.

Wardship. The custody of a ward; any form of the relation between guardian and ward.

Warehouse. In Part VII of the Merchant Shipping Act 1894 'unless the context otherwise requires includes all warehouses, buildings and premises in which goods, when landed from ships, may be lawfully placed' (see Merchant Shipping Act 1894, s 492).

Warehousing system. The system of allowing goods imported to be deposited in public warehouses, at a reasonable rent, without payment of the duties on importation if they are re-exported; or, if they are to be withdrawn for home consumption, then without payment of such duties until they are so removed.

Warlike operation means 'one which forms part of an actual or intended belligerent act or series of acts by combatant forces; that part may be performed preparatory to the actual act or acts of belligerency, or it may be performed after the actual act or acts of belligerency, but there must be a connection sufficiently close between the act in question and the belligerent act or acts to enable a tribunal to say with at least some modicum of common sense... that it formed part of acts of belligerency' (see *Clan Line Steamers Ltd v Liverpool and London War Risks Insurance Association Ltd* [1942] 2 All ER 367 at 374 (per Atkinson J)).

Warrant. 1 An order directed to an officer authorising him to arrest an offender to be dealt with according to law.
2 A writ conferring some right or authority.
3 A citation or summons.
See DOCK WARRANT; SEARCH WARRANT.

Warrantor. A person who warrants, or gives a warranty.
See WARRANTY.

Warranty. A promise or covenant offered by a bargainor, to warrant or secure the bargainee against all men in the enjoyment of anything agreed on between them. The word is used especially with reference to any promise (express or implied by law, according to the circumstances) from a vendor to a purchaser, that the thing sold is the vendor's to sell and is good and fit for use, or at least for such use as the purchaser intends to make of it.

In marine insurance an *express* warranty is an agreement expressed in the policy, whereby the assured stipulates that certain facts are or shall be true, or that certain acts shall be done relative to the risk. It may relate to an existing or past fact, or be promissory and relate to the future; and the fact or act warranted need not be material to the risk. A formal expression is not necessary to give effect to a warranty. An *implied* warranty is

such as necessarily results from the nature of the contract, e g that the ship is seaworthy (see Marine Insurance Act 1906, ss 33–41).
See SEAWORTHY.

In the sale of goods a warranty means an agreement with reference to goods which are the subject of a contract of sale, but collateral to the main purpose of such a contract, the breach of which gives rise to a claim for damages, but not a right to reject the goods and treat the contract as repudiated: Sale of Goods Act 1979, s 60(1).
See SALE OF GOODS, CONTRACT FOR; CONTRACT LAW.

Warranty, express. *See* EXPRESS WARRANTY.

Warranty, implied. *See* IMPLIED WARRANTY.

Warranty, promissory. *See* PROMISSORY WARRANTY.

Warranty of legality in marine insurance is an implied warranty that 'the adventure insured is a lawful one and that so far as the assured can control the matter the adventure shall be carried out in a lawful manner' (see Marine Insurance Act 1906, s 41).

Warranty of neutrality in marine insurance occurs where a ship or goods are expressly warranted neutral. If this is so, 'there is an implied condition that the property shall have a neutral character at the commencement of the risk, and that, so far as the assured can control the matter, its neutral character shall be preserved during the risk' (see Marine Insurance Act 1906, s 36(1)). 'Where a ship is expressly warranted neutral, there is also an implied condition that, so far as the assured can control the matter, she shall be properly documented, that is to say, that she shall carry the necessary papers to establish her neutrality, and that she shall not falsify or suppress her papers or use substituted papers. If any loss occurs through breach of this condition, the insurer may avoid the contract' (see ibid, s 36(2)).

Warsaw Convention. An international convention signed on 12th October 1929 relating to the unification of certain rules relating to international carriage by air, and subsequently amended. (See now Carriage by Air Act 1961).

Waste. 1 Spoil and destruction done or allowed to be done, by a tenant for life or other tenant, to houses, woods, lands, or other corporeal hereditaments, during

W

the continuance of his particular estate in them. Waste is either *voluntary*, if it is a matter of commission, eg by pulling down a house; or *permissive*, eg if a house is allowed to fall into ruins for want of necessary repairs.

2 *Waste of a manor* is the uncultivated or common ground, over which the tenants enjoyed rights of pasturage for their animals.

3 The verges at the sides of roads are called roadside wastes.
See VERGE.

Water. Under the word 'water', in a conveyance, it seems that a right of fishing will pass, but the soil will not pass. The term 'land' includes water, but the term 'water' does not include the land on which it stands.

Water bailiffs. 1 Officers in port towns for the searching of ships.

2 Keepers appointed under the Salmon Fishery Acts to prevent poaching.

Watercourse. A right which a man may have to the benefit of flow of a river or stream. This right includes that of having the course of the stream kept free from any interruption or disturbance to the prejudice of the proprietor, by the act of persons outside their own territory; whether owing to a diversion of the water, or to its obstruction or pollution.

Also used to describe the stream itself.

Water-gavil. A rent paid for fishing in, or other benefit received from a river.

Waterway. A lake, river, canal, etc, suitable for sailing, boating, bathing, or fishing (see the National Parks and Access to the Countryside Act 1949, s 114).

Way. *See* HIGHWAY; RIGHT OF WAY; WAYS.

Way-bill. A document setting out the names of passengers carried in a public conveyance or a description of goods sent with a carrier by land.

Way-going crop. *See* AWAY-GOING CROP.

Ways. 1 Paths. Of these there are various kinds: (i) a footway (Lat *iter*). (ii) a bridle road for horse and man (Lat *actus*). (iii) a cart-way, containing also the two preceding. (iv) a drift-way or a way for driving cattle. (v) a highway.
See HIGHWAY.

2 Rights of way: either private or public rights of way over a person's ground.
See RIGHT OF WAY.

Weapon. *See* OFFENSIVE WEAPON.

Wear and tear. The waste of any substance by the ordinary use of it. The words 'reasonable use, wear and tear excepted', or 'FAIR WEAR AND TEAR' are sometimes used in connection with the covenants in a lease.

Weather permitting working day. A working day which counts unless work is actually prevented by the weather (see *Magnolia Shipping Co Ltd of Limassol v Joint Venture of the International Trading and Shipping Enterprises and Kinship Management Co Ltd of Brussels: The 'Camelia' and 'Magnolia'* [1978] 2 Lloyd's Rep 182).

Weather working day. A term used in a charter-party to denote a working day on which the weather allows work to be done (see *Compania Naviera Azuero v British Oil and Cake Mills Ltd* [1957] 2 All ER 241 at 249 (per Pearson J)).

Welsh language. The Welsh language may be used in any court in Wales by any party, witness or other person who desires to use it (Welsh Language Act 1967, s 1(1)).

Welsh mortgage. A mortgage in which there is no condition or proviso for repayment at any specified time. The agreement is that the mortgagee, to whom the estate is conveyed, is to receive the rents until his debt is paid, and in such a case the mortgagor and his representatives are at liberty to redeem at any time.

Westminster, Statutes of. 1 A statute of Edward I, passed in 1275. It contains fifty-one chapters, each of which would in modern times be regarded as a separate Act of Parliament. In fact, it represents the whole of the legislation for the year 1275.

2 A later statute of Edward I, 1285. It contains fifty chapters, the first being the celebrated enactment *De Donis Conditionalibus*.

3 A third statute of Edward I, 1290, known as the statute of *Quia Emptores*.

4 A modern statute of 1931, with provisions relating to the Dominions.
See DOMINION.

Wharf means any wharf, quay, pier, jetty or other place at which sea-going ships can ship or unship goods or embark or disembark passengers: Harbours Act 1964, s 57(1).

Wharfage. Money paid for landing wares at a wharf, or for shipping or taking goods from there into a boat or barge.
See WHARF.

W

White book. Colloquial term for the former *Supreme Court Practice*, containing the Rules of the Supreme Court.
See GREEN BOOK.

White ensign. A white flag consisting of the cross of St George with a Union Jack described in a canton in the upper corner next to the staff. It is to be used by all HM ships in commission (see Order in Council, 8th July, 1894). By Admiralty warrant under the Merchant Shipping Act 1894, s 73(1) yachts belonging to members of the Royal Yacht Squadron are permitted on certain terms to carry the white ensign.

Whole blood. The relation between two persons descended from a pair of nearest common ancestors; as opposed to the relation of the half blood, in which there is but only one nearest common ancestor, whether male or female.

Whole life insurance. A type of life insurance policy which states that the sum insured shall be payable on the death of the person whose life is insured and not merely on the attainment by him of a specified age.

Will. The legal declaration of a person's intention which he wishes to be performed after his death. It is revocable during the testator's life.

No will made by a person under the age of 18 is valid: Wills Act 1837, s 7. No will is valid unless:
(i) it is in writing and signed by the testator, or by some other person in his presence and by his direction; and
(ii) it appears that the testator intended by his signature to give effect to the will; and
(iii) the signature is made or acknowledged by the testator in the presence of two or more witnesses present at the same time; and
(iv) each witness either
  (a) attests and signs the will; or
  (b) acknowledges his signature,
    in the presence of the testator (but not necessarily in the presence of any other witness
but no form of attestation is necessary: ibid, s 9.

Every will executed in the above manner is valid without any other publication: ibid, s 13.

In general, a will is revoked by the testator's marriage: ibid, s 18(1). But where it appears from a will that at the time it was made the testator was expecting to be married to a particular person and that he intended that the will should not be revoked by marriage, the will is not revoked by marriage to that person: ibid, s 18(3).

The wills of living persons may be deposited and registered at the Principal Registry of the Family Division of the High Court: Administration of Justice Act 1982, ss 23–25.

There are special provisions as to international wills, and those of servicemen.
See INTERNATIONAL WILL; MILITARY WILL.

Will, estate at. The estate of a tenant holding lands at the will of the lessor.
See ESTATE; TENANT AT WILL.

Winding up, voluntary. *See* VOLUNTARY WINDING UP.

Winding up an estate is the putting it in liquidation for the purpose of distributing the assets among the creditors and others who may be found entitled to them.

Winding up by the Court. A bringing to an end of the activities of a company by the Court. The Court may wind up a company where eg (i) it does not commence its business within a year from its incorporation; (ii) the number of members is reduced below 2; (iii) the company is unable to pay its debts; (iv) the Court is of opinion that it is just and equitable that the company should be wound up (see Insolvency Act 1986, s 122).

Winding up of a company. The process of the liquidation of a company. The winding up may be either voluntary or by the Court (see Insolvency Act 1986, s 73(1)).
See VOLUNTARY WINDING UP; WINDING UP BY THE COURT.

Winding-up order. An order by the Court bringing to an end the activities of a company.

With costs. A phrase which, when used with reference to the result of an action, means that the successful party is entitled to recover his costs from his opponent.
See COSTS.

Without day. *See* EAT INDE SINE DIE.

Without discount. *See* PAYMENT WITHOUT DISCOUNT.

Without impeachment of waste. A phrase used in a conveyance to tenants for life or other tenants, to indicate that the tenant is not to be held responsible for waste. At Common Law the tenant could not be impeached for any form of waste, but in equity he was liable if the waste was of a serious character, hence called *equitable waste*; ie, the commission of wanton injury, eg the pulling down of the family mansion house, or felling timber left standing for ornament.

See WASTE.

Without notice application. *See* EX PARTE APPLICATION.

Without prejudice to any matter in question means that a decision come to, or action taken, is not to be held to affect such question, but to leave it open. Thus, when a lawyer writes on behalf of a client to offer a compromise of a question in dispute, he guards himself from being supposed to make any admission, beyond the mere fact of his willingness to compromise, by stating that what he offers is without prejudice to any question in dispute.

Without recourse to me. *See* SANS RECOURS.

Without reserve. A term applied to a sale by auction, indicating that no price is reserved. In such a case the seller may not employ any person to bid at the sale, and the auctioneer may not knowingly take any bid from any such person (see Sale of Land by Auction Act 1867, and Sale of Goods Act 1979, s 58).

Witness. A person who, on oath or solemn affirmation, gives evidence in any cause or matter.

See EVIDENCE.

In general, any fact required to be proved at the trial of any action begun by the evidence of witnesses must be proved by the examination of the witnesses orally and in open court.

By the CIVIL PROCEDURE RULES 1998, the use at trial of 'witness statements', ie sworn written statements by a witness, has been expanded. In criminal cases evidence must almost always be given orally; sometimes evidence by deposition is accepted (see Magistrates' Courts Act 1980, s 105).

Witness statement. A written statement of the oral evidence which a party to civil proceedings intends to adduce on any issue of fact to be decided at the trial: Civil Procedure Rules 1998, Part 32.

Woolf reforms. *See* CIVIL PROCEDURE ACT 1997.

Woolsack. The seat of the Lord Chancellor in the House of Lords. It is not strictly within the House, for the Lords may not speak from that part of the chamber.

Words of limitation. Words following the name of an intended grantee or devisee under a deed or will, which are intended to 'limit' or 'mark out' the estate or interest taken by the party. See now Law of Property Act 1925, s 60 which abolishes technicalities in regard to conveyances and deeds and words of limitation.

See LIMITATION OF ESTATES.

Workman. *See* SERVANT.

Wounding. An aggravated type of assault and battery, consisting in one person giving another a dangerous wound. To constitute a wound, the continuity of the skin must be broken.

See ASSAULT.

Wreck, (Lat *Wreccum maris*) by the Common Law, was where any ship was lost at sea, and the goods or cargo were thrown on the land; in which case the goods so wrecked were adjudged to belong to the King.

In order to constitute a legal wreck the goods had (in the original sense) to come to land. The law distinguished goods lost at sea by the old names of *jetsam, flotsam* and *ligan*. By the Merchant Shipping Act 1894, s 510 'wreck' for the purposes of that Act includes *jetsam, flotsam, ligan* and *derelict*.

See JETSAM; FLOTSAM; LIGAN.

Provision is made by the Merchant Shipping Act 1970, ss 55, 56 for the holding of inquiries and investigations into shipping casualties.

Modern diving equipment has enabled people to explore the sea bed, and many 'wrecks' (in the sense of sunken ships which have remained, in some cases for centuries, beneath the sea) have been discovered. The Protection of Wrecks Act 1973 enables wreck sites within United Kingdom waters to be protected from unauthorised interference on account of their historic or archaeological importance.

Wreck commissioner. A person carrying out a formal investigation into a shipping casualty. The Lord Chancellor may appoint such number of persons as he thinks fit to be wreck commissioners and may remove any wreck commissioners appointed by him (see Merchant Shipping Act 1970, s 82(1)).

W

A wreck commissioner is paid such remuneration out of moneys provided by Parliament as the Lord Chancellor may with the consent of the Treasury determine (see ibid, s 83).

Writ. The Queen's precept, whereby any thing is commanded to be done touching a suit or action.

Writ of summons. *See* SUMMONS, 3; WRIT.

Writer to the Signet. The Writers to the Signet are the oldest body of law practitioners in Scotland. They perform in the superior Courts of Scotland duties corresponding to those of solicitors in England.

Wrong. That which is *wrung* or turned aside from the right or straight way to the desired end. It corresponds to the French *tort*, from the Latin *tortum*, twisted.

See TORT.

The words *wrong* and *tort* may be used in law to mean any injury; but they are used especially to denote such civil injuries as are independent of contract, and are not breaches of trust.

See CONTRACT; TRUST.

Wrongful dismissal. The unjustifiable dismissal of an employee in breach of a contract of service or before the expiration of a period of notice. The employee may sue for damages for loss of employment and wages or salary.

As to remedies for *unfair* dismissal (which include reinstatement or compensation) see Employment Protection (Consolidation) Act 1978, Part V.

Wrongful interference with goods means (i) conversion of goods; (ii) trespass to goods; (iii) negligence so far as it results in damage to goods or to an interest in them; and (iv) any other tort so far as it results in damage to goods or to an interest in them: Torts (Interference with Goods) Act 1977, s 1(1).

See INTERFERENCE WITH GOODS.

W

Y

Year. *See* OLD STYLE.

Year and day. 1 Where the law of Scotland requires any act to be performed within a year, a day is generally added *in majorem evidentiam*, so that it may appear with greater certainty that the year is completed.
2 The same reason will probably account for the frequent mention of the year and a day in English law; for instance, in reference to the time within which appeals might be brought; also in reference to the time within which death must follow on a fatal wound, in order to constitute the crime of murder, though by the Law Reform (Year and a Day Rule) Act 1996, this rule has been abolished in so far as it applies to liability for offences causing death; and in various other cases.

Year Books. Reports of cases in a regular series from the reign of King Edward I to the reign of King Henry VIII inclusive. They were taken down by the protonotaries, ie chief scribes of the courts, at the expense of the Crown, and published annually, when they were known under as *Year Books*.

Year to year. *See* TENANT FROM YEAR TO YEAR.

Years, estate for. An estate demised or granted for a term of years.
See TERM OF YEARS.

Yeomanry. The small freeholders and farmers. The name was also given to certain local forces raised by individuals with the approval of the King, who accepted their voluntary service. The name survives in some Territorial Army units e g City of London Yeomanry.

Yielding and paying. Words used at the beginning of the *reddendum* clause in a lease, with reference to the rent intended to be payable under the lease.
See REDDENDUM.

York–Antwerp Rules 1974. A standard set of rules relating to general average and usually incorporated into marine insurance policies and charter-parties. The name 'York–Antwerp' is derived from the places where conferences were held, which brought the Rules into existence, and was first given to the Rules formulated in 1877. They do not constitute a complete or self-contained code and need to be supplemented by bringing into the gaps provisions of the law applicable to the contract.
See GENERAL AVERAGE ACT; MARINE INSURANCE; CHARTER-PARTY.

Yorkshire deeds registries. The registries of documents and transactions relating to land first provided by Acts of Parliament for the ridings of the county of York. These Acts were repealed and re-enacted with certain modifications by the Yorkshire Registries Act 1884. Under the Law of Property Act 1925, s 11 it was necessary to register in the Yorkshire Registry only instruments which operated to transfer or create a legal estate; and, under s 197, this registration was deemed to constitute actual notice of the transfer or creation of the legal estate, or charge by way of legal mortgage, to all persons, and for all purposes whatsoever.

Further, it was provided by the Law of Property (Amendment) Act 1926, Schedule (amending the Land Charges Act 1925, s 10(6)), that the registration of a general equitable charge, restrictive covenant, equitable easement, or estate contract affecting land should be effected at the appropriate Registry in Yorkshire, and not at the Land Registry in London (see also Land Registration Act 1925, ss 135, 136).

The Yorkshire deeds registries were closed by the Law of Property Act 1969.

Young Offender Institution. A place for the detention of offenders sentenced to detention in such an institution: Prison Act 1952, s 43(1)(aa).

Young person. A person who has attained the age of fourteen years but who is under seventeen years (see Children and Young Persons Act 1933, s 107).

Younger Brethren. *See* TRINITY HOUSE.

Youth Courts. Courts for the trial of charges against children and young persons. (See Children and Young Persons Act 1933, ss 45–49). The public are excluded from such courts. Bona fide representatives of the Press may be present (s 47). There are restrictions on newspaper reports of proceedings (s 49). The courts were formerly known as 'Juvenile Courts'.

Y

Z

Zero-rating. Relief from payment of value added tax on the supply of certain goods and services, eg food (with exceptions), books and newspapers, coal, fuel, etc (see Value Added Tax 1983).